THE

POP, ROCK, SOUL

AND

READER

Histories and Debates

Third Edition

David Brackett

McGill University

New York   Oxford
OXFORD UNIVERSITY PRESS

Oxford University Press is a department of the University of Oxford.
It furthers the University's objective of excellence in research,
scholarship, and education by publishing worldwide.

Oxford   New York
Auckland   Cape Town   Dar es Salaam   Hong Kong   Karachi
Kuala Lumpur   Madrid   Melbourne   Mexico City   Nairobi
New Delhi   Shanghai   Taipei   Toronto

With offices in
Argentina   Austria   Brazil   Chile   Czech Republic   France   Greece
Guatemala   Hungary   Italy   Japan   Poland   Portugal   Singapore
South Korea   Switzerland   Thailand   Turkey   Ukraine   Vietnam

For titles covered by Section 112 of the US Higher Education
Opportunity Act, please visit www.oup.com/us/he for
the latest information about pricing and alternate formats.

Published by Oxford University Press
198 Madison Avenue, New York, NY 10016
www.oup.com

Oxford is a registered trademark of Oxford University Press.

Library of Congress Cataloging-in-Publication Data

Brackett, David.
The pop, rock, and soul reader : histories and debates / David Brackett.—Third editon.
    pages cm
ISBN 978-0-19-981170-0
1. Popular music—United States—History and criticism.   I. Title.
ML3477.B68 2013
781.6409—dc23   2013024079

Printing number: 9 8 7 6 5 4 3 2 1

Printed in the United States of America
on acid-free paper

Contents

Preface xiii

PART 1 **Before 1950**

1. **Irving Berlin in Tin Pan Alley** 1

   Charles Hamm, "Irving Berlin and the Crucible of God" 2

2. **Technology, the Dawn of Modern Popular Music,
   and the "King of Jazz"** 9

   Paul Whiteman and Mary Margaret McBride, "On Wax" 11

3. **Big Band Swing Music: Race and Power in the Music Business** 14

   Marvin Freedman, "Black Music's on Top; White Jazz Stagnant" 15

   Irving Kolodin, "The Dance Band Business: A Study in Black
   and White" 18

4. **Solo Pop Singers and New Forms of Fandom** 21

   Martha Weinman Lear, "The Bobby Sox Have
   Wilted, but the Memory Remains Fresh" 22

5. **Hillbilly and Race Music** 25

   Kyle Crichton, "Thar's Gold in Them Hillbillies" 26

6. ***Blues People* and the Classic Blues** 30

   LeRoi Jones, from *Blues People: The Negro Experience
   in White America and the Music that Developed from It* 32

7. **The Empress of the Blues** 39

   Nat Shapiro and Nat Hentoff, from *Hear Me Talkin' to Ya:
   The Story of Jazz as Told by the Men Who Made It* 40

8. **At the Crossroads with Son House** 44

   Jerry Gilbert, "Son House: Living King of Delta" 46

9. From Race Music to Rhythm and Blues: T–Bone Walker 48

*Kevin Sheridan and Peter Sheridan, "T-Bone Walker: Father
of the Blues"* 49

10. Jumpin' the Blues with Louis Jordan 51

Down Beat, "Bands Dug by the Beat: Louis Jordan" 52

*Arnold Shaw, from Honkers and Shouters: The Golden Years of
Rhythm and Blues* 53

11. On the Bandstand with Johnny Otis 56

*Johnny Otis, from Upside Your Head! Rhythm and Blues
on Central Avenue* 57

12. The Producers Answer Back: The Emergence of the "Indie"
Record Company 58

*Bill Simon, "Indies' Surprise Survival: Small Labels'
Ingenuity and Skill Pay Off"* 60

*Arnold Shaw, from Honkers and Shouters: The Golden Years
of Rhythm and Blues* 62

13. Country Music as Folk Music, Country Music as Novelty 65

*Billboard, "American Folk Tunes: Cowboy and Hillbilly Tunes
and Tunesters"* 66

Newsweek, "Corn of Plenty" 68

PART 2 The 1950s

14. Country Music Approaches the Mainstream 71

Rufus Jarman, "Country Music Goes to Town" 72

15. Rhythm and Blues in the Early 1950s: B. B. King 74

*Arnold Shaw, from Honkers and Shouters: The Golden Years of
Rhythm and Blues* 75

16. "The House that Ruth Brown Built" 77

*Ruth Brown (with Andrew Yule), from Miss Rhythm:
The Autobiography of Ruth Brown, Rhythm and Blues Legend* 78

17. Ray Charles, or, When Saturday Night Mixed It Up with Sunday Morning 82

*Ray Charles and David Ritz, from Brother Ray: Ray Charles'
Own Story* 83

18. Jerry Wexler: A Life in R&B 89

*Jerry Wexler and David Ritz, from Rhythm and the Blues:
A Life in American Music* 90

19. **The Growing Threat of Rhythm and Blues** 94

    Variety, "Top Names Now Singing the Blues as Newcomers
Roll on R&B Tide" 95

    Variety, "A Warning to the Music Business" 98

20. **From Rhythm and Blues to Rock 'n' Roll: The Songs of Chuck Berry** 100

    Norman Jopling, "Chuck Berry: Rock Lives!" 101

21. **Little Richard: Boldly Going Where No Man Had Gone Before** 104

    Charles White, from *The Life and Times of Little Richard:
The Quasar of Rock* 105

22. **Elvis Presley, Sam Phillips, and Rockabilly** 110

    Elizabeth Kaye, "Sam Phillips Interview" 112

23. **Rock 'n' Roll Meets the Popular Press** 118

24. **The *Chicago Defender* Defends Rock 'n' Roll** 120

    Rob Roy, "Bias Against 'Rock 'n' Roll' Latest Bombshell in Dixie" ... 121

25. **The Music Industry Fight Against Rock 'n' Roll: Dick Clark's
Teen-Pop Empire and the Payola Scandal** 123

    Peter Bunzel, "Music Biz Goes Round and Round:
It Comes Out Clarkola" 125

    New York Age, "Mr. Clark and Colored Payola" 128

PART 3   The 1960s

26. **The Brill Building and the Girl Groups** 131

    Charlotte Greig, from *Will You Still Love Me Tomorrow?
Girl Groups from the 50s On . . .* 133

27. **From Surf to *Smile*** 140

    Richard Cromelin, "Interview with Brian Wilson" 141

28. **Urban Folk Revival** 144

    Gene Bluestein, "Songs of the Silent Generation" 146

    Time, "Folk Singing: Sibyl with Guitar" 149

29. **Bringing It All Back Home: Dylan at Newport** 153

    Irwin Silber, "Newport Folk Festival, 1965" 156

    Paul Nelson, "Newport Folk Festival, 1965" 157

30. "For a Man to Be At Ease, He Must Not Tell All He Knows,
    Nor Say All He Sees" 160

    *John Cohen and Happy Traum, "Sing Out! 'An Interview
    with Bob Dylan'"* 161

31. From R&B to Soul 169

    *Jerry Wexler and David Ritz, from Rhythm and the Blues:
    A Life in American Music* 170

32. No Town Like Motown 173

    Harvey Kubernik, "Berry Gordy: A Conversation with Mr. Motown" 174

33. The Godfather of Soul and the Beginnings of Funk 178

    James Brown (with Bruce Tucker), from The Godfather of Soul 180

34. "The Blues Changes from Day to Day" 189

    Jim Delehant, "Otis Redding Interview" 190

35. Aretha Franklin Earns Respect 194

    *Phyl Garland, "Aretha Franklin—'Sister Soul':
    Eclipsed Singer Gains New Heights"* 195

36. The Beatles, the "British Invasion," and Cultural Respectability 200

    William Mann, "What Songs the Beatles Sang . . ." 201

    Theodore Strongin, "Musicologically . . ." 203

37. *A Hard Day's Night* and Beatlemania 205

    Andrew Sarris, "Bravo Beatles!" 205

    *Barbara Ehrenreich, Elizabeth Hess, and Gloria Jacobs,
    "Beatlemania: Girls Just Want to Have Fun"* 208

38. England Swings, and the Beatles Evolve on *Revolver*
    and *Sgt. Pepper* 213

    Richard Goldstein, "Pop Eye: On 'Revolver'" 214

    Jack Kroll, "It's Getting Better . . ." 217

39. The British Art School Blues 219

    Ray Coleman, "Rebels with a Beat" 221

40. The Stones versus the Beatles 225

    Ellen Willis, "Records: Rock, Etc.—the Big Ones" 226

41. If You're Goin' to San Francisco 231

    Ralph J. Gleason, "Dead Like Live Thunder" 233

42. **The Kozmic Blues of Janis Joplin** 235

   Nat Hentoff, "We Look at Our Parents and . . ." 237

43. **Jimi Hendrix and the Electronic Guitar** 240

   Bob Dawbarn, "Second Dimension: Jimi Hendrix in Action" 242

44. **Rock Meets the Avant-Garde: Frank Zappa** 244

   Sally Kempton, "Zappa and the Mothers: Ugly Can Be Beautiful" 245

45. **The Aesthetics of Rock** 249

   Richard Goldstein, "Pop Eye: Evaluating Media" 250

46. **Festivals: The Good, the Bad, and the Ugly** 254

   J. R. Young, "Review of Various Artists, *Woodstock*" 255

   George Paul Csicsery, "Altamont, California, December 6, 1969" 258

PART 4 The 1970s

47. **The Sound of Autobiography: Singer-Songwriters, Carole King** 261

   Robert Windeler, "Carole King: 'You Can Get to Know Me through My Music'" 263

48. **Exclusive Joni Mitchell Interview** 266

   Penny Valentine, "Joni Mitchell: An Interview (part 1)" 267

49. **Sly Stone: "The Myth of Staggerlee"** 270

   Greil Marcus, from *Mystery Train: Images of America in Rock 'n' Roll Music* 272

50. **Not-So-"Little" Stevie Wonder** 277

   Ben Fong-Torres, "The Formerly Little Stevie Wonder" 278

51. **Parliament Drops the Bomb** 283

   W. A. Brower, "George Clinton: Ultimate Liberator of Constipated Notions" 284

52. **Heavy Metal Meets the Counterculture** 290

   John Mendelsohn, "Review of Led Zeppelin" 292

   Ed Kelleher, "Black Sabbath Don't Scare Nobody" 294

53. **Led Zeppelin Speaks!** 299

   Dave Schulps, "The Crunge: Jimmy Page Gives a History Lesson" 300

54. "I Have No Message Whatsoever" 307

　Cameron Crowe, "David Bowie Interview" 308

55. Rock Me Amadeus 314

　Domenic Milano, "Keith Emerson" 316

　Tim Morse, from *Yesstories: Yes in Their Own Words* ... 319

56. The Global Phenomenon of Reggae 323

　Robert Hilburn, "Third-World Theme of Bob Marley" ... 324

57. Get On Up Disco 328

　Andrew Kopkind, "The Dialectic of Disco: Gay Music
　Goes Straight" 330

58. Punk: The Sound of Criticism? 339

　James Wolcott, "A Conservative Impulse in the New Rock
　Underground" 341

59. Punk Crosses the Atlantic 345

　Caroline Coon, "Rebels Against the System" 346

60. Punk to New Wave? 352

　Stephen Holden, "The B-52s' American Graffiti" 353

61. UK New Wave 355

　Allan Jones, "The Elvis (Costello, That Is) Interview" .. 356

PART 5 The 1980s

62. *Thriller* Begets the "King of Pop" 363

　Greg Tate, "I'm White! What's Wrong with Michael Jackson" ... 365

　Daryl Easlea, "Don't Stop 'Til You Get Enough: Bruce Swedien
　Remembers the Times with Michael Jackson" 368

63. Madonna and the Performance of Identity 372

　Camille Paglia, "Venus of the Radio Waves" 373

64. Bruce Springsteen: Reborn in the USA 377

　David Marsh, "Little Egypt from Asbury Park—and
　Bruce Springsteen Don't Crawl on His Belly, Neither" ... 378

　Simon Frith, "The Real Thing—Bruce Springsteen" ... 381

65. R&B in the 1980s: To Cross Over or Not to Cross Over? ... 388

　Nelson George, from *The Death of Rhythm and Blues* ... 389

66. **Heavy Metal Thunders On!** 395

    J. D. Considine, "Purity and Power—Total, Unswerving
Devotion to Heavy Metal Form: Judas Priest and the Scorpions" 396

67. **Metal in the Late Eighties: Glam or Thrash?** 399

    Richard Gehr, "Metallica" 400

68. **Parents Want to Know: Heavy Metal, the PMRC,
and the Public Debate over Decency** 405

    "Record Labeling: Hearing before the Committee on
Commerce, Science, and Transportation, United States Senate,
99th Congress, September 19, 1985" 408

69. **Postpunk Goes Indie** 415

    Al Flipside, "What Is This Thing Called Hardcore?" 416

70. **Hip-Hop, Don't Stop** 419

    Robert Ford, Jr., "B-Beats Bombarding Bronx: Mobile
DJ Starts Something with Oldie R&B Disks" 420

    Robert Ford, Jr., "Jive Talking N.Y. DJs Rapping Away in
Black Discos" 421

71. **"The Music Is a Mirror"** 423

    Harry Allen, "Hip Hop Madness: From Def Jams to Cold
Lampin', Rap Is Our Music" 425

    Carol Cooper, "Girls Ain't Nothin' but Trouble" 429

72. **Where Rap and Heavy Metal Converge** 431

    Jon Pareles, "There's a New Sound in Pop Music: Bigotry" 432

PART 6   The 1990s and Beyond

73. **Hip-Hop into the 1990s: Gangstas, Fly Girls,
and the Big Bling-Bling** 439

    J. D. Considine, "Fear of a Rap Planet" 441

74. **Nuthin' but a "G" Thang** 447

    Touré, "Snoop Dogg's Gentle Hip Hop Growl" 448

75. **Keeping It a Little Too Real** 452

    Sam Gideon Anso and Charles Rappleye, "Rap Sheet" 453

    Selwyn Seyfu Hinds, "Party Over" 454

    Natasha Stovall, "Town Criers" 455

76. Women in Rap 456
     Christopher John Farley, "Hip-Hop Nation" 458

77. The Beat Goes On 464
     Renee Graham, "Eminem's Old Words Aren't Hip-Hop's
     Biggest Problem" 465

78. From Indie to Alternative to . . . Seattle? 467
     Dave DiMartino, "A Seattle Slew" 468

79. Grunge Turns to *Scrunge* 471
     Eric Weisbard, "Over and Out: Indie Rock Values in the Age
     of Alternative Million Sellers" 473

80. "We Are the World"? 479
     George Lipsitz, "Immigration and Assimilation:
     Rai, Reggae, and Bhangramuffin" 482

81. Genre or Gender? The Resurgence of the Singer-Songwriter 490
     Robert L. Doerschuk, "Tori Amos: Pain for Sale" 492

82. Public Policy and Pop Music History Collide 496
     Jenny Toomey, "Empire of the Air" 498

83. Electronica Is in the House 501
     Simon Reynolds, "Historia Electronica Preface" 504

84. R&B Divas Go Retro 515
     Ann Powers, "The New Conscience of Pop Music" 516

85. Country in the Post–Urban Cowboy Era 520
     Mark Cooper, "Garth Brooks: Meet Nashville's New Breed
     Of Generously Stetsoned Crooner" 522
     Charles Taylor, "Chicks Against the Machine" 527

86. Performance as Simulacrum, Boy Bands, and Other
     21st-Century Epiphanies 534
     Joshua Clover, "Jukebox Culture: How I Learned to Stop
     Worrying and Love the Boy Band" 535
     Nina C. Ayoub, "Idol Pursuits" 537

87. Lady Gaga and the Triumph of Camp 540
     Sasha Frere-Jones, "Ladies Wild: How Not Dumb Is Gaga?" 541

88. **The End of History, the Mass-Marketing of Trivia, and a World of Copies without Originals** ... 544

Jay Babcock, "The Kids Aren't Alright ... They're Amazing" ... 546

Robert Everett-Green, "Ruled by Frankenmusic" ... 552

Eliot Van Buskirk, "Why File Sharing Will Save Hollywood, Music" ... 556

Selected Bibliography ... 561

Index ... 567

Preface

The music of a well-ordered age is calm and cheerful, and so is its government. The music of a restive age is excited and fierce, and its government is perverted. The music of a decaying state is sentimental and sad and its government is imperiled.
—Lu Be We, ancient Chinese philosopher[1]

It seems that music is used and produced [in one era] in the ritual in an attempt to make people forget the general violence; in another, it is employed to make people believe in the harmony of the world, that there is order in exchange and legitimacy in commercial power; and finally, there is one in which it serves to silence, by mass-producing a deafening, syncretic kind of music, and censoring all other human noises.
—Jacques Attali, contemporary French philosopher[2]

To some extent the genesis of this project can be blamed on my mother, who gave me a copy of *The Rolling Stone Record Review* (a collection of reviews from *Rolling Stone* from the years 1967–70) when I was 13. I became aware of an ongoing world of criticism with its own set of myths and assumptions about what was important in popular music. The contributors to the *Record Review* took popular music seriously, wrote about it literately, and seemed to share a sense of how the sound and style of popular music were bound up with contemporary social and political currents. I have continued to use that same, now-tattered paperback copy of the *Record Review* and its successor, *The Rolling Stone Record Review, Volume 2*, as a reference volume for the subsequent 30 years, and two reviews from the first volume (plus the epigraph by Lu Be We) made it into this book.

As is true of many things that happen during puberty, reading the *Record Review* had an impact that could not have been foreseen at the time. I subsequently morphed from music fan and fledgling musician to music student to professional musician to music academic, yet these early encounters with music criticism continued to exert a powerful fascination.

The Book's Approach

In the course of teaching classes on the history of 20th- and 21st-century (mostly) U.S. popular music for several years, I began to ponder ways to explore the interconnections among popular music, musical techniques, current events, and social identity in a way that would make popular music as exciting and powerful for students as it had become for me. I wanted to find material that could address several particularly compelling questions: How did the musicians who made the music explain it? What

---

1. *The Rolling Stone Record Review* (New York: Pocket Books, 1971), i.
2. Jacques Attali, *Noise: The Political Economy of Music*, trans. Brian Massumi (Minneapolis: University of Minnesota Press, 1985), 19.

did the music sound like? Who listened to it? Why did they listen to it? How did they react? What was the dominant impression made by the music to society at large? Why do some types of popular music still matter today?

Readings Offer Breadth and Flexibility

Over time, it became clear to me that one of the best ways to focus attention on these questions and, in some cases, to suggest possible answers to them was to assign source readings. Source readings challenge readers to re-create the context in which the first expressions of excitement and arguments about value in various genres occurred. This engagement with the social context is a large part of the reason why source readings tend to stimulate critical thinking and lively discussions, as readers relive the controversies and conflicts that accompanied significant events in the history of popular music. The wealth of entries means that readers and instructors using this book can pick and choose readings to correspond to a variety of interests and emphases.

Readings Provide Diverse Perspectives

A collection of source readings provides a different sense of history than do more conventional narrative histories, which tend to emphasize continuity. By contrast, the sense of history that emerges from an anthology of source readings is more disjunct in some respects, since different voices present authoritative versions of historical events that may compete or conflict with one another. This unresolved quality can be wonderfully stimulating. In this volume, for example, artists such as James Brown, Bob Dylan, the Beatles, and Jimi Hendrix can be seen through a prism of shifting perspectives consisting of critics writing at different times, as well as interviews and autobiographies of people involved in the creation of the music. This lack of resolution may also provide the impetus for classroom discussions.

Commentary Provides an Overarching Historical Backdrop

This book is a hybrid of sorts, differing from most other anthologies in that it furnishes its own sense of linear history. In addition to the usual sort of material found in headnotes (introductions to the entries), I have provided historical background about different artists, eras, and genres. This was necessitated by several factors: First, the large social and stylistic distances between genres grouped within the larger rubric of "popular music" made transitions between some entries difficult. It didn't seem right, for example, to go from an entry discussing the aesthetic innovation and cultural importance of disco to entries discussing the different aesthetic and social context of punk, with only a headnote to function as a transition. Second, these transitional historical passages allowed me to discuss a broader range of sources than I could include in the book as entries, and they opened the book up to a wider range of uses.

Organization Allows Broad Usage

The book is arranged chronologically by decades, with the first part of the book devoted to developments prior to the 1950s. Throughout this collection of source readings, I've woven in commentary that provides context preceding the articles and, on occasion, in the midst of them, thereby creating a hybrid text/reader. Thus the book can be used either as the main text for a course or as a supporting reader. In addition to courses on the history of 20th- and 21st-century popular music, the content applies to courses on American music, American studies, media studies, history, and sociology.

The Selections

The documents in this collection may be grouped into two large categories: the first includes articles from general-interest magazines, music magazines, newspapers, and music industry publications, and the second includes interviews and autobiographies of musicians and other participants in the music industry.

Journalism/Criticism

Works of journalism and criticism convey reactions to important musical developments at the moment they began to receive public attention. The interest in these pieces—often written with a tight deadline in mind and with little thought for creating enduring historical narratives—comes from a palpable sense of excitement as the pieces respond to, for example, the appearance of a new genre, the reinterpretation of an old genre as it finds a new audience, or the impact of new technology on production and reception. Journalistic criticism is particularly useful in communicating a sense of unfolding events, since critics fill an important role mediating between musicians, the music industry, and the audience.

Within the category of "criticism," I have included a variety of different types of writing about music, from articles and record reviews in magazines with a broad readership, to excerpts from underground "fanzines," to examples of "new journalism" in which the subjective impressions of the critic are highlighted. In deciding which pieces of criticism to select, I sought out examples of critics who have been historically influential, some of whom have played a role in the reception and meaning of the music itself. One of the clearest examples of this synergy between criticism, style, and meaning may be found in the debates that exploded in the late 1960s around rock aesthetics. These debates indicated a major shift in the reception of post–rock 'n' roll popular music and continue to illuminate debates that still rage whenever musicians and fans argue about their preferences. I also included accounts that are not particularly hip or influential in terms of popular music criticism, not in order to make fun of them or show how wrong the authors were, but because these articles are useful for conveying widespread attitudes about popular music at that time in a way that more specialized publications are not.

An interesting facet of working with journalistic sources is the variation in point of view and tone between different publications. This may be confusing for students because interpreting many of the entries often requires reading skills beyond those needed for gleaning facts from a standard textbook. The headnotes are intended to clarify some of the complicating factors. These include (to name only a few) the assumed readership of the publication, the ongoing dialogue with other critics in which the article might have been participating, and the larger issues in the music industry and/or society at large to which the article might have been alluding.

Interviews and Autobiographies

I looked for statements by musicians that focused on their social and musical backgrounds and on aspects of their music that had the greatest influence on others. I concentrated on artists who had a significant historical impact even if they were not necessarily the most popular in statistical terms during the period in which they worked. I also sought the views of "backstage" figures who played an important role in the history of popular music—it was often the vision of these entrepreneurs, record producers, and engineers that led to the formation of new musical alliances and the redrawing of the stylistic map. While it may be true that many of the interviews and autobiographies display the kind of self-serving revisionism that comes with first-person re-creations of events long past, even in their idealized form these recollections can still provide a good starting point for discussions.

I do not attempt to include every important personage in popular music during the period covered here. Some figures, such as Nat "King" Cole and Bill Haley, while they do not have entries devoted specifically to them, are mentioned in articles, headnotes, or interviews with and autobiographies of others. These omissions are not intended as a slight or an indication of what I think is important so much as they reflect the accessibility of primary materials that focus on these musicians. In the case of certain genres, such as doo-wop, I had difficulty tracking down source materials that I found acceptable. In other cases, I simply ran out of time, luck, money, or some combination of the three. At any rate, I welcome suggestions for future editions.

What's New in the Third Edition?

The third edition includes ten new entries, replacing the same number of entries from the second edition; these include the following:

- The global impact of Bob Marley and reggae
- Debates around censorship and content warnings in the 1980s
- Several essays focusing on the impact of technology and mass media on the circulation and social meaning of music, including topics such as auto-tune, filesharing, reality TV, *American Idol*, and the easy access to an ever-growing archive of past recordings
- Discussion of new stars such as Lady Gaga, whose rise to fame is inextricable from the new media, and a re-evaluation of the career of Michael Jackson in light of his death in 2009

So What, Exactly, Constitutes Popular Music?

The organization of this book reflects my long-time interest in issues of genre. This interest arose out of attempts to synthesize my experiences as a musician and as an academically trained music scholar; in other words, I sought a point of articulation between music analysis—the formal or technical description of music—and the social meanings and functions of music. Focusing on genre provides an ideal theoretical framework for exploring such an interest, since genre may be understood as a way of categorizing popular music so as to create a connection among musical styles, producers, musicians, and consumers. Genres also underline how meaning circulates in a kind of "feedback loop" that binds musicians, fans, and critics. Thus no one source rooted in any one of these groups can act as the ultimate arbiter of musical significance. The focus on genre in this book resembles that of a book like Philip Ennis's *The Seventh Stream*: one that relies on a model of popular music as an assemblage of several (or, as in Ennis's case, seven) simultaneous streams that cross, interweave, and diverge at different historical moments. Although one may quibble with what constitutes the boundaries of a stream at any given moment, the metaphor remains useful.

The main categorical or generic division, and one that occurs in every part of this book, is that between black popular music and white popular music. While there have certainly been moments of strong interconnection (the mid-1950s, for example), at other times these two large categories really do seem to exist in separate, although not necessarily equal, universes. This frequent sense of distance between musical categories and my desire to contextualize the categories are two of the driving forces behind what I referred to earlier as the "hybrid" nature of this anthology.

The presence of these multiple streams is reflected in my title: I avoided calling this book *The Rock 'n' Roll Reader* or *The Rock Reader* precisely because those terms seem somewhat more limited to me, especially in that they are frequently understood as not including the full range of African American popular music since World War II. The usage of "rock," for example, sometimes refers to all popular music after 1955; at other times the term refers to popular music made by (mostly) white, (mostly) male musicians after 1965. Neither "rock 'n' roll" nor the twin usages of "rock" do justice to the rich range of genres that have dominated popular music of the past 50 years. Dave Marsh's notion of "rock and soul music" comes close to capturing the complex range of styles discussed in this book and granting recognition to the importance of African American musicians, although I felt it necessary to expand "rock" and "soul" further by adding "pop."[3]

One question that readers are bound to raise concerns the boundaries of popular music itself. While my title, *The Pop, Rock, and Soul Reader*, may project capaciousness in terms of styles and genres, I am sure that despite my best efforts, the issue of inclusiveness will inevitably arise. It is, of course, not possible to include everything (imagine how large a book that would be!); nevertheless, I believe that the material presented here is diverse enough to encourage and enable the tracing of a variety of histories with different points of emphasis. The ability to refocus on a varying assortment of genres makes it possible to shift which dates, places, and personages seem important.

A Note on Chronology and Sources

That this anthology provides a variety of routes through history by allowing the reader to pick and choose from among the entries also underscores the fuzziness of generic borders, in that our perceptions of these borders may shift, depending on which points of view we consider. By the same token, a genre's temporal boundaries may also appear to be imprecise if we view them from different perspectives; therefore, the histories of genres will not necessarily begin or end clearly on specific dates. Acknowledging the lack of a specific point of origin for genres, however, does not preclude the possibility that certain types of historical emphases within genres will correspond more strongly than others to the perceptions of a particular socially or culturally situated group. For example, from the point of view of the first wave of baby boomers who came of age as fans in the 1950s, 1955 may seem like an obvious date for the transformation of popular music. On the other hand, this date may seem less important to those who formed strong attachments to popular music in the 1990s or 1930s. That the book goes back to the turn of the last century suggests that the intrageneric dialogue that we now associate with rock 'n' roll had already started by the early decades of the 20th century.

Although I was tempted, I decided not to divide chapters by dates that create the appearance of a significant point of arrival (e.g., 1955, 1964, and 1977) in order to open the use of the book to those who disagree about when significant breaks occur. Even the division by decades does not provide an easy solution, however, since many artists who are presented here through autobiography or interview had careers that spanned several decades, and their thoughts were inflected by the period in which they were written down, a period that may have occurred long after the time of the

---

3. The phrase "rock and soul" comes from Dave Marsh, *The Heart of Rock and Soul: The 1001 Greatest Singles Ever Made* (New York: Da Capo Press, [1989] 1999).

musical events they are describing. This historical untidiness sometimes means that readings referring to a single genre are spread out over two or more chapters.

This book is also very much a history of the different types of mass media and trade publications about popular music since 1920. The surge of writing in the late 1960s significantly altered the landscape of popular music criticism, a development that is reflected in this book. Prior to the late 1960s, sources consisted of music industry publications, such as *Billboard* and *Variety*; magazines that catered to jazz aficionados, such as *Down Beat* and *Metronome*; the occasional feature piece in a general-interest magazine or newspaper; and the odd interview or musician's autobiography (although it is interesting to note that many of the interviews and autobiographies dealing with events from before 1960 were actually published after 1970, a phenomenon facilitated by the same boom that produced an abundance of new publications). Whereas the problem with finding suitable material pre-1967 was its scarcity, or the lack of variety in the type of sources, the surfeit of riches after 1967 creates the opposite problem of having too much material and too many choices.

In a few cases I have included pieces of a more scholarly hue that are particularly illuminating about an issue occurring close in time to the publication of the piece, thus putting these essays in a context similar to that of the journalistic work or the trade publications. These scholarly works, along with several intensely researched pieces that could easily pass for academic work even if their conventional assignation falls into the category of "journalism" or "trade publication," emphasize how hazy the line can be between the scholarly and the nonscholarly. However, while some of the criticism here displays the thorough research and analysis that many would associate with scholarly work, many of these pieces do not provide the type of sustained analysis found in scholarship, nor do they usually contain in-depth descriptions of musical style like those found in musicological studies. The work of critics may seem remarkably prescient or spectacularly wrongheaded after the fact, but it almost always tells us something about how people felt at the time the events were happening. Scholars, with the benefit of hindsight, are able to work backward from questions that interest them in the present to shock, surprise, or comfort readers on the basis of how the authors perceive present-day attitudes toward their subjects. Although I am a musicologist rather than a critic, I have emphasized criticism and trade publications far more than scholarship because criticism better served the goals of this book. An impressive expansion occurred in academic studies of popular music in the 1980s and 1990s that would require a separate volume were I to attempt to do it justice. For those hankering for a greater proportion of academic work, references are given throughout to direct readers toward relevant scholarship.

Acknowledgments

In addition to thanking everyone I thanked in the first two editions, I would like to express my appreciation for my research assistants: Melvin Backstrom, Michael Ethen, Dana Gorzelany-Mostak, Mimi Haddon, Farley Miller, Sean Lorre, and Cedar Wingate, who helped track down the new entries and narrow the field of possibilities; and for the authors of the new entries in this edition for their permission to use their work.

The encouragement of my new editor, Richard Carlin, provided the necessary motivation down the homestretch. I can't resist repeating my thanks to two people mentioned in the acknowledgments of the second edition: first, to Jan Beatty, editor of the first two editions, whose dedication and enthusiasm for the project played a major role in its preparation; and second, to my partner Lisa Barg, guiding light in matters of the spirit and mind. Finally, I must mention my debt to our children,

Sophie and Fred, whose growing love of music and wide-open ears inspire me to keep listening and playing.

I extend my thanks to the following reviewers commissioned by OUP, who helped enormously with the preparation of the new edition, including

Eric Charry, Wesleyan University
Frank Gunderson, Florida State University
Clarence Hines, University of North Florida
Mark Katz, University of North Carolina–Chapel Hill
Mike Morrison, Purdue University
Tony Sheppard, Williams College
Joseph Taylor, James Madison University.

A Note on the Text

There are two kinds of footnotes in this anthology: those I prepared myself and those that are being reprinted from the original source readings. I have indicated my notes with numbers and the others with symbols.

PART 1

Before 1950

1. Irving Berlin in Tin Pan Alley

For most of the 19th century in North America and Western Europe, popular song publishing was built around a sheet-music trade aimed at home performers. In the United States during the 1890s, organizers of the variety entertainment known as vaudeville and theatrical producers increasingly consolidated their offices in New York City, which had already become the center of the music publishing business. Located first on West 28th Street in Manhattan and then moving uptown (eventually to the neighborhood between West 42nd and West 56th Streets), the area where the publishers set up shop became known as "Tin Pan Alley," a name that would later stand for the kind of songs created there. In the close connection between the stage and the publishing trade, both the vaudeville circuit and the Broadway show relied on Tin Pan Alley songwriters for their music; in turn, the stage, with its national circuits of theaters and touring attractions, popularized and circulated this music among customers who enjoyed listening to, singing, and playing it.

The decade of the 1890s dawned on a popular music scene dominated by Victorian-style ballads and waltz songs composed by European American songwriters such as Charles K. Harris, Paul Dresser, and Harry von Tilzer. Before the decade was over, however, a vigorous new style created by African American musicians called ragtime was introduced. Both types of song (as well as others) persisted through the years 1900–20, each developing in its own way. The classically trained Broadway composer Jerome Kern brought a cosmopolitan harmonic and melodic richness to the first type. As for ragtime, in the hands of the self-taught Russian immigrant songwriter Irving Berlin, rhythm and exuberance came to stand less for ethnic difference than for social liberation, especially as expressed in such new dances as the grizzly bear and the turkey trot. Songs from Tin Pan Alley (and from Broadway, its higher-toned relative) were heard live on stages and in

1

other entertainment venues across the country and overseas and on phonograph records and player-piano rolls, as well as in performances conducted at home.[1]

It is fitting that the first entry in this anthology is authored by Charles Hamm, a pioneering figure in the study of the popular music of the United States.[2] Hamm's work on Irving Berlin (1888–1989) stands as the definitive scholarly treatment of this major figure in American music, and the following excerpt from his book on Berlin illustrates well the turn-of-the-century milieu in which Berlin came of age and entered the music business. Hamm's account stresses the importance of ethnic identities—Jewish American, Irish American, African American, and others—in forging a Tin Pan Alley style that was perceived as distinctly "American" both within the United States and around the world; in Hamm's words, Berlin's songs "encode or reflect or perpetuate or shape or empower . . . the culture and values of this complex community." Other passages in this excerpt emphasize important distinctions in the way authorship functions in this type of popular music compared to classical music. Many of Berlin's songs were collaborations, not only with other songwriters, but with arrangers and "musical secretaries" who could transcribe his ideas into musical notation for him. And while Hamm describes the primacy of sheet music at this time for the circulation of commercial music, a medium that makes songs appear similar in formal terms, he stresses how the apparent standardized quality of these songs also enables a great deal of flexibility in performance, allowing the song to be rearticulated in a multitude of different contexts and genres. Differences in performance, in turn, strongly affect the reception and meaning of the songs.[3]

Irving Berlin and the Crucible of God
Charles Hamm

What little we know of his early life has been pieced together from scattered official documentation, journalistic coverage of his activities, an early biography by his

---

1. For more, see Richard Crawford, *America's Music Life: A History* (New York: Norton, 2001); and Alec Wilder, *American Popular Song: The Great Innovators, 1900–1950* (New York: Oxford University Press, 1972).

2. See Charles Hamm, *Yesterdays: Popular Song in America* (New York: W. W. Norton, 1979); idem., *Music in the New World* (New York: W. W. Norton, 1983); and idem., *Putting Popular Music in Its Place* (Cambridge, UK: Cambridge University Press, 1995).

3. For a fascinating case study of how performance affects genre, see Hamm, "Genre, Performance, and Ideology in the Early Songs of Irving Berlin," in *Putting Popular Music in Its Place,* pp. 370–80.

Source: IRVING BERLIN: SONGS FROM MELTING POT: THE FORMATIVE YEARS, 1907–1914 by Charles Hamm (1997): Extracts totaling 3700 words (pp. vi-viii, ix-x, 5, 7–8, 9, 11, & 12–18) © 1996 by Charles Hamm "By permission of Oxford University Press, USA"

friend Alexander Woollcott, the lyrics and music of his earliest songs, and general information about life and culture in the Lower East Side.* Born Israel Baline in Tumen in Western Siberia on 11 May 1888,† the youngest of the eight children of a cantor, Moses Baline, and his wife, Leah (Lipkin), he had come with his parents and five of his siblings to the New World, arriving in New York aboard the SS *Rhynland* on 13 September 1893. The family found temporary lodging in a basement apartment on Monroe Street in Manhattan's Lower East Side, then settled at 330 Cherry Street, in the southeastern corner of the Jewish quarter, in a flat that remained the family home until 1913.

The father was able to find only part-time employment, as a kosher poultry inspector and a manual laborer, and, as in so many immigrant families, everyone in the Baline household was expected to contribute to the family income. The mother became a midwife, three of the daughters found irregular employment wrapping cigars, the oldest son, Benjamin, worked in a sweatshop,‡ and young Israel peddled newspaper and junk in the streets while attending public school and receiving religious instruction at a *cheder*. With the death of the father in 1901, matters became even more difficult for the family, and Israel decided to strike out on his own:

> [Berlin] knew that he contributed less than the least of his sisters and that skeptical eyes were being turned on him as his legs lengthened and his earning power remained the same. He was sick with a sense of his own worthlessness. He was a misfit and he knew it and he suffered intolerably. Finally, in a miserable retreat from reproaches unspoken, he cleared out one evening after supper, vaguely bent on fending for himself or starving if he failed. In the idiom of his neighborhood, where the phenomenon was not uncommon, he went on the bum.§

Faced with the necessity of supporting himself, the fourteen-year-old Israel fell back on his one obvious talent: singing. According to Woollcott, he was paid for singing popular songs on Saturday nights at MacAlear's Bar, not far from Cherry Street, was hired briefly in the chorus of the road company for *The Show Girl*, which had opened in New York on 5 May 1902, and briefly plugged songs from the balcony at Tony Pastor's Music Hall. Most of the time, however, he was one of the company of buskers who, having learned the latest hit songs brought out by Tin Pan Alley publishers, "would appear in the bar-rooms and dance-halls of the Bowery and, in the words of Master Balieff, 'sink sat sonks' until the patrons wept and showered down the pennies they had vaguely intended for investment in more beer."¶

Early in 1904, Izzy, as he was now called, found a more secure position as a singing waiter at the Pelham Café, a saloon and dance hall at 12 Pell Street in Chinatown

---

*Alexander Woollcott, *The Story of Irving Berlin* (New York: Putnam, 1925). Later biographies include Michael Freedland, *Irving Berlin* (New York: Stein & Day, 1974) and *A Salute to Irving Berlin* (London: W. H. Allen, 1986); Ian Whitcomb, *Irving Berlin and Ragtime America* (London: Century Hutchinson, 1987); and Laurence Bergreen, *As Thousands Cheer: The Life of Irving Berlin* (New York: Viking, 1991). See also Charles Hamm, "Irving Berlin's Early Songs As Biographical Documents," *Musical Quarterly* 77/1 (Spring 1993): 10–34 and Vince Motto, *The Irving Berlin Catalog, Sheet Music Exchange* 6, no. 5 (October 1988) and 8, no. 1 (February 1990).

†According to research conducted recently by Berlin's daughters. See Mary Ellin Barrett, *Irving Berlin: A Daughter's Memoir* (New York: Simon & Schuster, 1994), pp. 98–99.

‡Bergreen, *As Thousands Cheer*, p. 11.

§Woollcott, *The Story of Irving Berlin*, p. 21.

¶Ibid., p. 27.

that was owned and operated by Mike Salter, a Russian Jewish immigrant whose dark complexion had earned him the nickname Nigger Mike. Salter capitalized on the location of his establishment in this sordid quarter to attract tourists, college students, and other "slummers" looking for vicarious thrills in the bowels of the city. In truth, though, "the sightseers usually outnumbered the local talent [at the Pelham], and the grand folk who journeyed eagerly from Fifth Avenue to Nigger Mike's seeking glimpses of the seamy side of life were usually in the predicament of those American tourists who retreat to some quaint village in France or Spain only to find its narrow streets clogged with not strikingly picturesque visitors from Red Bank, N.J., Utica, N.Y., and Kansas City, Mo."*

Izzy served drinks to the patrons of the Pelham Café and also entertained them by singing for coins tossed his way, specializing in "blue" parodies of hit songs of the day to the delight of both regular customers and tourists. In his free time he taught himself to play the piano, an instrument available to him for the first time in his life at the Pelham, and tried his hand at songwriting, his first attempt being "Marie From Sunny Italy," written in collaboration with the Pelham's resident pianist, Mike Nicholson. For reasons never fully explained, he chose to identify himself in the published sheet music of that first song as Irving Berlin, a name that he retained for the rest of his life.

His way with lyrics came to the attention of representatives of the popular music industry, who supplied him with the latest songs. Max Winslow, for instance, a staff member of the Harry Von Tilzer Company, came often to the Pelham to hear Izzy and was so taken with his talent that he attempted to place him in that publishing firm. As Von Tilzer described the episode in his unpublished autobiography:

> Max Winslow came to me and said, "I have discovered a great kid, I would like to see you write some songs with." Max raved about him so much that I said, "Who is he?" He said a boy down on the east side by the name of Irving Berlin. . . . I said, "Max, How can I write with him, you know I have got the best lyric writers in the country?" But Max would not stop boosting Berlin to me, and I want to say right here that Berlin can attribute a great deal of his success to Max Winslow. Max brought Berlin into my office one day shortly afterwards, and we shook hands, and I told him that I was glad to meet him and also said, "You have got a great booster in Winslow." Berlin told me that he had a song that he had written with Al Piantadosi and said he would like to have me hear it. I said I would be glad to hear it.†

Even though Von Tilzer agreed to publish the song, "Just Like The Rose," he didn't offer Berlin a position on his staff.

In 1908 Berlin took a better-paying position at a saloon in the Union Square neighborhood run by Jimmy Kelly, a one-time boxer who had been a bouncer at the Pelham, and moved into an apartment in the area with Max Winslow. Collaboration with such established songwriters as Edgar Leslie, Ted Snyder, Al Piantadosi, and George Whiting strengthened his ties with Tin Pan Alley, and in 1909, the year of the premiere of Zangwill's *The Melting-Pot*, he took a position as staff lyricist at the Ted Snyder Company. . . .

Even though Berlin had left home as a teenager to pursue a life unimaginable to his parents and their peers, he retained close ties with his family, as well as with their community of immigrant Eastern European Jews. When he was the featured performer at Hammerstein's vaudeville house in the fall of 1911, as the wealthy and world-famous writer of "Alexander's Ragtime Band" and dozens of other songs, the

---

*Ibid., pp. 49–50.

†Unpublished typescript, "Story of Harry Von Tilzer's Career," Library of Congress, p. 123.

New York *Telegraph* for 8 October reported that "a delegation of two hundred of his friends from the pent and huddled East Side appeared . . . to see 'their boy,' as one man among them expressed it, when he stopped the show long enough to tell the audience that 'Berlin was our boy when he wasn't known to Broadway, and he had never forgotten his pals during his success—and he is still our boy.'" The account goes on to say that "all the little writer could do was to finger the buttons on his coat and tears ran down his cheeks—in a vaudeville house!" In addition, according to the *Telegraph*, "the home [on Cherry Street] is envied by all who are invited into it from the original neighborhood where Berlin first saw the light. There his mother and sisters enjoy the benefits—all of them—of his first years' royalties." In 1913 he moved his mother into a new home at 834 Beck Street in the Bronx, in what was then a much more fashionable neighborhood, and on opening night of his first musical show, *Watch Your Step*, he shared his box at the New Amsterdam Theatre with his mother and his sisters.

In addition to maintaining his ties to his own community, Berlin was very much a part of New York City's radically multicultural milieu, which encompassed, in addition to his own group, Jews who had been in the United States for several generations; other recent immigrants to the New World from such places as Italy, Sicily, Portugal, and Turkey; Irish, Germans, and Scandinavians who had come over a generation or two ago; Americans of British heritage who had a much longer history in the United States and who had largely shaped the nation's political, educational, and cultural life; and some blacks, who were still very much on the fringes of American society. . . . Berlin had personal and professional association with many people outside his own ethnic group: Chuck Connors, a friend and protector during his early days in Chinatown; his first collaborator, Mike Nicholson; Edgar Leslie, born in Stamford, Connecticut, and a graduate of the Cooper Union; the Irish-American George M. Cohan and the Dublin-born Victor Herbert, who became mentors and friends. He associated as freely as was possible at the time with such black musicians as Eubie Blake. And he fell in love with and married Dorothy Goetz, a Catholic, and some years after her tragic early death married another Catholic.

Berlin, then, was a product of the multiethnic and predominantly immigrant/first-generation community of turn-of-the-century New York City, of which the Jewish enclave of Manhattan's Lower East Side was merely one component. His early songs, like those of his peers on Tin Pan Alley, encode or reflect or perpetuate or shape or empower—depending on how one views the social function of popular music—the culture and values of this complex community.

Remarkably, though, despite their regional origin and character, Tin Pan Alley songs came to be accepted far beyond the community in and for which they had been created. A parallel suggests itself. At exactly the same time, a quite different community, this one of African Americans, was forging its own body of popular music, created for and performed within its home community at first but eventually finding favor elsewhere as well. This music was jazz, and its acceptance by people outside its home community, like that of Tin Pan Alley song, seems to be explainable by this observation: Although it retained important aspects of the character and the distinctive musical style of the people who created it, it also accommodated and assimilated enough external aspects of America's older and more dominant culture to make it easily accessible to those outside the community as well.

Creation, Collaboration and Originality

. . . Writing a Tin Pan Alley song was both a complex and a corporate process. As Berlin described his own working method, he would begin with an idea for "either a title or a phrase or a melody, and hum it out to something definite. . . . I am working on songs all of the time, at home and outside and in the office. I gather ideas, and then I usually work them out between eight o'clock at night and five in the morning."* He would jot down lyrics as they came to him, on whatever material was at hand; some of his unpublished lyrics are written on scraps of paper or on hotel or business stationery, and others were typed out by a staff member of his publishing house.

In the next stage, words and music would be worked out more fully in collaboration with another songwriter and/or an arranger. Berlin's first biographer describes the genesis of Berlin's first song, "Marie From Sunny Italy":

> It was agreed that [Berlin and Mike Nicholson] must publish a song. Nick, of course, would invent the tune and [Berlin] must write the words, for which, they said, he had a knack because he was already famous in Chinatown for the amusing if seldom printable travesties he improvised as the new songs found their way downtown. . . .
>
> This masterpiece was wrought with great groaning and infinite travail of the spirit. Its rhymes, which filled the young lyricist with the warm glow of authorship, were achieved day by day and committed nervously to stray bits of paper. Much of it had to be doctored by Nick, with considerable experimenting at the piano and a consequent displeasure felt by the patrons at Nigger Mike's who would express their feelings by hurling the damp beer cloths at the singer's head. Truly it might be said that Berlin's first song was wrought while he dodged the clouts of his outraged neighbors.
>
> Finally the thing was done and then the two stared blankly at the bleak fact that neither of them knew how to record their work. Nick could read sheet music after a fashion but he had no notion how to reverse the process. . . . [W]hen the song was finally transcribed, the work was done by a young violinist who shall remain unidentified in this narrative because he has since clothed himself in the grandeur of a Russian name and betaken himself to the concert platform with the air of a virtuoso just off the boat from Paris.
>
> Next the masterpiece was borne with shaking knees to Tin Pan Alley, where it was promptly accepted by Joseph Stern for publication.[†]

Some songwriters were primarily lyricists, writing texts to which more musically adept collaborators added music, and at the beginning of his career Berlin was considered to be one of these. . . .

Berlin wrote both words and music for almost two thirds of his early songs, and in later years it became the exception for him to collaborate with another songwriter. He described the advantages of being both lyricist and composer this way:

> Nearly all other writers work in teams, one writing the music and the other the words. They either are forced to fit some one's words to their music or some one's music to their words. Latitude—which begets novelty—is denied them, and in consequence both lyrics and melody suffer. Writing both words and music I can compose them together and make them fit. I sacrifice one for the other. If I have a melody I want to use, I plug away at the lyrics until I make them fit the best parts of my music and vice versa.*

Even when Berlin was writing both words and music for a song, he was still engaged in collaboration. Like other songwriters of the day, he depended on someone else to take down his tunes in musical notation and to work out details of the

---

*Quoted in Bergreen, *As Thousands Cheer: The Life of Irving Berlin* (New York: Penguin, 1990), pp. 57–58.

†Alexander Woollcott, *The Story of Irving Berlin* (New York: Putnam), pp. 65–68.

Green Book Magazine (February 1915) cited in Bergreen, *As Thousands Cheer: The Life of Irving Berlin*, pp. 55–56.

piano accompaniment; as he put it, "when I have completed a song and memorized it, I dictate it to an arranger."[†] Though he has often been criticized for this, it was in fact standard procedure for Tin Pan Alley songwriters, even those fluent in musical notation, from Charles K. Harris on. . . .

The point of this discussion of the Tin Pan Alley mode of song production is not merely to justify the inclusion in the Berlin canon of pieces written by him in collaboration with others but, more important, to underline that the creation of a popular song is a vastly different process from the composition of a classical piece. And the difference between popular and classical music extends far beyond the mechanical details of how a new piece within each genre comes into being to such issues as the concept of "originality" and the relationship of music and its composers to the community for which it is created. . . .

The Material Form of Tin Pan Alley Songs

Tin Pan Alley songs were disseminated primarily in the material form of published sheet music. Production of such a piece began with its collaborative oral creation and its subsequent capture in musical notation, as described earlier, after which the song was sent off to be engraved. . . .

In their material form as published sheet music, Berlin's early songs appear to exhibit a high degree of uniformity, among themselves and also in relation to pieces by other songwriters. Structurally, virtually every one of them is made up of the same component parts:

1. a brief piano introduction, drawn usually from the final bars of the chorus or the beginning of the verse
2. a two- or four-bar vamp, with melodic and rhythmic material drawn from and leading into the verse
3. two (or sometimes more) verses, usually sixteen or thirty-two bars in length, depending on the meter of the song
4. a chorus, usually equal in length to the verse, with first and second endings. The first ending indicates a repeat of the chorus; the second gives instructions for either a da capo return to the introduction or a dal segno return to the vamp

The songs also appear to be quite uniform in melodic, harmonic, and rhythmic style. Texts are set in a predominantly syllabic fashion, to mostly diatonic tunes confined to a vocal range of an octave or less, with an occasional chromatic passing note. Harmonies are tonal and triadic, shaped into two- or four-bar phrases, with secondary dominants and other chromatic chords sometimes lending variety. Modulation may lead to another key for a phrase or two, and from early on Berlin had a mannerism of abruptly shifting a phrase to a key a third away from the tonic, without modulation.[*]

Most of what has been written about Berlin's early songs takes this sheet music as the primary (and often only) text, and most recent performances of these pieces are more or less literal readings from this text. But the songs were rarely performed just as they appear on the printed page. A literal reading from the sheet music results in a performance shaped as follows:

[†]*Green Book Magazine* (February 1915), cited in Bergreen, *As Thousands Cheer*, p. 57.

[*]For a general discussion of the musical style of these songs, see Hamm, *Irving Berlin: Early Songs*, vol. 1, pp. xxv–xxviii.

- piano introduction
- vamp
- first verse
- chorus with first ending
- repeat of chorus, with second ending
- vamp
- second verse
- chorus with first ending
- repeat of chorus, with second ending

But we know from period recordings and other evidence that this sequence was subject to change in performance. Only the first verse might be sung, or additional verses not found in the sheet music might be added. The chorus might be sung only once after each verse, "catch" lines of text might be interpolated into the second chorus, or there might be a completely different set of lyrics, not found in the sheet music, for the second chorus. The singer might alter notes in the melody or deliver the entire song in a semispoken way without precise pitches. The accompaniment might take over for a half or a full chorus without the singer(s), the instrumental introduction might be repeated after the last chorus, or the song might end with a coda not found in the sheet music. . . .

The problem with taking the notated form of these songs as the primary text, then, is that, unlike compositions of the classical repertory, which throughout the modern era were assumed to be "ideal objects with an immutable and unshifting 'real' meaning,"[†] a popular song may be "rearticulated" in any given performance.[‡] In other words, "dissemination of [a popular song] as printed sheet music was only the beginning of its history; it then became fair game for performers, who according to the conventions of the genre were free to transform [it] in details of rhythm, harmony, melody, instrumentation, words, and even overall intent."[§]

Throughout its history, popular music has been marked by the extraordinary flexibility with which its text has been treated by performers, and also by the variety of meanings that listeners have perceived in these songs. Stephen Foster's "Old Folks At Home" was sung by amateurs clustered around pianos in private parlors, performed on the minstrel stage in blackface, sung on the concert stage by famous performers of the classical repertory, interpolated into stage versions of *Uncle Tom's Cabin*, sung around campfires by groups of Civil War soldiers of both sides, reworked into elaborate display pieces for virtuoso pianists and trumpet players, paraphrased in classical compositions by Charles Ives and others, and quoted in Irving Berlin's "Alexander's Ragtime Band." In each instance, the overall shape, stylistic details, and the performance medium were different, as was the meaning of the song for its performers and listeners.[*]

[†]Carl Dahlhaus, *Foundations of Music History*, trans. J. B. Robinson (Cambridge: Cambridge University Press, 1983), p. 150.

[‡]See Richard Middleton, *Studying Popular Music* (Milton Keynes & Philadelphia: Open University Press, 1990), particularly pp. 16–32.

[§]Charles Hamm, review of *The Music of Stephen C. Foster: A Critical Edition*, ed. Steven Saunders and Deane L. Root, *Journal of the American Musicological Society* 45, no. 3 (1992): 525–26.

[*]For a book-length discussion of the varied and changing meanings of Foster's songs, see William Austin, *"Susanna," "Jeanie," and "The Old Folks at Home": The Songs of Stephen C. Foster from His Time to Ours* (New York: Macmillan, 1975).

Further Reading

Crawford, Richard. *America's Music Life: A History*. New York: W. W. Norton, 2001.

Furia, Philip. *America's Songs: The Stories behind the Songs of Broadway, Hollywood, and Tin Pan Alley*. New York: Routledge, 2007.

Hamm, Charles. *Yesterdays: Popular Song in America*. New York: W. W. Norton, 1979.

_____. *Putting Popular Music in Its Place*. Cambridge, UK: Cambridge University Press, 1995.

Jablonski, Edward. *Irving Berlin: American Troubadour*. New York: Henry Holt, 1999.

Sheed, Wilfrid. *The House that George Built: With a Little Help from Irving, Cole, and a Crew of About Fifty*. New York: Random House, 2007.

Van Vechten, Carl. "The Great American Composer." *Vanity Fair*, April 1917.

Wilder, Alec. *American Popular Song: The Great Innovators, 1900–1950*. New York: Oxford University Press, 1972.

Discography

Fitzgerald, Ella. *Ella Fitzgerald Sings the Irving Berlin Songbook, Vol. 1*. Polygram Records, 1990.

Irving Berlin: A Hundred Years. Sony, 1990.

The Melody Lingers On: 25 Songs of Irving Berlin. ASV Living Era, 1997.

Songs of Irving Berlin. Castle Pulse, 2004.

2. Technology, the Dawn of Modern Popular Music, and the "King of Jazz"

Prior to the 1920s, popular music in the United States mainly circulated as sheet music and in what we would now call live performance. The introduction of new technology in the 1920s for music consumers began a process that revolutionized the industry, leading to a shift from musical re-creation, featuring performances of sheet music in the home, to an emphasis on listening to recordings or broadcast performances. Record players and discs had become standardized enough by this time to permit several companies to produce compatible equipment on a mass scale. Radio broadcasting of music developed during the decade to become a popular source of domestic entertainment.

The music industry developed a classification system that affected what types of music were recorded and how they were distributed. A "popular" category emerged, in contrast to "classical" or "serious" music, that catered primarily to bourgeois, white, literate residents of urban areas. This category included music from dance bands (which began to be called "jazz" during this decade), as well as recordings of solo singers that ranged in style from vaudeville (Al Jolson, Sophie Tucker), to "crooning" (Gene Austin, Rudy Vallee), to torch singing (Helen Morgan, Libby Holman).

While the story of jazz as an autonomous history is not the central concern of this book, a few moments during which jazz and popular music intersected do warrant inclusion. From the early 1920s through the mid-1940s, the two categories were often synonymous. The decade of the 1920s is often referred to as the "Jazz Age"; however, the most popular music of the era—the music played by the high-society orchestras of Paul Whiteman (the "King of Jazz," 1890–1967) and Guy Lombardo, which is sometimes known as "syncopated dance music"—bears little resemblance to what contemporary listeners (or authors of jazz history books) would now recognize as jazz.[1] In the following excerpt from Whiteman's 1926 autobiography, the "King of Jazz" discusses his early recording career. Of particular interest is his discussion of the importance of keeping abreast of ever-changing dance fads and how the mysterious alchemy of the change in popular style occurs, fueled as it is by countless anonymous contributors. In his playful, self-deprecating writing style, Whiteman also describes the particular challenges of early "acoustic" recording and how changes in technology affected both the instrumentation heard on his recordings and the permanent makeup of his performing forces. Like many autobiographies by celebrity popular musicians, Whiteman and McBride assume an audience of fans who will associate the prose style with the public persona of the bandleader, which was, in this case, unassuming to

---

1. But for surveys that do not exclude this music, see Gunther Schuller, *The Swing Era: The Development of Jazz, 1930–1945* (New York: Oxford University Press, 1989), 632–769; and Michael Campbell, *And the Beat Goes On: An Introduction to Popular Music in America, 1840 to Today* (New York: Schirmer Books, 1996). For an examination of the eclectic repertoires (which often included "syncopated dance music") of bands that were later canonized as jazz pioneers, see Jeffrey Magee, "Before Louis: When Fletcher Henderson Was the 'Paul Whiteman of the Race,'" *American Music* 18, no. 4 (Winter 2000): 391–425.

say the least. Later denizens of dance music may be amused to hear of Whiteman's innovation in that area.

On Wax

Paul Whiteman and Mary Margaret McBride

When our first records came down from the laboratories of the Victor Company for their initial "audition," a visitor exploded, "What the dickens?"

Then he listened to a few bars—he was an experienced listener—and demanded: "Who is it?"

The one step was dying a natural death and in that death was becoming apotheosized into the fox trot. But our first record was different from either. Perhaps dancers in America who are old enough will remember it. It was a twelve-inch disc, the first I think of the dance variety ever made that size, and there was a one step on one side of it arranged from the "Dance of the Hours." On the other, was the legally immortalized "Avalon" which gave occupation for a time to the copyright lawyers of two continents under the theory that it had been plagiarized from "La Tosca." This was one of the greatest fox trots of the late "glide" period.

The companion record was that masterpiece of dance composition "The Japanese Sandman," ranking with the earlier "Havanola," which Rudolph Gans had had scored by the composer and played by the St. Louis Symphony Orchestra as an example of American music. The even more popular "Whispering" was on the other side.

For years before we began to record, it had been necessary for almost all recording laboratories to change the instrumentation of nearly all orchestral pieces. Certain instruments, notably the double basses, which were then used, the horn, the tympani, and in lesser degree, other instruments, failed to yield satisfactory results. The double basses frequently were discarded and replaced by a single tuba. Modifications also in the placing of the orchestra were necessary in order to make the volume of tone from a large number of instruments converge upon a tiny diaphragm whose vibrating needle inscribed, upon a disc of wax, the mysterious grooves, which, retraced by a second needle attached to a second diaphragm, gave back the voices and accents of music.

So for all our labor and study, we had to go into the recording room and learn all over. One of the changes we made when we found that ordinary drums could not be put on the record was to use the banjo as a tune drum. The tympani and snare drum record, but the regular drum creates a muddy and fuzzed-up effect when other music is going, although solo drums make very good records. It was at this time that I tried out the banjo for the ground rhythm and discovered the possibilities of that small instrument which until then had been kept in the back and hardly heard at all. We also discovered that almost every instrument has a treacherous or bad note and that when the score calls for that note the instrument had better stop playing. An extreme dissonance would mean that the record would be blasted. For all our troubles, however, we were told that fewer changes

Source: "On Wax," in Paul Whiteman and Mary Margaret McBride, (New York: *Jazz*, J. H. Sears & Company, 1926), 223–31.

had to be made in our scoring than in any dance records of the time. As a rule we made two records at a time, though once I believe we made nine in three days. Each record averages about an hour and a half or two hours, for there must first be a rehearsal and a test before the perfect record is passed upon by the company "hearing committee."

Recording is perhaps the most difficult task in the day's work—or the life-time's. A slip may pass unnoticed in concert, whether across the footlights or over the radio, and even if noticed, it may be forgiven, since living flesh and sensitive will cannot always achieve mechanical perfection. But a slip in a record after a time becomes the most audible thing in it. Everything else will be neglected to wait for the slip and to call the attention of someone else uninstructed in music to a great artist's false note. So every composition has to be recorded until it is perfect. If things go fine from the first, well and good; but if, from the three records of each number usually made, there is none which will quite pass the exacting standards of the committee, there must be another afternoon of making and remaking. Every faculty of the artist, emotional as well as physical, must be expended in producing a perfect result.

In late recording practice, with highly improved methods of capturing sound and with new scientific principles, it has grown more and more practicable to record large bodies of instruments without losing volume, without having a large quantity of tone dilute and diffuse itself before reaching the actual path of the recording apparatus.

In the laboratory, as we worked, the possibilities of the orchestra began to loom large and the original plan with a single player for each type of instrument began to expand. The saxophone, for instance, had always had a shadow or understudy. A third saxophone now was added and in time the orchestra developed the full Wagnerian quartette of instruments in this group. The one trumpet was reinforced by a second and the now popular combination "straight" and "comedy" trumpets came into existence. The banjo instead of just marking time began to make new excur-sions into the realms of rhythm and the fox trot began to change without, however, disturbing the pedestrian order of things.

Not all these changes took place, of course, in the laboratory. Most of the rehearsing and discussing and rescoring was done in consultations outside—consultations not always free of the heat of argument. The actual business of record-ing is a star chamber matter but it is no violation of a secret to admit that some of our early records were spoiled by men swearing softly at themselves before they learned the new adroitness which the delicate mechanism of the recording room required.

The records of our orchestra that I have liked particularly are fox trots like the "Song of India," with its burst of two part harmony, the "Waters of the Minnetonka," with its wood wind accompanimental figure and its swinging climax and the insidi-ously delicate "Oh, Joseph."

One sees all one's friends and some of one's enemies at the recording laborato-ries and the exchange of experience between the classicist and "coonshouter," the string quartette and the clarinet jazz band is illuminating for everybody.

Not long ago, Rosa Ponselle, Mischa Elman and I were all recording at the Victor, though in different laboratories. We had lunch together and regardless of the fact that the temperature was above 90, the great dramatic soprano demon-strated a dance step for us in the best Broadway style. Then we sat for our pictures, she in her bungalow apron, Elman minus collar and coat and I in plus four knick-erbockers.

It interested me that the singer should have been familiar with the current fox trot step, for with the almost weekly changes in the dance I had begun to believe that only orchestra leaders and college boys could possibly keep pace. We have even to anticipate the change and that has become our chief problem as the public is well aware. Dancers and musicians, as a rule, are harder to bring together than the various labor unions working on a big building. Ballroom dancers persistently refuse to conform to accepted or classical styles, or to any styles which they do not determine for themselves in the ballrooms of the hour. Any study of the long list of our fox trots will reveal peculiarities in tempo, rhythm and general style not to be accounted for on the basis of "individual variation," or the time-honored principle that "nature makes no two faces alike"; the simple truth of the matter is, that a dance, almost, is no sooner in the hands of the public than the style changes.

During the past half-dozen years there have been several powerfully marked variations in the ordinary, or "two-step" fox trot. The original "glide two-step" fox trot of the "Japanese Sandman" period soon was succeeded by the "radio roll" or the "scandal walk" (the two passed into one another) by the "blues," which was officially earlier but in point of fact later in the experience of many dancers than the "collegiate," which set up an entirely new style of dancing and called for an entirely new type of music. The "tango fox trot" prevailed in a few cities, the "military fox trot," and entirely local dances with fanciful, and in some cases meaningless, names, in others.

All of these changes of style or local and individual caprices in taste, have to be ministered to by a dance organization as large as ours, or we soon perish. Few new dances, except those for stage use, are ever brought forward by teachers; they are developed, in public, by persons of no particular skill, and with little or no knowledge of the dance as an art. It is avowed, and on excellent authority, that the "collegiate" sprang from the use of rubber-soled summer footwear and slow, sticky dance floors at public resorts, where the skate-like slides and pivots of the old-style dancer were impossible. With footwear of this sort it was possible to do little else than stamp up and down. From this developed a polka-like dance with crude hops and jumps, calling for agility, but with no great degree of sophisticated grace.

Small items like this determine the whole power of survival of an orchestra. When a method crystallizes or a dance is standardized, it is done. For the younger generation everywhere who invented it, without half knowing most of the time what they were about, are now through with it.

One phenomenon I noted when I was playing dance music at the Palais Royal on Broadway. A fox trot was played in a rhythm exactly that of the Habanera or Tango, but much swifter in time. The result was that the easy "chasse" skips peculiar to this type of dance became impossible to the dancers who thereby changed their rhythm from that of the tango to the easier two-step with the result that six hundred fox-trotters—not all of whom could be charged with profound musical knowledge—automatically were dancing in cross rhythm.

Further Reading

Campbell, Michael. *And the Beat Goes On: An Introduction to Popular Music in America, 1840 to Today*. New York: Schirmer Books, 1996.

Hamm, Charles. *Yesterdays: Popular Song in America*. New York: W. W. Norton, 1979.

Magee, Jeffrey. "Before Louis: When Fletcher Henderson Was the 'Paul Whiteman of the Race,'" *American Music* 18, no. 4 (Winter 2000): 391–425.

Schuller, Gunther. *Early Jazz: Its Roots and Musical Development*. New York: Oxford University Press, 1968.

Discography

Austin, Gene. *Voice of the Southland*. ASV/Living Era, 1997.
Etting, Ruth, and Helen Morgan. *More Than You Know*. Encore, 1996.
Holman, Libby. *Scandalous: Something to Remember Her By*. Jasmine, 2005.
Jolson, Al. *Best Of*. Universal Music Group, 2001.
Whiteman, Paul. *Greatest Hits*. Collector's Choice Music, 1998.
_____. *King of Jazz*. ASV/Living Era, 1996.

3. Big Band Swing Music
RACE AND POWER IN THE MUSIC BUSINESS

The music most canonized as jazz during the 1920s—the small, hot combos led by Louis Armstrong and the ragtime-influenced compositions of Jelly Roll Morton—was largely the province of African American listeners and white jazz connoisseurs and did not find a mass audience. This situation changed radically in the 1930s, when popular music and what is now heard as "real jazz" began to be closely intertwined. The period from the mid-1930s through the early 1940s is commonly referred to as "The Swing Era" or "The Big Band Era," named after the large ensembles that proliferated at that time and the type of jazz they played ("swing"). The two entries included here examine the racial politics of the Swing Era, demonstrating that contemporary writers were aware of how music that had initially been made largely by and for African Americans had been popularized mainly by white bandleaders.[1]

---

1. Both articles are discussed in Scott DeVeaux's excellent examination of the transformation of swing into bebop, *The Birth of Bebop: A Social and Musical History* (Berkeley: University of California Press, 1997).

Marvin Freedman's article appeared in *Down Beat,* one of the first publications in the United States to cater to jazz connoisseurs. Freedman discusses the distinction between "sweet" bands (e.g., Guy Lombardo, Sammy Kaye) and those that play a "hotter" type of "swinging" jazz (Count Basie, Duke Ellington, Benny Goodman, Artie Shaw). His valuation of black musicians over white ones may seem to counter common stereotypes about white superiority, yet some stereotypes are still at work in his article: Freedman identifies black musicians with the body and natural spontaneity, while he identifies whites with the mind, calculation, and "femininity" (after all, as he writes, "even college girls" like white swing bands, such as Jimmy Dorsey's). His history of the relationship between race and the ability to play jazz is overly simple at best: few would now agree that white musicians dominated jazz during the years 1927–31, though several of the greatest white jazz musicians produced fine music during that period. Clearly, Freedman recognizes that the relationship between race and musical style is important in jazz, but he never distinguishes whether these differences are social or biological, thus leading to a kind of stereotyping that modern cultural theorists might describe as "essentialist" (the notion that "black music" consists of a fixed repertoire of stylistic elements that is transmitted genetically), although he does state that a musician does not have to be black to sound black. The article is valuable in that it shows how public awareness of the racial politics of popular music is not necessarily of recent provenance. Freedman may have been one of the first white writers to recognize so explicitly how white musicians learn from and admire black musicians.

Black Music's on Top; White Jazz Stagnant
Marvin Freedman

Any good scientist will tell you there's no difference between the blood of a Negro and the blood of a white man. But you can still tell the color of a jazz musician by listening to the music he plays. There may be a lot of greys in between, but it's a long way from black to white.

The history of American music has been the story of two great conflicts. One of them, the fight between commercial dance music and jazz is all over. Some Guerilla warfare is going on, but the sweet corn has taken the Siegfried, Maginot, and Mannerheim lines. The other great fight, between white and black, is still in progress. Now, a good fight is worth any cause. So long as it's strictly man to man, and nixy on the brass knucks. There's conflict *inside* music. In classical music you call

Source: "Black Music's on Top; White Jazz Stagnant," Marvin Freedman. Courtesy of the *Downbeat* Archives.

it counterpoint. In American music you call it swing. The soloist swinging against the rhythm section is battling it so as not to get sucked into an "on beat" Busse solo. The rhythm section is shoving the soloist to prevent him from pulling them into a Joe Daniels "military" rhythm. A sweet band can't play music, because everyone in the sweet band is docilely going in the same direction with everyone else. You can't build musical structure by merely swelling your volume. There's got to be a conflict, swing, counterpoint. That's what's good about a jam session, an old fashioned "carving" session. Everyone fights everyone to give out or to give up—then you produce your best music. The fight between black and white is good because it keeps both sides on their toes.

Bix and Tesch Whites

Now, don't get the idea that white or black is just a difference in the color of the musician. It's a difference in the music itself. White jazz is colder, cleaner, more conscious; black music is richer, looser, more relaxed. Beiderbecke and Teschemacher were probably the whitest; Armstrong, Bechet, Hawkins probably the blackest. I can't tell you the difference. You either know it or you don't.

Right now, it's black on top, and white isn't climbing. Sure, there are a lot of white men playing jazz, but are they playing white or black? And when they play white is it good white?

Count Basie's band is the strongest influence in jazz. When Shaw's band beat out Goodman's, it did so by playing Basie music—weakened and commercialized Basie, but still the same black Kansas City style. Glenn Miller's band would probably fall off the stand if it heard itself swing a note, but it's getting by as a swing band, and it's black music again—Count Basie diluted some more. Charlie Barnet's band is as black a band as you'll ever hear, and that band is one of the idols of the growing white musicians. Ask Barnet if he doesn't think white men can swing only by imitating blacks.

Crosby "Canadian Capers"

There's no white vitality anywhere in jazz. Glen Gray stayed white, and stopped playing jazz. Crosby sounds like Canadian Capers except when it imitates black New Orleans style. Dorsey wears Lord Fauntleroy pants, and even college girls like his style. Goodman imitates Basie, or imitates the Goodman of five years ago, or doesn't swing. James wishes he was Louis Armstrong or Joe Smith. Is the great Teagarden as good as he used to be? Why does a fine old timer like Fud Livingston need a Stanley? Have the last 10 years done Krupa any good?

The white Chicagoans, Pee-Wee Russell, Freeman, Kaminsky, Joe Sullivan, Condon, are walking in the footprints they made 10 years ago. At their best they're almost as good as they were then. Spanier plays as well or better than ever, but the only thing white about his music is the color of the face behind the horn.

Meanwhile, men like Basie, Hawkins, Hines, Hampton are still going forward and upward. Not all the time, but every now and then a great colored musician comes out with something new that knocks you over. Louis Armstrong isn't trying any more, but every time you listen to him you'll come away with at least one new idea. Lionel Hampton is twice as good as he was five years ago. Chu Berry, Teddy Bunn, Frankie Newton, Al Morgan, Benny Carter, Cozy Cole—they're all growing.

Even old timers like Jelly Roll Morton and Sidney Bechet come out and put some of the finest jazz of all time on wax.

Harry James Plays Black Music

When young white musicians want to encourage themselves, they listen to black music. When a white arranger wants ideas he listens to Basie or Lunceford or Redman. In the last year or so you hear white musicians say that they've got to play like colored musicians, or their music doesn't swing. Even a great musician like Harry James forsakes the white cause, and carries out the ideas of colored musicians.

It wasn't always black music. A dozen years ago, white jazz was on top. The hottest music came from white men in Chicago. Teschemacher was probably the hottest musician alive. Bud Freeman was starting out, and full of energy, as were Krupa, Condon, Sullivan. Young musicians were getting their kicks from white music. From about 1927 until as late as 1931–32 (when Bix and Tesch died), colored musicians imitated the white style. And you can prove that by listening to Fletcher Henderson records of those times. White music was so far in front that bands like Red Nichols', playing pure white style, were tremendously popular. The public liked white jazz so much that even men like Whiteman let their men play some good jazz.

Goodman Took Up the Fight

Unfortunately for the white cause, they have no reserves. When Bix and Tesch died that took all of the strength out of white music. The white Chicagoans remained good (or great), but none of them had the necessary genius to lead a whole musical style. As white music got worse, the public and musicians discarded it. Goodman's band in about 1935 took up the fight again, and squeezed out some good white jazz. It wasn't enough, however, and I've told you the rest.

Maybe it doesn't matter. Music is music, black or white. But maybe it does. If Bix and Tesch had lived and if white music had developed (or if it develops anyway), it might have gotten (or it might get) better than Bix or Teschemacher, Louis, or any of them have done. Maybe white jazz could even conquer commercial dance music and Tin Pan Alley.

> Irving Kolodin's article touches on issues similar to those discussed by Freedman, framing them with an in-depth description of the network of live performances (frequently played in hotel ballrooms), radio broadcasts, and recordings that sustained the big bands at the apex of their success. By sticking to the different treatment received by black and white musicians, rather than trying to theorize why they sound different, Kolodin avoids some of the problems with stereotypes that haunt Freedman. The tone of the article was undoubtedly influenced by its inclusion in *Harper's*, a general-interest magazine, rather than one directed toward jazz fans, such as *Down Beat*. The article thus has more of the quality of a "human-interest" story in contrast to Freedman's essay, which conveys the passion of a fan participating in an ongoing debate.

The Dance Band Business: A Study in Black and White
Irving Kolodin

Those with a finger on the pulse of this capricious industry have an amazing instinct for estimating the moment when a band is truly "hot," in a sense unrelated to the kind of music it plays. It is at such a moment, when sales of records suddenly swing upward, and a fan club is started in Baton Rouge, and another leader tries to buy off the hitherto obscure arranger who has given the band its distinctive personality, and radio agents file requests for the band to audition, and even Winchell[2] recommends its performance, that a shrewd booker realizes that the time is at hand to tour the band on as long a series of one-nighters as the men can endure. In two months of the early summer of 1937 the Goodman band played a sequence of dates that carried it from New York to California and never found the band in the same town for two days. The Goodman share was nearly $90,000 in two months during what could hardly be called a boom period. How quickly (and mysteriously) a band can find itself in such a category is illustrated by the career of Glenn Miller. As recently as New Year's Day of 1939 Miller was playing an engagement (at union scale, or about $1,050 a week for the entire organization) at the Paradise Restaurant in New York, humbled to second billing below the clownish group known as Freddie "Schnickelfritz" Fisher and his orchestra. For purposes of economy Miller pared his band to thirteen dispensing with a guitar player—in this profession almost a confession of bankruptcy. In the few months that followed Miller played one-night engagements for as little as $400.

During the dismal stand at the Paradise, however, Miller had made a disk of his signature music which he called "Moonlight Serenade." It embodied a curious blending of reed instruments, in which two clarinets played the melody in unison with the saxophones, but an octave higher. And from this record, and the amazing vacillations of popular enthusiasms, Miller's rise may be traced. An engagement at Dailey's Meadowbrook during the late spring of the same year tested out Miller's new style, and through radio sustaining time,[3] impressed it on a wide public. When his manager told him, during the summer of 1939, that the band would never sell for less than $700 for a one-nighter thenceforth, Miller told him he was a dreamer with a perverted sense of humor.

But less than a year later Miller's band played two successive dates to a total of 13,000 people. On one night, in St. Louis, they drew 5,400; and on the following night, in Kansas City, Missouri, they broke every record (including the inaccurate ones) for attendance at such a public, unsponsored dance by attracting 7,800 people to the Kansas City Convention Hall. Miller received $4,680 for his night's work. "It's an inspiring sight," he recalls, "to look down from the balcony on the heads of 7,000 people swaying on a dance floor—especially when you are getting $600 for every thousand of them." Concurrently, Miller held a contract for three fifteen-minute broadcasts a week for Chesterfield, which brought him a quarter of a million dollars

---

2. Walter Winchell, famous theater and music critic based in New York City.

3. "Sustaining time": late-night radio broadcasts paid for by the hotel from which the performance originated rather than by the radio network.

in the first year and has recently been renewed for a second; and he was negotiating a contract for a moving picture (now in production) with $100,000 as the band's fee for eight weeks' work. It is not likely that Miller will ever use his Social Security card.

Now perhaps you can see why a band leader who has won his way to a second and a third engagement in a prominent New York hotel is rarely overjoyed with his situation. He is spending the hours from seven to two each night to earn a sum which will not cover his expenses; he is also aware that someone else might come along to take the money out of a territory he is eager to play before his popularity wanes. It might be someone as little known to the general public as Glenn Miller was at the Paradise when Goodman was blowing his clarinet in the Empire Room of the Waldorf. In this business the public does not merely want to be entertained—it wants to be entertained by a succession of new personalities, with a different instrument prominent in this year's "sensational" band than in the one they were ecstatic about the year before.

That it is possible to write a survey of this kind with no more than historic reference to the names of Paul Whiteman, Vincent Lopez, Fred Waring, Ted Lewis, Rudy Vallee, and other celebrities of the so-called Jazz Age is evidence that they have, substantially, been passed by. However, by less than the exalted standards of their highest popularity, they are not faring so badly. Waring, for example, very likely earns nearly as much now as he ever did, playing a series of brief, almost daily broadcasts for a cigarette company. Lopez still makes theater and dance-hall appearances and derives as well a moderate income from one of the lesser weekly radio shows. Vallee's radio career is momentarily in suspension, but his recent radio activities have had practically nothing to do with music anyhow. Lewis is still a person of consequence in the hinterlands, cavorting as ever with clarinet and silk hat, moaning "Is Everybody Happy?" and employing good musicians with traditional shrewdness. However, the infrequency of his appearances in New York is not altogether involuntary; what he has to offer now he is showman enough to realize is not for sophisticates. As for Whiteman, who has made the most eager effort to adapt himself to the new mode in music, he was last heard from in Florida (after a lapse from public prominence due to illness), organizing a new band, principally for radio work.

It is rather more curious that another group of names has been even less conspicuous in this inquiry, for it embraces musicians who are in no sense moribund, and very much a part of the contemporary jazz picture. It is a list which begins with the name of Duke Ellington, and continues with those of "Count" Basie, Jimmy [Jimmie] Lunceford, Louis Armstrong, Fletcher Henderson, Ella Fitzgerald, Cab Calloway, Teddy Wilson, Andy Kirk, John Kirby, Coleman Hawkins, Erskine Hawkins, Lionel Hampton, Roy Eldridge, and sundry others. They are names with a familiar echo even to a public unfamiliar with this subject; but they are almost never to be encountered in a prominent hotel, and never on a commercial radio program.

They are of course all Negro musicians—and rigorously excluded, as if by Congressional decree, from these two principal sources of prestige and financial reward. Thus, though each enjoys a serious repute among students of jazz music, and substantial income from records and theater engagements and dance-hall appearances, they can never hope to equal the fabulous earnings of Goodman, Shaw, or Glenn Miller. Nor can the working musicians in their bands hope to attain the degree of public prominence which Gene Krupa enjoyed when he received $500 a week from Benny Goodman.

A few Northern hotels have made an exception occasionally for a particular band—Duke Ellington has played in the Panther Room of the Hotel Sherman in Chicago several times, and the Ritz-Carlton in Boston has been hospitable to both Elling-ton and Basie. More recently, the Pump Room of the Ambassador East in Chicago has opened its doors to Teddy Wilson, John Kirby, and "Fats" Waller, of the glib piano and raucous voice, but this is a minor room in the hotel, with little social réclame.

The single effort of a New York hotel to take advantage of the undeniable popu-larity of Negro swing bands was so surrounded by compromises that it collapsed quickly under the burden of its own un-certainty. It was the roof-top Cocoanut Grove of the Park Central Hotel, which placed its premises at the disposal of the late "Chick" Webb and Ella Fitzgerald when the latter was still the "A-tisket A-tasket" girl two years ago. Instead of letting the band perform as it was accustomed to, the manage-ment encouraged a kind of exhibitionism which had a disastrous effect on the playing of the musicians. There was so much "Jim Crow" in the air, together with the kind of antics which the white public believes to be inseparable from the colored man's expression of his immortal soul, that the musicians were humiliated, the knowing public repelled, and the engagement a failure.

Considering the stratagems which a hotel manager will employ to attract busi-ness to his establishment, this avoidance of such established attractions as Ellington, Basie, Armstrong, Lunceford, and Calloway can only be regarded as pathological. There is a legend that the transient trade of the large "commercial" hotels in New York includes many persons from the South, and that they would be offended to find them-selves in a dining room where the musicians were colored. But the Goodman Trio and Quartet (with its Negro virtuosi Wilson, Hampton, and Christian) were ecstatically applauded when they appeared in the Empire Room of the Waldorf-Astoria though they were identified, somewhat disingenuously, as "special entertainers."

It is simply an exaggerated prejudice which no hotel manager has the enterprise to challenge or the courage to disregard. When one is driven to such a decision by such straits as influenced Weitman to experiment with bands at the Paramount it is probable that a vogue of Negro orchestras in hotels will ensue.

However the outlook is not too hopeful. Even a colored guest star on a dance band's radio commercial may bring angry mutterings from the South and one which regularly employs such musicians may write off, in advance, any hope of sales appeal in Georgia, Louisiana, and Mississippi.

If the swing fever is not what it was in 1938–39, there is still a substantial public for the orchestras which play music with precision and drive, life and flexibility—the qualities which were all but unknown in the dance music of commerce in the middle twenties and early thirties. The trend-followers and sensation-seekers who made of swing (and themselves) a public nuisance three years ago have gone on to some new enthusiasm. The youngsters who grew up with swing are sufficiently sure of their liking not to require the exhibitionistic simulation of it which made their older broth-ers and sisters subjects for the psychologists. Moreover, an increasingly large number of adults through the country have found swing and swing musicians an absorbing phase of general musical interest and will continue to be diverted by it regardless of its fate as a social phenomenon. Benny Goodman, Artie Shaw, Jack Teagarden, the Dorseys, Duke Ellington, and the rest continue to be important people in their lives.

Further Reading

DeVeaux, Scott. *The Birth of Bebop: A Social and Musical History*. Berkeley: University of California Press, 1997.
Hentoff, Nat. *At the Jazz Band Ball: Sixty Years on the Jazz Scene*. Berkeley: University of Cali-fornia Press, 2010.

Schuller, Gunther. *The Swing Era: The Development of Jazz 1930–1945*. New York: Oxford University Press, 1989.

Sheed, Wilfrid. *The House that George Built: With a Little Help from Irving, Cole, and a Crew of about Fifty*. New York: Random House, 2007.

Discography

An Anthology of Big Band Swing (1930–1955). Verve, 1993.

Basie, Count. *The Complete Decca Recordings*. GRP, 1997.

The Best of the Big Bands. Compendia, 1995.

Ellington, Duke. *Masterpieces: 1926–1949*. Proper, 2001.

Shaw, Artie. *Greatest Hits*. RCA/Victor, 1996.

4. Solo Pop Singers and New Forms of Fandom

Bing Crosby (1903–77), the most successful solo singer of the pre–rock 'n' roll era, skillfully combined many of the distinctive qualities of the preceding generation of popular singers: the energy and rhythmic vivaciousness of Al Jolson, the use of new amplification technology to project the sensitivity of crooners like Rudy Vallee, and the spontaneity and swing of Louis Armstrong. Crosby succeeded in all the media available to him at that time—records, radio, movies—to become the first international multimedia superstar. While he had first achieved prominence with Paul Whiteman's band in the late 1920s, Crosby was best known as a solo performer during the 1930s and 1940s, recording with studio orchestras (or occasionally smaller ensembles that had more in common with jazz groups), singing and acting in movies, and hosting his own network radio show. The only other star who could possibly rival him in the 1930s was Fred Astaire, who had an extraordinarily successful career as a dancer, actor, and singer. During World War II, a number of factors led to solo singers gradually supplanting the supremacy of big bands: the recording ban of 1943, the expense of operating a large band, the decrease in demand for dancing, and the increasing demand for sentimentality as the war progressed. The newfound dominance of solo singers also contributed to the increasing separation between popular music and jazz as solo singers relied less on swinging rhythm, improvisation, and blues tonality.

Frank Sinatra (1915–1998) began his career singing for big bands, first with Harry James, then, more notably, with Tommy Dorsey. Sinatra became one of the most popular big band singers during his stint with the Tommy Dorsey band, but it was not until he left the Dorsey band late in 1942 that he became a mass cultural phenomenon. Audiences and critics of the time understood him as a counterweight to Bing Crosby, as a singer formed by the musical styles of the thirties rather than the twenties (as with Crosby), Sinatra's musical (and cultural) sensibilities were more in tune with swing, and endeared him to a younger audience. So fervent was the response to Sinatra the solo singer that his popularity instigated one of the first known cases of sociological and psychological inquiries into popular music. These fans, known as "bobby soxers" were young, barely adolescent girls who represented a type of intense identification with popular music that became more common with the advent of the "teenager" (not yet a marketing category in the early 1940s) and rock 'n' roll. In the short first-person account that follows, Martha Weinman Lear recounts her experience as an archetypal bobby-soxer at a Sinatra show in Boston in the mid-1940s.[1]

The Bobby Sox Have Wilted, but the Memory Remains Fresh
Martha Weinman Lear

Ah, Frankie everlovin', here we are at the Garden dancing cheek to cheek and the lights are low and it's oh so sweet. We haven't been this close since the old days when I played hookey from school to come see you in the RKO-Boston. You remember me, don't you? I was the one in the bobby sox.

Lord, what that man meant to me. If you didn't go through it, you wouldn't believe it. Look at him now, what do you see? A paunch, a jowl, a toupee. What could have driven me so crazy—the cuff links? But no, in the beginning he was no sartorial splendor. Suits hung oddly on him. Suits with impossible shoulders jutting like angle irons from that frail frame. He used to make jokes about hanging on the microphone for support, Bob Hope–type jokes, badly delivered, which we found adorable. He had cabbage ears and the biggest damned Adam's apple you ever saw. It wobbled like a crow's when he sang. The voice was delicious, the phrasing superb. But listen, what did I know about phrasing? Those cabbage ears could

---

1. For a series of scholarly essays on Sinatra, see Stanislao G. Pugliese (ed.), *History, Identity, and Italian American Culture* (New York: Palgrave, 2004); particularly germane to these excerpts is the essay by Janice L. Booker, "Why the Bobby Soxers?," in *ibid.*, 73–81.

have been pure tin and it wouldn't have made any difference, not to me. So what drove me so crazy?

Sinatra at Madison Square Garden, last night and tonight, and I am a thirteen-year-old again, packing my peanut-butter sandwiches off to the RKO-Boston to shriek and swoon through four shows live, along with several thousand other demented teen-agers, while he crooned to some princess who wasn't even in the house. "Frankie!" we screamed from the balcony, because you couldn't get an orchestra seat unless you were standing on line at dawn, and how could you explain to Mom leaving for school before dawn? "Frankie, I *love you!*" And that glorious shouldered spaghetti strand way down there in the spotlight would croon on serenely, giving us a quick little flick of a smile or, as a special bonus, a sidelong tremor of the lower lip. I used to bring binoculars just to watch that lower lip. And then, the other thing: The voice had that *trick*, you know, that funny little sliding, skimming slur that it would do coming off the end of a note. It drove us bonkers. My friend Harold Schonberg, the *Times*'s music critic, says that it must have been what is called *portamento*, although he can't swear to it, he says, because he's never heard Sinatra sing. Elitist. Anyway, whatever it's called, it was an invitation to hysteria. He'd give us that little slur—"All . . . or nothing at *aallll* . . ."—and we'd start swooning all over the place, in the aisles, on each other's shoulders, in the arms of cops, poor bewildered men in blue. It was like pressing a button. It *was* pressing a button.

We loved to swoon. Back from the RKO-Boston, we would gather behind locked bedroom doors, in rooms where rosebud wallpaper was plastered over with pictures of The Voice, to practice swooning. We would take off our saddle shoes, put on his records and stand around groaning for a while. Then the song would end and we would all fall down on the floor. We would do that for an hour or so, and then, before going home for supper, we would forge the notes from our parents: "Please excuse Martha's absence from school yesterday as she was sick . . ."

We were sick, all right. Crazy. The sociologists were out there in force in those mid-forties, speculating about the dynamics of mass hysteria, blathering on about how his yearning vulnerability appealed to our mother instincts. What yo-yo's. Whatever he stirred beneath our barely budding breasts, it wasn't motherly. And the boys knew that and that was why none of them liked him, none except the phrasing aficionados. In school they mocked us, collapsing into each others' arms and shrieking in falsetto: "Oh-h-h, Frankie, I'm fainting I'm *fainting*." The hell with them. Croon, swoon, moon, spoon, June, Nancy with the Smiling Face, all those sweeteners notwithstanding, the thing we had going with Frankie was *sexy*. It was exciting. It was terrific.

I don't remember exactly when it stopped being terrific, but by the end of the decade he was bombing. His voice went bad. He sang terrible songs—he sang "Mairsy Doats," and on one record he barked like a dog, and I wept for the glory of the empire—and in movies he was developing into the loser incarnate, a bumpkin sailor boy who got to say dumb lines and kept losing Kathryn Grayson to somebody else. I mean, it was *over*. And so was his marriage to Nancy, and he was chasing around after Ava Gardner, whom he later (briefly) married, and in news photos there they were, Gardner gorgeous and Sinatra with a silly little mustache on his face; Beauty and the Schlep.

The comeback that began with his winning of an Oscar for *From Here to Eternity*, in 1953, must still stand as the most fantastic comeback in show-business history, because he really *had* been reduced to total schlephood, not only professionally, which we can forgive, but in the personal image, which we usually cannot. And to come back from that kind of rock-bottom takes—what? an extraordinary self-discipline. I suppose. What clicked in that head, what lights went on? All of a sudden the little loser was coming on like a bigger winner than we or he had ever dreamed, the voice sounding great and the man coming on cool, arrogant, exuberant, extravagant, *powerful*—the Swinger, *Il Padrone*, Chairman of the Board, all that business, with his pinkie rings flashing and his cuffs splendidly shot and his women and his starched $100 bills at the gambling tables in Las Vegas, with his own Rat Pack and his own Clan, his own court jesters, all those Dinos and Sammys and Joeys, his own myth in his own time. And even if only a fraction of it were true, what a myth!

And we were all grown up and our swoons were memories, but I tell you, the gravity was as powerful as ever. I remember, and still blush to remember, going to an opening night party that the film producer Norman Lear (a relative of mine by marriage), gave when *Come Blow Your Horn* opened here in New York City in the early sixties. I was standing around talking to some people, all adult and cool, right? when my husband came over and said, "Sinatra's just come in." *Wham!* A child again, beguiled again, zooming backward through time and space and I stood there shaking like a thirteen-year-old, hands clasped *tight* behind my back and wailing, "No, I *can't*." (And didn't.) "*What would I say to him?*" Oh, well. He probably wouldn't have remembered me, anyway.

A few years later, it started getting . . . seamy. Tacky. With the henchmen and the talk of mob connections, the mean-mouthed confrontations with the press, the public degrading of women, the spectacle of baggey-eyed, boozed-up, middle-aged men trying to make it New Year's Eve forever: We're gonna have fun if it *kills* us. The Kennedy White House, into whose Camelot he had drifted for a time, dropped him. The Clan faded, maybe of age. His third marriage, to nymphet Mia Farrow, broke up. A lifelong Democrat, he got chummy with Reagan and then, good grief, with Agnew. Not that it was hard to understand: two boys who had made it from nowhere, and possibly each longed for the other's brand of power. The gossip columns told us that his Palm Springs house was filled now with the good burghers of the Beverly Hills Establishment, with the Brissons, the Goetzes, people like that; just plain suburban folk.

But listen: The punch was still there. I can't explain it, but it was still there. It was just two years ago that the prominent portrait painter Aaron Shickler got a business call from Sinatra's office. His wife, Pete, answered the phone. Wait a minute, a voice at the other end said, we have Mr. Sinatra on the line. And, as Mrs. Shickler tells it, she damn near died. Her hand was unsteady, her breath came heavy. And then he said, "Hello," and here was this woman, mature, poised, veteran of a thousand cocktail-party ripostes—but she was one of us, you see, she had swooned at the Paramount when I was swooning at the RKO-Boston, and that is something you never quite get over—and what she said, her lips fluttering like wings around the mouthpiece, was this: "Oh, my goodness," she said, "It sounds *just like you*."

What I mean is, it's Ol' Blue Eyes, now, at fifty-nine, with the paunch and the jowl and the wig, and the hell with them. The blue eyes still burn, the cuffs are still incomparably shot, the style, the *style*, is still all there, and what's left of the voice still gets to me like no other voice, and it always will. Hey, out there in Boston. Hey, Rudi Litman, Therese O'Reilly, Nettie Holzman, Lillie Lefkovitz, and all the rest of that old RKO-Boston gang of mine: Are you listening? Could you swoon?

Further Reading

Crosby, Bing (as told to Pete Martin). *Call Me Lucky*. New York: Da Capo Press, 1953.

Fuchs, Jeanne, and Ruth Prigozy, eds. *Frank Sinatra: The Man, the Music, the Legend*. Rochester, N.Y.: University of Rochester Press, 2007.

Giddins, Gary. *Bing Crosby: A Pocketful of Dreams*. Boston: Little, Brown, 2001.

Keightley, Keir. "Music for Middlebrows: Defining the Easy Listening Era (1946–1966)," *American Music* (Fall 2008): 309–35.

Pugliese, Stanislao G. *Frank Sinatra: History, Identity, and Italian American Culture*. New York: Palgrave Macmillan, 2004.

Ulanov, Barry. *The Incredible Crosby*. New York: Whittlesey House, 1948.

Discography

Astaire, Fred. *The Essential Fred Astaire*. Sony Music, 2003.
Crosby, Bing. *Bing! His Legendary Years, 1931 to 1957*. MCA, 1993.
Jolson, Al. *Best Of*. Universal Music Group, 2001.
Sinatra, Frank. *A Voice in Time: 1939–1952*. Sony, 2007.
_____. *Sinatra Reprise: The Very Good Years*. Warner Bros., 1991.
_____. *The Capitol Years*. Capitol, 1990.
Vallée, Rudy. *The Vagabond Lover*. Pro Arte, 1993.

5. Hillbilly and Race Music

In addition to the category of popular music, during the 1920s the music industry developed categories for music that catered to African Americans and rural white Americans, dubbed "race" and "hillbilly," respectively. This article on the beginnings of these two latter categories appeared in *Collier's* in 1938. The faint tone of condescension found here would continue for many years in mainstream writing about these musics.[1] Astonishment mixed with condescension as writers conveyed their surprise at the success of musicians originating outside the ambit of New York's professional music circuit. Not discussed in this article is the phenomenon of the "Latin tinge" that crept into mainstream popular music during this time via novelty numbers such as Don Azpiazu's 1930 hit "El Manisero (The Peanut Vendor)."[2] The author does, however, mention in passing other ethnic sources of variety for the mainstream, such as "Calypso people in the West Indies, [and] the Cajuns of Louisiana."

---

1. "Hillbilly" did not become the predominant term until the 1930s. In the 1920s, the music industry tended to use "old-time tunes." A discussion of an assortment of bemused articles about "hillbilly" music may be found in David Brackett, *Interpreting Popular Music* (Berkeley: University of California Press, [1995] 2000), 101–05.

2. For more on the Latin tinge in American popular music, see John Storm Roberts, *The Latin Tinge: The Impact of Latin American Music on the United States*, 2nd ed. (New York: Oxford University Press, [1979] 1999).

Thar's Gold in Them Hillbillies
Kyle Crichton

The young man with the Adam's apple seemed out of place in a New York elevator. Very definitely he was not a New Yorker and in addition he was not welcome in the crowded car because he carried under his arm a case that looked like a rough box for a horse.

"Will y'all pahdon me?" he said plaintively. "Ah'm havin' some trouble with this here git-tar."

He carried the trouble with him when he got off at the eleventh floor and was presently in a room before a microphone having an audition for phonograph records. He said, with some hesitation, that he would do imitations of Jimmie Rodgers and started in a thin wailing voice to do Blue Yodel, No. 1, which has for its theme: "T for Texas, T for Tennessee and T for Thelma." It seemed that Thelma had made a bum out of somebody and was to receive a bullet from a .44 through her middle—"just for to see her jump and fall."

This was the rare thing of a New York audition for hillbilly songs and race records. The general practice is to take a recording outfit into the territory where such songs grow and out of this endeavor have come such classics as The Wreck of Old 97, Floyd Collins in the Cave, Little Old Log Cabin in the Lane, The Old Hen Cackles and The Rooster's Goin' ta Crow, Crazy Blues, Jimmie Rodgers and his Blue Yodels (Nos. 1 to 12), That Thing Called Love, Just Because, Deep Elam Blues, The Prisoner's Song, Comin' Round the Mountain, Hand Me Down My Walkin' Cane, Casey Jones, Twenty-one Years, and hundreds of others.

South of a point that might roughly be regarded as St. Albans, West Virginia, the grapevine system of news distribution still beats anything known to modern science. A hint from New York that David Kapp of Decca or Eli Oberstein of Victor is headed South will find the tidings flying over mountains and the result will be that when the city slickers arrive they will be unable to get into their hotels for the presence of mouth organ virtuosos, yodelers, blues singers and specialty bands equipped with instruments made up of tissue paper on combs, washboards, assorted saws and rutabaga gourds.

If there needs to be another picture at this point, the camera can leap agilely to such distant parts of South African and Australia where the native bushmen are busily humming a little number written by Jimmie Davis of Shreveport, Louisiana, and entitled Nobody's Darling but Mine. In short, no matter what the citizens of the United States think about their native songs, the world ranks the hillbilly ballads among the folk-tune wonders of the universe.

It started back in 1921 when Ralph S. Peer was with Okeh records. Sophie Tucker had agreed to do You Can't Keep a Good Man Down but it was found at the last moment that another contract prevented her from working for Okeh. In this crisis Perry Bradford, who was a colored song plugger for W. C. Handy (St. Louis Blues, Memphis Blues, etc.), informed Mr. Peer that he could furnish a girl who was as good as Sophie. She turned out to be Mamie Smith, a colored girl who was working as [sic] cleaning woman in a theatre. She made the Good Man song, and for the other side of the record did That Thing Called Love. Mamie had a loud raucous voice and there was great difficulty with recordings in that day of poor equipment, but the Okeh people knew they had something when the record sold 75,000 copies the first month.

Source: "Thar's Gold in Them Hillbillies," Kyle Crichton, *Collier's* (April 30, 1938), pp. 26–27.

Mamie was forthwith yanked back into the studio and this time she brought with her a horrendous five-piece band known as Mamie Smith's Jazz Hounds. They made Crazy Blues and It's Right Here for You.

A Market Nobody Thought Of

Bert Williams, the colored comedian, had been making records for Columbia for many years but the companies never imagined that the Negroes themselves might be a market for Negro records. In fact, the companies carefully hid the fact that colored singers were being used. About this time, dealers in New York began to report a curious trend in the business. It seemed that Negro Pullman porters on trains going South invariably left New York with as many as twenty-five records apiece under their arms. Since the records cost one dollar each, the business was big stuff and Mr. Peer went South to investigate. He found (a) that the Negroes were buying records of their own people in great quantities and (b) that the Negroes of Richmond, Virginia, invariably referred to themselves as The Race.

"We had records by all foreign groups," says Mr. Peer. "German records, Swedish records, Polish records, but we were afraid to advertise Negro records. So I listed them in the catalogue as 'race' records and they are still known as that."

About this time the vogue of Mamie Smith at Okeh was swamped by the arrival of the great Bessie Smith on Columbia records. Bessie Smith has now become almost a legendary figure and her records have lately been reissued in a new form and are considered classics in blues singing by the experts. Her most famous was Gold Coast Blues, which originally sold into the millions. It may be remarked that at the present day a sale of 100,000 records is held to be sensational in any field.

With Bessie Smith being so successful, Okeh was under the necessity of digging up a new sensation, and Mr. Peer took a portable recording outfit to Atlanta and began looking around. For some reason Atlanta is the worst town in the South for Negro talent (then and now), and Mr. Peer was soon stumped. At the suggestion of a local dealer who guaranteed to sell enough records to cover the cost, he did a few recordings by Fiddler John Carson, a white mountaineer who arrived for the recordings in overalls. Old John had been a ballyhoo man with a circus, had a repertory of hillbilly songs that never ended, and he could sing a bit with his fiddling. He made Little Old Log Cabin in the Lane, and The Old Hen Cackles and The Rooster's Goin' ta Crow.

"It was so bad that we didn't even put a serial number on the records, thinking that when the local dealer got his supply, that would be the end of it," says Mr. Peer. "We sent him 1,000 records, which he received on a Thursday. That night he called New York on the phone and ordered 5,000 more sent by express and 10,000 by freight. When the national sale got to 500,000, we were so ashamed we had Fiddler John come up to New York and do a re-recording of the numbers."

The matter of the name arose again in this connection. It was obviously impossible to list them under the designation of each section (mountaineer, "Georgia Cracker," etc.) and Mr. Peer, who had come from Kansas City and was well acquainted with the Ozarks, named them hillbilly records. The result is that the word has come to have a general application, and mountaineers of all sections are now known as hillbillies.

The greatest success of all time was made by The Prisoner's Song, which was introduced almost as an afterthought by Vernon Dalhart, who had done The Wreck of Old 97 and was desperate for something for the other side of the record. It eventually sold 2,500,000 records for the Victor company. It cost the company seven cents to make the record (all expenses included) and the wholesale price they received was thirty-seven cents a record.

The Singing Brakeman

The greatest of all romances in the hillbilly business centers about Jimmie Rodgers, the little railroad brakeman who fought desperately against poverty and the ravages of tuberculosis until Mr. Peer discovered him in Bristol, Tennessee, and started him on a career that was fabulous even in the phonograph industry. It is estimated that the Blue Yodel records sold over 5,000,000 copies. Jimmie Rodgers is now dead and his records do not have the fame with collectors that has come to those of Bessie Smith, but he has left a mark on all hillbilly music.

When David Kapp goes out to Dallas now for Decca to record hillbilly and race records, he will do as many as 325 selections in fifteen days. The big stars now are Jimmie Davis, clerk of the Criminal Court in Shreveport, Louisiana, and Gene Autry, the singing cowboy of the movies. Another favorite group is the Carter Family of Maces Springs, Virginia, who sing and play and make marvelous didos with such instruments as the guitar and autoharp, which is really a zither with keys.

The best colored singer since Bessie Smith is said to be Georgia White, and it is in this field that some of the most remarkable records are made. There are colored numbers so strictly African and special that nobody but a Negro could understand them or appreciate them. When Sleepy John Estes does his own Negro compositions, they seem to be in another language. The melodies are strange, the words are like something out of a voodoo chant and the manner of delivery is such that they make no sense whatever to the untrained white mind. The recordings by Petie [sic] Wheatstraw come in the same class, and when Kokomo Arnold does the "sebastapool" on his guitar, effects are made that seem unearthly.

Unless the artist is also the writer of his own material and hence shares in the royalty for composers, the rewards of recording are not great, being on an average of $25 a "side." The payment is outright and there is no bookkeeping.

Among the novelty records are those made by the Calypso people in the West Indies, the Cajuns of Louisiana and Corny Allen Greer and his band.

The loyalty of the hillbilly audience to its heroes can be seen in the titles of the songs. When Jimmie Davis wrote Nobody's Darling But Mine, he immediately made a sequel entitled An Answer to Nobody's Darling. That was followed by A Woman's Answer to Nobody's Darling. Bob and Joe Shelton, who also come from Shreveport, wrote Just Because in collaboration with Leon Chappalear. When it became a success, they followed *that* with Just Because III. It is quite possible that the thing could go on forever.

Students are convinced that Bessie Smith and particularly the players who accompanied Bessie Smith on her records have had a great part in stimulating that disease known as swing music, which has now gripped the nation. Bessie had such men doing her accompaniments as Louis Armstrong, Fletcher Henderson, Joe Smith, Fred Longshaw, Charlie Green and the late James P. Johnson, one of the most spectacular of the hot pianists. Musicians are the keenest people in the world at admiring new talent and just as Benny Goodman will sit goggle-eyed now listening to the "hotteties" of Count Basie, the colored demon of Kansas City, so did the orchestra leaders of ten years ago go insane over the berserk playing of Bessie Smith's boys. From that interest came the change in orchestra music that is now so pronounced in the work of Goodman, Tommy Dorsey, Glen Gray, Jimmy Dorsey and others.

The traditional folk songs of the Southern mountaineers and the spirituals have not been included in this discussion because they occupy a special position in the art of song. In the strictest sense the mountaineer ballads are old English folk songs, some of them even traceable to old Gregorian chants; and as such they are not strictly American products. New York was recently visited by the Rev. John William Dawson, pastor of the Dry Fork Primitive Baptist Church of Morehead, Kentucky, who sang Lord, Spare Me for Another Year and The Wayfaring Stranger. The words seemed to have grown out of local legends of the mountains but the tunes stemmed back to the earliest days of American history when the first settlers crossed from the old country. Most strictly in the American tradition are the songs of Aunt Molly Jackson of Harlan County, Kentucky, who has told the story of the labor struggles of that section. Her songs are richly evocative and thrilling, carrying the troubadour quality of old.

Fans Are Delighted

But it's when Sleepy John Estes on his guitar and Hammie Nix on his mouth organ get wound up that the newfound fans start yammering with delight. There are isolated groups in all sections of the world prepared to fight to the death to prove that Maxine Sullivan, from the Onyx Club, is a greater artist than Lily Pons. Miss Sullivan became the storm center of radio controversy as the first person to swing Loch Lomond and other old ballads. There are strange individuals who wouldn't give a Georgia White and Rhubarb Red (guitar) record for anything made by Caruso.

The cult of the hillbillies may be a passing fancy but it is significant that Ambrose, the swankiest orchestra conductor in London, has made an arrangement of Nobody's Darling But Mine. When the St. Louis Blues is made into a Metropolitan Opera, the truth will finally be evident. In the meanwhile, the nasal-voiced boys and girls of the hinterlands who have most curious things to say about love and My Gal Sal. There seems to be an awful lot of double-crossing done by the ladies in the "mountings," and they invariably pay for it. This makes art.

Further Reading

Lange, Jeffrey. *Smile When You Call Me a Hillbilly: Country Music's Struggle for Respectability, 1939–1954*. Athens: University of Georgia Press, 2004.
Malone, Bill C. *Country Music U.S.A.* 2nd rev. ed. Austin: University of Texas Press, 2002.
Miller, Karl Hagstrom. *Segregating Sound: Inventing Folk and Pop Music in the Age of Jim Crow*. Durham, N.C., and London: Duke University Press, 2010.
Roberts, John Storm. *The Latin Tinge: The Impact of Latin American Music on the United States*. 2nd ed. New York: Oxford University Press, 1999.
Russell, Tony. *Blacks, Whites, and Blues*. New York: Stein and Day Publishers, 1970.
Southern, Eileen. *The Music of Black Americans: A History*. 3rd ed. New York: W. W. Norton, 1997.

Discography

The Anthology of American Folk Music. Smithsonian Folkways, [1952] 1997.
Azpiazu, Don. *Don Azpiazu and His Havana Casino Orchestra*. Harlequin, 1994.
Great Race Record Labels Vols. 1–3. Windsong, 2000.
Rodgers, Jimmie. *The Singing Brakeman*. ASV/Living Era, 2006.
Roots N' Blues: Retrospective 1925–1950. Sony, 1992.

6. *Blues People* and the Classic Blues

As indicated in the preceding article, from the 1920s through the 1940s, the music industry classified most of the music made by and directed toward African Americans as "race music." Notwithstanding this practice of musical segregation, several notable African American bands were marketed in the "popular" category and broadcast on network radio shows; they included swing bands led by Duke Ellington, Count Basie, and Jimmie Lunceford, and some of the close harmony groups such as the Mills Brothers and the Ink Spots. The "race music" category, on the other hand, included blues, gospel tunes, piano boogie-woogies, small jazz groups, and the funkier swing bands unknown to the white public. During the 1920s, the category of race music also included types of music that would later not be closely associated with African Americans, such as music for jug bands and string bands.[1]

The name of the category itself, "race music," probably carried pejorative connotations to the executives who coined it, yet for African Americans during this period, it also carried positive meanings. In the Harlem Renaissance of the 1920s up through the 1940s, to be a "race man" was to be active in the fight for equal rights and the recognition of black achievement and ability; this designation was obviously not limited to the "Negroes of Richmond, Virginia" as implied by the previous article.

The previous article from *Collier's* also mentioned how the late 1920s witnessed the growing importance of newly composed gospel music in addition to secular music. Thomas Dorsey, a pianist and songwriter who had provided material and worked as an accompanist for Ma Rainey, began to write sacred material and to work with female singers such as Mahalia Jackson and Willie Mae Ford Smith.

---

1. For an excellent assortment of "race" and "hillbilly" recordings from the late 1920s, see the now-classic *Anthology of American Folk Music,* compiled by Harry Smith (Smithsonian Folkways Recordings, [1952] 1997). For a discussion of the diversity of traditions issued on race records, see Paul Oliver, *Songsters and Saints: Vocal Traditions on Race Records* (Cambridge, UK: Cambridge University Press, 1984). The usefulness of the term "race music" for understanding post-1940 forms of African American popular music is explored by Guthrie P. Ramsey, Jr., in *Race Music: Black Cultures from Bebop to Hip-Hop* (Berkeley: University of California Press, 2003).

Dorsey, known as the "Father of Gospel Music," was a major force in the development of modern gospel music and its rise to prominence in a network of African American Baptist churches across northern and midwestern cities. As gospel developed into an important component of the "race" records category, gospel quartets like the Golden Gate Quartet and the Five Blind Boys made successful recordings throughout the 1930s and 1940s. This style of gospel performance would play a major role in the development of "doo-wop" a capella singing, which would, in turn, play a major role in rhythm and blues, beginning in the late 1940s, and later in early rock 'n' roll. While sacred and secular music had been intertwined previously, the vitality of gospel music provided a major resource (and training ground) to which African American popular musicians continually returned.

Amiri Baraka, widely known as a poet, playwright, and associate of the Beat writers, wrote what was arguably the first social history of African American music in the early 1960s (when he was known as LeRoi Jones). His *Blues People* has been much debated, its theses argued and disputed, but Jones's strong views of his subject continue to encourage readers to focus on the political aspects of this history.[2] Baraka's account is valuable both for its perspective on the relationship between changing social conditions and the development of the classic blues and for his discussion of the historical linkages among classic blues, minstrelsy, and vaudeville. Many have argued that Baraka's views of the "whitening" of African American genres is overly simplistic and that his ideas about the connections between racial identity and musical style betray traces of essentialism.[3] He may also be faulted now for his use of the "reflection" theory between culture and art that posits a straightforward and direct relationship between social change and musical change, and others have challenged his scholarly assertions. Nonetheless, the passion and moral authority with which Jones asserts his analysis and the imaginative way in which he illuminates the aural manifestations of social forces all continue to make knowledge of this text invaluable for the student of American popular music.

2. The most famous rejoinder came from Ralph Ellison; see his "Blues People," in *Shadow and Act* (New York: Vintage Books, [1964] 1972), 247–58.

3. Baraka modified this notion himself with the development of the idea of black music as a "changing same." See Amiri Baraka, "The Changing Same (R&B and New Black Music)," in *Black Music* (New York: William Morrow, 1967), 180–211.

from Blues People: The Negro Experience in White America and the Music that Developed from It

LeRoi Jones

What has been called "classic blues" was the result of more diverse sociological and musical influences than any other kind of American Negro music called blues. Musically, classic blues showed the Negro singer's appropriation of a great many elements of popular American music, notably the music associated with popular theater or vaudeville. The instrumental music that accompanied classic blues also reflected this development, as it did the Negro musician's maturing awareness of a more instrumental style, possibly as a foil to be used with his naturally vocal style. Classic blues appeared in America at about the same time as ragtime, the most instrumental or nonvocal music to issue from Negro inspiration. Ragtime is also a music that is closely associated with the popular theater of the late nineteenth and early twentieth centuries. Although ragtime must be considered as a separate kind of music, borrowing more European elements than any other music commonly associated with Negroes, it contributed greatly to the development of Negro music from an almost purely vocal tradition to one that could begin to include the melodic and harmonic complexities of instrumental music.

Socially, classic blues and the instrumental styles that went with it represented the Negro's entrance into the world of professional entertainment and the assumption of the psychological imperatives that must accompany such a phenomenon. Blues was a music that arose from the needs of a group, although it was assumed that each man had his *own* blues and that he would sing them. As such, the music was private and personal, although the wandering country blues singers of earlier times had from time to time casual audiences who would sometimes respond with gifts of food, clothes, or even money. But again it was assumed that *anybody* could sing the blues. If someone had lived in this world into manhood, it was taken for granted that he had been given the content of his verses, and as I pointed out earlier, musical training was not a part of African tradition—music like any art was the result of natural inclination.[4] Given the deeply personal quality of blues-singing there could be no particular method for *learning* blues. As a verse form, it was the lyrics which were most important, and they issued from life. But classic blues took on a certain degree of professionalism. It was no longer strictly the group singing to ease their labors or the casual expression of personal deliberations on the world. It became a music that could be used to entertain others *formally.* The artisan, the professional blues singer, appeared; blues-singing no longer had to be merely a passionately felt avocation, it could now become a way of making a living. An external and sophisticated idea of performance had come to the blues, moving it past the casualness of the "folk" to the conditioned emotional gesture of the "public."

This professionalism came from the Negro theater: the black minstrel shows, traveling road shows, medicine shows, vaudeville shows, carnivals, and tiny circuses

---

4. This is an example of one of Baraka's assertions that would be hotly questioned by contemporary scholars.

all included blues singers and small or large bands. The Negro theater, in form, was modeled on the earlier white minstrel shows and traveling shows which played around America, especially in rural areas where there was no other formal entertainment. The Negro theater did not, of course, come into being until after the Civil War, but the minstrel show is traceable back to the beginning of the nineteenth century. White performers using blackface to do "imitations of Negro life" appeared in America around 1800, usually in solo performances. By the 1840's, however, blackface was the rage of the country, and there were minstrel shows from America traveling all over the world. It was at least thirty more years before there were groups of traveling entertainers who did not have to use burnt cork or greasepaint.

It is essential to realize that minstrelsy was an extremely important sociological phenomenon in America. The idea of white men imitating, or caricaturing, what they consider certain generic characteristics of the black man's life in America to entertain other white men is important if only because of the Negro's reaction to it. (And it is the Negro's *reaction to* America, first white and then black and white America, that I consider to have made him such a unique member of this society.)

The reasons for the existence of minstrelsy are important also because in considering them we find out even more about the way in which the white man's concept of the Negro changed and why it changed. This gradual change, no matter how it was manifested, makes a graph of the movement of the Negro through American society, and provides an historical context for the rest of my speculations.

I suppose the "childlike" qualities of the African must have always been amusing to the American. I mentioned before how the black man's penchant for the supernatural was held up for ridicule by his white captors, as were other characteristics of African culture. Also, I am certain that most white Americans never thought of the plight of the black man as tragic. Even the Christian Church justified slavery until well into the nineteenth century. The "darky" at his most human excursion into the mainstream of American society was a comic figure. The idea that somehow the slavery of the black man in America was a tragic situation did not occur to white Americans until the growth of the Abolition movement. But it is interesting that minstrelsy grew as the Abolition movement grew. I would say that as the "wild savage" took on more and more of what New England Humanists and church workers considered a human aspect, there was also more in his way of life that Americans found amusing. (And who has not laughed at the cork-faced "Negro" lawmakers in D. W. Griffiths' *Birth of a Nation?* It is a ridiculous situation, ignorant savages pretending they know as much as Southern senators.) As the image of the Negro in America was given more basic human qualities, e.g., the ability to feel pain, perhaps the only consistent way of justifying what had been done to him—now that he had reached what can be called a post-bestial stage—was to demonstrate the ridiculousness of his inability to act as a "normal" human being. American Negroes were much funnier than Africans. (And I hope that Negro "low" comedy persists even long after all the gangsters on television are named Smith and Brown.)

The white minstrel shows were, at their best, merely parodies of Negro life, though I do not think that the idea of "the parody" was always present. It was sufficiently amusing for a white man with a painted face to attempt to reproduce some easily identifiable characteristic of "the darky." There was room for artistic imprecision in a minstrel show because it wasn't so much the performance that was side-splitting as the very idea of the show itself: "Watch these Niggers." Among the typical "Negro" material performed by the white minstrels are these two songs which perhaps indicate the nature of the parody white minstrelsy proposed to make of Negro life:

The Traveling Coon

Once there was a traveling coon
Who was born in Tennessee.
He made his living stealing chickens
. . . And everything else he could see.
Well, he traveled and he was known for miles around,
And he didn't get enough, he didn't get enough,
Till the police shot him down.

The Voodoo Man

I've been hoodooed, hoodooed
Hoodooed by a negro voodoo;
I've been hoodooed, hoodooed,
Hoodooed by a big black coon.

A coon for me had a great infatuation;
Wanted for to marry me but had no situation.
When I refused, that coon he got wild.
Says he, "I'm bound for to hoodoo this child."

He went out and got a rabbit's foot and burned it with a frog
Right by the road where I had to pass along.
*Ever since that time my head's been wrong.**

The black minstrel shows were also what might be called parodies, or exaggerations, of certain aspects of Negro life in America. But in one sense the colored minstrel was poking fun at himself, and in another and probably more profound sense he was poking fun at the white man. The minstrel show was appropriated from the white man—the first Negro minstrels wore the "traditional" blackface over their own—but only the general form of the black minstrel show really resembled the white. It goes without saying that the black minstrels were "more authentic," and the black shows, although they did originate from white burlesques of Negro mores, were given a vitality and solid humor that the earlier shows never had.

The minstrel shows introduced new dance steps to what could then be considered a mass audience. The cakewalk was one of the most famous dance steps to come out of minstrelsy; it has been described as "a take-off on the high manners of the white folks in the 'big house.'" (If the cakewalk is a Negro dance caricaturing certain white customs, what is that dance when, say, a white theater company attempts to satirize it as a Negro dance? I find the idea of white minstrels in blackface satirizing a dance satirizing themselves a remarkable kind of irony—which, I suppose, is the whole point of minstrel shows.)

Early Negro minstrel companies like the Georgia Minstrels, Pringle Minstrels, McCabe and Young Minstrels, provided the first real employment for Negro entertainers. Blues singers, musicians, dancers, comedians, all found fairly steady work with these large touring shows. For the first time Negro music was heard on a wider scale throughout the country, and began to exert a tremendous influence on the mainstream of the American entertainment world; a great many of the shows even made extensive tours of England and the Continent, introducing the older forms of blues as well as classic blues and early jazz to the entire world.

---

*From Newman Ivey White, ed., *The Frank C. Brown Collection of North Carolina Folklore* (Durham, N.C.: Duke University Press, 1962), 88–89.

Classic blues is called "classic" because it was the music that seemed to contain all the diverse and conflicting elements of Negro music, plus the smoother emotional appeal of the "performance." It was the first Negro music that appeared in a formal context as entertainment, though it still contained the harsh, uncompromising reality of the earlier blues forms.[5] It was, in effect, the perfect balance between the two worlds, and as such, it represented a clearly definable step by the Negro back into the mainstream of American society. Primitive blues had been almost a conscious expression of the Negro's *individuality* and equally important, his *separateness*. The first years after the Civil War saw the Negro as far away from the whole of American society as it was ever possible for him to be. Such a separation was never possible again. To the idea of the meta-society is opposed the concept of integration, two concepts that must always be present in any discussion of Negro life in America.

The emergence of classic blues indicated that many changes had taken place in the Negro. His sense of place, or status, within the superstructure of American society had changed radically since the days of the field holler. Perhaps what is so apparent in classic blues is the sense for the first time that the Negro felt he was a *part* of that superstructure at all. The lyrics of classic blues become concerned with situations and ideas that are recognizable as having issued from one area of a much larger human concern. Classic blues is less obscure to white America for these reasons, less involuted, and certainly less *precise*. Classic blues attempts a universality that earlier blues forms could not even envision. But with the attainment of such broad human meaning, the meanings which existed in blues *only for Negroes* grew less pointed. The professionalism of classic blues moved it to a certain extent out of the lives of Negroes. It became the stylized response, even though a great many of the social and emotional preoccupations of primitive blues remained. Now large groups of Negroes could sit quietly in a show and listen to a performer re-create certain serious areas of their lives. The following blues was written by Porter Grainger and sung by Bessie Smith:

Put It Right Here or Keep It Out There
I've had a man for fifteen years, give him his room and board;
Once he was like a Cadillac, now he's like an old, worn-out Ford;
He never brought me a lousy dime and put it in my hand;
So there'll be some changes from now on, according to my plan

He's got to get it, bring it, and put it right here,
Or else he's goin' to keep it out there;
If he must steal it, beg it, or borrow it somewhere,
Long as he gets it, I don't care.

I'm tired of buyin' porkchops to grease his fat lips,
And he has to find another place for to park his old hips;
He must get it, and bring it, and put it right here.
Or else he's goin' to keep it out there.

The bee gets the honey and brings it to the comb,
Else he's kicked out of his home sweet home.
To show you that they brings it, watch the dog and the cat;
Everything even brings it, from a mule to a gnat.

---

5. By "earlier blues forms," I am assuming Jones is referring to what blues scholars would term the "country blues" or the "downhome blues." These blues genres are discussed later in Part 1.

The rooster gets the worm and brings it to the hen;
That oughta be a tip to all you no-good men.
The groundhog even brings it and puts it in his hole,
So my man is got to bring it—dog gone his soul.

The "separate society" was moving to make some parallels with the larger world. An idea of theater had come to the blues, and this movement toward performance turned some of the emotional climate of the Negro's life into artifact and entertainment. But there was still enough intimacy between the real world and the artifact to make that artifact beautiful and unbelievably moving.

Classic blues formalized blues even more than primitive blues had formalized earlier forms of Negro secular music. Just as the wandering primitive blues singers had spread a certain style of blues-singing, the performers of classic blues served as models and helped standardize certain styles. Singers like Gertrude "Ma" Rainey were responsible for creating the classic blues style. She was one of the most imitated and influential classic blues singers, and perhaps the one who can be called the *link* between the earlier, less polished blues styles and the smoother theatrical style of most of the later urban blues singers. Ma Rainey's singing can be placed squarely between the harsher, more spontaneous country styles and the somewhat calculated emotionalism of the performers. Madame Rainey, as she was sometimes known, toured the South for years with a company called the Rabbit Foot Minstrels and became widely known in Negro communities everywhere in America. It was she who taught Bessie Smith, perhaps the most famous of all the classic blues singers. Both these women, along with such performers as Clara Smith, Trixie Smith, Ida Cox, Sarah Martin, Chippie Hill, Sippie Wallace, brought a professionalism and theatrical polish to blues that it had never had before. They worked the innumerable little gin towns with minstrel shows.

By the turn of the century there were hundreds of tiny colored troupes, and some larger ones like The Rabbit Foot, Silas Green's, Mahara's. There were medicine shows, vaudevilles, and circuses when minstrel shows finally died. By the early twenties there were also certain theater circuits that offered tours for blues singers, jazz bands, and other Negro entertainers. One of the most famous, or most infamous, was the old T.O.B.A. (Theatre Owners' Booking Agency), or as the performers called it, "Tough On Black Artists" (or "Asses"). Tours arranged by these agencies usually went through the larger Southern and Midwestern cities.

While the country singers accompanied themselves usually on guitar or banjo, the classic blues singers usually had a band backing them up. They worked well with the jazz and blues bands, something the earlier singers would not have been able to do. Classic blues was much more an instrumental style; though the classic singers did not lose touch with the vocal tradition, they did augment the earlier forms in order to utilize the more intricate styles of the jazz bands to good effect.

The great classic blues singers were women. Ma Rainey, Bessie Smith, and the others all came into blues-singing as professionals, and all at comparatively early ages. (Ma Rainey started at fourteen, Bessie Smith before she was twenty.) Howard W. Odum and Guy B. Johnson note from a list of predominantly classic blues titles, taken from the record catalogues of three "race" companies. "The majority of these formal blues are sung from the point of view of woman . . . upwards of seventy-five per cent of the songs are written from the woman's point of view. Among the blues singers who have gained a more or less national recognition there is scarcely a man's name to be found."* However, the great country blues singers, with exceptions like Ida May Mack or Bessie Tucker, were almost always men. But the country blues singers were not recorded until much later, during the great swell of blues and "race" recordings when the companies were willing to try almost any black singer or musician because they were still ecstatic about their newly discovered market. The first recordings of blues were classic blues; it was the classic singers who first brought blues into general notice in the United States.

There were several reasons why women became the best classic blues singers. Most of the best-known country singers were wanderers, migratory farm workers, or men who went from place to place seeking employment. In those times, unless she traveled with her family it was almost impossible for a woman to move about like a man. It was also unnecessary since women could almost always obtain domestic employment. Until the emergence of the Negro theater, Negro women either sang in the church (they were always more consistent in their churchgoing) or sang their own personal sadnesses over brown wood tubs. In the slave fields, men and women worked side by side—the work songs and hollers served both. (Given such social circumstance, one must assume that it was only the physiological inequality of the black woman, e.g., not infrequent pregnancies, that provided some measure of superiority for the male, or at least some reticence for the female.)

> *I'm a big fat mama, got the meat shakin' on my bones*
> *I'm a big fat mama, got the meat shakin' on my bones*
> *And every time I shake, some skinny gal loses her home.*

Only in the post-bellum society did the Christian Church come to mean social placement, as it did for white women, as much as spiritual salvation. (Social demeanor as a basic indication of spiritual worth is not everybody's idea. Sexual intercourse, for instance, is not thought filthy by a great many gods.) It was possible to be quite promiscuous, if it came to that, and still be a person capable of "being moved by the spirit." But in post-bellum Negro society, Christianity did begin to assume the spirituality of the social register; the Church became an institution through which, quite sophisticatedly, secular distinction was bestowed. The black woman had to belong to the Church, even if she was one of the chief vestals of the most mysterious cult of Shango, or be thought "a bad woman." This was a legacy of white American Protestantism. But the incredibly beautiful Jesus of Negro spirituals is so much a man of flesh and blood, whether he is sung of by the church women or those women who left the Church to sing the "devil songs."

> *Dark was de night an' cold was de groun'*
> *On which de Lawd had laid;*
> *Drops of sweat run down,*
> *In agony he prayed.*

> *Would thou despise my bleedin' lam'*
> *An' choose de way to hell,*
> *Still steppin' down to de tomb,*
> *An' yet prepared no mo'?*

Negro Workaday Songs (Chapel Hill, University of North Carolina Press, 1926), p. 38.

I love Jesus,
I love Jesus,
I love Jesus,
O yes, I do,
*Yes, Lawdy.**

Minstrelsy and vaudeville not only provided employment for a great many women blues singers but helped to develop the concept of the professional Negro female entertainer. Also, the reverence in which most of white society was held by Negroes gave to those Negro entertainers an enormous amount of prestige. Their success was also boosted at the beginning of this century by the emergence of many white women as entertainers and in the twenties, by the great swell of distaff protest regarding women's suffage. All these factors came together to make the entertainment field a glamourous one for Negro women, providing an independence and importance not available in other areas open to them—the church, domestic work, or prostitution.

The emergence of classic blues and the popularization of jazz occurred around the same time. Both are the results of social and psychological changes within the Negro group as it moved toward the mainstream of American society, a movement that tended to have very significant results. The Negro's idea of America as the place where he lived and would spend his life was broadened; there was a realization by Negroes (in varying degrees, depending upon their particular socio-economic status) of a more human hypothesis on which to base their lives. Negro culture was affected: jazz is easily the most cosmopolitan of any Negro music, able to utilize almost any foreign influence within its broader spectrum. And blues benefited: it was richer, more universal, and itself became a strong influence on the culture it had depended upon for its growth.

Ragtime, dixieland, jazz, are all American terms. When they are mentioned anywhere in the world, they relate to America and an American experience. But the term *blues* relates directly to the Negro, and his *personal* involvement in America. And even though ragtime, dixieland, and jazz are all dependent upon blues for their existence in any degree of authenticity, the terms themselves relate to a broader reference than blues. *Blues* means a Negro experience, it is the one music the Negro made that could not be transferred into a more general significance than the one the Negro gave it initially. Classic blues differs a great deal from older blues forms in the content of its lyrics, its musical accompaniment, and in the fact that it was a music that moved into its most beautiful form as a *public entertainment,* but it is still a form of blues, and it is still a music that relates directly to the Negro experience. Bessie Smith was not an American, though the experience she relates could hardly have existed outside America; she was a Negro. Her music still remained outside the mainstream of American thought, but it was much closer than any Negro music before it.

Further Reading

Jones, LeRoi. *Blues People: The Negro Experience in White America and the Music that Developed from It.* New York: William Morrow, 1963.
Oliver, Paul. *Songsters and Saints: Vocal Traditions on Race Records.* Cambridge, UK: Cambridge University Press, 1984.
Ramsey, Guthrie P., Jr. *Race Music: Black Cultures from Bebop to Hip-Hop.* Berkeley: University of California Press, 2003.

*From *Negro Workaday Songs,* p. 196.

Discography

Blues Masters, Vol. 11: Classic Blues Women. Rhino, 1993.

Jackson, Mahalia. *Gospels, Spirituals, and Hymns.* Sony Jazz, 1998.

Kings of the Gospel Highway: The Golden Age of Gospel Quartets. Shanachie, 2000.

Lost Sounds: Blacks and the Birth of the Recording Industry 1891–1922. Archeophone Records, 2005.

Precious Lord: The Great Gospel Songs of Thomas A. Dorsey. Sony, 1994.

Smith, Willie Mae Ford. *Mother Smith and Her Children.* Yazoo, 1990.

7. The Empress of the Blues

Amiri Baraka concludes his discussion of the classic blues with a reference to Bessie Smith (1894–1937), the "Empress of the Blues," the most popular and influential of the classic blues singers and one of the most popular recording artists of the 1920s. Gaining her experience from traveling vaudeville shows, Smith developed a powerful voice that could project in large spaces without amplification. Unlike the country and Delta blues singers, many of her songs were tailor-made for her by professional songwriters. Thus, while she incorporates conventional blues phrasing and harmonic patterns into her singing, she also incorporates formal devices from contemporary popular song as well (this is true of "St. Louis Blues," the most famous song associated with her). The persona projected by Smith—strong, sassy, sensual—has become almost an archetype in representations of classic blues.[1] Her influence on subsequent female blues, jazz, and rock singers was strong and was felt by everyone from Billie Holiday to Dinah Washington to Janis Joplin.

---

1. For more on issues of sexuality and place in the classic blues, see Hazel V. Carby, "'It Jus' Be's Dat Way Sometime': The Sexual Politics of Women's Blues," *Radical America* 20, no. 4 (1986): 9–24, reprinted in Robert Walser, ed., *Keeping Time: Readings in Jazz History* (New York: Oxford University Press, 1999), 351–65; see also Daphne Duval Harrison, *Black Pearls: Blues Queens of the 1920s* (New Brunswick, N.J.: Rutgers University Press, 1988); and Angela Y. Davis, *Blues Legacies and Black Feminism: Gertrude "Ma" Rainey, Bessie Smith, and Billie Holiday* (New York: Vintage Books, 1999).

In the following discussion from Nat Shapiro and Nat Hentoff's classic oral history of jazz, *Hear Me Talkin' to Ya,* we hear from Frank Walker (a record company executive who was a central figure in the development of both "race" and "hillbilly" categories), Danny Barker and Buster Bailey (musicians who accompanied her), Mezz Mezzrow (a jazz musician of the period), and Alberta Hunter (a songwriter and blues singer in her own right).

from Hear Me Talkin' to Ya: The Story of Jazz as Told by the Men Who Made It

Nat Shapiro and Nat Hentoff

Frank Walker

I don't think there could have been more than fifty people up North who had heard about Bessie Smith when I sent Clarence Williams down South to get her. Clarence did a lot of work for me then. He was very important in coaching and teaching and working on our artists. He could somehow manage to get the best out of them, and to this day hasn't received the credit he really deserves.

Clarence really wasn't much of a pianist though, he'll tell you that himself. When he was back home in New Orleans he played piano in one of those honky-tonks and could only play by ear—maybe knowing a half a dozen songs. Then some inebriate might come in and ask for a song he didn't know, and Clarence would say, "Come back tomorrow night." The next day he'd go down to the five-and-ten-cent store, to the sheet music counter, and pull out the song for the piano player to demonstrate. He would hear it once and know it. If that customer came back, Clarence would play the song and maybe pick up a dime tip. It was like some of our hillbilly artists say about songs, "I can write them down, but I can't note them."

Anyway, I told Clarence about the Smith girl and said, "This is what you've got to do. Go down there and find her and bring her back up here."

He found her, and I'm telling you that the girl he brought back looked like anything *but* a singer. She looked about seventeen—tall and fat and scared to death—just awful! But all of this you forgot when you heard her sing, because when Bessie sang the blues, she meant it. Blues were her life. She was blues from the time she got up in the morning until she went to bed at night. Oh, she had a sense of humor all right, and she could laugh too. But it didn't last long.

Her first record was *Down Hearted Blues* and it was a tremendous hit. And there was one line in that blues that did it. It was the first time it was used and it made that record a hit. It was "Got the world in a jug, got the stopper in my hand."

I don't know that there was anyone closer to Bessie than I was. She came to me for advice; I took care of her money and bookings (at one time she was probably the highest-paid Negro performer in vaudeville—next to Bert Williams, that

Source: Hear Me Talkin to Ya: The Story of Jazz as Told by the Men Who Made It, Nat Shapiro and Nat Hentoff, © 1955 Dover Publications.

is).[2] She knew that we looked at her and treated her as a human being and not a piece of property.

It was all a matter of feeling with her. It was inside. Not that there was any repression. It all came out in her singing. Almost all of the blues she sang told sort of a story, and they were written especially for her. I don't want to give you the idea that Bessie Smith was incapable of writing her own blues, not at all. She probably could have. She would get an idea, then we would discuss it. But once she started to sing, nobody told her what to do. Nobody interfered. That was one of the reasons she liked Fletcher Henderson so much. He was quiet and never butted in. He did what Bessie told him to.

I suppose that lots of people remember and think of Bessie as a rough-and-tumble sort of person. Still, that wasn't the only side of her. They didn't know about things like her buying a rooming house for her friends to live in, and hundreds of other little things which cost her barrels of money. Yes, Bessie had a heart as big as all outdoors, but she gave it all away.

Later on, when the blues began to spread out and became established, new people were coming along and Bessie began to lose heart. You might say she didn't have a hitching post to tie her horse to. She began to lose interest in life. She had no heart left and was singing differently.

There was bitterness in her, and, you know, the blues aren't bitter.

Danny Barker

Bessie Smith was a fabulous deal to watch. She was a pretty large woman and she could sing the blues. She had a church deal mixed up in it. She dominated a stage. You didn't turn your head when she went on. You just watched Bessie. You didn't read any newspapers in a night club when she went on. She just upset you. When you say Bessie—that was it. She was unconscious of her surroundings. She never paid anybody any mind. When you went to see Bessie and she came out, that was it. If you had any church background, like people who came from the South as I did, you would recognize a similarity between what she was doing and what those preachers and evangelists from there did, and how they moved people. The South had fabulous preachers and evangelists. Some would stand on corners and move the crowds from there. Bessie did the same thing on stage. She, in a sense, was like people like Billy Graham are today. Bessie was in a class with those people. She could bring about mass hypnotism. When she was performing, you could hear a pin drop.

Buster Bailey

Bessie Smith was a kind of roughish sort of woman. She was good-hearted and big-hearted, and she liked to juice, and she liked to sing her blues slow. She didn't want no fast stuff. She had a style of phrasing, what they used to call swing—she had a certain way she used to sing. I hear a lot of singers now trying to sing something like that. Like this record that came out a few years ago—*Why Don't You Do Right?*—they're trying to imitate her.

We didn't have any rehearsals for Bessie's records. She'd just go with us to the studio around Columbus Circle. None of us rehearsed the things we recorded with her. We'd just go to the studio; Fletcher would get the key. This, by the way, applied

---

2. Bert Williams was the most famous black minstrel performer of the period.

not only to Bessie but to almost all the blues singers. The singers might have something written out to remind them what the verse was but there was no music written on it. On a lot of the records by Bessie you'll see lyrics by Bessie Smith and music by George Brooks. That was Fletcher.

We recorded by the horn. You know the way they used to record in those days. We'd monkey around until we had a good balance and we'd make two or three but we never made more than two masters on a tune. We'd make only two sides in a session and at that time we got more money for that than we do now.

For Bessie, singing was just a living. She didn't consider it anything special. She was certainly recognized among blues singers—a shouter, they called her. They all respected her because she had a powerful pair of lungs. There were no microphones in those days. She could fill up Carnegie Hall, Madison Square Garden, or a cabaret. She could fill it up from her muscle and she could last all night. There was none of this whispering jive.

Mezz Mezzrow

Bessie was a real woman, all woman, all the femaleness the world ever saw in one sweet package. She was tall and brown-skinned, with great big dimples creasing her cheeks, dripping good looks—just this side of voluptuous, buxom, shapely as a hourglass, with a high-voltage magnet for a personality.

You ever hear what happened to that fine, full-of-life female woman? You know how she died? Well, she went on for years, being robbed by stinchy managers who would murder their own mothers for a deuce of blips, having to parade around in gaudy gowns full of dime-store junk and throwaway her great art while the lushes and morons made cracks about her size and shape. She drank a lot, and there must have been plenty of nights when she got the blues she couldn't lose, but she went on singing, pouring out the richness and the beauty in her that never dried up. Then one day in 1937 she was in an automobile crash down in Mississippi, the Murder State, and her arm was almost tore out of its socket. They brought her to the hospital but it seemed like there wasn't any room for her just then—the people around there didn't care for the color of her skin. The car turned around and drove away, with Bessie's blood dripping on the floor mat. She was finally admitted to another hospital where the officials must have been color-blind, but by that time she had lost so much blood that they couldn't operate on her, and a little later she died. *See that lonesome road, Lawd, it got to end*, she used to sing. That was how the lonesome road ended up for the greatest folk singer this country ever heard—with Jim Crow directing the traffic.

Buster Bailey

Alberta Hunter was another singer of the type I mean. She didn't need a mike. Bricktop was also in that gang. She was a good singer and she could dance. You had to sing and dance in those days. Bricktop was the one who later had a club of her own in Paris and now has one in Rome. Ma Rainey was good—you can't leave her out. But they all considered Bessie the best, like they put Louis on top. Bessie was the Louis Armstrong of the blues singers. She had more original ideas for blues and things than the others did.

Alberta Hunter

The blues? Why the blues are a part of me. To me, the blues are—well, almost religious. They're like a chant. The blues are like spirituals, almost sacred. When we sing blues, we're singin' out our hearts, we're singin' out our feelings. Maybe we're hurt and just can't answer back, then we sing or maybe even hum the blues. Yes, to us, the blues are sacred. When I sing:

> *"I walk the floor, wring my hands and cry.*
> *"Yes, I walk the floor, wring my hands and cry. . . ."*

what I'm doing is letting my soul out.

Blues are a part of me, and when I knew nothing about music, or even about such a thing as music being written down, I was singing blues and picking them out on the piano with one finger. I was less than eleven years old when I started writing *Down Hearted Blues*, just before I ran away from home. Later on, I recorded it for Paramount Records and it was a tremendous hit. That was before Frank Walker sent for Bessie Smith. Bessie made it after it had been recorded on almost all the labels and even on piano rolls. We thought that it was exhausted, but it was Bessie's first record and it sold 780,000 copies!

No, they don't have blues singers now like they had then, except maybe Dinah Washington. There was Sara Martin, Ida Cox, Chippie Hill, Victoria Spivey, Trixie Smith, and Clara Smith and Mamie Smith, who made it possible for all of us with her recording of *Crazy Blues*, the first blues record.

But Bessie Smith was the greatest of them all. There never was one like her and there'll never be one like her again. Even though she was raucous and loud, she had a sort of a tear—no, not a tear, but there was a misery in what she did. It was as though there was something she had to get out, something she just had to bring to the fore. Nobody, least of all today, could ever match Bessie Smith.

Further Reading

Carby, Hazel V. "'It Jus' Be's Dat Way Sometime': The Sexual Politics of Women's Blues." *Radical America* 20 (1986): 9–24. Reprinted in Robert Walser, ed., *Keeping Time: Readings in Jazz History*, 351–65. New York: Oxford University Press, 1999.

Davis, Angela Y. *Blues Legacies and Black Feminism: Gertrude "Ma" Rainey, Bessie Smith, and Billie Holliday*. New York: Vintage Books, 1999.

Harrison, Daphne Duval. *Black Pearls: Blues Queens of the 1920s*. New Brunswick, N.J.: Rutgers University Press, 1988.

Discography

Smith, Bessie. *The Empress of the Blues: 1923–1933*. Jazz Legends, 2004.

8. At the Crossroads with Son House

Of the many musical forms associated with African Americans, the country blues, along with work songs and the religious ring shout, has most often been linked with West African musical practices such as those used by the *jali* singers of the Gambia region.[1] While both *jalis* and blues singers are frequently troubador-like solo singers who accompany themselves on stringed instruments while telling stories, crucial differences exist as well: a *jali* sings about the history of his or her people while a blues singer describes personal experiences, and the blues musician uses Western musical techniques such as harmonic progressions and instruments based on equal temperament. Nonetheless, some view the expressive note-bending and the use of multi- or polyrhythms in the blues as musical connections to *jalis* in particular and West African music-making in general.

In contrast to the classic blues, country blues singers tended to be men from the rural South who accompanied themselves most often on guitar. The earliest recordings date from the 1920s, not too long after the first classic blues recordings, but no country blues singer ever enjoyed the widespread success of a Bessie Smith or Ma Rainey. Of the country blues artists who recorded in the 1920s, the best-known, most influential, and perhaps most successful was Blind Lemon Jefferson (1897–1930), who sang in a high-pitched wailing style, accompanied himself on the guitar with a mixture of single-note runs and chords, and featured an extremely flexible rhythmic sense in recordings such as "Matchbox Blues," "Black Snake Moan," and "See That My Grave Is Kept Clean."

---

1. For the connection between the country blues and the music of the *jalis,* see Paul Oliver, *Savannah Syncopators: African Retentions in the Blues* (New York: Stein and Day, 1970); and Samuel Charters, *The Roots of the Blues: An African Search* (New York: Da Capo, 1981). For more in-depth accounts of the *jali* tradition, see Sidia Jatta, "Born Musicians: Traditional Music from the Gambia," in *Repercussions: A Celebration of African-American Music,* ed. Geoffrey Haydon and Dennis Marks (London: Century, 1985); and Eric Charry, *Mande Music: Traditional and Modern Music of the Maninka and Mandinka of Western Africa* (Chicago: University of Chicago Press, 2000).

The Delta blues was a specific variety of country blues that developed in the Mississippi Delta and featured greater rhythmic intensity and a more extroverted style of blues than that recorded by singers such as Blind Lemon Jefferson, who hailed from Texas. Other innovations such as bottleneck, or "slide," guitar and blues harmonica also first became widespread in the Delta region. Of these Delta blues musicians, none had more impact or influence than Robert Johnson (1911–38). Johnson, who left behind a mere 29 recorded songs, wrote and recorded some of the most well-known blues songs, including "I Believe I'll Dust My Broom," "Sweet Home Chicago," "Cross Road Blues," and "Come On in My Kitchen." The release of his collected recordings by Columbia in the early sixties helped spur the blues revival of the 1960s and was one of the most important events in the development of blues-rock in England during that time. Although he played unamplified guitar, Johnson's style influenced numerous electric blues artists who were instrumental in the later development of the Chicago blues, such as Muddy Waters and Elmore James. The complexity of his guitar playing and the emotional fervor of his singing were also undoubtedly responsible for the continuing popularity and influence of his recordings on subsequent generations of blues aficionados.

Accounts of Johnson's music have often presented him as almost *sui generis*, a unique creative force propelled by inner demons, and as a locus of Romantic desire. Some recent blues historians have begun to provide alternative perspectives, stressing Johnson's position within a creative and cultural network in which he participated as an amalgamator of current African American popular styles, albeit a particularly skilled one.[2] His sources included then-contemporary popularizers of the blues such as Peetie Wheatstraw and Kokomo Arnold, as well as earlier Delta musicians like Charlie Patton and Son House. The following reading is an interview with the latter and portrays House during a revival of his career that occurred during the 1960s. House recalls his earlier contemporaries and discusses his bottleneck technique (which influenced Johnson). The interview also includes a brief reminiscence of House's encounter with Robert Johnson and the impression made on House by both Johnson's music and his temperament.

---

2. For the classic accounts of Johnson and the country/Delta blues, see Samuel B. Charters, *The Country Blues* (New York: Da Capo, [1959] 1975); David Evans, *Big Road Blues: Tradition and Creativity in the Folk Blues* (New York: Da Capo, 1982); Greil Marcus, "Robert Johnson," in *Mystery Train: Images of America in Rock 'n' Roll Music*, 4th rev. ed. (New York: Penguin, [1975] 1990), 19–38; Paul Oliver, *Blues Fell This Morning: Meaning in the Blues* (Cambridge: Cambridge University Press, [1960] 1997); and Robert Palmer, *Deep Blues* (New York: Viking, 1981). For revisionist histories of Johnson, see Elijah Wald, *Escaping the Delta: Robert Johnson and the Invention of the Blues* (New York: Amistad, 2004); and David Brackett, "Preaching Blues," *Black Music Research Journal* 32, no. 1 (2012): 113–36.

"Son House: Living King of Delta"
Jerry Gilbert

"All ma old boys has left me by myself; they's all dead and gone—Charley Patton, Blind Lemon, Willie Brown, Skip James. I'm 69 now and it won't be long before I'm 70; I may be old but you know I still have young ideas." . . .

He was particularly fascinated by early bottleneck players around his home town of Clarksdale, and he adopted his own method of producing the whine up the treble strings—a copper ring which was to become the trademark of his music. Son is now using a piece of copper tubing, and has been known to use other implements including a penknife.

"I was born and raised in Clarksdale but Charley [Patton] was living in Jackson, Mississippi when I first ran into him. I couldn't play the blues like him by just learning straight off. So I stayed around with him for a little while, then I moved on and ran into Willie Brown. We started playing together, Bill and me, and soon after that Charley was recording for Paramount and he wanted someone to play with him.

"I think Charley had heard people braggin' on me, so me and Willie was talked into going down. So then there was Willie, me and Louise McGhee. Blind Lemon was way up ahead of us, and he left us there."

Patton, Brown and House all recorded for Paramount at Grafton, Wisconsin in May 1930. House's sides included versions of "My Black Mama," "Preachin' The Blues," "Dry Spell Blues," "Clarksdale Moan," "Mississippi County Farm Blues" and "What Am I To Do Blues."

Muddy Waters, who also came from Clarksdale, is reported to have told Paul Oliver that Son was the best blues-man to play the jukes around Clarksdale. Muddy recalled that Son came from a plantation east of Clarksdale and played with the neck of a bottle over his little finger. Muddy admits to getting the idea from Son House, but felt that Son never came over as well on record as his live performances.

"A man from Jackson wanted us to make some records and he thought we was all sanctified folks, but we was just whiskey drinkers," mused Son.

"Then Charley died of pneumonia and me and Willie was up in Robinsonville at the time, and they wrote us a special; but there wasn't nothing we could do nohow, so we just stayed right on and didn't go [to] the funeral."

Around August 1941, Son and Willie recorded at Lake Cormorant for the Library of Congress, and House's "Shetland Pony Blues," "Fo' Clock Blues," "Camp Hollers," "Delta Blues" and "Going To Fishing" were subsequently released.

Son cut a further eight sides for Alan Lomax at the General Store in Robinsonville in 1942, which were among his best sides. Six of these were reissued recently on an Xtra album with Jaydee Short. The sides are "Sun Going Down," "I Ain't Goin' To Cry No More," "This War Will Last You For Years," "Was I Right Or Wrong," "My Black Woman" and "County Farm Blues." The other titles, Son's famous "Jinx Blues" and "The Pony Blues," a variant of his earlier "Shetland Pony Blues" have recently been reissued on Roots. But most of the tracks have been retitled since they were originally recorded.

Source: "Son House (part 1): Living King of the Delta" by Jerry Gilbert, originally published in *Sounds*, 10 October 1970, © Jerry Gilbert/Rock's Backpages.

It appears that Son was given time off from the plantation to record for the Library of Congress: "I was a tractor driver for six or seven dollars a week but it didn't matter what you went out and did to yourself at the weekends so long as you was there ready to start on Monday morning. Willie and me had moved back from Jackson about 25 miles south of Memphis, Tennessee; we weren't making much money and I was drivin' the tractors and plowing the mules. At the weekends we played the juke joints and rent parties. We didn't sleep on Saturday night, then we'd play on all day Sunday and Sunday night, and then it was Monday." . . .

Because of the mystique surrounding that other great Delta bluesman, Robert Johnson, Son House has tended to be slightly overshadowed. Thus it was interesting to hear first hand of Son's encounter with Robert and a further aid to understanding the chromatics and semantics of the blues environment.

"I first met Robert in 1933, I think in Robinsonville. I got friendly with his mother and father, and he was blowing Jew's harp. Why, even then he could blow the pants off just about anyone, but he wanted to play guitar. When he grabbed a guitar, the people would ask why don't he stop; he was driving 'em all crazy with his noise. Then he slipped off to Arkansas somewhere, but sure enough he came back and he found us. We was asking if he remembered we'd showed him, but then he showed us something, and we didn't believe what we saw. I said to old Bill 'that boy's good.'

"But Robert was too quick to get excited and he'd believe everything the girls say; they'd be saying things to him and he'd be thinking they was meanin' it; but we told him they didn't mean no good, and he went and got killed on the levee camp."

Further Reading

Charters, Samuel B. *The Country Blues*. New York: Da Capo Press, [1959] 1975.
_____. *The Roots of the Blues: An African Search*. New York: Da Capo Press, 1981.
Guralnick, Peter. *Searching for Robert Johnson*. New York: Plume, [1982] 1989.
Oliver, Paul. *Savannah Syncopators: African Retentions in the Blues*. New York: Stein and Day, 1970.
Palmer, Robert. *Deep Blues*. New York: Viking Press, 1981.
Pearson, Barry Lee, and Bill McCulloch. *Robert Johnson: Lost and Found*. Urbana: University of Illinois Press, 2003.
Schroeder, Patricia R. *Robert Johnson, Mythmaking, and Contemporary American Culture*. Urbana: University of Illinois Press, 2004.
Wald, Elijah. *Escaping the Delta: Robert Johnson and the Invention of the Blues*. New York: Amistad, 2004.

Discography

Back to the Cross-Roads: The Roots of Robert Johnson. Yazoo 2070, 2004.
Johnson, Robert. *The Complete Recordings*. Sony Jazz, 1996.
Martin Scorsese Presents the Blues: Son House. Hip-O Records, 2003.

9. From Race Music to Rhythm and Blues

T-BONE WALKER

The migration of a large number of African Americans to northern and western cities also led to new contexts for the performance of blues and sacred music. Singers such as Muddy Waters, who moved from Mississippi to Chicago in the 1940s, were increasingly accompanied by small ensembles that included electrically amplified guitars, harmonica, bass, and drums. The widespread popularity of big band swing during the years 1935–45 also encouraged blues musicians to add saxophones and brass instruments to their bands and to incorporate techniques of jazz arranging. Finally, some jazz musicians, many of whom had played in big bands, began to play in smaller groups and to simplify some of the harmonic and rhythmic devices of jazz in order to adapt to less favorable economic conditions for big bands and to provide danceable music. All these elements began to coalesce in the mid- to late 1940s in a new genre known as "rhythm and blues": a blues-based music that used jazz elements but was designed to meet the dancing and partying needs of an urban, African American audience. While this sound had been anticipated during the 1930s by some of the small groups led by jazz pianist and bandleader William "Count" Basie and by the boogie-woogie piano craze, the sides waxed in the early 1940s by Louis Jordan and Nat "King" Cole (both jazz musicians) demonstrated that blues performed in an urbane style could find the same kind of widespread success as the classic blues.

In 1949, *Billboard* magazine began to use the term "rhythm and blues" for all black secular popular music, conflating genres now recognized as urban blues, Chicago blues, doo-wop, small-band jazz, and rhythm and blues. The name, now shortened to "R&B," still persists as the name for the industry category and consumer genre associated with black popular music.

T-Bone Walker (1910–75) was one of the first blues guitar players to exploit the possibilities of the electric guitar opened up by the great jazz guitarist Charlie Christian. Walker's fusion of downhome blues with jazzy, single-note lines backed by a horn section set the stage for the development of "urban blues" musicians such as B. B. King and Otis Rush. The following article, written shortly after Walker's death, discusses his early influences and the development of his guitar style

48

and includes the recollections of a number of his contemporaries. The emphasis on Walker's guitar technique springs from the publication of this article in *Guitar Player*, one of a number of magazines directed toward a specialized audience of music practitioners that began to develop in the late 1960s and early 1970s.

T-Bone Walker: Father of the Blues
Kevin Sheridan and Peter Sheridan

"It's awful late, isn't it?" Blues singer Jimmy Witherspoon pauses and lets the disappointment in his statement sink in.

"It's a shame all those trade magazines didn't even write nothing about this man before he died," declares Spoon [who later recorded with Walker on *Evenin' Blues* (Prestige, 7300)]. "Most black artists are victims of this shit. I'm not being paranoid either. It's pitiful, man, it's a damn shame. A lot of these artists could have helped people like T-Bone—exposed them to a lot of youngsters by putting them on the bill with themselves. A lot of pop English groups, a lot of pop American groups—at least they could give each other exposure and let people hear you."

In 1939 a young Witherspoon went to a club, Little Harlem, in East Los Angeles where T-Bone was playing. "I always wanted to sing," he recalls. "I told him I wanted to sing, and he called me up. I was just an amateur, and he let me sing. All I can say is that he's the Charlie Parker of guitars when it comes to blues. And in jazz guitarists, he's right with Charlie Christian. No one else can touch T-Bone in the blues on guitar."

The respect evident in Witherspoon's tone is almost consistent to a man when it comes to the subject of T-Bone Walker "He brought the blues guitar back in style," blues guitarist Lowell Fulson states with the resolve to set the record straight. "Blues guitar players wasn't much back in those days; if you couldn't blow a horn, why, you was just out. And T-Bone came out with 'Bobby Sox Blues' in '46, then guitar players were able to work a little more, get a decent price. I always give him credit, because he's the first man brought the blues guitar—matter of fact, brought the *guitar* back in style, playing lead.

"Back in those times," Fulson goes on, "the average guitar player, if he was pretty positive into music, he wanted to be a Charlie Christian. When T-Bone brought the blues guitar out, you ought to have seen the guys going back and studying and playing and really trying to get their licks in, because the man was the only one being talked about."

Oklahoma-born Lowell Fulson met T-Bone in 1944 while in the Navy. At that time Lowell was playing guitar but not regularly; "just a little playing off the base on liberty." T-Bone was in San Diego at the Silver Slipper, and as Lowell puts it, "I never seen nobody like him at that time. Since, either."

Lowell didn't see Walker again until 1949, four years after his discharge. Bone was well on his way to legend while Lowell was just beginning to break into touring, having cut "Everyday I Have The Blues." Fulson recounts, "As I improved, agents began getting a package together called the Battle Of The Blues. It seemed at the time, me and T-Bone was pretty good drawing cards for promoters. I'll never forget— they used to call us The Big Three: me, T-Bone, and Big Joe Turner. We'd each play

Source: "T-Bone Walker: Father of the Blues," © Kevin Sheridan and Peter Sheridan, *Guitar Player*/Wright's Media/New Bay Media.

a separate set. I was the newest in the game, so I'd open the show. Well, Joe Turner, he didn't play an instrument, so he'd come on in the middle (instead of having both guitars together). Then T-Bone played on the end. On the last set we'd all get together and have a jam session. I really enjoyed working with those men.

"Bone used to tell me, 'Swing the blues a little more, Fulson. You can play it, swing it a little more. Put a little life into it, a little pep; rock into it. Tap your foot off of what you're doing.' It was wonderful advice; then I began to get into better houses, playing."

Lowell leans back in his chair and smiles. "He used to knock me out, because he was the only guy I'd seen play the guitar behind his head and do the splits with it. He'd tear the house up!"

T-Bone was indeed a master showman—the best according to his present peers and disciples. He did the splits without missing a beat, played leads behind his head (more than a decade before Jimi Hendrix brought the trick to rock audiences). He repeatedly excited crowds, whose women reacted by throwing purses, clothing, and even their husbands' paychecks onto the stage.

In 1942, at the age of sixteen, Riley B. King first heard T-Bone on a 78 in a jukebox. "I lived in the country, and I went to town that particular day, to this little cafe, and heard this record playing, I went to the jukebox and saw the name 'T-Bone Walker.' And I've never forgotten it; it seems like yesterday."

By that time, T-Bone's distinctive sound was well in hand, and he was playing the rocking blues with a swing touch as he would continue to do for the next three decades. "I don't think it was any particular amp," states B.B., in reference to Walker's one-of-a-kind tone; "T-Bone would play any guitar, any amp, and he would get the same sound. It was the man. I have no idea how he got his sound, but I remember Bone later telling me that he used to play banjo. I guess that was one of the things that started him playing single strings. But he was the first guy I ever heard play blues using a 9th chord."

Bone even held his guitar "different than anybody else," adds King; always slanted out, away from his body, with his chording hand curling around the neck. "I think it's kind of like Wes Montgomery playing with his thumb," explains B.B. "It was comfortable for him. The only people I saw playing guitar like T-Bone played his, I saw a few guys playing steel guitar, had it around their neck. They played with the left hand free, with the bar. But to actually note it, to fret with the left hand, I haven't seen anybody else do that."

Lowell Fulson elaborates, "He was the only guitar player I've ever seen hold his guitar flat and watch his whole hand. I don't know how that man could hold his wrist over like that, playing the guitar, and not miss a note. He laid it flat like you were going to play piano or keyboards. That's the one thing other guys couldn't do. Oh, they tried to put the guitar behind their heads and do the splits—some of the younger players came up and could do that pretty good—but they never could hold the guitar out like that, so they finally let that alone.

"All his lead playing he did like that." Lowell continues, "and when he got ready to riff, he'd drop it down so he could swing his box, you understand. But when he really got down to playing, he'd turn it up, push it out from him, and go to work on it."

"His touch was so clear," B.B. states with envy. "I don't think he did much up-and-down strokes; I think he mostly picked down. Whenever he hit the strings he hit them with authority. It was almost a measured touch. You don't find too many people who have that kind of control, especially in the blues; you find it more in jazz."

Inevitably, when anyone sits down to reminisce about T-Bone Walker—guitarists, bluesmen, whomever—the conversation turns to his classic "Stormy Monday."

"To me, 'Stormy Monday' tells such a good story," stresses B.B. King, "especially for the working man. It's a very unique song."

"It's true everyday life," declares Fulson, "about the average guy. It's smooth. It goes between a ballad and a blues. It's a type of tune that will fit in any kind of club. I rate it along with 'St. Louis Blues'—you can sing it anywhere, if you can sing."

Jimmy Witherspoon is even more emphatic about his love for the tune: "It's just like a national anthem; it tells the truth. It tells the strife of working people getting paid on Friday, Saturday they go out and have a ball."

"Everybody tried to do it," adds Pee Wee Crayton, putting things into perspective, "can't anybody do it like him."

Bone's importance, concludes Spoon, lies in the fact that "he's one of the few people who put dignity into the blues. That the right word, dignity."

Further Reading[1]

Dance, Helen Oakley. *Stormy Monday: The T-Bone Walker Story*. Foreword by B. B. King. Baton Rouge: Louisiana State University Press, 1987.

O'Neal, Jim, and Amy Van Singel. *The Voice of the Blues: Classic Interviews from* Living Blues *Magazine*. New York: Routledge, 2002.

Ramsey, Guthrie P., Jr. *Race Music: Black Cultures from Bebop to Hip-Hop*. Berkeley: University of California Press, 2003.

Discography

Martin Scorsese Presents the Blues: A Musical Journey. Hip-O Records, 2003.

Walker, T-Bone. *Blues Masters: The Very Best of T-Bone Walker*. Rhino, 2000.

10. Jumpin' the Blues with Louis Jordan

Louis Jordan's (1908–75) role in the transition of race music to rhythm and blues is second to none. His group, the Tympany Five (which usually consisted of seven members), established the concept of the swinging

---

1. Almost all the chapters from this point onward can be supplemented by chapters from *The Rolling Stone Illustrated History of Rock and Roll: The Definitive History of the Most Important Artists and Their Music*, ed. Anthony DeCurtis and James Henke with Holly George-Warren (New York: Random House, 1992).

small band with rhythm section (piano, bass, drums, and occasionally guitar) and a horn section consisting of two saxophones and one or two trumpets. Jordan's use of simplified swing rhythm (which became known as "shuffle rhythm"), blues harmonic patterns, and witty, vaudeville-influenced lyrics led him to achieve unprecedented popularity for an African American artist during the years 1942–49. While reviews from the period and statements from musicians who were his contemporaries stress his musicianship and his professionalism, Jordan departed from other jazz-oriented players of the day in his emphasis on pleasing audiences and his unabashed embrace of commercialism.

The following article from *Down Beat* comes from a period when Jordan was beginning to broaden his audience. The anonymous reviewer notes how Jordan is merging aspects of jazz, blues, and pop with novelty and "jump numbers." Although the writer criticizes Jordan for monotony, he acknowledges that Jordan's emphasis on entertainment results in a crowd-pleasing show. He also looks somewhat askance at those stage mannerisms that Jordan retained from his days as a vaudeville-minstrel entertainer. *Down Beat*, as mentioned earlier, was one of the first magazines to cater to jazz fans. As such, the criticisms of Jordan allude to ongoing debates among jazz critics about the relationship between jazz and commercialism.[1]

Bands Dug by the Beat: Louis Jordan
Down Beat

Dynamic is the word for Jordan's compact jazz machine. One of the strongest contributing factors to Jordan's phenomenal success has been his unrelenting insistence on a continuous performance. The band came on the Savoy bandstand at ten and played one number on top of the other until two ayem [*sic*] with only a twenty-minute intermission. This group really works hard and manages to keep the same tension intact all through their appearance. Another very important factor contributing to the shining of Jordan's star has been those innumerable juke box sides. Playing this dance job, they took advantage of the nickel grabbers and played their recorded repertoire, most of which features the leader vocally. Louis gave with his usual gestures and rolling of the eyes but did not bother to don any stage garb to depict *Deacon Jones*. In fact,

---

1. These debates over value in the jazz press have received a fair amount of scholarly attention; for two studies, see Bernard Gendron, "Moldy Figs and Modernists," in *Between Montmartre and the Mudd Club: Popular Music and the Avant-Garde* (Chicago: University of Chicago Press, 2002), 121–42; and Scott DeVeaux, "Constructing the Jazz Tradition: Jazz Historiography," *Black American Literature Forum* 25, no. 3 (Fall 1991): 525–60.

Source: "Bands Dug by the Beat: Louis Jordan," *Downbeat*, Courtesy of the Downbeat Archives.

he kept the pure novelty numbers at a minimum and featured blues to a great extent with a very fine reception from the Savoy throng. Consequently there was a good deal of jazz played with Louis himself playing fine alto and some quite acceptable tenor plus a little clarinet.

The group is closely knit and jumps like mad when really wound up. Louis' vocal on every number tended to slow up the winding however. When Eddie Roane, a fine trumpet, got a break he made the most of it and played some amazing things. His wah-wah muting accompaniment to the blues vocals showed a variety of ideas for that type of playing. His open horn is clean and full-toned. Both Louis and Eddie worked over a full and driving beat furnished by the rhythm trio, which in itself is stellar. The original Jordan pianist, Arnold Thomas, played relaxed and his fillins are well worth listening to. Al Morgan, considered one of the finest bass men still slapping the bass, fitted into the rhythm trio perfectly. Wilmore (Slick) Jones, the late Fats Waller's favorite drummer, also helped keep the rhythm going at [a] terrific pace.

Louis Jordan has versatility and one feature is some good jazz playing. One criticism, however, is the fact that every number played in jump tempo with Louis' singing is likely to become monotonous. His renditions of *G. I. Jive, Straighten Up and Fly Right*, and *Is You Is Or Is You Ain't My Baby* all sound alike. Although the band is versatile in presenting novelties, blues, jump numbers and pops, it still retains a sameness in the style of playing various types.

> In the next entry, Jordan describes his background in minstrel shows and large swing bands and his role in the development of "jump blues," a genre using a small band, blues-based forms, and shuffle rhythms. Throughout his recollections, Jordan shows a concern for the makeup of his audience, and although he recognized that he needed to please white audiences to achieve commercial success, he also believed that much of the vitality of his music came from his continued connection with black listeners. This belief is apparent in Jordan's telling account of an engagement he shared with the Mills Brothers, a band with much less connection to blues and jazz.

from Honkers and Shouters: The Golden Years of Rhythm and Blues
Arnold Shaw

"It was a saxophone in a store window. I could see myself in the polished brass—that started me off. I ran errands all over Brinkley [Arkansas] until my feet were sore, and I saved until I could make a down payment on that shiny instrument. My father taught me music. I was still a teen-ager when I played my first gig. It was vacation time, and I blew with Rudy Williams—he was known as 'Tuna Boy' Williams. It was

Source: Honkers and Shouters: The Golden Years of Rhythm and Blues, Arnold Shaw © Arnold Shaw and Ghita Shaw

at The Green Gables in Hot Springs. That was about 150 miles west of Brinkley where I was born. Little Rock is in between, and about 100 miles from my hometown. I went to Arkansas Baptist College there and majored in music.[2]

"My first professional job was with The Rabbit Foot Minstrels. Ma Rainey was once the star, and Bessie Smith got her start with them. I played clarinet and danced all through the South. Around 1932, I went North, settled in Philadelphia and got connected with Charlie Gaines's band. I had eyes, you know, on the Big Apple—New York City. But it took several years before I could get a union card in Local 802.

"I worked with several bands. Joe Marshall was one. He was a drummer with Fletcher Henderson. We played the Elks Rendezvous in Harlem for a while. Around 1936 I joined Chick Webb at The Savoy. Played alto, sang, and announced numbers. Chick was a little man, hunchback, but a great drummer. He had big ears for talent—like Ella Fitzgerald, whom he adopted so she could sing with the band. But he was no showman and some people thought I was the leader because I introduced numbers.

"I loved playing jazz with a big band. Loved singing the blues. But I really wanted to be an entertainer—that's me—on my own. I wanted to play for the people, for millions, not just a few hep cats.

"When Chick died in 1938, I cut out and formed my own band. Nine pieces, and we had a regular gig at the Elks Rendezvous. Four-sixty-four Lenox Avenue was the address. Also played club dates 'off nights.' Those were nights when a band was off. I played up and down Swing Street, Fifty-second Street. After a while, I cut the nine pieces down to six. Later I added a guitar and made it seven. Once I got known as Louis Jordan and His Tympany Five, I kept the name. But I always had seven or eight men.

"After that Fifty-second Street bit, I started playing proms, like at Yale and Amherst. That's when friends began saying, 'Why don't you get out of New York, Louis? It's taking too long for you to get started.' So they came and asked me if I would play with the Mills Brothers in Chicago. The Capitol Lounge was for white folks. It was across the alley from the Chicago Theater. Not many Negroes came because they felt they weren't welcome. They wanted me to play intermission for the Mills Brothers. I started not to go—that was a big mistake.

"At first I was doing ten minutes; then they raised me to fifteen; then I got to half an hour. The Mills Brothers went over big. 'Cause the people who came to hear them and Maurice Rocco—he was the third act—they had *their* following and he had *his*. And after a while, I had *my* following. The Capitol Lounge couldn't hold two hundred people. But they would have a hundred twenty sittin' down and maybe a hundred eighty standin' at the bar. After that booking, I was gone!

"The Fox Head in Cedar Rapids was a great turning point in my career. It was there I found 'If It's Love You Want, Baby, That's Me' and a gang of blues—'Ration Blues,' 'Inflation Blues,' and others. Now, it was just a beer joint. It ran from a street to an alley. Beer was fifteen cents. The owner was a ham radio operator. He insisted that I stay at his house. He was a wonderful man.

"After my records started to sell, we drew mixed audiences to clubs like The Tick Tock in Boston, Billy Berg's Swing Club in Los Angeles, The Garrick in Chicago and The Top Hat in Toronto. The first time I played the Adams Theatre in Newark, I played with a fellow who sings like Perry Como. He was in Vic Damone's bag. And the second time I played there, I appeared with a society band like Meyer Davis. I was the Negro part, and they played the white part. That's how we did it in the early forties, so that we drew everybody. I was trying to do what they told me: straddle the fence.

---

2. While Jordan wanted to attend college, he was never able to for financial reasons despite many statements to the contrary. See John Chilton, *Let the Good Times Roll: The Story of Louis Jordan and His Music* (Ann Arbor: University of Michigan Press, 1997), 17.

"I made just as much money off white people as I did off colored. I could play a white joint this week and a colored next. The Oriental Theatre in Chicago was a white theater for the hep crowd. The State Theatre in Hartford was the same. It drew the college crowd. Same with the Riverside Theatre in Milwaukee. Any time I played a white theater, my black following was there. The Paradise Theatre in Detroit was on the borderline. The Negroes lived on that side of Woodward, and the whites on this side. Oh yeah, the Royal in Baltimore was a colored theater. But white people came to see me. The Beachcomber in Omaha was basically a Negro place. When I played there, I had white audiences. Many nights we had more white than colored, because my records were geared to the white as well as colored, and they came to hear me do my records.

"For Negroes, there were three basic theaters: Howard in Washington, Regal in Chicago, and Apollo in Harlem. In the big years, we played the Paramount on Broadway—a four-week engagement every year—and the Apollo twice a year. We appeared at the Regal in Chicago every Easter week and the Apollo every Christmas week.

"Not all of my hits was written by Negroes. 'Knock Me a Kiss' was by a white man, Mike Jackson, though Andy Razaf wrote some special words. Two white guys came up with 'Choo Choo Ch' Boogie.' I believe that Vaughn Horton and Denver Darling were really country-western writers. The song was played to me in the studio. We were recording with Milt Gabler, who handled all my Decca sessions. He brought the words and asked what I could do with them. At that time I had Wild Bill Davis playing piano. All of my things are based on the blues, twelve-bar blues. So I asked Bill to play some blues in B-flat. I was using the shuffle boogie then. He started shuffling off in B-flat, a twelve-bar phrase—and that's how we got the record together.

"'Blue Light Boogie' was by a colored woman, Jessie Mae Robinson. She was the best-oriented colored songwriter. She didn't write white songs. 'Don't Worry 'bout That Mule' was written by colored. 'Beans and Cornbread' was by a colored boy, Freddie Clark. 'The Chicks I Pick Are Slender, Tender, and Tall,' 'What's the Use of Getting Sober?,' 'Somebody Done Changed the Lock on My Door,' 'That'll just about Knock You Out,' started from a white man in Grand Forks, North Dakota. The boss of the place had a husky voice. [Imitating] He'd say it all the time. That's where we wrote the song from.

"'Saturday Night Fish Fry' was the work of a colored girl. 'Let the Good Times Roll' was by Sam Theard, a black comedian. 'Mama Blues' was by a black writer, and so was 'Small Town Boy.' That was written by Dallas Bartley, my bass man, who comes from a small town. But 'Five Guys Named Moe' was by a white guy. It was done with a Negro feel. [Sings lyrics and some of the instrumental licks] 'Beware, Brother, Beware' and 'Buzz Me' were both written by white guys. 'Early in the Mornin' was by a mixed group—Leo Hickman, a white man; Dallas Bartley, my bassman; and me.

"I had five tunes that sold a million records, and 'Is You Is, or Is You Ain't (Ma' Baby)?' was by a white man. I was playing at Lakota's Lounge on Wisconsin Avenue in Milwaukee. He was a little humpback fellow about the size of Chick Webb. He'd come in every night and talk to this girl. They'd have dinner and stay for lunch. He just loved me and he'd hang around so long as I was there. She'd be talkin' to someone else and he'd say to her, 'Is you is or is you ain't ma baby?' And he was strictly Caucasian—no black blood in him at all. Soon I started sayin' it. And he said, 'Let's write a song.' You can't say because of color or race that a person would not say a thing or would not do a thing.

"'Caldonia' was by a black writer, meaning me. Fleecie Moore's name is on it, but she didn't have anything to do with it. That was my wife at the time, and we put it in her name. She didn't know nothin' about no music at all. Her name is on this song and that song, and she's still getting money."

Further Reading

Ake, David. "Jazz Historiography and the Problem of Louis Jordan." In *Jazz Cultures*, 42–61. Berkeley and Los Angeles: University of California Press, 2002.

Chilton, John. *Let the Good Times Roll: The Story of Louis Jordan and His Music*. Ann Arbor: University of Michigan Press, 1997.

Discography

Jordan, Louis. *Saturday Night Fish Fry: The Original and Greatest Hits*. Jasmine, 2000.

_____. *Louis Jordan and His Tympani Five*. JSP Records, 2001.

11. On the Bandstand with Johnny Otis

Although not well known to many rock 'n' roll fans, Johnny Otis (b. 1921) was a major force in rhythm and blues from the late 1940s through the 1950s. He worked as a bandleader, record producer, disc jockey, and entrepreneur. Otis's collaborators included Willie Mae "Big Mama" Thornton (Otis played drums and produced her recording of "Hound Dog"), Little Esther, and Etta James, among others. After numerous rhythm and blues hits throughout the 1950s, in 1958 he led a recording of "Willie and the Hand Jive," which used a rhythm common throughout the African diaspora (sometimes rendered as "shave and a haircut, six bits") and became a crossover hit when revived by Eric Clapton in 1974.[1] Otis's involvement in rhythm and blues for over 50 years is remarkable for another reason; although biologically white, Otis identified with African Americans from an early age, becoming culturally, if not

---

1. In addition to the uses of this rhythm in African American music, which are described in the following excerpt, this rhythm, in slightly varied form, also forms the basic clave rhythm of the Cuban *son*, which, in turn, provides the rhythmic underpinning for much salsa. For a concise exploration of this connection, see Peter Manuel, *Caribbean Currents: Caribbean Music from Rumba to Reggae* (Philadelphia: Temple University Press, 1995).

racially, black. His life serves as an important reminder of the instabil-
ity of racial categories. As dedicated to social causes as he is to music,
Otis continues to be a sterling advocate of African American popular
music and political interests. Otis is also a master storyteller, and his
autobiography, *Upside Your Head!* deserves to be read in its entirety.

from Upside Your Head! Rhythm and Blues on Central Avenue
Johnny Otis

From my vantage point on the drummer's stool in the Club Alabam, I could see the
music that was to be named rhythm and blues taking shape. First in Harlan Leonard's Kansas City Rockets and later, with my own big swing band, the blues and
jazz elements were coming together. Neither Harlan's band nor mine could have
been described as rhythm and blues, but the acts we were backing at the Alabam in
the early and mid-forties were certainly the forerunners of the R&B style. Wynonie
Harris, Jo Jo Adams, Marion Abernathy, T-Bone Walker, Little Miss Cornshucks, and
Mabel Scott were the kind of artists who headlined the shows. Each of them and the
many other blues-oriented performers who starred at the Alabam in those years, had
a down-to-earth, uninhibited approach that set them apart from the more formal and
formatted jazz and swing performers of the preceding era.

These new show stoppers grew out of the Lionel Hampton, Louis Jordan, Ray
Nance, Jimmy Rushing, Illinois Jacquet tradition. The high-spirited exuberance of the
African American church tradition and of the little honky-tonk clubs around America was being felt on the stages of the larger, more prestigious Black entertainment
rooms. They were demonstrating that artistry, energy, and fun could coexist in Black
music without sacrificing artistic integrity. Louis Armstrong had always performed
in this way, and now, more and more, the deadpan stiff concept was giving way to a
freer, bluesier, more entertaining form. Even in the more conservative world of bebop
music, the great Dizzy Gillespie began to use dancing, good humor, and earthiness
as a kind of act of love, and his burgeoning popularity among both the music experts
and the general public proved him commercially and artistically correct.

During the thirties and forties and perhaps as far back as the 1920s, there evolved
an interesting breed of musicians. They inhabited that musical never-never land
that exists somewhere between southern blues and so-called jazz. Usually working
for peanuts, in small undistinguished clubs, they made up for whatever technical
shortcomings they may have had with enthusiasm and showmanship. They probably regarded themselves as "jazz" players and singers but could be tagged more
accurately barrel-house or jump music stylists. A typical jazz musician wouldn't
have lasted five minutes in those clubs. The customers weren't interested in musical

subtlety or even virtuosity—they wanted spirited entertainment and fun. The bigger the beat, the stronger the boogie woogie flavor, and the bawdier the lyrics, the better.

Of course, bawdy by those standards would hardly raise an eyebrow today. An example of a very daring lyric for that time was the blues Count Otis Matthews sang when we played in those West Oakland greasy spoon dives. It went, "Oohwee, baby, I ain't gonna' do it no more, 'Cause every time I do it, it makes my wee wee sore!" The audience would squeal with delight.

One night in 1941, at the Peavine Club—a tacky Black joint in Reno, Nevada—Count Otis sang his risqué little verse, and a burly, white plainclothes cop materialized out of the shadows and snarled, "Sing one more dirty, filthy song and I'm taking all you niggers down!" After that, our most daring number was "Mama Bought a Chicken."

Further Reading

Lipsitz, George. *Midnight at the Barrelhouse: The Johnny Otis Story*. Minneapolis: University of Minnesota Press, 2010.

Otis, Johnny. *Upside Your Head! Rhythm and Blues on Central Avenue*. Hanover, N.H.: University Press of New England, 1993.

Discography

Otis, Johnny. *Jukebox Hits: 1946–1954*. Acrobat, 2007.

_____. *The Godfather of Rhythm and Blues, and the R&B Caravan*. EP Musique, 2003.

12. The Producers Answer Back

THE EMERGENCE OF THE "INDIE" RECORD COMPANY

The article reproduced in Chapter 5, "Thar's Gold in Them Hillbillies," discussed the position of the "race" and "hillbilly" categories in relation to mainstream "popular" music during the 1920s and 1930s. What that article did not really discuss or analyze was how the structure of the music industry in the United States discriminated against popular musicians outside the mainstream. Radio was dominated by national network shows (somewhat analogous to network television), which played a broad range of programs: music variety, dramas, comedies, news, concerts, and so forth. The music featured on these shows tended to consist of songs written by professionals employed in Tin Pan Alley. These songwriters also were responsible for the vast majority of Broadway (and, after 1930, Hollywood) musicals. The main organization responsible for securing royalties for songwriters was a publishing-rights organization known as the American Society of Composers and Publishers (ASCAP). ASCAP had stringent rules about who they would accept as a composer, and most composers of hillbilly and race music did not fit their guidelines. These songwriters were thus excluded both from receiving exposure via radio broadcasts and from collecting revenue from their songs (which might accrue from either jukebox play, sales of recordings, public performance, or radio broadcasts).[1]

This situation began to change on several fronts in the late 1930s. A publishing-rights organization, Broadcast Music Incorporated (BMI), formed with somewhat looser guidelines than ASCAP about what constituted an acceptable composition and what type of people might qualify as acceptable composers. Small local radio stations that began to play "hillbilly" music proliferated (stations devoted to "race" music developed a bit later). "Barn Dance" shows, such as the Grand Ole Opry, and the WLS *National Barn Dance*, both of which had been broadcasting since 1925, reached larger audiences, and the Grand Ole Opry even procured a half-hour Saturday night slot on the NBC radio network. Recording bans during 1942 and 1943 increased radio networks' interest in alternative sources for recordings, a development that also facilitated crossovers and cover tunes of both hillbilly and race music. And immediately following the war, the number of independent record companies catering to these types of music grew at an unprecedented rate. All these developments set the stage for a massive shift in the role played by hillbilly and race music in popular music.

The following article demonstrates the music industry's awareness of the growing role of independent record companies. During the late 1940s, four major companies dominated record sales: RCA Victor, Columbia, Decca, and Capitol. Nevertheless, the percentage of sales controlled by the "majors" slipped between 1948 and 1955, presaging a major decentralization of record sales by the late 1950s.[2] This article

1. See John Ryan, *The Production of Culture in the Music Industry: The ASCAP-BMI Controversy* (New York: Rowman and Littlefield, 1985); Russell Sanjek and David Sanjek, *Pennies from Heaven: The American Popular Music Business in the Twentieth Century* (New York: Da Capo Press, 1996); and Philip T. Ennis, *The Seventh Stream: The Emergence of Rocknroll in American Popular Music* (Hanover, N.H.: University Press of New England, 1992).

2. For an in-depth analysis of record companies during this period, see Richard A. Peterson and David G. Berger, "Cycles in Symbol Production: The Case of Popular Music," *American Sociological Review* 40 (1975), reprinted in *On Record: Rock, Pop, and the Written Word*, ed. Simon Frith and Andrew Goodwin, 140–59 (New York: Pantheon, 1990).

was published in *Billboard*, the leading music industry weekly, whose editorial policy took for granted the centrality and superiority of music originating in Tin Pan Alley. While somewhat condescending, the author nonetheless recognizes the entrepreneurial skill and organizational advantages (which include flexibility, underpaying recording artists, and smaller expenses for "disc jockey promotion"[3]) held by small companies in "nonmainstream" categories, such as polka, Polish, Latin, rhythm and blues, and country and western.

Indies' Surprise Survival: Small Labels' Ingenuity and Skill Pay Off

Bill Simon

It's almost a year ago that James C. Petrillo signed with the record companies to end his historic recording ban. At that time most prognosticators foresaw the early demise of the indie companies as the majors threatened to grab their proven artists and methods in all categories. It was reasoned then that distribution and exploitation power, plus slicker recording facilities would spell the end to the indie era. Now it appears that a number of indie label producers have by creative ability, ingenuity and sharp business acumen, carved special niches in the market and actually outsold the majors in several fields. Many indie-produced disks have racked sensational sales figures despite the fact that the artists and tunes were unknown, distribution spotty and exploitation funds virtually nonexistent.

It has become more and more obvious that the gimmick makes the hit, and these indies have been able to come up with the gimmicks. The hit then makes its own distribution. The indie topper, who usually acts as artists-repertoire chief, recording director, business manager and promotion man has got out in the field to dig up new talent with that different, provocative sound. And he's kept his door open to all sorts of new writers and performers. Since overhead is low, and he's not expected to pay the kind of fees a major pays a name artist, he can afford to take chances. And he often has the boldness and the imagination to do so.

Some of the small diskeries have taken advantage of the majors' weakness in certain departments such as rhythm-blues, folk, Latin-American and Polish, and by clever concentration have nabbed the leadership in the various markets. They have consistently attracted the salable new talent and tunes. They have learned their field thoroly [*sic*], and maintain a close contact with the buying public. They have set up their distribution where it counts.

---

3. This practice, acknowledged openly at this point, later became the focus of a backlash against early rock 'n' roll when certain disc jockeys were prosecuted for accepting such "promotional fees," which were subsequently labeled "payola." See Chapter 27 for articles documenting this late 1950s "scandal."

Source: "Indies' Surprise Survival: Small Labels' Ingenuity and Skill Pay Off," *Billboard* / Author: Bill Simon / published December 3, 1949, pg 3, 13, 18.

With low talent and recording costs and with the low, or non-existent royalty rates that are paid out for original material, the indie can usually get off his recording nut with a sale of 5,000 records. A major usually has to go three times that figure to break even. Where the majors pay $275,000 or even more annually for disk jockey promotion, some of the indies will go no higher than $150 a month, usually divided between a couple of key jocks. Some send out vinylites but they know exactly which spinners can use them, and few are wasted.

Rhythm and Blues

In the rhythm-and-blues field, such indies as Atlantic, King, Alladin, Miracle, Supreme, and Savoy have come up sensational sellers. Most of their sides have displayed an acute awareness of their market's ephemeral predictions. Savoy's Herman Lubinsky and Teddy Reig have led the way on many occasions, and the label's original waxing of *The Hucklebuck* is reported to have hit around 500,000. Atlantic's Herb Abramson, who once came up with an *Open the Door, Richard* for National, and also waxed that label's big sides with The Ravens and Billy Eckstine, has come up with a new star, Ruth Brown, on his own label. Her first record, *So Long*, has been out three months and sold 65,000. The label's big click was Stick McGhee's *Drinkin' Wine Spo-Dee-O-Dee*, released in March and, according to publisher's statement, hitting 170,000 at the end of the last quarter. It's now up to about 200,000 and is enjoying a late spurt. Joe Morris's small combo disking of *Beans and Corn Bread* has done 70,000 to date. The diskery anticipates a total sale of 950,000 disks this year.

Sensation, another rhythm-blues outfit, has had several platters hit between 70,000 and 100,000 sales this year. A Crystalette sleeper, *Ain't She Sweet?*, by Mr. Goon Bones, has sold close to 500,000. The Tempo etching of *Margie*, by the original Mr. Bones, hit 376,000 between the first of the year and the end of the last quarter. This platter, which retails at $1.05, was the first of the gimmicked "Bones" novelties to hit.

Hillbillies Score

King, 4-Star, Imperial and several more are racking up startling figures in Country-Western territories. The original disking of *Why Don't You Haul Off and Love Me?*, cut for King by Wayne Raney, has hit 250,000 and versions are now available on all major labels. None of these, however, has approached Raney's mark. Another King disk, *Blues Stay 'Way From Me?*, by the Delmore Brothers, is close to 125,000 in six weeks, and the other companies have just begun to cover the tune. King, masterminded by Sid Nathan, virtually dominated the folk field during some months of this year.

> One of the unsung heroes of early R&B and rock 'n' roll, and one of a handful of African Americans with some clout in the recording industry at this time, Henry Glover was a songwriter, arranger, producer, and A&R (artists and repertoire) director at King Records, an independent label located in Cincinnati specializing in rhythm and blues and country music (discussed at the end of the previous article). Glover was the musical brain behind King who helped label owner Syd Nathan realize his goal of having country artists record rhythm and blues songs and

rhythm and blues artists record country songs—usually they would have one artist from each category record the same song. Glover's arrangements and skills as a producer enabled these ideas to work musically.[4] Here Glover recounts King Records' crossover strategy.

from Honkers and Shouters: The Golden Years of Rhythm and Blues
Arnold Shaw

"Sam Phillips has received great recognition because he did the novel thing of recording R&B with white country boys. He deserves credit, considering that Elvis Presley, Jerry Lee Lewis, Roy Orbison, Carl Perkins, and Johnny Cash all emerged from the Sun label. But the fact is that King Records was covering R&B with country singers almost from the beginning of my work with Syd Nathan. We had a duo called The York Brothers who recorded many of the day's R&B hits back in '47–'48. They sounded something like the Everly Brothers, whom they probably influenced. We were more successful in doing the reverse—covering C&W hits with R&B singers. In '49, as you already know, Bull Moose Jackson's hit "Why Don't You Haul Off and Love Me" was a cover of a Wayne Raney country hit. And Wynonie Harris's "Bloodshot Eyes"—on R&B charts in '51—was originally a Hank Penny country record. I'll confess that we didn't think we were doing anything remarkable. It's just that we had both types of artists, and when a song happened in one field, Syd Nathan wanted it moved into the other.

"You see it was a matter of Cincinnati's population. You couldn't sell Wynonie Harris to country folk, and black folk weren't buying Hank Penny. But black folk might buy Wynonie Harris doing a country tune. And since Syd published most of the tunes we recorded, he was also augmenting his publishing income and building important copyrights. He was a smart businessman and didn't miss a trick."

Cofounder of rhythm and blues independent Atlantic label, Ahmet Ertegun was one of the most important behind-the-scenes personages in the development of the "uptown" R&B that began to cross over to white audiences. His career intersected with many of the leading names of not only 1950s, but 1970s rock as well. Near the end of this

---

4. For more on the literature on rhythm and blues with an emphasis on the role of producers, A&R men, and record company owners, see David Sanjek, "One Size Does Not Fit All: The Precarious Position of the African American Entrepreneur in Post–WWII American Popular Music," *American Music* 15, no. 4 (Winter 1997): 535–62. For a longer interview with Glover, see John Rumble, "The Roots of Rock and Roll: Henry Glover of King Records," *Journal of Country Music* 14, no. 2 (1992): 30–42.

entry, Ertegun claims that part of Atlantic's success was due to the loyalty of the artists engendered through generous contracts and the creation of a sense of "family." It is interesting to compare Ertegun's recollections with Ruth Brown's account (in Chapter 16) of how she and other Atlantic artists from that period were treated.

"When I was studying for my doctorate at Georgetown University in Washington, D.C., I hung around a record store not far from the Howard Theatre. That's where I got my doctorate in black music, at the Howard Theatre. What I learned at Max Silverman's Quality Music Shop was that black people didn't buy jazz. They bought country blues singers like Washboard Sam; they bought city blues men like Charles Brown; and they bought rhythm-and-bluesmen like The Ravens. My Atlantic partner, Herb Abramson, had been making these records on National. When we cut Brownie McGhee's brother, Stick McGhee, doing an old blues, our direction was set. 'Drinkin' Wine, Spo-Dee-O-Dee' was our first R&B hit in 1949.

"Black people were clamoring for blues records, blues with a sock dance beat. Around 1949, that was their main means of entertainment. Harlem folks couldn't go downtown to the Broadway theaters and movie houses. Downtown clubs had their ropes up when they came to the door. They weren't even welcome on Fifty-second Street where all the big performers were black. Black people had to find entertainment in their homes—and the record was it.

"Even radio was white oriented. You couldn't find a black performer on network radio. And when it came to disk jockeys on the big wattage stations, they wouldn't play a black record. We had a real tough time getting our records played—even Ruth Brown, who didn't sound particularly black. All the jocks had to see was the Atlantic label and the name of the artist and we were dead. We'd say, 'Just listen and give your listeners a chance to listen.' But they had a set of stock excuses: 'Too loud'; 'Too rough'; 'Doesn't fit our format.' They'd never say, 'We don't play black artists.' But then they'd turn around and play a record of the very same song that was a copy of our record, only it was by a white artist.

"The breakthrough didn't come, as you might expect, in the North. No, it was 'prejudiced' white Southerners who began programming R&B. They began playing Fats Domino, Ivory Joe Hunter, Roy Milton, Ruth Brown, Amos Milburn because young white teen-agers heard them on those top-of-the-dial stations and began requesting them. What the hell was Elvis listening to when he was growing up?

"From the beginning, our records were really accessible to white listeners. Our artists weren't down-home bluesmen. They didn't come from red-clay country. And our backup groups were either studio musicians or jazzmen. Working with these sophisticated cats, we did try to get an authentic blues feeling. And how could you beat a polished performance of down-to-earth blues material? It has mass appeal, white as well as black.

"We worked at getting a strong and clean rhythm sound. This was partly a matter of engineering. We were among the first independents to mike instruments in the rhythm section separately—a separate mike for drums, bass, and guitar. But to get that clean rhythmic punch, we found it necessary to use written arrangements. This was a major departure in R&B recording. Experienced black arrangers like Jesse Stone, Howard Biggs, Budd Johnson, Bert Keyes, and Teacho Willshire, later white arrangers like Ray Ellis and Stan Applebaum, helped develop a blues arranging style. Some writers have described the Atlantic Sound as R&B with strings or arranged R&B, and there's some merit in that.

"In later years, the Atlantic Sound acquired what Jelly Roll Morton spoke of as 'the Spanish tinge.' Leiber and Stoller introduced a shuffling Latin beat in some of The Drifters' records. Bert Berns also had a big feeling for Spanish music. W. C. Handy used the habanera rhythm in his 'St. Louis Blues.' In the late fifties the samba beat, guaracha, baion, and other Afro-Cuban rhythms added color and excitement to the basic drive of R&B.

"Atlantic grew and survived when most other independents disappeared because it had great flexibility and responded to change. A record company needs engineers, creative producers, and smart promoters. But more than anything else, it needs artists. We established a reputation early for paying established artists top royalty—and did pay. This trade secret attracted many performers to our doors. And after we signed them, we worked to make them feel at home and to search out the best material we could find for recording. We're probably too big now to cultivate the family feeling that was ours for years, but we still like to think of ourselves as a big, happy, soulful family."

Further Reading

Ennis, Philip H. *The Seventh Stream: The Emergence of Rocknroll in American Popular Music.* Hanover, N.H.: University Press of New England, 1992.

Peterson, Richard A., and David G. Berger. "Cycles in Symbol Production: The Case of Popular Music." *American Sociological Review* 40 (1975); reprinted in *On Record: Rock, Pop, and the Written Word*, ed. Simon Frith and Andrew Goodwin, 140–59. New York: Pantheon, 1990.

Rumble, John. "The Roots of Rock and Roll: Henry Glover of King Records." *Journal of Country Music* 14, no. 2 (1992): 30–42.

Ryan, John. *The Production of Culture in the Music Industry: The ASCAP-BMI Controversy.* Lanham, Md.: University Press of America, 1985.

Sanjek, David. "One Size Does Not Fit All: The Precarious Position of the African American Entrepreneur in Post–WWII American Popular Music." *American Music* 15, no. 4 (Winter 1997): 535–62.

Sanjek, Russell, and David Sanjek. *Pennies from Heaven: The American Popular Music Business in the Twentieth Century.* New York: Da Capo Press, 1996.

Discography

Atlantic Rhythm and Blues 1947–1974. Atlantic, 1991.

The Black and White Roots of Rock 'n' Roll. Indigo, 2004.

Fifty Years of Country Music from Mercury. Polygram, 1995.

King R&B Box Set. King, 1996.

Mercury Blues 'n' Rhythm Story 1945–1955. Polygram, 1996.

13. Country Music as Folk Music, Country Music as Novelty

Several articles have already touched upon the position of country (or "hillbilly") music within the post-1920 music industry. Country music, in its modern, commercial, mechanically reproducible form, began in the 1920s as a conglomeration of separate genres: ballads derived from traditional music of the British Isles, string band music, fiddle tunes, hymns, and blues. As the inclusion of "blues" in the preceding list indicates, musical elements that would later be associated exclusively with African Americans formed a powerful part of the mix. The early music industry name for this category of music, "hillbilly," was a pejorative term used by rural, white southerners in the spirit of affectionate self-deprecation; however, its use by music executives in New York City arose from a misunderstanding and conveyed a supercilious attitude toward the music.[1]

New genres of country music developed in the 1930s in response to changing performance contexts and increasing contact with other popular idioms. One new genre, Western Swing, arose from a conjunction of fiddle-led, string band dance music and big band swing. Breaking with country music tradition by using drums, Western Swing also featured amplified guitars, horns, and piano alongside bass and fiddle. From the rough barrooms of the rural South came another new genre, "honky-tonk" music, named after the venues in which it was featured. Honky-tonk also featured amplfied guitars and produced stars in the late 1930s and early 1940s such as Ernest Tubb, Cliff Bruner, and Ted Daffan.

In the early 1940s, both Western Swing and honky-tonk produced "crossover" hits: songs that appeared on the popular music charts and were heard on national network radio broadcasts. Songs like "New San Antonio Rose" by Bob Wills, "Born to Lose" by Ted Daffan, and "Walking the Floor Over You" by Ernest Tubb found large audiences that cut across the demographic spectrum, a development aided by pop artists such as Bing Crosby, who recorded their own "cover" versions of the songs. Country music, in turn, was influenced by mainstream popular music in

---

1. For a more thorough description of the history of this term, see Bill Malone, *Country Music U.S.A.*, rev. ed. (Austin: University of Texas Press, 1985); and Archie Green, "Hillbilly Music: Source and Symbol," *Journal of American Folklore* 78 (July–September 1965): 204–28.

terms of songwriting conventions, instrumentation, and rhythm (as in the "swing" of Western Swing).

Beginning in 1939, the popularity of country music began to be tracked in the music industry publication, *Billboard*, in a chart initially titled "hillbilly." The number of songs represented in this chart increased throughout the 1940s as the name vacillated, changing to "American folk" in 1945, before finally settling down to "country and western" in 1949. This name reflected what were perceived at the time as two different types of music: "country" included honky-tonk music and music descended from fiddle tunes, ballads, waltzes, and novelty tunes, while "western" referred to Western Swing and cowboy songs.

The unsigned article that begins this chapter marks an increase of interest in country music in music industry publications. The author correctly points out the link between country music of the 1940s and the traditional music of Euro-Americans (particularly in the rural South) prior to the advent of recording. The tone is faintly apologetic, as if anticipating a skeptical readership, which, since the article was appearing in *Billboard*, was not unreasonable. The explanation that the spread of country music's popularity reflects demographic shifts has some validity but implies that the music could appeal only to southerners (or their friends), an explanation that turned out to be overly pessimistic. The article also refers to a phenomenon that was only beginning: the writing of country tunes by Tin Pan Alley tunesmiths.

American Folk Tunes: Cowboy and Hillbilly Tunes and Tunesters

Billboard

People's Music

Folk music, tho highly sectional, has always been the music of the people as a whole. Plaintive or catchy, the melodies are easily remembered and easily sung. Written from the heart, the words more often than not are imperfect grammatically, but they express the feeling of the people more clearly than would even perfect poetry. To be sure, many folk tunes have been written by commercial writers and some corrupted by the South American influence, but the majority are written by people who find music as the outlet for their thoughts and emotions. They stress the ordinary sorrows and joys of people which are experienced by everyone, be he rich or poor. Love, hate, loyalty, infidelity, all have their place in folk music. Early American folk music told the tales of heroes, good and bad. Sung by people as they pioneered the country, the songs were a means of spreading news. The story of many a famous battle has been told in a folk song. Today's folk music has changed but little from the early songs.

Source: "American Folk Tunes: Cowboy and Hillbilly Tunes and Tunesters," *Billboard*/Published August 17, 1946, pg 120.

While they are no longer need [*sic*] to carry news the basic components have remained the same.

Another major factor in the increasing popularity of folk music was the migration of country dweller to the city during the war. The country dweller demanded the music with which he was familiar at night clubs, theaters, dance halls and amusement parks. He organized square dances, jamborees and hayrides, and as a result of this activity, the city dweller, once too sophisticated for the simple music, found himself enjoying it as he attended the square dances in the company of his country friends.

A third factor was the cognizance of the trend by show business. Ever on the alert for the changing moods of its audiences, show business eagerly complied with the request for folk music. Folk artists were imported from country fairs to theaters and night clubs. Entertainers in the popular and concert fields included folk music on their programs. Radio increased its folk shows. Motion pictures included folk artists and folk music in pictures other than Westerns. Thus more and more people became acquainted with folk music and the interest in it spread from coast to coast.

That this rise in popularity of folk tunes will continue is certain, for today efforts are being made to catalog, categorize and compile folk music for the first time in its history. Whether or not folk music will ever entirely supplant the so-called popular music is not certain. At any rate, folk music is here to stay.

In the late 1940s, the profile of country music among the general public continued to increase. However, the most successful recordings of country tunes in the "popular" category during this period were not songs by country artists, but "cover tunes" of country songs by pop artists or pseudo-country songs written by Tin Pan Alley songwriters.[2] In 1950, the phenomenon of country music's crossover success reached an apex: "The Tennesse Waltz," recorded and composed by country artist Pee Wee King in 1948, was released in a cover version by pop singer Patti Page in 1950 and became one of the best-selling recordings up to that time, spawning an additional six cover versions by pop artists that made the best-seller charts during 1951.[3]

By 1949, the presence of tunes originating in the country field had grown to the point where mass circulation magazines such as *Newsweek* felt the need to give their readers some background on the phenomenon. The title of the following article, "Corn of Plenty," tells readers all they need to know about the cultural status of the music under discussion (and shows how impressions of country music had changed little since the 1938 *Collier's* article reprinted in Chapter 5). The article refers to

---

2. This phenomenon is noted in the following entry and was the focus of an article in the *New York Times Magazine*: "Tin Pan Alley's Git-tar Blues," *New York Times Magazine,* July 15, 1951, 8, 36, 37.

3. For a more in-depth account of "Tennessee Waltz" and its significance for both the country and popular music fields, see James M. Manheim, "B-side Sentimentalizer: 'Tennessee Waltz' in the History of Popular Music," *Musical Quarterly* 76, no. 3 (Fall 1992): 37–56.

the increasing prominence of country tunes on the popular Hit Parade and discusses the prominence of Eddy Arnold in particular. Because of the prevalence of cover versions, Arnold's songs were heard by the popular music audience in recordings by pop singers, despite the fact that his own versions sold over a million copies. The overall impression conveyed by this article is the sense of a vacuum in mainstream popular music that the music industry ("in its chronic fluttery state") is filling with country music and other sorts of "simpler songs."

Corn of Plenty
Newsweek

"The corn is as high as an elephant's eye—and so are the profits." A hard-bitten Tin Pan Alley character shook his head in amazement, for he was talking about hillbilly songs—the current wonder of the music world.

Always a steady factor in record and sheet sales, hillbilly music is now such a vogue that it is "just about pushing popular tunes, jazz, swing, bebop, and everything else right out of the picture," noted *Down Beat* magazine. While the rest of the music business remained in its chronic fluttery state, the hillbilly output remained fairly constant. But the demand for it has multiplied fivefold since the war. This week the industry was still moving in concentric circles and nothing was dependable—except hillbilly music.

Out of the Hills

Ten years ago, if a hillbilly record sold 10,000 copies, it was a hit; today a 50,000 sale is mediocre. Once a specialty product marketed in the Deep South, it now has a nationwide sales field. The South is still lapping it up (some radio stations play hillbilly music eighteen hours a day), but Pennsylvania and New York are right behind. City slickers are square-dancing from Ciro's in Hollywood to the Pierre in New York, and the cowpoke "Riders in the Sky" is the most popular song in the nation.

With the war, hillbilly music quickly came out of the hills. Most of the large training camps were in the South, and GI's who might have never been exposed to this relatively unfamiliar music heard it constantly. They liked it—and brought the songs home with them. Postwar shifts in population helped spread it; and disk jockeys followed through and aired "country" music to a widening audience. It all tied in with the current trend toward simpler songs—and nothing is simpler than country music.

Rich Soil

From the plains, prairies, and hills the songs are now coming—ballads (love stories), narratives, sacred songs, and dance tunes. Titles range from "My Daddy Is Only a Picture" to "Life Gits Tee-jus, Don't It?" Songs celebrating news events pop up overnight. For example, only three days after little Kathy Fiscus of San Marino, Calif., died in an abandoned well, the record companies were swamped with songs about her. And no Tin Pan Alley tunesmith can turn out songs faster than country-song writers—men like Fred Rose, Bob Miller, and Carson Robison.

But country music has spilled over into the more conventional popular field, and many numbers are being recorded in both straight and country styles. Jo Stafford's raucous hayseed version of "Timtayshun" undoubtedly started something, and it would seem that all a singer needs is a hoedown fiddle, a steel guitar, a mandolin, and new inflection in his voice—and he's set for the bonanza. Dinah Shore did just that and changed the schmaltzy European waltz "Forever and Ever" into a backwoods ditty.

Back in 1930 country singers started going highly commercial when Gene Autry pioneered the way. Following him came a long procession of names, led today by Hank Williams, George Morgan, Red Foley, Roy Acuff, Jimmy Wakely—and the kingpin of them all—Eddy Arnold.

Barefoot Boys

In New Orleans last February, Eddy Arnold guest-starred on the Spike Jones show. Laying aside his guitar, he did a skit in which he was murdered by a storekeeper. As Arnold sagged dying to the floor, Jones bawled to the other actor: "You just killed RCA Victor's biggest asset!"

He wasn't far wrong, for Eddy Arnold ranks with Perry Como and Vaughn Monroe among RCA's top popular names. Just another country boy five years ago, today he is the pace setter in the whole country-music field.

Arnold was born on his father's farm near Henderson, Tenn., 30 years ago. As a child, he picked cotton and husked corn on land that barely gave his family enough to eat. "I figured," he recalls, "there must be a better way of makin' a livin'."

When he was 10, his cousin gave him an old Sears, Roebuck guitar, and Arnold started fooling around with it. Soon he was good enough to play with local outfits. At 15 he took four lessons at 75 cents apiece from an itinerant musician—the only music lessons he ever had.

Pay Dirt

By the time he was 18, he signed up with Pee Wee King and His Golden West Cowboys, and from there he struck out on his own. On a six-day-a-week stint over Station WSM at Nashville, the 6-foot, drawling baritone sang, played the guitar, and called himself "The Tennessee Plowboy"—a sobriquet he still uses. There RCA heard him and signed him up in 1944.

In 1946 along came "That's How Much I Love You," and the ball started rolling. It picked up momentum with "I'll Hold You in My Heart" and last year's "Bouquet of Roses," which sold a million and a half records and is still going strong. Ever since Arnold made the big time, no record of his has sold less than 400,000 copies. His current number, "One Kiss Too Many," hit the 250,000 mark last week—with only six weeks' sales.

Arnold is tied up with RCA Victor until 1956. He also has a radio show on Mutual and a two-picture deal with Columbia. He is now star-gazing in Hollywood while making "Hoedown," but somehow, "I'm real downright homesick for my wife an' kids an' my mom back home."

Today the barefoot boy has an annual gross income of $250,000, a great cure for homesickness.

Further Reading

La Chapelle, Peter. *Proud to Be an Okie: Cultural Politics, Country Music, and Migration to South-ern California*. Berkeley: University of California Press, 2007.

Malone, Bill C. *Country Music, U.S.A*. 2nd ed. Austin: University of Texas Press, 2002.

Pecknold, Diane. *The Selling Sound: The Rise of the Country Music Industry*. Durham, N.C.: Duke University Press, 2007.

Peterson, Richard A. *Creating Country Music: Fabricating Authenticity*. Chicago: University of Chicago Press, 1997.

Russell, Tony. *Country Music Originals: The Legends and the Lost*. New York: Oxford University Press, 2007.

Discography

Acuff, Roy. *King of Country Music*. Proper Box UK, 2004.

Daffan, Ted and His Texans. *Born to Lose*. Jasmine, 2004.

Foley, Red. *Hillbilly Fever*. Blaricum, 2005.

The Smithsonian Collection of Classic Country Music. PS 15640, 1981.

Tubb, Ernest. *The Definitive Collection*. MCA Nashville, 2006.

Wills, Bob. *The Essential Bob Wills*. Sony, 1992.

PART 2

The 1950s

14. Country Music Approaches the Mainstream

In contrast to the bemused accounts in the late 1940s in publications such as *Billboard* and *Newsweek,* country music had so succeeded by 1953 that it earned a feature story in a business magazine. The period 1949 to 1953 witnessed numerous cover versions of country songs (especially those written and recorded by Hank Williams) that succeeded on the pop charts, as well as some crossover hits by country stars such as Red Foley and Tennessee Ernie Ford. While this article shares with the earlier entries a somewhat condescending tone (note especially the description of the audience), it nevertheless enthusiastically discusses the spread of country music to Europe and Asia. Another important focus is the history provided of that enduring institution, the Grand Ole Opry, and its development in tandem with the rest of the Nashville-based country music industry (which is, after all, what one may expect to find in a business magazine). The article concludes with a brief interview with Hank Williams (1923–53), arguably the most significant songwriter and performer in country music during this period and one of the most influential musicians in country music history. An unwritten requirement of any piece on Williams is that it must include a reference to Tee-Tot, an African American guitarist and street musician who was an early mentor of Williams.

Country Music Goes to Town
Rufus Jarman

What brought this homely music out of the back-roads and into great popularity nationally—and now internationally—was radio in general and in particular station WSM, owned by the National Life & Accident Insurance Company. Through country music, Nashville is now a phonograph-recording center comparable to New York and Hollywood. WSM has become the "big time" to country musicians, as the old Palace once was to vaudeville. The *Wall Street Journal* has estimated that country music in Nashville now amounts to a $25,000,000-a-year industry.

What baffles conservative Nashvillians are the crowds that swarm into town each week to see the program, which lasts four and one-half hours. All of it is broadcast over WSM's powerful, clear-channel station, and 30 minutes of it has been broadcast for a dozen years over the NBC network, sponsored by Prince Albert Tobacco. Red Foley is the master of ceremonies. In addition to the music of bands and quartets, there are two immensely popular comedians, Red Brasfield of Hohenwald, Tenn., and Cousin Minnie Pearl, a product of Centerville, Tenn.

Only the network portion of the show is rehearsed and that only once, for timing. About 125 stars and their "side men" take part in this whole jamboree, which is marked by great informality. Performers, some in outlandish costumes, stroll about the stage, join in with their instruments with units of the show other than their own, and occasionally toss one another playfully into a tub of iced drinks that is kept on the stage at all times.

The audience ranges from a few people who think the term "Opry" means they should come formal to those who take off their shoes and nurse their babies during the show. Many of them come in trucks.

In Nashville hotels, they often bed down eight to a room, and bring along their food. They clean their hotel rooms, never having heard of maid service. Many of them never heard of tipping either. Bellboys and elevator operators, when the management isn't looking, may make up for this over-sight by charging ten cents per elevator ride.

Besides their radio programs and records, the Opry stars constantly manifest themselves to their followers through personal appearances, arranged by the WSM Artist Service Bureau, under Jim Denny. Every night one or more troupes of Opry stars are appearing in some city about the land. They have crammed Carnegie Hall in New York and played before sellout audiences in white ties and tails in Constitution Hall in Washington. More often they appear on Sundays in picnic groves in Pennsylvania, Illinois or Ohio. Not long ago, one troupe played to 65,000 persons in four days in Texas.

To fill this schedule, the Opry stars live a hard life. They usually leave Nashville in their cars on Sundays, and drive hard from one engagement to another, heading back to Nashville in time for Saturday. Often they don't sleep in a bed for nights on end, but take turns driving.

They keep their car radios tuned to hillbilly broadcasts at all times, and when they hear some local rustic singer who sounds promising, they tip off Jack Stapp, the Opry's program director.

Source: "Country Music Goes to Town," Rufus Jarman, originally published February 1953.
Reprinted by permission, uschamber.com, July 2012. Copyright © 1953 U.S. Chamber of Commerce.

The touring stars have simple living tastes. One observer who has travelled with them reports that some stars, making hundreds of thousands of dollars a year will eat the same meal three times a day—fried potatoes, fried eggs and fried pork chops. For, in spite of their fancy clothes, big cars and abundant money, the Opry stars remain simple people who "were raised hard and live hard," as one of them has said. Some of them do not know a note of music, but their great appeal as entertainers is in the rawness of their emotions and their sincerity in conveying them.

Hank Williams was discussing that shortly before his death in January. Williams was a lank, erratic countryman who learned to play a guitar from an old Negro named Teetot in his home village of Georgiana, Ala.

"You ask what makes our kind of music successful," Williams was saying. "I'll tell you. It can be explained in just one word: sincerity. When a hillbilly sings a crazy song, he feels crazy. When he sings, 'I Laid My Mother Away,' he sees her a-laying right there in the coffin.

"He sings more sincere than most entertainers because the hillbilly was raised rougher than most entertainers. You got to know a lot about hard work. You got to have smelt a lot of mule manure before you can sing like a hillbilly. The people who has been raised something like the way the hillbilly has knows what he is singing about and appreciates it.

"For what he is singing is the hopes and prayers and dreams and experiences of what some call the 'common people.' I call them the 'best people,' because they are the ones that the world is made up most of. They're really the ones who make things tick, wherever they are in this country or in any country.

"They're the ones who understand what we're singing about, and that's why our kind of music is sweeping the world. There ain't nothing strange about our popularity these days. It's just that there are more people who are like us than there are the educated, cultured kind.

"There ain't nothing at all queer about them Europeans liking our kind of singing. It's liable to teach them more about what everyday Americans are really like than any thing else."

Further Reading

Ching, Barbara. *Wrong's What I Do Best: Hard Country Music and Contemporary Culture.* New York: Oxford University Press, 2001.

Green, Archie. "Hillbilly Music: Source and Symbol." *Journal of American Folklore* 78 (July–September 1965): 204–28.

Malone, Bill. *Country Music U.S.A.* 2nd rev. ed. Austin: University of Texas, 2002.

Peterson, Richard. *Creating Country Music: Fabricating Authenticity.* Chicago: University of Chicago Press, 1997.

Discography

Classic Country, vols. 1 and 2. Time-Life Music, Sony, 1999.

Foley, Red. *Hillbilly Fever: 24 Greatest Hits.* Blaricum, 2005.

Ford, Tennessee Ernie. *Vintage Collections Series.* EMI Special Products, 1997.

The Smithsonian Collection of Classic Country Music. PS 15640, 1981.

Wells, Kitty. *My Cold, Cold Heart Is Melted Now.* Decca, 1954.

Williams, Hank. *Original Singles Collection . . . Plus.* Mercury Nashville, 1992.

15. Rhythm and Blues in the Early 1950s

B. B. KING

The music industry category of rhythm and blues included within it a great diversity of distinct musical genres. The three musicians examined more closely in this and subsequent chapters—B. B. King, Ruth Brown, and Ray Charles—represent three important strands of R&B that emerged during the early 1950s: the transformation of the country blues into urban blues, the development of a more carefully arranged form of R&B, and the increasing use of vocal techniques derived from solo gospel singing.

Riley "B. B." ("Blues Boy") King (b. 1925) already appeared as an interviewee in the article about T-Bone Walker in Chapter 9. One of the most popular rhythm and blues performers of the 1950s and early 1960s, B. B. King was responsible for spreading and popularizing many of Walker's innovations: the jazzy, single-note improvisations on guitar; the gospel-influenced vocal style; and the large band arrangements featuring horns.[1] A widely imitated guitarist, King became known to many fans of rock music through his influence on rock guitarists such as Eric Clapton and through the tributes paid to him by Clapton and other white artists. Despite the acclaim generated by such attention and by successful albums like *Live at the Regal* (1964), King had to wait until 1970 for his greatest mainstream success with "The Thrill Is Gone." In this interview, recorded in 1978, King talks about how he learned to entertain audiences, some unsuspected relationships between sacred and secular music, and what the blues mean to him. King comments on the shifting nature of music industry classifications and how in many ways they seem determined more by sociological factors than musical ones.

---

1. A fascinating account of King during this period can be found in Charles Keil, *Urban Blues* (Chicago: University of Chicago Press, 1966).

from Honkers and Shouters:
The Golden Years of Rhythm and Blues
Arnold Shaw

"I left Indianola in 1946, hitchhiking to Memphis. I had been singing with a gospel quartet called the St. John Gospel Singers. There were a lot of groups around, and material would pass from group to group so that we did some new gospel songs. We picked most of our material from what we heard on records, radio, jukeboxes. Poor people were beginning to afford a radio and they got to know the name [of] groups and their songs. CBS and a few of the networks were presenting groups like The Trumpeteers and the Golden Gate Quartet. Then, out of Nashville, we could hear the Fairfield Four. The Soul Stirrers came into our area, and that was when I first met Sam Cooke—around 1948, I guess.

"The distinctions that I hear writers make between blues and rhythm and blues I regard as artificial. Most of the people that we hear playing the blues came from the same area, even though they may be living in other areas. We hear of the Chicago blues because many of the Mississippi crowd lives in Chicago. When I was on the radio in Memphis, we used to get *Billboard, Cash Box,* and they classed things that Louis Jordan was doing as rhythm and blues. Or they would call it 'race.' And that's how you could distinguish what he and others like him did from so-called pop. But today, for instance, James Brown is considered rhythm and blues. Aretha Franklin is considered soul or rhythm and blues—and I am considered blues. [Chuckling] In Memphis, I was considered rhythm and blues. I personally think that it's all rhythm and blues because it's blues and it has rhythm. I guess that you could break it down if you wanted to. I remember that Dinah Washington was considered R&B or 'race.' But Dinah sang anything that anybody else sang. She just sang it her own way. She was doing all of the popular tunes of the late forties and early fifties. So were Ella Fitzgerald, Nat Cole, and Louis Armstrong—these were the top black recording artists. Louis Jordan, too, and The Ink Spots. But they were classed differently. Ella was more pop than most of the black female singers, but she still covered most of the bluesy tunes. But Dinah stayed with them, and Louis Jordan stayed with them, and they came up with some very big records. I remember Dinah covering 'Three Coins in a Fountain.' Mercury Records was using her to sell records to black record buyers. But when she did these pop tunes in her way, they were classed as rhythm and blues.
    "It's true that after the big band era, blues singers started being accompanied by horns and rhythm groups instead of just guitar and harp. But the reason that this happened was because, before that, blues singers just could not afford to be backed by bands. They wanted it. In the delta, there was a band called the Red Caps that had all kinds of instruments. They were playing like Jimmie Lunceford. They were stationed right there in Greenville, Mississippi. They were among the lucky few that could afford band instrumentation. Incidentally, the Red Caps I'm talking about were not the Red Caps of Steve Gibson that had 'Wedding Bells Are Breaking Up That Old Gang of Mine.' But they played the socials around Greenville, and they had a very varied repertoire. They played bluesy things and jazz.

What I'm trying to say is that if we had the money or even a music store where we could borrow instruments—why we had to go twenty-five miles to the nearest music store. We did not have one in Indianola, Greenwood or Greenville was the nearest place. And when you went to one of these stores, you had to pay cash. They didn't know you, and you didn't have any credit. At that time, a horn was costing like $100. Gosh, in those days, it would take me five months to make $100. Out of the twenty-two fifty a week I was making, after you bought groceries and other necessities, you could save only seven to eight dollars. So you bought whatever instrument you could afford—and that was the guitar. As for a piano, you could forget about that. Or an organ. But my aunt had one that you had to paddle with your feet. It's so funny to see people now playing notes on an organ with their feet. Well, then you had to use your feet to get air flowing through the organ pipes. I don't know how she got that organ. My aunt was one of those people who said that a person had to have something for themselves. And she did. She had a phonograph, or as we called them, a Victrola. When I was a good boy—and I stayed a good boy around her—she would let me play the Victrola. And that's how I got into those old blues records like Lemon Jefferson. I had a chance to fool with the organ, and that's how I learned to play a few chords.

"My first hit record was Lowell Fulson's tune, 'Three O'Clock Blues.' I always did like his work. In fact, I idolized Lowell. But I probably like his singing better than his playing. It's nice of him to say that I do 'Every Day I Have the Blues' better than he does, but he had a hit on it. Several of us had hits on that Memphis Slim tune. But Lowell was the one who influenced me to do the tune. He and Joe Williams. You know, a lot of people don't know that Williams cut 'Every Day I Have the Blues' before he made it with Basie. He first made it with King Kolak's band. That was the one, along with Lowell's record, that made me think that I could get a hit on it. And luckily I did. But then, when Joe Williams got with Basie, he did it again, and that was the master one. But Lowell is a great artist. He is one of the sleeping giants in the blues.

"When I first started performing, it was me alone. Then I got a trio on the radio: Johnny Ace on piano, Earl Forest on drums. It was hard to keep a bass player. Later on is when I got Billy Duncan on tenor sax. That's when I made 'Three O'Clock Blues.' We recorded our first hit in the YMCA in Memphis. One of my biggest hits, 'Darling, I Love You,' was recorded at Tuff Green's home, the same fellow that made the first record with me.

"By 1955 I was pretty well known, and we were booked for like five to seven hundred dollars a day. That was our guarantee. Then it went up to a thousand and, if we were lucky, twelve hundred. But then I had my own bus and a very big group. We ran it up to about thirteen pieces, and we kept that until I went broke. [Chuckling] Then I dropped down to five: organ, drums, tenor, trumpet, and alto. Kept that for a while, and when things started to pick up, we added more men. I like the big band sound. I guess one of the reasons is my being brought up in the church. I can always hear the choir singing behind me, and that's what I hear when the horns are playing behind me. The little tricky things they do, like rhythms within rhythms—this is what puts spice on. Blues is usually slow, melancholy, and if you have some little figures going on with the horns, it makes it more interesting.

"The blues is the blues. They don't change. But sounds do change. And I've just had to make some changes in my band after working with some men for many years. For some time, I've been asking them to listen to the sounds behind

James Brown, behind Aretha, behind Wilson Pickett. Audiences feel the difference. But it was like I wasn't saying anything. Each year, I give my men four weeks off, two with pay and two without. This was to give them a chance to make a change if they wanted to. And this year, I felt that I had to. It wasn't easy, especially since some of the men are Memphis friends from way back. I understand their feelings. But you either change with the times or you find yourself looking at empty seats. . . ."

Further Reading

Keil, Charles. *Urban Blues*. Chicago: University of Chicago Press, 1966.

Kostelanetz, Richard. *The B. B. King Reader: Six Decades of Commentary*. Milwaukee: Hal Leonard Corp., 2005.

Shaw, Arnold. *Honkers and Shouters: The Golden Years of Rhythm and Blues*. New York: Macmillan, 1986.

Discography

King, B. B. *King of the Blues*. Geffen, 1992.

_____. *Live at the Regal*. Geffen, [1964] 1997.

16. "The House that Ruth Brown Built"

Ruth Brown (b. 1928), along with Dinah Washington, was the biggest female R&B star of the 1950s. Like other R&B and soul stars, Brown's formative musical experiences occurred in the church, and her early musical influences also included field hollers and blues. By the time she began to sing professionally, she had also been exposed to a great variety of music via records and radio and had acquired a background in jazz and mainstream popular music. In 1948, she signed with manager Blanche Calloway, who helped arrange a contract with Atlantic Records. Shortly after signing with Atlantic, Brown was hobbled by a serious auto accident. Nevertheless, she began recording as soon as she possibly could, and her first session resulted in a major R&B

hit, "So Long." Subsequent sessions were marked by eclecticism and uncertainty about how to repeat the success. The search for a follow-up was finally rewarded when Brown, in tandem with arranger Jesse Stone and producers Ahmet Ertegun and Herb Abramson, began to develop a style that fused elements of blues, jazz, and pop. As Brown further refined this fusion into a trademark form of smooth "uptown" rhythm and blues, her continuing success led to Atlantic being known as "The House that Ruth Brown Built."[1]

In her autobiography, *Miss Rhythm*, Ruth Brown describes her contributions to Atlantic, the origins of her biggest hits, and the development of her business relationship with Atlantic. Brown devotes a lot of space to detailing how companies such as Atlantic exploited her and other rhythm and blues artists of the time. One of the factors that gave the companies almost unlimited leverage in withholding royalties was the onerous practice of charging "session fees" to the leader of the date. She also describes the difficulties of touring in the Jim Crow South, a hardship compounded by being the only woman in the entourage as well as the star of the show. Brown's autobiography offers an insightful view of the relationship between rhythm and blues artists in the fifties and the owners of independent companies like Atlantic.

from Miss Rhythm: The Autobiography of Ruth Brown, Rhythm and Blues Legend
Ruth Brown (with Andrew Yule)

On April 6, [1949], still on crutches and wearing a leg brace, I hobbled into the Apex Studio at the tail end of a John "Texas Johnny" Brown session, with Amos Milburn sitting hunched over the piano. I sang "Rain Is a Bringdown," a tune I'd doodled in the hospital just to give Ahmet and Herb an idea of how my voice came over on disc. Then Herb began to talk material, mentioning "So Long," the bluesy ballad we all knew from Little Miss Cornshuck's version. We talked a little bit about the tempo and treatment, and Herb said he'd have an arrangement worked out by the time we were set to record at WOR the following month. We recorded the song with Eddie Condon's orchestra on May 25, and after listening to the playback Ahmet and Herb decided the track was strong enough for my first A-side. "It's Raining" formed the B-side.

---

1. This phrase is a play on the description of Yankee Stadium as "The House that Ruth Built."

Within a few weeks of its release "So Long" was selling well, climbing to number six on Billboard's R-and-B chart. It was only the company's second hit after Sticks McGhee's "Drinkin' Wine, Spo-dee-o-dee," and everybody at Atlantic was thrilled to see the company's name back on the charts. Me too, believe it! This time they were determined it would be no one-hit wonder.

After four of my follow-up releases to "So Long" went nowhere however, it was time for a reappraisal. The problem on Atlantic's side was they couldn't figure out what to do with me. I was recorded with the Delta Rhythm Boys, singing spirituals, even flirting with Yiddish songs in English. *"Too* darn versatile," I heard Herb mutter more than once. The problem I posed, in turn, was my resistance to singing anything but my first love, ballads. I wanted to tell stories in songs, to explore emotions, to the lush sounds of velvety string accompaniments I'd always conjured up when dreaming of recording. A solution had to be found; meanwhile I was working regularly, and for decent money, although I was hampered by the legacy of that car crash.

The house writer that broke the dry spell after "So Long" was Rudolph "Rudy" Toombs. The song Rudy composed especially for me, "Teardrops from My Eyes," took me to the top of the R-and-B chart in October 1950. And there it stayed for eleven solid weeks, with a total chart run of twenty-six weeks. One-hit wonder? Not me, baby! The disc also became a tiny piece of history, being Atlantic's first record made available on seven-inch 45-rpm vinyl as well as the standard ten-inch 78-rpm shellac.

Rudy was my good friend, a man who was simply bursting with life, as effervescent as any of his songs. The things he did for me were different rhythmically from what I was into, but I finally had to give in to the fact that Ahmet, Herb and their team were a step ahead of the accepted sound of the day. Taking a deep breath, I went along with it. Although I had no right of veto in my contract, that did not stop me from fighting if I wasn't happy with what came up. On most issues we reached common ground, with Ahmet and Herb resigned to my singing the occasional ballad, if only for a B-side. Although Herb was the man in charge of my sessions, many of the decisions regarding material were made by Ahmet and arranger Jesse Stone, whose remarkable body of compositions ranged from "Smack Dab in the Middle" all the way to "Shake, Rattle and Roll." He was the man behind so many of the great things that came out of Atlantic, together, of course, with the engineering wizard, Tom Dowd. Tommy had impeccable intuition and was a fixture in the control booth with Ahmet and Herb.

A couple of times during early morning sessions, with sunshine streaming through the windows, I remember protesting it was the wrong time of day to capture a blue mood. "Ruth, just sing like you've got tears in your eyes," Herb would direct me. Another time it would be, "Give me that million-dollar squeal." There were occasions when my throat felt sore, or what I used to call "rusty." "I *like* your sound when it's like that," Herb would enthuse. "It has an earthy quality, a sexiness." *"Down,* boy!" I'd kid him.

Soon I felt like the Queen of the One-Nighters, with dates stretching through the Litchman Theater chain from New York to Washington, Baltimore, Richmond, and near home again at the Booker T in Norfolk. One-night dance dates followed into the Carolinas and all the way down to Georgia, Alabama and Tennessee, bringing me face to face with all those racial problems, rubbing my nose in them. We did close on seventy one-nighters on the trot, spending most days riding the tour bus. When we hit Atlanta we set up camp and made excursions to neighboring towns like Columbus and Augusta, and in Atlanta itself there were lots of clubs to work.

On stage I took to wearing multicolored petticoats and accordion-pleated skirts, featuring all the colors of the rainbow, and from the brighter end of the spectrum: peacock blue, surprise pink, sunshine yellow, orange and lavender. Apart from fellow performers, you had the audiences to compete with, who came along dressed to the nines. Our dates were once-in-a-lifetime-style affairs, a big night out, with posters up months before we arrived. In the South it was even trickier; you had to watch in case a member of the audience was wearing the same dress as you and took offense.

Some people to this day call Atlantic "The House that Ruth Brown Built," and even if this is an exaggeration, few would deny that I contributed a solid portion of the foundation as well as quite a few of the actual bricks. No doubt the cement was the matchless team at the company, Ahmet, Herb, Jesse and Tommy, together with the incredible mix of outstanding musical talent they employed and nurtured.

Rudy Toombs was responsible for the next smash I enjoyed. His original title was "5-10-15 Minutes (Of Your Love)" until Herb coolly informed him that "minutes" was no longer enough now that we were in the era of Billy Ward and the Dominoes' *Sixty-Minute Man*. Presto, it became "5-10-15 Hours (Of Your Love)." The song followed "Daddy, Daddy" into the R-and-B chart in '52 and lodged at number one for seven weeks. Ruth Brown? Hotter than a pistol!

Caught up in the euphoria of having a contract to sign at all, I had taken no advice beyond a quick word with Blanche before signing with Atlantic. Ahmet had a great pitch that settled any questions: "Only Bing Crosby gets five percent at Decca." Ruth Brown on the same percentage as Der Bingle? Sure sounded good to me, although I knew I was starting at the bottom as far as advances were concerned—I'm sure Bing had long since worked his way past sixty-nine dollars a side. I also understood that I was responsible for certain production costs, but how big a deal could they be if I sold enough records?

Strangely enough, despite my continuing chart success, I had to ask every time I needed cash. Any real money I made came from touring, and I was always out there promoting the records. Back then any record by a black artist needed every ounce of help it could get. The expression "R-and-B chart" was another way in the late forties and early fifties to list "race and black" as well as "rhythm and blues" records. And the reason so few discs by black artists crossed over to Billboard's mainstream chart was simple: it was compiled from white-owned radio station playlists featuring music by white artists, with our list confined to stations catering to blacks. As Jerry Wexler, Herb's successor at Atlantic, put it when asked if it was difficult to get R-and-B records played on general-audience stations in the early fifties, "*Difficult* would have been easy. It was *impossible*."

It very gradually became less so, of course, as R-and-B artists broke through the barriers by the sheer strength and quality of their music. But it took time, and throughout my biggest hit-making period I was forced to stand by as white singers like Georgia Gibbs and Patti Page duplicated my records note for note and were able to plug them on top television shows like *The Ed Sullivan Show,* to which I had no access.

Chuck Willis wrote "Oh, What a Dream" especially for me, and it was my favorite song, but it was Patti Page, with an identical arrangement, who got to sing it on national television. Even topical stuff like my "Mambo Baby" had a Georgia Gibbs duplicate rushed out. My labelmate and good friend LaVern Baker, who joined Atlantic in '53, suffered the same fate on her original of "Tweedle Dee"— another note-for-note copy by Her Nibs Miss Gibbs. There was no pretense, either, that they were anything but duplicates. Mercury actually called up Tommy Dowd on the day they were cutting "Tweedle Dee" and said, "Look, we've got the same arrangement, musicians and tempo, we might as well have the same sound engineer too."

It was tough enough coming up with hit sounds, therefore doubly galling to see them stolen from under our noses. Few seemed to stop and question the morality of this, least of all the publishers, to whom it was a case of the more the merrier. LaVern for one did, protesting to her congressman over her treatment at Mercury's hands, but then as now, there was no copyright protection on arrangements.

I was denied sales abroad as well, although I knew nothing of this at the time. "Abroad," as far as the feedback from Atlantic's accounting department was concerned, could have been the moon. Having made number three on Billboard's R-and-B chart in the States, and actually crossing over to their pop charts as well, reaching number twenty-five, my version of "Lucky Lips" was ignored in Britain.

It was because of Willis[2] that I couldn't relate to "Mama, He Treats Your Daughter Mean" when it was first presented to me at Atlantic. Maybe it reminded me of a past relationship I wanted to forget, maybe I felt that singing it would put a jinx on us. I had to be coaxed into it by Herb, who upped the tempo from the slow ballad it had been. The tune had been written by two friends of mine, Herb Lance and Johnny Wallace (brother to a young fighter named Coley, who played the champion in *The Joe Louis Story*). There was a lot of joking around the night we recorded it, for everyone present knew I was less than keen. And Willis was absent, off doing a session of his own. "Does *your man* treat you mean, Ruthie?" drummer Connie Kay inquired, mock-anxiety written all over his teasin' face. "Anybody here seen Gator?" trumpeter Taft Jordan chimed in. I tell you, spitfires can be a target themselves sometimes.

During the first playback Herb and the others all looked at me expectantly. Although I still didn't like it, there was something so comical about their concern that I had to smile and relax into the second take. This time we hit it just right. I can't put my finger on what was so special about that record, for the rhythm pattern was similar to a lot of stuff that was out there, but boy, did it take a trick. I was never so wrong about any piece of material in my life.

Further Reading

Brown, Ruth, and Andrew Yule. *Miss Rhythm: The Autobiography of Ruth Brown, Rhythm and Blues Legend*. New York: Da Capo Press, 1999.
Deffaa, Chip. *Blue Rhythms: Six Lives in Rhythm and Blues*. New York: Da Capo Press, 2000.
Hoskyns, Barney. "Ruth Brown." *Mojo*, March 1995.
Whiteis, David. "Ruth Brown." *Living Blues*, February 2007, 69–71.

Discography

Brown, Ruth. *Miss Rhythm (Greatest Hits and More)*. Atlantic/WEA, 1989.
_____. *The Best of Ruth Brown*. Atlantic/WEA, 1996.

---

2. The "Willis" in question is Willis "Gator Tail" Jackson, tenor saxophonist on many Atlantic recordings from the period, including Brown's, and the person Brown describes as "the love of her life."

17. Ray Charles, or, When Saturday Night Mixed It Up with Sunday Morning

Ray Charles (1930–2004) was almost bewilderingly talented: a pianist, singer, songwriter, arranger, saxophonist, and bandleader, he was also an extraordinarily eclectic musician, skilled in jazz, gospel, blues, country, pop, and classical musics. After initial experiences playing jazz and country music in Florida, Charles moved to Seattle in 1948 and began playing clubs and recording in a sophisticated rhythm and blues style indebted to Nat "King" Cole and Charles Brown. Charles's real breakthrough came in 1953–55 when he developed an earthy adaptation of gospel music that fused the melodies, singing style, and harmonic and rhythmic patterns of gospel with secular lyrics and rhythm and blues instrumentation.

Prior to Charles, the first rhythm and blues singer to attract attention for his indebtedness to gospel technique was Clyde McPhatter, who had been the lead singer on many hit recordings made in the early to mid-1950s with Billy Ward and the Dominoes and with the Drifters. These recordings featured McPhatter's impassioned melismas and call-and-response alternations between him and the other singers in the band to a greater extent than had been evident in previous R&B recordings. What distinguished McPhatter from singers in earlier gospel-derived male groups, such as the Ink Spots and the Mills Brothers, was the way in which he adopted the dynamic solo style of female singers such as Mahalia Jackson and Clara Ward for songs with gospel-derived harmonic progressions in which the change of a single word ("Have Mercy Baby" to "Have Mercy Lord") could transform the song back into a gospel number. Also important during the late 1950s was McPhatter's successor in the Dominoes, Jackie Wilson, a dynamic performer who employed gospel-derived vocal techniques in a pop-oriented idiom.

It was Charles, however, who brought many of McPhatter's innovations to fruition in a series of recordings beginning in 1954. Thinly veiled adaptations of gospel songs, such as "I've Got a Woman" (1954), "This Little Girl of Mine" (1955), "Drowning in My Own Tears" (1956), and "Hallelujah, I Love Her So" (1956), became major rhythm and blues hits while raising charges of blasphemy in the African American community. On these recordings, Charles sings in a raspy, exuberant tone full of whoops, cries, bent notes, melismas, and shouts, engaging in call-and-response patterns with either the horns (a combination of saxophones, trumpets, and trombones) or a female backup trio named the Raelettes, and accompanying himself with gospel-style piano. The apotheosis of this approach comes in Charles's 1959 recording "What'd I Say," which not only imported musical elements from gospel music, but also produced a condensed simulation of an African American Holiness religious service. Charles succeeded with yet another innovative fusion in 1962 with his *Modern Sounds in Country and Western Music.* Although it caught his fans and the music industry off guard, he was merely bringing sounds together that he had been hearing and performing since his childhood.

Ray Charles's autobiography, *Brother Ray*, conveys his charming and irascible personality and details the rise of a poor, blind, African American country boy in the Deep South to become one of the world's most successful entertainers. The path to this success was paved by his voracious appetite for diverse styles and his ability to synthesize them. The passages reproduced here focus on the years during which he developed his proto-soul sound and address the controversy aroused by his adaptation of preexisting gospel material. Throughout these passages, Charles displays a keen sensitivity to the relationship between his style and the makeup of his audience, enabling him to explain quite clearly the difference between the music he was making in the mid-1950s and early rock 'n' roll.

from Brother Ray: Ray Charles' Own Story
Ray Charles and David Ritz

These are the years—'53, '54, '55—when I became myself. I opened up floodgates, let myself do things I hadn't done before, created sounds which, people told me afterward, had never been created before. If I was inventing something new, I wasn't aware of it. In my mind, I was just bringing out more of me. I started taking gospel lines and turning them into regular songs.

Now, I'd been singing spirituals since I was three, and I'd been hearing the blues for just as long. These were my two main musical currents. So what could be more natural than to combine them? It didn't take any thinking, didn't take any calculating. All the sounds were there, right at the top of my head.

Many of those first tunes were adaptations of spirituals I had sung in quartets back in school. "You Better Leave That Woman Alone" was originally something called "You Better Leave That Liar Alone." "Lonely Avenue" was based on a spiritual that Jess Whitaker used to sing with the Pilgrim Travelers. "Talkin' 'Bout You" was another song which I had been singing my whole life in another form.

Source: Brother Ray: Ray Charles' Own Story, Ray Charles and David Ritz, Aaron M. Priest Literary Agency.

None of the spirituals had copyrights. How could they? Black folk had been singing 'em through the hollow logs as far back as anyone could remember. And often my new tunes would be based on three or four gospel numbers—not just one.

But the basic line, the basic structure, the basic chord changes were throwbacks to the earliest part of my life on earth. Nothing was more familiar to me, nothing more natural.

Imitating Nat Cole had required a certain calculation on my part. I had to gird myself; I had to fix my voice into position. I loved doing it, but it certainly wasn't effortless. This new combination of blues and gospel was. It required nothing of me but being true to my very first music.

Now with my band I could rebuild my own little musical world that I first heard in Greensville. In fact, this was the heaviest writing period of my life. When Ahmet Ertegun or Jerry Wexler at Atlantic sent me songs they thought I should record, I often didn't like them. That inspired me to begin writing more tunes of my own.

Atlantic let me record anything I wanted to. They never said, "No, do our songs, not yours." They trusted me and left me alone.

The same thing had been true with Jack Lauderdale when I was recording for Swingtime. And it would be no different years later when I would start making records for ABC.

I've never had what they call a producer to oversee me. I've always produced myself. And during my Atlantic days, I always came into the studio with the tunes already picked and the arrangements already written. There was nothing left for a producer to do.

You might ask: How could a young kid like me—at twenty-two or twenty-three or twenty-four—have that kind of power? I still wasn't much of a name. And I certainly didn't have any right to go round demanding or dictating a goddamn thing. Well, these record people saw that I was developing and that I needed space to find myself. Even though I was young and tender, they let me make my own mistakes, let me produce my own small triumphs.

Only one time at Atlantic—and that was a very minor incident—did one of the cats suggest that I listen to Fats Domino and maybe do something on the style of "Blueberry Hill." I told the guy that I was *for* Fats, but that I wasn't Fats. I was Brother Ray. That quieted him down.

So I was lucky. Lucky to have my own band at this point in my career. Lucky to be able to construct my musical building to my exact specifications. And lucky in another way:

While I was stomping around New Orleans, I had met a trumpeter named Renolds Richard who by this time was in my band. One day he brought me some words to a song. I dressed them up a little and put them to music. The tune was called "I Got a Woman," and it was another one of those spirituals which I refashioned in my own way.

"I Got a Woman" was my first real smash, much bigger than "Baby, Let Me Hold Your Hand." This spiritual-and-blues combination of mine was starting to hit.

But even though this record, made toward the end of 1954, was very big, that didn't mean I was making very big money. It was like that story I told before about Joe Morris. He had a hit, but he still had to hustle like crazy. Well, now *I was* Joe Morris. The success of my record meant I'd get to work more often. But the black promoters—the men I dealt with—still paid very little. And as for royalties, well, they took a long, long time to start coming in, and when they did I used the money for things like new tires for the car.

At the time this was happening, not everyone approved. I got letters accusing me of bastardizing God's work. A big-time preacher in New York scolded me before his congregation. Many folks saw my music as sacrilegious. They said I was taking church songs and making people dance to 'em in bars and nightclubs.

Must tell you that none of those reactions bothered me. I'd always thought that the blues and spirituals were close—close musically, close emotionally—and I was happy to hook' em up. I was determined to go all out and just be natural. Everything else would spring from that. I really didn't give a shit about that kind of criticism.

After "I Got a Woman," my three big records were "A Fool for You," "Drown in My Own Tears" and "Hallelujah, I Love Her So." These were the songs which caught on, the tunes which kept me working.

"Hallelujah" was probably the most important. I did it in late 1955, at the same session as "Drown," and, as far as I was concerned, it was just another number I'd written. I didn't ascribe any great importance to it, and actually the lyrics were a little more lighthearted than the ones I usually wrote.

When I was writing songs, I concentrated on problems or feelings everyone could understand. I wouldn't call the tunes biographical; I just made' em up. But I always tried to stick to common themes—love heartaches, money heartaches, pleasures of the flesh and pleasures of the soul.

"Hallelujah" clicked. It sold big among blacks, and I guess it was my first record to enjoy some popularity among whites.

If these early hits sold two hundred thousand copies, I was pleased. That was almost all in one market—the black market—and two hundred thousand were a lot of records in those days. Oh, sure, there'd be whites who bought my sides—even *sneak* and buy 'em if they had to—but up until "Hallelujah," the overwhelming majority of those listening to me were black.

When I stopped imitating Nat Cole and slid into my own voice, I saw that my successes were exclusively at black clubs and black dances. My music had roots which I'd dug up from my own childhood, musical roots buried in the darkest soil. Naturally it was music blacks could immediately take to heart.

Little by little, though, beginning around 1956, I saw that my music had appeal beyond my own people. I saw it breaking through to other markets, and now and then there'd be a date in a city auditorium where whites would come along with blacks. It probably took me longer to digest this gradual change than it would have taken someone else. I couldn't see the increasing number of white faces.

It meant more work and more money. But it wasn't going to change my music, and it wasn't going to change me. The more people there were who liked my stuff, the happier I was. But at this point in my life that only convinced me to stick to my guns and follow my program. Most of the material the band was playing was our own. Ninety-five percent of everything we did in those years was written by me. There were the original songs—maybe fifteen or twenty that we played. And there were also Latin numbers and hard-driving jazz tunes which I arranged. I remember writing a chart of Dizzy's "Manteca," and we also did a bolero thing on "In a Little Spanish Town" and "Frenesi."

I might write arrangements on ballads like "Funny Valentine" or "If I Had You." I loved old standards and always had them in the book. From the first days the band was together, we played a mixture of the different music I found myself drawn to.

The cats in the band could play the blues. That came first. Show me a guy who can't play the blues and I'm through with him before he can get started. If you can't get nasty and grovel down in the gutter, something's missing.

It's not that the blues are complicated. They're not; they're basic. There are hundreds of versions of the same blues—the same changes, the same patterns—just as there are hundreds of versions of the same spirituals. The music is simple. But the feeling—the low-down gut-bucket feeling—has to be there or it's all for nothing.

My cats could also play serious jazz. Donald Wilkerson, for example, could kick the ass of almost any tenor player in the country. For my money, he's one of the best saxophonists of the century. Fathead[1] was right there next to him, playing with a lyricism and a sweetness which Donald lacked. Fathead didn't have Donald's speed and maybe not as much fire, but he could make his sax sing the song like no one else.

In this period, I loved to watch Donald attack Fathead on the stand. Course that was good for David, and it brought out the best in both cats. When someone tries to stomp on you, naturally you're going to respond. And together—blowing out in front of the band—they'd be burning up the place.

Most of my original compositions—the ones with my own words and my own music—found their way to the recording studio, but I'd guess there must have been three times that number of songs—maybe as many as a hundred—which I arranged and never recorded.

I like to think I'm a half-ass composer. I ain't no Duke Ellington, but I *can* write. There isn't that much to making a song—jazz or otherwise. There are lyrics, and then there are notes, melody lines which you set up.

As I told you before, I could write on demand—especially when we were about to go into the studio. And I suspect that if you asked me tonight to write you a song, and if I wasn't too sleepy, I'd have it done by morning.

I noticed some interesting developments in popular music. White singers were picking up on black songs on a much more widespread basis. They had always done it, but now it was happening much more frequently. Georgia Gibbs and Pat Boone and Carl Perkins and Elvis were doing tunes which originally had been rhythm-and-blues hits.

It didn't bother me. It was just one of those American things. I've said before that I believe in mixed musical marriages, and there's no way to copyright a feeling or a rhythm or a style of singing. Besides, it meant that White America was getting hipper.

Something else happened in this time slot: rock 'n' roll. I have a hard time defining schools of music, and I've never been one to even try. I've been arguing against labels my whole life—I hate it when they're slapped on me—but finally they become so popular that even I have to use them.

I never considered myself part of rock 'n' roll. I didn't believe that I was among the forerunners of the music, and I've never given myself a lick of credit for either inventing it or having anything to do with its birth.

When I think of the true rock 'n' roll, cats like Chuck Berry and Little Richard and Bo Diddley come to mind. I think they're the main men. And there's a towering difference between their music and mine. My stuff was more adult. It was more difficult for teenagers to relate to; so much of my music was sad or down.

A tune like Little Richard's "Tutti Frutti" was fun. Less serious. And the kids could identify with it a lot easier than my "A Fool for You" or "Drown in My Own Tears."

---

1. "Fathead" was David Newman, Charles's long-time tenor sax player.

I don't want to put down the others, and I don't want to butter myself up. Richard and Chuck and Bo sold millions of records, and they helped the whole industry. They did some spirited music and it broke through some thick barriers. Those guys sold a hell of a lot more records than I did back then. They sold to whites by the truckloads. Fats Domino had huge hits in the white market—"Blueberry Hill" and "Ain't It a Shame"—and I wasn't even in the same league.

Rock 'n' roll was also music that the teenagers were able to play themselves. Little Richard's or Jerry Lee Lewis's piano style—taking your thumb and scraping all the way up the keyboard—had a flare and a sound that the kids loved. And which they could duplicate. I sang some happy songs, and I played tunes with tempos that moved. But if you compare, let's say, my "Don't You Know, Baby?" to Little Richard's "Long Tall Sally," you'll hear the difference; my music is more serious, filled with more despair than anything you'd associate with rock 'n' roll.

Since I couldn't see people dancing, the dance crazes passed me by. I didn't try to write any jitterbugs or twists. I wrote rhythms which moved me and figured they'd also make other folk move.

I've heard the Beatles say that they listened to me when they were coming up. I believe them, but I also think that my influence on them wasn't nearly as great as these other artists. I was really in a different world, and if any description of me comes close, it's the tag "rhythm and blues." I've fooled around in the same way that blacks have been doing for years—playing the blues to different rhythms.

The style requires pure heart singing. Later on they'd call it soul music. But the names don't matter. It's the same mixture of gospel and blues with maybe a sweet melody thrown in for good measure. It's the sort of music where you can't fake the feeling.

Earlier I was telling you how I never test songs on the public before I record them. I've always been my own private testing service. But there was one exception to this rule, even though I didn't mean for it to happen the way it did. I'm talking about the accidental birth of "What I Say."

We happened to be playing one of my last dances—somewhere in the Midwest—and I had another twelve minutes to kill before the set closed. A typical gig of that kind lasted four hours, including a thirty-minute intermission. We played from 9:00 till 11:30, took a half-hour break, and then did the final hour.

It was nearly 1:00 A.M., I remember, and we had played our whole book. There was nothing left that I could think of, so I finally said to the band and the Raeletts, "Listen, I'm going to fool around and y'all just follow me."

So I began noodling. Just a little riff which floated up into my head. It felt good and I kept on going. One thing led to another, and suddenly I found myself singing and wanting the girls to repeat after me. So I told 'em, "Now."

Then I could feel the whole room bouncing and shaking and carrying on something fierce. So I kept the thing going, tightening it up a little here, adding a dash of Latin rhythm there. When I got through, folk came up and asked where they could buy the record. "Ain't no record," I said, "just something I made up to kill a little time."

The next night I started fooling with it again, adding a few more lyrics and refining the riffs for the band. I did that for several straight evenings until the song froze into place. And each time I sang it, the reaction was wild.

I called Jerry Wexler from the road and told him that I was coming to New York with something new to record. "I've been playing it," I said, "and it's pretty nice." That was further than I usually went with Jerry. I don't believe in giving myself advance notices, but I figured this song merited it.

We made the record in 1959, and it became my biggest hit to date. Like "Hallelujah," it sold to whites and blacks alike, although not everyone dug it. It was banned by several radio stations. They said it was suggestive. Well, I agreed. I'm not one to interpret my own songs, but if you can't figure out "What I Say," then something's wrong. Either that, or you're not accustomed to the sweet sounds of love.

Later on, I saw that many of the stations which had banned the tune started playing it when it was covered by white artists. That seemed strange to me, as though white sex was cleaner than black sex. But once they began playing the white version, they lifted the ban and also played the original.

These bans didn't bother me none, mainly 'cause I could see, feel, and smell royalties rolling in. At this point, it was bread I really needed.

The biggest of the concept albums involved country-and-western music. And it came about because I had been planning it for years. If I had remained on Atlantic, I would have done the country thing a year or two earlier. I knew, however, that ABC thought of me as a rhythm-and-blues singer, and I didn't want to shock the label too badly or too quickly. So I waited till the beginning of 1962. That seemed like a reasonable time.

My contract was up for its three-year renewal and, to my way of thinking, I had done well for ABC. They hadn't hassled me before, and I had no reason to believe they would bother me now. Still, my country music idea might have hit them as half-cocked and completely crazy.

What better time to test their faith in me? If they were really behind me, they'd let me do what I wanted. And if they weren't with me all the way, I'd get to learn that right now.

I called Sid Feller and asked him to gather up the great country hits of all time. He sounded a little bewildered, but he was nice enough to do what I asked. Later on, the ABC executives mildly protested—but all in good taste.

They told me how this might injure my career. They told me how all my fans had been loyal to me. They explained how I might irritate some people, how I might lose my following. And even though I listened and understood what they were saying, I ignored them and made the record anyway. We had no contract problems.

I didn't plan on making a killing on the country stuff; I had no commercial scheme in mind. I just wanted to try my hand at hillbilly music. After all, the Grand Ole Opry had been performing inside my head since I was a kid in the country.

To show you how naive I was about the sales potential of this material, I put "I Can't Stop Loving You" as the fifth song on the B side. I called the album *Modern Sounds in Country and Western Music.*

I had no special plans for the arrangements. In fact, I set some of the songs against strings with a choir, the way I was doing much of my material then. Other tunes were done with a big band—my big band—which had just been formed.

I was only interested in two things: being true to myself and being true to the music. I wasn't trying to be the first black country singer. I only wanted to take country songs and sing them my way, not the country way. I wasn't aware of any bold act on my part or any big breakthrough.

It was just blind luck that the tunes—"I Can't Stop Loving You," "Born to Lose," and later, "Take These Chains," "You Are My Sunshine," "Busted," and "You Don't Know Me"—hit with such impact. These country hits wound up giving me a bigger white audience than black, and today when I play concerts, there are still usually more whites than blacks.

At the same time, "I Can't Stop Loving You" was a big song among blacks. It didn't get the initial air play that it might have, but that's 'cause it wasn't the kind of song black jocks normally programmed. And also I was led to believe by some of these cats that they just didn't like ABC. They told me that they played my songs only because it was me. Finally, "I Can't Stop Loving You" made the black stations simply cause they had no choice; the record was too important to be ignored.

Further Reading

Charles, Ray, and David Ritz. *Brother Ray: Ray Charles' Own Story.* New York: Dial Press, 1978.

Cooper, B. Lee. "Ray Charles (1930–2004): Reflections on Legends." *Popular Music and Society* 28 (February 2005): 111–12.

Lydon, Michael. *Ray Charles: Man and Music.* New York: Routledge, 2004.

Phinney, Kevin. *Souled American: How Black Music Transformed White Culture.* New York: Billboard Books, 2005.

Discography

Charles, Ray. *The Birth of Soul: The Complete Atlantic Rhythm and Blues Recordings, 1952–1959.* Atlantic/WEA, 1991.

———. *The Complete Country and Western Recordings, 1959–1986.* Rhino/WEA, 1998.

18. Jerry Wexler
A LIFE IN R&B

A colorful character who had a hand in recording numerous R&B and soul greats, Jerry Wexler (1917–2008), along with Ahmet Ertegun, ran Atlantic Records from the mid-1950s through the 1960s. These excerpts from his autobiography look both backward—to "race" records of the 1940s—and forward—to the transformation of rhythm and blues into rock 'n' roll. Wexler describes the situation at Atlantic Records when he joined as codirector with Ahmet Ertegun and presents his analysis of the social and historical context of the early 1950s in which R&B recordings began to appeal to white teenagers. Always engaging and opinionated, Wexler offers his views on cross-cultural collaboration, the "White Negro" syndrome,[1] and the relationship between commercialism and notions of expressive sincerity (or "authenticity"). Not surprisingly, both he and Ertegun take a rather different view of Atlantic's relationship with its artists than the artists themselves do.

from Rhythm and the Blues: A Life in American Music
Jerry Wexler and David Ritz

The early catalogue [at Atlantic] was eclectic. There were Eddie Safranski's Poll Cats; Stan Kenton band members like Art Pepper, Shelly Manne, Pete Rugolo, and Bob Cooper. There were guitarist Tiny Grimes; Swing Era jazzmen like Rex Stewart; vocal groups like the Delta Rhythm Boys, the Clovers, and the Cardinals; pianists Erroll Gamer and Mal Waldron; boppers Howard McGhee, James Moody, and Dizzy Gillespie; scat singers Jackie and Roy; Sarah Vaughan; blues legends Leadbelly and Sonny Terry; Mary Lou Williams; clarinetist Bamey Bigard; cafe society singers Mabel Mercer and Bobby Short; Billie Holiday–based Sylvia Syms; boogie-woogie virtuoso Meade Lux Lewis. In short, there was everything.

At the same time, nothing was selling big except for that single Stick McGhee hit—"Drinkin' Wine Spo-Dee-O-Dee"—and some Ruth Brown and Joe Turner. In spite of a noble attempt to represent a broad spectrum of jazz and jazz-tinged music, it was rhythm and blues and rhythm and blues alone that paid the rent—a situation that wouldn't change for a long time to come.

So when I came along, the agenda was already set. Ahmet ran it down to me in no uncertain terms. "Here's the sort of record we need to make," he explained. "There's a black man living in the outskirts of Opelousas, Louisiana. He works hard for his money; he has to be tight with a dollar. One morning he hears a song on the radio. It's urgent, bluesy, authentic, irresistible. He becomes obsessed. He can't live without this record. He drops everything, jumps in his pickup, and drives twenty-five miles to the first record store he finds. If we can make that kind of music, we can make it in the business."

It's interesting that Ahmet's decree makes no mention of cross-over—the notion of selling black music to whites. That idea wasn't yet in the air. When I started working at Atlantic, I certainly had no such notions. I knew that the postwar rhythm-and-blues phenomenon had been spearheaded by independent labels. The war had caused a scarcity in shellac, and the majors were recording only their big-selling white acts and very few blacks. Thus black buyers' demand for black records was

---

1. The "White Negro" syndrome refers to a famous article by Normal Mailer, "The White Negro: Superficial Reflections on the Hipster," *Dissent,* Summer 1957, 276–93. Wexler discusses Mailer's article in this excerpt.

great. That's the slot the indies filled in the forties. And to a large extent, in the early fifties that was still the deal.

It happened before, I wrote in an essay for *Cashbox* in 1954. "It happened in the twenties when Perry Bradford and Spencer Williams were as hot as Irving Berlin; it happened when Bessie Smith and Ethel Waters sold their records into millions of white parlors. Now it's happening again. The blues will get stronger before the blues get weaker. Regardless of its impact on the pop field, the blues will surely go on."

I was talking about the present state of rhythm and blues and the beginnings of rock 'n' roll. In significant numbers, white people were listening to, buying, and playing black music. Atlantic's black-and-red label carried the slogan "Leads the Field in Rhythm and Blues," but it was clear that our market, once exclusively black, was expanding.[2]

The first hint came when my friend Howie Richmond called to say that something new was happening in the South and Southwest. They were calling it "cat music," the pre-rock-'n'-roll handle for rhythm and blues selling to whites. Immediately I glommed on to the name, and we started a "Cat" subsidiary label. That had two advantages: first, I hoped the name would pick up on the trend; and secondly, another label allowed us to use other distributors in major markets. (We usually made exclusive agreements with a single distributor in each city, when in fact there were any number of excellent distributors.) We had black artists on Cat—Little Sylvia Vanderpool (later of Mickey and Sylvia), Mike Cordon and the El Tempos, and the Chords, whose record of "Sh-Boom" would be copied (and buried) by the Crewcuts, a white group.

A picture was beginning to emerge: Kids, especially kids down South, were taking newly invented transistor radios to the beach. White Southerners, I believe, in spite of the traditional aura of racial bigotry, have always enjoyed the most passionate rapport with black music, itself a Southern phenomenon. And in the fifties, white Southern teenagers started the charge towards ballsy rhythm and blues. As the Eisenhower decade became more conformist, the music became more rebellious, more blatantly sexual, climaxing in the remarkable persona of Elvis Presley, a Memphis boy raised on the pure sounds of the black South.

In the wake of postwar prosperity, teenagers were becoming a market of their own. Their buying power was real, their emotional needs immediate, their libidinous drive no longer reflected by the dead-and-gone fox-trots of their parents. Suddenly there was another force at work—old but new, primal yet complex, a music informed by the black genius for expressing pent-up frustration, joy, rage, or ecstasy in a poetic context marked by hip humor and irresistible rhythm.

Ahmet had already anticipated this evolution, the best example being his seminal work with Joe Turner. Big Joe was the blues-shouting bartender from Kansas City whom I'd heard back in my student days. A mountain of a man, his voice was among the most powerful in the history of the form. History had placed him in a niche with Pete Johnson, his boogie-woogie-piano-playing partner, and Count Basie, whose band he'd joined when Ahmet caught him at the Apollo in the early fifties.

"Joe took Jimmy Rushing's place," says Ahmet, "but unlike Jimmy, Joe didn't fit. Musically, he and Basie were fighting each other, and it was depressing. The crowd

---

2. This assertion is borne out by a spate of articles that appeared in music industry publications around this time; see Bob Rolontz and Joel Friedman, "Teen-Agers Demand Music with a Beat, Spur Rhythm-Blues: Field Reaps $15,000,000; Radio, Juke Boxes Answer Big Demands," *Billboard,* April 24, 1954, 1, 18, 24, 50; and other articles reprinted or cited later.

didn't like it, Joe didn't like it, and afterwards I found him in a bar where he told me Columbia had dropped him from the label. Joe really had the blues. 'I think you're the greatest blues singer in the world,' I told him. 'All you need is fresh material. Sign with Atlantic and we'll make hits.'"

Ahmet's "Chains of Love" hit the charts in 1951, followed by "Sweet Sixteen," "Honey Hush," and "TV Mama." It was "Shake, Rattle and Roll," though, that opened the floodgates for Joe. The song was written by Jesse Stone, a brilliant black arranger with roots back to Jelly Roll Morton. Jesse's musical mind had as much to do as anyone's with the transformation of traditional blues to pop blues—or rhythm and blues, or cat music, or rock 'n' roll, or whatever the hell you want to call it. Jesse was a master, and an integral part of the sound we were developing. He had the unique gift of maintaining a hang-loose boogie-shuffle feel in the context of a formal chart. Jesse was a record producer's dream come true. I always felt he viewed me with a slightly jaundiced eye, as though I might sign the checks but was in on a pass, not knowing shit about the music. Jesse seemed to know everything.

He'd written hits for Jimmy Dorsey. He'd written "Idaho," whose sophisticated chord structure became a favorite vehicle for the beboppers. In "Shake, Rattle and Roll," under the pseudonym of Charles Calhoun, he also wrote, "you wear those dresses, the sun comes shining through, I can't believe my eyes, all that mess belongs to you"—one of my favorite images of erotic poetry. In Bill Haley's white cover, whose sales outstripped Turner's version, the sex was stripped off, the lyrics bleached clean. No matter; Joe's reading remains a gem.

Highly imitated as innovators, Jesse Stone and Howard Biggs (another fabulous arranger) were absolutely essential to the good rockin' feel of our early-fifties hits. Howard is gone, but Jesse is still with us. In his eighties, he is living in Florida, alert and in full possession of all his faculties.

Those first couple of years at Atlantic had me flying high. With the aid of Miriam Abramson, who shared my zeal for the nitty-gritty of daily detail, the business side was clean-cut and straight-ahead. Ahmet was cooking in the studio, and I was at his side soaking up the make-it-up-as-you-go-along recipes.

Luckily, my arrival came at that fortunate point in American music when the lines between black and white were starting to fade. Things were getting blurry in a hurry, and Atlantic both benefited from and contributed to that breakdown. Hip disc jockeys—white guys who talked black—were starting to play black music to an audience that was increasingly white. Cats like Zenas "Daddy" Sears in Atlanta, George "Hound Dog" Lorenz in Buffalo, Hunter Hancock in Los Angeles, Bob "Wolfman Jack" Smith in Shreveport and Del Rio, Ken "Jack the Cat" Elliott and Clarence "Poppa Stoppa" Hamman in New Orleans, Gene Nobles and John Richbourg and Hoss Allen in Nashville, not to mention a man destined for national prominence, Alan "Moondog" Freed in Cleveland—these were all white guys who broadcasted black, speaking with the timing and rhyming of the ghetto. Both in the existential sense of Norman Mailer's term ("The source of Hip is the Negro," he wrote, "for he has been living on the margin between totalitarianism and democracy for two centuries") and in the sense of pure entertainment, these were White Negroes. Their significance cannot be overemphasized. These sons-of-bitches not only pointed to the future of American popular music but were also the makers and the breakers of our records.

The black style represented a diverting departure from the mid-fifties blahs. You could segregate schoolrooms and buses, but not the airwaves. Radio could not resist the music's universality—its intrinsic charm, its empathy for human foibles, its direct application to the teen-age condition.

The hip of my generation, who were teenagers in the thirties, had always been drawn to black culture. In fact, I had always known White Negroes, not pretenders or voyeurs but guys who had opted to leave the white world, married black women, and made Harlem or Watts their habitat. These guys *converted.* Clarinetist Mezz Mezzrow—of the famous joints—was the most colorful example; Teddy Reig, the three-hundred-pound soul man who managed Count Basie and Chuck Berry and produced Charlie Parker, was another. Symphony Syd, jazz voice of the night in New York City; Johnny Otis, pioneering rhythm-and-blues band leader, creator of "Willie and the Hand Jive," discoverer of Esther Phillips and Etta James in Los Angeles; Monte Kay, bebop impresario, manager of the Modern Jazz Quartet, whose kinky coif might have been the first Jewfro in hair-fashion history—these were all friends.

I dug cross-cultural collaborations and craved commercial success, which is maybe why Ahmet and I got on so well. We could have developed a label along the lines of Blue Note, Prestige, Vanguard, or Folkways, fastidious documentarians of core American music. Bobby Weinstock, Alfred Lion, Moe Ash, Orrin Keepnews, Manny Solomon, and the other keepers of the flame were doing God's work. Ahmet and I, however, didn't feature ourselves as divinely elected. We weren't looking for canonization; we lusted for hits. Hits were the cash flow, the lifeblood, the heavenly ichor—the wherewithal of survival. While we couldn't divorce ourselves from our tastes and inclinations, neither could we deny our interest in income. Nor could we stand still; we believed to our souls that the way of the independent label was either growth or death. Every month, it seemed, another indie would hit the dust. Our competitors in commercial black music—Lew Chudd at Imperial, Sam and Hymie Weiss at Old Town, Syd Nathan at King, Art Rupe at Specialty, Don Robey at Duke/Peacock, Jules and Saul Bihari at Modern, Bess Berman at Apollo, Herman Lubinsky at Savoy, Phil and Leonard Chess—weren't exactly pushovers. If we slipped, these sweethearts would be right behind us picking up the pieces. This was a pushy, get-to-the-distributor, get-to-the-deejay, get-the-goddamn-song-on-the-air business.

Consequently, the term "commercial" was not a pejorative for me—wasn't then, isn't now. If "commercial" meant a song with a strong hook, an inviting refrain, melodic variety, and a rhythm pattern with a walloping bass line—well, give me commercial and lots of it. The merry jingle of cash registers was music to my ears. As a kid, I might have been cavalier about money. But this was a different deal. I had a family to support; people were working for me. Fear of bankruptcy was always around the corner—deep-depression, nothing-to-eat, nowhere-to-sleep fear. Given my high level of chain-smoking anxiety, I still wonder that I didn't develop ulcers early on.

Yet the tonic wasn't money; it was music. Substantial financial rewards wouldn't come until well into the sixties. In the precarious fifties, my fascination with the glories of the music seemed to push me beyond my own limitations. If now and then Ahmet or I might begin to worry during a session, unnecessarily afraid that LaVern or Ray was getting too hoarse or the drummer was dragging, the natural abilities of our artists would eventually pull things together. We also had the benefit of Dowd's engineering talents, arrangers like Jesse, and a large pool of New York City session musicians, many of whom—drummers Connie Kay and Panama Francis, tenor men Budd Johnson and Sam Taylor, pianists Hank Jones and Dick Hyman—were jazz musicians of the first order.

Further Reading

Mailer, Norman. "The White Negro: Superficial Reflections on the Hipster." *Dissent,* Summer 1957, 276–93.

Rolontz, Bob, and Joel Friedman. "Teen-Agers Demand Music with a Beat, Spur Rhythm-Blues: Field Reaps $15,000,000; Radio, Juke Boxes Answer Big Demands." *Billboard,* April 24, 1954, 1, 18, 24, 50.

Wexler, Jerry, and David Ritz. *Rhythm and the Blues: A Life in American Music.* New York: Alfred A. Knopf, 1993.

Discography

Atlantic Rhythm and Blues 1947–1974. Atlantic/WEA, 1991.

19. The Growing Threat of Rhythm and Blues

While the early 1950s witnessed numerous crossovers and cover versions of country songs, such developments occurred more slowly in rhythm and blues. As described by Jerry Wexler and Ruth Brown, however, by 1954 people in the music industry were aware of the broadening appeal of R&B. The expanding audience for R&B began to be reflected in a growing number of pop cover versions of R&B hits, as well as in the occasional crossover, such as "Crying in the Chapel" by the Orioles in July 1953 or "Gee" by the Crows in March 1954, both "doo-wop"–style vocal numbers. Diverse factors played a role in heightening public awareness of black popular music: the spread of R&B to jukeboxes and record stores in white neighborhoods, the integrated audiences at rhythm and blues shows emceed by Alan Freed, new technology (the introduction of the inexpensive and durable "45," affordable tape recorders, transistor radios), and a growing number of radio shows devoted to R&B.

In early 1955, a series of articles appeared in *Variety* (one of the three most important music industry publications, along with *Billboard* and

Cashbox) describing the effect of the increasing popularity of rhythm and blues on popular music. These articles generally lamented the incursion of R&B, citing the difficulties created for old-fashioned pop tunes and the music-publishing business. As one article observed, "R&B is strictly a sound phenom"—that is, it is the particular sound of a recorded performance of an R&B record that listeners find attractive, rather than the more abstract sense of melody and harmony provided by sheet music that may retain its appeal through numerous competing recordings or performances (as in the pop tunes of the Tin Pan Alley era).[1]

As the weeks went by, the sense of panic in *Variety*'s pages increased. The following article provides evidence of this tone in its assertions of the displacement of pop vocalists by rhythm and blues artists. *Variety*'s own popularity charts contradict this, however, as cover versions were far more popular than the original versions of these tunes. For example, Georgia Gibbs's version of "Tweedle-Dee" (discussed in the following article) ranked number nine, while LaVern Baker's (R&B) version was not listed at all during the week this article was published. At any rate, regardless of whether its assertions were well grounded, *Variety* clearly found the presence of *any* R&B recordings or covers on the pop charts profoundly *upsetting*.

Top Names Now Singing the Blues as Newcomers Roll on R&B Tide
Variety

Like the major disk companies, the established pop vocalists are finding the current rhythm & blues phase of the music biz to be tough sledding. At the present time, the only veteran names in the topselling brackets are Perry Como and Georgia Gibbs. Both are rolling with the cycle and have turned r&b tunes, such as "Ko Ko Mo" and "Tweedle Dee," into top hits.

The major diskers are not finding it easy to crack the r&b formula. For one thing, most of the artists & repertoire chiefs frankly can't recognize a potential r&b hit when they hear one. As a result, they are all waiting for the tunes to break through on the indie labels and then they decide to cover.

However, unlike a straight pop tune on which a major could usually take the play away from an indie, this does not necessarily hold true of r&b tunes. The kids not only are going for the tunes and the beat, but they seem to be going for the original

---

1. "Music Biz Now R&B Punchy: Even Hillbillies Are Doing It," *Variety*, February 9, 1955, 51, 54.

interpretations as well. Several covers of r&b tunes by pop names have not been able to gain ground because they lacked that authentic low-down quality accented on the indie labels.

The major labels are not only being knocked over by the r&b cycle, but by the general demand for offbeat stuff. Femme vocal groups, which used to be a drug on the market only a few month ago, are now hitting big. Such combos as the McGuire Sisters, Fontane Sisters, and DeJohn Sisters are one, two, three disk attractions currently.

The Crew-Cuts is another combo mopping up in the current tune trend, as is Bill Haley & His Comets. The Penguins, on the indie Dootone label, have also been clicking with their original r&b interpretation of "Earth Angel," although the Crew-Cuts are outpacing them in sales.

Like the influx of hillbilly names into the pop market about four years ago, the r&b cycle is turning up its share of new combos and singers. These include The Charms, The Five Keys, Lavern Baker, Fats Domino, Gene & Eunice, the Moonglows, and a flock of other such combos.

Topsyturvy nature of the current disk biz is spotlighted by the dominance of the small labels among the top 10 or 15 disks. Companies like Dot, Cadence, Coral, Epic and Mercury are riding roughshod over the Big Four of Victor, Columbia, Decca and Capitol.

That there's no completely uniform pattern to the music biz is revealed by the presence of an oldie ballad like "Melody of Love" among the topsellers. Also a legitimate tune like "That's All I Want From You" continues to hold up despite the demand for the "Ko Ko Mos" and "Tweedle-Dees."

> *Variety's* anxiety reached its shrillest pitch in the following editorial, which appeared the same week as the preceding article. "Abel" (the pseudonym used by the author of this piece) seems particularly upset about companies that are irresponsibly pursuing the "filthy fast buck" by foisting R&B on an unsuspecting public. This idea, which verges on a conspiracy theory, implies the unlikely historical scenario whereby the music business, prior to its defilement by popular music sporting "leer-ics," was engaged in a philanthropic, rather than a capitalistic, activity. Abel blames payola, even though independent companies spent less money on "promotion" (the official term for payola) than the majors did.[2]
>
> The following week's edition of *Variety* printed letters from several prominent people in the entertainment industry who supported the editorial, along with one anonymous writer who argued in favor of the independent record companies.[3] That the writers who favored the editorial were allied with the superstructure supporting old-style pop music—ASCAP, a major record company, and a Broadway

---

2. For more on panics surrounding early rock 'n' roll concerts, see "'Rock & Roll' to Get Ofay Theatre Showcasing; Freed Set for Par, B'kln," *Variety*, February 1955, 47; "Cleve. Cats Are Clipped by Cops' Crackdown on Jock's Jive Jamboree," *Variety*, February 9, 1955, 58; "Jocks Junk Payola Platters," *Variety*, February 16, 1955, 39.

3. "Trade Execs Generally Support Stand vs. Indigo R&B Lyrics," *Variety*, March 2, 1955, 51.

theater—should not be too surprising. None of these people stood to profit from the expansion of rhythm and blues into the pop market. Though never overt, the issue of race informs the editorial and the responses to it: the concern about the inroads made by R&B is unimaginable without the widely held associations between race and certain categories of popular music and the way in which the structure of popular music at that time mirrored the segregation of U.S. society (as the editorial reminded its readers, "this sort of lyric was off in a corner by itself. It was the music underworld—not the main stream").[4]

Of greater interest, though, and a bit more perplexing, is that Abel doesn't provide examples of offending songs. Which particular "leer-ic" does he have in mind? Two somewhat salacious songs had experienced a minor degree of crossover success in the preceding year: Joe Turner's "Shake, Rattle, and Roll" and the Midnighters' "Work with Me Annie," both of which were huge R&B hits (another suggestive song, "Sixty-Minute Man," had followed a similar pattern three years earlier). However, as Jerry Wexler noted in his autobiography, another version of "Shake, Rattle, and Roll," a cover by Bill Haley that toned down the lyrics of the Joe Turner version, had been much more successful on the pop charts.[5] On the other hand, nothing in the lyrics of songs of other recent crossovers from this period, such as "Earth Angel" and "Tweedle-Dee," explains why they might cause offense. The plentiful cover songs on the charts at the time of the editorial also offer no explanation for this fear of an invasion of "euphemisms which are attempting a total breakdown of all reticences about sex." One can only speculate that this panic was being driven by fears about aspects of the music style, the threat to the established structure of the music industry, and the breakdown of extant social barriers that would accompany an unprecedented integration of African American performers into white society. Despite the fact that these reactions seem out of proportion to what was actually going on in the popular music of the time, they proved remarkably prescient. By 1956, African American artists playing what would by then be termed "rock 'n' roll" were thoroughly integrated into the mainstream pop charts.

---

4. I discuss the moment in greater detail in "Music," in *Key Terms in Popular Music and Culture*, ed. Bruce Horner and Thomas Swiss, 124–40 (Malden, Mass.: Blackwells, 1999). For an in-depth account, see Trent Hill, "The Enemy Within: Censorship in Rock Music in the 1950s," *South Atlantic Quarterly* 90, no. 4 (Fall 1991): 675–708. Charles Hamm also discusses this editorial and the series of articles in *Variety* in *Yesterdays: Popular Song in America* (New York: W. W. Norton, 1979), 401–02.

5. The original recording of "Shake, Rattle, and Roll," by Joe Turner reached 22 in the pop jukebox charts and spent a total of two weeks in the Top 30 during August 1954. "Work with Me Annie" performed similarly in the pop charts in June 1954. After Etta James had an R&B hit with a reply song, "The Wallflower (Roll with Me Henry)," Georgia Gibbs had a huge hit with a watered-down version, entitled "Dance with Me Henry," in April 1955.

A Warning to the Music Business
Variety

Music "leer-ics" are touching new lows and if the fast-buck songsmiths and music makers are incapable of social responsibility and self-restraint then regulation—policing, if you will—have to come from more responsible sources. Meaning the phonograph record manufacturers and their network daddies. These companies have a longterm stake rather than a quick turn-around role. It won't wash for them to echo the cheap cynicism of the songsmiths who justify their "leer-ic" garbage by declaring "that's what the kids want" or "that's the only thing that sells today."

What are we talking about? We're talking about "rock and roll," about "hug," and "squeeze," and kindred euphemisms which are attempting a total breakdown of reticences about sex. In the past such material was common enough but restricted to special places and out-and-out barrelhouses. Today "leer-ics" are offered as standard popular music for general consumption, including consumption by teenagers. Our teenagers are already setting something of a record in delinquency without this raw musical idiom to smell up the environment still more.

The time is now for some serious soul-searching by the popular music industry. This is a call to the conscience of that business. Don't invite the Governmental and religious lightning that is sure to strike. Forget the filthy fast buck. Nor is it just the little music "independents" who are heedless of responsibility.

The major diskeries, with the apparently same disregard as to where the blue notes may fall, are as guilty. Guiltier, perhaps, considering the greater obligation—their maturer backgrounds—their time-honored relations with the record-buying public.

The most casual look at the current crop of "lyrics" must tell even the most naive that dirty postcards have been translated into songs. Compared to some of the language that loosely passes for song "lyrics" today, the "pool-table papa" and "jellyroll" terminology of yesteryear is polite palaver. Only difference is that this sort of lyric then was off in a corner by itself. It was the music underworld—not the main stream.

For the music men—publishers and diskeries—to say that "that's what the kids want" and "that's the only thing that sells nowadays," is akin to condoning publication of back-fence language. Earthy dialog may belong in "art novels" but mass media have tremendous obligation. If they forget, they'll hear from authority. Seemingly that is not the case in the music business.

Before it's too late for the welfare of the industry—forgetting for the moment the welfare of young Americans—VARIETY urges a strong self-examination of the record business by its most responsible chief executive officers. A strong suspicion lingers with VARIETY that these business men are too concerned with the profit statements to take stock of what's causing some of their items to sell. Or maybe they just don't care. A suspicion has been expressed that even the network-affiliated and Hollywood-affiliated record companies brush things off with "that's the music business." This is illogical because it is morally wrong and in the longrun it's wrong financially.

Today's "angles" and sharp practices in the music business are an intra-trade problem. Much of it, time-dishonored. The promulgation and propagation of a pop song, ever since there was a Tin Pan Alley, was synonymous with shrewdness, astuteness and deviousness that often bordered on racketeering in its subornation of talent, subsidy, cajolery and out-and-out bribery.

In its trade functions no trade paper, VARIETY included, wants to be accused of "blowing the whistle." But the music business is flirting with the shrill commands of an outer influence if it doesn't wake up and police itself. This is not the first time VARIETY has spotlighted the pyramiding evils of the music business as it operates today. One of the roots is the payola. If some freak "beat" captures the kids' imagination, the boys are in there quick, wooing, romancing, cajoling the a&r men.

Here is where the responsible chief officers of the major diskeries should come in. They can continue to either blind themselves, as apparently seems to be the case, or they can compel their moral obligations to stand in the way of a little quick profit. This has an accumulative force, because their own radio outlets can limit the exploitation of this spurious stuff. Not only the commodities of their own affiliation, but others.

Some may argue that this is a proposal of "censorship." Not at all. It is a plea to ownership to assume the responsibilities of ownership and eliminate practices which will otherwise invite censorship. In short, chums, do it yourself or have it done for you. You're not going to get or have it done for you.

Abel.

Further Reading

Brackett, David. "Music." In *Key Terms in Popular Music and Culture*, ed. Bruce Horner and Thomas Swiss, 124–40. Malden, Mass.: Blackwell, 1999.

Hamm, Charles. *Yesterdays: Popular Song in America*. New York: W. W. Norton, 1979, 401–02.

Hill, Trent. "The Enemy Within: Censorship in Rock Music in the 1950s." *South Atlantic Quarterly* 90, no. 4 (Fall 1991): 675–708.

Discography

Baker, LaVern. *The Platinum Collection*. WEA International, 2007.

The Crew Cuts. *Best of the Crew Cuts*. Polygram International, 2001.

Domino, Fats. *Greatest Hits: Walking to New Orleans*. Capitol, 2007.

Founding Fathers of the Rock 'n' Roll Hall of Fame. Orpheus Records, 2001.

Gibbs, Georgia. *Her Nibs*. ASV Living Era, 2006.

The McGuire Sisters. *The Anthology*. MCA, 1999.

Miami Rockin' Doowop from the Chart Label. Ace Records UK, 2000.

The Penguins. *Earth Angel*. Ace Records UK, 1990.

20. From Rhythm and Blues to Rock 'n' Roll
THE SONGS OF CHUCK BERRY

Earlier in this chapter, in one of the excerpts from his autobiography, Ray Charles described several factors that defined the difference between himself, a rhythm and blues artist, and rock 'n' rollers such as Chuck Berry and Little Richard; these included the intended audience for his recordings (more adult for R&B, more teenage for rock 'n' roll) and the level of emotional seriousness (rock 'n' roll featured more unadulterated "fun" while rhythm and blues was more "serious"). During 1955, Chuck Berry, Little Richard, Bo Diddley, and Fats Domino all developed a new form of rhythm and blues that lent itself to being marketed to an interracial teenage market.[1] Of these three, Chuck Berry (b. 1926) in many ways represents the prototypical rock 'n' roller because of his abilities as a singer, songwriter, and guitarist (the quality that separates him from Little Richard and Fats Domino, both pianists). More than the other two, Berry was also a master of creating stories directed toward teenagers that described experiences that were widespread enough to transcend most social boundaries (cars, dating, and the frustrations of high school). This does not mean that Berry was motivated solely by a desire to cross over. Musically, he remained rooted in blues and the guitar styles of Muddy Waters, T-Bone Walker, and Charlie Christian, although he experimented early on with incorporating influences from country and pop music, developing a fusion that would prove important to his success. He also occasionally wrote lyrics that expressed subtle social commentary ("Too Much Monkey Business") and even racial pride ("Brown-Eyed Handsome Man").

The following discussion with British music critic Norman Jopling catches up with Berry in 1967, around the time that he changed record companies from Chess to Mercury. In the article, Berry describes how he had recently re-recorded many of his earlier hits for Mercury at the same time that Chess was releasing a now-historic compilation of his

---

1. Some might argue that of the three, Fats Domino's success resulted the least from a change of style, as he had been recording songs similar in sound since the late forties. In this case, changes in the audience and the popular music mainstream may have been more responsible for his sudden success in the pop market.

greatest hits, *Chuck Berry's Golden Decade*. Berry also reveals the inspiration behind many of his most famous lyrics and the important role of
country music in the formation of his style.[2] Beyond his songs and his
recordings of them, however, Berry's legacy lives on in the numerous
rock 'n' roll artists who owe a large part of their style to him, including
the Beach Boys, Beatles, and Rolling Stones, to name only the most
famous. Learning his trademark guitar licks and boogie-style accompaniment has become a rite of passage for every would-be rock guitarist,
and his songs still feature prominently in many country and rock 'n' roll
bar bands.[3]

"Chuck Berry: Rock Lives!"
Norman Jopling

Chuck Berry has become a musical institution in the eleven years that he has been
making hit records. Since his first American hit single "Maybellene" in 1955 (before
Elvis Presley scored HIS first American hit), Chuck has endeared himself to the hearts
of all types of pop music admirers—from never-say-die side-burned drape-jacketed
rockers, to trendy mini-skirted young ladies.

Just how much has Chuck himself changed in that considerable amount of time,
musically? (to go back to Presley, think how much HE has changed!)

"Then was then, and now is now," Chuck replied; "I re-cut my old tunes for this
new Mercury album, but they're different from on the old albums. I doubt if I could
play them the same now. When I listen to my old tunes I'm never completely satisfied
with them. I won't say I'm unsatisfied—just not completely satisfied. New songs?
Well, I've written seven, no, eight songs in six months. Five of them I've recorded
and sent to Mercury—the others are lying there in my brief-case. One was released—
'Club Nitty Gritty.' The other album I have here is just a re-issue from Chess." The
Chess LP was a double-album set, containing most of Chuck's biggest hits, ranging from "Maybellene" and the early hits, to "No Particular Place To Go" and "You
Never Can Tell," his later hits for Chess. Why did Chuck leave Chess after ten years
recording with them? Was there any ill-feeling?

---

2. Berry provides much more detail on these subjects in his autobiography, *Chuck Berry: The
Autobiography* (New York: Simon & Schuster, 1987). For excerpts that focus on the formation of
his musical style and the background of his early recordings and most famous songs, see "From
Rhythm and Blues to Rock 'n' Roll: The Songs of Chuck Berry," in *The Pop, Rock, and Soul Reader:
Histories and Debates*, 2nd ed., ed. David Brackett, 107–12 (New York: Oxford University Press,
2009).

3. For more on Berry's guitar style, see Steve Waksman, *Instruments of Desire: The Electric
Guitar and the Shaping of Musical Experience* (Cambridge, MA: Harvard University Press, 1999),
148–66; and R. Vito, "The Chuck Berry Style: A Modern Rocker Pays Tribute to the Master," *Guitar
Player* (June 1984): 72–75.

Source: "Chuck Berry: Rock Lives!" by Norman Jopling, originally published in *Record Mirror*, 4
March 1967. © Norman Jopling/Rock's Backpages.

"Oh no, there were no bad feelings. We just shook hands and they wished me good luck. The change-over was just a business deal. The first Mercury album will be released . . . in March or April."

One thing which fascinates most people about Chuck Berry are the lyrics of his songs. All about life—cars, school, real romance. What has Chuck to say about the words of his songs?

"The car songs—I had a phase of about four or five years of writing songs about cars. Because this was a yearning which I had since I was aged seven to drive about in a car. I first started driving at 17—one year earlier than I should have. It was my fascination for the roads, for driving, motoring, which prompted me to write those songs.

"I have written about my cars, and about my school. I can't write about something which I haven't experienced. I wrote 'Sweet Little Sixteen' at a concert when I saw a little girl running around backstage collecting autographs. She couldn't have seen one act on the show—unless it was mine! When I wrote 'Memphis,' I had known couples who had divorced and the tragedies of the children.

"You can associate these songs with life—for instance when I wrote 'Maybellene' just about every farmer must have been driving about in Fords, station wagons etc. But then Chevrolet got wise and started a big advertising campaign with the farmers!"

I wondered how much notice Chuck took of the charts. How much does he follow them, and consequently how much is his music influenced by current trends and other artists?

"I don't study the charts—I observe them," he replied. "Of course I've been influenced, by everyone from Bing Crosby to the Beatles. I don't let my music be consciously affected by anything. What do I think of the Beatles versions of two of my songs? Very nice. But they recorded them two, three years ago now. In fact it's only now that I'm beginning to feel the benefits of them—those songs 'Roll Over Beethoven' and 'Rock And Roll Music' are now on an upward trend.

"Talking about the Beatles, three or four of their songs are amongst the best ever written in pop music. Especially 'I Wanna Hold Your Hand.' I put that one with songs like my 'Sweet Little Sixteen'—and I'm not saying that just because I wrote it. I'll never write another song like that.

"And of course there's the Everly Brothers 'Wake Up Little Susie.' That's really one of my favorite songs. Those three songs I've named—they have virtue and freshness. It doesn't matter who sings them."

On the personal side there are a couple of popular misconceptions about Chuck. He stated, "When I meet people they say, 'Wow, we thought you were a short man.'" (Chuck is well over six feet tall.) "I guess it's because of the name. Chuck, it's small, you know! And another thing, I have this popular image of being quiet, and people wonder why, because of my stage act I suppose in which I go pretty wild. Well, you can't expect me to be leaping around when I come off stage, and talking extra-fast!"

Apart from the musical side, Chuck Berry has developed into a very successful businessman. He has his own music corporation, music publishers, amusement park, and several other highly-successful money-making projects. Why, I wondered, had Chuck chosen of all things an amusement park (called Berry Park) to make money from?

"It goes a long way back. When I was a child I lived opposite a park but my father forbade me to go there. We moved somewhere else, and the same thing happened. You see, it's a psychological thing. When I bought the land to develop it was just wheat land. It was winter at the time, and of course there was no wheat growing. The first thing I built there was a swimming pool, and I charged 25¢ admission. Now there are many more things to do and I charge more. I have groups there, Western and Rock. That's the music people want to listen to—they don't want jazz. After all who wants to learn and study music when they go to an amusement park—people just want something to entertain them.

"Myself, when I feel like dancing then I play rock music. If I'm in a sentimental mood, then Western music. And of course I do play jazz because that's the only music you can learn something from."

I ventured to suggest that it was strange that Chuck, hero of the rock and roll set, should like Country and Western music. Especially as his own brand of sound was so different.

"Oh no! You're wrong there. 'Maybellene' was very much a country song, with country lyrics. Maybe a little faster but basically it was country. You ask me if I would have made money if I hadn't been an entertainer. Yes!"

Finally, just how much work does Chuck do now, and will he be appearing in any more rock films?

"I take about 60 per cent of the work that's offered to me. That means I work about three days a week. I'm offered work for about four or five days of the week. But I won't do the kind of tours that I used to. They were eighty day tours . . . really something. I like to do different kind of venues—colleges, concert halls, different avenues of work. The reason I haven't made any films for a long while is because I haven't been offered any. I wouldn't be averse to making films at all."

And a final point of interest—Chuck reads a lot. He reads works on psychology and science. Nothing else. No fiction. And he says, "I write fiction, I don't read it. . . ."

Further Reading

Berry, Chuck. *Chuck Berry: The Autobiography*. New York: Random House, 1987.

Taylor, Timothy D. "His Name Was in Lights: Chuck Berry's Johnny B. Goode." In *Reading Pop: Approaches in Textual Analysis in Popular Music,* ed. Richard Middleton, 165–82. Oxford, UK: Oxford University Press, 2000.

Vito, R. "The Chuck Berry Style: A Modern Rocker Pays Tribute to the Master." *Guitar Player* (June 1984): 72–75.

Waksman, Steve. *Instruments of Desire: The Electric Guitar and the Shaping of Musical Experience*. Cambridge, Mass.: Harvard University Press, 1999.

———. "The Turn to Noise: Rock Guitar from the 1950s to the 1970s." In *The Cambridge Companion to the Guitar*, ed. Victor Coelho, 109–21. Cambridge, UK: Cambridge University Press, 2003.

Discography

Berry, Chuck. *The Great Twenty-Eight*. MCA, 1990.

———. *Johnny B. Goode: His Complete '50s Chess Recordings*. Hip-O Select, 2007.

Diddley, Bo. *I'm a Man: The Chess Masters, 1955–1958*. Hip-O Select, 2007.

Legends Collection: Rock 'n' Roll Teenagers. Legends Collection, 2002.

21. Little Richard

Compared to Chuck Berry, Little Richard (b. 1932) came from a far more rural and humble background, and his early experiences in a back-woods Pentecostal church played a stronger role in shaping his musical style than they did Berry's. Little Richard's extroverted and energetic singing, piano playing, and songwriting made him one of the biggest stars of the rock 'n' roll era. His vocal style, in particular, had an impact on many subsequent musicians, including James Brown, Otis Redding, Paul McCartney, and John Fogerty (of Creedence Clearwater Revival). After making several unsuccessful recordings in the early 1950s, he recorded "Tutti Frutti" in September 1955, which rose high on both the R&B and pop charts. "Tutti Frutti" set the tone for the hits that followed between 1956 and 1958: Over a fast boogie-shuffle rhythm with many stop-time breaks, Richard would sing playful double entendres near the top of his range in a searing timbre interspersed with trademark falsetto whoops. His piano playing derives from boogie-woogie style, emphasizes the upbeat, and features a great many glissandi. In performance, Richard would frequently leave the piano to dance exuberantly, occasionally on top of the piano itself.

In addition to his uninhibited presence as a singer, pianist, and dancer, Richard's visual appearance added to the sense of his out-rageousness: with his large pompadour, liberal use of makeup, and gaudy clothing, he raised the spectre of cross-dressing and ambiguous sexuality at a time when such issues were strictly taboo. In pondering the improbability of Richard's mass acceptance at the time, one pos-sible explanation suggests itself: his outrageous performance style camouflaged (and perhaps deflected and deflated) whatever threat he posed to heterosexual norms. After several more hits and appearances in three films (*Don't Knock the Rock* and *The Girl Can't Help It,* both in 1956, and *Mister Rock 'n' Roll,* in 1957), Richard decided abruptly to quit his career for the ministry because of a vision he had during a flight back to the States from Australia.

The following excerpts come from an "oral history" of Little Richard, rather than an autobiography. Thus, in addition to Richard's voice, we hear from Bumps Blackwell, a famous A&R (artist and repertoire) man for Specialty Records (an independent record company specializing in

African American sacred and secular music). An academically trained composer, Blackwell, along with Henry Glover and Jesse Stone, was one of the few African American A&R men at the time. His astute comments derive from the important role that he played in Little Richard's early recordings: in addition to producing, he cowrote many of Richard's best-known songs. Richard presents his own views on how his music mapped racial relations, the interesting origins of "Lucille," and Alan Freed.

from The Life and Times of Little Richard: The Quasar of Rock
Charles White

You'd hear people singing all the time. The women would be outside in the back doing the washing, rubbing away on the rub-boards, and somebody else sweeping the yard, and somebody else would start singing "We-e-e-ll . . . Nobody knows the trouble I've seen. . . ." And gradually other people would pick it up, until the whole of the street would be singing. Or "Sometimes I feel like a motherless child, a long way from home. . . ." Everybody singing. I used to go up and down the street, some streets were paved, but our street was dirt, just singing at the top of my voice. There'd be guitar players playing on the street—old Slim, Willie Amos, and my cousin, Buddy Penniman. I remember Bamalama, this feller with one eye, who'd play the wash-board with a thimble. He had a bell like the school-teacher's, and he'd sing, "A-bamalam, you shall be free, and in the mornin' you shall be free." See, there was so much poverty, so much prejudice in those days. I imagine people had to sing to feel their connection with God. To sing their trials away, sing their problems away, to make their burdens easier and the load lighter. That's the beginning. That's where it started.

We used to have a group called the Penniman Singers—all of us, the whole family. We used to go around and sing in all the churches, and we used to sing in contests with other family groups, like the Brown Singers, in what they called the Battle of the Gospels. We used to have some good nights. I remember one time. I could always sing *loud* and I kept changing the key upward. Marquette said it ruined his voice trying to sing tenor behind me! The sisters didn't like me screaming and singing and threw their hats and purses at us, shouting "Hush, hush, boys—hush!" They called me War Hawk because of my hollerin' and screamin' and they stopped me singing in church.

From a boy, I wanted to be a preacher. I wanted to be like Brother Joe May, the singing evangelist, who they called the Thunderbolt of the West. My daddy's father, Walter Penniman, was a preacher, and so was my mother's brother, Reverend Louis Stuart, who's now pastor of a Baptist church in Philadelphia. And I have a cousin, Amos Penniman, who's a minister in the Pentecostal Church. I have always been basically a religious person—in fact most of the black people where I'm from was. I went to the New Hope Baptist Church, on Third Avenue, where my mother was a member. My daddy's people were members of Foundation Templar AME Church, a Methodist church on Madison Street, and my mother's father was with the Holi-

Source: THE LIFE AND TIMES OF LITTLE RICHARD, by Charles White © 1985.

ness Temple Baptist Church, downtown in Macon. So I was kind of mixed up in it right from the start. Of all the churches, I used to like going to the Pentecostal Church, because of the music.

Clint Brantley set up a tour around Georgia and Tennessee—Nashville, Knoxville, Milledgeville, Sparta, Fitzgerald, and Tallahassee, places like that. We used to draw the crowds all the time. The places were always packed. I was popular around those states before Chuck and Lee Diamond joined the band. I got two sax players and named the band the Upsetters. It made me outstanding in Macon at that time, to have this fantastic band in a little town like this. The other bands couldn't compete. So when it said "Little Richard and the Upsetters" everybody wanted to come. We had a station wagon with the name written on it, and I thought it was fantastic.

We were each making fifteen dollars a night, and there was a lot you could do with fifteen dollars. We would play three, four nights a week—that's fifty dollars. And sometimes we would play at a place on the outskirts of Macon at a midnight dance. That would pay ten dollars and all the fried chicken you could eat. We were playing some of Roy Brown's tunes, a lot of Fats Domino tunes, some B. B. King tunes, and I believe a couple of Little Walter's and a few things by Billy Wright. I really looked up to Billy Wright. That's where I got the hairstyle from and everything. "Keep Your Hand on Your Heart," that was one of them. We'd play all around Georgia, Tennessee, and Kentucky, cos we had a big name around those places. We would draw packed houses every place and we'd get a guarantee and a percentage of the take over the guarantee. We were making a darned good living. One song which would really tear the house down was "Tutti Frutti." The lyrics were kind of vulgar, "Tutti Frutti good booty—if it don't fit don't force it. . . ." It would crack the crowd up. We were playing without a bass and Chuck would have to bang real hard on his bass drum in order to get a bass-fiddle effect.

BUMPS BLACKWELL: When I got to New Orleans, Cosimo Matassa, the studio owner, called and said, "Hey, man, this boy's down here waiting for you." When I walked in, there's this cat in this loud shirt, with hair waved up six inches above his head. He was talking wild, thinking up stuff just to be different, you know? I could tell he was a mega-personality. So we got to the studio, on Rampart and Dumaine. I had the Studio Band in—Lee Allen on tenor sax, Alvin "Red" Tyler on baritone sax, Earl Palmer on drums, Edgar Blanchard and Justin Adams on guitar, Huey "Piano" Smith and James Booker on piano, Frank Fields, bass, all of them the best in New Orleans. They were Fats Domino's session men.

Let me tell you about the recording methods we used in those days. Recording technicians of today, surrounded by huge banks of computer-controlled sound technology, would find the engineering techniques available in the 1950s as primitive as the *Kitty Hawk* is to the space shuttle. When I started there was no tape. It was disk to disk. There was no such thing as overdubbing. Those things we did at Cosimo's were on tape, but they were all done straight ahead. The tracks you heard were the tracks as they were recorded from beginning to end. We would take sixty or seventy takes. We were recording two tracks. Maybe we might go to surgery and intercut a track or cut a track at the end or something, but we didn't know what overdubbing was. The studio was just a back room in a furniture store, like an ordinary motel room. For the whole orchestra. There'd be a grand piano just as you came in the door. I'd have the grand's lid up with a mike in the keys and Alvin Tyler and Lee Allen would be blowing into that. Earl Palmer's drums were out of the door, where I had one mike, as well. The bassman would be way over the other side of the studio. You see, the bass would cut and bleed in, so I could get the bass.

The recording equipment was a little old quarter-inch single-channel Ampex Model 300 in the next room. I would go in there and listen with earphones. If it didn't sound right I'd just keep moving the mikes around. I would have to set up all those things. But, you see, once I had got my sound, my room sound, well then I would just start running my numbers straight down. It might take me forty-five minutes, an hour, to get that balance within the room, but once those guys hit a groove you could go on all night. When we got it, we got it. I would like to see some of these great producers today produce on monaural or binaural equipment with the same atmosphere. Cos the problem is, if you're going to get a room sound with the timbre of the instruments, you can't put them together as a band and just start playing. All of a sudden one horn's going to stick out. So I had to place the mikes very carefully and put the drummer outside the door.

Well, the first session was to run six hours, and we planned to cut eight sides. Richard ran through the songs on his audition tape. "He's My Star" was very disappointing. I did not even record it. But "Wonderin'" we got in two takes. Then we got "I'm Just a Lonely Guy," which was written by a local girl called Dorothy La Bostrie who was always pestering me to record her stuff. Then "The Most I Can Offer," and then "Baby." So far so good. But it wasn't really what I was looking for. I had heard that Richard's stage act was really wild, but in the studio that day he was very inhibited. Possibly his ego was pushing him to show his spiritual feeling or something, but it certainly wasn't coming together like I had expected and hoped.

The problem was that what he looked like, and what he sounded like didn't come together. If you look like Tarzan and sound like Mickey Mouse it just doesn't work out. So I'm thinking, Oh, Jesus . . . You know what it's like when you don't know what to do? It's "Let's take a break. Let's go to lunch." I had to think. I didn't know what to do. I couldn't go back to Rupe[1] with the material I had because there was nothing there that I could put out. Nothing that I could ask anyone to put a promotion on. Nothing to merchandise. And I was paying out serious money.

So here we go over to the Dew Drop Inn, and, of course, Richard's like any other ham. We walk into the place and, you know, the girls are there and the boys are there and he's got an audience. There's a piano, and that's his crutch. He's on stage reckoning to show Lee Allen his piano style. So WOW! He gets to going. He hits that piano, didididididididididi . . . and starts to sing "Awop-bop-a-Loo-Mop a-good Goddam—Tutti Frutti, good booty. . . ." I said, "WOW! That's what I want from you, Richard. That's a hit!" I knew that the lyrics were too lewd and suggestive to record. It would never have got played on the air. So I got hold of Dorothy La Bostrie, who had come over to see how the recording of her song was going. I brought her to the Dew Drop.

Dorothy was a little colored girl so thin she looked like six o'clock. She just had to close one eye and she looked like a needle. Dorothy had songs stacked this high and was always asking me to record them. She'd been singing these songs to me, but the trouble was they all sounded like Dinah Washington's "Blowtop Blues." They were all composed to the same melody. But looking through her words, I could see that she was a prolific writer. She just didn't understand melody. So I said to her, "Look. You come and write some lyrics to this, cos I can't use the lyrics Richard's got." He had some terrible words in there. Well, Richard was embarrassed to sing the song and she was not certain that she wanted to hear it. Time was running out, and I *knew* it could be a hit. I talked, using every argument I could think of. I asked him if he had a grudge against making money. I told her that she was over twenty-one, had

---

1. Art Rupe, owner of Specialty Records.

a houseful of kids and no husband and needed the money. And finally, I convinced them. Richard turned to face the wall and sang the song two or three times and Dorothy listened.

Break time was over, and we went back to the studio to finish the session, leaving Dorothy to write the words. I think the first thing we did was "Directly from My Heart to You." Now that, and "I'm Just a Lonely Guy," could have made it. Those two I could have gotten by with—just by the skin of my teeth. Fifteen minutes before the session was to end, the chick comes in and puts these little trite lyrics in front of me. I put them in front of Richard. Richard says he ain't got no voice left. I said, "Richard, you've *got* to sing it."

There had been no chance to write an arrangement, so I had to take the chance on Richard playing the piano himself. That wild piano was essential to the success of the song. It was impossible for the other piano players to learn it in the short time we had. I put a microphone between Richard and the piano and another inside the piano, and we started to record it. It took three takes, and in fifteen minutes we had it. "Tutti Frutti."

BUMPS BLACKWELL: The white radio stations wouldn't play Richard's version of "Tutti Frutti" and made Boone's cover number one. So we decided to up the tempo on the follow-up and get the lyrics going so fast that Boone wouldn't be able to get his mouth together to do it! The follow-up was "Long Tall Sally." It was written by a girl named Enortis Johnson and the story of how she came to us seems unbelievable today.

I got a call from a big disk jockey called Honey Chile. She *had* to see me. Very urgent. I went, because we relied on the jocks to push the records, and the last thing you said to them was no. I went along to this awful downtown hotel, and there was Honey Chile with this young girl, about sixteen, seventeen, with plaits, who reminded you of one of these little sisters at a Baptist meeting, all white starched collars and everything. She looked like someone who's just been scrubbed—so out of place in this joint filled with pimps and unsavory characters just waiting to scoop her up when she's left alone, you know?

So Honey Chile said to me, "Bumps, you got to do something about this girl. She's walked all the way from Appaloosa, Mississippi, to sell this song to Richard, cos her auntie's sick and she needs money to put her in the hospital." I said okay, let's hear the song, and this little clean-cut kid, all bows and things, says, "Well, I don't have a melody yet. I thought maybe you or Richard could do that." So I said okay, what *have* you got, and she pulls out this piece of paper. It looked like toilet paper with a few words written on it:

> Saw Uncle John with Long Tall Sally
> They saw Aunt Mary comin,
> So they ducked back in the alley

And she said, "Aunt Mary is sick. And I'm going to tell her about Uncle John. Cos he was out there with Long Tall Sally, and I saw 'em. They saw Aunt Mary comin' and they ducked back in the alley."

I said, "They did, huh? And this is a song? You walked all the way from Appaloosa, Mississippi, with this piece of paper?" (I'd give my right arm if I could find it now. I kept it for years. It was a classic. Just a few words on a used doily!)

Honey Chile said, "Bumps, you gotta do something for this child." So I went back to the studio. I told Richard. He didn't want to do it. I said, "Richard, Honey Chile will get mad at us. . . ." I kept hearing "Duck back in the alley, duck back in the alley." We kept adding words and music to it, to put it right. Richard started to sing it—and all of a sudden there was "Have some fun tonight." That was the hook. Richard loved it cos the hottest thing then was the shuffle.

Richard was reciting that thing. He got on the piano and got the music going and it just started growing and growing. We kept trying, trying it, and I pulled the musicians in and we pulled stuff from everybody. That's where Richard's "Ooooooh" first came in. That's what he taught to Paul McCartney. Well, we kept rerecording because I wanted it faster. I drilled Richard with "Duck back in the alley" faster and faster until it burned, it was so fast. When it was finished I turned to Richard and said, "Let's see Pat Boone get his mouth together to do *this* song."* That's how it was done, and if you look at the copyright you'll see it's Johnson, Penniman, and Blackwell.

LITTLE RICHARD: We were breaking through the racial barrier. The white kids had to hide my records cos they daren't let their parents know they had them in the house. We decided that my image should be crazy and way-out so that the adults would think I was harmless. I'd appear in one show dressed as the Queen of England and in the next as the pope.

They were exciting times. The fans would go really wild. Nearly every place we went, the people got unruly. They'd want to get to me and tear my clothes off. It would be standing-room-only crowds and 90 percent of the audience would be white. I've always thought that Rock 'n' Roll brought the races together. Although I was black, the fans didn't care. I used to feel good about that. Especially being from the South, where you see the barriers, having all these people who we thought hated us, showing all this *love*.

A lot of songs I sang to crowds first to watch their reaction, that's how I knew they'd hit, but we recorded them over and over again. "Lucille" was after a female impersonator in my hometown. We used to call him Queen Sonya. I just took the rhythm of an old song of mine called "Directly from My Heart to You" slowed down and I used to do that riff and go "Sonya!" and I made it into "Lucille." My cousin used to live in a place called Barn Hop Bottom in Macon, right by the railway line, and when the trains came past they'd shake the houses—*chocka-chocka-chocka*—and that's how I got the rhythm for "Directly from My Heart" and "Lucille." I was playing it way before I met Bumps. I was playing "Lucille" and "Slippin' and Slidin'" in my room in Macon way before I started recording for Specialty. I'd make up the music while I was making the words fit.

"Good Golly Miss Molly" I first heard a D.J. using that name. His name was Jimmy Pennick, but you know it was Jackie Brenston that gave me the musical inspiration. Jackie Brenston was a sax player with Ike Turner's Kings of Rhythm when he did "Rocket 88" and "Juiced," and Ike Turner's band backed him, but they didn't take any credits because of their contracts. I always liked that record, and I used to use the riff in my act, so when we were looking for a lead-in to "Good Golly Miss Molly" I did that and it fitted.

---

*Boone did cover "Long Tall Sally." An anemic version in which he reverses the Midas touch and turns gold into dross, managing to sound as though he is not quite sure what he is singing about. It sold a million.

Further Reading

Altschuler, Glenn C. *All Shook Up: How Rock 'n' Roll Changed America*. New York: Oxford University Press, 2003.
White, Charles, Richard Wayne Penniman, and Robert Blackwell. *The Life and Times of Little Richard: The Quasar of Rock*. New York: Random House, 1984.

Discography

Boone, Pat. *Pat's 40 Big Ones*. Connoisseur Collection, 2001.
_____. *The Singles+*. Br Music Holland, 2003.
Little Richard. *Little Richard: Eighteen Greatest Hits*. Rhino/WEA, 1985.
_____. *Greatest Gold Hits*. Mastercuts Lifestyle, 2004.
_____. *The Explosive Little Richard*. Edsel Records, UK, 2007.

22. Elvis Presley, Sam Phillips, and Rockabilly

As the most successful artist of the mid-1950s rock 'n' roll explosion, Elvis Presley (1935–77) had a profound impact on popular music. His sense of style, both musical and personal, was both the focal point of the media reaction to early rock 'n' roll and the inspiration for some of the most important rock musicians to follow. The narrative of his meteoric rise and subsequent decline amid mysterious and tawdry circumstances fueled many myths both during his life and after his death at 42.[1]

The earliest musical experiences of Presley, who was raised in poverty in the Deep South, came in the Pentecostal services of the First Assembly of God Church.[2] Other formative influences included popular

---

1. The mythologizing after his death has been prolific enough to spawn at least two books that are devoted to understanding it, as well as numerous articles; see Gilbert Rodman, *Elvis after Elvis: The Posthumous Career of a Living Legend* (New York: Routledge, 1996); and Greil Marcus, *Dead Elvis: A Chronicle of a Cultural Obsession* (New York: Doubleday, 1991).

2. C. Wolfe, "Presley and the Gospel Tradition," in *The Elvis Reader: Texts and Sources on the King of Rock 'n' Roll*, ed. K. Quain, 13–27 (New York: St. Martin's Press, 1992).

tunes of the day, country music, blues, and rhythm and blues. Although he had little experience as a performer, in 1954, at age 19, he came to the attention of Sam Phillips, owner of a Memphis recording company, Sun Records. Phillips teamed Presley, who sang and played guitar, with local country and western musicians Scotty Moore (guitar) and Bill Black (bass). During their first recording session in June 1954, the trio recorded a single with "That's All Right, Mama" (originally recorded in 1946 by blues singer Arthur "Big Boy" Crudup) on one side and "Blue Moon of Kentucky" (originally recorded in 1946 by bluegrass pioneer Bill Monroe) on the other. The group's style blended elements of country and rhythm and blues without being identifiable as either; the distinctive sound included Moore's rhythmically oriented lead guitar playing, Black's slapped bass, and Presley's forceful, if crude, rhythm guitar, with the recording swathed in a distinctive electronic echo effect. Presley's voice, however, attracted the most attention: swooping almost two octaves at times, changing timbre from a croon to a growl instantaneously, he seemed not so much to be synthesizing preexisting styles as to be juxtaposing them, sometimes within the course of a single phrase.[3] While the trio's initial record provoked enthusiastic responses immediately upon being broadcast on Memphis radio, it confused audiences, who wondered if the singer was white or black. And although white musicians' music had incorporated African American instrumental and vocal approaches since the earliest "hillbilly" recordings of the 1920s, no previous white singer had so successfully forged an individual style clearly rooted in a contemporaneous African American idiom.

Presley, Moore, and Black released four more singles on Sun during 1954–55; each one featured a blues or rhythm and blues song backed with a country-style number. Presley's uninhibited, sexually charged performances throughout the Southeast provoked frenzied responses and influenced other musicians: by the end of 1955, performers such as Carl Perkins and Johnny Cash had emerged with a style (coined "rockabilly") that resembled Presley's.

Presley's growing popularity attracted the attention of promoter "Colonel" Tom Parker, who negotiated the sale of Presley's contract to RCA Records for the then-unheard-of sum of $35,000. Presley's first recording for RCA, "Heartbreak Hotel" (released in March 1956), achieved the unprecedented feat of reaching the Top 5 on the pop, rhythm and blues, and country charts simultaneously. This recording and the songs that followed in 1956 all combined aspects of his spare Sun recordings with increasingly heavy instrumentation—including piano, drums, and background singers—that moved the sound closer to that of mainstream pop. Both sides of his third RCA single "Hound Dog"/"Don't Be Cruel" hit number one on all three charts. "Hound Dog" radically transformed

---

3. These aspects of Presley's style are described in Richard Middleton, "All Shook Up," in *The Elvis Reader*, 3–12.

Willie Mae "Big Mama" Thornton's 1952 R&B hit, while "Don't Be Cruel" was a more pop-oriented recording written specifically for Presley by Otis Blackwell. Presley's vocal style already showed signs of mannerism, trading the unpredictable exchanges of different voices of the early recordings for a single affect throughout each song.

Although Elvis Presley did participate in some interviews throughout his career, the questions and his answers in these interviews tended toward the perfunctory (e.g., in response to questions about rock 'n' roll, Elvis responded, "It's hard to explain rock 'n' roll. It's not what you call folk music. It's a beat that gets you. You feel it.").[4] In contrast, Presley's first producer, Sam Phillips, has reflected at length on those early recording sessions and the conditions that gave rise to rockabilly. Prior to recording Presley's first five singles and the appearance of Elvis's rockabilly successors at Sun such as Carl Perkins, Jerry Lee Lewis, Johnny Cash, and Roy Orbison, Phillips recorded local blues and R&B musicians like B. B. King, Ike Turner, and Howlin' Wolf, including a session that resulted in the important proto–rock 'n' roll recording, Jackie Brenston's "Rocket 88" (with a band led by Turner) in 1951. Phillips is also a natural-born storyteller, as revealed by many of the anecdotes in this interview.

Sam Phillips Interview
Elizabeth Kaye

There are many stories about how Elvis came to Sun in 1954. I'd like to hear your version of it.
He was working for Crown Electric. I'd seen the truck go back and forth outside, and I thought, "They sure are doing a hell of a lot of business around here." But I never saw it stop anywhere. So Elvis had . . . he had cased the joint a long time before he stopped the truck and got out. And there's no telling how many days and nights behind that wheel he was figuring out some way to come in and make a record without saying, "Mr. Phillips, would you audition me?" So his mother's birthday gave him the opportunity to come in and make a little personal record. [Elvis claimed he was making the record for his mother, but her birthday was, in fact, months away, so perhaps he had other motives.]

The first song he recorded was "My Happiness." What do you think when you heard it?
There wasn't anything that striking about Elvis, except his sideburns were down to here [*gestures*], which I kind of thought, well, you know, "That's pretty cool, man. Ain't nobody else got them that damn long." We talked in the studio. And

---

4. This quote comes from Mick Farren and Pearce Marchbank, *Elvis in His Own Words* (London: Omnibus Press, 1977), 27.

Source: Elizabeth Kaye, "Sam Phillips Interview," Rolling Stone, 13 February 1986, pp. 54–58, 86–88.

I played the record back for him in the control room on the little crystal turntable and walked up front and told Marion [Phillips's assistant, Marion Keisker] to write down Elvis' name and a number and how we can get ahold of him.

You called him back to cut a ballad called "Without You." That song was never released. What went wrong?

We got some pretty good cuts on the thing, but I wanted to check him out other ways before I made a final decision as to which route we were going to attempt to go with him.

And I decided I wanted to look at things with a little tempo, because you can really hang yourself out on ballads or when you go up against Perry Como or Eddie Fisher or even Patti Page, all of those people. I wasn't looking for anything that greatly polished.

After that, you put Elvis with a band, Scotty Moore on guitar and Bill Black on bass. Why did you choose them?

The two of them, they'd been around the studio, Lord, I don't know how many damned times, you know? Scotty had been playing with different bands, and although he hadn't ever done a session for me, I knew he had the patience and he wasn't afraid to try anything, and that's so important when you're doing laboratory experiments.

Scotty was also the type of person who could take instruction real good. And I kidded him a lot. I said, "If you don't quit trying to copy Chet Atkins, I'll throw you out of this damn place." And Bill, he was just Bill Black, and the best slap bass player in the city.

What were you trying to achieve with Elvis?

Now you've got to keep in mind Elvis Presley probably innately was the most introverted person that came into that studio. Because he didn't play with bands. He didn't go to this little club and pick and grin. All he did was set with his guitar on the side of his bed at home. I don't think he even played on the front porch.

So I had to try to establish a direction for him. And I had to look into the market, and if the market was full of one type of thing, why try to go in there? There's only so many pieces in a pie. That's how I figured it. I knew from the beginning that I was going to have to do something different and that it might be harder to get it going. But if I got it going, I might have something.

How did you come to cut "That's All Right"?

That night we had gone through a number of things, and I was getting ready to fold it up. But I didn't want to discourage the damn people, you understand? I knew how enthusiastic Elvis was to try to do something naturally. I knew also that Scotty Moore was staying there till he dropped dead, you know? I don't remember exactly what I said, but it was light hearted. I think I told him, "There ain't a damn song you can do that sounds worth a damn," or something like that. He knew it was tongue in cheek. But it was getting to be a critical time, because we had been in the studio a lot. Well, I went back into the booth. I left the mikes open, and I think Elvis felt like, really, "What the hell have I got to lose? I'm really gonna blow his head off, man." And they cut down on "That's All Right," and hell, man, they was just as instinctive as they could be.

It's said that you heard him singing it, and you said, "What are you doing?" and he said, "I don't know," and you said, "Do it again." Is that true?

I don't remember exactly verbatim. But it was something along the lines that I've been quoted.

Scotty Moore says that when he heard the playback he thought he'd be run out of town. How did you feel when you heard it?

First of all, Scotty wasn't shocked at any damned thing I attempted to do. Scotty isn't shockable. And for me, that damned thing came through so loud and clear it was just like a big flash of lightning and the thunder that follows. I knew it was what I was looking for for Elvis. When anybody tells you they know they've got a hit, they don't know what the hell they're talking about. But I knew I had it on "That's All Right." I just knew I had found a groove. In my opinion. And that's all I had to go on, honey. I mean I let people hear it. But I didn't ask them their damn opinions.

Then what happened?

I let Scotty, Bill and Elvis know I was pretty damn pleased. Then I made an acetate dub of it and took it up to [Memphis disc jockey] Dewey Phillips and played him the tape. And Daddy-O Dewey wanted to hear it again. "Goddamn, man," he says, "I got to have it." Red, hot and blue. You'd have to know Dewey.

And two nights later he played that thing, and the phones started ringing. Honey, I'll tell you, all hell broke loose. People were calling that station, and it really actually surprised me, because I knew nobody knew Elvis. Elvis just didn't have friends, didn't have a bunch of guys he ran with or anything, you know? Anyway, it was just fantastic. To my knowledge, there weren't any adverse calls.

Why did you decide to back "That's All Right" with "Blue Moon of Kentucky"?

This was before anybody thought of young people being interested in bluegrass. But we did this thing, and it just had an intrigue. And that's the one where I thought maybe there was a good possibility of getting run out of town, 'cause hey, man, you didn't mess with bluegrass. Bluegrass is kind of sacred, you know.

Once the record was released, there was an incredible furor. How did it affect you?

Rock & roll probably put more money in the collection boxes of the churches across America than anything the preacher could have said. I certainly know that to be a fact. Not only them. Disc jockeys broke the hell out of my records. Broke 'em on the air. Slam them over the damn microphone. Now if I *hadn't* affected people like that, I might have been in trouble.

Do you remember the session for "Good Rockin' Tonight"?

Oh, God, we all loved that song, man. I took Bill, and I said, "I don't want none of this damned slapping. I want you to pull them damned strings, boy."

Your contract with Elvis had him completely locked up, so the only way Colonel Parker could have become involved was as a concert booker. Why did you decide to sell his contract just a year and a half after he started with you?

I had looked at everything for how I could take a little extra money and get myself out of a real bind. I mean, I wasn't broke, but man, it was hand-to-mouth. I made an offer to Tom Parker, but the whole thing was that I made an offer I didn't think they'd even consider—$35,000, plus I owed Elvis $4000 or $5000.

So you thought the offer was so high no one would take it?

I didn't necessarily want them *not* to take it.

Did you realize how much Elvis was worth?

Hell, no. I didn't have any idea the man was going to be the biggest thing that ever happened to the industry.

Were you ever sorry you let him go?

No. That was the best judgment call I could make at the time, and I still think it is. And Sun went on and did many, many things. I hoped the one thing that wouldn't happen to me was that I would be a one-artist or a one-hit label.

Did you give Elvis any advice when he left Sun?

The one real ammunition I gave him was "Don't let them tell you what to do. Don't lose your individuality."

Then how did you feel when he started making the type of movies he made?

They were just things that you could make for nothing and make millions off of, and Elvis didn't have anything to do with it. That was Colonel Tom Parker and the moguls at the different studios. I think it was almost sinister, I really do.

Did you ever think of becoming a manager?

I'm insane. But I'm not that insane.

Once Elvis was gone, were you banking Sun's future on Carl Perkins?

Absolutely. And there was another one of those instincts. I was giving up some kind of a cat, man, but, sure enough, I sold him, and that's what financed "Blue Suede Shoes."

Steve Sholes of RCA called you at the time "Blue Suede Shoes" was climbing the charts. RCA couldn't get anything going with Elvis, and Sholes asked you, "Did we buy the wrong guy?" What did you tell him?

I told him, "You haven't bought the wrong person." And I gave him the reasons. Number one, Elvis certainly had the talent. And unlike Carl, he was single and had no children and was a helluva-looking man. He said, "Well, would you be mad at us if we put out 'Blue Suede Shoes'?" Man, that staggered me. I said, "Steve, you all are big enough to kill me, you know." But they didn't put it out as a single. They released it as an EP.

Did it outsell Perkins' version?

Hell, no. Well, I guess over the years when it was put in nineteen packages. But the only reason Carl is not recognized for "Blue Suede Shoes" is that Elvis became so mammothly big.

When did you realize how big Elvis would be?

Not when I heard "Heartbreak Hotel." That was the worst record. I knew it when I heard "Don't Be Cruel." I was driving back from the first vacation I'd had in my life, and it came on the radio, and I said, "Wait a minute. Jesus, he's off and gone, man." I'd like to run off the road.

Were you jealous?

Hell, no, 'cause when I heard "Heartbreak Hotel," I said, "Damned sons of bitches are going to mess this man up." Then, boy, I heard "Don't Be Cruel," and I was the happiest man in the world.

What was the difference in what you were trying to achieve first with Elvis, then with Perkins?

With Elvis I kind of wanted to lean more toward the blues. I wanted to get Carl more into modifying country music.

What was your favorite Perkins song?

This is the craziest thing, but one of the cutest songs I ever heard was his "Movie Magg." And "Boppin' the Blues."

Do you remember when you first heard Jerry Lee?
It was the day after I first heard "Don't Be Cruel." Jerry had come to Memphis with his cousin, staying at his house. He was a pretty determined person, and he made up his mind he was going to see Sam Phillips. Jack Clement [Sun's producer] was at the studio, and Jerry didn't even want to audition for him. But they cut this little audition tape. And when I went to the studio, Jack says, "Man, I got a cat I want you to hear." Well, I had been looking for somebody that could do tricks on the piano as a lead instrument. Lo and behold, man, I hear this guy and his total spontaneity.

Then, when you met Jerry Lee and he played for you, you're supposed to have told him, "You are a rich man."
I probably did. Not in the connotation of money, but of talent.

You've said that Jerry Lee was the most talented person you ever worked with but that you don't think he could have been bigger than Elvis. Why is that?
That gets into the thing of the total effect of the person. There is no question that the most talented person I ever worked with is Jerry Lee Lewis. Black or white. But Elvis had a certain type of total charisma that was just almost untouchable by any other human that I know of or have ever seen.

But this is a tough comparison for me to make. It looks like I'm drawing lines between two of the most talented people in the world, and I don't like to do that. But I would say that if they were both at their peak, and Elvis was booked for a show but Jerry Lee showed up, no one would be disappointed. Is there a better answer you can think of than that?

What do you remember about recording "Great Balls of Fire"?
That was the toughest record I ever recorded in my life. Otis Blackwell had done the demo.[5] When I heard it, I said, "What in the hell are they doing sending me a record like this? It ought to be out." He'd written the damn thing on a napkin in a bar he owed a lot of money to. And we worked our ass off because those breaks . . . with Jerry having to do his piano, it had to be exactly synced with his voice.

You didn't do any overdubbing on it?
Hell, no. We didn't have nothing to overdub with.

When Elvis died, you said that he died of a broken heart. Can you amplify that?
When you really don't have something to look forward to with a good, sweet, beautiful attitude, you're in trouble. I don't care who you are. You're also in trouble if you're in bondage in any way. I'm talking about emotional entrapment. That's deep stuff. And it's serious stuff. And no matter what happens to you in this world, if you don't make it your business to be happy, then you may have gained the whole world and lost your spirit and maybe even your damned soul.

But wasn't Elvis entrapped by circumstance?
Absolutely.

What could he have done differently?
Been hardheaded like me and said, "I will break your damned neck, I don't care—you can't scare me. Monetary factors can't scare me. Starvation can't scare me. Threats can't scare me." I mean you have to have that attitude.

---

5. Blackwell also wrote many songs for Presley, including "Don't Be Cruel," "All Shook Up," and "Jailhouse Rock."

Elvis also knew that success wasn't enough. It's like Mac Davis said, man, and I think this is one of the greatest quotes, Bible included: "Stop and smell the roses." Now that's where we can all find ourselves if we don't stop and smell the roses.

And the sad thing about it is dying before you actually physically die. I mean, you know, bless his heart.

Further Reading

Farren, Mick, and Pearce Marchbank. *Elvis in His Own Words.* London: Omnibus Press, 1977.

Guralnick, Peter. *Last Train to Memphis: The Rise of Elvis Presley.* Boston: Little, Brown, 1994.

_____. *Careless Love: The Unmaking of Elvis Presley.* Boston: Little, Brown, 1999.

Marcus, Greil. *Mystery Train: Images of America in Rock 'n' Roll Music.* 3rd rev. ed. New York: Plume, [1975] 1990.

Middleton, Richard. "All Shook Up." In *The Elvis Reader: Texts and Sources on the King of Rock 'n Roll*, ed. Kevin Quain, 3–12. New York: St. Martin's Press, 1992.

Rodman, Gilbert. *Elvis after Elvis: The Posthumous Career of a Living Legend.* New York: Routledge, 1996.

Wolfe, Charles. "Presley and the Gospel Tradition." In *The Elvis Reader: Texts and Sources on the King of Rock 'n Roll*, ed. Kevin Quain, 13–27. New York: St. Martin's Press, 1992.

Discography

Legendary Sun Records Story. Castle/Pulse, 2003.

Legends Collection: Rock 'n' Roll Teenagers. Legends Collection, 2002.

Orbison, Roy. *The Essential Roy Orbison.* Sony, 2006.

Presley, Elvis. *Elvis Presley.* RCA Victor, 1956.

_____. *Elvis.* RCA Victor, 1956.

_____. *Loving You.* RCA Victor, 1957.

_____. *Elvis 30 #1 Hits.* BMG/Elvis, 2002.

_____. *Elvis at Sun.* BMG/Elvis, 2004.

_____. *The Essential Elvis Presley.* BMG/Elvis, 2007.

Thornton, Big Mama. *Hound Dog: The Peacock Recordings.* MCA, 1992.

23. Rock 'n' Roll Meets the Popular Press

Beginning in 1956—after the first wave of national hits by Fats Domino, Chuck Berry, Little Richard, and Elvis Presley, and amidst a torrent of cover versions of R&B songs and increasing numbers of integrated rock 'n' roll revues—articles on rock 'n' roll began appearing in mainstream newspapers such as the *New York Times* and in magazines such as *Time*, *Newsweek*, and *Life*. These articles recall and amplify some of the topics present in the series of *Variety* articles included earlier in this volume: the tone, by and large, is condescending, making frequent references to the connections between rock 'n' roll and sex, violence, and juvenile delinquency. In particular, descriptions abound of audiences and performers trespassing societal norms, and this aberrant behavior (one article describes "snake-dancing around town and smashing windows"[1]) is typically linked to the influence of the beat or rhythm of the music.

For example, in an article entitled "Rock-and-Roll Called Communicable Disease," a "noted psychiatrist," Dr. Francis J. Braceland of Hartford, Connecticut, "called rock-and-roll a 'cannibalistic and tribalistic' form of music. He was commenting on the disturbances that led to eleven arrests during the week-end at a local theatre." Dr. Braceland explains further: "It is insecurity and 'rebellion' . . . that impels teenagers to affect 'ducktail' haircuts, wear zoot-suits and carry on boisterously at rock-and-roll affairs."[2]

Roughly three months later, *Time* stoked similar fears, commencing an article with the evocative title "Yeh-Heh-Heh-Hes, Baby" with a description of a concert that blends images of a riot with those of a menagerie:

> When [the names of the stars] appear on theater and dance-hall marquees announcing a stage show or "record hop," the stampede is on. The theater is jammed with adolescents from the 9 a.m. curtain to closing and it rings and shrieks like the jungle bird house at the zoo. If one of the current heroes is announced—groups

---

1. This phrase comes from "Yeh-Heh-Heh-Hes, Baby," *Time*, June 18, 1956, 54. Part of this article is reprinted here, but not this particular passage.

2. "Rock-and-Roll Called Communicable Disease," *New York Times*, March 28, 1956, 33.

such as Bill Haley and His Comets or The Platters or a soloist such as Elvis Presley—the shrieks become deafening.[3] The tumult completely drowns the sound of the spastically gyrating performers despite fully powered amplification. Only the obsessive beat pounds through, stimulating the crowd to such rhythmical movements as clapping in tempo and jumping and dancing in the aisles. Sometimes the place vibrates with the beat of music and stamping feet, and not infrequently kids have been moved to charging the stage, rushing ushers and theater guards.

The article continues with the warning that rock 'n' roll is as "suggestive as swing." The effect it elicits from listeners is apparently involuntary, and the gyrations of Elvis's pelvis were sufficient to raise the moral hackles of policemen in Oakland, California:

There is no denying that rock 'n' roll evokes a physical response from even its most reluctant listeners, for that giant pulse matches the rhythmical operations of the human body, and the performers are all too willing to specify it. Said an Oakland, Calif. policeman, after watching Elvis Presley last week: "If he did that in the street we'd arrest him."

This article closes with a clincher: the seductive call of rock 'n' roll is compared by anonymous "psychologists" to the calls of the leader of National Socialism (Nazism), the spectre of which would have still been relatively fresh in 1956: "Psychologists feel that rock 'n' roll's deepest appeal is to the teeners' need to belong; the results bear passing resemblance to Hitler mass meetings."

Show business personalities from the realms of both high and low culture could not resist weighing in on the impact of rock 'n' roll. Herbert von Karajan, the conductor of the Berlin Philharmonic at the time, offered this medico-musical explanation, recalling passages from the *Time* article quoted previously: "Strange things happen in the blood stream when a musical resonance coincides with the beat of the human pulse."[4] Frank Sinatra's comments merged aesthetics with the then-popular sociological discourse on delinquency when he averred that "rock 'n' roll smells phony and false. It is sung, played and written for

---

3. Elvis Presley, in fact, became a focus of the media's reaction to rock 'n' roll's "lewdness" and "degeneracy." For examples of early responses to Elvis's TV performances, see "Teeners' Hero," *Time*, May 14, 1956; and Jack Gould, "TV: New Phenomenon—Elvis Presley Rises to Fame as Vocalist Who Is Virtuoso of Hootchy-Kootchy," *New York Times*, June 6, 1956, 67.

4. "Rock 'n' Roll's Pulse Taken," *New York Times*, October 27, 1956, 58.

the most part by cretinous goons and by means of its almost imbecilic reiteration and sly, lewd, in plain fact, dirty lyrics, it manages to be the martial music of every sideburned delinquent on the face of the earth."[5]

Further Reading

Gould, Jack. "TV: New Phenomenon—Elvis Presley Rises to Fame as Vocalist Who Is Virtuoso of Hootchy-Kootchy." *New York Times*, June 6, 1956, 67.
"Teeners' Hero." *Time*, May 14, 1956, 53–54.

24. The *Chicago Defender* Defends Rock 'n' Roll

The landmark U.S. Supreme Court decision of 1954, *Brown v. Board of Education,* which in effect mandated integration of public schools, sent shockwaves through U.S. society. The struggles around civil rights for African Americans that intensified after this decision received considerable media attention from the mid-1950s through the 1960s. The following article attests to the interconnection between early rock 'n' roll and the increasing public pressure to end racial segregation, an interconnection that was especially important to those who were most concerned with resisting integration. While Asa Carter (head of the North Alabama White Citizens Council) made claims that may seem extreme in the context of previous media reactions (e.g., rock 'n' roll pulls "the white man down to the level of the Negro"), these statements brought out what was implicit in the earlier "Warning to the Music Business" published in *Variety*. In lighthearted fashion, Rob Roy (the author of this article) makes overt the linkages between the threats of both rock 'n' roll and integration

---

5. Gertrude Samuels, "Why They Rock 'n' Roll—And Should They?," *New York Times Sunday Magazine*, January 12, 1958, 19–20.

to U.S. social conventions of the era. The publication of this article in the African American newspaper the *Chicago Defender* indicates some of the issues related to rock 'n' roll that concerned the black community at the time.

Roy's experiences in Alabama were hardly unique; nor were they the most extreme instance of harassment: three days after this article was published, an attack on Nat "King" Cole during a concert in Birmingham by the White Citizens Council illustrates the lengths to which such groups could go. This attack led to the cancellation of the remainder of Cole's southern tour. Cole was certainly not a rock 'n' roller by any stretch of the imagination, representing the persistence of older-style pop music into the late 1950s (and 1960s), but he was also assuredly African American, obviously a factor that was more important to the White Citizens Council than the type of music he was playing.[1]

Bias Against "Rock 'n' Roll" Latest Bombshell in Dixie
Rob Roy

In a small town in Alabama not so many moons ago, and after several "moonshines" (at a rear bar) this corner [i.e., the author] attempted to play a number on [a] juke box that was situated near a front bar. The bartender yelled, "No, no, no" so no music was played. That will not happen again.

One of the reasons is factual—this corner will hardly be in a position to reach a juke box in that little town again. Then there is the other reason: Should council leader Asa Carter of Birmingham have his way there will be no Rock 'N' Roll numbers on the juke box and of course no reason for this corner to wish to spend his dime. Even in Birmingham a dime is a dime.

Councilman Asa Carter says "Rock 'N' Roll" music is nothing but a plot by [the] NAACP to lower American youth's morals. He indicates he'll ask blacklisting of juke box operators who carry "Rock 'N' Roll" records on their vendors. Only thing wrong here is Mr. Carter, if successful, wouldn't be hurting the NAACP or the customers who wish to play the music but the juke box operators and the tavern owners.

Fancy if you can, a group of youngsters, patronizing a dancehall tavern and having to waltz each number that isn't a fox trot. "What, no jitterbugging?" they'd say on the way out of the place. In that case who would be hurt? Of course Mr. Carter would hardly be hurt. One must feel that he does not operate a tavern. Nor is it likely that his accomplishments include the jitterbug or rugcutting dance. To do either one must be alert of limb, fast, think what is the next move just naturally, and a few more sensible things. If Asa's feet match his expressed mind and actions they are too sluggish and out of line for even a dancer. Just an old story? "Free schools yet dumb people."

---

1. For a report on this incident, see "Alabamans Attack 'King' Cole on Stage," *New York Times*, April 11, 1956, 1, 27.

Source: "Bias Against 'Rock 'n' Roll' Latest Bombshell in Dixie," Rob Roy, *Chicago Defender*.

Carter, executive secretary of the powerful pro-segregation group, declared that citizen's councils through the state were circulating petitions demanding that "rock and roll" music be banned from jukeboxes.

He said in an interview that what he called "this generate music" was being encouraged by the NAACP and other pro-integration groups, adding:

"The NAACP uses this type of music as a means of pulling the white man down to the level of the Negro."

He declared that "rock and roll" as well as other forms of jazz, was undermining the morals of American youth with its "degenerate, anamalistic [sic] beats and rhythms." He added:

"This savage and primitive type of music which comes straight from Africa brings out the base things in man."

"Rock and Roll" music, he said, got its start in Negro night clubs and Negro radio broadcasts and its influence was spread by the NAACP.

"Instead of opposing it in an attempt to raise the morals of the Negro," he said, "the NAACP encouraged it slowly for the purpose of undermining the morals of white people."

He estimated that 300,000 signatures would be collected by the petitions and added:

"If jukebox operators hope to stay in business they better get rid of these smutty records with their dirty lyrics."

Further Reading

"Alabamans Attack 'King' Cole on Stage." *New York Times*, April 11, 1956, 1, 27.
Gourse, Leslie. *Unforgettable: The Life and Mystique of Nat King Cole.* New York: Cooper Square, 2000.

Discography

Cole, Nat King. *After Midnight: The Complete Session.* Blue Note Records, 1956.
_____. *The Greatest Hits.* Capitol, 1994.

25. The Music Industry Fight Against Rock 'n' Roll

DICK CLARK'S TEEN-POP EMPIRE AND THE PAYOLA SCANDAL

The 1950s ended on a bum note for rock 'n' roll: Chuck Berry was on the verge of being convicted for having transported a minor across state lines; Elvis was in the army; Little Richard had left popular music for the ministry; Jerry Lee Lewis had effectively been blacklisted for having married his 13-year-old cousin; and Buddy Holly, Richie Valens, and the Big Bopper (all of whom had scored major hits during 1957–58) had died in a plane crash. As early as 1956, defenders of pop music's old guard, represented by ASCAP officials and songwriter-performers associated with ASCAP, mounted an attack on rock 'n' roll by linking it to the rise of BMI and accusing BMI of manipulating public taste owing to its undue influence in the broadcast media. Several rounds of public hearings resulted.[1] The repeatedly asserted link between BMI and radio stations was specious: all broadcasters at that time had licenses from both BMI and ASCAP that required them to pay a fee for using music affiliated with those organizations, and even radio stations that owned stock in BMI did not receive dividends. No, the battle's focus truly lay in a conjunction of aesthetics and politics.[2] The old guard were defending their business interests, as well as their taste in music. The analyses of BMI's power, while inaccurate, could have been applied quite fairly to the position of ASCAP before BMI-affiliated music began making inroads in the pop music mainstream during the late 1940s.[3]

---

1. For a summary and analysis of these hearings, see Trent Hill, "The Enemy Within: Censorship in Rock Music in the 1950s," *South Atlantic Quarterly* 90, no. 4 (Fall 1991) 1: 675–708. The hearings lasted from 1956 into 1958. For accounts in the press, see "Rock 'n' Roll Laid to B. M. I. Control: Billy Rose Tells House Unit That 'Electronic Curtain' Furthers 'Monstrosities,'" *New York Times*, September 19, 1956, 75; Val Adams, "Networks Held Biased on Music: Senate Unit Hears Charges that They Promote Products of Their Own Affiliates," *New York Times*, March 12, 1958, 63; Val Adams, "Hanson Decries Hillbilly Music: Tells Senate Unit Hearing Tunes Heard on Air Are 'Madison Ave.' Version," *New York Times*, March 14, 1958, 51.

2. See Reebee Garofalo, *Rockin' Out: Popular Music in the USA* (Boston: Allyn and Bacon, 1997), 172; and Russell Sanjek, "The War on Rock," *Downbeat Music '72 Yearbook* (Chicago: Maher, 1972).

3. See Richard A. Peterson and David G. Berger, "Cycles in Symbol Production: The Case of Popular Music," in *On Record: Rock, Pop, and the Written Word* (New York: Pantheon Books, 1990), 140–59.

The payola hearings (which grew out of congressional hearings on crooked practices on television quiz shows) represented yet another official intervention into the business and media practices associated with early rock 'n' roll. In media accounts of payola, one is struck by how politicians were so quick to believe that the popularity of rock 'n' roll was due to either a conspiracy with BMI or payola; in other words, they thought that the music was so horrible that there had to be some form of external coercion involved for people to want to listen to it.

A new form of rock 'n' roll emerged that was designed to please both politicians and teenagers. The main variety of this new rock 'n' roll, "teen pop," was promoted by a nationally syndicated television show, *American Bandstand*, hosted by Dick Clark, a figure at once youthful and nonthreatening. Teen pop adopted older techniques of pop music production, incorporating aspects of rock 'n' roll while reinstating the separate roles of songwriter, instrumentalist, and singer that had been collapsed by artists like Chuck Berry and Little Richard. *American Bandstand* largely featured the stars of teen pop, known as "teen idols": good-looking young people from the Philadelphia area (where *American Bandstand* originated) singing music with a vague resemblance to rock 'n' roll.

Equally striking as the official, public response to rock 'n' roll were the disparate fates of Alan Freed and Dick Clark. The Jewish Freed rose to success by playing black popular music to white kids and by promoting concerts at which both performers and audiences were integrated. The clean-cut, all-American Clark's signature show, *American Bandstand,* featured a virtually all-white audience and was cautious about integration on the air.[4] Freed's career was effectively ended by the scandal; Clark hosted *American Bandstand* until 1989 and continued to make appearances on television, most notably as the host for *New Year's Rockin' Eve,* until his death on April 18, 2012.[5]

The following article from *Life* describes the payola hearings of late 1959–early 1960 and focuses on Clark. This article reproduces many of the criticisms and stereotypes found in early media reports on rock 'n' roll, even suggesting in the opening paragraph that a teenager murdered his mother because she refused to let him watch *American Bandstand*. More evenhanded than some other mainstream reports of the time, however, the article gives space to the views of fans of the show in order to explain why they like it. And while the familiar con-

4. That this was recognized by African American viewers is substantiated by the article from the African American newspaper *New York Age,* reprinted in this chapter.

5. For a thorough history of *American Bandstand,* see John A. Jackson, *American Bandstand: Dick Clark and the Making of a Rock 'n' Roll Empire* (New York: Oxford University Press, 1997).

descending tone is present, most of the comments critical of rock 'n' roll are ascribed to the members of the Senate committee. Along the way, a history and explanation of payola is presented and contrasted with the specifics of Clark's business operation so as to anticipate his ultimate exoneration.

Music Biz Goes Round and Round: It Comes Out Clarkola
Peter Bunzel

Back in September 1958 a roly-poly Tulsa boy named Billy Jay Killion came home from high school and wanted to watch Dick Clark's television program, *American Bandstand*. His mother, who didn't particularly care for rock 'n' roll music, was all set to watch a different program, so she told Billy "No." He seethed the whole night long. Then in the morning Billy took out a rifle and shot his mother dead.

Millions of American teen-agers feel just as strongly about Dick Clark, though no others have vented their feelings so violently. Last week their loyalty was put to the supreme test, for Clark was up before Congress to answer for mayhem of another kind. For six months the Harris Committee had been investigating payola in music and broadcasting, and had developed a greedy image of the whole industry. A long succession of disk jockeys admitted taking payments from music companies. But the one man the committee had always been gunning for was Dick Clark, the biggest disk jockey of all and a symbol, in giant screen, of the whole questionable business.

"I have never," Clark told the committee, "agreed to play a record in return for payment in cash or any other consideration." This statement seemed more and more astonishing to the committee as Clark went on to admit that in the last three years he had parlayed his position into a whopping personal fortune of $576,590. "Plugola," "royola" and "Clarkola," the committeemen variously called it.

But their skepticism did not alter Clark's mien as he sat on the stand giving off the same air of proper respectability he does on TV. He wore a blue suit, button-down shirt and black loafers. Every strand of his hair was neatly lacquered into place. His voice had the bland, dulcet tone of the TV announcer that he is.

A Most Important Commercial

His tone was appropriate, for 30-year-old Richard Wagstaff Clark was delivering the most important commercial of his life. He is out to sell his highly select adult audience the same moralistic image of himself that he has convincingly sold to the nation's teen-agers. It was an image he had peddled not only on the air but in a book of adolescent etiquette called *Your Happiest Years*. In this work he made a strong pitch for neatness and good manners, pausing briefly for little homilies: "Don't make the mistake of thinking those TV cameras are branches of the United States mint. Contrary to popular opinion, dollar bills don't come out of them like bread from a bakery oven."

Clark himself made the mistake he warned his public against, but it turned out fine for him. After all, he was in a unique spot to profit by his error. Most disk jockeys perform on radio. Clark is on TV. Most others are only on local stations. He is on a national network and he reaches some 16 million people with his stock in trade, rock 'n' roll. This form of music is alien to most adults, for whom it has all the soothing charm of a chorus of pneumatic drills. "But we love it," said a teen-age girl from Charleston, W. Va., who attended the Clark hearings. "When I hear a Beethoven symphony, I don't feel anything. When I hear our kind of music, I feel something way down deep, like oatmeal."

Payola as a Compliment

The same adults who disparage rock 'n' roll unwittingly helped get it going. When long-playing records came in, grown-ups stopped buying single records. Manufacturers of singles had to aim their products at teen-age taste and rock 'n' roll became the staple. The singles are easy and cheap to make and 600 record companies are expelling a constant flow. But the big problem is selling them.

First the records get a test run in such "break-out" cities as Cleveland, Boston or Detroit to see which can be sold—or which the public can be conned into buying. A sure way to boost the songs has been to put money on the line to disk jockeys. Many deejays were proud to be bribed, for, in their curious little fraternity, payments became a status symbol. "Payola comes to the top disk jockeys, not the others," said one. "If you are in show business, don't you want to be at the top? Isn't this the greatest compliment?"

A large number of fraternity brothers felt the same way, for the Federal Trade Commission estimates that 250 disk jockeys accepted the compliment. Generally the recipients deny that there is any connection between paying and playing. But remarked Congressman John Moss of the committee, "Some kind of telepathic communication seems to take place. By intellectual osmosis between the disk jockey and the record manufacturer, money is passed and records get played."

Actually the committee should not be so surprised at payola. It is old stuff in the music business. In Victorian England, before he teamed up with William Gilbert, a young composer named Arthur Sullivan dashed off a song called *Thou'rt Passing Hence*. He got it performed in public by giving a share of the royalties to Sir Charles Santley, a leading baritone of the time. Sir Charles was still collecting his payoff when the tune was played at Sullivan's funeral.

In the U.S., in the 1890s, the music publishers paid to have their songs played in beer gardens. Later, top stars like Al Jolson and Eddie Cantor were offered enormously tempting payola deals—and in the '30s maestros of big-name bands got a cut of the royalties for playing new tunes on network radio.

Until the payola scandals broke, disk jockeys had no pangs of conscience about benefiting from a practice with such a tradition. Payola was simply the way they did business and they imagined that everyone else did it that way too. "This seems to be the American way of life," said Boston's Stan Richards, "which is a wonderful way of life. It is primarily built on romance: 'I'll do for you. What will you do for me?'"

What Dick Clark did for music people was to give them a pre-sold market and what they gave him in return was a windfall. He did not rely on conventional cash payola but worked out a far more complex and profitable system. It hinged on his numerous corporate holdings which included financial interests in three record companies, six music publishing houses, a record pressing plant, a record distributing firm and a company which manages singers. The music, the records and the singers involved with these companies gained a special place in Clark's programs, which the committee said gave them systematic preference.

A statistical breakdown showed how his system worked. In a period of 27 months Clark gave far less air time to a top star like Elvis Presley than to a newcomer named Duane Eddy, one of the several singers whom he has helped make into a star. Clark had no stake in Presley. But firms in which he held stock both managed and recorded Eddy. During the same 27 months Clark played only one record by Bing Crosby (the almost mandatory *White Christmas*) and none at all by Frank Sinatra. "You sought to exploit your position as a network personality," said Moss. "By almost any reasonable test records you had an interest in were played more than the ones you didn't." Replied Clark, "I did not consciously favor such records. Maybe I did so without realizing it."

"You Laid It On"

Nor did Clark neglect revenues from copyright ownership. He owned 160 songs, and of these 143 came to him as outright gifts, much as Gilbert's *Thou'rt Passing Hence* came to Santley. "Once you acquired an interest," said Moss, "then you really laid it on."

A shining example was a record called *16 Candles*. Before getting the copyright, Clark spun it only four times in 10 weeks, and it got nowhere. Once he owned it, Clark played it 27 times in less than three months and it went up like a rocket. Each time the record was purchased Clark shared in the profits to the merry tune of $12,000. This pattern was duplicated with a song called *Butterfly*—and for his trouble the publisher gave him $7,000.

Many of his deals afforded Clark a special tax break. In May 1957 he invested $125 in the Jamie Record Company, which was then $450 in the red. Once he was a stockholder, Clark found Jamie records very attractive. By plugging them on his show he helped make many of them hits. When he sold out last December for $15,000, Clark had a cool profit of $11,900, and he could declare it all as capital gains. Clark granted the accuracy of these figures but explained, "I followed the ground rules that existed." He was familiar with the rules from another angle. Although he denied *he* had taken payola he admitted, paradoxically, that one of his record companies had passed out payola to get its wares plugged.

Coming back again and again to rock 'n' roll, the committee members strongly implied that Clark had deliberately foisted it on teen-agers. "I don't know of any time in our history when we had comparably bad, uniformly bad music," said Moss. Clark replied, "Popular music has always become popular because of young people. You can't force the public to like anything they don't want. If they don't want it, it won't become a hit."

Clark's soft sell made him an effective, if slippery, witness. At the end Chairman Oren Harris remarked, "You're not the inventor of the system or even its architect. You're a product of it." Then showing as much perspicacity as any 15-year-old, the congressman added, "Obviously you're a fine young man."

This encomium was sweet music to teen-agers who came to the hearing to see their hero in his hour of travail. Seated in the front row were two sisters from West Orange, N.J., whose parents had brought them to Washington to view the sights. To them the loveliest sight of all was Dick Clark.

"I don't care if he took payola," said Karen Katz, 13. "He gets to us as kids. The reason *16 Candles* took off is because we liked it. They say he didn't play enough Bing Crosby. Look, his show isn't for grandmothers. And Frank Sinatra, who needs him?"

The final verdict on Clark rests in part with teen-agers like Karen, but even more with his many sponsors. If they decide that his value as a pitchman has been hurt, then they will drop him like a cracked record. Already the danger signals are up. "We aren't happy about this thing," said the account executive for Hollywood Candy Bars, "and neither are any of the other ad agencies. We want to keep our noses clean."

The American Broadcasting Company is playing it cautious, waiting to see which way the wind will blow. Its stake in Clark is huge, for the network carries both of his shows, and each year they bring $6 million in advertising revenue. At least one disk jockey, a Miami man, says that ABC has already lined him up as Clark's replacement, just in case—and he is waiting for word to catch the next plane north.

But the sponsors had better think twice before dropping Clark. The teen-agers feel an almost fanatical bond with him. An investigator for the committee named James Kelly ran into this fanaticism right in his own family. Kelly's wife has a 15-year-old sister and they used to be great pals. But ever since Kelly started prying into Dick Clark's affairs, the girl has cut him absolutely dead.

> The concluding article for this chapter, published in the *New York Age*, an African American newspaper, explores an aspect of *American Bandstand*'s "all-American" appeal ignored by the previous article.

Mr. Clark and Colored Payola
New York Age

With all of the publicity focusing on disc jockey payola, we are concerned about another matter which has never seemed to bother many people. This is the question of Negro participation on the various TV bandstand programs.

If there's one shining star in the constellation of Alan Freed's career, it has been his determined, quiet, but effective war on racial bigotry in the music business. Largely as a result of his efforts, several Negro singing groups are top successes today because of his encouragement and fairness.

At the same time, his "Big Party" has always had Negro kids right in there putting down a tough "slop" with the best of them.

Have you even seen Negro kids on Dick Clark's program? Perhaps, a few times, but the unspoken rule operates—Negro kids simply have been quietly barred from the "American Bandstand."

Somebody should raise the question as to whether there was ever any payola to keep Negro kids off of Dick Clark's American Bandstand TV program.

Further Reading

Adams, Val. "Networks Held Biased on Music: Senate Unit Hears Charges that They Promote Products of Their Own Affiliates." *New York Times*, March 12, 1958, 63.

_____. "Hanson Decries Hillbilly Music: Tells Senate Unit Hearing Tunes Heard on Air Are 'Madison Ave.' Version." *New York Times*, March 14, 1958, 51.

Blitz, Stanley, and John Pritchard. *Bandstand the Untold Story: The Years before Dick Clark*. Phoenix: Cornucopia Publications, 1997.

Source: "Mr. Clark and Colored Payola" © *New York Age*.

Clark, Dick. *The History of American Bandstand.* New York: Ballantine Books, 1985.

Hill, Trent. "The Enemy Within: Censorship in Rock Music in the 1950s." *South Atlantic Quarterly* 90, no. 4 (Fall 1991): 675–708.

Jackson, John A. *American Bandstand: Dick Clark and the Making of a Rock 'n' Roll Empire.* New York: Oxford University Press, 1997.

Peterson, Richard A., and David G. Berger. "Cycles in Symbol Production: The Case of Popular Music." In *On Record: Rock, Pop, and the Written Word*, ed. Simon Frith and Andrew Goodwin, 140–59. New York: Pantheon Books, 1990.

"Rock 'n' Roll Laid to B.M.I. Control: Billy Rose Tells House Unit that 'Electronic Curtain' Furthers Monstrosities." *New York Times*, September 19, 1956, 75.

Discography

The 50's Decade: Teen Idols. St. Clair Records, 2001.

Avalon, Frankie, and Fabian. *Collector's Edition: Frankie and Fabian—Teen Idols.* Madacy Records, 2000.

The Official American Bandstand Library of Rock and Roll. Atlantic/WEA, 2000.

The Rock 'n' Roll Era: Teen Idols. Time Life/Warner, 1989.

Teenage Idols. Disky, 2001.

Wolfman Jack's: Teen Idols. St. Clair Records, 2001.

PART 3

The 1960s

26. The Brill Building and the Girl Groups

The payola hearings, one of the most publicized aspects of popular music at the end of the 1950s and the beginning of 1960s, highlighted some of the dominant trends in the mainstream: the early wave of rock 'n' roll, represented by Alan Freed and promoted by independent recording companies, lay dormant while teen idols coexisted with continuations of previous popular styles embodied in soundtrack themes and new versions of standards.[1] Until recently, histories of popular music describing this period tended to trace an arc of declining quality as authentic, virile rock 'n' roll was supplanted by mass-produced schlock.

A closer inspection of popular music circa 1960, however, leads one to resist such tidy characterizations. It is true that music industry centers such as the Brill Building in New York City did revive some of the production practices of Tin Pan Alley, but not all their efforts can be dismissed as "schlock-rock." A breed of young songwriters combined the youthful energy of rock 'n' roll with the sophisticated harmonic and melodic techniques of earlier popular music to create new forms of soulful, dance-oriented popular music. These songwriters—who included among their ranks newcomers such as the teams of Carole

---

1. Reebee Garofalo and Steve Chapple use the term "schlock-rock" to refer to the music developed around teen idols; see *Rock and Roll Is Here to Pay* (Chicago: Nelson-Hall, 1977). By the mid-sixties, recordings of pre–rock 'n' roll pop music led to the creation of a new category, "easy listening," alternately referred to as "middle-of-the-road" or even "good" music. Despite the lack of attention paid in this book and almost every history of popular music to this type of music after the 1950s, it continued to be extremely popular; soundtracks and original cast recordings of musicals remained among the best-selling albums up through the late 1960s.

King and Gerry Goffin, Barry Mann and Cynthia Weil, Ellie Greenwich and Jeff Barry, and Burt Bacharach and Hal David, along with seasoned pros like Jerry Leiber and Mike Stoller—created new syntheses while working with young singers, many of whom were African American and female. Thus, the period 1961–63 witnessed the emergence and success of numerous "girl groups," marking the first time that female subjectivity had been so widely represented, perhaps because many of the people just noted who were involved with the songwriting and production of the girl groups were women (also a new development). Production teams in New York and Philadelphia also participated in the creation and promotion of dance crazes: songs based in R&B and rock 'n' roll that named and described a particular dance (e.g., the "jerk," the "limbo," the "mashed potatoes"). The most successful of these songs was "The Twist," which became a number one hit for Chubby Checker *twice*, in 1960 and 1961.

The frequent collaborations of Brill Building songwriters, most of whom were Jewish, with young African American female singers marked the most recent reemergence of a partnership observed in Chapter 1 in the discussion of Irving Berlin's career. While most of the earlier writers on the girl groups quite rightly trace the emergence of "girl" vocal groups back to 1958 and the Chantels' hit "Maybe," the particular convergence of production-songwriting teams based in the Brill Building with female vocal groups first came to prominence in the Shirelles' late-1960 hit, "Will You Love Me Tomorrow," which initiated one of the dominant trends of the era. More hits followed by the Shirelles and other artists, such as the Marvelettes and the Crystals, in which a particular approach to vocal arrangement and a typical range of subjects coalesced.[2] Vocal arrangements relied on a modified call-and-response approach, adapted primarily from African American gospel practice, with the lyrics frequently arranged to simulate a dialogue between lead and backing vocalists.

Lest the forgoing description of the participants in the genre appear monolithic, it is important to note that many girl group recordings occurred outside the orbit of the Brill Building, that some of the singers were white (e.g., the Angels, the Shangri-Las), that some of the songwriters and producers were black (e.g., Luther Dixon), and that some recordings that are now understood as part of the girl group phenomenon because of their musical arrangements were then credited to

---

2. For more on the relationship between this approach to vocal arrangement and young female identity, see Barbara Bradby, "Do-Talk and Don't-Talk: The Division of the Subject in Girl-Group Music," in *On Record: Rock, Pop and the Written Word*, ed. Simon Frith and Andrew Goodwin, 341–69 (New York: Routledge, 1990); for a more comprehensive study of the girl group genre, see Jacqueline Warwick, *Girl Groups, Girl Culture: Popular Music and Identity in the 1960s* (New York: Routledge, 2007).

individuals (e.g., Little Eva, Leslie Gore). The following passage from Charlotte Greig's book focuses on the experience of songwriters such as Carole King and Ellie Greenwich and underscores the flexibility of the working arrangements at the Brill Building, where songwriters could quickly assume the role of producer and/or performer.

from Will You Still Love Me Tomorrow? Girl Groups from the 50s On . . .
Charlotte Greig

The Shirelles, as the first popular rock 'n' roll girl group, were largely responsible for introducing what we think of as "pop" music to a wide public. In the fifties, there had been two very separate strands of popular music: on the one hand, rock 'n' roll, and on the other, the showbiz songs written by the professional songwriters of Tin Pan Alley. The mostly Jewish songwriters of Tin Pan Alley traditionally looked to Italian Americans, with their suitably romantic good looks and operatic vocal style, as performers of their songs. The imitation-Elvis, teen-boy pop idols of the late fifties and early sixties were essentially a continuation of this tradition. At the same time, however, the music industry was changing. The songwriters of Tin Pan Alley were no longer all middle-aged men churning out novelty songs; a new breed of young men and women songwriters was coming up who looked to black artists to perform their songs. Pete Waterman explains:

> What happened in the early sixties is that white guys, people like Barry Mann, and white girls like Carole King met, for the first time, black artists. So you had black artists singing doo wop, but you had white songwriters writing white melodies. Suddenly, there was an interpollination of black voices with white melodies; and most of the writers at that time were of Jewish descent, so of course you got very different chordal structures. There were these amazing black girls singing Jewish melodies that didn't quite work out; here was a new form of music. Because of the white element, girls like Carole King, arrangers put strings on the records which doo-wop bands could never have afforded. You had major companies like Liberty and Roulette making records with full orchestras! They would pay the money, and they were white; the only black thing about the records was the artists and the management. Suddenly you had this dichotomy of cultures; and it worked, it worked perfectly.

These cultures were being forged together not just by a happy blending of musical styles, however; the essential element that bound the black artists and the white songwriters and producers together was that they were young. They were, however directly or indirectly, part of a teen culture built on the legacy of fifties' rock 'n' roll whose tendencies towards "aural miscegenation"—as Gerry Hirshey calls it in her book *Nowhere to Run*—had so disturbed the establishment both morally and, in the music business, financially. In a sense, the girl groups who were used to effect the

---

Source: "Will You Still Love Me Tomorrow? Girl Groups from the 50s On," Charlotte Greig/ Virago Press Ltd.

mass crossover of black music into white pop in the early sixties represented Tin Pan Alley's attempt to co-opt and control rock 'n' roll; but because the songwriters and producers involved were so young and so much part of rock 'n' roll themselves, their very attempt to sweeten up and sanitize the black sound to appeal to a teenage public brought with it something genuine: a new, female-centred pop sensibility that was wonderfully fresh.

Carole King entered the music business in New York as a teenage songwriter at a time when the industry had recognized the huge profits to be made out of selling pop records to teenagers. She was hired by a music publisher, Don Kirshner, one of the first to gear his whole output towards the teenage market. Aldon, as his company was called, was part of the Brill Building on Broadway, where virtually everyone in the music business congregated. There was a frantic atmosphere of wheeling and dealing in the building, almost like that of the stock exchange; songs were written, demos were cut, and tracks were recorded and released, all at a speed which now seems quite incredible; a song could be written in the morning, recorded in the afternoon and released a few days later on one of the many small labels that operated out of the Brill. It was a production line, as Carole King pointed out to writer Paula Taylor in 1976:

> We each had a little cubby hole with just enough room for a piano, a bench, and maybe a chair for the lyricist—if you were lucky. You'd sit there and write, and you could hear someone in the next cubby hole composing some song exactly like yourself.

In the offices of another publisher, Leiber and Stoller, plans were also being made to cash in on the teen boom. Ellie Greenwich was one of the star songwriters the duo hired to give them those teen hits, and she did, coming up with such classics as "Da Doo Ron Ron," "Then He Kissed Me," "Doh Wah Diddy" and "Chapel of Love."

Today Ellie lives in a New York apartment not far from Broadway. A big brass musical note adorns her front door, and the theme is continued throughout the apartment, even to treble and bass clefs on the wallpaper in the bathroom and piano-key motifs on the toilet seat. Still working in the music business, and looking a million dollars with a Dusty Springfield hairdo, Ellie beams warmly at me, welcomes me like an old friend and settles back to entertain me with stories of those early days. Chain smoking her way through a heavy cold, which only improves her husky New York tones, she remembers the past with affection:

> I went to Leiber and Stoller's office to wait for my appointment. They thought I was Carole King, so they went, "Hey, Carole, come on in." I told them who I was and started playing away, a nervous wreck. They offered me a job writing, $75 a week. I said, no, $100, and they agreed. Wow! I thought. A hundred bucks a week! I'm flying here. And I have my own cubby hole where I can write my stuff to my heart's content, and who knows who I might meet. . . .
>
> There were many small labels in the Brill Building that offered you the opportunity to just run up there and say, "Hey, listen to this song." There was a spontaneity there, the doors were easy to walk through. If you played a song and they liked it, they'd say, "Let's think. Do we know anyone who can do this? Do you?" So then you could go out and look for an artist, and a record label would give you a shot to produce a single. If it did well, great, you started getting a name for yourself. If it didn't, so what, no big deal. Not any more. Now it's album, album . . . nobody would hire you just like that.
>
> It was a happy time. Monetarily stupid, maybe, but on a creative level you just weren't bothered with any problems. All you did was come in and hone in on your craft. We were very grateful to be signed to a music publisher and get our weekly lit-

tle paycheck. We always got our royalties. But we never knew to ask about retaining songs. So I didn't finally make $200,000. I got $25,000. Fine. Who knew those songs would live on?

By 1962, when Ellie joined Leiber and Stoller, Carole King was already making a name for herself as a songwriter after her success with "Will You Love Me Tomorrow?" In partnership with lyricist Gerry Goffin, an ex-chemistry student she married at the age of eighteen, Carole was now writing for white teen idols like Bobby Vee. A whole industry was by this time building up around TV shows like American Bandstand, which not only introduced a never-ending stream of wooden boy idols to the nation's teenagers but also created hundreds of dance crazes. When the Goffins came up with "The Locomotion," a new dance tune, they asked their babysitter—who had inspired the song by her style of dancing—to cut the demo for them. Kirschner liked the demo so much that he released it as it was on his new Dimension label, and in no time, "The Locomotion" had reached the number-one spot. Little Eva, as she was now called, became an overnight sensation; such a huge success by an unknown artist on a new label was extraordinary. Yet her subsequent records, like "Let's Turkey Trot" did not match "The Locomotion." Her sister Idalia was pulled in to make a record, a track called "Hula Hoppin"; but by now the label was flogging a dead horse. Having been fêted in Europe and America, in less than two years Eva's career was over.

The tale of Little Eva showed the industry both at its best and at its worst. In the Brill Building, individuals, often working freelance, could set up a series of loose relationships: songwriters could sell their songs to different publishers or record labels, producers could look for songs amongst the many publishers, and so on. Often, a single individual would perform some or all of these functions; many songwriters set up their own labels, produced, and even sang on the records. The speed at which all this happened meant that a trend could be quickly spotted and exploited. The sheer volume of records that such a system produced made it likely that a certain percentage at least would chart.

The advantages of the system were that it allowed for an extraordinary degree of creative flexibility and a fast response to an ever-changing market so that the small labels could make it. Monolithic recording corporations like RCA Victor, although they had all the financial muscle, simply could not keep up with what was going on. But there were clear disadvantages for the artists, as the Shirelles had already seen. Singers were at the very bottom of the hierarchy. Producers could take their pick from the many talented young black singers who were desperate to succeed and sold their skills cheap. For these singers, the world of entertainment was the only way out from a life of poverty, unemployment or hard labour; they would characteristically record songs for nothing, or for a flat fee, in order to get their start.

Also, because the functions of singing and songwriting were completely split at the time, so that singers seldom wrote or recorded their own songs, their voices came to be regarded virtually as sounds only, for the producer to use as he wished. Thus for any singer who wanted to build a career in the music industry, the situation was a disaster.

Little Eva at least had her moment of fame. The other girls that King and Goffin were writing for did not fare so well. The Cookies were a trio who provided backing vocals for many of the releases on Aldon's label, and who also recorded songs written for them by Goffin and King. Some of these did well at the time: "Chains" and "Don't Say Nothin' Bad About My Baby" were hits for the Cookies, while Earl-Jean, their lead singer, charted with "I'm Into Something Good." The follow-up to "Don't Say Nothin' Bad," "Will Power," didn't do so well, but it is interesting as an example of the kind of powerful, contained sexuality that the supposedly over-naive, romantic girl groups actually presented their teenage listeners with:

> It's been an hour since we reached my door
> I really ought to say goodnight
> It's been an hour since you said
> won't you give me five minutes more
> don't you see that I hardly even know you yet
> I should be playing hard to get
> oh baby what you do
> to my will power

The doo-wah, doo-wah choruses and the young, sweet voices of the Cookies disguised the fact that what was being described here were not the joys of coy femininity but its awful restrictions.

As with Little Eva, Aldon was keener to make the most of the Cookies while the going was good than to help the group sustain its popularity over the long term. The group never got the attention they deserved, and soon disappeared from view. Their songs are now best remembered for the cover versions they inspired: the Beatles' "Chains" and Herman's Hermits' "I'm Into Something Good." In the space of two years, the sudden rise of black girl singers, whether singly or in groups, and their equally sudden fall from popularity as they released a string of soundalike records after their initial hit, was fast becoming a time-honoured tradition of Teen Pan Alley.

* * *

Over at Leiber and Stoller's, Ellie Greenwich was beginning to rival Carole King as the songwriting queen of teen pop. She had arrived in the business in 1962, later than Carole King, and began by teaming up with several different writers until she settled into a partnership with Jeff Barry. In the early days, she remembers:

> Most of the women in the industry were background singers or lyricists. There were very few women that played piano, wrote songs and could produce a session, go into a studio and work those controls.
>
> The studio would be booked from two to five and those singers would go in there and read off the songs; maybe they'd do seventeen songs in three hours. I couldn't do that. I'd write a song and go in and put the background parts on myself; I learnt about overdubbing and laying down tracks, so a different sound started coming out.

Ellie had not set out to be a producer, but she soon found herself becoming one:

> Myself and Carole King . . . we came into an industry strictly as songwriters. We also sang. So we'd go in and make demos on our songs and they sometimes sounded great. The publishers would take the demo off to a record label who would say, "OK, let's put this out." And then they'd ask, "Who produced this?" Well, Carole King, or Jeff and I . . . we didn't think about being producers; it sort of happened to us, we came in through the back door.

Not only was Ellie the songwriter finding herself in the position of producer, she was also effectively becoming an artist too. Since record companies were beginning to release the demos they got from publishers as records, Ellie soon became the voice behind a host of fictitious teen groups:

> A case like that was the Raindrops, which was just myself and Jeff doing all the voices. We did this demo for a group called the Sensations; it was a song called

"What A Guy," which we thought would be great for them. We made the demo, and the publishers said, "This could be a record." I said, "What do you mean? There is no group." But there had to be a group. So we released it as a record by "The Raindrops." Back then, a lot of labels put out "dummy groups." We'd throw a few people together and have them go out and lip synch the record. There really wasn't a Raindrops. . . .

As the tales of Little Eva and her sister Idalia and of groups like the Shirelles and the Cookies demonstrate, the creative flexibility of the Brill Building could work to the disadvantage of the singers. The fate of recordings such as "Let's Turkey Trot" and "Hula Hoppin'" showed that singers were often viewed as interchangeable parts. It is also difficult to ignore how the racial identities of the actors involved reproduced disparities in the larger society, even though a few of the tunes, such as the Crystals' "Uptown," hinted at the heightened awareness, fostered by the civil rights movement, of racial inequities (the song was written in 1962 by Mann and Weil and begins "He gets up each mornin' and he goes downtown/Where ev'ryone's his boss and he's lost in an angry land").

In what is probably not a paradox, the most widely celebrated figure connected with the singer-songwriter genre was male: producer-songwriter Phil Spector (b. 1939). Spector developed a trademark sonic quality on his recordings, known as the "Wall of Sound," that featured a dense, reverberant texture filled with instruments that were often difficult to separate from one another and undergirded by an R&B rhythm section, an approach that found fruition in his productions from 1962 onward with artists such as the Crystals, Bob B. Soxx and the Blue Jeans, Darlene Love, and the Ronettes. Although this sound has often been inaccurately compared (occasionally by Spector himself) to the textural approach of European Romantics, such as Richard Wagner, what Spector shared with Wagner was a grandiosity of vision and a tendency toward self-aggrandizement. Taking the exploitation of singers that we have already noted to an extreme, Spector assumed complete power and economic control over the female artists who appeared in his productions.[3] While a case can be made that Spector's achievements have been overglorified in historical narratives about popular music, his recent well-publicized personal travails make him a tempting and all-too-easy object of ridicule as well.[4] His sound was widely influential, and Spector represented a shift of power in the music business to people who were of the same generation as the audience,[5] a trend that intensified with the alignment of songwriter and

3. A particularly disturbing case occurred with Ronnie Bennett, lead singer of the Ronettes, who later married Spector; she presents her account in Ronnie Spector (with Vince Waldron), *Be My Baby: How I Survived Mascara, Miniskirts, and Madness or My Life as a Fabulous Ronette* (New York: HarperPerennial, 1990).

4. I am referring to his arrest for the murder of Lana Clarkson on February 3, 2003, and the subsequent trial that ended with a verdict of "mistrial" on September 26, 2007. These events seemed to cap years of revelations about Spector's bizarre behavior.

5. This is a point made by Tom Wolfe in his celebrated profile of Spector, "The First Tycoon of Teen," in *The Kandy-Kolored Tangerine-Flake Streamline Baby* (New York: Pocket Books, 1966), 47–61.

performer that came to dominate American popular music in the wake of the girl groups.

Darlene Love (b. 1938) sang on many of Spector's best-known record-ings, including the first number one hit he produced, "He's a Rebel." However, as she makes clear, she benefited little from the prominent role she played in Spector's success. While Spector allowed her to make recordings under her own name, she also appeared on recordings attrib-uted to any number of other groups whose names existed as trademarks controlled by Spector. Both the structure of the music business and the anonymity-by-design of the performers make it little wonder, then, that Spector's notoriety has far outstripped that of the people who sang (and played and arranged and engineered) on the recordings that are associated with him.

"He's A Rebel" was the highest point of the Crystals' career; but it was also one of the lowest. Here, Darlene Love takes up the story. When I visited her, she was liv-ing in style at the Royal Shakespeare Company in Stratford on Avon, during the first run of the musical *Carrie,* which later bombed on Broadway. We sat in her dressing room overlooking the river, and she told me:

> I first met Phil in Los Angeles through his partner Lester Sill, because I was doing a lot of sessions for Lester singing back-up. I was called in to do "He's A Rebel." I went in, he showed me the song, and within three or four days, we had recorded it.

But why did Phil Spector choose Darlene rather than the real Crystals back in New York to do the song?

> Something had happened with their friendship at the time. Phil owned the name of the Crystals. During that time, producers owned groups' names so they could record anyone they wanted under any name. Phil gave me my name, in fact; at that time I was called Darlene Wright. He asked me if I liked the name "Love"—there was a gospel singer called Dorothy Love that he admired—and I said yes . . . so I became Darlene Love.
>
> During the sixties, the scale for "after" background singers, for three or less, was $22.50 an hour. I told Phil I'd do "He's A Rebel" for him if he paid me triple scale. So I got about 1,500 dollars.
>
> I was nineteen when I met Phil, and I was a professional singer. That probably gave me the edge on the rest of the girls he was working with, because they were really young, about thirteen up. He always had to pay me because, as professionals, me and the Blossoms went through the union; we always got paid session fees, but not necessarily royalties. The only money I ever made in those days was through sessions.
>
> After "He's A Rebel," I wanted a contract. I wanted royalties—they were three cents a record in those days, or something ridiculous like that. Well, I never got what I felt was due to me.

Meanwhile, back in New York, the real Crystals were astonished to find themselves with their first number-one hit, a record that they had not even made. There was nothing they could do; indeed, they were helpless without Spector. To this day, Dee Dee Kennibrew of the Crystals, who did finally manage to retrieve the group's name from Spector and work under it, refuses to acknowledge Darlene Love's part in the Crystals' career.

Darlene's story is, however, that Spector, like so many other producers in the business, paid no regard to anyone's names, including her own:

When we went to record with Phil we never knew which record was going to be by who. After "He's A Rebel," the next thing he wanted was another record for the Crystals. I said, this time you're going to pay me a royalty, not just no $1,500. But I didn't get it. Well, the next record was "He's Sure the Boy I Love" which was supposed to be my Darlene Love record—I was going to record it under my own name. But no. When I heard it on the radio, they announced that it was by the Crystals.

I asked for a contract again with "Da Doo Ron Ron." Phil said OK, but I wasn't convinced and I never gave him a clean finish of the song so he brought La La Brooks in from the Crystals and put her voice on top of what I had already done. We didn't sign contracts in the end until after "Da Doo Ron Ron."

Clearly, Spector's by now very powerful role as the Boy Wonder of the pop industry gave him carte blanche to override the inconvenient demands of his young singers. Records were issued by fictitious groups, mere names dreamed up by Spector; polished, experienced session singers like Darlene would be brought in to record, and then they or others who looked the part would pose for publicity shots. To all intents and purposes, groups like the Crystals appeared only to exist now in Spector's imagination as concepts for the next single.

The public did not seem to mind or notice what was going on. The Crystals—whoever they were—scored big hits in 1963 with "He's Sure the Boy I Love," "Da Doo Ron Ron" and "Then He Kissed Me." The records were now usually in the confident, romantic boy-meets-girl-they-fall-in-love-and-marry vein that had replaced the plaintive, adolescent uncertainties of the early girl groups, but writers like Barry Mann and Cynthia Weil still held out for a bit of social realism in songs like "He's Sure the Boy I Love":

> He doesn't hang diamonds round my neck
> all he's got is an unemployment check
> He sure ain't the boy I've been dreaming of, but
> He's sure the boy I love

Besides recording as the Crystals, Darlene also then became—with Bobby Sheen and Fanita James of the Blossoms—Bob B. Soxx and the Blue Jeans:

Phil had this idea of recording "Zip-A-Dee-Doo-Dah." We thought that was the funniest thing we'd ever heard; everybody knew that song, what could he possibly do with it? But it was a huge hit, and we became Bob B. Soxx and the Blue Jeans. After that, I finally recorded as Darlene Love. Nobody knew who I was at all. They were trying to figure out if there was one person doing all the singing on Phil's records. They thought it was Barbara Alston of the Crystals.

Darlene's wonderful voice put her solo recordings, like "Today I Met the Boy I'm Gonna Marry" and "Christmas (Baby Please Come Home)," in a class of their own amongst Spector's by now unbelievably successful teen pop discs. Yet she still did not emerge as a solo artist in her own right:

I didn't really push my career as Darlene Love. I was a very successful back-up singer, and that was important, because I had something to fall back on; it was a job, like being a secretary. I didn't just depend on Phil, I had my own career. Also, I had children and I didn't want to tour. I've had a very full career; in the sixties, I sang with all kinds of people, including Elvis on his comeback special in 1968. From 1972 to 1981 I sang back-up for Dionne Warwick. In the eighties, my career has really taken off; I got a part in "Lethal Weapon," then there was *Carrie*, and my new album is coming out too.

You know, I started off in 1959, and in 1981 I started a solo career. That's kind of unusual. It helps that no one has ever really seen me. I'm a fresh idea.

Further Reading

Bradby, Barbara. "Do-Talk and Don't-Talk: The Division of the Subject in Girl-Group Music," in *On Record: Rock, Pop and the Written Word*, ed. Simon Frith and Andrew Goodwin, 341–69. New York: Routledge, 1990.

Brown, Mick. *Tearing Down the Wall of Sound: The Rise and Fall of Phil Spector*. New York: Alfred A. Knopf, 2007.

Clemente, John. *Girl Groups: Fabulous Females that Rocked the World*. Iola, Wisc.: Krause Publications, 2000.

Emerson, Ken. *Always Magic in the Air: The Bomp and Brilliance of the Brill Building Era*. New York: Viking, 2005.

Spector, Ronnie (with Vince Waldron). *Be My Baby: How I Survived Mascara, Miniskirts, and Madness or My Life as a Fabulous Ronette*. New York: Harper Perennial, 1990.

Warwick, Jacqueline. *Girl Groups, Girl Culture: Popular Music and Identity in the 1960s*. New York: Routledge, 2007.

Wolfe, Tom. "The First Tycoon of Teen," in *The Kandy-Kolored Tangerine-Flake Streamline Baby*, 47–61. New York: Pocket Books, 1966.

Discography

The Best of the Girl Groups, Vols. 1 and 2. Rhino/WEA, 1990.

The Chantels. *The Best of the Chantels*, Rhino. 1990.

Spector, Phil (with various artists). *Back to Mono (1958–1969)*. Abcko, 1991.

27. From Surf to *Smile*

Concurrent with the dance crazes and girl-group phenomenon, the American imagination increasingly shifted westward to the land of fruit and nuts, as California rapidly became the most populous and economically important of the 50 states. Out of the sun-drenched expanses of the rapidly growing suburbs in Southern California came surf music, with its litany of beaches, blondes, and Bonneville sport coupes. Initially an instrumental genre led by guitarist Dick Dale (a real, live surfer) and guitar-dominated instrumental bands such as the Ventures, surf came to be associated most strongly with the Beach Boys, a band that developed a distinctive, contrapuntal, falsetto-led vocal style.

The group was a family affair, consisting of three Wilson brothers (Brian, Carl, and Dennis), cousin Mike Love, and pal Al Jardine. The eldest brother, Brian (b. 1942), was the musical mastermind of the group, concocting a potent brew of multipart harmony singing (derived from 1950s vocal groups such as the jazz-influenced Four Freshmen and the Hi-Los), Chuck Berry riffs, trebly guitar timbres (a holdover from surf instrumental groups), and lyrics extolling the ennui of beach-loving, middle-class white teens. The early hits of 1962–63 all hewed close to these themes in one way or another, although the emotional range and harmonic palette expanded in ballads like "Surfer Girl" and "In My Room." Their first major national hit, "Surfin' U.S.A.," owed so much to Chuck Berry's "Sweet Little Sixteen" that Berry was eventually awarded songwriting credit for it.

The following excerpts from Brian Wilson's autobiography describe a period after Wilson suffered a nervous breakdown in 1964 and subsequently stopped touring, a move that enabled him to devote more energy to songwriting and production. While his songs had continuously increased in musical complexity beginning with the Beach Boys' first recordings in 1962, the Beatles' *Rubber Soul*, released in December 1965, inspired Wilson to try and surpass his earlier efforts. The result? *Pet Sounds*, one of the first "concept" albums and one of the first to feature overt studio experimentation (including elaborate overdubbing and mixing, unusual instruments, and songs with multiple tempi). Although *Pet Sounds* did not equal the success of earlier Beach Boys albums (managing nevertheless to reach the Top 10), it, and the commercially successful single that followed, "Good Vibrations," subsequently established critical highwater marks for the band. Here, Wilson describes the creation of these recordings.[1]

"Interview with Brian Wilson"
Richard Cromelin

Pet Sounds, the masterpiece, was the first instance of commercial decline for the Beach Boys, and it also marked a division between Brian, holed up in Beverly Hills, working

---

1. For a portrait of Wilson during the period following "Good Vibrations" while he worked on *Smile*, the imploding follow-up to *Pet Sounds*, see Jules Siegel, "A Teen-age Hymn to God," in *Rock and Roll Is Here to Stay: An Anthology*, ed. William McKeen, 387–99 (New York: W. W. Norton, [1967] 2000).

Source: "Brian Wilson, part 1" by Richard Cromelin, originally published in *Sounds*, 31 July 1976. © Richard Cromelin/Rock's Backpages.

his alchemy on the Spector sound, and the rest of the group, touring the world with their surf music. . . .

Brian's version of the *Pet Sounds* encounter: "I think they thought it was just for Brian Wilson only. I think the problem was that they knew that Brian Wilson was gonna be a separate entity, something that was a force of his own. . . . So with *Pet Sounds* there was resistance in that I was doing most of the artistic work on it, and for that reason there was a little bit of inter-group (sic) struggle. . . .

"Well, it resolved in the fact that they figured, 'Well, sure, it's a showcase for Brian Wilson, but it's still the Beach Boys.' In other words—" here he flashes a cagey smile—"they gave in. They gave in to the fact that I had a little to say myself, so they let me have my stint. . . .'"

Since 1961, when he and Mike Love concocted the first surf song, everything Brian Wilson has touched has attained mythic proportions: The Beach. The California Consciousness. The Beach Boys, once again, and probably for good, an American Rock institution. And Brian Wilson himself, the enigmatic genius whose shrouded presence pervades popular music. The prodigious weight of those myths, you feel, is one of the adversaries in his silent struggle, but at the same time his pride in their creation is certainly one of the forces that accounts for his emergence.

"Well, it grows on," he reflects softly. "It grows on and on. At first it was the thing of surfing, where we were the only things coming up with this new Chuck Berry–orientated sound. And legends grew. Legends grew about *Pet Sounds*, legends have grown about a lot of our music. 'Good Vibrations' was a legend. I'm proud that we have created several different legends. . . . It's a unique quality we have, which I'm very proud of. The fact that we can be leaders at times—we have at least gone through periods where we're leaders. . . ."

As for the elevation of Brian's Spectorian *Pet Sounds* to masterpiece status, Wilson gives and takes credit where due. "Well, I felt that the production was a masterpiece," he says, somehow not sounding boastful. "*Pet Sounds* is an offshoot of the Phil Spector production technique, and it was considered a masterpiece because it was masterful in the tradition of Phil Spector records. . . . My contribution was adding the harmonies, learning to incorporate harmonies and certain vocal techniques to that Spector production concept.

"I hope that he enjoyed some of the techniques we used, and some of the sounds that were created. That word 'Pet Sounds,' I think we wanted to get across the point that this album was a concept in sound. . . . We wanted to show that you could display instruments richly combined together. In other words, it was a concept in mixing instruments together, to combine as one sound. . . . Yeah, there were some good songs, but the basic concept was in production, and we're very proud of the continuity of the production."

Smile, set to follow *Pet Sounds* but never completed, was conceived as a different sort of theme album. "That," explains Brian, "was a concept in humour. The humourous aspect of each of the tracks. Some of the tracks, we left laughing on the tracks, where Carl would go—" Brian sings a line and breaks into a huge guffaw. "Dylan did that in one of his songs. Which one was it?"

"'All I Really Want To Do,'" I help.

"Yeah! He laughed in that damn thing and I laughed my head off! I thought it was really funny. We did the same thing. Yeah, it was a concept in humour, like 'She's Goin' Bald,' obviously that's a humour idea. . . ."

Mention of the *Surf's Up* album evokes a cryptic response. "That I like, but I don't like discussing. I don't know why." After a pause, though, he offers a few comments:

" 'Surf's Up,' itself was a masterpiece of a song which Van Dyke and I wrote. I thought it rambled beautifully and I thought it really said a lot, at the end. A children's song, you know, a song of freedom: 'I heard the word, a wonderful thing, a children's song,' you know, and I went into a high—" Brian emits an awkward, atonal falsetto noise, like a seagull's eerie cry—"You know, that kind of childlike sound in my voice.

"That album marked the first time the guys actually could produce, actually follow through with dubbing down, producing the tracks, getting the instruments on themselves separate from me. So I think it began a series of things where the guys became independent of me. That was a good move."

Of all his recordings, though, Brian reserves the most pride for what was, strangely enough, the Beach Boys' only million-selling single. "My mother used to talk about vibrations a lot when I was a kid," he says, "and she told me a lot about that. . . . She told me that dogs bark at some people and don't bark at others, and she said this can be attributed to the fact that vibrations are picked up by dogs—and by people, she said.

"And so I learned that, and then some 10 or 15 years later I came up with a song, 'Good Vibrations,' which was about that very concept, about people picking up vibrations from other people.

"It had a pocket symphony effect, and it was a series of intricate harmonies and of mood changes. Using a cello for the first time in rock 'n' roll that way—the use of the cello in that respect was an innovation. . . . The song took about a month to develop. It was a long time structuring that song. We threw away a lot of pieces and bits, and did some 10 different sessions on that song. . . .

"Yes, I had a feeling all along that we were in the midst of developing quite an interesting piece of music, an interesting structure, that had something new and fresh. I'm very proud of that. I'm very proud of the effects it had on it too, that brought about that feeling."

Brian sounds like a big, rhythmic bee as he hums the familiar, charging-cello riff. "It was kind of denoting the pulsations of vibrations, you know," he explains. "So it really kind of said it. It *said* something, that record said something." . . .

The brisk cadence of Brian's conversational pace accelerates as he continues, and his words seem to be whipping up some immense, if erratic energy inside his imposing frame as he talks about the Brian Wilson competitive spirit: "I'd call up the guys and say, 'You guys, you think the last one was good, well wait till you hear this one.'

"I was a better-better-better type, what's that called? One-upmanship, yeah. I was glued to that aspect. I though that was the way. And that *is* the way. The way to think is that what you're doing now is the best."

Spector, it seems, isn't the only egomaniac roaming the hills above the Los Angeles plain. "Oh yeah," Brian admits, "I was considered an egomaniac myself. I'm like Spector in that I have the egomaniac attitude for myself. I always consider myself great and I pat myself on the back every day.

"I wake up in the morning and say, 'You're the greatest, you're this and someday you're gonna be this, and someday people are gonna hear about this and that.' I'm that way. I'm just not as profound an egomaniac," he adds with a hearty laugh that turns into a dangerous-sounding cough spasm.

The Beach Boys' greatest rivalry occurred a decade ago, and if they lost that round, just look who's working today and who isn't. "I think we had a lot of competition with the Beatles," says Brian, "and I think we held our own. It was an overflood of airplay. Totally unfair airplay. It was unfair to a lot of American acts. Some of the great artists of the mid-60s were neglected.

"With the Beatles, both of us too being on the same label made it even more competitive. Both of our names started with B-E-A and both on the same label. I thought that was very amusing.

"I think it was a very simple competition. I don't think we competed directly because they were making their completely own kind of records. Thank God that we weren't making similar kinds of records or it would have really been a competitive thing."

Further Reading

Gaines, Steven. *Heroes and Villains: The True Story of the Beach Boys.* New York: New American Library, 1986.
Lambert, Philip. *Inside the Music of Brian Wilson: The Songs, Sounds, and Influences of the Beach Boys' Founding Genius.* New York: Continuum, 2007.
Wilson, Brian (with Todd Gold). *Wouldn't It Be Nice: My Own Story.* New York: Harper Collins, 1991.

Discography

Beach Boys. *Pet Sounds.* Capitol, 1966.
_____. *Good Vibrations: Thirty Years of the Beach Boys.* Capitol, 1993.

28. Urban Folk Revival

The whole notion of "urban folk" summons a number of paradoxes: If we take "folk music" to mean music that survives in an oral, rather than a written, tradition, preserved in face-to-face encounters between people who recognize one another as belonging to the same community, then the idea of "urban folk," in which the music exists among widely dispersed city dwellers and is shared through mass-mediated technology, seems at least somewhat contradictory. If we try to retain some sense of American folk music as connected to the rural folk in a premodern era, the term "urban folk" similarly involves a suspension of disbelief.

The idea of urban folk music first gathered momentum in the 1930s. Many of the early performers were either black or white southerners who had been brought (or encouraged to come) to New York City by folklorist-musicologists who were associated with the leftist Popular Front political movement, such as John and Alan Lomax and Charles Seeger.[1] While early urban folk performers did include African American blues singers like Leadbelly (Huddie Ledbetter) and Josh White among their ranks, the dominant musical style derived in large part from the ballad tradition of white, rural Southerners and thus shared qualities with the "hillbilly" music of the period. Many of the differences between "hillbilly" and "folk" were, in fact, more sociological than musicological: rather than the utilitarian, overtly commercial aims of 1920s and 1930s hillbilly music, urban folk used the associations of rural, traditional music to evoke a sense of timeless purity.

Of all the performers who are associated with the urban folk movement, Woody Guthrie (1912–67) became the most recognized. Born and raised in Oklahoma, Guthrie wrote original songs (using melodies with strong connections to traditional tunes) that chronicled the tribulations of Dust Bowl refugees—"Okies" like those memorialized in John Steinbeck's *Grapes of Wrath*—and the hardships endured by the common "folk." Guthrie's lyrics were pro-labor and pro–working class, but sufficiently populist so that people from various political perspectives could adopt a song like "This Land Is Your Land," especially when the most explicitly left-wing verses were excised. For example, the often-deleted fourth verse of "This Land Is Your Land" protests the negative effects of land ownership: "Was a high wall there that tried to stop me/A sign was painted said: Private Property."[2] Guthrie also developed a ramblin', gamblin' persona in many witty talking blues that had much in common with personae developed later by Beat writers such as Jack Kerouac, and that influenced many male singers of the 1960s.

In 1941, Guthrie joined the Almanac Singers, a group that included among its members Pete Seeger (b. 1919), son of the noted musicologist Charles Seeger. The Almanac Singers continued to stress political and social issues, such as the importance of civil rights and labor unions. Seeger then formed the Weavers, a group that continued to be associated with the liberal themes of the Almanac Singers, while their richly harmonized (and thickly orchestrated) versions of songs, such as Leadbelly's "Goodnight Irene" (number one for 13 weeks in 1950!) and Guthrie's "So Long It's Been Good to Know You" (number four in 1951) were sufficiently successful to enter the popular music mainstream. Although the Weavers' hits eschewed strong political messages, their left-wing views brought them to the attention of Joseph McCarthy and the House

---

1. For more on the popular front and the urban folk revival, see Michael Denning, *The Cultural Front: The Laboring of American Culture in the Twentieth Century* (New York: Verso, 1997); Robert Cantwell, *When We Were Good: The Folk Revival* (Cambridge, Mass.: Harvard University Press, 1996); Benjamin Filene, *Romancing the Folk: Public Memory and American Roots Music* (Chapel Hill: University of North Carolina Press, 2000); and Bryan Carman, *A Race of Singers: Whitman's Working-Class Hero from Guthrie to Springsteen* (Chapel Hill: University of North Carolina Press, 2000).

2. The sixth verse of this song, also usually omitted, describes the devastating effects of poverty in the United States.

Un-American Activities Committee, the proceedings of which led to the group's demise in 1953.

Despite their blacklisting, the Weavers and other folk musicians like Burl Ives planted seeds for the popularity of urban folk music that led some of their fans to an awareness of Guthrie, Leadbelly, Josh White, and others. Although the McCarthy hearings effectively suppressed urban folk music, artists like Harry Belafonte—who found success with several Caribbean-flavored recordings in 1956–57—and the Kingston Trio—whose "Tom Dooley" went to number one in 1958—maintained the mass-mediated presence of folk music, and the music gained popularity among college-age audiences. Urban folk music also maintained its paradoxical stature as the anticommercial form of popular music and was heard by many as the antidote to mainstream pop music and early rock 'n' roll.

The article that follows describes the links between many of the artists associated with the urban folk music of the 1930s and 1940s and their successors in the late 1950s and early 1960s. The article notes how, from the late 1950s onward, urban folk reasserted its political connotations (which for many it had never lost) and how distinctions were already being made between overtly commercial folk groups (the Kingston Trio) and artists who were viewed (rightly or wrongly) as making few, if any, concessions to mass taste. The civil rights movement provided the strongest public cause for this new confluence of folk music (dubbed by historians the urban folk music *revival*) and politics, and, as the article notes, the fight for civil rights provided the strongest motivation for the "nonconformity" exhibited by folk music fans. It is significant that, despite the prominence of several African American performers within the movement and its strong commitment to civil rights, the vast majority of the performers and audience members were white, college educated, and middle class, thereby forming another link with the 1930s urban folk scene.

Songs of the Silent Generation
Gene Bluestein

Mademoiselle, the magazine which specializes in telling smart young women what the bright young men of Madison Avenue think they ought to know, got around to explaining (in its December 1960 issue) what the "folksong fad" is all about. Notwithstanding a brief nod in the direction of anthropology and social psychology (folksinging provides students with a sense of "togetherness," it helps them channelize

---

Source: "Songs of the Silent Generation," Gene Bluestein

their feelings toward a "brutal and threatening" world), what *Mademoiselle* wants to emphasize is the fact that this generation of college students are "hungry for a small, safe taste of an unslick, underground world" and folksong, like pizza and popcorn, takes the edge off their appetites.

Mademoiselle's description of the college "folkniks" as a "student middle class" which has adapted "the trappings and tastes of a Bohemian minority group" is based on the assumption that the students draw their main inspiration from the bearded "beatniks" who inhabit the countless coffee houses which have sprung up around the country. But as Kenneth Rexroth has been pointing out from the beginning, the "beatnik" is the creature of Time, Inc; it is a popular view of the artist as irresponsible, incomprehensible, and "maladjusted." And, as in the case of the new young poets, the analogy is false.

Neither does the college folksong addict flip over the antics of commercial folksong groups which have become standard property in the stables of such bigtime operators as RCA Victor, Decca, and Columbia. (The Kingston Trio was so out of place at the first Newport Folk Festival that it did not appear at the second one.) The repertoires of these groups do consist mainly of traditional songs but they are adapted, dislocated, expurgated or, when the occasion is right, turned into popular songs. Often the appeal of the big time night club singers comes less from their vocal or instrumental skill than from the patter *in between* the songs; the routines are second-rate imitations of the humor developed by the "sick" comics.

But the interest of large numbers of college students in folksong goes far beyond the limits of wisecracks accompanied by banjo and guitar. Even *Mademoiselle* noticed this, for its reporter can't quite understand what attracts these middle class kids to a music which evokes "the ideas and emotions of the downtrodden and the heartbroken, of garage mechanics and mill workers and miners and backwoods farmers"—a lineup of materials which reflects neither the world of the beats nor of the slick trios.

Here is where a little historical perspective would help. As Harold Taylor has pointed out recently, this generation of college students has begun to react against being treated like adolescents. If they have not been ideological, Mr. Taylor points out, they have been willing to associate themselves with non-conformist movements, despite warnings by parents and teachers that such activities will endanger their personal as well as their job security. The moral leadership for this so-called "silent generation," Mr. Taylor notes, was "established by the Negro students in the South who quietly and courageously began to assert their rights with the sit-in strikes at lunch counters." And as TV coverage of events in the South has revealed, the passive resistance movement of young people and adults is a singing movement as well.

Martin Luther King's meetings with Negro college students almost always conclude with a song—a popular one has its roots in the spiritual: "We shall overcome—Oh Lord, Deep in my heart, I do believe, we shall overcome some day." A Huntley-Brinkley special on the sit-ins showed students singing a West Indian work song which they had sung in jail—"Daylight's comin' and I wanna go home." The same program featured snatches of a song which told how the "cops went wild over me, and they locked me up and threw away the key." The words were up to date, but it was unmistakably the IWW protest song called the "Popular Wobbly." Earlier, the bus-boycotters in Mongomery, Alabama, had sung, "Walk Along Together."

That spirituals, work songs, and other protest songs should figure prominently in the expression of the students in the South is not surprising. What is significant is that the main stream of the song traditions that interest college students in general derive from similar materials. Almost fifty years ago, John Lomax told a meeting of academic folklorists that the significance of American folksong was to be seen not in transplanted ballads, but in songs of the miners, lumbermen, Great Lakes sailors, railroad men, cowboys, and Negroes. (A special category singled out "songs of the down and out classes—the outcast girls, the dope fiend, the convict, the jail bird and the tramp.") It was a shocking revision of the academic approach to American folksong, for in 1913, as today, the professional folklorist tends to be concerned mainly with ballads, and especially the relationship between American and British ballads. But as Lomax continued to collect in the field the vitality of non-ballad traditions impressed upon him. With the help of his son Alan, John Lomax explored the prisons of the South, uncovering such singers as Huddie Ledbetter (Lead Belly), Vera Hall, Dock Reed; they were impressed by the songs of the dust bowl songmaker, Woodie Guthrie, but especially by "the singers who have moved us beyond all others that we have heard . . . the Negroes, who in our opinion have made the most important and original contributions to American folksong . . ."

Long before folksongs became commercially profitable, singers like Guthrie, Lead Belly, and Pete Seeger were spreading the Lomax gospel on picket lines, at union meetings, and through the recordings made by quixotic Moses Asch, whose supreme devotion to traditional material kept his record companies producing even when he had neither a large audience nor a source of capital. Through the thirties and forties Guthrie kept a constant stream of songs flowing like an underground river—about the dust bowl, hoboes, folk heroes (including the Oklahoma Robin Hood, Pretty Boy Floyd), the Grand Coulee Dam, New York City, mining disasters, as well as a Whitmanesque catalogue about America called "This Land Is Your Land." Lead Belly popularized such songs as "Good Night Irene," "The Midnight Special," The Rock Island Line," and dozens of blues including "Bourgeois Blues," based on his attempt to find housing in Jim Crow Washington, D.C. Seeger, whose sensitivity to vocal and instrumental traditions is unrivalled, has been, since the early forties, a Johnny Appleseed encouraging his audience to pick up a banjo and make music.

Lead Belly died in 1949, just before the Weavers put "Good Night Irene" at the top of the hit parade, paving the way for a mass folksong audience. But like other serious arts in America, folksongs resist the mass production and standardization of tin-pan alley. (Lee Hays, who sings bass with the Weavers, commented that the success of "Good Night Irene" made tin-pan alley believe America was ready for a waltz revival!) Guthrie has become seriously ill and is unable to appreciate fully the response to his songs and his artistry which has developed among enthusiasts in America and in England. Pete Seeger is today the most sought after performer on college campuses, more often through the insistence of student groups than the promotion by official university concert bureaus. With obvious respect for his materials and the people who produced them, Seeger continues in the tradition of the Lomaxes, Guthrie and Leadbelly.

This is still a young movement, composed of students who are filled with the stubborn idealism that permeates the songs of Negro slaves, miners, hoboes, and blues singers. If the Kennedy administration is serious in its proposal to recruit them into a corps which will work to push the new frontiers, they will respond en masse and bring their guitars with them.

> In a manner curiously redolent of the girl group trend, the urban folk music revival was also more egalitarian in terms of gender than many genres that preceded and/or followed it. Notable females in the folk

revival included Judy Collins, Peggy Seeger, Odetta, Carolyn Hester, Mary (of Peter, Paul, and Mary), and Sylvia (of Ian and Sylvia), but by far the best known (and most successful as a solo performer) was Joan Baez (b. 1941). The following article from *Time* focuses on Baez and makes plain that she was beloved by purists even as her success superseded all but a handful of other folk artists.[3] The beginning of the article draws parallels among the "purity" of Baez's voice, her unadorned appearance, and her commitment to "authentic" folk music; the focus on her appearance and personal life sets the stage for a profile in which the article's anonymous author struggles to make sense of Baez's persona within the existing range of available roles for women. While space is given to Baez's own comments, which touch on some of her political concerns, the overall tone of the article downplays her musical and political activities, using the focus on her lifestyle, romantic life, clothes, and appearance to accent her eccentricity.

This feature article on Baez in *Time*, one of the weekly publications with the widest circulation in the United States, illustrates the high profile of the folk revival at the time. Indeed, not long after this article appeared, a weekly show, *Hootenanny*, began its run on U.S. national television and lasted from April 1963 to September 1964.

Folk Singing: Sibyl with Guitar
Time

Removed from its natural backgrounds, folk singing has become both an esoteric cult and a light industry. Folk-song albums are all over the bestseller charts, and folk-singing groups command as much as $10,000 a night in the big niteries. As a cultural fad, folk singing appeals to genuine intellectuals, fake intellectuals, sing-it-yourself types, and rootless root seekers who discern in folk songs the fine basic values of American life. As a pastime, it has staggeringly multiplied sales of banjos and guitars; more than 400,000 guitars were sold in the U.S. last year.

The focus of interest is among the young. On campuses where guitars and banjos were once symptoms of hopeless maladjustment, country twanging has acquired new status. A guitar stringer shows up once a week at the Princeton University Store.

The people who sit in the urban coffeehouses sipping mocha java at 60¢ a cup are mainly of college age. They take folk singing very seriously. No matter how bad a performing singer may be the least amount of cross talk will provoke an angry shhhh.

These cultists often display unconcealed, and somewhat exaggerated, contempt for entertaining groups like the Kingston Trio and the Limeliters. Folk singing is a

---

3. For an account of the folk music revival that focuses on divisions within the movement, see Dick Weissman, *Which Side Are You On? An Inside History of the Folk Music Revival in America* (New York: Continuum, 2006); for a history that connects the earlier urban folk movement with its revival, see Ronald D. Cohen, *Rainbow Quest: The Folk Music Revival and American Society, 1940–1970* (Amherst and Boston: University of Massachusetts Press, 2002).

religion, in the purists' lexicon, and the big corporate trios are its money-changing De Milles. The high pantheon is made up of all the shiftless geniuses who have shouted the songs of their forebears into tape recorders provided by the Library of Congress. These country "authentics" are the all but unapproachable gods. The tangible sibyl, closer to hand, is Joan Baez.

Her voice is as clear as air in the autumn, a vibrant, strong, untrained and thrilling soprano. She wears no makeup, and her long black hair hangs like a drapery, parted around her long almond face. In performance she comes on, walks straight to the microphone, and begins to sing. No patter. No show business. She usually wears a sweater and skirt or a simple dress. Occasionally she affects something semi-Oriental that seems to have been hand-sewn out of burlap. The purity of her voice suggests purity of approach. She is only 21 and palpably nubile. But there is little sex in that clear flow of sound. It is haunted and plaintive, a mother's voice, and it has in it distant reminders of black women wailing in the night, of detached madrigal singers performing calmly at court, and of saddened gypsies trying to charm death into leaving their Spanish caves.

Impresarios everywhere are trying to book her. She has rarely appeared in nightclubs and says she doubts that she will ever sing in one again; she wants to be something more than background noise. Her LP albums sell so well that she could hugely enrich herself by recording many more, but she has set a limit of one a year. Most of her concerts are given on college campuses.

She sings Child ballads with an ethereal grace that seems to have been caught and stopped in passage in the air over the 18th century Atlantic. *Barbara Allen* (Child 84) is one of the set pieces of folk singing, and no one sings it as achingly as she does. From *Lonesome Road* to *All My Trials*, her most typical selections are so mournful and quietly desperate that her early records would not be out of place at a funeral. More recently she has added some lighter material to create a semblance of variety, but the force of sadness in her personality is so compelling that even the wonderful and instructive lyrics of *Copper Kettle* somehow manage to portend a doom deeper than a jail sentence:

> *Build your fire with hickory—*
> *Hickory and ash and oak.*
> *Don't use no green or rotten wood,*
> *They'll get you by the smoke.*
> *While you lay there by the juniper,*
> *While the moon is bright,*
> *Watch them jugs a-filling*
> *In the pale moonlight.*

That song is a fond hymn to the contemplative life of the moonshiner, but Joan Baez delivers it in a manner that suggests that all good lives, respectable or not, are soon to end.

The people who promote her records and concerts are forever saying that "she speaks to her generation." They may be right, since her generation seems to prefer her to all others. If the subtle and emotional content of her attitude is getting through to her contemporaries, she at least has an idea of what she is trying to say to them and why they want to hear it. "When I started singing, I felt as though we had just so long to live, and I still feel that way," she says. "It's looming over your head. The kids who sing feel they really don't have a future—so they pick up a guitar and play. It's a desperate sort of thing, and there's a whole lost bunch of them."

Resentful Stones

After she finished high school, the family moved to Boston, where her father had picked up a mosaic of jobs with Harvard, M.I.T., Encyclopaedia Britannica Films, and the Smithsonian Institution. They had scarcely settled when Dr. Baez came home one night and said, "Come, girls, I have something to show you." He took them to Tulla's Coffee Grinder, where amateur folk singers could bring their guitars and sing.

Joan was soon singing there and in similar places around Boston. She spent a month or so at Boston University studying theater—the beginning and end of college for her—and she met several semipro folk singers who taught her songs and guitar techniques. She never studied voice or music, or even took the trouble to study folklore and pick up songs by herself. Instead, she just soaked them up from those around her. She could outsing anybody, and she left a trail of resentful stepping-stones behind her.

She sang in coffeehouses in and around Harvard Square that were populated by what might be called the Harvard underworld—drifters, somewhat beat, with Penguin classics protruding from their blue jeans and no official standing at Harvard or anywhere else. They pretended they were Harvard students, ate in the university dining halls and sat in on some classes. Joan Baez, who has long been thought of as a sort of otherworldly beatnik because of her remote manner, long hair, bare feet and burlap wardrobe, actually felt distaste for these academic bums from the start. "They just lie in their pads, smoke pot, and do stupid things like that," she says.

They were her first audiences, plus Harvard boys and general citizens who grew in number until the bums were choked out. She was often rough on them all. She ignored their requests if she chose to. When one patron lisped a request to her, she cruelly lisped in reply. When another singer turned sour in performance, Joan suddenly stood up in the back of the room and began to sing, vocally stabbing the hapless girl on the stage into silence.

Sometime Thing

She made one friend. His name is Michael New. He is Trinidad English, 23 years old, and apparently aimless—a sulky, moody, pouting fellow whose hair hangs down in golden ringlets. He may go down in history as the scholar who spent three years at Harvard as a freshman. "I was sure it would only last two weeks as usual," says Joan. "But then after three weeks there we were, still together. We were passionately, insanely, irrationally in love for the first few months. Then we started bickering and quarreling violently." Michael now disappears for months at a time. But he always comes back to her, and she sometimes introduces him as her husband.

In the summer of 1959, another folk singer invited her to the first Folk Festival at Newport, R.I. Her clear-lighted voice poured over the 13,000 people collected there and chilled them with surprise. The record-company leg-and-fang men closed in. "Would you like to meet Mitch, Baby?" said a representative of Columbia Records, dropping the magic name of Mitch Miller, who is Columbia's top pop artists-and-repertory man when he isn't waving to his mother on TV.

"Who's Mitch?" said Joan.

The record companies were getting a rude surprise. Through bunk and ballyhoo, they had for decades been turning sows' ears into silk purses. Now they had found a silk purse that had no desire to become a sow's ear. The girl did not want to be exploited, squeezed, and stuffed with cash. Joan eventually signed with a little outfit called Vanguard, which is now a considerably bigger outfit called Vanguard.

Cats and Doctors

Somewhere along the line Joan Baez' family became Quakers, but Joan herself is not a Friend. "Living is my religion," she says. She practices it currently on California's rugged coast. She has lived there for more than a year, including eight months in the Big Sur region in a squalid cabin with five cats and five dogs. The cabin was a frail barque adrift on a sea of mud, and sometimes when Joan opened the front door, a comber of fresh mud would break over the threshold and flow into the living room. When she couldn't stand it any more, she moved to cleaner quarters in nearby Carmel.

She does not like to leave the area for much more than a short concert tour, for her psychiatrist is there and she feels that she must stay near him. He is her fourth "shrink," as she calls analysts, and the best ever. Mercurial, subject to quickly shifting moods, gentle, suspicious, wild and frightened as a deer, worried about the bugs she kills, Joan is anything but the harsh witch that her behavior in the Cambridge coffeehouses would suggest. Sympathetic friends point out that her wicked manner in those days was in large part a cover-up for her small repertory. She could not have honored most requests if she had wanted to. Actually, friends insist, she is honest and sincere to a fault, sensitive, kind and confused. She once worked to near exhaustion at the Perkins School for the Blind near Boston.

Segregation and Sentiment

Like many folk singers, she is earnestly political. She has taken part in peace marches and ban-the-bomb campaigns. Once in Texas she broke off singing in the middle of a concert to tell the audience that even at the risk of embarrassing a few of them, she wanted to say that it made her feel good to see some colored people in the room. "They all clapped and cheered," she says. "I was so surprised and happy."

She is a lovely girl who has always attracted numerous boys, but her wardrobe would not fill a hatbox. She wears almost no jewelry, but she has one material bauble. When a Jaguar auto salesman looked down his nose at the scruffily dressed customer as she peered at a bucket-seat XK-E sports model, she sat down, wrote a giant check, and bought it on the spot. Wildly, she dashes across the desert in her Jaguar, as unsecured as a grain of flying sand. "I have no real roots," she says. "Sometimes, when I walk through a suburb with all its tidy houses and lawns, I get a real feeling of nostalgia. I want to live there and hear the screen door slam. And when I'm in New York, it sometimes smells like when I was nine, and I love it. I look back with great nostalgia on every place I've ever lived. I'm a sentimental kind of a goof."

Further Reading

Cantwell, Robert. *When We Were Good: The Folk Revival*. Cambridge, Mass.: Harvard University Press, 1996.

Carman, Bryan. *A Race of Singers: Whitman's Working-Class Hero from Guthrie to Springsteen*. Chapel Hill: University of North Carolina Press, 2000.

Cohen, Ronald D. *Rainbow Quest: The Folk Music Revival and American Society, 1940–1970*. Amherst and Boston: University of Massachusetts Press, 2002.

Dunaway, David King. *Singing Out: An Oral History of America's Folk Music Revivals*. New York: Oxford University Press, 2010.

Filene, Benjamin. *Romancing the Folk: Public Memory and American Roots Music*. Chapel Hill: University of North Carolina Press, 2000.

Hajdu, David. *Positively 4th Street: The Lives and Times of Joan Baez, Bob Dylan, Mimi Baez Fariña, and Richard Fariña*. New York: Picador, 2011.

La Chapelle, Peter. *Proud to Be an Okie: Cultural Politics, Country Music, and Migration to Southern California.* Berkeley and Los Angeles: University of California Press, 2007.

Weissman, Dick. *Which Side Are You On? An Inside History of the Folk Music Revival in America.* New York: Continuum, 2006.

Discography

Alan Lomax Collection Sampler. Rounder Select, 1997.

The Almanac Singers. *Talking Union and Other Union Songs.* Smithsonian Folkways, 2007.

Baez, Joan. *Joan Baez.* Vanguard Records, 1960.

———. *The First Ten Years.* Vanguard Records, 1990.

Folk Hits of the '60s. Shout Factory, 2003.

Guthrie, Woody. *The Asch Recordings* (4 vols.). Smithsonian Folkways, 1999.

The Kingston Trio. *The Essential Kingston Trio.* Shout Factory, 2006.

In the Wind: The Folk Music Collection. Varese Fontana, 2003.

Peter, Paul, and Mary. *Peter, Paul, and Mary.* Warner Brothers, 1962.

———. *The Very Best of Peter, Paul, and Mary.* Rhino/WEA, 2005.

Seeger, Pete. *Pete Seeger's Greatest Hits.* Sony, 2002.

Van Ronk, Dave. *Inside Dave Van Ronk.* Fantasy, 1991.

29. Bringing It All Back Home

DYLAN AT NEWPORT

Early in 1961, Bob Dylan (b. 1941) left Minneapolis, arrived in New York City's Greenwich Village, and quickly made his way to the forefront of the folk music scene there. Early signs of outward encouragement came in September 1961 with a glowing review from the *New York Times* critic Robert Shelton[1] and a contract from Columbia Records (the largest record company at the time) that resulted in his first album, the eponymous *Bob Dylan*, recorded in November 1961 and released in March 1962. In keeping with the practice of the folk revival at the time, the album relied heavily on preexisting material, containing only two originals, both of which were heavily indebted to Dylan's idol Woody Guthrie. The other songs on the album reveal what set Dylan apart from the rest of the folk performers: an eclectic mixture of material, which included renditions of hard-driving country blues that were first recorded by Blind Lemon Jefferson and Bukka White.

In fact, Dylan's performance style at this time owed a lot to the high-energy performances of the musicians he had emulated in high school: Little Richard, Jerry Lee Lewis, and Hank Williams. This performance style, which he combined with Chaplinesque physical humor and a moodiness derived from the image of James Dean, makes it easy in retrospect to see what made Dylan appear much hipper than the other "pure" folkies, who tended to project a kind of somber earnestness. Furthermore, in another atypical move for a "folky," Dylan never denied the influence of overtly commercial musicians, and he moved quickly toward writing the majority of the songs he performed.

The political orientation of many folksingers was directly implicated in the development of the protest song movement, which sought to express the folk revival's political concerns through newly composed songs that addressed topical matters. Here, Seeger was again a pioneer: he had written songs with topical themes dating back to the 1940s—"I Had a Hammer," cowritten by Seeger and Weavers bandmate Lee Hays in 1949, was a hit for Peter, Paul, and Mary in 1962—and several of his songs, such as "Where Have All the Flowers Gone" and "Turn, Turn, Turn," figured prominently in the new wave of politically inspired material. Many of Dylan's earliest songs fell into the protest genre but stood out from other songs of their ilk in their use of allusion, rather than straightforward description, a quality evident in his most famous song in this mode, "Blowin' in the Wind."

Peter, Paul, and Mary's recording of "Blowin' in the Wind" provided a commercial breakthrough for Dylan, albeit as a songwriter, rather than as a performer. The trio followed with another hit recording of Dylan's "Don't Think Twice, It's Alright," and Dylan himself performed in front of 200,000 people at one of the keystones of the civil rights movement in August 1963—the March on Washington, an event that featured Dr. Martin Luther King's famous "I Have a Dream" speech. These events sealed an image of Dylan with the public as the conscience of his generation.[2]

With the arrival of the Beatles and other British groups, along with the emergence of Motown in 1964, folk music slipped from its 1963 peak of popularity even as it retained its core audience. However, the album Dylan recorded early in 1965, *Bringing It All Back Home*, along with the single released from it, "Subterranean Homesick Blues," constituted a serious threat to the aesthetic and political beliefs of the folk movement. Many of Dylan's new songs featured a rock 'n' roll beat, and his lyrics had become increasingly surrealistic, drawing from the Beat

1. "Bob Dylan: A Distinctive Folk-Song Stylist," *New York Times*, September 29, 1961.

2. For a vivid portrait of this period, see David Hajdu's account of the relationships among Dylan; Joan Baez; Baez's sister, Mimi (a folksinger in her own right); and Richard Fariña, husband of Mimi and author of *Been Down So Long It Looks Like Up to Me* (David Hajdu, *Positively Fourth Street: The Lives and Times of Joan Baez, Bob Dylan, Mimi Baez Fariña, and Richard Fariña* [New York: Farrar, Straus and Giroux, 2001]). And, for an almost hagiographical depiction of Dylan and Baez circa 1964, see Fariña's article, "Baez and Dylan: A Generation Singing Out," *Mademoiselle*, August 1964.

poets, Walt Whitman, and the French symbolist Arthur Rimbaud. While the songs did not directly address any recognizable political causes, their sarcastic and bizarrely imaginative humor contained a critique of society, albeit a fairly abstract one. Rather than specific causes, the targets were now the moral fabric and cultural assumptions of Western society itself, including sexual repression; materialism; received notions of "normality"; and the taken-for-granted beliefs in "reality," "truth," and "rationality."

In June 1965, Dylan followed *Bringing It All Back Home* with "Like a Rolling Stone," which featured the organ and electric guitar–led backing that would be most associated with him during this period. "Rolling Stone" ran over six minutes long, an unheard-of length for a single, and became his biggest hit, reaching number two on the pop charts. "Rolling Stone" had been preceded onto the charts by an electrified version of Dylan's "Mr. Tambourine Man," recorded by the Los Angeles–based rock band the Byrds. While Dylan's recording of "Tambourine Man" had appeared on *Bringing It All Back Home* with a muted electric guitar added to Dylan's voice, acoustic guitar, and harmonica, the Byrds added a rhythm used in recent hits such as the Beach Boys' "Don't Worry Baby" and overlaid it with leader Roger McGuinn's electric 12-string guitar and the distinctive harmony singing of David Crosby. The music industry and mass media recognized the combined impact of these recordings with the swiftly coined label, "folk-rock." Numerous cover versions of Dylan songs with electric backing, as well as countless imitations, swiftly appeared, all with "deep" and "relevant" lyrics—the most commercially successful of these imitations was "Eve of Destruction," recorded by Barry McGuire and written by P. F. Sloan (August 1965).[3]

As the folk-rock craze was gathering momentum, Dylan appeared in late July at the Newport Folk Festival, accompanied by members of the Butterfield Blues Band. A storm of controversy followed: the folk movement could no longer ignore Dylan's "defection," nor could certain contradictions in folk music's opposition to commerce be ignored. Dylan's hit single and his use of a rock 'n' roll band seemed to embody the very commercial forces to which the folk revival had seen itself in revolt.

The following two articles appeared in *Sing Out*, a major publication devoted to folk music, and they chart the reaction to Dylan's Newport appearance and a subsequent appearance in August at Forest Hills, New York. To folk purists, Dylan's move toward amplification and rock 'n' roll smacked of a "sellout"; to supporters of his new style, Dylan's music was becoming more personalized and conveyed a truer picture of the contemporary world. However, as the descriptions of the other performers

---

3. For a contemporary overview of some of these recordings, see Robert Shelton, "On Records: The Folk-Rock Rage," *New York Times,* January 30, 1966, 17–18.

at Newport indicate, even the split between "pure" folk and pop music revealed unsuspected complexity: all was not well with the urban folk music world's equation of simple acoustic music with left-wing politics.

Newport Folk Festival, 1965
Irwin Silber

The Festival's most controversial scene was played out on the dramatically-lit giant stage halfway through the final night's concert when Bob Dylan emerged from his cult-imposed aura of mystery to demonstrate the new "folk rock," and [*sic*] expression that has already begun to find its way into the "Top Forty" charts by which musical success is measured. To many, it seemed that it was not very good "rock," while other disappointed legions did not think it was very good Dylan. Most of these erupted into silence at the conclusion of Dylan's songs, while a few booed their once-and-former idol. Others cheered and demanded encores, finding in the "new" Dylan an expression of themselves, just as teen aged social activists of 1963 had found themselves summed up in the angry young poet's vision.

Shocked and somewhat disoriented by the mixed reaction of the crowd, a tearful Dylan returned to the stage unelectrified and strained to communicate his sense of unexpected displacement through the words and music of a song he made fearfully appropriate, "It's All Over Now, Baby Blue."

But if the audience thought that the Dylan scene represented a premature climax to the evening, more was yet to come. A double finale (presumably a Newport tradition by now) saw hordes of singers, musicians, self-appointed participants and temporary freaks take over the stage in a tasteless exhibition of frenzied incest that seemed to have been taken from a Hollywood set. One singer called it a "nightmare of pop art," which was one of the more apt and gentle of the comments heard in the audience. The stage invasion took place during the singing of Mrs. Fannie Lou Hamer, one of that incredible band of Mississippi heroines who are in the process of reshaping America for us all. It seemed as though everyone wanted to make sure they were in on the big "civil rights act," and a moment that might have become the highpoint of the entire weekend was suddenly turned into a scene of opportunistic chaos—duplicated once again after the inevitable Peter, Paul and Mary finale and reducing the meaning of Newport to the sense of a carnival gone mad.

At the height of the frenzy, it was easy to forget the music and the conviction that had come before. There were many who thought they sensed a feeling of revulsion even among some of the Newport directors who were themselves participating in the debacle. And when the end finally came, the crowd filed out to the sound of a mournful and lonesome harmonica playing "Rock of Ages." It was the most optimistic note of the evening.

Here is a second account of the 1965 Newport Folk Festival.

Source: "Newport Folk Festival, 1965," Irwin Silber, *Sing Out!*

Newport Folk Festival, 1965
Paul Nelson

For all its emphasis on tradition and its quiet highpoints (Roscoe Holcomb and Jean Ritchie singing "Wandering Boy" was my favorite among many), Newport is still a place for the Big Moment, the Great Wham, that minuscule second of High Drama that freezes the blood and sparks the brain into the kind of excitement that stays forever in one's memory. Nothing approaching such a moment happened at Newport in 1964 (it was a dull circus), but Bob Dylan provided it on Sunday night this year: the most dramatic scene I've ever witnessed in folk music.

Here are two accounts of it, the first sketched quickly in my notebook at the time:

"Dylan doing his new R&R, R&B, R&? stuff knocked me out. . . . I think his new stuff is as exciting as anything I've heard lately in any field. The Newport crowd actually booed the electric guitar numbers he did, and there followed the most dramatic thing I've seen: Dylan walking off the stage, the audience booing and yelling 'Get rid of that electric guitar,' Peter Yarrow trying to talk the audience into clapping and trying to talk Dylan into coming back, Yarrow announcing that Dylan was coming back, George Wein asking Yarrow in disbelief '*Is* he coming back?' Dylan coming back with tears in his eyes and singing 'It's All Over Now, Baby Blue,' a song that I took to be his farewell to Newport, an incredible sadness over Dylan and the audience finally clapping now because the electric guitar was gone, etc." (Dylan did only his first three numbers with electric guitar and band.)

The second account is from a long report on Newport by Jim Rooney of Cambridge, Massachusetts:

"Nothing else in the festival caused such controversy. His (Dylan's) was the only appearance that was genuinely disturbing. It was disturbing to the Old Guard, I think, for several reasons. Bob is no longer a neo-Woody Guthrie, with whom they could identify. He has thrown away his dungarees and shaggy jacket. He has stopped singing talking blues and songs about 'causes'—peace or civil rights. The highway he travels now is unfamiliar to those who bummed around in the thirties during the Depression. He travels by plane. He wears high-heel shoes and high-style clothes from Europe. The mountains and valleys he knows are those of the mind—a mind extremely aware of the violence of the inner and outer world. 'The people' so loved by Pete Seeger are 'the mob' so hated by Dylan. In the face of violence, he has chosen to preserve himself alone. No one else. And he defies everyone else to have the courage to be as alone, as unconnected . . . as he. He screams through organ and drums and electric guitar, 'How does it feel to be on your own?' And there is no mistaking the hostility, the defiance, the contempt for all those thousands sitting before him who aren't on their own. Who can't make it. And they seemed to understand that night for the first time what Dylan has been trying to say for over a year—that he is not theirs or anyone else's—and they didn't like what they heard and booed. They wanted to throw him out. He had fooled them before when they thought he was theirs. . . . Pete (Seeger) had begun the night with the sound of a newborn baby crying, and asked that everyone sing to that baby and tell it what kind of a world it would be growing up into. But Pete already knew what he wanted others to sing. They were going to

---

Source: "Newport Folk Festival, 1965," Paul Nelson, *Sing Out!*

sing that it was a world of pollution, bombs, hunger, and injustice, but that PEOPLE would OVERCOME. . . . (But) can there be no songs as violent as the age? Must a folk song be of mountains, valleys, and love between my brother and my sister all over this land? Do we allow for despair only in the blues? . . . (That's all) very comfortable and safe. But is that what we should be saying to that baby? Maybe, maybe not. But we should ask the question. And the only one in the entire festival who questioned our position was Bob Dylan. Maybe he didn't put it in the best way. Maybe he was rude. But he shook us. And that is why we have poets and artists."

Indeed, that's why we have poets and artists. Newport 1965, interestingly enough, split apart forever the two biggest names in folk music: Pete Seeger, who saw in Sunday night a chance to project his vision of the world and sought to have all others convey his impression (thereby restricting their performances), and Bob Dylan, like some fierce young Spanish outlaw in dress leather jacket, a man who could no longer accept the older singer's vague humanistic generalities, a man who, like Nathaniel West, had his own angry vision to project in such driving electric songs as "Like a Rolling Stone" and "Maggie's Farm."

And, like it or not, the audience had to choose. Whether, on the one hand, to take the word of a dignified and great humanitarian whose personal sincerity is beyond question but whose public career more and more seems to be sliding like that other old radical Max Eastman's toward a *Reader's Digest* Norman Rockwell version of how things are (Pete's idea of singing peace songs to a newborn baby makes even the most middlebrow *Digest* ideas seem as far-out as anything William Burroughs ever did!); or whether to accept as truth the Donleavy-Westian-Brechtian world of Bob Dylan, where things aren't often pretty, where there isn't often hope, where man isn't always noble, but where, most importantly, there exists a reality that coincides with that of this planet. Was it to be marshmallows and cotton candy or meat and potatoes? Rose colored glasses or a magnifying glass? A nice guy who has subjugated and weakened his art through his constant insistence on a world that never was and never can be, or an angry, passionate poet who demands his art to be all, who demands not to be owned, not to be restricted or predicted, but only, like Picasso, to be left alone from petty criticisms to do his business, wherever that may take him?

Make no mistake, the audience had to make a clear-cut choice and they made it: Pete Seeger. They chose to boo Dylan off the stage for something as superficially silly as an electric guitar or something as stagnatingly sickening as their idea of owning an artist. They chose the safety of wishful thinking rather than the painful, always difficult stab of art. They might have believed they were choosing humanity over a reckless me-for-me attitude, but they weren't. They were choosing suffocation over invention and adventure, backwards over forwards, a dead hand instead of a live one. They were afraid, as was Pete Seeger (who was profoundly disturbed by Dylan's performance), to make a leap, to admit, to consider, to think. Instead, they took refuge in the Seeger vision as translated by the other less-pure-at-heart singers on the program, indeed, by all other than Seeger: the ghastly second half of Sunday night's program, where practically all forms of Social Significance ran completely out of control in a sickening display of egomania and a desperate grasping for publicity and fame [see Irwin Silber's account earlier in this chapter]. The second half of Sunday night (from all reports) was more ugly and hysterical than anything in a Dylan song; and, remember, the impetus for it was not Dylan at all, but Pete Seeger. (Ironically, although the audience chose the Seeger vision, it was a hollow victory for Pete, who felt he'd failed badly.)

It was a sad parting of the ways for many, myself included. I choose Dylan, I choose art. I will stand behind Dylan and his "new" songs, and I'll bet my critical reputation (such as it may be) that I'm right.

Further Reading

Bromell, Nick. *Tomorrow Never Knows: Rock and Psychedelics in the 1960s*. Chicago and London: University of Chicago Press, 2000.

Cott, Jonathan, ed. *Bob Dylan, The Essential Interviews*. New York: Wenner Books, 2006.

Dettmar, Kevin J. H., ed. *The Cambridge Companion to Bob Dylan*. Cambridge, UK: Cambridge University Press, 2009.

Dylan, Bob. *Chronicles: Volume One*. New York: Simon & Schuster, 2004.

Hajdu, David. *Positively 4th Street: The Life and Times of Joan Baez, Bob Dylan, Mimi Baez Fariña, and Richard Fariña*. New York: Farrar, Straus and Giroux, 2001.

Heylin, Clinton. *Bob Dylan: Behind the Shades, Revisited*. New York: William Morrow, 2001.

Marcus, Greil. *Invisible Republic: Bob Dylan's Basement Tapes*. New York: Henry Holt, 1997.

_____. *Like a Rolling Stone: Bob Dylan at the Crossroads*. New York: Public Affairs, 2005.

McGregor, Craig, ed. *Bob Dylan: The Early Years, A Retrospective*. New York: Da Capo, [1972] 1990.

Scaduto, Anthony. *Bob Dylan: An Intimate Biography*. New York: Signet Books, 1973.

Teehan, Mark. "The Byrds, 'Eight Miles High,' the Gavin Report, and Media Censorship of Alleged 'Drug Songs' in 1966: An Assessment." *Popular Musicology Online* 4 (2010).

Unterberger, Richie. *Turn! Turn! Turn! The '60s Folk-Rock Revolution*. San Francisco: Backbeat Books, 2002.

Discography

Dylan, Bob. *Bob Dylan*. Columbia, 1962.

_____. *The Freewheelin' Bob Dylan*. Columbia, 1963.

_____. *Bringin' It All Back Home*, Bob Dylan, Columbia, 1965.

_____. *Highway 61 Revisited*. Columbia, 1965.

30. "For a Man to Be At Ease, He Must Not Tell All He Knows, Nor Say All He Sees"

One amusing result of the sudden increase in public interest in Dylan, much of it by media who had previously avoided popular music or condescended to it, was a vast increase in the number of interviews given by Dylan. These media performances throughout 1965 and 1966 grew increasingly surreal as Dylan took a creative approach to the interview situation. Because his lyrics were more "serious" and "poetic" than those found in previous pop songs, he was barraged with questions about what the songs meant, which he steadfastly refused to answer. One of the most famous interviews from that period, conducted by Nat Hentoff (a famous jazz critic, social commentator, and writer not likely to ask naïve questions), provides a particularly amusing exchange on the subject of "message songs." When asked why he thought message songs were vulgar, Dylan replied, "You've got to respect other people's right to also have a message themselves. Myself, what I'm going to do is rent Town Hall and put about 30 Western Union boys on the bill. I mean, then there'll *really* be some messages. People will be able to come and hear more messages than they've ever heard before in their life."[1]

The following interview comes from 1968, a few years after the highpoint of Dylan's surrealist interview phase. The fact that the interviewers, John Cohen and Happy Traum, were long-time participants in the Greenwich Village folk scene comes through in exchanges that reflect a long acquaintance and numerous shared experiences with Dylan.[2] Cohen begins by asking Dylan to reflect on one of his poetic epics, "A Hard Rain's Gonna Fall" from 1962, in order to assess how far songwriting and the folk/pop music audience had come since that time. This question leads into a discussion of Dylan's literary influences and how these helped Dylan find his own voice, one that was different from that of earlier songwriters he admired, like Woody Guthrie. Dylan paints himself as a kind of naif, or at least as semi-literate,

---

1. Nat Hentoff, "The *Playboy* Interview: Bob Dylan—A Candid Conversation with the Iconoclastic Idol of the Folk-Rock Set," *Playboy*, March 1966; reprinted in *Bob Dylan: The Early Years: A Retrospective*, ed. Craig McGregor, 132–33 (New York: Da Capo Press, Inc., [1972] 1990).

2. Cohen was a founding member of the New Lost City Ramblers, a group devoted to re-creating the sound of 1920s old-time music, as well as a noted documentary filmmaker (and the husband of folksinger Peggy Seeger, sister of Pete), while Traum recorded with Dylan on several occasions.

but this image is contradicted by his own later accounts, like the one presented in his autobiography *Chronicles: Volume One* (Simon & Schuster, 2004).

Somewhat later in the interview, Cohen expresses surprise at Dylan's notion of "training," but Dylan provides an excellent account of how popular musicians acquire their craft through aural and oral tradition. Cohen's reaction may also be due to the widespread perception of Dylan as a primitive, as he was often portrayed as someone lacking any sort of technique, and the interview recapitulates reactions about his voice and lack of musicianship that would have been very familiar to Dylan's fans and critics.

Other exchanges make it evident that the readers of *Sing Out!* (the publication in which this interview first appeared, and one that was directed largely toward the folk music audience) were still interested in Dylan's opinion of rock music, making it appear as though the "sell-out" controversy of 1965 had not yet died out completely. Cohen and Traum also press Dylan about his political involvement, both hearkening back to the sense of disappointment his fans had felt three years earlier and reflecting the political turmoil of the late sixties in general, of which 1968 is generally recognized as the highpoint.

This interview also follows fairly closely upon the release of Dylan's eighth album, *John Wesley Harding* (December 1967), which was widely perceived as a huge shift in style from *Highway 61 Revisited* and *Blonde on Blonde*, featuring, as it does, Dylan on guitar or piano backed for the most part by only bass and drums. The songs themselves are more concise and parable-like, and many heard them as an implicit riposte to the baroque intricacies of psychedelia that had dominated the world of rock during 1967. *John Wesley Harding* was also Dylan's first official release since his motorcycle accident in June 1966 and thus was viewed as a major cultural event. A year and a half between albums may not seem like much nowadays, but when one considers that Dylan's previous three albums had been released in a span of 14 months, the 19 months between *Blonde on Blonde* and *John Wesley Harding* constituted a major hiatus to an audience starved for Dylan-related information of any kind.

Sing Out! "An Interview with Bob Dylan"

John Cohen and Happy Traum

JC: *I recall a conversation we had in 1962 . . . I don't know if I was seeing something, or wishing something on you—but I had just come back from Kentucky and you showed me "Hard Rain," at Gerde's or upstairs from the Gaslight. . .*
I believe at the time, you were wondering how it fit into music. How I was going to sing it.

Source: Interview with John Cohen and Happy Traum, *Sing Out!* October/November 1968

JC: *That was my initial reaction. That's really ancient history now because a whole aesthetic, a whole other approach has come into music since then, to make it very possible to sing that kind of song.*

Yes, that's right.

JC: *Before then it wasn't so possible. The question I asked you on seeing this stream of words was, if you were going to write things like that, then why do you need Woody Guthrie? How about Rimbaud? And you didn't know Rimbaud . . . yet.*

No, not until a few years ago.

JC: *Back then, you and Allen Ginsberg met.*

Al Aronowitz, a reporter from the *Saturday Evening Post,* introduced me to Allen Ginsberg and his friend Peter Orlovsky, above a bookstore on 8th street, in the fall of '64 or '65. I'd heard his name for many years. At that time these two fellas had just gotten back from a trip to India. Their knapsacks were in the corner and they were cooking a dinner at the time. I saw him again at Washington Square, at a party. . . .

JC: *At that time, for you, was there a stronger leaning towards poetry, and the kind of thing that Allen had dealt with? . . . as opposed to what Woody had dealt with.*

Well, the language which they were writing, you could read off the paper, and somehow it would begin some kind of tune in your mind. I don't really know what it was, but you could see it was possible to do more than what . . . not more . . . something different than what Woody and people like Aunt Molly Jackson and Jim Garland did. The subject matter of all their songs wasn't really accurate for me; I could see that they'd written thousands of songs, but it was all with the same heartfelt subject matter . . . whereas that subject matter did not exist then, and I knew it. There was a sort of semi-feeling of it existing, but as you looked around at the people, it didn't really exist the way it probably existed back then, there was no real movement, there was only organized movement. There wasn't any type of movement which was a day by day, livable movement. When that subject matter wasn't there anymore for me, the only thing that was there was the style. The idea of this type of song which you can live with in some kind of way, which you don't feel embarrassed twenty minutes after you've sung it; that type of song where you don't have to question yourself . . . where you're just wasting your time.

JC: *I don't know which was the cart and which was the horse, but people were asking about your music (and Phil Ochs' and others'), "Is this stuff poetry or is this song?"*

Yes, well you always have people asking questions.

JC: *What I'm trying to get at is whether you were reading a lot then, books, literature? Were your thoughts outside of music?*

No, my mind was with the music. I tried to read, but I usually would lay the book down. I never have been a fast reader. My thoughts weren't about reading, no . . . they were just about that feeling that was in the air. I tried to somehow get ahold of that, and write that down, and using my musical training to sort of guide it by, and in the end, have something I could do for a living.[1]

JC: *Training!*

Yes, training. You have to have some. I can remember traveling through towns, and if somebody played the guitar, that's who you went to see. You didn't necessarily go to meet them, you just went necessarily to watch them, listen to them, and if possible, learn how to do something . . . whatever he was doing.

---

1. Dylan's non-interest in literature is contradicted by passages in *Chronicles: Volume 1.*

And usually at that time it was quite a selfish type of thing. You could see the people, and if you knew you could do what they were doing with just a little practice, and you were looking for something else, you could just move on. But when it was down at the bottom, everyone played the guitar, and when you knew that they knew more than you, well, you just had to listen to everybody. It wasn't necessarily a song; it was technique and style, and tricks and all those combinations which go together—which I certainly spent a lot of hours just trying to do what other people have been doing. That's what I mean by training.

JC: *It's hard for me, because this is an interview and can't be just a conversation . . . like the tape recorder is the third element . . . I can't just say to your face that you did something great, that I admire you. . . .*

Well in my mind, let me tell you John, I can see a thousand people who I think are great, but I've given up mentioning names anymore. Every time I tell somebody who I think is pretty good, they just shrug their shoulders . . . and so I now do the same thing. Take a fellow like Doc Watson, the fellow can play the guitar with such ability . . . just like water running. Now where do you place somebody like that in the current flow of music? Now he doesn't use any tricks. But that has to do with age, I imagine, like how long he lives.

JC: *I think it's also got to do with the age he comes from, he doesn't come from yours or mine.*

No, but I'm a firm believer in the longer you live, the better you get.

JC: *But Doc is different from you and me. I know people who hate your voice. They can't stand that sound, that kind of singing, that grating. The existence of your voice and people like you, like Roscoe Holcomb, it challenges their very existence. They can't conceive of that voice in the same breath as their own lives.*

Well my voice is one thing, but someone actually having hate for Roscoe Holcomb's voice, that beautiful high tenor, I can't see that. What's the difference between Roscoe Holcomb's voice and Bill Monroe's?

JC: *I don't think Bill likes Roscoe's voice. Bill sings with such control. Roscoe's voice is so uncontrolled.*

Well Bill Monroe is most likely one of the best, but Roscoe does have a certain untamed sense of control which also makes him one of the best.

JC: *I don't think Doc Watson's voice and your voice are compatible, it doesn't bother me.*

No, no . . . maybe some day, though.

* * *

JC: *I'd like to talk about the material in the songs.*

All right.

JC: *Well, I mean your music is fine, it's complete . . . but what I'm asking about is the development of your thoughts . . . which could be called "words." That's why I was asking about your poetry and literature. Where do these things come upon a person? Maybe nobody asks you that.*

No, nobody does, but . . . who said that, it wasn't Benjamin Franklin, it was somebody else. No, I think it was Benjamin Franklin. He said (I'm not quoting it right) something like, "For a man to be—(something or other)—at ease, he must not tell all he knows, nor say all he sees." Whoever said that certainly I don't think was trying to cover up anything.

JC: *I once got a fortune cookie that said "Clear water hides nothing." . . . Three or four years ago, there was an interview with you in Playboy. One particular thought stuck with me. You said it was very important that Barbara Allen had a rose grow out of her head, and that a girl could become a swan.*

That's for all those people who say, "Why do you write all these songs about mystery and magic and Biblical implications? Why do you do all that? Folk music doesn't have any of that." There's no answer for a question like that, because the people who ask them are just wrong.

JC: *They say that folk music doesn't have this quality. Does rock and roll music have it?*

Well, I don't know what rock and roll music is supposed to represent. It isn't that defined as a music. Rock and roll is dance music, perhaps an extension of the blues forms. It's live music; nowadays they have these big speakers, and they play it so loud that it might seem live. But it's got rhythm. . . . I mean if you're riding in your car, rock and roll stations playing, you can sort of get into that rhythm for three minutes—and you lose three minutes. It's all gone by and you don't have to think about anything. And it's got a nice place; in a way this place is not necessarily in every road you turn, it's just pleasant music.

JC: *You're part of it aren't you? Or it's part of you.*

Well, music is a part of me, yes.

JC: *From what I saw in that film Eat the Document, you were really in it.*

I was in it because it's what I've always done. I was trying to make the two things go together when I was on those concerts. I played the first half acoustically, second half with a band, somehow thinking that it was going to be two kinds of music.

JC: *So acoustic would mean "folk" and band would mean "rock and roll" at that moment?*

Yes, rock and roll is working music. You have to work at it. You just can't sit down in a chair and play rock and roll music. You can do that with a certain kind of blues music, you can sit down and play it . . . you may have to lean forward a little.

JC: *Like a ballad, or one of your "dreams"?*[2]

Yes, you can think about it, you don't necessarily have to be in action to think about it. Rock and roll is hard to visualize unless you're actually doing it. . . . Actually, too, we're talking about something which is for the most part just a commercial item; it's like boats and brooms, it's like hardware, people sell it, so that's what we're talking about. In the other sense of the way which you'd think about it, it's impossible.

JC: *But the kids who are getting into it today, they don't want to sell brooms.*

It's an interesting field . . .

JC: *Could we talk about your new record John Wesley Harding?*

There were three sessions: September, October, and December, so it's not even a year old. I know that the concepts are imbedded now, whereas before that record I was just trying to see all of which I could do, trying to structure this and that. Every record was more or less for impact. Why, I did one song on a whole side of an

---

2. This question about one of Dylan's "dreams" probably refers two songs that Dylan wrote with "Dream" in the title: "Bob Dylan's Dream" (from his 1963 album *The Freewheelin' Bob Dylan*) and "Bob Dylan's 115th Dream" (from his 1965 album *Bringing It All Back Home*). As these two songs are very different structurally, it is difficult to interpret Cohen's question: these songs hardly constitute a formal type, such as a blues, or the "talking blues" that was featured regularly on Dylan's early albums.

album![3] It could happen to anybody. One just doesn't think of those things though, when one sees that other things can be done. It was spontaneously brought out, all those seven record albums. It was generously done, the material was all there. Now, I like to think that I can do it, do it better, on my own terms, and I'll do whatever it is I can do. I used to slight it off all the time. I used to get a good phrase or a verse, and then have to carry it to write something off the top of the head and stick it in the middle, to lead this into that. Now as I hear all the old material that was done, I can see the whole thing. I can't see how to perfect it, but I can see what I've done. Now I can go from line to line, whereas yesterday it was from thought to thought. Then of course, there are times you just pick up an instrument—something will come, like a tune or some kind of wild line will come into your head and you'll develop that. If it's a tune on the piano or guitar—you'll just be uuuuhhhh [hum] whatever it brings out in the voice, you'll write those words down. And they might not mean anything to you at all, and you just go on, and that will be what happens. Now I don't do that anymore. If I do it, I just keep it for myself. So I have a big lineup of songs which I'll never use. On the new record, it's more concise. Here I am not interested in taking up that much of anybody's time.

JC: *That's why I gave you Kafka's Parables and Paradoxes, because those stories really get to the heart of the matter, and yet you can never really decipher them.*

Yes, but the only parables that I know are the Biblical parables. I've seen others. Khalil Gibran perhaps. . . . It has a funny aspect to it—you certainly wouldn't find it in the Bible—this type of soul. Now Mr. Kafka comes off a little closer to that. Gibran, the words are all mighty but the strength is turned into that of a contrary direction. There used to be this disc jockey, Rosko. I don't recall his last name. Sometimes at night, the radio would be on and Rosko would be reciting this poetry of Khalil Gibran. It was a radiant feeling, coming across it on the radio. His voice was that of the inner voice in the night.

JC: *When did you read the Bible parables?*

I have always read the Bible, though not necessarily always the parables.

JC: *I don't think you're the kind who goes to the hotel, where the Gideons leave a Bible, and you pick it up.*

Well, you never know.

JC: *What about Blake, did you ever read . . . ?*

I have tried. Same with Dante, and Rilke. I understand what's there, it's just that the connection sometimes does not connect. . . . Blake did come up with some bold lines though . . .

JC: *A feeling I got from watching the film—which I hadn't considered much before folk music and rock and roll got so mixed together—is about this personal thing of put ons, as a personal relationship. Like with the press, they ask such idiotic questions that they are answered by put ons.*

The only thing there, is that that becomes a game in itself. The only way to not get involved in that is not to do it, because it'll happen every time. It even happens with the housewives who might be asked certain questions.

JC: *It's become a way of imparting information. Like someone will come with an idea, a whole thesis, and then they'll ask, "Is this so?" and you might not have thought about it before, but you can crawl on top of it.*

---

3. This comment refers to "Sad Eyed Lady of the Lowlands" from *Blonde on Blonde*.

It's this question and answer business, I can't see the importance of it. There's so many reporters now. That's an occupation in itself. You don't have to be any good at it at all. You get to go to fancy places. It's all on somebody else.

JC: *Ridiculous questions get ridiculous answers, and the ridiculous response becomes the great moment.*

Yes, well you have to be able to do that now. I don't know who started that, but it happens to everybody.

JC: *I wouldn't have mentioned it, but to me, you've moved away from it . . . gotten beyond it.*

I don't know if I've gotten beyond it. I just don't do it anymore, because that's what you end up doing. You end up wondering what you're doing.

JC: *Hey. In the film, was that John Lennon with you in the car, where you're holding your head? He was saying something funny, but it was more than that . . . it was thoughtful.*

He said "Money." . . .

JC: *Do you see the Beatles when you go there or they come here? There seems to be a mutual respect between your musics—without one dominating the other.*

I see them here and there.

JC: *I fear that many of the creative young musicians today may look back at themselves ten years from now and say "We were just under the tent of the Beatles." But you're not.*

Well, what they do . . . they work much more with studio equipment, they take advantage of the new sound inventions of the past year or two. Whereas I don't know anything about it. I just do the songs, and sing them and that's all.

JC: *Do you think they are more British or International?*

They're British I suppose, but you can't say they've carried on with their poetic legacy, whereas the Incredible String Band who wrote this "October Song" . . . that was quite good.

JC: *As a finished thing—or did it reach you?*

As a finished song it's quite good.

JC: *Is there much music now that you hear, that reaches you?*

Those old songs reach me. I don't hear them as often as I used to. But like this other week, I heard on the radio Buell Kazee and he reached me. There's a lot . . . Scrapper Blackwell, Leroy Carr, Jack Dupree, Lonnie Johnson, James Ferris, Jelly Roll Morton, Buddy Bolden, Ian and Sylvia, Benny Ferguson, Tom Rush, Charley Pride, Porter Wagoner, The Clancy Brothers and Tommy Makem. . . . Everything reaches me in one way or another.

JC: *How do you view the music business?*

I don't exactly view it at all. Hearing it and doing it, I'll take part in that—but talking about it . . . there's not much I can contribute to it.

JC: *I recall in 'Billboard,' a full page ad of you with electric guitar like in the movie. . . .*

Sure, I was doing that.

JC: *I'm interested in how you talk of it in the past tense, as if you don't know what's coming next.*

Well, I don't in a sense . . . but I've been toying with some ridiculous ideas—just so strange and foreign to me, as a month ago. Now some of the ideas—I'll tell you about them—after we shut off this tape recorder.

* * *

JC: *I was pleased that you know the music of Dillard Chandler, and that you were familiar with some unaccompanied ballads on a New Lost City Ramblers record. Do you think you'll ever try to write like a ballad?*

Yes, I hope so. Tom Paxton just did one called "The Cardinal," quite interesting . . . it's very clean . . . sings it unaccompanied. The thing about the ballad is that you have to be conscious of the width of it at all times, in order to write one. You could take a true story, write it up as a ballad, or you can write it up in three verses. The difference would be, what are you singing it for, what is it to be used for. The uses of a ballad have changed to such a degree. When they were singing years ago, it would be as entertainment . . . a fellow could sit down and sing a song for a half hour, and everybody could listen, and you could form opinions. You'd be waiting to see how it ended, what happened to this person or that person. It would be like going to a movie. But now we have movies, so why does someone want to sit around for a half hour listening to a ballad? Unless the story was of such a nature that you couldn't find it in a movie. And after you heard it, it would have to be good enough so that you could sing it again tomorrow night, and people would be listening to hear the story again. It's because they want to hear that story, not because they want to check out the singer's pants. Because they would have conscious knowledge of how the story felt and they would be a part of that feeling . . . like they would want to feel it again, so to speak.

JC: *It must be terrific to try to write within those dimensions.*

Well once you set it up in your mind, you don't have to think about it any more. If it wants to come, it will come.

JC: *Take a song like "The Wicked Messenger." Does that fit?*

In a sense, but the ballad form isn't there. Well, the scope is there actually, but in a more compressed sense. The scope opens up, just by a few little tricks. I know why it opens up, but in a ballad in the true sense, it wouldn't open up that way. It does not reach the proportions I had intended for it.

JC: *Have you ever written a ballad?*

I believe on my second record album, "Boots of Spanish Leather."

JC: *Then most of the songs on John Wesley Harding, you don't consider ballads.*

Well I do, but not in the traditional sense. I haven't fulfilled the balladeer's job. A balladeer can sit down and sing three ballads for an hour and a half. See, on the album, you have to think about it after you hear it, that's what takes up the time, but with a ballad, you don't necessarily have to think about it after you hear it, it can all unfold to you. These melodies on the *John Wesley Harding* album lack this traditional sense of time. As with the third verse of "The Wicked Messenger," which opens it up, and then the time schedule takes a jump and soon the song becomes wider. One realizes that when one hears it, but one might have to adapt to it. But we are not hearing anything that isn't there; anything we can imagine is really there. The same thing is true of the song "All Along the Watchtower," which opens up in a slightly different way, in a stranger way, for we have the cycle of events working in a rather reverse order.

HT: *Has anyone picked up on your new approach—like on the album, clear songs and very personal, as opposed to the psychedelic sounds?*

I don't know.

HT: *What do you know?*

What I do know is that I put myself out of the songs. I'm not in the songs anymore, I'm just there singing them, and I'm not personally connected with them. I write them all now at a different time than when I record them. It used to be, if I would sing, I'd get a verse and go on and wait for it to come out as the music was there, and sure enough, something would come out, but in the end, I would be deluded in those songs. Besides singing them, I'd be in there acting them out—just pulling them off. Now I have enough time to write the song and not think about being in it. Just write it for somebody else to sing, then do it—like an acetate. At the moment, people are singing a simpler song. It's possible in Nashville to do that.

JC: *I heard "Blowin' in the Wind" played on the radio after the most recent assassination.*
By who?

JC: *It was Muzak style . . . music to console yourself by.*
Airplane style.

JC: *Do you think you'll ever get a job playing for Muzak? The best musicians do that work, Bob.*
Well I'd give it a try if they ask.

JC: *No one calls you into the studio to "Lay down some music" as they say.*
Before I did the new album, I was waiting to meet someone who would figure out what they would want me to do. Does anybody want any songs written about anything? Could Bob be commissioned, by anybody? Nobody came up with anything, so I went ahead and did something else.

JC: *For a while a number of years ago, the songs you were writing, and that others were writing along similar lines, were played a lot on popular radio. Today it's not completely disappeared, but it certainly is going in some other direction.*
You just about have to cut something tailor-made for the popular radio. You can't do it with just half a mind. You must be conscious of what you're involved in. I get over-anxious when I hear myself on the radio, anyway. I don't mind the record album, but it's the record company, my A & R man, Bob Johnston—he would pick out what's to be played on the radio.

HT: *Did you ever make a song just to be a single?*
Yes I did. But it wasn't very amusing because it took me away from the album. The album commands a different sort of attention than a single does. Singles just pile up and pile up; they're only good for the present. The trend in the old days was that unless you had a hit single, you couldn't do very well with an album. And when you had that album, you just filled it up. But now albums are very important.

Further Reading

See Chapter 29.

Discography

Dylan, Bob. *Blonde on Blonde.* Columbia, 1966.
_____. *Bob Dylan Live, 1966: The "Royal Albert Hall Concert."* Sony, 1998.

31. From R&B to Soul

The mid-1950s represented a time of relative rapprochement between rhythm and blues and mainstream pop that found its greatest expression in early rock 'n' roll. Despite the overlapping of the two categories, however, rhythm and blues did maintain a distinct style, as well as its own audience and set of connotations. As Ray Charles noted in the excerpt from his autobiography in Chapter 18, before the release of "What'd I Say" in 1959, his music had not been programmed on Top 40 radio, nor had it found much support among the portion of the rock 'n' roll audience constituted by white teenagers. The same is true of numerous other R&B stars, including Dinah Washington and James Brown, who enjoyed a succession of hits on the R&B charts but rarely, if ever, crossed over.[1] These singers' styles were heavily indebted to gospel music, and the singers continued to embrace themes in their lyrics that were not obviously directed toward teenagers. The use of gospel vocal technique in secular music, as pioneered by Charles and Clyde McPhatter, was increasingly adopted by R&B singers as the 1950s waned, and was one of the main musical factors involved in the gradual acquisition of a new name for R&B: soul music. In addition to its association with a cluster of musical practices, the ascendancy of the term "soul music" is inextricably linked to the growth of the civil rights movement.

Along with Ray Charles and James Brown (who began recording in 1956), two other artists form an important link between the gospel-influenced R&B of the 1950s and soul music of the 1960s: Sam Cooke (1935–64) and Jackie Wilson (1934–84). Although both artists experienced crossover success in the late 1950s and early 1960s, Cooke's career formed an early template for the extensive mainstream success of the African American singers who were to follow. Cooke used the smooth and sophisticated vocal technique that he developed in the popular gospel group the Soul Stirrers to record a major crossover hit in 1957, "You Send Me," as well as numerous other hits. Cooke's approach to ballads, which conveyed an understated spirituality and sensuality, was a major influence on soul singers of the 1960s and 1970s, such as Otis Redding and Al Green, while his involvement in the management of his own career also established an important precedent for subsequent black stars.

---

1. Dinah Washington did enjoy several pop hits beginning in the late fifties until her death in 1963 after she started recording with increasingly lush arrangements.

It was a number of newcomers, however, who signaled the stir-rings of a recognizable soul genre when they began in the early 1960s to record songs that merged spiritual fervor with secular topics. Among the many emerging talents were Solomon Burke ("Cry to Me," 1962), Wilson Pickett ("I Found a Love," with the Falcons, 1962), Otis Redding ("These Arms of Mine," 1962), and Etta James (who, after an early hit as a teenager with "The Wallflower," racked up a string of hits in the early 1960s). In addition to the melismas, bent notes, and wide range of timbres employed by these singers, their hit recordings from this period (almost all of which were in a slow tempo) prominently featured triplet subdivisions that were often articulated in arpeggiations played by piano or guitar; they also frequently featured interjected "sermons" that usually took the form of romantic advice addressed to the audi-ence. Many of these artists recorded for either Atlantic or Stax, which had a distribution deal with Atlantic for a time.

While it may seem as if no genre could make stronger claims about cultural purity than soul music, Solomon Burke describes the unique blend—"multicultural" before the phrase existed—that contributed to the Atlantic sound:

Ahmet would come in to a session and ask you if you wanted a pastrami sandwich. He'd order it from the Jewish deli, then start yakking in French on another phone. Some wheezy cat from Bogalusa's on tenor sax, working at a carton of takeout Cantonese. A pleasant Jewish man name of Wexler is cussing out a late drummer with some mighty greasy Lenox Avenue jive. Me, the black preacher, the apprentice mortician from Philadelphia, standing at the mike. Singing country and western. Now what would I call those years at Atlantic? Broadway fricassee.[2]

Because of his position of importance at Atlantic, Jerry Wexler held a good vantage point for recounting central events in the R&B world dur-ing the early to mid-1960s. In this excerpt from his autobiography, he describes his work with Wilson Pickett and Stax Records and the memo-rable occasion of the recording of "In the Midnight Hour."

from Rhythm and the Blues: A Life in American Music
Jerry Wexler and David Ritz

Pickett was a pistol. I called him the Black Panther even before the phrase was politi-cal. He had matinee-idol looks, flaming eyes, lustrous ebony skin, a sleek, muscular

---

2. Gerri Hirshey, *Nowhere to Run: The Story of Soul Music* (New York: Penguin Books, [1984] 1985), 80.

torso. His temperament was fire, his flash-and-fury singing style a study in controlled aggression, his blood-curdling scream always musical, always in tune. In the mid-sixties Wicked Wilson Pickett mainlined American music with a hefty dose of undiluted soul. Three decades later, his steel-belted hits like "Funky Broadway," "Mustang Sally," "In the Midnight Hour," and "Midnight Mover" have lost none of their tread.

Pickett told me he wanted to be on Atlantic when we met in my Broadway office in 1964. This was only a year after the fight over "If You Need Me"—Wilson Pickett versus Solomon Burke—and I asked if that hadn't pissed him off.[3]

"Fuck that," he said. "I need the bread."

I sent Wilson into the studio with Bert Berns . . . but all I got back was a single, a seven-thousand-dollar production bill (outrageous for those days), and no hits. Pickett was obstreperous, and Bert abrasive; the chemistry couldn't work. So I took it upon myself to find the songs; but what I liked, Wilson didn't, and vice versa. For a year we did the dance of the fireflies. We couldn't get it together. I knew what a powerhouse singer he was, and it was killing me.

Finally I got an idea—not for a song but for a trip: me and Pickett to Memphis, whose freshness just might give us the edge. And instead of trying to provide material, I urged him—with local genius Steve Cropper—to create his own. I put the two of them in a hotel room with a bottle of Jack Daniel's and the simple exhortation—"Write!"—which they did. When we got in that beat-up old movie theater on East McLemore, the place was rocking, the speakers nearly blown by the power of Wayne Jackson's punctuated horns. One of the songs was "In the Midnight Hour." I loved the lyric and the gospel fervor; Cropper inspired Pickett's truest passion. Originally from Prattville, Alabama, the Wicked One was back home, raising hell.

I was taken with everything but the rhythm pattern. Jim Stewart was at the board setting knobs, and I was working the talkback, directing the vocal, when I suddenly realized I was on the wrong side of the glass.

"Jerry amazed us," Cropper told Jann Wenner for a piece in *Rolling Stone*. "He ran out of the booth and started dancing."

"The bass thing was Wexler's idea," Duck Dunn said. "We were going another way when Jerry started doing the jerk dance."

I was shaking my booty to a groove made popular by the Larks' "The Jerk," a mid-sixties hit. The idea was to push the second beat while holding back the fourth—something easier demonstrated than explained. The boys caught it, put it in the pocket, and sent Pickett flying up the charts. "Midnight Hour" was a stone smash, Wilson's vocal a cyclone of conviction. The song became a bar-band anthem; the MG's incorporated the little rhythm variation into their playing from then on.

Further Reading

George, Nelson. *The Death of Rhythm and Blues*. New York: E. P. Dutton, 1989.

Guralnick, Peter. *Sweet Soul Music: Rhythm and Blues and the Southern Dream of Freedom*. New York: Harper & Row, 1986.

Hirshey, Gerri. *Nowhere to Run: The Story of Soul Music*. New York: Penguin Books, 1984.

Ward, Brian. *Just My Soul Responding: Rhythm and Blues, Black Consciousness, and Race Relations*. Berkeley and Los Angeles: University of California Press, 1998.

---

3. The previous year, Wexler and Atlantic Records had released a cover of Pickett's "If You Need Me," recorded by Solomon Burke, that surpassed the sales of Pickett's recording.

Wexler, Jerry, and David Ritz. *Rhythm and Blues: A Life in American Music*. New York: Alfred A. Knopf, 1993.

Discography

Atlantic Rhythm and Blues 1947–1974. Atlantic, 1991.
Cooke, Sam. *The Best of Sam Cooke*. RCA Victor, 1962.
_____. *Portrait of a Legend 1951–1964*. Abkco, 2003.
James, Etta. *At Last!* Chess, 1961.
_____. *The Definitive Collection*. Geffen, 2006.
Wilson, Jackie. *The Ultimate Jackie Wilson*. Brunswick, 2006.

32. No Town Like Motown

As the term "soul music" began to enter mainstream usage, black popular music increasingly cut its ties with 1950s rhythm and blues to establish a distinctive sixties "soul" genre. At the same time, differences began to emerge between a down-home, "southern" soul style—identified with the Stax and Atlantic recording companies and studios based in Memphis and Muscle Shoals, Alabama—and a "northern," "smooth," or "uptown" soul style identified primarily with Motown Records, based in Detroit.

The story of Motown is so remarkable that it has become the stuff of myth: begun by aspiring songwriter Berry Gordy (b. 1929 and the writer of Jackie Wilson's biggest hit, "Lonely Teardrops") on a family loan of $700 in 1959, Gordy's keen ear for catchy tunes and infectious rhythms, his deft judgment of personnel, and his business sense combined to establish Motown as both the most successful independent record company and the most successful black-owned business in the United States by the mid-1960s.

Initially, Motown's musical style blended in with other developments in R&B and pop with its successful recordings of girl groups (e.g., the Marvellettes' "Please Mr. Postman" [1961]) and soulful ballads (e.g., the Miracles' "You Really Got a Hold on Me" [1963]). Gradually a distinctive style began to coalesce, for which "Heat Wave" (1963) by Martha and the Vandellas provides a template: written and produced by the songwriting team of Holland-Dozier-Holland (the most successful of such teams at the company), the recording features Martha Reeves's gospel-influenced vocal over an irresistibly danceable groove and an instantly memorable melody. Between 1964 and 1972, Motown produced an extraordinary number of hits, and its artist roster included many of the leading names of 1960s soul: in addition to those already noted, the Supremes, the Four Tops, the Temptations, Marvin Gaye, Mary Wells, Junior Walker and the All Stars, Smokey Robinson (songwriter and leader of the Miracles), Stevie Wonder, the Isley Brothers, and Gladys Knight and the Pips. The Motown sound, while frequently stereotyped as being only "sweet" and "pop," actually ranged from the pop stylings of the Supremes ("Where Did Our Love Go?," "Baby Love," "Come See About Me"—all from 1964–65) to the downright funkiness of Junior Walker and the All Stars ("Shotgun" [1965]).[1]

<hr>

The following interview with Gordy took place in 1995. Here, he discusses his early career as the owner of a jazz record store and his eventual conversion to rhythm and blues. He describes the importance of the Funk Brothers, Motown's house band, and profiles many of the record company's luminaries, from early collaborator and singer-songwriter Smokey Robinson to his last major "discovery," Michael Jackson.[2]

"Berry Gordy: A Conversation with Mr. Motown"
Harvey Kubernik

Goldmine: Goldmine readers might not know you had a life from age 18–29, before Motown began. You talk about it in the book. The 3D Record Mart, writing songs, a 10-year period where being in the real world probably paid advantages later.

Berry Gordy: The real world. I learned a lot. If I hadn't worked in the factory at Lincoln-Mercury I wouldn't have had the assembly line idea, I wouldn't have written a lot of songs. I wouldn't have been locked into a place where I had to write a lot of thoughts I had. I saw what the real world was like and I saw what I wanted and what I didn't want.

Goldmine: After you were discharged from the Korean War, you opened a record shop, 3D Record Mart–House Of Jazz, that stocked exclusively jazz records in 1953.

Berry Gordy: Yes, that's all we stocked. I did know a lot about the blues. I did hear the old people playing it on the weekends. They had these parties, these house parties on the weekends, drink beer, and the blues was wailing in the bars on Hastings Street. B. B. King, you know? I was aware of it but it was beneath us, my little group. We [liked] "The Bird," Charlie Parker. If you weren't hip to "The

<hr>

1. For more on the stylistic range of Motown, see Jon Fitzgerald, "Motown Crossover Hits 1963–1966 and the Creative Process," *Popular Music* 14, no. 1 (1995): 1–12; and, for a less-than-flattering account of the company, see Nelson George, *Where Did Our Love Go? The Rise and Fall of the Motown Sound* (New York: St. Martin's Press, 1985). A major new work on Motown is forthcoming: Andrew Flory, *I Hear a Symphony: Listening to the Music of Motown* (Ann Arbor: University of Michigan Press).

2. A recent documentary, Standing in the Shadows of Motown (2002) seeks to redress this neglect of the Funk Brothers. George's Where Did Our Love Go also gives the musicians their due.

Source: "Berry Gordy: A Conversation with Mr. Motown" by Harvey Kubernik, originally published in *Goldmine*, 3 March 1995. © Harvey Kubernik/Rock's Backpages.

Bird," man, or Miles Davis could soothe you to death. I can still hear it today. I really did love jazz.

So when I went in the record business I opened up a jazz record store. The people in our neighborhood were factory workers and things like that and they did not know jazz, nor care about it. They were older, and I said, "I've got a major job to do. I'm gonna help these people with their life. I'm gonna teach them about jazz. These people are ignorant about jazz." And so I started telling them about Charlie Parker and they keep saying, "You got Muddy Waters? Jimmy Reed?" I said, "No. If you want that stuff you'll have to go down Hastings Street."

And I'd say, "Here's jazz, let me explain it to you." They did not want to hear it. They wanted the blues. And so, anyway, when we started going out of business, started losing money, I decided maybe I better listen to some of this blues stuff, and then just get some stock around.

So that's when I met the Mad Russian, who was a card, who was great, and I had to communicate. But see, there again, it was communication. I communicated with him. And I started buying boxes of records that I thought would hit.

Goldmine: He had a mark-up.

Berry Gordy: Five cents. He was a one-stop. He went to distributors and he could buy 'em from Chicago before they ever got here [Detroit] or he'd buy them all out from the distributors. And when a record would come out that was unique or different, by the Midnighters or something like that, you wouldn't be able to find them from the distributors. You'd like to go to four or five distributors for different labels. He was a one-stop. He had them all. He only charged a nickel more but he was this crazy guy that walked around there but he was crazy like a fox. Because when you talked about buying a box, all of a sudden he wasn't crazy no more. "You want two? You want three? What do you want?" And then you'd say, "I want a box of so-and-so." "Okay." Then he was kind of sane.

Goldmine: In the book you discuss the Motown session musicians. Some had played with Dizzy Gillespie, and had a jazz background. There were a lot of jazz chops goin' on.

Berry Gordy: Absolutely. We had a big story in there [the book] about me and [bassist] James Jamerson when I threatened him and gave him an ultimatum and I was praying he would . . . I could have put him out. I wanted control of all the guys 'cause I was the boss and I wanted to make sure they knew that, because otherwise I couldn't have any order. And Jamerson, I mean, he came very close to me having a confrontation, but neither of us . . . he loved what he was doin' and I loved him being there. But I still wanted him to have freedom in the restriction and he took it and he was great.

Goldmine: What was your first impression of Smokey Robinson?

Berry Gordy: Well, Smokey Robinson, my first impression was he was a great, a great poet, but he didn't know how to really write songs or put songs together. When he learned how to put stuff together and he really understood, Smokey was incredible. When I turned down his first 100 songs, he got more excited with every song. I said, "This guy has to be either crazy or one of the most special people I'll ever meet." He was incredible. He turned out to be one of the most special people I ever met.

Goldmine: And with an angelic voice.

Berry Gordy: Oh, yes. Pure. And then, he got it and understood it. So now Smokey has succeeded at the cycle of success. It takes a lot of character, because you are tempted along the way. The cycle of success is a vicious cycle. It takes you into places. People offer you things never offered before. To succeed and be successful is tough so it takes a lot of character. You got to keep your same values. So Smokey has done that. The Four Tops have done that. And most of the Motown artists have it drilled into them and they were all very tight.

Goldmine: The Four Tops?

Berry Gordy: The epitome of loyalty, integrity, class. They've been together for 40 years, the same four members. That is unheard of, impossible, and I just admire them so much. I admire them the most of any of the artists.

Goldmine: The Temptations?

Berry Gordy: Legends. They've managed to keep their look and their style all these years and they've changed members constantly, but Otis and Melvin have done just an amazing job of finding one major talent after another. Because they are legends, people want to be with the Temptations, and they have proven that the group is stronger than any of its parts. I don't care how great that part was, the Temptations are an institution.

Goldmine: Diana Ross?

Berry Gordy: Diana . . . Special, magic, sensitive. When she does a song like "Somewhere" in front of an audience she still cries. I mean, I've never seen her do "Somewhere" without crying. In fact, we used to stop her from doing it every night in the week. The Bernstein song from *West Side Story*. She was so dramatic and then she did the second ending and it was too much on her emotionally. She's so emotional and she gives all to her audience and she is sincere about it and serious about it.

Goldmine: Marvin Gaye?

Berry Gordy: The truest artist I've ever known. Whatever he was going through in his life he put on records. So if you want to know Marvin just listen to one of his records.

Goldmine: Stevie Wonder?

Berry Gordy: Innovative. The most innovative person that I've ever known. But also unique with his tones and his voice quality and all that. He was as close to a genius, and I don't like to use the word genius for any of them because, you know, Marvin could have been a genius. I don't like to throw it around, but Stevie is one of those kind of special, special, special people that had a sound, and he's quick. He's creative and can make up something very quick.

Goldmine: And he is involved in technological developments.

Berry Gordy: That's what I'm saying. Contraptions. He would take technology. He was the first in technology. He's an innovator.

Goldmine: Michael Jackson?

Berry Gordy: Greatest entertainer in the world and one of the smartest people and businessmen in the world. He conducted his own career, basically. He knew what he wanted. And from nine years old he was a thinker. And I called him "Little Spongy," because he was a sponge and he learned from everybody.

He not only studied me, but he studied James Brown, Jackie Wilson, Marcel Marceau, Fred Astaire . . . Walt Disney. And, he bought the Beatles' catalog. Michael is nobody's fool. Very bright. Very smart.

Goldmine: Jackie Wilson. People are rediscovering Jackie due to some of the repackages.

Berry Gordy: The most natural artist that I've ever seen in terms of dancing, vocals. His voice was the strongest. He could do opera, he could do rock, he could do blues and he created the most creative singer that I'd known. As I said in the book, he never sang a bad note. Maybe a bad song, but never a bad note . . . one of the most talented artists I've ever seen. 'Cause I'm talking about all great people here. So when I say talented in another way, I mean he was the most natural.

Goldmine: Was he more dynamic live than on record?

Berry Gordy: Yes, of course. He was more dynamic live than he was on record. And he could dance, and could do flips and splits and stuff like that. Different than Michael. Michael studied a lot of people who did a lot of things. Jackie did not study anybody but Jackie. Jackie was Jackie, the most natural, innate performer, probably, that I've ever seen. He had nobody to study that I know of. Jackie was an original. Probably the most original artist that I've ever seen.

And he *should* be rediscovered. Because he created stuff and he could wink on cue. I said it in the book. He could do things, do a spin, and then wink at the girls.

Goldmine: The Holland, Dozier and Holland production and songwriting team?

Berry Gordy: H-D-H was phenomenal. They came up with hit after hit. They started a thing. They had a lock on the Supremes and they took them, and they did stuff on Marvin. H-D-H was absolutely brilliant. The three of them were different and they all complemented each other.

Eddie [Holland] did mostly vocals, Brian [Holland], I always thought was the most talented, creative person. He was my protege for many years. I thought Lamont [Dozier] was also a good writer, and he was good on backgrounds and this and that and so forth. But Brian would do something, like he had their own assembly line. And they were tremendous.

Goldmine: Norman Whitfield?

Berry Gordy: Norman to me was probably the most underrated of all the producers, because he was producing by himself. And he would deal with different sounds, different beats, change with the times and write his stuff, and also Barrett Strong would work with him as a writer on many of his things. Norman was innovative and he had *fire*. And he had a different kind of style. His beat was different and could go from "Cloud Nine," "Psychedelic Shack," "Papa Was A Rolling Stone," to "Just My Imagination." He was sensitive and I think he could do so many different types of things. Then he'd come right back with "War" and then "Ain't Too Proud To Beg."

He could take one chord, like on "Papa Was A Rolling Stone," and play the same chord and do all these different beautiful melodies and stuff that many people could not really imagine this guy doin'. And I would watch him and he did it all by himself as a producer. He would work with five guys in the Temps and he would change leads on each one. He would pick the right lead for the right song, ya know, and he'd utilize all five of those leads in a song that was just incredible.

When I listen to 'em today, now that I have time to listen to 'em, I'm saying, "Wow! This guy was probably the most underrated producer we had."

Goldmine: My favorite Motown/Jobete song is the Supremes' "Up The Ladder To The Roof."

Berry Gordy: Frank Wilson [the producer]. That's one of those 95 percent. That was Jean Terrell.

Further Reading

Coffey, Dennis. *Guitars, Bars, and Motown Superstars*. Ann Arbor: University of Michigan Press, 2004.

Early, Gerald. *One Nation Under a Groove: Motown and American Culture*. Ann Arbor: University of Michigan Press, 2004.

Gordy, Berry. *To Be Loved: The Music, the Magic, the Memories of Motown: An Autobiography*. New York: Warner Books, 1994.

Neal, Mark Anthony. *What the Music Said: Black Popular Music and Black Popular Culture*. New York, Routledge, 1999.

Ward, Brian. *This Is My Soul Responding: Rhythm and Blues, Black Consciousness, and Race Relations*. Berkeley: University of California Press, 1998.

Warwick, Jacqueline. *Girl Groups, Girl Culture: Popular Music and Identity in the 1960s*. New York: Routledge, 2007.

Werner, Craig. *A Change Is Gonna Come: Music, Race and the Soul of America*. Ann Arbor: University of Michigan Press, 2006.

Discography

The Four Tops. *Reach Out*. Motown, 1967.

Hitsville USA, The Motown Singles Collection, 1959–1971. Motown, 1992.

Martha and the Vandellas. *Heatwave*. Gordy, 1963.

The Marvelettes. *Please Mr. Postman*. Tamla, 1961.

The Supremes. *Where Did Our Love Go*. Motown, 1964.

The Temptations. *The Temptations Sing Smokey*. Gordy, 1965.

Wonder, Stevie. *The 12 Year Old Genius*. Tamla, 1963.

33. The Godfather of Soul and the Beginnings of Funk

James Brown (1933–2006) stands out as one of the most influential and successful musicians in the history of R&B. While his innovations as a singer, performer, composer, arranger, and bandleader virtually defined the genre of funk and contributed mightily to the development of hip-hop, his achievements cannot be measured only in terms of his musical contributions: during the height of his popularity, he became a cultural icon in the African American community, exploring the limits of economic self-determination for a black performer and demonstrating how crossover success could be achieved without forswearing the black vernacular.

Born into extreme poverty in the rural South (in Barnwell, South Carolina, near Augusta, Georgia), Brown began his career as a professional musician with the gospel-based Flames in the early 1950s. By 1956, the group had recorded the R&B hit "Please, Please, Please" and changed its name to "James Brown and the Famous Flames." This early recording established what was to become a stylistic trademark: insistent repetition of a single phrase (in this case, the song's title) resulting in a kind of ecstatic trance. This trademark and Brown's characteristic raspy vocal timbre and impassioned melismas display his debt to the African American gospel tradition. His stage shows, dancing, and inspired call-and-response interactions with the audience also convey the fervor of a sanctified preacher.

The subsequent highpoints of his career are numerous: the surprising smash success of his 1962 recording *Live at the Apollo;* his development of funk during the years 1964–65 with three successive hits, "Out of Sight," "Papa's Got a Brand New Bag," and "I Got You (I Feel Good)"; and his continued crossover success with a string of recordings—including "Cold Sweat," "Say It Loud (I'm Black and I'm Proud)," "Superbad," "Hot Pants"—that further defined the funk genre during the years 1967–72. In recordings such as "Cold Sweat," verse-chorus structures were replaced by sections of irregular length, defined by densely overlapping ostinati played by all the instruments. Brown's lyrics grew increasingly impressionistic, celebrating black vernacular speech (often creating slang in the process) and emphasizing racial pride.[1]

In a book organized by decades, where does one place a musician who was active and influential in three of them (the 1950s, 1960s, and 1970s) and who continued to perform and record until his death? While funk will be discussed at greater length in Part 4, I chose to place Brown in this chapter because it was during the 1960s that he developed the innovations that were felt and continue to be felt across a broad musical spectrum.

The following excerpts come from Brown's autobiography, *The God-father of Soul,* and detail his early experiences and eclectic influences, his indebtedness to gospel music and charismatic preaching styles, the importance of audience-performer interaction (also learned in church), his firsthand experience of the ring shout, and the somewhat surprising link between minstrel shows (and professional wrestling!) and the later

---

1. For an essay exploring how Brown's funk expressed an African American aesthetic in its conjunction of music and lyrics, see David Brackett, "James Brown's 'Superbad' and the Double-Voiced Utterance," *Interpreting Popular Music* (Berkeley: University of California Press, [1995] 2000), 108–56.

development of his stage act. He also charts the development of soul and funk, the circumstances of the famous *Live at the Apollo* album, and his business philosophy, and profiles several of the well-known musicians who worked for him.

from The Godfather of Soul
James Brown (with Bruce Tucker)

I liked gospel and pop songs best of all. I got all the Hit Parade books and learned all the pop tunes—Bing Crosby's "Buttermilk Sky," Sinatra's "Saturday Night Is the Loneliest Night of the Week," "String of Pearls." I also admired Count Basie's "One O'Clock Jump," but I couldn't play piano good enough to do it.

I heard a lot of church music, too, because I went to all the different churches with a crippled man named Charlie Brown who lived in one of the shacks in Helmuth Alley. He had to walk with two sticks or with somebody on each side holding his arms. On Sundays when we weren't shining shoes, Junior and I walked Mr. Charlie to one or another of the churches because they'd take up collections for people like him.

At the churches there was a lot of singing and handclapping and usually an organ and tambourines, and then the preacher would really get down. I liked that even more than the music. I had been to a revival service and had seen a preacher who really had a lot of fire. He was just screaming and yelling and stomping his foot and then he dropped to his knees. The people got into it with him, answering him and shouting and clapping time. After that, when I went to church with Mr. Charlie, I watched the preachers real close. Then I'd go home and imitate them because *I* wanted to preach. I thought that was the answer to it.

Audience participation in church is something the darker race of people has going because of a lot of trials and tribulations, because of things that we understand about human nature. It's something I can't explain, but I can bring it out of people. I'm not the only person who has the ability, but I *work* at it, and I'm sure a lot of my stage show came out of the church.

One thing I never saw in the churches was drums until I went to Bishop Grace's House of Prayer. Those folks were sanctified—they *had* the beat. See, you got sanctified and you got holy. Sanctified people got more fire; holy people are more secluded—sort of like Democrats versus Republicans. I'm holy myself, but I have a lot of sanctified in me.

Bishop Grace was a big man, the richest and most powerful of that kind of preacher in the country, bigger than Father Divine or any of 'em. He had houses of prayer in more than thirty cities in the East and South, and he had these "Grace Societies" that just took in the money. Every year when he came back to Augusta there was a monstrous parade down Gwinnett Street for him, with decorated floats and cars and brass bands. Everybody in the Terry[2] turned out for it, and other people

---

2. The name for the African American neighborhood where Brown lived.

came from as far away as Philadelphia to march in it. You could join in it with your car or, if you had a musical instrument, you could fall in with one of the bands.

He was called "Daddy" Grace, and he was like a god on earth. He wore a cape and sat on a throne on the biggest float, with people fanning him while he threw candy and things to the children. He had long curly hair, and real long fingernails, and suits made out of money.

His House of Prayer on Wrightsboro Road in Augusta resembled a warehouse. A sign over the door said: "Great joy! Come to the House of Prayer and forget your troubles." And everybody *did* come at one time or another, even people who didn't believe in him, because he put on such a show. Inside there were plank benches, a dirt floor covered with sawdust, and crepe paper streamers on the ceiling. At one end there was a stage where Daddy Grace sat on a red throne.

He'd get to preaching and the people would get in a ring and they'd go round and round and go right behind one another, just shouting. Sometimes they'd fall out right there in the sawdust, shaking and jerking and having convulsions. The posts in the place were padded so the people wouldn't hurt themselves. There was a big old tin tub sitting there, too, and every time they went by the tub, they threw something in it. See who could give the most. Later on he had various big vases out there, like urns, one for five-dollar bills, one for tens and twenties, and one for hundreds. It seemed like the poorest people sacrificed the most for him.

Daddy Grace had to be a prophet, but seeing him I knew I was an outsider because I couldn't believe in him. I believed in God so that made me an outsider right away.

The Lenox [Theater in Augusta] was where I first saw films of Louis Jordan performing. Louis Jordan and His Tympany Five. They played a kind of jumping R&B and jazz at the same time, and they were something else. They did a lot of comedy, but they could play a blues if they had to, or anything in between. The films were shorts of Louis doing whatever his latest song was, and they showed them before the regular picture. He played alto sax *real* good and sang *pretty* good. Louis Jordan was the man in those days, though a lot of people have forgotten it. His stuff was popular with blacks *and* whites, and he usually had several hits at one time, a lot of 'em that sold a million. "Choo Choo Ch'Boogie," "Early in the Morning," "Saturday Night Fish Fry," and "Ain't Nobody Here but Us Chickens" were all his. When I first saw him I think he had out "G. I. Jive" and "Is You Is, or Is You Ain't (Ma' Baby)?" but the one that knocked me out was "Caldonia, What Makes Your Big Head So Hard?" especially the way he'd go up real high; Cal-don-*ya*! I learned the words as quick as I could, picked it out on the piano, and started playing it and singing it whenever I got the chance.

"Caldonia" was a song you could really put on a show with, and I guess that Louis Jordan short is what first started me thinking along those lines. That and the preachers. The circus and the minstrel shows that came through town played a part, too.

Johnny J. Jones was my favorite circus. Junior and I used to crawl through a hole in the fence in the back of the fairgrounds to see him. Since he stayed for a whole week, they called it a fair, but it was really a circus. A circus is supposed to do all its stuff in one night and then move on to the next town, the way I did with my show years later.

We had to pay to get into the minstrel shows, but only because we couldn't figure out a way to sneak in. Silas Green from New Or-leans was the best. He presented a complete varied program with singers, dancers, musicians, and comics. That's what I tried to do fifteen years later when I put together the James Brown Revue.

It's strange: Even though I'd seen just about everything there was to see in the house on Twiggs Street,[3] I thought the short dresses on Silas Green's girls were unbelievable. To me, those brown skinned models were the prettiest things in the world. I saw some top talent in those shows, too, like Willie Mae Thornton, who first did "Hound Dog." I saw a lot of great comedians, too. In those days the comics still worked in blackface, but like everybody else I just thought it was funny.

Ever since the Uptown we'd worked on our closing routine with "Please." I'd fall to my knees and out would come the coat to go around my shoulders. At first, we used anybody's coat that was laying around. Might belong to one of the Flames or one of the fellas in the band. It worked fine until people started hiding their coats; cleaning bills were mounting up, and didn't nobody want their coat to be the one. So they started bringing me a towel, like for a boxer. That was effective, too. Then one night in Chattanooga on a bill with B. B. King and Bobby "Blue" Bland they brought me the towel, and after a little bit I threw it into the audience. They loved it, so we did it that way for a good while.

Later on in that tour, when we were in Atlanta, we sat around the hotel one day watching wrestling on television. Gorgeous George was on, and when he got through killing whoever he was killing, he started walking around the ring taking his bows. A handler followed him and threw a robe over his shoulders. Gorgeous shook it off, went to another side of the ring, and took another bow. The fella threw the robe over him again, and George shook it off and took another bow. Watching it, I said, "We got to get a robe." So we went out and got some store-bought robes. Later on we got capes that I signed and had tailor-made, but the whole thing really started coming together while watching Gorgeous George.

Willie John or somebody might have said we were using more tricks to get over, but they didn't understand that everything was developing at once—the stage show, the band, the dancing, the music. There were a lot of different aspects to what we were doing. I wanted people to appreciate them so I decided to record the band on an instrumental and kind of popularize the mashed potatoes at the same time. Most entertainers today never really understand that show business means just that, show business.

You can hear the thing starting to change on the records I put out during the beginning of 1960. I was changing before that, but that's when you can *hear* it. "I'll Go Crazy" came out in January; "Think" and "You've Got the Power" were released in May. "I'll Go Crazy" is a blues, but it's a different kind of blues, up-tempo, a kind of jazz blues. "Think" is a combination of gospel and jazz—a rhythm hold is what we used to call it. Soul really started right there, or at least my kind did. See when people talk about soul music they talk only about gospel and R & B coming together. That's accurate about a lot of soul, but if you're going to talk about mine, you have to remember the jazz in it. That's what made my music so different and allowed it to change and grow after soul was finished.

Once Mr. [Syd] Nathan [owner of King Records] saw I was going to go ahead with the live recording [from a performance at the Apollo in 1962], he started cooperating. Mr. Neely took care of getting the equipment from A-1 Sound in New York, the only ones who had portable stuff—Magnacorders, I think. Matter of fact, Mr. Nathan

---

3. The "house on Twiggs Street" refers to the whorehouse where Brown spent many of his formative years.

started cooperating *too* much. He sent word that he wanted us to use cue cards to direct the audience participation. I said, "Now if y'all are going to pay for it, then I'll do it the way y'all want to, but if I'm going to pay for it, then please leave it alone. All I want y'all to do is tape the stuff."[4] That was the end of it.

We had opened on the nineteenth and were building up to recording on the twenty-fourth, a Wednesday, which meant amateur night. I wanted that wild amateur-night crowd because I knew they'd do plenty of hollering. The plan was to record all four shows that day so we'd have enough tape to work with. I think Mr. Neely and Chuck Seitz, the engineers, had six or eight mikes, two crowd monitors in front, one above the crowd, and then the mikes on me, the band, and the Flames.

The other acts on the bill were Olatunji, the Sensations, Curley Mays, and Pigmeat Markham. Yvonne Fair had a solo spot, and so did Baby Lloyd. On the twenty-fourth I was going around backstage telling the Flames and the band not to get nervous, and I guess I was probably the most nervous of all. I wasn't worried about performing; I was worried about the recording coming off good. I had a lot riding on it, not just my own money but my reputation because here I was having to prove myself to Mr. Nathan and them all over again, just like when I had to demo "Try Me." I was standing in the wings thinking about all this when Fats stepped up to the microphone and did his intro:

"So now, ladies and gentlemen, it is startime. Are you ready for startime?" *Yeah!* "Thank you and thank you very kindly. It is indeed a great pleasure to present to you at this particular time, nationally and internationally known as the *Hardest* Working Man in Show Business, the man that sings, 'I'll Go Crazy'" . . . *a fanfare from the band: Taaaaa!* "'You've Got the Power'" . . . *Taaaaa!* "'Think'" . . . *Taaaaa!* "'If You Want Me'" . . . *Taaaaa!* "'I Don't Mind'" . . . *Taaaaa!* "'Bewildered'" . . . *Taaaaa!* "million-dollar seller 'Lost Someone'" . . . *Taaaaa!* "the very latest release, 'Night Train'" . . . *Taaaaa!* "Let's everybody 'Shout and Shimmy'" . . . *Taaaaa!* "Mr. Dynamite, the amazing Mr. 'Please Please' himself, the star of the show . . . James Brown and the Famous Flames."

Then the band went into the chaser—the little up-tempo vamp we used between songs—and I hit the stage. As soon as I was into "I'll Go Crazy" I knew it was one of those good times. That's a hard feeling to describe—being on stage, performing, and knowing that you've really got it that night. It feels like God is blessing you, and you give more and more. The audience was with me, screaming and hollering on all the songs, and I thought, "Man, this is really going to do it."

It's a funny thing, though. When I'm up on stage I'm very aware of everything that's going on around me—what the band and the backup singers are doing, how the audience is reacting, how the sound system's working, all that. When you work small clubs you watch the door, check out how rough the crowd looks, listen for little pitch changes in your one little amplifier that tell you it's about to blow out. You can't just be thinking about the song or how pretty you look up there. You learn to be aware.

As the show went along I started noticing little things and filing them away in my mind. Every now and then the band made a mistake or the Flames were a half tone off. Sometimes I hollered where I usually didn't in the song, and some of the audience down front was too enthusiastic. A little old lady down front kept yelling, "Sing it motherf——r, sing it!" She looked like she must have been seventy-five years old. I could hear her the whole time and knew the overhead crowd mike was right above her. Mr. Neely had strung it on a wire between the two side balconies. Most

---

4. Brown was paying for the recording because of Nathan's initial objections.

times none of those things would've mattered, but we were recording and I was thinking, "Oh, Lord, this take's ruined."

During a quiet stretch of "Lost Someone" the woman let out a loud scream, and the audience laughed right in the middle of this serious song. I thought "Well, there goes that song, too." Then I thought I had better try to fix it some kind of way so I started preaching: "You know we all make mistakes sometimes, and the only way we can correct our mistakes is we got to try one more time. So I got to sing this song to you one more time." I stretched out the song, hoping we could get something we could use; then I went into "Please."

Mr. Neely brought the tape into a back room between the first two shows and played it for us on a little tape recorder. As soon as we heard the little old lady, we all busted out laughing. He didn't understand. All he could hear was her high piercing voice, but he didn't really understand what she was saying even though it was clear as a bell. Finally, somebody told him. *Then* he understood.

"Oh no," he said. "I can't have that. I have to get it out of there and make sure she's not here for the other shows, too. This is terrible."

He was getting all worked up, while all the cats were listening to it over and over, laughing, having a great time, and getting other cats to listen to it. After a while, watching everybody carry on, Mr. Neely settled himself down and said, "Hey, maybe we've got something here."

He found the lady down front and told her he'd buy her candy and popcorn and give her $10 if she'd stay for the other three shows—he didn't tell her why. He moved the overhead mike so it wouldn't pick her up so strong. We were using two-track, which meant practically mixing as we went along. She stayed for the next three shows and hollered the same thing every time I did a spin or something she liked. It was like it was on cue. I think the shows got even better as the day went along. By the end of the last one we had four reels of tape. Mr. Neely was so excited he brought the master up to the dressing rooms and passed around the headphones for us to listen. None of us had ever heard ourselves live like that. It sounded fantastic. We knew we really had something.

By this time we had completely forgotten about the finale, where all the acts change clothes and come out on stage together to close the show. Everybody else had changed and was waiting backstage, but we were listening to the tape over and over. Never did do that finale.

A lot of people don't understand about the hollering I do. A man once came up to me in a hotel lobby and said, "So you're James Brown. You make a million dollars, and all you do is scream and holler."

"Yes," I said, very quiet, "but I scream and holler on key."

I was branching out in a lot of directions. At the end of 1962 I formed my own song publishing company, Jim Jam Music, and got King to give me my own label, Try Me. I had already been producing on Federal and King and Dade and wanted to bring it all together on Try Me. I wasn't content to be only a performer and be used by other people; I wanted to be a complete show business person: artist, businessman, entrepreneur. It was important to be because people of my origin hadn't been allowed to get into the *business* end of show business before, just the *show* part.

By this time Mr. Neely had finished editing the *Live at the Apollo* tape. He had a good mix of the performance and the audience, and he had fixed all the cussing so it wasn't right up front. He figured it would become an underground thing for people who knew what the lady was screaming; he was right too. He worked on the tape a long time and did a fantastic job of mixing it.

When Mr. Nathan finally heard the tape he hated it. "This is not coming out," he said. "We have a certain standard, and we're going to stick with it." What he didn't like now was the way we went from one tune to another without stopping. He just couldn't understand that. I guess he was expecting exact copies of our earlier records, but with people politely applauding in between. He had all kinds of theories about how records should be. He wanted the hook right up front because he knew that disc jockeys auditioned hundreds of records every week by putting the needle down and playing only the first fifteen or twenty seconds. If that didn't grab them, they went on to the next record. The same thing happened in record stores, where they usually let you hear fifteen or twenty seconds on a player on the counter. A lot of my things were more like stage numbers, and he couldn't understand that. After more conversation, he finally agreed to put the album out. I think Mr. Neely was the one who finally sold him on it.

After all the editing and all the arguing it was January 1963 before *Live at the Apollo* was finally released. Then discussion began about what singles to release off it. Byrd thought "Think" should be spun off it, especially since the live version was so different from the version we'd put out before. Some people thought "Try Me" was going to do it again, some people had faith in "Lost Someone."

The idea of a smash *album* was far from anybody's mind. Those were the days when most popular albums had only one hit on them plus filler. Mr. Nathan was waiting to see which tune the radio stations were going to play from the album, and then he would shoot it out as a single. I said, "What do you mean? We're not going to take any singles off it. Sell it the way it is."

"James," he said, "all the money I've made in this business I made off singles. That's how it's done. As soon as we get the reports from the radio stations, we're going to start releasing singles."

"Nosir, Mr. Nathan," I said. "No singles."

"You've been paid. You have no say in it anymore, James."

I didn't give him no more argument. I still had faith in the album. While he was waiting to see what would break off the album, King put out the "Prisoner of Love" single in April; it crossed over into the pop market and made it to the top twenty. It was very different from the raw stuff on the *Live* album, which was starting to build momentum.

When Mr. Nathan checked the radio stations to see what was being played off the album, he got a surprise; they told him that there *wasn't* a tune the stations were playing. They were playing the whole album. It was unheard of for a station to play a whole album uninterrupted, but a lot of stations with black programming were doing it. You could tune in at a certain time each night to some of them and they would be playing it. Mr. Nathan couldn't believe it, but it convinced him to let the album keep going on its own.

Meantime, it was a standoff between King Records and Mercury.[5] I started to think there was something funny about it; Mercury seemed more interested in putting Mr. Nathan out of business than in recording me on vocals. The doors at King were all but closed; they had beat him, he had nothing to fight with. I felt bad about it, so I went to Arthur Smith's studio in Charlotte, North Carolina, cut "Papa's Got a

---

5. Brown had tried to get out of his contract with King and had released a single on Mercury. This single, "Out of Sight," was an important precursor to "Papa's Got a Brand New Bag" (see *The Godfather of Soul*, 148–49, and Brown's up-tempo performance of the song in the famous *T.A.M.I. Show* from late 1964).

Brand New Bag," and sent the tape to Mr. Nathan. It was done underground—I had
to sneak the tape to him.

The song started out as a vamp we did during the stage show. There was a little
instrumental riff and I hollered: "Papa's got a bag of his own!" I decided to expand
it into a song and cut it pretty quick to help Mr. Nathan, so when we went into the
studio I was holding a lyric sheet in my hand while I recorded it. We were still going
for that live-in-the-studio sound, so we cranked up and did the first take.

It's hard to describe what it was I was going for; the song has gospel feel, but
it's put together out of jazz licks. And it has a different sound—a snappy, fast-
hitting thing from the bass and the guitars. You can hear Jimmy Nolen, my guitar
player at the time, starting to play scratch guitar, where you squeeze the strings
tight and quick against the frets so the sound is hard and fast without any sustain.
He was what we called a chanker; instead of playing the whole chord and using
all the strings, he hit his chords on just three strings. And Maceo played a fantastic
sax solo on the break. We had been doing the vamp on the show for a while, so
most of it was fine, but the lyrics were so new I think I might have gotten some
of them mixed-up on the take. We stopped to listen to the playback to see what
we needed to do on the next take. While we were listening, I looked around the
studio. Everybody—the band, the studio people, *me*—was dancing. Nobody was
standing still.

Pop said, "If I'm paying for this, I don't want to cut any more. This is it."

And that *was* it. That's the way it went out. I had an acetate made and took it to
Frankie Crocker, a deejay in New York. He thought it was terrible, but he put it on the
air and the phones lit up. Then he admitted I was right about it.

"Papa's Bag" was years ahead of its time. In 1965 soul was just really getting popular. Aretha and Otis and Wilson Pickett were out there and getting big. I
was still called a soul singer—I still call myself that—but musically I had already
gone off in a different direction. I had discovered that my strength was not in the
horns, it was in the rhythm. I was hearing everything, even the guitars, like they
were drums. I had found out how to make it happen. On playbacks, when I saw
the speakers jumping, vibrating a certain way, I knew that was it: deliverance. I
could tell from looking at the speakers that the rhythm was right. What I'd started
on "Out of Sight" I took all the way on "Papa's Bag." Later on they said it was the
beginning of funk. I just thought of it as where my music was going. The title told
it all: I had a new bag.

My music was changing as fast as the country. The things I'd started doing in "Papa's
Bag" and "Cold Sweat," and other tunes around that time, I was taking even further
now. In the middle of 1967 Nat Jones left the band and was replaced by Alfred "Pee
Wee" Ellis as musical director. He was really in sync with what I was trying to do. He
played alto, tenor, and some keyboards. Maceo, after a hitch in the army, came back
in April that year. I still had St. Clair Pinkney and L. D. Williams on saxes. Joe Dupars
and Waymond Reed played trumpets; Jimmy Nolen and Alphonso Kellum gave me
that distinctive scratch guitar sound; and John "Jabo" Starks and Clyde Stubblefield
were two of the funkiest drummers you could find. They did it to *death*.

I started off 1968 by buying my first radio station. I got into the radio business
because of all the things going on in the country. I believed in human rights—not civil
rights, *human* rights of *all* people everywhere—and I loved my country. But I would
speak out for my people, too. That was part of loving my country. I thought we
needed pride and economic power and, most important of all, education. So I bought
WGYW which I changed to WJBE, in Knoxville, Tennessee.

I know people might not believe it but I didn't go into it to make money. First, I thought black communities need stations that really served them and represented them. The station I bought in Knoxville had been a black-oriented station, but it had gone off the air. When I put it back on I kept a format of soul and gospel and jazz—the whole spectrum of black music. We had talk shows, too, and editorials and programs directed at the kids to get them to stay in school. We directed a lot of it at their parents, too, encouraging them to give their kids the support they needed.

Second, I wanted my station to be a media training ground so black people could do more than just be jocks. I wanted them to learn advertising, programming, and management at all levels. Third, as owner I wanted to be a symbol of the black entrepreneur. All three of these reasons were, to me, part of education. That was real black power.

Eventually I bought two more radio stations, WEBB in Baltimore and WRDW in Augusta. At that time there were around five hundred black-oriented radio stations in the country, but only five of them were owned by black people—three of those were mine. I did the same thing with my other two stations that I did in Knoxville. We used to joke that WEBB really stood for "We Enjoy Being Black." WRDW was really special because that was in my hometown.

We did many political things on the stations, editorials that irritated a lot of people. Sometimes I would cut an editorial and just say what I was really thinking. I wasn't a radio professional, so some of 'em were a little too raw for the FCC and they got on us every now and then. With the war in Vietnam and the unrest at home, you couldn't avoid politics during that time.

> Brown re-formed his band in 1970. New members included bassist "Bootsy" Collins and his brother, guitarist "Catfish" Collins. Bootsy later went on to fame with Parliament-Funkadelic and with his own Rubber Band.

Bootsy and the others turned out to be the nucleus of a very good band. They were studio musicians so when I hummed out solos and things they knew how to give me what I wanted. I think Bootsy learned a lot from me. When I met him he was playing a lot of bass—the ifs, the ands and the buts. I got him to see the importance of the *one* in funk—the downbeat at the beginning of every bar. I got him to key in on the dynamic parts of the one instead of playing all around it. Then he could do all his other stuff in the right places—*after* the one.

I think the first thing of my own I recorded with the new band was "Hot Pants (She Got to Use What She Got to Get What She Wants)," and it was one of my biggest records.[6] It came out in July 1971 and went to number 1 on the soul charts and number 15 on the pop charts. At the same time I recorded another live album at the Apollo, *Revolution of the Mind*, a two-record set that came out in December. In August I followed up "Hot Pants" with "Make It Funky," which went to number 1 on the soul chart, and with "I'm a Greedy Man," which went to number 7. Those songs did well on the pop charts, too. Most of my music right on through the mid-seventies did, but a funny thing was happening to music on the radio then. It was

---

6. The "new band" referred to here is the one Brown formed after the Collins brothers departed and included Fred Wesley as arranger and trombonist.

starting to get segregated again, not just by black and white but by *kinds:* country, pop, hard rock, soft rock, every kind you could name. Radio formats became very rigid. Because of that and because of my political thing, about 80 percent of the popular stations in the country would not play James Brown records. But my sales were so strong to Afro-Americans and some hip whites that they couldn't keep me off the pop charts. Matter of fact, in all of the seventies I tied with Elvis for the most charted pop hits—thirty-eight. The bad thing about it is that I was making some of my strongest music during that period, and I think most whites have been deprived of it.

Because of my stuff, Polydor was really starting to hit the charts for the first time. My first album for them, *Hot Pants,* came out soon after I signed. *Revolution of the Mind* came out in December. At the beginning of 1972 I released "Talkin' Loud and Sayin' Nothing" and "King Heroin," which was a rap song like "Get Up, Get Into It, Get Involved" and "America Is My Home." But, really the very first rap in my career was a thing I did back in 1963 called "Choo-Choo (Locomotion)." We were in the studio at King one night recording it and it just wasn't happening. It was about two or three in the morning, and Mr. Neely said, "Why don't you just play conductor and call off the names of the towns and talk about them?" So that's what I did.

In August 1972 I opened the Festival of Hope at Roosevelt Raceway on Long Island. It was the first rock festival held to help an *established* charity, the Crippled Children's Society. It was a big show: us, Chuck Berry, Ike and Tina Turner, Billy Preston, Sly and the Family Stone, Stephen Stills, Jefferson Airplane, Commander Cody, and so on. The festival didn't bring in as much money as everybody hoped, but it was worth it if it brought in anything. I had visited an Easter Seal summer day camp in Albertson, New York, and my heart went out to those kids.

Right before the festival I put out "Get on the Good Foot." Afrika Bambaataa says it's the song that people first started break dancing to. I feel solidarity with the breakers and rappers and the whole hip hop thing—as long as it's clean. Their stuff is an extension of things I was doing for a long time: rapping over a funky beat about pride and respect and education and drugs and all kinds of issues. I did what I said in the songs: I got up, got into it, and got involved. I was determined to have a say, and I thought anybody with a big following had a responsibility to speak out like I'd done with "America Is My Home" and with "Black and Proud."

By the middle of 1975 disco had broken big. Disco is a simplification of a lot of what I was doing, of what they *thought* I was doing. Disco is a very small part of funk. It's the end of the song, the repetitious part, like a vamp. The difference is that in funk, you dig into a groove, you don't stay on the surface. Disco stayed on the surface. See, I taught 'em everything *they* know, but not everything *I* know.

Disco was easy for artists to get into because they really didn't have to do anything. It was all electronic sequencers and beats-per-minute—it was done with machines. They just cheated on the music world. They thought they could dress up in a Superfly outfit, play one note, and that would make them a star. But that was not the answer. It destroyed the musical basis many people worked so hard to build up in the sixties. The record companies loved disco because it was a producer's music. You don't really need artists to make disco. They didn't have to worry about an artist not cooperating; machines can't talk back and, unlike artists, they don't have to be paid. What disco became was a lawyer's recording; the attorneys were making records.

Disco hurt me in a lot of ways. I was trying to make good hard funk records that Polydor was trying to soften up, while people were buying records that had no substance. The disco people copied off me and tried to throw me away and go with young people. You can't do that. You have to come back to the source. Disco hurt live music in general. The black concert business was already hurting. Whites wouldn't come even if the black artist had big record sales. Black America was in a serious recession; there was just no money in the black community. Later on, that situation hurt records sales, too. For everybody.

Further Reading

Brackett, David. "James Brown's 'Superbad' and the Double-Voiced Utterance." In *Interpreting Popular Music*, 108–56. Berkeley: University of California Press, [1995] 2000.

Brown, Geoff. *The Life of James Brown*. London: Omnibus Press, [1996] 2008.

Brown, James (with Marc Eliot). *I Feel Good: A Memoir of a Life of Soul*. New York: New American Library, 2005.

Danielsen, Anne. *Presence and Pleasure: The Funk Grooves of James Brown and Parliament*. Middletown, Conn.: Wesleyan University Press, 2006.

Ramsey, Guthrie P., Jr. *Race Music: Black Cultures from Bebop to Hip-Hop*. Berkeley: University of California Press, 2003.

Stewart, Alexander. "'Funky Drummer': New Orleans, James Brown and the Rhythmic Transformation of American Popular Music." *Popular Music* 19 (2000): 293–318.

Wolk, Douglas. *James Brown's* Live at the Apollo *(33 1/3)*. New York: Continuum, 2004.

Discography

Brown, James. *Live at the Apollo Theater*. King/Polydor, 1963.

_____. *Star Time*. Polydor/UMGD, 1991.

The J. B.s. *Pass the Peas: The Best of the J. B.'s*. Polydor, 2000.

34. "The Blues Changes from Day to Day"

During 1965–66, the Southern Soul sound gained prominence in tandem with Motown. Southern Soul recordings tended to eschew some of the complexities of Motown arrangements, emphasizing (like

James Brown) the gospel roots of the music and presenting a looser, more spontaneous-seeming sound. Among these artists, Otis Redding (1941–67), from Macon, Georgia, achieved a special sort of notoriety with the white counterculture by being the only soul artist to appear at the Monterey Pop Festival in 1967. While Redding had been one of the most consistently successful artists associated with Stax and a staple on the R&B radio for years, his exposure to the white audience had been fairly limited up to that time. His greatest commercial triumph, "(Sittin' on) The Dock of the Bay" (number one on the pop and R&B charts early in 1968), followed his death in a plane crash in December 1967. The following interview from 1967 reflects the newfound interest in Redding among the pop and rock audiences and touches on Redding's views about the musical relationships between black and white performers, as well as the differences between Motown and Stax. The initials "J. D." stand for Jim Delehant, the editor of *Hit Parader* who conducted the interview in the summer of 1967.

Otis Redding Interview
Jim Delehant

J.D: *What do you dislike about England?*

Otis: Nothing. I loved England from head to toe. I love the weather, the people. I was there in the summer and it was nice. The people are so groovy; they treated me like I was somebody. They took me wherever I wanted to go. I loved Paris too.

J.D: *Did you find any language problems with your audiences in Paris?*

Otis: No, they sang along with almost all the songs. But England is a beautiful country. If I were to leave the U.S., I'd live in England. But I'd never leave the U.S. I own a 400-acre farm in Macon, Georgia. I raise cattle and hogs. I own horses too. I love horses as much as singing. I'd like to hunt on horseback.

J.D: *Tell us about the album you recorded with Carla Thomas.*

Otis: Carla and I worked on this album for three days. We do things like "It Takes Two" that Marvin Gaye and Kim Weston did. And we do "Tramp" by Lowell Fulsom. I wrote an original called "Oo Wee Baby." We do "Tell It Like It Is." There's a lot of great stuff on it.

J.D: *Your voices are so different. Did you have any problems working together?*

Otis: My voice right today is hoarse from working on the album. We didn't have any problems working at all. I went in first and sang my part, and then she came in and overdubbed her part. We used Booker T. & MG's too. Booker played both the piano and the organ. We cut eleven songs in three days.

J.D: *How did you write "Respect"?*

Otis: That's one of my favorite songs because it has a better groove than any of my records. It says something too: "What you want, baby you got it. What you need

Source: "Otis Redding Interview," by Jim Delehant, includes Otis My Favorite Records, May 1967 H.P. "Tell the Truth" license notes July 1970.

baby, you got it. All I'm asking for is a little respect when I come home." The song lyrics are great. The band track is beautiful. It took me a whole day to write it and about twenty minutes to arrange it. We cut it once and that was it. Everybody wants respect, you know.

J.D: *Why did you choose to do "Satisfaction"?*

Otis: That came from Steve Cropper and Booker. We were all in the studio one day to record an album and they suggested I do "Satisfaction." They asked me if I had heard the new Rolling Stones song but I hadn't heard it. They played the record for me and everybody liked it except me. If you notice, I use a lot of words different from the Stones' version—that's because I made it up.

J.D: *Were you in the music business before you joined Stax?*

Otis: No, I used to be a well driller. I made a $1.25 an hour drilling wells in Macon, Georgia. One day I drove a friend of mine, Johnny Jenkins, up to do a recording session. They had thirty minutes left in the studio and I asked if I could do a song, "These Arms of Mine." They did it and it sold about 800,000 copies. I've been going ever since. I wrote that song in 1960 when I wasn't even thinking about the music business. I recorded it in November, 1962. I tried the song out with a small recording company but it didn't do anything. I knew it was saying something though. I dug the words.

J.D: *What was the first music you heard that impressed you deeply?*

Otis: My mother and father and I used to go to parties when I was a kid. We used to go out to a place called Sawyer's Lake in Macon. There was a calypso song out then called "Run, Joe." My mother and daddy used to play that for me all the time. I just dug the groove. Ever since then I've been playing music. As I was growing up, I did a lot of talent shows. I won fifteen Sunday nights straight in a series of talent shows in Macon. I showed up the sixteenth night and they wouldn't let me go on anymore. Whatever success I had was through the help of the good Lord.

J.D: *What do you think of people like Muddy Waters and Jimmy Reed?*

Otis: I dig them because they give me a lot of ideas. I listen to them a lot.

J.D: *Do you like harmonica?*

Otis: Yes, I love harmonica. I haven't done one on record, yet, but I might try. I play it a little. It's easy. I play piano too—the chords. I write songs with my guitar.

J.D: *How many pieces do you have in your band?*

Otis: I used to have ten, but now I have eight. I cut it down because it was getting away from my sound. I have two trumpets, two tenors, guitar, bass, drums and organ.

J.D: *What do you think of Sam and Dave and the Righteous Brothers?*

Otis: I'll tell you. When I first heard the Righteous Brothers, I thought they were colored. I think they sing better than Sam and Dave. But Sam and Dave are much better showmen. Sam and Dave have been together for ten or twelve years. I think Sam and Dave are my favorites.

J.D: *Why do you think white blues performers are so much more successful than the originals?*

Otis: Because the white population is much larger than the colored. I like what these rock and roll kids are doing. Sometimes they take things from us, but I take things from them too. The things that are beautiful, and they do a lot of beautiful things.

J.D: *What do you think of Eric Burdon?*

Otis: Now, Eric is one of the best friends I have. He's a great guy. I like the way he works. I like the way he sings, too. He's a good blues performer. I've seen him work in a club in England. This boy came on stage with a blues song and he tore the house up. They called me up on stage after he finished and I wouldn't go up. I knew I couldn't do anything to top it. Eric can really sing blues.

J.D: *Any blues by the Stones you like?*

Otis: No. I like their uptempo songs. They really groove on "Satisfaction." It's too much. I like their original things better. They can't do anybody else's songs.

J.D: *You're a producer and manager now, aren't you?*

Otis: I have an artist that just came out on Atlantic Records named Arthur Conley. He does one of my songs, "Sweet Soul Music." It's uptempo and he does it beautifully. I manage him and record him. My band is on the record too.

J.D: *What's the difference between rock and roll and rhythm and blues?*

Otis: Everybody thinks that all the songs by colored people are rhythm and blues but that's not true. Johnny Taylor, Muddy Waters and B. B. King are blues musicians. James Brown is not a blues singer. He has a rock and roll beat and he can sing slow pop songs. My own songs "Respect" and "Mr. Pitiful," aren't blues songs. I'm speaking in terms of the beat and structure of the music. A blues is a song that goes twelve bars all the way through. Most of my songs are soul songs. When I go in to record a song, I only have the title and maybe a first verse. The rest I make up as we're recording. We'll cut it three or four times and I'll sing it different every time. You know, once I cut a song, I can't pantomime it on a TV show. I've goofed TV shows every time. I missed the lyrics. I'd be going my own way but then I'd catch up.

J.D: *What's the difference between the Stax sound and the Motown sound?*

Otis: Motown does a lot of overdubbing. It's mechanically done. At Stax the rule is whatever you feel, play it. We cut everything together—horns, rhythm, and vocals. We'll do it three or four times, go back and listen to the results and pick the best one. If somebody doesn't like a line in the song, we'll go back and cut the whole song over. Until last year, we didn't even have a four-track tape recorder. You can't overdub on a one-track machine. Like yesterday, we cut six songs in five hours for my album with Carla. They were perfect songs, and they'll all be in the album.

J.D: *Do you think R&B has changed a great deal?*

Otis: Yes, I'd like to say something to the R&B singers who were around ten years ago. They've got to get out of the old bag. Listen to the beat of today and use it on records. Don't say we're gonna go back ten years and use this old swing shuffle. That's not it. I know what the kids want today, and I aim all my stuff at them. I'd like to see all those singers make it again. I'd like to take Fats Domino, Little Richard, Big Joe Turner, Clyde McPhatter and bring them into the bag of today. They'd have hits all over again. The blues changes from day to day. It all depends on what the kids will be dancing to, what they're moving to. I watch people when I sing. If they're stompin' their foot, or snappin' their fingers, then I know I got something. But if they don't move, then you don't have anything. Five years from now, I know the kids are going to be tired of my singing. If I can keep a good mind with the help of the good Lord, I'm gonna keep producing records. You can't have anything else on your mind but the music business. When I go into the studio, I'm strictly for business. I can go in there any time of the day and cut six songs if I want to. I don't like any fooling around in the studio.

J.D: *Do you like country and western music?*

Otis: Oh yeah. Before I started singing, maybe ten years ago, I loved anything that Hank Williams sang. Eddy Arnold does some groovy things, too. Everybody's got their own bag and if they're doing something good, I can hear it.

J.D: *From your experience, what's the best advice you could give to someone who wants to get in the business?*

Otis: If you want to be a singer, you've got to concentrate on it 24 hours a day. You can't be a well driller, too. You've got to concentrate on the business of entertaining and writing songs. Always think different from the next person. Don't ever do a song as you heard somebody else do it. Concentrate and practice every single day. It took me four years to get into show business in a big way. Also I think it's very important to write your own songs.

Further Reading

Bowman, Rob. *Soulsville, U.S.A.: The Story of Stax Records.* New York: Schirmer Books, 1997.

Freeman, Scott. *Otis!: The Otis Redding Story.* New York: St. Martin's Griffin, 2002.

Guralnick, Peter. *Sweet Soul Music: Rhythm and Blues and the Southern Dream of Freedom.* New York: Harper & Row, 1986.

Ware, Vron, and Les Back. *Out of Whiteness: Color, Politics, and Culture.* Chicago: University of Chicago Press, 2002.

See also "Further Reading" for Chapter 34.

Discography

Booker T. and the M.G.s. *The Definitive Soul Collection.* Atlantic, 2006.

Redding, Otis. *Pain in My Heart.* Stax, 1964.

_____. *The Great Otis Redding Sings Soul Ballads.* Stax, 1965.

_____. *The Dock of the Bay.* Stax, 1968.

_____. *The Very Best of Otis Redding.* Elektra/WEA, 1992.

_____ and Carla Thomas. *King and Queen.* Stax, 1967.

35. Aretha Franklin Earns Respect

In 1967–68, Aretha Franklin's version of Otis Redding's "Respect" and James Brown's "Say It Loud (I'm Black and I'm Proud)" signaled soul music's entry into a new phase of political engagement. The emergence of Aretha Franklin (b. 1942), one of the first solo female stars in the genre, had a huge impact: her tremendous range, mastery of all aspects of gospel singing technique, and sturdy gospel piano playing, applied to consistently excellent material (some of which she wrote or cowrote), resulted in a series of brilliant recordings in 1967–70, during which time she sold more records than any other African American artist. Her recordings from the late 1960s include, in addition to "Respect," such anthems as "I Never Loved a Man (the Way I Love You)," "Natural Woman (You Make Me Feel Like a)," "Chain of Fools," and "Think." While her other recordings did not have quite the broad political resonance of "Respect," these hits did convey a sense of pride and strength not previously expressed by black female singers.

Aretha Franklin's success brought with it media coverage from a wide range of publications. The following article from *Ebony* seeks to present Franklin to a then-growing black middle-class readership. This orientation may be responsible for the emphasis on Franklin's "homebody" persona in the article, although it should be noted that other articles and subsequent profiles on her also tend toward superficiality, perhaps because she is a famously reticent interviewee. The opening passage of the piece emphasizes the connection between Franklin and her audience, evoking gospel music's ritualistic power in a secular setting—in the words of the author Phyl Garland, Franklin exudes a "magnetic appeal that exceeds simple entertainment." Garland details Franklin's background in the Baptist church and the impact of the church on her development as a musician, ranging from her father's career as a famous preacher to her own early experiences as a teenage gospel singer; in one revealing passage, she reflects on the importance of timing in her music and observes how she owes this sense of timing to her father's singing and, perhaps a bit more surprising, to his preaching. Her father's position as a famous minister also brought Franklin into early contact with several musicians who influenced her, from famous gospel singers such as James Cleveland and Clara Ward to gospel singers who achieved fame in popular music like Sam Cooke and Lou Rawls. This piece also underscores the importance of Franklin's switch from Columbia to Atlantic Records and the simultaneous move from an "easy listening" pop-jazz style to one based more on her gospel roots.

The relationship of soul music and "soul" in general to the black church and to changing notions of black racial self-consciousness is another focus of the article, which came at a moment when racial politics were assuming a higher and more militant profile, and as public awareness about black nationalism and the black power movement was increasing. These larger political currents form (at least part of) the context that enabled recordings like "Respect" and "Think" to resonate so strongly with African American audiences.[1]

Aretha Franklin—"Sister Soul": Eclipsed Singer Gains New Heights
Phyl Garland

It had been an ordinary evening, so far as the noisy, star-crowded events called jazz festivals are concerned. Some considerate deity seemingly had answered the promoter's prayer that it wouldn't rain as more than 35,000 fans huddled in the stands or rocked their folding chairs on the grass of Downing Stadium on Randall's Island, a little bit of New York rising in the East River within walking distance of Harlem. In a relaxed atmosphere suggestive of an evening picnic, they elbowed their way through clusters of competitors for a dwindling supply of hot dogs and beer, grumbled about defects in the sound system, talked loudly during acts that were not their favorites, and, above all, awaited the top-billed performers in a show heavily steeped in gospel-flavored funk. They were pleased enough, but some singer or instrumentalist had yet to unleash their full capacity to enjoy. Then the moment came when a full-bodied young woman with a chocolate-brown face offset by a pink brocade gown came onto the stage to be greeted by a chorus of expectant shouts, cheers and applause that were soon transformed into frenzied hand-clapping and foot-tapping. It was the sort of unbridled response that is accorded only a star, a favorite, an entertainer possessing the uncommon ability to electrify an audience.

For the singer, Aretha Franklin, the piano-plunking, earthy-sounding daughter of a Detroit minister, it was a resounding "amen" to all the words and emotions she

---

1. For accounts of Franklin's first recordings for Atlantic, a momentous event in the history of recent popular music, see the following: Jerry Wexler and David Ritz, *Rhythm and the Blues: A Life in American Music* (New York: Alfred A. Knopf, 1993), 208–11; Peter Guralnick, *Sweet Soul Music: Rhythm and Blues and the Southern Dream of Freedom* (New York: Harper and Row, 1986), 339–42; and Aretha Franklin (and David Ritz), *Aretha: From These Roots* (New York: Villard, 1999), 109–10, 123–24.

has projected in a series of top-selling record hits that have added a new dimension to her precocious but uneven career. Within less than a year, the one-time gospel singer has returned from near obscurity to achieve a level of popularity where she is regarded by many a fan as "sister soul herself." Under a contract negotiated with Atlantic Records in late 1966, she has released three consecutive million-selling singles. Her first album on that label, *I Never Loved a Man the Way I Love You*, is a certified million-seller, with a second album, *Aretha Arrives*, nosing its way up on the charts. Triumph in the recording world has, in turn, brought honors from the arbiters of public taste—three awards from the National Association of Radio Announcers for being the top female vocalist who produced the top single record and top album for 1967; recognition from Record World, Billboard and Cashbox magazines as a leading artist.

However, her success can be measured in more than monetary terms, for Aretha's version of the Otis Redding composition *Respect* stands, week after week, at the head of JET magazine's Soul Brothers Top 20 Tunes poll and is considered by far more than a few of those "brothers" to be "the new Negro national anthem." Due to this magnetic appeal that exceeds simple entertainment, Dr. Martin Luther King's Southern Christian Leadership Conference presented her with a special citation at the organization's convention in Atlanta, Ga., this summer.

All this sudden adulation might overwhelm some, but not Aretha, who endured the experience of almost making it once before, only to become a comet that apparently burnt out too soon. A reticent person whose basic shyness might be mistaken for hostility or indifference, she is aware of where she has been and where she wants to go. "I don't feel very different," she states with a quiet simplicity that belies her ebullience in song. "People ask for my autograph now and that's real nice, but I don't think it puts you up on any pedestal. You can't get carried away with it." She is quick to acknowledge the ups and downs that came in the wake of her earlier success, in 1961, when John Hammond, the man credited with discovering Billie Holiday, said she had "the best voice I've come across in 20 years," and signed her to an exclusive contract with Columbia Records.

Though some of her recordings from that period gained critical favor, namely *Today I Sing the Blues*, *Try a Little Tenderness* and *Skylark*, she failed to break into the top money-making level of the big hits and, after a while, her public following began to fade. "Things were kinda hungry then," she says of the interim years, adding, "I might just be 25, but I'm an old woman in disguise . . . 25 goin' on 63."

If the appeal of her music can be linked to the sum of her experiences as a human being, a significant portion of it lies in her early background. She was born in Memphis, Tenn., one of three daughters and two sons of a Baptist minister father, the Rev. C. L. Franklin, who went on to become a noted radio and recording artist, and a musically gifted mother who died when Aretha was a child. Though the family soon moved to Buffalo, N.Y., and later Detroit, Mich., the South left an imprint on her speech with its softened endings on words. When Aretha was "about eight or nine," she began trying to teach herself how to play the piano by listening to Eddie Heywood records, "just bangin', not playin', but finding a little somethin' here and there." Her father noticed her efforts and hired a piano teacher whose approach was scorned by the young Aretha. "When she'd come, I'd hide," she recalls. "I tried for maybe a week, but I just couldn't take it. She had all those little baby books and I wanted to go directly to the tunes." This failure was overcome, shortly afterwards, by the arrival of James Cleveland, the noted gospel singer, who came to live with the family. "He showed me some real nice chords and I liked his deep, deep sound," Aretha remembers. "There's a whole lot of earthiness in the way he sings, and what he was feelin', I was feelin', but I just didn't know how to put it across. The more

I watched him, the more I got out of it." Cleveland helped Aretha, her older sister Erma and two other girls form a gospel group that appeared at local churches but lasted only eight months because "we were too busy fussin' and fightin.'" But in this group, Aretha got her first public experience as a singer and sometime pianist. Another gospel artist who left a deep impression on Aretha was Clara Ward. "I wasn't really that conscious of the gospel sound," she explains, "but I liked all Miss Ward's records. I learned to play 'em because I thought one day she might decide she didn't want to play and I'd be ready."

The Franklin household was a fertile one for the development of musical talent. Because of her father's prominence as an evangelist, Aretha had an opportunity to meet artists of more than one genre. Mahalia Jackson, Arthur Pryscock, B. B. King, Dorothy Donegan and the late Dinah Washington were likely houseguests. She met Lou Rawls when he was an unknown singer with the Pilgrim Travelers and became a friend of the late Sam Cooke when he appeared at her father's church with the Soul Stirrers. She remembers Cooke as being "just beautiful, a sort of person who stood out among *many* people." Along with Sam Cooke, James Cleveland and Clara Ward, one of the celebrities who impressed Aretha tremendously with "the way he could just sit down and play" was the blind jazz pianist Art Tatum. "I just cancelled that out for me and knew that I could never do that, but he left a strong impression on me as a pianist and a person." Above all others, Aretha credits her father with having the greatest artistic influence on her in his singing style and his more broadly acknowledged fusion of rhythm and words in preaching. "Most of what I learned vocally came from him," she readily admits. "He gave me a sense of timing in music and timing is important in everything."

Before entering her teens, Aretha had become a member of the youth choir at New Bethel Baptist Church, which Rev. Franklin pastors in the heart of Detroit's black ghetto. Occasionally she was soloist and during four important years of her adolescence, she toured the country with her father's evangelistic troupe. During one of those tours, she recorded her version of *Never Grow Old* and *Precious Lord, Take My Hand*, which are still regarded as classics in the gospel vein and established her reputation as a child singer. However, at the time, she had no dreams of becoming a star or an entertainer of any sort. Her primary ambition was to become "just a housewife."

Fate didn't play it that way.

When Aretha was 18, yet another friend, Major "Mule" Holly, bassist for the jazz pianist Teddy Wilson, convinced her that she had a certain basic style that could be commercially salable if applied to jazz or popular music. Though rumors persist that the religiously oriented elder Franklin opposed his daughter's pursuit of a secular career, he actually escorted her to New York City when she made her first demonstration records to be presented to commercial firms. His opinion has been that "one should make his own life and take care of his own business. If she feels she can do what she is doing as successfully as she does it, I have nothing against it. I like most kinds of music myself." He observes that in his congregation there was "at first a quiet and subdued resentment, but now they acclaim her in loud terms."

For Aretha, the experience of being thrust into a different milieu was, if not traumatic, somewhat difficult. As she attended classes in New York that were intended to polish her as a performer and personality, she was confronted with the problems that face most fledgling entertainers. She was ensnarled in hassles with booking agents and managers that earned her a reputation for being difficult to handle. As the first glimmer of success began to vanish, she retreated into silence, returning to Detroit and a personal life that she secludes from the public. In 1963, she did appear at the Newport Jazz Festival and the Lower Ohio Jazz Festival, and in subsequent years played Bermuda, the Bahamas and Puerto Rico. Yet the plum of a major success had not come her way. There was some enthusiasm for a European tour, but her current personal manager, Ted White, who is also her husband, contends that "Her earnings wouldn't have made it possible to take along the musicians who could back her up and show off her talents in the best way. Even in this country, you have to work for practically nothing if you don't have a hit, so she just worked less."

White, a native Detroiter whose experience in show business before his alliance with Aretha was as "a sandlot" promoter not in the major leagues, contends that part of his wife's lag in her previous professional outing was due to the fact that her Columbia recordings were not geared to the rhythm and blues or rock 'n' roll market and, therefore, received limited jukebox and radio attention. A five-year contract with a one-year option precluded any drastic change in approach. "We waited out those years," says White, "but when the time came to move, we were ready. We knew we had something to offer."

When the time did come for a change, Ted and Aretha got a helping hand from Jimmy Bishop, a Philadelphia deejay, and his wife, Louise, who had access to the interested ear of Jerry Wexler, vice-president of Atlantic Records. A new contract resulted and ever since that momentous day, Aretha has been waxing hit after hit. If there is any key to her resurgence, Wexler believes that it is based on the magnitude of her talent as a singer, pianist and prolific song writer.

I'd say that she's a musical genius comparable to that other great musical genius, Ray Charles," says the bearded recording executive who has specialized in "soul" artists for 15 years, having been involved with Wilson Pickett, Solomon Burke, Ruth Brown and Charles during his earlier efforts. He believes that many parallels can be drawn between Aretha and Ray Charles. "Both play a terrific gospel piano, which is one of the greatest assets one can have today," he states. "Since they have this broader talent, they can bring to a recording session a total conception of the music and thus contribute much more than the average artist." According to Wexler, Aretha's recordings evolve out of "head arrangements." She sets the tone for the whole session. Afterwards, strings and other instrumental trappings can be built around her effort. On her first album, Aretha accompanies herself at the piano, though an arm injury sustained during a tour with the Jackie Wilson show early this year prevented her from following through on many of the tunes on her second album. Unknown to much of the public, she was backed, on most of her hit records, through a process of over-dubbing, by a vocal group consisting of Aretha herself and her two sisters, Erma, a recording artist in her own right, and Carolyn, a singer-composer. On other outings, the Sweet Inspirations shared the spotlight. The combination seems to work and the proof is in the success of the sound.

For some artists, the "soul" sound might be a mere artifice, but for Aretha Franklin, it is an element deeply imbedded in herself. She has never learned how to be pretentious enough to build a false image and deeply identifies with people on all levels who hear her music. "Everybody who's living has problems and desires just as I do," she remarks. "When the fellow on the corner has somethin' botherin' him, he feels the same way I do. When we cry, we all gonna cry tears, and when we laugh, we all have to smile." She is not eager to adopt any image of herself as a new queen of the blues and asserts, "The queen of the blues was and still is Dinah Washington." Though her future engagements will include some of the nation's top nightclubs, one-nighters are more suited to her as a rather withdrawn personality. "I dig playin' at night and leavin' in the morning,'" says Aretha.

Away from the public, she shuns crowds, admitting, "When I'm not workin', I like to come in the house and sit down and be very quiet. Sometimes nobody even knows I'm home. I don't care too much about goin' out. By the time I get home, I've had enough of nightclubs."

Her essential tastes are for the same "soul" things she sings about, and she makes no bones about the fact that chitterlings are her favorite food, "with maybe some hot water cornbread and greens or ham."

In the flush of a new affluence that might reap for her a gross income of $500,000 this year, she anticipates, more than anything, moving into a new house she and Ted have purchased in a quiet, tree-shaded section of Detroit that is fast becoming a haven for middle-class Negroes. "I just want a big, comfortable house," she says, "where we can lock the door and have a lot of family fun." There she hopes to pursue a peaceful private life with her mate and her three sons.

While the lure of public acclaim is enticing and she wants to continue selling a million on all her records, Aretha is, underneath it all, a homebody with interests that she refuses to compromise in order to comply with public demands. During a previous phase of her career, she provoked controversy by appearing, in 1963, before an audience in Philadelphia, though eight months pregnant. The shadows of scandal that enshrouded her at the time were fanned by the fact that her secret marriage to her manager, Ted White, had not yet been revealed.

To those who might question anything she does onstage or off, she supplies a single answer: "I must do what is real in me all ways. It might bug some and offend others, but this is what I must live by, the truth, so long as it doesn't impose on others."

Further Reading

Awkward, Michael. *Soul Covers: Rhythm and Blues Remakes and the Struggle for Artistic Identity: Aretha Franklin, Al Green, Phoebe Snow.* Durham, N.C.: Duke University Press, 2007.

Dobkin, Matt. *I Never Loved a Man the Way I Love You: Aretha Franklin, Respect, and the Making of a Soul Music Masterpiece.* New York: St. Martin's Press, 2004.

Franklin, Aretha (and David Ritz). *Aretha: From These Roots.* New York: Villard, 1999.

Guralnick, Peter. *Sweet Soul Music: Rhythm and Blues and the Southern Dream of Freedom.* New York: Harper & Row, 1986.

Wexler, Jerry, and David Ritz. *Rhythm and the Blues: A Life in American Music.* New York: Alfred A. Knopf, 1993.

Discography

Franklin, Aretha. *Aretha.* Columbia, 1961.

_____. *Lady Soul.* Atlantic, 1967.

_____. *I Never Loved a Man the Way I Love You.* Atlantic, 1968.

_____. *Aretha Live at Fillmore West.* Atlantic, 1971.

_____. *The Definitive Soul Collection.* Atlantic/WEA, 1993.

36. The Beatles, the "British Invasion," and Cultural Respectability

The Beatles' music emerged with such distinctiveness from the other popular music of the time that the band's popularity became a media sensation, first in the United Kingdom during 1963, then in the United States in 1964. In the United States, the novelty of a *British* pop group contributed to their singularity and set them apart. The energy and enthusiasm conveyed by their recordings and performances, the variety of repertoire, the musicality and skill of the singing and playing, all conveyed with an irreverence toward establishment figures—these qualities created an effect of overwhelming charisma, especially for the white, middle-class teenagers who made up the bulk of their early audience.

The Beatles consisted of four members: rhythm guitarist John Lennon (1940–80) and bass guitarist Paul McCartney (b. 1942) wrote most of the songs and sang most of the lead vocals, while lead guitarist George Harrison (1943–2001) occasionally contributed songs and sang, with drummer Ringo Starr (Richard Starkey, b. 1940) rounding out the group. In combining the functions of songwriting, singing, and playing, the band recalled some of the pioneers of rock 'n' roll, particularly Chuck Berry, with the important innovation that they were a *band* whose recordings reproduced almost uncannily their sense of camaraderie (in this, they were preceded to some extent by the girl groups and the Beach Boys). The producer of all but one of their albums, George Martin, was also an unusually sympathetic partner; he ensured that the recordings possessed remarkable clarity, gave them a classically trained ear to help with arrangements, and had a knack for recognizing and capturing peak performances.[1] Martin also contributed much to the originality of the Beatles' use of orchestral instruments when they began to use them in 1965. Despite the importance of his contribution, skeptics of the Beatles who assign all credit for their success to Martin are surely overstating their case.

In light of the Beatles' impressive originality, it is easy to lose sight of where they came from. Somewhat in the manner of earlier international multimedia superstars such as Bing Crosby and Elvis Presley, at least some of that originality resulted from the synthesis of preexisting

---

1. Close listening to the Beatles' *Anthology* (three double-CD albums filled with rare recordings and alternate takes) sets provokes few quibbles about whether the best take of a given song was included on the official release.

strains of popular music that had been kept more or less separate. From their start in "skiffle" (a form of folk music performed in a highly rhythmic manner borrowed from "trad" jazz, a British adaptation of New Orleans–style jazz), the Beatles' early performing repertory in numerous nightclub and dance performances consisted of liberal doses of 1950s rhythm and blues (especially Chuck Berry and Little Richard), rockabilly (especially Elvis, Carl Perkins, and the Everly Brothers), Brill Building–produced pop music (especially the songs and arrangements of the girl groups), and the songs and performing style associated with Motown. The Beatles also occasionally included "standards" from pre–rock 'n' roll pop music, especially those that had been recently rere-corded by other artists, and influences from British music hall, a style dating back to the 19th century, also occasionally appeared in their compositions. The Beatles' first two albums, *Please Please Me* and *With the Beatles,* released in the United Kingdom in 1963, mixed cover tunes of their nightclub repertory with original compositions.

The significance of the Beatles extends far beyond their popularity or their ability to create something fresh from a synthesis of previous styles: the Beatles, along with Bob Dylan, did more than any other pop musicians to shift the perception of popular music in the mainstream media.[2] The early article presented here—originally printed unsigned but later attributed to the London *Times* music critic William Mann—shows how critics were taking the Beatles seriously even during the first year of their popularity. Mann, with his musicological terminology, compares the Beatles' musical processes to those used by Austrian composer Gustav Mahler (1860–1911). While some of their most dedi-cated fans may dispute the appropriateness of this terminology for the Beatles' music, the fact that a music critic for the London *Times* would deign to analyze the music in this way (and approvingly, at that) was significant and a harbinger of things to come.

What Songs the Beatles Sang . . .
William Mann

The outstanding English composers of 1963 must seem to have been John Lennon and Paul McCartney, the talented young musicians from Liverpool whose songs

---

2. Bernard Gendron termed this phenomenon "cultural accreditation." This chapter on the Beatles is much indebted to the chapters in Gendron's book dealing with the band; see *From Montmartre to the Mudd Club: Popular Music and the Avant-Garde* (Chicago: University of Chicago Press, 2002), chaps. 8–9.

have been sweeping the country since last Christmas, whether performed by their own group, The Beatles, or by the numerous other teams of English troubadours that they also supply with songs.

I am not concerned here with the social phenomenon of Beatlemania, which finds expression in handbags, balloons and other articles bearing the likenesses of the loved ones, or in the hysterical screaming of young girls whenever the Beatle Quartet performs in public, but with the musical phenomenon. For several decades, in fact since the decline of the music-hall, England has taken her popular songs from the United States, either directly or by mimicry. But the songs of Lennon and McCartney are distinctly indigenous in character, the most imaginative and inventive examples of a style that has been developing on Merseyside during the past few years. And there is a nice, rather flattering irony in the news that The Beatles have now become prime favourites in America too.[3]

The strength of character in pop songs seems, and quite understandably, to be determined usually by the number of composers involved; when three or four people are required to make the original tunesmith's work publicly presentable, it is unlikely to retain much individuality or to wear very well. The virtue of The Beatles' repertory is that, apparently, they do it themselves; three of the four are composers, they are versatile instrumentalists, and when they do borrow a song from another repertory, their treatment is idiosyncratic—as when Paul McCartney sings "Till there was you" from *The Music Man,* a cool, easy, tasteful version of this ballad, quite without artificial sentimentality.

Their noisy items are the ones that arouse teenagers' excitement. Glutinous crooning is generally out of fashion these days, and even a song about "Misery" sounds fundamentally quite cheerful; the slow, sad song about "This boy," which figures prominently in Beatle programmes, is expressively unusual for its lugubrious music, but harmonically it is one of their most intriguing, with its chains of pandiatonic clusters, and the sentiment is acceptable because voiced cleanly and crisply. But harmonic interest is typical of their quicker songs too, and one gets the impression that they think simultaneously of harmony and melody, so firmly are the major tonic sevenths and ninths built into their tunes, and the flat—submediant key—switches, so natural is the Aeolian cadence at the end of "Not a second time" (the chord progression which ends Mahler's *Song of the Earth*).

Those submediant switches from C major into A-flat major, and to a lesser extent mediant ones (e.g. the octave ascent in the famous "I want to hold your hand") are a trademark of Lennon-McCartney songs—they do not figure much in other pop repertories, or in The Beatles' arrangements of borrowed material—and show signs of becoming a mannerism. The other trademark of their compositions is a firm and purposeful bass line with a musical life of its own; how Lennon and McCartney divide their creative responsibilities I have yet to discover, but it is perhaps significant that Paul is the bass guitarist of the group. It may also be significant that George Harrison's song "Don't bother me" is harmonically a good deal more primitive, though it is nicely enough presented.

I suppose it is the sheer loudness of the music that appeals to Beatles admirers (there is something to be heard even through the squeals), and many parents must have cursed the electric guitar's amplification this Christmas—how fresh and euphonious the ordinary guitars sound in The Beatles' version of "Till there was you"—but parents who are still managing to survive the decibels and, after

---

3. This statement was a bit premature when this article was published; no Beatles' recordings entered *Billboard*'s Hot 100 until January 11, 1964.

copious repetition over several months, still deriving some musical pleasure from the overhearing, do so because there is a good deal of variety—oh, so welcome in pop music—about what they sing.

The autocratic but not by any means ungrammatical attitude to tonality (closer to, say, Peter Maxwell Davies's carols in *O Magnum Mysterium* than to Gershwin or Loewe or even Lionel Bart); the exhilarating and often quasi-instrumental vocal duetting, sometimes in scat or in falsetto, behind the melodic line; the melismas with altered vowels ("I saw her yesterday-ee-ay") which have not quite become mannered, and the discreet, sometimes subtle, varieties of instrumentation—a suspicion of piano or organ, a few bars of mouth-organ obbligato, an excursion on the claves or maracas; the translation of African blues or American Western idioms (in "Baby, it's you," the Magyar 8/8 meter too) into tough, sensitive Merseyside.

These are some of the qualities that make one wonder with interest what The Beatles, and particularly Lennon and McCartney, will do next, and if America will spoil them or hold on to them, and if their next record will wear as well as the others. They have brought a distinctive and exhilarating flavour into a genre of music that was in danger of ceasing to be music at all.

> The following article by Theodore Strongin (music critic for the *New York Times*), published two months after Mann's piece, demonstrates how the intellectual apparatus of high culture could be marshaled against pop music. Strongin's article perpetuates a tradition that goes back to dismissive academic descriptions of jazz and swing.[4]

Musicologically . . .
Theodore Strongin

"You can tell right away it's the Beatles and not anyone else," is the opinion of a 15-year-old specialist on the subject who saw the Beatles on the Ed Sullivan show last night. The age of 15 or 16 or 14 or 13 is essential in a Beatles expert.

Taking the above axiom as gospel, this listener made an attempt to find out just what is musically unique about the British visitors.

The Beatles are directly in the mainstream of Western tradition: that much may be immediately ascertained. Their harmony is unmistakably diatonic. A learned British colleague, writing on his home ground, has described it as pandiatonic, but I disagree.

The Beatles have a tendency to build phrases around unresolved, leading tones. This precipitates the ear into a false modal frame that temporarily turns the fifth of the scale into a tonic, momentarily suggesting the Mixylydian [*sic*] mode. But everything always ends as plain diatonic all the same.

---

4. For numerous examples of such descriptions, see Robert Walser, *Keeping Time: Readings in Jazz History* (New York and Oxford: Oxford University Press, 1999).

Meanwhile, the result is the addition of a very, very slight touch of British countryside nostalgia with a trace of Vaughan Williams to the familiar elements of the rock and roll prototype. "It's just that English rock and roll is more sophisticated," explained the 15-year-old authority.

As to instrumentation, three of the four Beatles (George Harrison, Paul McCartney, and John Lennon) play different sizes of electronically amplified plucked-stringed instruments. Ringo Starr ("He's just like a little puppy, he's so cute," said our specialist) plays the drums. The Beatles vocal quality can be described as hoarsely incoherent, with the minimal enunciation necessary to communicate schematic texts.

Two theories were offered in at least one household to explain the Beatles' popularity. The specialist said "We haven't had an idol in a few years. The Beatles are different, and we have to get rid of our excess energy somehow."

The other theory is that the longer parents object with such high dudgeon, the longer children will squeal so hysterically.

Further Reading

The Beatles (John Lennon, Paul McCartney, George Harrison, and Ringo Starr). *The Beatles Anthology*. San Francisco: Chronicle Books, 2000.

Bromell, Nick. *Tomorrow Never Knows: Rock and Psychedelics in the 1960s*. Chicago: University of Chicago Press, 2000.

Davies, Hunter. *The Beatles: The Authorized Biography*. New York: McGraw-Hill, 1968.

Everett, Walter. *The Beatles as Musicians: Revolver through the Anthology*. New York: Oxford University Press, 1999.

_____. *The Beatles as Musicians: The Quarry Men through Rubber Soul*. New York: Oxford University Press, 2001.

Gendron, Bernard. *Between Montmartre and the Mudd Club: Popular Music and the Avant-Garde*. Chicago: University of Chicago Press, 2002.

Rorem, Ned. "The Music of the Beatles." *Music Educators Journal* 55 (1968): 33–34, 77–83.

Spitz, Bob. *The Beatles: The Biography*. Boston: Little, Brown, 2005.

Thomson, Elizabeth, and David Gutman, eds. *The Lennon Companion: Twenty-Five Years of Comment*. New York: Schirmer Books, 1987.

Wenner, Jann. *Lennon Remembers: The Rolling Stone Interviews*. New York: Popular Library, 1971.

Womack, Kenneth, ed. *The Cambridge Companion to the Beatles*. Cambridge, UK: Cambridge University Press, 2009.

Discography

The Beatles. *Please Please Me*. Parlophone, 1963.

_____. *With the Beatles*. Parlophone, 1963.

_____. *A Hard Day's Night*. Parlophone, 1964.

_____. *Beatles for Sale*. Parlophone, 1964.

_____. *Help!* Parlophone, 1965.

_____. *Rubber Soul*. Parlophone, 1965.

_____. *Yesterday and Today*. Capitol, 1966.

_____. *Revolver*. Capitol, 1966.

_____. *Sgt. Pepper's Lonely Hearts Club Band*. Capitol, 1967.

_____. *1962–1966*. Capitol, 1993.

_____. *1967–1970*. Capitol, 1993.

_____. *Anthology 1*. Capitol, 1995.

_____. *Anthology 2*. Capitol, 1996.

37. *A Hard Day's Night* and Beatlemania

The Beatles' third British album, *A Hard Day's Night* (1964, also the title of their first movie), was their first to consist entirely of original compositions. The movie, however, rather than the album, won them a whole legion of new converts among high-middlebrow cultural authorities and audiences. Andrew Sarris's review is indicative of the pleasantly surprised reception that greeted *A Hard Day's Night* from the intelligentsia, and Sarris was not alone in applauding the film for its incorporation of sophisticated cinematic style derived, at least partly, from the French *nouvelle vague* (or "New Wave").[1]

Bravo Beatles!
Andrew Sarris

A Hard Day's Night is a particularly pleasant surprise in a year so full of unexpectedly unpleasant surprises. I have no idea who is the most responsible—director Richard Lester or screenwriter Alun Owen or the Messrs John Lennon, Paul McCartney, George Harrison, and Ringo Starr, better known collectively as The Beatles. Perhaps it was all a happy accident, and the lightning of inspiration will never strike again in the same spot. The fact remains that *A Hard Day's Night* has turned out to be the *Citizen Kane* of jukebox musicals, the brilliant crystallisation of such diverse cultural particles as the pop movie, rock 'n' roll, *cinéma vérité*, the *nouvelle vague*, free cinema, the affectedly hand-held camera, frenzied cutting, the cult of the sexless subadolescent, the semi-documentary, and studied spontaneity. So help me, I resisted The Beatles as long as I could. As a cab driver acquaintance observed, "So what's new about The Beatles? Didn't you ever hear of Ish Kabibble?" Alas, I had. I kept looking for openings to put down The Beatles. Some of their sly crows' humour at the expense of a Colonel Blimp character in a train compartment is a bit too deliberate. "I fought the war for people like you," sez he. "Bet you're sorry you won," sez they. Old Osborne ooze, sez I. But just previously, the fruitiest looking of the four predators had looked up enticingly at the bug-eyed Blimp and whimpered "Give

1. For another, even more surprised-sounding review, see Bosley Crowther, "The Four Beatles in 'A Hard Day's Night,'" *New York Times*, August 12, 1964, 41.

us a kiss." Depravity of such honest frankness is worth a hundred pseudo-literary exercises like Becket.

Stylistically, *A Hard Day's Night* is everything Tony Richardson's version of *Tom Jones* tried to be and wasn't. Thematically, it is everything Peter Brook's version of *Lord of the Flies* tried to be and wasn't. Fielding's satiric gusto is coupled here with Golding's primordial evil, and the strain hardly shows. I could have done with a bit less of a false sabre-toothed, rattling wreck of an old man tagged with sickeningly repetitious irony as a "clean" old man. The pop movie mannerisms of the inane running joke about one of the boys' managers being sensitively shorter than the other might have been dispensed with at no great loss.

The foregoing are trifling reservations, however, about a movie that works on every level for every kind of audience. The open-field helicopter-shot sequence of The Beatles on a spree is one of the most exhilarating expressions of high spirits I have seen on the screen.[2] The razor-slashing wit of the dialogue must be heard to be believed and appreciated. One as horribly addicted to alliteration as this otherwise sensible scribe can hardly resist a line like "Ringo's drums loom large in his legend."

I must say I enjoyed even the music enormously, possibly because I have not yet been traumatised by transistors into open rebellion against the "Top 40" and such. (I just heard "Hello, Dolly" for the first time the other day, and the lyrics had been changed to "Hello, Lyndon.") Nevertheless I think there is a tendency to underrate rock 'n' roll because the lyrics look so silly in cold print. I would make two points here. First, it is unfair to compare R&R with Gershwin, Rodgers, Porter, Kern, et al., as if all pre-R&R music from Tin Pan Alley was an uninterrupted flow of melodiousness. This is the familiar fallacy of nostalgia. I remember too much brassy noise from the big-band era to be stricken by the incursions of R&R. I like the songs The Beatles sing despite the banality of the lyrics, but the words in R&R only mask the poundingly ritualistic meaning of the beat. It is in the beat that the passion and togetherness is most movingly expressed, and it is the beat that the kids in the audience pick up with their shrieks as they drown out the words they have already heard a thousand times. To watch The Beatles in action with their constituents is to watch the kind of direct theater that went out with Aristophanes, or perhaps even the Australian bushman. There is an empathy there that a million Lincoln Center Repertory companies cannot duplicate. Toward the end of *A Hard Day's Night* I began to understand the mystique of The Beatles. Lester's crane shot facing the audience from behind The Beatles established the emotional unity of the performers and their audience. It is a beautifully Bazinian deep-focus shot of hysteria to a slow beat punctuated by the kind of zoom shots I have always deplored in theory but must now admire in practice. Let's face it. My critical theories and preconceptions are all shook up, and I am profoundly grateful to The Beatles for such a pleasurable softening of hardening aesthetic arteries.

As to what the Beatles "mean," I hesitate to speculate. The trouble with sociological analysis is that it is unconcerned with aesthetic values. *A Hard Day's Night* could have been a complete stinker of a movie and still be reasonably "meaningful." I like The Beatles in this moment in film history not merely because they

---

2. This scene, accompanied by "Can't Buy Me Love" on the soundtrack, was one of the clearest antecedents of post-MTV music video and contemporary rock film scoring; see Jeff Smith, *The Sounds of Commerce: Marketing Popular Film Music* (New York: Columbia University Press, 1998), 159–60.

mean something but rather because they express effectively a great many aspects of modernity that have converged inspiredly in their personalities. When I speak affectionately of their depravity, I am not commenting on their private lives, about which I know less than nothing. The wedding ring on Ringo's finger startles a great many people as a subtle Pirandellian switch from a character like Dopey of the Seven Dwarfs to a performer who chooses to project an ambiguous identity. It hardly matters.

What interests me about The Beatles is not what they are but what they choose to express. Their Ish Kabibble hairdos,[3] for example, serve two functions. They become unique as a group and interchangeable as individuals. Except for Ringo, the favourite of the fans, the other three Beatles tend to get lost in the shuffle. And yet each is a distinctly personable individual behind their collective façade of androgynous selflessness—a façade appropriate, incidentally, to the undifferentiated sexuality of their sub-adolescent fans. The Beatles are not merely objects, however. A frequent refrain of their middle-aged admirers is that The Beatles don't take themselves too seriously. They take themselves seriously enough, all right; it is their middle-aged admirers and detractors they don't take too seriously. The Beatles are a sly bunch of anti-Establishment anarchists, but they are too slick to tip their hand to the authorities. People who have watched them handle their fans and the press tell me that they make Sinatra and his clan look like a bunch of rubes at a county fair. Of course, they have been shrewdly promoted, and a great deal of the hysteria surrounding them has been rigged with classic fakery and exaggeration. They may not be worth a paragraph in six months, but right now their entertaining message seems to be that everyone is "people." Beatles and squealing sub-adolescents as much as Negroes and women and so-called senior citizens, and that however much alike "people" may look in a group or a mass or a stereotype, there is in each soul a unique and irreducible individuality.

> Previous articles on the Beatles mentioned the remarkable reaction of the audience to their performances; for the most part, these references are deprecatory—"hysterical screaming of young girls" (Mann), "squealing adolescents" (Sarris), and "children [who] squeal so hysterically" (Strongin)—and gendered (hysteria has had clear associations with femininity at least since Freud's earliest theories). In the next essay, Barbara Ehrenreich, Elizabeth Hess, and Gloria Jacobs note that this intensity had its precedents in the reaction of fans to Frank Sinatra (see Chapter 4) and Elvis Presley, but they then explain what separates Beatlemania from these previous phenomena in terms of both the audience and the mass media response.[4] In brief, they contend that the "experts" were slow to recognize the sexual dimension of the fans' excitement because asserting an active, powerful sexuality was revolutionary and because the received wisdom of the day dictated that the life of the middle-class, white American left nothing to be discontent about. Yet later in this essay (in a passage not reprinted here), the authors connect the intensity of Beatlema-

---

3. Ish Kabibble was a trumpeter and novelty singer with Kay Kyser's swing band during the 1930s and 1940s. Kabibble wore a distinctive "pudding basin"–style haircut.

4. The title of this essay refers to Cyndi Lauper's 1983 recording of the same name.

nia to an emerging form of female awareness that began to rebel against the twin dangers of sexuality for middle-class girls: that of being either too sexual or too puritanical. If "publicly advertis[ing] this hopeless love [represented by Beatlemania] was to protest the calculated, pragmatic sexual repression of teenage life," then it mattered that the Beatles were "while not exactly effeminate, at least not easily classifiable in the rigid gender distinctions of middle-class American life."[5] It is also surely significant that this androgynous image was a product of the gay sensibility of the Beatles' manager, Brian Epstein, providing yet another twist on the strict heterosexual dichotomies that ruled public perceptions of sexuality.[6] In other, more general terms, the Beatles represented the freedom the girls wished they could have, even as these girls celebrated their power in creating Beatlemania.

Beatlemania: *Girls Just Want to Have Fun*
Barbara Ehrenreich, Elizabeth Hess, and Gloria Jacobs

> . . . witness the birth of eve—she is rising she was sleeping she is fading in a naked field sweating the precious blood of nodding blooms . . . in the eye of the arena she bends in half in service—the anarchy that exudes from the pores of her guitar are the cries of the people wailing in the rushes . . . a riot of ray/dios . . .
> —Patti Smith, "Notice," in *Babel*

The news footage shows police lines straining against crowds of hundreds of young women. The police look grim; the girls' faces are twisted with desperation or, in some cases, shining with what seems to be an inner light. The air is dusty from a thousand running and scuffling feet. There are shouted orders to disperse, answered by a rising volume of chants and wild shrieks. The young women surge forth; the police line breaks . . .

Looking at the photos or watching the news clips today, anyone would guess that this was the sixties—a demonstration—or maybe the early seventies—the beginning of the women's liberation movement. Until you look closer and see that the girls are not wearing sixties-issue jeans and T-shirts but bermuda shorts,

---

5. Barbara Ehrenreich, Elizabeth Hess, and Gloria Jacobs, "Beatlemania: *Girls Just Want to Have Fun*," in *Re-making Love: The Feminization of Sex* (Garden City, N.Y.: Doubleday, 1987), 27, 34.

6. A history remains to be written on the impact of gay style on British rock of the 1960s, whether it be through managers such as Brian Epstein and Andrew Loog Oldham or the artists themselves, such as Ray Davies of the Kinks (in a song like "See My Friends") or, a little bit later, David Bowie and Elton John.

high-necked, preppie blouses, and disheveled but unmistakably bouffant hairdos. This is not 1968 but 1964, and the girls are chanting, as they surge against the police line, "I love Ringo."

Yet, if it was not the "movement," or a clear-cut protest of any kind, Beatlemania was the first mass outburst of the sixties to feature women—in this case girls, who would not reach full adulthood until the seventies and the emergence of a genuinely political movement for women's liberation. The screaming ten- to fourteen-year-old fans of 1964 did not riot *for* anything, except the chance to remain in the proximity of their idols and hence to remain screaming. But they did have plenty to riot against, or at least to overcome through the act of rioting: In a highly sexualized society (one sociologist found that the number of explicitly sexual references in the mass media had doubled between 1950 and 1960), teen and preteen girls were expected to be not only "good" and "pure" but to be the enforcers of purity within their teen society—drawing the line for overeager boys and ostracizing girls who failed in this responsibility. To abandon control—to scream, faint, dash about in mobs—was, in form if not in conscious intent, to protest the sexual repressiveness, the rigid double standard of female teen culture. It was the first and most dramatic uprising of *women's* sexual revolution.

Beatlemania, in most accounts, stands isolated in history as a mere craze—quirky and hard to explain. There had been hysteria over male stars before, but nothing on this scale. In its peak years—1964 and 1965—Beatlemania struck with the force, if not the conviction, of a social movement. It began in England with a report that fans had mobbed the popular but not yet immortal group after a concert at the London Palladium on October 13, 1963. Whether there was in fact a mob or merely a scuffle involving no more than eight girls is not clear, but the report acted as a call to mayhem. Eleven days later a huge and excited crowd of girls greeted the Beatles (returning from a Swedish tour) at Heathrow Airport. In early November, 400 Carlisle girls fought the police for four hours while trying to get tickets for a Beatles concert; nine people were hospitalized after the crowd surged forward and broke through shop windows. In London and Birmingham the police could not guarantee the Beatles safe escort through the hordes of fans. In Dublin the police chief judged that the Beatles' first visit: was "all right until the mania degenerated into barbarism."* And on the eve of the group's first U.S. tour, *Life* reported, "A Beatle who ventures out unguarded into the streets runs the very real peril of being dismembered or crushed to death by his fans."†

When the Beatles arrived in the United States, which was still ostensibly sobered by the assassination of President Kennedy two months before, the fans knew what to do. Television had spread the word from England: The approach of the Beatles is a license to riot. At least 4,000 girls (some estimates run as high as 10,000) greeted them at Kennedy Airport, and hundreds more laid siege to the Plaza Hotel, keeping the stars virtual prisoners. A record 73 million Americans watched the Beatles on "The Ed Sullivan Show" on February 9, 1964, the night "when there wasn't a hubcap stolen anywhere in America." American Beatlemania soon reached the proportions of religious idolatry. During the Beatles' twenty-three-city tour that August, local promoters were required to provide a minimum of 100 security guards to hold back the crowds. Some cities tried to ban Beatle-bearing craft from their runways; otherwise it took heavy deployments of local police to protect the Beatles from their fans and the fans from the

---

*Frederick Lewis, "Britons Succumb to 'Beatlemania,'" *New York Times Magazine*, December 1, 1963, p. 124.

†Timothy Green, "They Crown Their Country with a Bowl-Shaped Hairdo," *Life*, January 31, 1964, p. 30.

crush. In one city, someone got hold of the hotel pillowcases that had purportedly been used by the Beatles, cut them into 160,000 tiny squares, mounted them on certificates, and sold them for $1 apiece. The group packed Carnegie Hall, Washington's Coliseum and, a year later, New York's 55,600-seat Shea Stadium, and in no setting, at any time, was their music audible above the frenzied screams of the audience. In 1966, just under three years after the start of Beatlemania, the Beatles gave their last concert—the first musical celebrities to be driven from the stage by their own fans.

In its intensity, as well as its scale, Beatlemania surpassed all previous outbreaks of star-centered hysteria. Young women had swooned over Frank Sinatra in the forties and screamed for Elvis Presley in the immediate pre-Beatle years, but the Fab Four inspired an extremity of feeling usually reserved for football games or natural disasters. These baby boomers far outnumbered the generation that, thanks to the censors, had only been able to see Presley's upper torso on "The Ed Sullivan Show." Seeing (whole) Beatles on Sullivan was exciting, but not enough. Watching the band on television was a thrill—particularly the close-ups—but the real goal was to leave home and meet the Beatles. The appropriate reaction to contact with them—such as occupying the same auditorium or city block—was to sob uncontrollably while screaming, "I'm gonna die, I'm gonna die," or, more optimistically, the name of a favorite Beatle, until the onset of either unconsciousness or laryngitis. Girls peed in their pants, fainted, or simply collapsed from the emotional strain. When not in the vicinity of the Beatles—and only a small proportion of fans ever got within shrieking distance of their idols—girls exchanged Beatle magazines or cards, and gathered to speculate obsessively on the details and nuances of Beatle life. One woman, who now administers a Washington, D.C.–based public interest group, recalls long discussions with other thirteen-year-olds in Orlando, Maine:

> I especially liked talking about the Beatles with other girls. Someone would say, "What do you think Paul had for breakfast?" "Do you think he sleeps with a different girl every night?" Or, "Is John really the leader?" "Is George really more sensitive?" And like that for hours.

This fan reached the zenith of junior high school popularity after becoming the only girl in town to travel to a Beatles' concert in Boston: "My mother had made a new dress for me to wear [to the concert] and when I got back, the other girls wanted to cut it up and auction off the pieces."

To adults, Beatlemania was an affliction, an "epidemic," and the Beatles themselves were only the carriers, or even "foreign germs." At risk were all ten- to fourteen-year-old girls, or at least all white girls; blacks were disdainful of the Beatles' initially derivative and unpolished sound. There appeared to be no cure except for age, and the media pundits were fond of reassuring adults that the girls who had screamed for Frank Sinatra had grown up to be responsible, settled housewives. If there was a shortcut to recovery, it certainly wasn't easy. A group of Los Angeles girls organized a detox effort called "Beatlesaniacs, Ltd.," offering "group therapy for those living near active chapters, and withdrawal literature for those going it alone at far-flung outposts." Among the rules for recovery were: "Do not mention the word Beatles (or beetles)," "Do not mention the word England," "Do not speak with an English accent," and "Do not speak English."* In other words, Beatlemania was as inevitable as acne and gum-chewing, and adults would just have to weather it out.

---

* "How to Kick the Beatle Habit," *Life*, August 28, 1964, p. 66.

But why was it happening? And why in particular to an America that prided itself on its post-McCarthy maturity, its prosperity, and its clear position as the number one world power? True, there were social problems that not even *Reader's Digest* could afford to be smug about—racial segregation, for example, and the newly discovered poverty of "the other America." But these were things that an energetic President could easily handle—or so most people believed at the time—and if "the Negro problem," as it was called, generated overt unrest, it was seen as having a corrective function and limited duration. Notwithstanding an attempted revival by presidential candidate Barry Goldwater, "extremism" was out of style in any area of expression. In colleges, "coolness" implied a detached and rational appreciation of the status quo, and it was de rigueur among all but the avant-garde who joined the Freedom Rides or signed up for the Peace Corps. No one, not even Marxist philosopher Herbert Marcuse, could imagine a reason for widespread discontent among the middle class or for strivings that could not be satisfied with a department store charge account—much less for "mania."

In the media, adult experts fairly stumbled over each other to offer the most reassuring explanations. The *New York Times Magazine* offered a "psychological, anthropological," half tongue-in-cheek account, titled "Why the Girls Scream, Weep, Flip." Drawing on the work of the German sociologist Theodor Adorno, *Times* writer David Dempsey argued that the girls weren't really out of line at all; they were merely "conforming." Adorno had diagnosed the 1940s jitterbug fans as "rhythmic obedients," who were "expressing their desire to obey." They needed to subsume themselves into the mass, "to become transformed into an insect." Hence, "jitter*bug*," and as Dempsey triumphantly added: "Beatles, too, are a type of bug . . . and to 'beatle,' as to jitter, is to lose one's identity in an automatized, insectlike activity, in other words, to obey." If Beatlemania was more frenzied than the outbursts of obedience inspired by Sinatra or Fabian, it was simply because the music was "more frantic," and in some animal way, more compelling. It is generally admitted "that jungle rhythms influence the 'beat' of much contemporary dance activity," he wrote, blithely endorsing the stock racist response to rock 'n' roll. Atavistic, "aboriginal" instincts impelled the girls to scream, weep, and flip, whether they liked it or not: "It is probably no coincidence that the Beatles, who provoke the most violent response among teen-agers, resemble in manner the witch doctors who put their spells on hundreds of shuffling and stamping natives."*

Not everyone saw the resemblance between Beatlemanic girls and "natives" in a reassuring light however. *Variety* speculated that Beatlemania might be "a phenomenon closely linked to the current wave of racial rioting."† It was hard to miss the element of defiance in Beatlemania. If Beatlemania was conformity, it was conformity to an imperative that overruled adult mores and even adult laws. In the mass experience of Beatlemania, as for example at a concert or an airport, a girl who might never have contemplated shoplifting could assault a policeman with her fists, squirm under police barricades, and otherwise invite a disorderly conduct charge. Shy, subdued girls could go berserk. "Perky," ponytailed girls of the type favored by early sixties sitcoms could dissolve in histrionics. In quieter contemplation of their idols, girls could see defiance in the Beatles or project it onto them. *Newsweek* quoted Pat Hagan, "a pretty, 14-year-old Girl Scout, nurse's aide,

---

*David Dempsey, "Why the Girls Scream, Weep, Flip," *New York Times Magazine*, February 23, 1964, p. 15.

†Quoted in Nicholas Schaffner, *The Beatles Forever* (New York: McGraw-Hill, 1977), p. 16.

and daughter of a Chicago lawyer . . . who previously dug 'West Side Story,' Emily Dickinson, Robert Frost, and Elizabeth Barrett Browning: 'They're tough,' she said of the Beatles. 'Tough is like when you don't conform. . . . You're tumultuous when you're young, and each generation has to have its idols.'"* America's favorite sociologist, David Riesman, concurred, describing Beatlemania as "a form of protest against the adult world."†

There was another element of Beatlemania that was hard to miss but not always easy for adults to acknowledge. As any casual student of Freud would have noted, at least part of the fans' energy was sexual. Freud's initial breakthrough had been the insight that the epidemic female "hysteria" of the late nineteenth century—which took the form of fits, convulsions, tics, and what we would now call neuroses—was the product of sexual repression. In 1964, though, confronted with massed thousands of "hysterics," psychologists approached this diagnosis warily. After all, despite everything Freud had had to say about childhood sexuality, most Americans did not like to believe that twelve-year-old girls had any sexual feelings to repress. And no normal girl—or full-grown woman, for that matter—was supposed to have the libidinal voltage required for three hours of screaming, sobbing, incontinent, acute-phase Beatlemania. In an article in *Science News Letter* titled "Beatles Reaction Puzzles Even Psychologists," one unidentified psychologist offered a carefully phrased, hygienic explanation: Adolescents are "going through a strenuous period of emotional and physical growth," which leads to a "need for expressiveness, especially in girls." Boys have sports as an outlet; girls have only the screaming and swooning afforded by Beatlemania, which could be seen as "a release of sexual energy."‡

For the girls who participated in Beatlemania, sex was an obvious part of the excitement. One of the most common responses to reporters' queries on the sources of Beatlemania was, "Because they're sexy." And this explanation was in itself a small act of defiance. It was rebellious (especially for the very young fans) to lay claim to sexual feelings. It was even more rebellious to lay claim to the *active*, desiring side of a sexual attraction: The Beatles were the objects; the girls were their pursuers. The Beatles were sexy; the girls were the ones who perceived them as sexy and acknowledged the force of an ungovernable, if somewhat disembodied, lust. To assert an active, powerful sexuality by the tens of thousands and to do so in a way calculated to attract maximum attention was more than rebellious. It was, in its own unformulated, dizzy way, revolutionary.

Further Reading

See Chapter 36.

Discography

See Chapter 36.

---

*"George, Paul, Ringo and John," *Newsweek*, February 24, 1964, p. 54.

†"What the Beatles Prove About Teen-agers," *U.S. News & World Report*, February 24, 1964, p. 88.

‡"Beatles Reaction Puzzles Even Psychologists," *Science News Letter*, February 29, 1964, p. 141.

38. England Swings, and the Beatles Evolve on *Revolver* and *Sgt. Pepper*

The album *A Hard Day's Night,* along with the two that followed—*Beatles for Sale* (1964) and *Help!* (1965, also the title of their second movie)—featured a steady expansion of musical and technological resources. The Beatles had begun to use four-track recording on *A Hard Day's Night,* which increased the possibilities of overdubbing (i.e., layering vocal and instrumental parts in succession, rather than recording everything at once). The expansion of instrumentation was modest on these albums but nonetheless significant as more songs featured acoustic guitars, additional percussion instruments, and piano and organ, as well as unusual instrumental effects, such as the guitar feedback that opens "I Feel Fine" (1964, from *Beatles for Sale*). One song from *Help!,* "Yesterday," was the first Beatles' song to feature orchestral instruments. Compared to the thick texture found in most pop recordings employing orchestral instruments, the chamber ensemble texture of the string quartet on "Yesterday" produced a novel and relatively transparent sound.

The modest sense of evolution found in the Beatles' early albums, regardless of its novelty for a rock 'n' roll group, did little to prepare the public for what was to happen next. On *Rubber Soul,* released late in 1965, the combination of subtle instrumentation with introspection of lyric content and an "artsy" cover photo was novel within the pop music context of the time.[1] The U.S. version of the album enhanced the effect of seriousness by deleting several of the songs with clearer ties to rock 'n' roll and adding some quieter acoustic tracks that had been left off the U.S. release of *Help.*[2] Many listeners shared Brian Wilson's reaction to *Rubber Soul.* On the eve of the explosion of media attention to the counterculture and psychedelia, *Rubber Soul* and its successor *Revolver* (1966), along with the concurrent albums of Bob Dylan, convinced many that rock could

---

1. One recent article described the cover of *Rubber Soul* as "the first suggestion of psychedelia . . . with its hallucinatory photo of the band and distorted Art Nouveau-derived lettering." See Steve Jones and Martin Sorger, "Covering Music: A Brief History and Analysis of Album Cover Design," *Journal of Popular Music Studies* 11–12 (1999–2000): 68–102.

2. British albums typically contained 14 songs, rather than the 12 that were on U.S. albums, resulting in different versions of albums released on both sides of the Atlantic.

be the music of adults, even those with intellectual inclinations. While Dylan had primarily brought notions of artistic sincerity with him from the folk music movement, where such notions were con- nected to creating a sense of community between performer and audience, the Beatles achieved their sense of authenticity through their allusions to high art. Sarris's review in Chapter 37 described how *A Hard Day's Night* helped accomplish this cultural accredita- tion, but many of the songs released in 1965–66 achieved a sense of artiness musically via formal complexity, textural variety, and lyri- cal introspection.

With Richard Goldstein's review of *Revolver,* we enter the realm of a new form of criticism that arises from a sensibility and milieu similar to that of the music it describes. While earlier critics such as Robert Shelton, Nat Hentoff, and Ralph J. Gleason had written sympatheti- cally about popular music, their critical sensibilities were honed in the 1940s and 1950s on jazz and folk music. Goldstein was among the first of a new breed of critic who had come of age with "rock music" (now distinct from the earlier "rock 'n' roll") and were trying to articulate an alternative aesthetic that might correspond with the new music. Goldstein asserts his belief in the validity of aesthetic contemplation for rock when he writes, "We will view this album in retrospect as a key work in the development of rock 'n' roll into an artistic pursuit." That Goldstein (and other early rock critics) devoted a lot of space to the Beatles was not fortuitous: he wrote in a later piece (on *Sgt. Pepper*) that "without [the Beatles] there could be no such discipline as 'rock criticism.' The new music is their thing."[3]

Pop Eye: On "Revolver"
Richard Goldstein

SWINGING LONDON, August 17—As though displaying unswerving loyalty to its idols, British youth has flipped completely over the new Beatles album "Revolver." The single chosen from these songs—"Yellow Submarine b/w Eleanor Rigby"—came on the charts one week ago at number four. Today it is number one. The entire album is in the top twenty. Large record stores and tiny street stalls feature mass displays of the art-nouveau-ish album jacket. The sound of "Revolver" blares from window after window. John harmonizes with Paul in greengrocers and boutiques. George plays

---

3. Richard Goldstein, "Pop Eye: I Blew My Cool through the *New York Times*," *Village Voice,* July 20, 1967, 14, 25–26.

Source: "Pop Eye: On 'Revolver'" © Richard Goldstein/*Village Voice.*

his sitar from cars stalled in traffic. Ringo ricochets from the dome of St. Paul's. The Beatles are harder to avoid than even the Americans.

But there is more than mere adulation behind the sudden conquest of Britain by this particular LP. "Revolver" is a revolutionary record, as important to the expansion of pop territory as was "Rubber Soul." It was apparent last year that the 12 songs in "Rubber Soul" represented an important advance. "Revolver" is the great leap forward. Hear it once and you know it's important. Hear it twice, it makes sense. Third time around, it's fun. Fourth time, it's subtle. On the fifth hearing, "Revolver" becomes profound.

If "Rubber Soul" opened up areas of baroque progression and Oriental instrumentation to pop commercialization, "Revolver" does the same for electronic music. Much of the sound in this new LP is atonal, and a good deal of the vocal is dissonant. Instead of drowning poor voices in echo-chamber acoustics, "Revolver" presents the mechanics of pop music openly, as an integral part of musical composition. Instead of sugar and sex, what we get from the control knobs here is a bent and pulverized sound. John Cage move over, the Beatles are now reaching a super-receptive audience with electronic sound.

Resemble Mantra

The key number on the album is that last track, "Tomorrow Never Knows." No one can say what actually inspired the song, but its place in the pantheon of psychedelic music is assured. The lyrics resemble a mantra in form and message:

> *Turn off your mind*
> *Relax and float downstream*
> *This is not dying*
> *This is not dying*
>
> *Lay down all thought*
> *Surrender to the void*
> *It is shining*
> *It is shining*
>
> *That you may see*
> *the meaning of within*
> *It is being*
> *It is being*
>
> *Love is all*
> *and love is everyone*
> *It is knowing*
> *It is knowing . . .*

While not unprecedented, the combination of acid-Buddhist imagery and rock beat had never before been attempted with such complexity. At first, the orchestration sounds like Custer's last stand. Foghorn-like organ chords and the sound of bird-like screeching overshadows the vocal. But the overall effect of this hodge-podge is a very effective suspension of musical reality. John's vocal sounds distant and God-like. What he is saying transcends almost everything in what was once called pop music. The boundaries will now have to be re-negotiated.

"Revolver" also represents a fulfillment of the raga-Beatle sound. A George Harrison composition, "Love You To," is a functioning raga, with a natural beat and an engaging vocal advising: "Make love all day long/Make love singing songs."

"Eleanor Rigby" is an orchestrated ballad about the agony of loneliness. Its characters, Eleanor herself and Father McKenzie, represent sterility. Eleanor "died in the church and was buried along with her name." The good father writes "words to the sermon that no one will hear. No one comes near." As a commentary on the state of modern religion, this song will hardly be appreciated by those who see John Lennon as an anti-Christ.[4] But "Eleanor Rigby" is really about the unloved and un-cared for. When Eleanor makes up, the narrator asks: "Who is it for?" While the father darns his socks, the question is: "What does he care?"

More Next Door

"Yellow Submarine" is as whimsical and child-like as its flip side is metaphysical. Its subject is an undersea utopia where "our friends are all aboard / many more of them live next door," and where "we live a life of ease / Every one of us has all he needs."

"For No One" is one of the most poignant songs on the record. Its structure approaches madrigal form—with an effective horn-solo counterpoint. Its lyrics are in an evocative Aznavour bag.

"Taxman" is the album's example of political cheek, in which George enumerates Britain's current economic woes. At one point, the group joins in to identify the villains. "Taxman—Mr. Wilson . . . Taxman—Mr. Heath." They lay it right on the non-partisan line.

There is some mediocre material on this album. But the mystique forming around "Revolver" is based on more than one or two choice tracks—it encompasses the record as a whole.

It is a bit difficult to gauge the importance of "Revolver" from this city, where it has become gospel and where other beat groups are turning out cover copies like Guttenberg Bibles. But it seems now that we will view this album in retrospect as a key work in the development of rock 'n' roll into an artistic pursuit.

If nothing else, "Revolver" must reduce the number of cynics where the future of pop music is concerned—even on the violent side of the Atlantic.

> The Beatles' critical acceptance reached new heights with the release of their next album, *Sgt. Pepper's Lonely Hearts Club Band* (1967). The album was a loosely organized "concept" album, simulating a concert given by the Beatles' alter egos—the namesake of the album. The album made extensive use of the recording studio, incorporating numerous sound effects, tape collages, orchestral instruments, and sound processing. The brief article that follows appeared in *Newsweek* and documents how *Sgt. Pepper* won over even those middlebrow publications that had maintained a condescending stance toward popular music until that point, although the author cannot completely relinquish the patronizing tone of yore adopted by such publications. While the album won new admirers for the Beatles' music, and most rock fans and critics were dazzled, not all agreed. One of the disenchanted, Richard Goldstein, published a review of the album and a defense of the review; in both cases, he argued that innovations in

---

4. This is probably a reference to Lennon's remarks, published in March 1966, that the Beatles were "more popular than Jesus," a comment that when repeated in the United States caused a furor on the eve of their 1966 tour.

instrumentation and recording techniques were leading formal innovations in songwriting, rather than the other way around, much to the
detriment of the Beatles' music.[5] The release of *Sgt. Pepper* coincided
with the Beatles' withdrawal from "live" performance, a coincidence
that suggested to Goldstein that performance has the potential to
rein in excesses that result from the pursuit of dazzling effects in the
recording studio.

It's Getting Better . . .
Jack Kroll

The problem of choosing Britain's new Poet Laureate is easy. The obvious choice is
the Beatles. They would be the first laureates to be really popular since Tennyson—
their extraordinary new LP, "Sgt. Pepper's Lonely Hearts Club Band," has been out
for two weeks and has already sold 1.5 million copies in the U.S. alone. And the
Beatles' recent LP's "Rubber Soul," "Revolver," and now "Sgt. Pepper" are really
volumes of aural poetry in the McLuhan age.[6]

Indeed, "Sgt. Pepper" is such an organic work (it took four months to make) that
it is like a pop "Façade," the suite of poems by Edith Sitwell musicalized by William
Walton. Like "Façade," "Sgt. Pepper" is a rollicking, probing language-and-sound
vaudeville, which grafts skin from all three brows—high, middle, and low—into a
pulsating collage about mid-century manners and madness.

The vaudeville starts immediately on the first track, in which the Beatles, adding several horn players, create the "persona" of the album—Sgt. Pepper's band,
oompahing madly away with the elephant-footed rhythm, evoking the good old
days when music spoke straight to the people with tongues of brass, while dubbed
in crowds cheer and applaud as the Beatles make raucous fun of their own colossal
popularity.

After this euphoric, ironic, nostalgic fanfare, the Beatles leave Sgt. Pepper
polishing his coronet in the wings and go on with the show, creating little lyrics,
dramas, and satires on homely virtues, homely disasters, homely people and all the
ambiguities of home. "She's leaving home," sing John and Paul, as a harp flutters,
a string group makes genteel aspidistra sounds and a lugubrious cello wraps the
soggy English weather around the listener's ears. The song is a flabby family fiasco
in miniature, spiking the horrors of the British hearth like a stripped down Osborne
play. "Me used to be an angry young man," sings Paul in "Getting Better," and adds
"it's getting better all the time," as the group sarcastically repeats "get-ting bet-ter,
get-ting bet-ter" in those Liverpudlian accents.

---

5. Richard Goldstein, "We Still Need the Beatles, but . . . ," *New York Times*, June 18, 1967,
sec. II, 24; and idem., "Pop Eye: I Blew My Cool through the *New York Times*," *Village Voice*, July
20, 1967, 14, 25–26.

6. This reference to Marshall McLuhan echoes remarks made by Richard Goldstein in an
article reprinted in Chapter 45; see "Pop Eye: Evaluating Media," *Village Voice*, July 14, 1966, 6–7.

Vision

Getting better? Well, there's John's vision of a vinyl Arcadia, with it's Sitwellian images: "Cellophane flowers of yellow and green . . . Plasticine porters with looking-glass ties" which turns Wordsworth's idealized Lucy into a mod goddess, "Lucy in the sky with diamonds." And then there's Paul announcing "I'm painting my room in the colorful way / And when my mind is wandering / There I will go / And it really doesn't matter if I'm wrong I'm right / Where I belong I'm right." But even this manifestation of psychedelic individualism is undercut as George's sitar boings one note relentlessly like a giant mocking frog.

"Within You Without You" is George Harrison's beautiful new cuddle-up with Mother India. Backed by three cellos, eight violins, three tambouras, a dilruba, a tabla, and a table-harp, George plays the sitar as he chants Vedantic verities such as "The time will come when you see we're all one, and life flows on within you and without you." These Himalayan homilies are given powerful effect by the wailing, undulating cascade of sound which turns the curved, infinite universe of Indian music into a perfect tonal setting for the new pantheism of the young. But even here, the Beatles, like Chaplin, deflate their own seriousness as the song ends—to be followed by a crowd laughing.

Some critics have already berated the Beatles for the supersophisticated electronic technology on this record. But it is useless to lament the simple old days of the Mersey sound. The Beatles have lost their innocence, certainly, but loss of innocence is, increasingly, their theme and the theme of a more "serious" new art from the stories of Donald Barthelme to the plays of Harold Pinter.

The new Beatles are justified by the marvelous last number alone: "A Day in the Life," which was foolishly banned by the BBC because of its refrain "I'd love to turn you on." But this line means many things, coming as it does after a series of beautifully sorrowful stanzas in which John confronts the world's incessant bad news sighing "Oh boy" with a perfect blend of innocence and spiritual exhaustion. Evoking the catatonic metropolitan crown (like Eliot's living dead flowing across London Bridge), John's wish to "turn you on" is a desire to start the bogged-down juices of life itself. This point is underscored by an over-whelming musical effect, using a 41-piece orchestra—a growling, bone-grinding crescendo that drones up like a giant crippled turbine struggling to spin new power into a foundered civilization. This number is the Beatles' "Waste Land," a superb achievement of their brilliant and startlingly effective popular art.

Further Reading

See Chapter 36.

Discography

See Chapter 36.

39. The British Art School Blues

The Beatles hailed from Liverpool, a seaport on England's northwest coast. Liverpool had long had access to the latest releases from the United States, and, consequently, other bands (in addition to the Beatles) developed a blend of rockabilly, pop, and R&B for playing in local dance halls and nightclubs, resulting in a style dubbed "Merseybeat" by the British music press. In the wake of the Beatles, other Merseybeat artists, such as Gerry and the Pacemakers, Billy J. Kramer and the Dakotas, and Peter and Gordon (not from Liverpool but with a song written by Lennon and McCartney), had hits in the United States, thus inspiring the media to coin the term "British Invasion" to describe the phenomenon. It had been rare for any British artists to penetrate the American pop market until that time, and this sudden success set off a fad for all things British.

Concurrent with the pop-oriented Merseybeat artists, a more blues-oriented music scene was thriving down in London, fueled by record enthusiasts and collectors, along with refugees from British art schools. The role of art schools cannot be underestimated in the development of a distinctive form of British rock 'n' roll: with no real equivalent in the United States, art schools in Britain filled a gap somewhere between university (which during the 1950s and 1960s was still a fairly exclusive affair) and technical or trade schools. Better-than-average students with some vague artistic inclination were often sent to art school, where they would presumably learn a trade, such as graphic design. These schools became hotbeds for aspiring pop musicians, some of whom even absorbed some fashionable theories about art along the way.[1] The Rolling Stones' lead guitarist Keith Richards (b. 1942) memorably described his experience:

I mean in England, if you're lucky, you can get into art school. It's somewhere they put you if they can't put you anywhere else. If you can't saw wood straight or file metal. It's where they put me to learn graphic design because I happened to be good at drawing apples or something. Fifteen . . . I was there for three years and meanwhile I learned how to play guitar. Lotta guitar players in art school. A lot of terrible artists too. It's funny.[2]

---

1. For an extensive study of the impact of British art schools on the development of British rock, see Simon Frith and Howard Horne, *Art into Pop* (London: Methuen, 1987).

Several groups from the London blues and British art school scenes achieved commercial success during this period, most notably the Kinks, the Who, the Yardbirds, and the Rolling Stones. The Kinks scored three hits in a row in the United States in late 1964–early 1965 with "You Really Got Me," "All Day and All of the Night," and "Tired of Waiting." The first two of these songs were proto–heavy metal, constructed around primal riffs played on a highly distorted electric guitar. Subsequent Kinks' recordings saw them developing a style based on British music hall influences and ironic, detached personae ("Well Respected Man," "Sunny Afternoon"), presenting an interesting antithesis to the "authentic" ethos so prevalent during the era. Many have viewed this self-consciousness and the nonblues sound of their later music as peculiarly representative of a British-identified pop, with main songwriter Ray Davies (b. 1944) seen as particularly responsible for this sensibility.

The Yardbirds, on the other hand, came out of the same London blues scene as the Rolling Stones and recorded numerous covers of American blues recordings, especially songs associated with the Chicago blues. Their American hits included both bluesy songs such as "I'm a Man" and the more pop-oriented "For Your Love." The Yardbirds are also notable for having featured a succession of guitarists who eventually became famous on their own or as leaders of other groups: Eric Clapton (b. 1945), Jeff Beck (b. 1944), and Jimmy Page (b. 1944).

The Who had a main songwriter, Pete Townshend (b. 1945), who did time in art school. The band was associated with the Mods, a London subculture of the mid-1960s that worshipped American R&B and had a particular fondness for motor scooters, smart clothes, and amphetamines. The Who's music included blues influences at times, along with generous dollops of ironic self-consciousness. Master manipulators of mass cultural symbols, the band began wearing clothing redolent of "old England" years before *Sgt. Pepper*. They were also practitioners of performance art—their stage act featured a kind of highly theatricalized violence, which for a time included the destruction of their equipment. Pete Townshend became one of the more articulate spokespeople for understanding 1960s rock through the prism of modernist theories about art. The Who's music presented two somewhat opposing tendencies: an emphasis on performance and the enduring values of early rock 'n' roll and the blues, and an exploration of extended forms associated with art music, which reached its apogee in the "rock opera" *Tommy*.[3]

---

2. Robert Greenfield, "Keith Richard: Got to Keep It Growing," in *The Rolling Stone Interviews, Vol. 2* (New York: Straight Arrow, 1973), 218; first published in *Rolling Stone* in August 1971.

3. For Pete Townshend's witty appraisal of the Who's career from 1965 to 1971, see Peter Townshend, "Review of 'The Who: *Meaty, Beaty, Big, and Bouncy*,'" *Rolling Stone*, December 7, 1971, 36–38.

The Rolling Stones were the most famous band to emerge from the early 1960s London blues scene, and they had roots in art school as well. The Stones were quickly pegged in the press as a scruffy foil to the Beatles' bohemian charm. The following article is one of the earliest in the British music press to seize upon the rebellious image of the Stones, an image that seemed to flaunt its artificiality. The music press did little to hide its complicity in the production of this image: an article appearing a month later, in March 1964, featured a headline screaming, "Would You Let Your Sister Go with a Rolling Stone?"; the headline, however, had little to do with the content of the article, which was little more than a profile of "life on the road" with the band.[4] The article reprinted here appeared in *Melody Maker,* one of the two leading British popular music magazines, along with the *New Musical Express*. At a time when no real equivalents existed in the United States, these magazines mixed informative profiles with tabloid-style sensationalism. The author, Ray Coleman, who later went on to write respectable biographies of pop musicians, seems to be writing with tongue firmly placed in cheek.

Rebels with a Beat
Ray Coleman

"Wasn't that the Rolling Stones you just left?" asked the taxi driver as I left a restaurant in London's Mayfair.

"Yes. What do you think of them?"

"A bunch of right 'erberts!" he replied with the cutting pertinence so typical of the London cabbie. "'Ere, aren't they the boys they say are trying to knock the Beatles off the top?"

While cab drivers are often noted for their lack of tact, some have rare perception. Had I been an agent or a record chief, I would probably have signed that taxi driver immediately as my trends adviser.

The Rolling Stones might have had other ideas, like punching him on the nose. Because they deeply resent any suggestion that they are attempting to overtake the Beatles.

Yet if the Beatles are to be knocked from their perch in the future, by a British group, the popular notion is that the Rolling Stones could easily be their successors.

Why? Their image is perfect . . . five disheveled rebels who have already made a firm imprint on the hit parade, who have gained a huge following among young people, who never wear stage uniforms, and who JUST DON'T CARE.

There are even rumblings inside show business of a swing against the Beatles in favor of the Rolling Stones. Many observers endorse the view of an alert writer to Melody Maker's Mailbag.

---

4. Ray Coleman, "Would You Let Your Sister Go with a Rolling Stone?" *Melody Maker,* March 14, 1964, 8. Note that this article was written by the same author as, and appeared in the same magazine a mere month later than, the article reprinted in this anthology.

Source: "Rebels with a Beat," Ray Coleman © IPC Media.

She asserted that young pop fans instinctively turn against an idol whom their parents endorse, like the Beatles. Fans actually enjoy hearing their elders spurning their worship of their heroes. That way, there is an outlet for their emotional involvement.

Horrors

That taxi driver we met earlier was aged 42. He loathed the Rolling Stones. Like certain others he considers them downright scruffy, hairy horrors who need a severe talking-to from Lord Montgomery.

I have no psychiatric or sociological qualifications, but I think I can confirm that the Rolling Stones are 100 percent human beings, acutely aware of what is going on.

They have no leader, but Mick Jagger, 19-year-old ex-economics student (lead singer, harmonica) and Keith Richard (19, ex-art student, guitarist) do most of the talking.

The others are Brian Jones, aged 20 (harmonica, guitar), whom the rest describe as an ex-layabout; Bill Wyman (22, bass guitarist, former electronics man); and 22-year-old drummer Charlie Watts, a man of few words who claims to have been a brilliant advertising executive before turning to music.

They all come from Southern England, and have a close association with Richmond, where they played a seven-month residency when started under their present title 18 months ago.

"Yes!" replied Jagger when I asked if they were jealous of the Beatles' success. "No!" said the others. With that formality over, we switched to talk of images and money, untidiness and fans.

Jagger spoke: "Yeah, we know about the image. I think most groups need one. You see, you can get so far without an image in people's minds, but as soon as you make a not-so-hot record, you feel it.

"If you've got an image, you sell the records on the image, if you see what I mean, and you can always rely on a following whatever you do.

Strange

"But we didn't all sit down and say 'right, let's be untidy and let's not have uniforms and let's grow our hair long like the Beatles' or anything like that'."

Wyman said: "The image was a thing that just happened. We always carried on like this. People thought, when we started, that we were so strange to look at. Now we're lumbered with the image."

The difference [between the Stones and the Beatles] is that Keith and Mick do not write their own material, but work on orders for songs from other groups and solo artists.

Visually, the Rolling Stones are not the prettiest quintet in the land. Although they deny it, the truth is that they are angry young rebels who scorn conformity.

Groan

"We're not deliberately untidy," says Keith. "We think a lot of this 'rebel' thing has been brought up by people thinking too much about it. People like you come up to us and say 'are you rebels?' The answer's no."

To which one could reply that they are either rebels or blatant exhibitionists.

Said Charlie Watts: "We like it this way—we like to please ourselves what we do. We don't like this 'big star' bit. We get treated by the fans as just ordinary blokes, and that's good. There's none of this 'fab gear' and all that."

I asked how much they earned today and how much they earned when they started. At once, their publicist and co-manager, 20-year-old Andrew Oldham, joined the conversation.

"It's about 20 times more than we got when we started," Mick Jagger stated.

"About £1,500 a week for personal appearances, that's between them, and excluding record royalties," said Andrew, who now sports a Rolling Stone-type hair style.

And what about that hair style? There was a groan of horror at the mere suggestion that it had been described as Beatle-ish.

"Look," said Keith, "These hair styles had been quite common down in London long before the Beatles and the rest of the country caught on. At art school and years ago, ours had always been the same."

"Look at Jimmy Savile," urged Jagger. "He had his like it is long before others started that style. It's the same with us."

"And Adam Faith," added Bill Wyman. "He had hair like the Beatles years ago, didn't he?"

"I dunno," Richard said to Wyman. "I reckon your style came direct from the Three Stooges."

They talked about extravagancies now they had money, and disclosed that they had few. "Nobody's gone really mad with money," said Keith, "except that Charlie's bought a blue suede coat."

"I spend a lot of money on records," said Wyman. "Six new LPs a week." "You can't," declared Keith. "There aren't six good LPs issued a week." "Well, I do, and that's where the money goes," said Bill.

"Charlie likes jazz," said Jagger. "He's the only one in the group who does, really." Wyman said he preferred R&B from Chuck Berry, Jerry Lee Lewis, "and Fats Waller." "I go for singers like Ben E. King" said Jagger. "So do I," said Keith. "And Muddy Waters."

Mates

Do the Stones call themselves an R&B group? "We claim to be R&B as much as anyone," Richard said. "We were playing R&B material long before this beat craze got going.

"You know, the beat craze that's going on at the moment will last longer than a lot of people think. Kids realize that having four or five stars, like a group, is better than having one star, and groups are improving tremendously all the time.

"The Searchers' 'Needle and Pins' is the best record they ever made."

Was there any prejudice from promoters because of their dress habits? "Sometimes," said Keith. "They used to have this attitude of 'that scruffy lot from London who don't turn up on time and are nasty to look at.'"

"But once we appear, we always get re-booked."

"They just think we're layabouts," added Wyman.

"Well, they can lump it," announced Keith.

"They call us the ugliest pop group in the country," admitted Wyman. "We could name a few uglier people in the business," said Jagger, whose face creases into a mammoth smile at the slightest provocation. "Yes, quite a few more. . . ."

"Do you know," said Wyman, "some places we go, they bill us as London's answer to the Beatles. They don't like it when we say we don't do 'Twist and shout.'"

"Yes," said Jagger. "And whatever you do, don't write that article saying we're knocking the Beatles. They're good mates of ours. We like 'em and they've done so much good for the whole scene see?"

"The cancer business doesn't scare me," said Wyman, lighting up. They all smoke about 20 a day and drink moderately. "We not boozers," said Richard, "but we enjoy a drink and fags like anybody else."

"No, it doesn't scare me at all," affirmed Wyman. "Let's face it, if you have got to go, you have got to go."

"I'll probably die of electric shock," said Keith, the guitarist. He lit up. They all trailed out of the restaurant.

People eating lunch looked up, aghast at such a sight. Unkempt the Rolling Stones may be, but their music has vitality and they are mentally sharp.

AND COMMERCIAL.

Further Reading

Booth, Stanley. *The True Adventures of the Rolling Stones.* Chicago: Chicago Review Press, 2000.

Frith, Simon, and Howard Horne. *Art into Pop.* London: Methuen, 1987.

Groom, Bob. *The Blues Revival.* London: Studio Vista, 1971.

Jagger, Mick, Keith Richards, Charlie Watts, and Ronnie Wood. *According to the Rolling Stones,* ed. Dora Loewenstein and Philip Dodd. San Francisco: Chronicle Books, 2003.

Kitts, Thomas. *Ray Davies: Not Like Everybody Else.* New York: Routledge, 2007.

Marsh, Dave. *Before I Get Old: The Story of the Who.* New York: St. Martin's Press, 1983.

Marten, Neville, and Jeff Hudson. *The Kinks.* London: Bobcat Books, 2007.

Discography

The Kinks. *The Kinks.* Pye, 1964.

_____. *The Singles Collection.* Sanctuary UK, 2004.

The Rolling Stones. *Hot Rocks, 1964–1971.* Abkco, [1972] 2002.

_____. *More Hot Rocks: Big Hits and Fazed Cookies.* Abkco, [1972] 2002.

The Who. *My Generation.* Brunswick, 1965.

_____. *Tommy.* Polydor, 1969.

_____. *Thirty Years of Maximum R&B.* MCA, 1994.

The Yardbirds. *Having a Rave Up with the Yardbirds.* Epic, 1965.

_____. *The Yardbirds—Greatest Hits, Vol. 1: 1964–1966.* Rhino/WEA, 1990.

40. The Stones versus the Beatles

The preceding chapter described some of the ways in which the Rolling Stones, especially lead singer Mick Jagger (b. 1942), projected an ironic detachment, arrogance, and aggressive sexuality that made them seem as if they were the opposite of the cuter, more polite public image of the Beatles. The rawer, blues-based sound of the Stones also seems at odds with the polished, more conventionally melodic pop of the Beatles. This apparent difference masked many similarities: both bands were influenced by the rock 'n' roll of the 1950s (the Stones more by Chicago blues, the Beatles more by rockabilly) and the soul music of the early 1960s (the Stones more by "downhome" singers, such as Solomon Burke, and the Beatles more by Motown). As the Stones began writing their own material, the Beatles' influence became clearer. Although they tended to retain a less polished sound, the Stones followed the Beatles closely in the use of strings ("As Tears Go By," late 1965, after "Yesterday"), the sitar ("Paint It Black," 1966, after "Norwegian Wood"), and psychedelia (*Their Satanic Majesties Request,* late 1967, after *Sgt. Pepper*). Following *Satanic Majesties,* the Stones began developing their own brand of hard rock; "Jumpin' Jack Flash" (1968) stands as both the inaugural and archetypal song in this style, with its hypnotic syncopated riff based on a fragment of the blues scale.

The following article by Ellen Willis dates from 1969 and explicitly compares what were then the two latest releases of the Stones and Beatles, *Beggars Banquet* and *The Beatles* (aka, "The White Album"). Willis captures well the Stones' appeal and uniqueness within the pop context. She also refers to debates about the Stones' imitations of the Beatles that were rampant at that point and discusses the connection between rock and politics, another hot topic among critics, fans, and musicians. Both bands had produced songs that had brought political involvement into the foreground—the Stones with "Street Fighting Man," the Beatles with "Revolution"—during 1968, the year when the relationship between the counterculture and politics began to become more pressing and contentious. The sources of this shift were numerous: the growth of the antiwar movement, riots at the Democratic convention in Chicago, and the assassinations of Dr. Martin Luther King, Jr., and Robert Kennedy all played a role.

225

A curious aspect of this article, in retrospect, is Willis's failure to mention the Stones' misogyny, something she was to comment upon later. Willis was one of the first female rock critics, and the lack of consciousness on this subject was symptomatic of the lack of feminism within the counterculture at this time. The paradox becomes more palpable in that Willis subsequently became better known as a writer about cultural politics and feminism than as a rock critic.[1]

Records: Rock, Etc.—the Big Ones
Ellen Willis

It's my theory that rock and roll happens between fans and stars, rather then between listeners and musicians—that you have to be a screaming teen-ager, at least in your heart, to know what's going on. Yet I must admit I was never much of a screaming teen-ager myself. I loved rock and roll, but I felt no emotional identification with the performers. Elvis Presley was my favorite singer, and I bought all his records; just the same, he was a stupid, slicked-up hillbilly, a bit too fat and soft to be really good-looking, and I was a middle-class adolescent snob. Jerry Lee Lewis? More revolting than Elvis. Buddy Holly? I didn't even know what he looked like. Fats Domino? He was *comic*—and black. When I went to rock shows, I screamed, all right, but only so I wouldn't be conspicuous. Actually, I grooved much more easily with records than with concerts, which forced me to recognize the social chasm separating me from the performers (and, for that matter, from much of the audience). The social-distance factor became more acute as I got older; that was one reason I defected to folk music. By the time the Beatles came on the scene, I wasn't paying much attention to rock. Naturally, I was *aware* of them, but I didn't have the slightest inkling of their importance. Their kookiness had the same effect on kids that Elvis's dirtiness had had; as far as I was concerned, the two phenomena were identical, and neither had much to do with me. I didn't realize that Elvis was to the Beatles as a Campbell Soup can is to an Andy Warhol replica. (Of course, the Beatles probably didn't realize it, either.) At first, I reacted to the Stones with equal incomprehension. Mick Jagger had his gimmick: he was a hood. The j.-d. [juvenile delinquent] image was a familiar one, though Mick played the role with more than the usual élan. He was so aggressively illiterate, his sexual come-on was so exaggerated and tasteless that it never occurred to me he might be smart. (I didn't know then that he'd gone to the London School of Economics.) But his songs, which had all the energetic virtues of rock and roll,

---

1. Curiously, this issue had been debated in a series of articles on the Stones in the Marxist *New Left Review*. See Alan Beckett/Richard Merton, "Stones/Comment," in *The Age of Rock: Sounds of the American Cultural Revolution*, ed. Jonathan Eisen, 109–17 (New York: Random House, 1969); and Michael Parsons, "Rolling Stones," in *The Age of Rock*, 118–20. These articles originally appeared in the *New Left Review* in 1968, issues 47 and 48. For more of Willis's writings, see *Beginning to See the Light: Sex, Hope, and Rock-and-Roll* (Hanover, N.H.: Wesleyan University Press and University Press of New England, 1992).

Source: "Records: Rock, Etc.—The Big Ones," © Ellen Willis/ *The New Yorker*.

also displayed the honesty and clear-headedness I expected only from blues. I loved both rock and blues, but in each case my response was incomplete: rock was too superficial, blues too alien. The Stones' music was the perfect blend. And, I came to realize, so was Mick's personality; he was an outcast, but he was also thoroughly indigenous to mass society. Because he was so unequivocally native, he touched a part of me that the black bluesmen and alienated folk singer could never reach. And because I couldn't condescend to him—his "vulgarity" represented a set of social and aesthetic attitudes as sophisticated as mine, if not more so—he shook me in a way Elvis had not. I became a true Stones fan—i.e., an inward screamer—and I've been one ever since.

As a fan, I feel ambivalent about "Beggars Banquet." It's a good album—the Stones have never put out a bad one—but something of an anti-climax. This is the first Stones L.P. in a year, and there have been no major performances since 1966. When stars have as little contact with their public as this, everyone's fantasies get so baroque that the eventual reality rarely satisfies. (Bob Dylan has got away with this sort of thing twice; if he tries it again, he'll be pressing his luck.) Besides, "Beggars Banquet" had an unusually long gestation—the rumors of its imminent appearance began back in August. Through the fall, I followed the Stones' hassle with (British) Decca over that men's-room-with-graffiti-album cover. I took it for granted they'd win. The cover was really pretty innocent, and, anyway, what mere record company could thwart the Rolling Stones? But they lost. For the first time, I had to think of the Stones as losers. So even before I heard the record the reality—that black and white jacket designed to look like an engraved invitation—was a letdown from the fantasy.

There's another reason, also having to do with contact, that "Beggar's Banquet" doesn't quite make it: I have the feeling that Jagger is responding more to the Beatles than to the world, and that the album gets to us only after bouncing off John Lennon. In a very general way, the Stones' sensibility has always been—at least in part—a revision of and a reaction to the Beatles. But the symbiosis—or, rather, the competition—has become more pronounced and specific since "Sergeant Pepper" forced them to respond with "Their Satanic Majesties Request." I'm not putting down "Satanic Majesties" as a mere imitation, or parody, or comment. There was nothing mere about that album. The Stones showed they could do the studio thing; they did it with just the right amount of extravagance and wit, and with beautiful songs. Anyway, they could scarcely have ignored an event of "Sergeant Pepper's" magnitude. But "Satanic Majesties" was a special record for a special time. In practice it was good, in principle very dangerous. While "Satanic Majesties" was still in the works, the Beatles released "All You Need Is Love," and the Stones countered with "We Love You," a better-conceived and more powerful song. Now the best track on "Beggars Banquet" is "Street Fighting Man," which is infinitely more intelligent than "Revolution." I sense an unworthy effort to expose John as callow. (Callowness is part of his charm anyway.) It may be that anything the Beatles do, the Stones can do better, but it never pays to work on someone else's terms. In this case, there is a special risk. What has made the Stones the Stones, more than anything else, is a passionate, thrusting ego. The Beatles' identity is collective, but the Stones are Mick Jagger. The Beatles' magic inheres in their glittering surface, the Stones' in Jagger's genius for visceral communication. Yet in this album, as in "Satanic Majesties," Mick is—the only word for it is "leashed." "Parachute Woman" and "Stray Cat Blues" do show traces of the old self-assertion, but in both of them bad production has made the lyrics nearly impossible to catch. In the other songs that have an "I" at all, it is weak, even passive—"Take me to the station,/And put me on a train./I've got no expectations/To pass through here again," or "But what can a poor boy do/'Cept to sing for a rock-and-roll band?/ Guess in sleepy London town there's just no place for a street fighting man"—or else, as in "Sympathy for the Devil," it belongs to a stock character. Most of the songs are impersonal artifacts. The "Factory Girl" is just described, not loved or sneered at. "Salt of the Earth" is positively alienating, in the Brechtian sense. What can it mean for Mick Jagger to toast the workers? Is he being sarcastic? Is the song just a musical exercise? Or is he making a sincere, if rather simple-minded, political statement? Like the Beatles, the Stones play with forms: "Prodigal Son," flawless folk blues (another political statement?); "Dear Doctor," a rather overdone parody of country music; "Jig-Saw Puzzle," proof that Jagger (or Richard) can write lyrics exactly like Dylan's. My response to these songs is purely cerebral. "Street Fighting Man" is my favorite, because it really gets down to the ambiguous relation of rock and roll to rebellion. It does with politics what early rock did with sex. (Are they deliberately using the tradition, or unconsciously re-creating it?) The lyrics of the old songs had to be bland enough to be played on the radio, but the beat and arrangements that emphasized a phrase out of context here, a double-entendre there got the message across. Taken together, the words of "Street Fighting Man" are innocuous. But somehow the only line that comes though loud and clear is "Summer's here, and the time is right for fighting in the streets." Then, there's the heavy beat and all that chaotic noise in the background. So Mick leaves no doubt where his instincts are. (And he didn't fool the censors, either; the single of "Street Fighting Man" was virtually boycotted by AM stations, though "Revolution" was played constantly.) But what can a poor boy do—if he wants to make some bread—'cept to sing for a rock and roll band? There it is. Rock is a socially acceptable, lucrative substitute for anarchy; being a rock and roll star is a way of beating the system, of being free in the midst of unfreedom. And I know Jagger understands the ironies involved and has no illusions about himself. (Which isn't to say he's cynical—I suspect that his famous cynicism has always been more metaphor than fact.) Still, there was a time when he applied equal energy to having no illusions about other people. It's the direct link between subject and object that I miss.

Apparently, the Stones, too, are worried that all is not right; I hear they're planning an American tour in the spring. Whether that decision stems from a desire for artistic renewal or from nervousness about declining sales doesn't matter. It's wonderful news. The Stones were never meant to be studio recluses. They need to get out and face the people.

The Beatles have also found it necessary to define themselves politically. But unlike the Stones, they have little insight into their situation. Instead, they have taken refuge in self-righteousness, facile optimism, and status mongering (revolution isn't hip, you'll scare away the chicks). Not that I believe the Beatles have any obligation to be political activists, or even political sophisticates. There are many ways to serve mankind, and one is to give pleasure. Who among the Beatles' detractors has so enriched the lives of millions of kids? No, all I ask of the Beatles is a little taste. When Bob Dylan renounced politics, he also renounced preaching. "Revolution," in contrast, reminds me of the man who refuses a panhandler and then can't resist lecturing him on the error of his ways. It takes a lot of chutzpah for a millionaire to assure the rest of us, "You know it's gonna be alright." And Lennon's "Change your head" line is just an up-to-date version of "Let them eat cake"; anyone in a position to follow such advice doesn't need it.

We may as well face it. Deep within John Lennon, there's a fusty old Tory struggling to get out. Yet I think "Revolution" protests too much. It had been obvious for a while—ever since all the Beatles grew beards and/or mustaches and George announced "We're tired of that kiddie image"—that they're suffering growing pains from the who-am-I-and-where-am-I-going-and-how-do-my-money-and-my-fame-fit-in variety. When they were four silly kids jumping around on a stage, making tons of money was a rebellious act—they were thumbing their noses at the Protestant ethic. But once Leonard Bernstein had certified them as bona-fide artists they began in the eyes of society to *deserve* all that money. They could no longer accept it as part of the lark. It's no accident that the Maharishi was not only a believer in transcendental meditation but a believer in the virtue of material things. And would John have needed to write "Revolution" if on some level he hadn't felt a little defensive? He can see that all those student revolutionaries are sufficiently well-off to do more or less what he's done, if on a less spectacular scale—that is, to find a personal solution within the system—yet, they've chosen a far less comfortable route. I notice that in the album version of "Revolution" he has put the ambivalence right into the song: "Don't you know that you can count me out—in?" And he admitted to a *Rolling Stone* reporter that if he were black, he might not be so "meek and mild." Good.

Everybody has to grow up, but few people have done it as late and publicly as Lennon. Though Dylan also went through a protracted adolescence in front of a mass audience, he at least battled the media for every scrap of his private life. John takes us through all the changes—LSD, religion, politics, broken marriage, love affair.[2] In the context of this openness, the nude pictures of him and Yoko are very touching. I'm sure he didn't analyze what he was doing—isn't everyone undressing these days?—But he certainly gets my most-inspired-whim-of-the-year-award. What makes the pictures beautiful is that the bodies *aren't* beautiful; by choosing to reveal them, John is telling his fans that celebrities aren't gods, that people shouldn't be ashamed of their bodies just because they're imperfect, that even a Beatle can love a woman who isn't a pinup. When I think of both of them looking so vulnerable, I don't resent "Revolution" so much. How can I expect someone to be right all the time?

About the new album. To get it over with, here's what I *don't* like:

1. Calling the album "The Beatles" and packaging it in a white cover. Everyone's going back to the basics, and it's getting boring. The right cover should have been John and Yoko, clothed.
2. The slowed-down version of "Revolution." Aside from the lyrics, the song was fine: good, heavy hard rock. You could even dance to it. Why do it at half the speed? So that we can hear the words better?
3. "Revolution 9." Though I know nothing about electronic music, it sounds to me like the worst kind of pretentious nonsense. Friends who are more knowledgeable than I am concur.

---

2. Lennon discussed these topics at great length in a famous interview published in *Rolling Stone* following the Beatles' breakup. See Jann Wenner, *Lennon Remembers: The Rolling Stone Interviews* (New York: Popular Library, 1971). This interview is also important in that Lennon goes to great lengths to debunk what he already saw as the dominant myth of the sixties as a period dominated by an ethos of "peace and love." For another contemporary debunking (albeit an allegorical one), see the "fictional review" by J. R. Young reprinted in Chapter 46.

4. The album is just a bit too in-groupy. It parodies Bob Dylan, Tiny Tim, the Beach Boys, fifties gospel, rock, blues, and music-hall songs; a whole song is devoted to discussing the Beatles' previous work; and one of the songs on the record alludes to another. But it's all done so well that this is a minor criticism.

Otherwise, this album is very satisfying. The Beatles have always blended sentimentality with irreverence. Lately, the sentimentality has become fantasy and the irreverence a whimsical disregard of linguistic conventions. Whether or not it has anything to do with their politics, "The Beatles," even more than "Magical Mystery Tour," belongs to a private world. And what doesn't work in life works fine as art. By "private" I don't mean exclusive; the Beatles' world is one anybody can get into. "The Beatles" is a terrific children's album—much better than Donovan's "For the Little Ones"—yet there is nothing prohibitively childish about it. The songs are funny (especially "Piggies" and "Why Don't We Do It in the Road?"), moving ("I'm So Tired" and "Julia"), clever ("Rocky Raccoon"), singable ("Ob-la-di, Ob-la-da" and "Back in the U.S.S.R."). For sheer fun with language, none of the lyrics quite come up to "I Am the Walrus," but the general level is high. A special treat is Ringo Starr's first song, "Don't Pass Me By." It's beautiful, especially the verse that goes, "I'm sorry that I doubted you,/I was so unfair./You were in a car crash,/And you lost your hair." Ringo, you keep us all sane. The Beatles might still be with the giggling guru if you hadn't turned up your nose at the curry. "Don't Pass Me By" makes up for all George Harrison's Indian songs, plus "The Fool on the Hill." The screaming teenager in me wants to know how your Beatle museum is coming along, and sends her love to Maureen and the kids—and to you.

Further Reading

Burke, Patrick. "Rock, Race, and Radicalism in the 1960s: The Rolling Stones, Black Power, and Godard's *One Plus One*." *Journal of Musicological Research* 29, no. 4 (Oct–Dec 2010): 275–94.

Eisen, Jonathan, ed. *The Age of Rock: Sounds of the American Cultural Revolution*. New York: Random House, 1969.

MacPhail, Jessica Holman Whitehead. *Yesterday's Papers: The Rolling Stones in Print, 1963–1984*. Ann Arbor, Mich.: Pierian Press, 1986.

See also Chapters 36 and 39.

Discography

The Beatles. *The Beatles*. Apple, 1968.

The Rolling Stones. *Aftermath*. Decca, 1966.

_____. *Their Satanic Majesties Request*. Decca, 1967.

_____. *Beggars Banquet*. Decca, 1968.

41. If You're Goin' to San Francisco . .

Psychedelic rock provided rock critics with more evidence (in addition to the work of Dylan and the Beatles) for their belief that rock music had become a form of "art." Taking its cue from a hodgepodge of elements derived from early 20th-century modernism, psychedelic rock was particularly enamored with notions of the unconscious derived from Freud. The Symbolist poetry of Rimbaud and Baudelaire, filtered through Beat writers such as Jack Kerouac and Allen Ginsberg; "stream of consciousness" writing as practiced by James Joyce and Virginia Woolf; existentialist philosophy as espoused by Jean-Paul Sartre and Albert Camus; visual imagery drawn from surrealism and expressionism; Eastern philosophy: all were cultural threads that the counterculture and psychedelic music drew upon. The first flowering of psychedelic rock occurred in San Francisco, also one of the geographic centers for the Beat movement and the place where liberal politics and the lack of a "blue-blood" social hierarchy conjoined to encourage artistic experimentation.

The lyric style of psychedelic rock, while drawing on the literary influences just noted, was filtered most directly through Dylan's work of 1965–66. In musical terms, psychedelic rock drew from many sources, most notably from the emphasis on improvisation found in blues, jazz, and South Asian classical music, particularly that of the North Indian, or Hindustani, tradition. The earliest songs recognized as psychedelic, such as the Byrds' "Eight Miles High" or the Beatles' "Tomorrow Never Knows" (both recorded early in 1966), combined surrealistic lyrics with drones and modal improvisation influenced by Indian classical music. "Tomorrow Never Knows" used *musique concrète* (recorded sounds manipulated with a tape recorder), a technique borrowed from avant-garde art music, to create an "otherworldly" effect, a technique soon adopted by many other bands.[1] Dissonance and atonality were other musical elements derived from avant-garde

---

1. The Mothers of Invention were probably the pioneers in the use of *musique concrète* in popular music, since their *Freak Out!* was released prior to *Revolver* (the Beatles' album containing "Tomorrow Never Knows"). Despite this, it is safe to say that the Beatles did the most to expose the public (and other pop musicians) to this practice. See Richard Goldstein's review of *Revolver,* reprinted in Chapter 38.

jazz and classical music that came to connote the "psychedelic" within the rock music context.

Psychedelic rock, as it developed in the San Francisco Bay Area, London, Los Angeles, and elsewhere, was connected to local hippie sub-cultures through large outdoor concerts and other, more experimental performance practices. These performances incorporated multimedia approaches from the avant-garde and included light shows, projections, and film. In San Francisco, many of these events were connected to mass "dosings" of LSD, in which much of the audience ingested the hallucinogen. Author Ken Kesey (*One Flew Over the Cuckoo's Nest*) and his gang of cohorts, the Merry Pranksters, were important organizers of many of these events, dubbed the "Acid Tests."[2] The "Human Be-In," a public concert held in San Francisco's Golden Gate Park in January 1967, brought these happenings into public awareness. The three-day-long Monterey Pop Festival (held in June 1967)[3] demonstrated some of the commercial potential of such gatherings and impressed even the "straight" press with how peaceful the participants were.

The San Francisco psychedelic rock scene was one of the first popular music movements ever to receive attention by the mass media before many people had heard the music or before much of it had even been recorded. The first group to record, the Jefferson Airplane, was also the first to achieve commercial success; after an initial album, *The Jefferson Airplane Takes Off* (1966), failed to attract many buyers, the second, *Surrealistic Pillow* (1967), sold several million copies and, much to the surprise of the group and its followers, generated two Top 10 singles, "Somebody to Love" and "White Rabbit."

The Airplane, with their backgrounds in folk music and blues; their modal harmonies and dissonant, contrapuntal textures; and their charismatic female vocalist, Grace Slick, were only the most public face of the San Francisco scene. The colorful names of other San Francisco bands caught the fancy of the national media: the Grateful Dead, the Quicksilver Messenger Service, Moby Grape, Country Joe and the Fish, Big Brother and the Holding Company. Of these, the Grateful Dead enjoyed the most sustained success and influence, surviving as primarily a concertizing unit until leader Jerry Garcia's death in 1995.

The entry on psychedelic rock that follows is an article by Ralph J. Gleason. Gleason was the jazz and pop music critic for the *San Francisco Chronicle* from the 1940s through the 1960s and one of the first established critics to write about rock music with the seriousness previously accorded jazz. Gleason became an advocate of the San Francisco bands and cofounded *Rolling Stone* with Jann Wenner in 1967. Gleason's essay portrays the Grateful Dead circa 1967 and reflects on the development of their style and the San Francisco psychedelic scene in general.

2. This scene was memorably recorded by Tom Wolfe in his *Electric Kool-Aid Acid Test*.

3. Commemorated in a documentary by D. A. Pennebaker, *Monterey Pop*.

Dead Like Live Thunder
Ralph J. Gleason

San Francisco has become the Liverpool of America in recent months, a giant pool of talent for the new music world of rock.

The number of recording company executives casing the scene at the Fillmore and the Avalon is equaled only by the number of anthropologists and sociologists studying the Haight-Ashbury hippy culture.

Nowhere else in the country has a whole community of rock music developed to the degree it has here.

At dances at the Fillmore and the Avalon and the other, more occasional affairs, thousands upon thousands of people support several dozen rock 'n' roll bands that play all over the area for dancing each week. Nothing like it has occurred since the heyday of Glenn Miller, Benny Goodman, and Tommy Dorsey. It is a new dancing age.

The local band with the greatest underground reputation (now that the Jefferson Airplane has gone national via two LP's and several single records) is a group of young minstrels with the vivid name, The Grateful Dead.

A Celebration

Their lead guitar player, a former folk musician from Palo Alto named Jerry Garcia and their organist, harmonica player and blues singer Pig Pen (Ron McKernan) have been pictured in national magazines and TV documentaries. Richard Goldstein in the *Village Voice* has referred to the band as the most exciting group in the Bay Area and comments, "Together, the Grateful Dead sound like live thunder."

Tomorrow The Grateful Dead celebrate the release of their first album on the Warner Brothers label. It's called simply "The Grateful Dead" and the group is throwing a record promotion party for press and radio at Fugazi Hall.

The Dead's album release comes on the first day as their first single release, two sides from the album—"Golden Road" and "Cream Puff War."

The Dead, as their fans call them, got their exotic name when guitarist Garcia, a learned and highly articulate man, was browsing through a dictionary. "It just popped out at me. The phrase—'The Grateful Dead.' We were looking for a name at the time and I knew that was it."

The Grateful Dead later discovered the name was from an Egyptian prayer: "We grateful dead praise you, Osiris. . . . "

Garcia, who is a self-taught guitarist ("my first instrument was an electrical guitar; then I went into folk music and played a flat-top guitar, a regular guitar. But Chuck Berry was my influence!") is at a loss to describe the band's music, despite his expressiveness.

The Grateful Dead draws from at least five idioms, Garcia said, including Negro blues, country and western, popular music, even classical. (Phil Lesh, the bass player, is a composer who has spent several years working with serial and electronic music.)

"He doesn't play bass like anybody else; he doesn't listen to other bass players, he listens to his head," Garcia said.

Source: "Dead Like Live Thunder," Ralph J. Gleason/ *San Francisco Chronicle.*

Pig Pen, the blues vocalist, "has a style that is the sum of several styles," Garcia pointed out, including that of country blues singers such as Lightnin' Hopkins, as well as the more modern, urban blues men.

"When we give him a song to sing, it doesn't sound like someone else, it comes out Pig Pen's way." Pig Pen's father, by the way, is Phil McKernan, who for years had the rhythm and blues show on KRE, the predecessor of KPAT in Berkeley.

Bill Sommers [usually known as Bill Kreutzmann], the drummer, is a former jazz and rhythm and blues drummer. "He worked at the same music store I did in Palo Alto. I was teaching guitar and he was teaching drums," Garcia said. He is especially good at laying rhythms under a solo line played by the guitars. Bob Weir, the rhythm guitarist, "doesn't play that much straight rhythm," Garcia said, "he thinks of all these lovely, pretty things to do."

The Dead (they were originally known as the Warlocks) have been playing together for over two years now. They spend at least five or six hours a day rehearsing or playing or "just fooling around," Garcia continued.

"We're working with dynamics now. We've spent two years with loud, and we've spent six months with deafening! I think we're moving out of our loud stage. We've learned after these past two years, that what's really important is that the music be groovy, and if it's groovy enough and it's well played enough, it doesn't have to be too loud."

Dance Band

The Dead's material comes from all the strains in American music. "We'll take an idea and develop it; we're interested in form. We still feel that our function is as a dance band and that's what we like to do; we like to play for dancers. We're trying to do new things of course, but not arrange our material to death. I'd say we've stolen freely from everywhere, and we have no qualms about mixing our idioms. You might hear some traditional style classical counterpoint cropping up in the middle of some rowdy thing, you know!"

The eclectic electric music has won the Dead its Warner Brothers contract, offers of work in films, a dedicated group of fans who follow them faithfully and the prospect of national tours, engagements in New York and elsewhere. But Garcia, who is universally loved by the rock musicians and fans, is characteristically calm about it all. "I'm just a student guitar player," he concluded, "I'm trying to get better and learn how to play. We're all novices."

Further Reading

Burke, Patrick. "Tear Down the Walls: Jefferson Airplane, Race, and Revolutionary Rhetoric in 1960s Rock." *Popular Music* 29, no. 1 (January 2011): 61–79.

Dodd, David G., and Diana Spaulding. *The Grateful Dead Reader*. New York: Oxford University Press, 2000.

Gleason, Ralph J. *The Jefferson Airplane and the San Francisco Sound*. New York: Ballantine Books, 1969.

Lesh, Phil. *Searching for the Sound: My Life with the Grateful Dead*. New York: Back Bay Books, 2006.

Meriwether, Nicholas G., ed. *All Graceful Instruments: The Contexts of the Grateful Dead Phenomenon*. Newcastle, UK: Cambridge Scholars Press, 2007.

O'Dair, Barbara. *Trouble Girls: The Rolling Stone Book of Women in Rock*. New York: Random House, 1997.

Perry, Charles. *The Haight-Ashbury: A History*. New York: Wenner Publications, [1984] 2005.

Tamarkin, Jeff. *Got a Revolution! The Turbulent Flight of Jefferson Airplane*. New York: Atria Books, 2003.

Unterberger, Richie. *Eight Miles High: Folk-Rock's Flight from Haight-Ashbury to Woodstock*. San Francisco: Backbeat Books, 2003.

Wolfe, Tom. *The Electric Kool-Aid Acid Test*. New York: Farrar, Straus and Giroux, 1968.

Discography

Big Brother and the Holding Company. *Cheap Thrills*. Columbia, 1968.

Country Joe and the Fish. *Electric Music for the Mind and Body*. Vanguard, 1967.

The Grateful Dead. *The Grateful Dead*. Warner Brothers, 1967.

_____. *Anthem of the Sun*. Warner Brothers, 1968.

_____. *Live Dead*. Warner Brothers, 1970.

Jefferson Airplane. *Surrealistic Pillow*. RCA Victor, 1967.

_____. *After Bathing at Baxter's*. RCA Victor, 1967.

Moby Grape. *Moby Grape*. Columbia, 1967.

Quicksilver Messenger Service. *Happy Trails*. Capitol, 1969.

42. The Kozmic Blues of Janis Joplin

Although she first gained prominence as the lead singer with the San Francisco psychedelic band Big Brother and the Holding Company, Janis Joplin's (1943–70) fame soon superseded her band's. She departed Big Brother in 1968, following a successful year that included a critically acclaimed performance at the Monterey Pop Festival, a major recording contract with Columbia Records, and a pop hit with the single "Piece of My Heart." The career of this dynamic, blues-influenced singer was riddled with contradictions: Joplin was labeled the first "hippie poster girl," yet was claimed by progressive writers as a proto-feminist for her assertive performing style, extroverted public persona, and status as a bandleader.

Often described as the "the best white blues singer of all time," she clearly modeled her style after blues and R&B singers in contrast to the more folk-influenced vocal approach favored by other popular white female singers of the era (with the obvious exception of Grace Slick, with whom she was often compared). These influences also

contrasted with the effort by some of the San Francisco bands to distance themselves from African American sources.[1] The perception of
her performances as completely uninhibited was reinforced by her
hard-living, hard-drinking image, which she emphasized on stage and
in interviews. Another contradiction surfaces in the contrast between
this "one-of-the-boys" image and the image of Joplin as a "victim,"
an image promoted by the tales of suffering outlined in many of her
songs and by reports of her personal life.[2] Regardless of these aspects
of her persona, her brief recording career, which included four albums
released between 1967 and 1971, displays increasing vocal refinement
from the all-out, larynx-shattering performance of "Ball and Chain"
on *Cheap Thrills* with Big Brother and the Holding Company (1968;
also captured in the film *Monterey Pop*, 1967) to the carefully nuanced
buildup in her most commercially successful recording, "Me and Bobby
McGee," recorded shortly before her death in 1970 and released post-
humously in 1971 on *Pearl*.

The article that follows charts the broadening public awareness of Joplin and her reception in New York early in 1968 shortly before her split
with Big Brother and the Holding Company. This portrayal of Joplin by
Nat Hentoff is based on an interview in which Joplin discusses her influences, the connection between "soul" and race, and her approach to
performing. Hentoff's role in the criticism of rock music resembles that
of Ralph J. Gleason's in that Hentoff was well known initially as a jazz
critic in the 1950s; the "oral history" of Bessie Smith in Chapter 7 is
excerpted from a volume coedited by him. Hentoff's relationship with
jazz musicians was less adversarial than that of many white critics,
sharing close personal relationships with musicians otherwise known
for their irascible personalities, such as Charles Mingus. Hentoff moved
into writing about other forms of popular music somewhat earlier than
Gleason, however, writing a well-known profile of Bob Dylan in 1964 and
conducting one of the most-celebrated interviews of Dylan late in 1965.[3]

---

1. For examples of this "anxiety of (African American) influence," see the following: the
exchange between Ralph Gleason and Nick Gravenites in *Rolling Stone* over white bluesman Mike
Bloomfield's "cultural authenticity"—Gleason, "Perspectives: Stop This Shuck, Mike Bloomfield,"
Rolling Stone, May 11, 1968, 10; and Gravenites, "Gravenites: Stop This Shuck, Ralph Gleason,"
Rolling Stone, May 25, 1968, 17; Ed Ward's review of *The Worst of the Jefferson Airplane*, *Rolling
Stone*, February 4, 1971; and many of Gleason's comments and questions in *The Jefferson Airplane
and the San Francisco Sound* (New York: Ballantine Books, 1969). In the piece reprinted here, Joplin
betrays her own anxieties about seeming to be *too* influenced by black singers.

2. These aspects of Joplin's persona are brilliantly addressed by Ellen Willis in "Janis Joplin,"
in *Beginning to See the Light: Sex, Hope, and Rock-and-Roll* (Hanover, N.H.: Wesleyan University
Press and University Press of New England, [1976] 1992), 61–67.

3. Nat Hentoff, "The Crackin', Shakin', Breakin', Sounds," *New Yorker*, October 24, 1964,
reprinted in *Bob Dylan: The Early Years—A Retrospective*, ed. Craig McGregor (New York: Da Capo,
1990), 44–65; Hentoff, "The *Playboy* Interview," *Playboy*, March 1966, reprinted in *Bob Dylan: The
Early Years—A Retrospective*, ed. Craig McGregor (New York: Da Capo, 1990), 124–45.

Clearly, Hentoff had a gift for earning the trust of musicians who were wary of journalists. His empathy for Joplin is clearly apparent in the profile that follows.

We Look at Our Parents and . . .
Nat Hentoff

The only girl in the group (Big Brother and the Holding Company), Janis Joplin has exploded the increasingly mandarin categories of rock music by being so intensely, so jovially herself. Her singing with that unit is a celebration—her voice and body hurled with larruping power that leaves her limp and this member of her audience feeling that he has been in contact with an overwhelming life force. Part of that force is an open sensuality, with no tinge of coyness or come-on. It's not that she is beautiful by ordinary standards (a phrase that makes her wince). Rather, she brings *all* of herself into a performance. "The sex thing they keep trying to lay on me," Miss Joplin says, "is always in the receiver's head, which is where it should be. If I turn on anyone that way—great! Because that's what it's all about."

The triumphs of Janis Joplin began last June when she lifted a huge audience at the Monterey International Pop Festival to a standing ovation. The glory of her abandon has continued to draw open-mouthed attention as she and the group travel more and more widely from their San Francisco base, most recently having touched here at Generation, a new rock cellar room in Greenwich Village. The hosannas from the most flinty of the rock critics sound like hyperbole until you see her—"the best rock singer since Ray Charles"; "the best popular stylist since Billie Holiday, and certainly the most impressive woman on the rock scene"; "the major female voice of her generation."

The best single description of Janis Joplin I've seen appeared in Cashbox, not usually a source of memorable metaphor: "She's a kind of a mixture of Leadbelly, a steam engine, Calamity Jane, Bessie Smith, an oil derrick, and rot gut bourbon funneled into the 20th century somewhere between El Paso and San Francisco." Not entirely complete: her drink of preference is Southern Comfort, not bourbon, and that choice also indicates the gentleness at the core of her corybantic devotions.

Having seen her at Fillmore East on Second Avenue a few weeks ago, I wanted to know more. More than the biological facts—born in Port Arthur, Texas; a dropout from four colleges; a singer of country music in Texas and blues in San Francisco; a drifter until she found a molten center of gravity in Big Brother and the Holding Company two years ago.

We met in the darkly uninviting bar of the Chelsea Hotel, where she stays when she is in New York. Her long hair is brown, her eyes blue-gray, her figure trim, and her hands are always moving. When she's not wielding a microphone, her voice is soft but not guarded; and her face, as on stage, is a kaleidoscope of swiftly changing emotions. I asked her, because I was concerned, how long her voice can hold out since she spends it without stint in performance. "I was worried about that for a while," she grinned, "and so for a couple of weeks, I consciously held back—like maybe a third of what I could do. And it was *nothing*! I'm not doing that anymore.

Source: "We Look at Our Parents and . . . ," 2/21/1968 "We Look at Our Parents and . . . " Hentoff, Nat (1928 words), *New York Times*/Pars International Corp.

Maybe I won't last as long as other singers, but I think you can destroy your now by worrying about tomorrow. If I hold back, I'm no good *now*, and I think I'd rather be good sometimes than holding back all the time. I'm 25 and, like others of my generation and younger, we look back at our parents and see how they gave up and compromised and wound up with very little. So the kids want a lot of something now rather than a little of hardly anything spread over 70 years."

She frowned, "But that's what *I* think. I'm still not used to being asked about my opinions, I'm still not used to all this attention. Nobody gave a damn about me before the Monterey Festival. Look, I'm not a spokesman for my generation. I don't even use acid. I drink." She laughed. "The reason I drink," she had had enough of the generation talk, "is that it loosens me up while the guys are tuning their instruments. I close my eyes and feel things. If I were a musician, it might be a lot harder to get all that feeling out, but I'm really fortunate because my gig is just feeling things." She laughed, again. "I'm really lucky. It doesn't always happen the way I want. It's not always a supreme emotional experience, but when everything is together—the band, me, the audience, it's boss! It's just like magic. I don't think I could ever feel that way about a man. It seems to be the kind of feeling a woman would like to have about a man. I hope I do someday."

New York had gotten in the way of that boss feeling for a while. "At first," she shook her head in exasperation, "this city seemed to have made us all crazy; it was dividing the unity of the band." Miss Joplin hadn't received quite the drink she'd ordered and I waved to the waiter. Slowly, grumblingly, he acceded to the request. "The first three weeks here," she went on, "we all got superaggressive, separate, sour. Something like that waiter there. San Francisco's different. I don't mean it's perfect, but the rock bands there didn't start because they wanted to make it. They dug getting stoned and playing for people dancing. Here they want to MAKE it. What we've had to do is learn to control success, put it in perspective and not lose the essence of what we're doing—the music. Well, we played a gig in Philadelphia recently, and the minute we walked offstage after the first set, it all fell back into place. We all looked at each other, like 'Remember me?' We all remembered what it was all about. We're learning how to handle New York."

San Francisco had been a saving place for her. "In Texas, I was a beatnik, a weirdo, and since I wasn't making it the way I am now, my parents thought I was a goner. Now my mother writes and asks what kinds of clothes a 1968 blues singer wears. That's kind of groovy, since we've been on opposite sides since I was 14. Texas is O.K. if you want to settle down and do your own thing quietly, but it's not for outrageous people, and I was always outrageous. I got treated very badly in Texas." She smiled grimly. "They don't treat beatniks too good in Texas."

Janis Joplin didn't get into music until she was 17, when hard, basic blues changed her from being a painter. "It was Leadbelly first. I knew what it was all about from the very front. I was right into the blues." She moved into a bluegrass band in Austin, dug Bob Dylan and Woody Guthrie, but the blues were always her base. She went to San Francisco to stay in 1962, and sang in folk clubs and bars until she joined the Holding Company.

I told her that she was the first white blues singer (female) I'd heard since Teddy Grace who sang the blues out of black influences but had developed her own sound and phrasing. She'd never heard of Teddy Grace, also a Southern girl, but she beamed. "God, I'm glad you think that. I keep trying to tell people that whites have soul too. There's no patent on soul. It's just feeling things. I sure loved Otis Redding, and Bessie Smith before him, but I don't think I copy anybody much. I've got country in my music too, but what changed things was singing with an electric band. All that power behind you—that pulsating power. I had to react to what was behind me, and my style got different. You can't sing a Bessie Smith vocal with a rock band, so I had to make up my own way of doing it."

Do you categorize yourself at all? I asked. Would you call yourself a jazz singer? "No, I don't feel quite free enough with my phrasing to say I'm a jazz singer. I sing with a more demanding beat, a steady rather than a lilting beat. I don't riff over the band; I try to punctuate the rhythm with my voice. That's why Otis Redding is so great. You can't get away from him; he pounds on you; you can't help but *feel* him. He was a man! Still is! Categories? I regard myself as a blues singer but then I regard myself as a rock singer. Actually, I don't feel there's any separation now. I'm a chick singer, that's what I am."

We had another drink. "You know how that whole myth of black soul came up? That only they have soul?" She wasn't asking, she was telling. "Because white people don't allow themselves to feel things. Housewives in Nebraska have pain and joy; they've got soul if they'd give in to it. It's hard. And it isn't all a ball when you do. Me, I never seemed to be able to control my feelings, to keep them down. When I was young, my mother would try to get me to be like everybody else. 'Think before you speak.' 'Learn how to behave yourself.' And I never would. But before getting into this band, it tore my life apart. When you feel that much, you have superhorrible downs. I was always victim to myself. I'd do wrong things, run away, freak out, go crazy. Now, though, I've made feeling work for me, through music, instead of destroying me. It's superfortunate. Man, if it hadn't been for the music, I probably would have done myself in."

She looked tired, not so much from present feeling as from an all-night record session the night before. Being made for Columbia, the album, due this spring, will be the first to fully reflect—she hopes—what Big Brother and the Holding Company are all about. (A previous, poorly recorded set, made much earlier, was issued despite the group's vehement protests.) "Making this record hasn't been easy," she said. "We're not the best technicians around. We're not the kind of dispassionate professionals who can go into a studio and produce something quick and polished. We're passionate; that's all we are. And what we're trying to get on record is what we're good at—insisting, getting people out of their chairs."

"What also makes it hard for John Simon, who's producing the album, is that we're kinda sloppy at the same time as we're happy. Last night he was trying to get something done and said 'Come on, who's the head of this band?' There was a pause because, well, no one is. We vote on things. We're democratic. But I think we're getting what we want into the recording." She sighed. "We've got complete control over this one, and if it's no good, it's our fault."

Janis leaned back, smiled again. "Like I said, it's hard to be free, but when it works, it's sure worth it."

Further Reading

Dalton, David. *Piece of My Heart: A Portrait of Janis Joplin*. New York: Da Capo Press, 1991.

Echols, Alice. *Scars of Sweet Paradise: The Life and Times of Janis Joplin*. New York: Holt Paperbacks, 2000.

Joplin, Laura. *Love, Janis*. New York: Villard, 1992.

Reynolds, Simon. *The Sex Revolts: Gender, Rebellion, and Rock'n'roll*. Cambridge, Mass.: Harvard University Press, 1995.

Willis, Ellen. "Janis Joplin," in *Beginning to See the Light: Sex, Hope, and Rock-and-Roll*, 61–67. Hanover, N.H.: University Press of New England, 1992.

Discography

Big Brother and the Holding Company. *Cheap Thrills*. Columbia, 1968.
_____. *Live at Winterland '68*. Columbia Legacy, 1998.
Joplin, Janis. *I Got Dem Ol' Kozmic Blues Again Mama!* Columbia, 1969.
_____. *Pearl*. Columbia, 1971.
_____. *Box of Pearls*. Sony Legacy, 1999.

43. Jimi Hendrix and the Electronic Guitar

Like Janis Joplin, Jimi Hendrix (1942–70) first achieved prominence through a form of highly amplified blues merged with psychedelic rock. Hendrix's path to that point, however, followed a very different trajectory from Joplin's: an African American raised in Seattle, Hendrix toured as a sideman for R&B artists such as Wilson Pickett and Little Richard before he moved to London, where he launched his solo career. While clearly steeped in the blues, Hendrix made the most significant contribution of any guitarist of his generation toward conceiving of the electric guitar as an electronic instrument, rather than merely an amplified guitar. Distortion no longer occurred as a byproduct of turning up an amplifier: Hendrix made sustain and feedback an integral part of his technique, and he pioneered the use of electronic devices such as fuzztones and wah-wah pedals (he may not have been the first to use these, but he was the first to incorporate them fully as more than gimmicks).

Again, like Joplin, Hendrix first came to the attention of American audiences during the 1967 Monterey Pop Festival. Early commentaries (including those about this festival) all center on his highly theatrical stage performance, which involved playing the guitar behind his head and with his teeth, licking it (all techniques used by earlier blues and R&B musicians, such as T-Bone Walker), lighting it on fire, and finally destroying it (in a gesture perhaps adopted from the Who's Peter Townshend). The highly sexualized performance of a black man in front of a white band and (mostly) white audience also attracted attention and evoked some uncomfortable contradictions within the counterculture, which (as I discussed earlier) was almost entirely white, despite a professed ethos of inclusion.[1]

Hendrix's compositions drew not only on blues and R&B, but also on psychedelic innovations in sound and recording, as well as on Dylan's approach to lyrics; as such, he was an innovator and synthesizer with few previous peers among rock musicians.[2] Hendrix freely acknowledged his indebtedness to Dylan, both in interviews and by recording Dylan's "Like a Rolling Stone" (at Monterey Pop) and "All Along the Watchtower" (which Dylan later said he preferred to his own version). His performance of the "Star Spangled Banner" was a highlight of the Woodstock festival; Hendrix used his guitar wizardry to simulate exploding bombs and sky-diving aircraft, turning the U.S. national anthem into an antiwar protest song. Some of his comments to interviewers and his abandonment of the Jimi Hendrix Experience (which was two-thirds white) toward the end of his career revealed that Hendrix was wrestling with the relationship of his music to his identity as an African American.[3] He died in September 1970 in his sleep from an accidental overdose of barbiturates.

The critical response to Jimi Hendrix during his life featured much debate about whether the highly theatrical performances early in his career were a "gimmick" or not. Also common in the press were comparisons to Eric Clapton and Cream, who achieved prominence at roughly the same time with the same trio format and also featured long, blues-based improvisations. While all writers conceded the quality of Hendrix's guitar playing, many criticized his singing and his ability as a lyricist. The English music press viewed him as part of the London scene (as indeed he was for several years), and this article from the British music magazine *Melody Maker* provides a good example of that perspective. The article also shows Hendrix in transition from the flashy theatrics of his trio and reveals his awareness of earlier criticisms. Like so many articles from this period (and after), this article raises the opposition of art to mass culture. Because the author accepts the terms of this opposition, "showmanship" of the kind associated with Hendrix must result from an artistic compromise—appealing to teenyboppers—rather than from continuity with previous African American approaches to performance.

---

1. For a fuller discussion of these issues, see Steve Waksman, *Instruments of Desire: The Electric Guitar and the Shaping of Musical Experience* (Cambridge, Mass.: Harvard University Press, 1999), 167–206.

2. See Greg Tate's comments in his interview with George Clinton in *Flyboy in the Buttermilk: Essays on Contemporary America* (New York: Fireside/Simon and Schuster, 1992), 39–40, 92–93.

3. Again, see Waksman, *Instruments of Desire*, for a discussion of Hendrix in the context of the black arts movement; and Samuel A. Floyd, *The Power of Black Music: Interpreting Its History from Africa to the United States* (New York: Oxford University Press, 1995), for a discussion that includes Hendrix within a broader, theoretically informed conception of "black music."

Second Dimension: Jimi Hendrix in Action
Bob Dawbarn

Jimi Hendrix—like Eric Clapton, the Nice, the Pink Floyd and many others—is faced with one major problem.

He is trying to produce music with claims to permanent value, yet the outlets for that music are the mass media which, as yet, seem unable to distinguish between a Jimi Hendrix or a Donald Peers.

This means that a Hendrix must continually compromise in order to conform to the patterns demanded by his means of communication.

To stay in business he must make singles, he finds he is forced into acts of showmanship to get his music across, he must make use of publicity machines geared to the needs of teenyboppers.

Before his Albert Hall concert last Tuesday he told me: "I just hope the concert turns out all right. We haven't played in a long time and we concentrate on the music now.

"As long as people come to listen rather than to see us, then everything will be all right. It's when they come to expect to see you doing certain things on stage that you can get hung up."

Jimi dislikes miming on TV. "If you play live, nobody can stop you or dictate what you play beyond setting a time limit."

A good example was his recent appearance on the Lulu show when he surprised everybody in the studio by suddenly shifting from "Hey Joe" into "Sunshine Of Your Love" as a tribute to Cream.

"It was the same old thing," explained Jimi, "with people telling us what to do. They wanted to make us play 'Hey Joe.' I was uptight about it, so I caught Noel's and Mitch's attention and we went into the other thing.

"I dream about having our own show where we would have all contemporary artists as guest stars. Everybody seems to be busy showing what polished performers they are and that means nothing these days—it's how you feel about what you are doing that matters.

"I just cross off people who are just in it for their own ego scene instead of trying to show off another style of music."

Jimi admits that he feels a little restricted by the Trio format.

"It restricts everybody—Noel and Mitch, too," he said. "Now and then I'd like to break away and do a bit of classic blues. Mitch wants to get into a jazz thing and Noel has this thing with Fat mattress and wants to go on an English rock thing—how about Anglo Rock. A patriotic blues-rock music."

As a performer, Hendrix seems to be going through a period of change at the moment leaning towards extended performances.

Personally, I find his playing has great impact when disciplined by a four minute track. The longer things on the "Electric Ladyland" album don't always come off, his ideas seem to get diffused. But this is no doubt a time of transition.

Nobody is better at conveying an atmosphere in a few phrases—there was the menace of "Purple Haze," the raw, immensely masculine "Hey Joe," the blues influence of "Foxy Lady." And listen to the way guitar and voice complement each other on something like "51st Anniversary." Or the way he shows blues can be utterly contemporary on "Voodoo Chile."

"You have to make people identify with the music," explains Jimi. "You make a record in the hope that the public may want to buy it, so you have to make it presentable in some way. They have to have an identification mark.

"The trouble is that a single has to be under six minutes—it used to be under three, which was a real hang-up. It's like you used to be able to give them just one page of a book, now you can give them two or three pages—but never the whole book.

"The music is what matters. If an audience are really digging you on a show, then naturally you get excited and it helps. But a bad audience really doesn't bother me that much because then it is a practice session, a chance to get things together.

"I always enjoy playing, whether it's before ten people or 10,000. And I don't even care if they boo, as long as it isn't out of key.

"I don't try to move an audience—it's up to them what they get from the music. If they have paid to see us then we are going to do our thing.

"If we add a bit of the trampoline side of entertainment then that is a fringe benefit but we are there to play music. If we stand up there all night and play our best and they don't dig it, then they just don't dig us and that's all there is to it."

Jimi is rather underrated as a songwriter—the imagery of the lyric of "The Wind Cries Mary," for example, could not have been written by anyone else.

"I've not written too many heavy things recently," he told me. "Most of what I have done will come out on the next LP in the late summer. I don't try to make a thing about my songs when I put them on record. I try to make them honest and there doesn't seem too much point in talking about them.

"The people who listen to them are the ones who will know whether they are successful or not."

One of the things Jimi seems to be cutting out of his personal appearances is playing guitar with his teeth.

"The idea of doing that came to me in a town in Tennessee," he recalled. "Down there you have to play with your teeth or else you get shot. There's a trail of broken teeth all over the stage.

"It was another way of letting out things and you have to know what you are doing or you might hurt yourself. The trouble was audiences took it as something they must see or they don't enjoy the show. So I don't do it much any more. We don't do too much of anything any more, except play music."

Jimi says it is usually the lyrics that attract him to a song.

"Maybe a lyric has only five words and the music takes care of the rest," he said. "I don't mean my lyrics to be clever. What I want is for people to listen to the music and words together, as one thing. Sometimes you get wrapped up in the words and forget the music—in that case I don't think the song can be completely successful.

"Generally, I don't do other people's songs unless they really say something to me."

Jimi laughed when I said I thought I could detect church music influences in some of his things.

"Spiritual music, maybe," he said. "But if you say you are playing electric church music people go 'gasp, gasp' or 'exclaim, exclaim.'"

"The word church is too identified with religion and music is my religion. Jesus shouldn't have died so early and then he could have got twice as much across.

"They killed him and then twisted so many of the best things he said. Human hands started messing it all up and now so much of religion is hogswash.

"So much of it is negative—Thou Shalt Not. Look at sex. It's been screwed around so much I'm surprised babies are still being born.

"Don't get me wrong. I'm not trying to stop people going to church. But as long as I'm not hurting anybody else I don't see why they should tell me how to live and what to do."

Further Reading

Chenoweth, Lawrence. "The Rhetoric of Hope and Despair: A Study of the Jimi Hendrix Experience and the Jefferson Airplane." *American Quarterly* 23 (1971): 25–45.

Cross, Charles R. *Room Full of Mirrors: A Biography of Jimi Hendrix*. New York: Hyperion, 2005.

Murray, Charles Shaar. *Crosstown Traffic: Jimi Hendrix and the Post-War Rock 'N' Roll Revolution*. New York: St. Martin's Press, 1991.

Waksman, Steve. *Instruments of Desire: The Electric Guitar and the Shaping of Musical Experience*. Cambridge, Mass.: Harvard University Press, 1999.

Zak, Albin J., III. "Bob Dylan and Jimi Hendrix: Juxtaposition and Transformation: 'All along the Watchtower.'" *Journal of the American Musicological Society* 57 (2004): 599–644.

Discography

The Jimi Hendrix Experience. *Are You Experienced*. Track Records, 1967.

_____. *Axis: Bold as Love*. Track Records, 1967.

_____. *Electric Ladyland*. Reprise, 1968.

_____. *Band of Gypsies*. Capitol, 1970.

44. Rock Meets the Avant-Garde
FRANK ZAPPA

Frank Zappa's (1940–93) persona presents an imposing conundrum: immensely talented and witty to his fans, unbearably obnoxious to his detractors. After involvement in a diverse range of musical activities and genres, Zappa formed the Mothers of Invention, signed a recording contract with Verve Records (known primarily as a jazz label), and recorded *Freak Out!* (released in August 1966), one of the first, if not *the* first, album to be organized around a concept, rather than simply presenting an assemblage of songs (the other contender for this distinction is the Beach Boys' *Pet Sounds,* released in May 1966). *Freak Out!* was also one of the first rock albums to feature classical avant-garde approaches to composition, electronics, and sound—in fact, even describing the album as "rock" demonstrates the breadth of that generic label. Other artists, primarily the Beatles, received more attention for their incorporation of such techniques, primarily because their music was heard by a larger audience, but none pursued the use of such experimentation within a rock context as zealously as Zappa.

Zappa's use of parody also stands out in the context of the time: he seemed simultaneously to belong to the counterculture and to mock it. Although it is doubtful that a figure like Zappa could have emerged at any other time and found an audience even as large as the one he had (meaning that he owed something to the social context of the time, and, hence, to the counterculture), the parodic aspects of his music and his separation from the counterculture became more obvious with the release of successive albums. His incorporation of an avant-garde classical performance approach also became more aggressive over time, as did his guitar pyrotechnics. While not really part of the (mostly British) progressive- or art-rock genre per se, Zappa's concern with integrating art music approaches to rock overlaps to some extent with that of such progressive rock bands as King Crimson and Yes.

This 1968 article captures Frank Zappa's role in his band, the Mothers of Invention, as analogous to that of a conductor of a classical music ensemble and comments upon and provides examples of Zappa's ironic verbal style. The description of Zappa as a modernist is apt, particularly with regard to his disdain of the audience; his attitude seems to personify the modernist credo—"if it's popular, it must be bad." Nevertheless, the tone of general approval in the article reveals the increasing acceptance of such high-art notions within the public discourse of rock music. At this moment, the rock audience, writ large, was understood to have room for highly intellectualized parodies of itself.

Zappa and the Mothers: Ugly Can Be Beautiful
Sally Kempton

It is 1 A.M. on a Friday night and the Mothers of Invention are recording part of the soundtrack for their forthcoming movie. Ian is playing the harpsichord and Bunk is playing the flute. They huddle together in a cluster of microphones, Bunk leaning

Source: "Zappa and the Mothers: Ugly Can Be Beautiful" © Sally Kempton/*Village Voice.*

over Ian's shoulder to read the music propped up on the harpsichord stand. Bunk wears a goatee and a matching moustache, and his long thick hair is gray (in the studio light it looks like a powered [sic] wig). Resembling a figure in an old etching, he bends closer to Ian, his flute poised, and Ian straightens his back and places his fingers on the harpsichord keys. Poised like musicians at a nineteenth-century musicale, they wait for a signal to begin. One feels they are waiting to play a Mozart sonata.

Inside the control booth Frank Zappa, wearing a T-shirt bearing the legend "Herzl Camp, Garner, Wisconsin," is fiddling with knobs on the control board. "You're going to have to do the parody notes more staccato, Ian," he says through the intercom.

"You want a little bebop vibrato on that too?" calls Ian.

"Yeah, a little bebop a go go," says Frank. Dick Cunk, the engineer, flips the "record" switch.

"OK, for fame and stardom," says Frank. "You ready?"

Ian and Bunk begin to play a series of dissonant, rhythmic, oddly beautiful chords. The people in the control booth listen intently.

"This is going to be a nice soundtrack," someone says.

Frank Zappa is bent over a music sheet, writing out the next piece. "Yeah," he says. "This is one the folks can enjoy listening to at home."

Frank Zappa is an ironist. He is also a serious composer, a social satirist, a promoter, a recording genius, but his most striking characteristic is his irony. Irony permeates his music, which is riddled with parodies of Charles Ives and Guy Lombardo, of Bartók and the Penguins and Bo Diddly and Ravel and Archie Shepp and Stravinsky and a whole army of obscure fifties rhythm and blues singers. It permeates his lyrics, which are filled with outlandish sexual metaphors and evocations of the culture of the American high school and the American hippie.

Irony is the basis of his public image. In pursuit of absurdity he has had himself photographed sitting naked on the toilet. His latest album is titled *We're Only in It for the Money.* And he has appeared on television speaking in well-rounded periods about music and society and The Scene, all the while emanating a kind of inspired freakishness. Zappa's is the sort of irony which arises from an immense self-consciousness, a distrust of one's own seriousness. It is the most modernist of defense mechanisms, and Zappa is an almost prototypically modernist figure; there are moments when he seems to be living out a parody of the contemporary sensibility.

And now he and his group are teenage idols, or anti-idols, and Zappa's irony, which, because it is so often expressed through contemporary clichés, is the most accessible part of his musical idiom, turns on audiences and makes the Mothers, in addition to everything else, a splendid comedy act. Until recently Zappa's voice, the paradigm California voice, could be heard on the radio doing "greasy teen-age commercials" for Hagstrom Guitars. During the Mothers' live appearances he sits on a stool, his expression deadpan above his bandillero moustache, and occasionally he will lean over and spit on the floor under the bandstand, saying to the audience: "Pigs!"

"Actually, we don't turn on audiences," he said the other day. "Not in the sense that other groups do, anyway. I think of that sort of thing as the strobes going and everybody dancing and love-rock-at-the-Fillmore bullshit—if anybody felt like that about us it'd be for the wrong reasons. Last week we were playing in Philadelphia and we got seven requests, so we played them all at once. It was fantastic. Sherwood was playing the sax part to one song: the whole thing, even the rests. It was really great. But nobody knew what we were playing. They couldn't even tell the songs apart. Half the time, when we're really doing something, the audience doesn't know what it is. Sometimes the guys in the band don't know."

But the Mothers' first album sold a quarter of a million copies and the second has done almost as well. And when they played a long stretch at the Garrick last summer they were beset by loyal groupies. Perhaps the groupies sensed the presence of a governing intelligence, perhaps they simply dug perversity. In any case, the Mothers have an audience.

Frank Zappa is twenty-seven years old. He was born in Baltimore and began playing drums in a rock-and-roll band in Sacramento when he was fifteen.

"It's almost impossible to convey what the r and b scene was like in Sacramento," he says. "There were gangs there, and every gang was loyal to a particular band. They weren't called groups, they were called bands. They were mostly Negro and Mexican, and they tried to get the baddest sound they could. It was very important not to sound like jazz. And there was a real oral tradition of music. Everybody played the same songs, with the same arrangements, and they tried to play as close as possible to the original record. But the thing was that half the time the guys in the band had never heard the record—somebody's older brother would own the record, and the kid would memorize it and teach it to everybody else. At one point all the bands in Sacramento were playing the same arrangement of 'Okey Dokey Stomp' by Clarence Gatemouth Brown. The amazing thing was that it sounded almost note for note like the record."

Zappa was lying in bed, eating breakfast and playing with his three-month-old baby. He lives with his wife, Gail, and the baby, in a long basement apartment in the West Village. The apartment has a garden and its walls are papered with posters and music sheets and clippings from magazines; there is a full-length poster of Frank in the hall and a rocking chair in the living room with a crocheted cover that says "Why, what pigs?"

Frank was in bed because he had been up all night before, recording. "The reason I can stand New York is because I spend all my time here or at the studio," he said.

"Mostly at the studio," said his wife, smiling.

"Let's see, my life," he said. "Well, when I was sixteen my father moved us to a little town out in the country. That was terrible, I hated it. I was used to Sacramento, you see. I was the strangest thing that ever hit that high school. They were so anxious to get rid of me they even gave me a couple of awards when I graduated. After that my father wanted me to go to college. I said no, I was interested in music, I didn't want to go to college. So I hung out at home for awhile, but there was nobody to talk to, everybody else being at college, so I finally decided I should go too. That was very ugly. I stayed for a year. In the meantime I had shacked up with this girl and married her. We stayed married for five years during which time I held a number of jobs" (he listed the jobs). "Then in 1963 we were living in Cucamonga and there was a recording studio there which I bought for $1000, also assuming the former owner's debts. He had hundreds of tapes, among them such big hits as" (he named three or four obscure songs) "and I took the tapes and the equipment and began fooling around. About that time I got divorced and moved into the studio. I spent all my time experimenting; a lot of stuff the Mothers do was worked out there."

A year later the studio was torn down to make room for a widened road, but by that time he had gotten the Mothers together. "We were playing at local beer joints for like six dollars a night. I finally decided this would not do, so I began calling up all the clubs in the area. This was in 1965, and to get work you had to sound like the Beatles or the Rolling Stones. You also had to have long hair and due to an unfortunate circumstance all my hair had been cut off. I used to tell club managers that we sounded exactly like the Rolling Stones. Anyway we finally got a booking in a club in Pomona, and were something of a hit. It was more because of our act than because of our music. People used to go away and tell their friends that here was this group that insulted the audience.

"Then M-G-M sent someone around to sign us to a contract. Their guy came into the club during a set of 'Brain Police' and he said, 'Aha, a protest rhythm and blues group,' so they paid us accordingly. The fee we got for signing was incredibly small, particularly considering the number of guys in the group."

Nowadays, of course, Zappa runs something of an empire. He has an advertising agency ("mostly to push our own products, at least so far"), and a movie coming out which someone else shot but for which they are going to do the soundtrack. The movie is a surrealistic documentary called "Uncle Meat"; it is shot in a style Zappa refers to as "hand-held Pennebaker bullshit," and it will be edited to fit the music.

"Then we're going to do a monster movie in Japan—Japan is where they do the best monster work. And we're starting our own record company. We'll record our own stuff and also some obscure new groups."

It was time for him to go to the studio. The Mothers have rented Apostolic Studios on Tenth Street for the entire month of January. "One hundred and eighty hours—not as much time as the Beatles use, of course, we can't afford that"—and that is where Zappa spends most of his time. He puts on a brown leather greatcoat, pulls a red knitted cap over his ears, and sets out, talking about his music as he walks.

"Stockhausen isn't really an influence," he says. "That is, I have some of his records but I don't play them much. Cage is a big influence. We've done a thing with voices, with talking that is very like one of his pieces, except that of course in our piece the guys are talking about working in an airplane factory, or their cars."

"It was very tough getting the group together in the beginning. A lot of guys didn't want to submit to our packaging. They didn't like making themselves ugly, but they especially didn't like playing ugly. It's hard getting a musician to play ugly, it contradicts all his training. It's hard to make them understand that all that ugliness taken together can come out sounding quite beautiful."

The studio, when he arrived, was nearly deserted, except for Mother Don Preston, who sat at the organ wearing earphones and playing a piece audible only to himself. "Can you run a playback on the violins?" he asked when Frank came in.

"Sure," said Frank. "We recorded this thing last night. I found some violins in a closet and I gave them to three of the guys. None of them had ever played a violin before. They were making all these weird sounds on them, and then in the middle I got them to add some farts. It's a concerto for farts and violins."

But instead of playing back the violin thing, Dick put on a tape of "Lumpy Gravy," one of the Mothers' new records, an instrumental piece, framed at the beginning and end with cocktail music, and interspersed with quiet, hollow, surreal voices talking behind a continuous hum of resonating piano strings. The music has overtones of Bartòk and Ives, but by some stylistic alchemy it ends by sounding like nothing but Zappa. It is an impressive record. Three or four people had drifted into the control room while it was playing, and after it was over someone said, "I love that piece."

"Yeah, but will the kids go for it," said Frank.

"It's good to have it out," said Don, "so people will know what you can do."

"No, no," Frank said. "It's good to have it out so I can take it home and listen to it."

Further Reading

Ashby, Arved. "Frank Zappa and the Anti-Fetishist Orchestra." *The Musical Quarterly* 83 (1999): 557–606.

Kostelanetz, Richard. *The Frank Zappa Companion: Four Decades of Commentary*. New York: Schirmer Books, 1997.

Lowe, Kelly Fisher. *The Words and Music of Frank Zappa*. Westport, Conn.: Praeger, 2006.

Watson, Ben. *Frank Zappa: The Negative Dialectics of Poodle Play*. New York: St. Martin's Press, 1995.

Wragg, David. "'Or Any Art at All?' Frank Zappa Meets Critical Theory." *Popular Music* 20 (2001): 205–22.

Discography

The Mothers of Invention. *Freak Out!* Verve, 1966.

Zappa, Frank, and the Mothers of Invention. *Lumpy Gravy*. Verve, 1967.

_____. *We're Only in It for the Money*. Verve, 1968.

_____. *Weasels Ripped My Flesh*. Bizarre Records, 1973.

45. The Aesthetics of Rock

An important part of a history in documents about popular music is the way in which writing about popular music changes over time. Prior to the 1960s, one period in particular stands out for the amount of print expended on popular music: the late 1930s and early 1940s witnessed the birth of several publications devoted to jazz, precisely at the moment when debates about "authenticity" and "commercialism" in jazz were becoming more common. The aesthetic and historical issues in the mid-1960s were similar in many respects. As I mentioned earlier, music criticism devoted to rock blossomed parallel to a shift in the seriousness of the audience for popular (especially rock) music. Several new publications appeared in response to these changes in reception. *Crawdaddy!* led the way early in 1966 and was quickly followed by *Rolling Stone* in 1967 and *Creem* in 1968. In addition to these, several older, more established publications published articles by critics that discussed popular music in a tone previously reserved for classical music and jazz (some of these articles appeared earlier in Part 3). The *Village Voice* earned the distinction of being the first established publication to hire a member of the counterculture, Richard Goldstein, as its rock critic in 1966. Other publications followed suit: *Cheetah* hired Robert Christgau in 1967; the tony *New Yorker* broke down in 1968 and hired Ellen Willis, one of the first female rock critics. Meanwhile, other notables of rock criticism such as Greil Marcus, Jon Landau, and Dave Marsh were getting their start at one or the other of the above-named countercultural publications.[1]

Compared to the previous generation of critics and mainstream publications such as *Time* and *Newsweek*, these countercultural writers brought with them a new sensibility. What follows is an article that explicitly addresses the notion of rock aesthetics—in other words, what is it that makes rock music good or beautiful? And how does the specificity of late sixties rock demand a different approach to answering these questions compared to other types of music?

The following is an early article by Richard Goldstein that takes Marshall McLuhan's ideas about the effects of electronic media on communications as its point of departure. One of the first attempts to articulate why rock music demanded a new way of listening and a new context for evaluation, this article aligns rock with McLuhan's "cool media," which, according to McLuhan, counteract the serial, unitary logic of hot media (such as print) with an "intuitive mosaic of instantaneous communication" (McLuhan uses television as an example of the latter).[2] Goldstein's innovative move here is to apply McLuhan's often-quoted statement "the medium is the message" to rock music in the service of developing a type of criticism specific to it. Part of the urgency of this project for Goldstein stems from a reaction to the modernist tendency to dismiss pop because of its inescapable association with commerce.

Pop Eye: Evaluating Media
Richard Goldstein

The most disturbing thing about Marshall McLuhan's "Understanding Media" to most readers of this column will be its insistence that those who attempt to impose standards upon the "cool" electronic media based on their aesthetic experiences with

---

1. For a more in-depth account of the development of rock criticism, see Bernard Gendron, *From Montmartre to the Mudd Club: Popular Music and the Avant-Garde* (Chicago: University of Chicago Press, 2002) (Gendron discusses the debates about jazz aesthetics in the early 1940s as well); Steve Jones and Kevin Featherly, "Re-Viewing Rock Writing: Narratives of Popular Music Criticism," in *Pop Music and the Press*, ed. Steve Jones, 19–40 (Philadelphia: Temple University Press, 2002; and other essays in *Pop Music and the Press*. Richard Meltzer, another critic who began with *Crawdaddy!*, authored a book with the same title as this section, *The Aesthetics of Rock* (New York: Something Else Press, 1970).

2. See Marshall McLuhan, *Understanding Media: The Extensions of Man* (New York: Signet Books, 1964).

Source: "Pop Eye: Evaluating Media" © Richard Goldstein/*Village Voice*

the printed word are cultural illiterates. They are as far from understanding radio, television, cinema, or mixed media discotheques as non-literate cultures are from comprehending the scope of literature.

Many of those absorbed in criticizing these new media "are typically book-orientated individuals who have no competence in the grammars of newspaper or radio or film but who look askew and askance at all non-book media," according to McLuhan. Such critics would be hard pressed to understand why "Death of a Salesman" could be an "evening of exalted theatre" (to quote Jack Gould of the Times) and still be mediocre television, while a series like "I Spy," with no literary aspirations, can use the spontaneous and informal qualities of television to maximum advantage.

What McLuhan's oft-quoted and oft-vilified statement—"the medium is the message"—means to criticism is that no longer can aestheticians separate form from content. McLuhan differentiates between "hot" media, which provide a maximum amount of information to one specific sense, and "cool" media, which provide low definition images and invite the audience to fill in the gaps.

To tell a professor of literature that Marvel Comics are artistic extensions of the comic book form is probably futile because few professors choose to consider the possibility that the cartoon—which McLuhan calls a "cool" pictorial form—can be artistic. To speak of the New Journalism is useless because, many critics will maintain, reporting facts in a mosaic rather than a sequential fashion cannot possibly be artistic.

To tell the connoisseur that a happening is a "cool" or participational approach to theatre is an impudence. To discuss seriously recent exhibits such as the USCO show, which combined throbbing light, oscilloscopic patterns, flashing color sparks, and electronic music to create an intimate "psychedelic" art-experience is self-defeating. Such approaches will be considered irrelevant to the real stuff of art by those whose academic backgrounds have enabled them to "appreciate" only the hot techniques in painting, music, and especially the printed word.

McLuhan refers to the "ancient book" and places our literary standards in opposition to the newer pop arts. "Genteel art," he claims, "is a kind of repeat of the specialized acrobatic feats of an industrialized world. Popular art is the clown reminding us of all the life and faculty that we have omitted from our daily routines. . . . The highbrow, from Joyce to Picasso, has long been devoted to American popular art because he finds in it an authentic imaginative reaction to official action."

Pop aestheticism has found its maximum support among the young intellectuals because its emergence as a meaningful experience can best be appreciated by those who have been nursed on the 24-inch flickering box. For the great majority of our youth, pop culture becomes a pervasive reality long before the age of artistic discrimination. McLuhan tells us that "every American home has a Berlin Wall" between its youthful and adult occupants.

The dichotomy between classic and pop, between hot and cool, between high and low art forms, is especially apparent in the area of popular music. Adult intellectuals may never be able to comprehend why Bob Dylan is worshipped by legions of pubescent "teeny-boppers" and, at the same time, considered a major American poet by many serious students. These parochial critics face a practically insurmountable obstacle in their unwillingness to accept the fact that a poet can work in a medium such as rock 'n' roll—that this is an age of electronic troubadours.

They reply that rock 'n' roll cannot possibly be artistic because it is self-limiting in form, because it is not musically complex, because it has traditionally been commercial and therefore anti-artistic. When we mention that rock 'n' roll is musical television, that it is the language of the streets and increasingly of the campus, that it comes closest to being a universal means of communication, we are met with impatient snickering from those who inhabit the other side of the wall.

Just as reprehensible as the widespread ignorance of the classics among the young is the widespread ignorance of the current among adults. Yet, many of those churning out words and music to feed the sensibilities of our youth are becoming particular about the product they produce. A sure sign of this new sense of potential is the trend toward censorship of pop music by radio officials. Pop, we are told, is warping the tastes of our young. We are confronted with songs about pre-marital sex, the drug experience, war and peace, poverty, and lack of communication, and many, many shades of love. The basic Italian sound which came out of Philadelphia in the late 50's—the sound of Fabian, Frankie Avalon, and Connie Francis, among others—has nearly disappeared from popular view. In its place we have more variation in pop-sounds than ever before.

From the Negro ghettos of the North comes soul, with its gospel flavor. And from the South comes the Chuck Berry heritage of "hard" rhythm-and-blues. Far removed from the basic soul approach is the Motown sound, from Negro Detroit. It features a smooth, driving beat, reliance upon heavy orchestration, and a syrupy vocal quality. The lyrics are repetitive and rarely present any poetic ideas; the beauty is in the "sound."

The surf-sound from California presents us with loud, direct harmonies and subject matter that is materialistic and happy. By way of contrast, the California folk sound—exemplified by the Mamas and the Papas and new groups from the San Francisco Bay Area—is spiritual and often "psychedelic."

Psychedelic music—the most controversial sound—emphasizes melodic ambiguity, a free association approach to lyrics, and many electronic and atonal touches. It encompasses performers like the new Bob Dylan, Simon and Garfunkel, Bob Lind, and groups such as the Lovin' Spoonful, the Byrds, the Yardbirds, and the Fugs.[3]

Jazz-rock, a new hybrid, has enabled groups like the Ramsey Lewis Trio, the Blues Project, and the Alan Price Set to experiment with sound-stretching. Folk-rock is, by now, an almost meaningless generalization since it labels the diverse work of the protest writers, the balladeers, and almost anyone who accompanies himself on a guitar. But any number of folk purists have made the electronic discovery that the big beat can be ethnic. Joan Baez has just recorded a rock album; three years ago, she parodied rock regularly in her concerts.

The English Renaissance did much more than add a broad "a" to pop music; it brought to the fore a number of angry young troubadours who sing, almost obsessively, of the struggles between the poor and the rich, young and old, boss and worker. The Rolling Stones, the Animals, and the Kinks specialize in scathing putdowns. They sing Clifford Odets with an echo chamber.

And, of course, there are the Beatles. Their ascendancy covers almost every style mentioned above. They initiated Baroque-rock—making the classical style an inte-

---

3. This is an early description of "psychedelic" music and differs considerably from later appraisals. Some of the other descriptions also diverge considerably from estimations that were current at the time and were to become prominent shortly thereafter (e.g., Motown and Southern Soul).

gral part of their sound rather than the flourishing touch it has always been to rock 'n' roll. They are widely credited with awakening an interest in Eastern music and instrumentation which goes under the lamentable name of Raga-Rock. In their latest releases, the Beatles too seem to be drifting in the direction of electronic feedback and atonal rock and roll.

There are hacks working in pop music, but there is mediocrity on both sides of the wall. Rock 'n' roll may not be the most flexible form, but it is the one most with us today and the form most of our youth chooses to participate in. True artists are always aware of the limitations in their form. But they must receive an intense satisfaction in the realization that they are reaching a wider, more receptive, and more diversified audience through rock 'n' roll than ever before. And they are making money at it.

Their craft—rock 'n' roll—needs a critic. McLuhan complains that our educational apparatus educates principally with regard to the printed word. We learn to tell Dostoevsky from Spillane, but we know nothing about the flicks. We learn to tell Rembrandt from Keane, but we know nothing about advertising. We learn to deal with classical music and legitimate theater but we know nothing about the sights and sounds which bombard us perpetually in the name of pop.

And pop is not mere entertainment; it is anything but passive and conventional. Television, radio, advertising and cinema have radically changed the perceptions of every man on any street. The question now is how to deal with pop—how do we screen the fallout from Madison Avenue? How do we evaluate our responses to the electronic waves racing through our living room? How do we tell what is noise and what is good, even artistic, rock 'n' roll?

A pop critic needs his eyes, his ears, a typewriter, and an impressive German vocabulary. But most important, he needs his youth. Understanding media is hardly enough; we must learn to evaluate as well. And, in rock 'n' roll at least, the child may be father to the man.

Further Reading

Gendron, Bernard. *Between Montmartre and the Mudd Club: Popular Music and the Avant-Garde.* Chicago: University of Chicago Press, 2002.

Jones, Steve, ed. *Pop Music and the Press.* Philadelphia: Temple University Press, 2002.

Lindberg, Ulf, Gestur Gudmundsson, Morten Michelsen, and Hans Weisethaunet. *Rock Criticism from the Beginning: Amusers, Bruisers, and Cool-Headed Cruisers.* New York: Peter Lang, 2005.

Meltzer, Richard. *The Aesthetics of Rock.* New York: Da Capo Press, [1970] 1987.

46. Festivals

THE GOOD, THE BAD, AND THE UGLY

While stadium concerts featuring several bands had been occurring since at least 1964, the Monterey Pop Festival in the summer of 1967 inaugurated a new era in which a "rock festival" spanned several days and somehow managed to connote antimaterialism within what were still basically capitalist enterprises. The decade ended with two major festivals. Woodstock, held in August 1969, was widely viewed as a successful event by the national media, and attendance became a kind of retroactive litmus test for hipness (if not hippieness). The idea of the "Woodstock Nation" gained widespread currency among hippies and media observers and became a metonym for the "new age" of peace and love that many hoped the change in lifestyles would bring.

Less than four months later, however, the Altamont "festival" (actually a one-day event) brought such fantasies to a crashing halt. Organized at the behest of the Rolling Stones as the finale of their tour late in 1969, the concert took place near the San Francisco Bay Area and featured local bands such as the Grateful Dead, the Jefferson Airplane, and Santana. The Hell's Angels were hired as security and were at least partially responsible for the feelings of paranoia that many audience members remember as characterizing the event.[1]

Some of the most thoughtful accounts of Woodstock discuss the contradictions between the peace-and-love ethos projected by the event and the effort required by entrepreneurs to produce that effect. At the same time, few writers could resist an optimistic interpretation of Woodstock,

---

1. It is interesting to compare the films from all three of these events: *Monterey Pop* and *Woodstock* both seem in sympathy with the hippie milieu. *Woodstock*, in particular, coordinated as it was with the release of a triple album (perhaps the first of its kind), ran over three hours in length, meaning that consumption of both the album and the movie required feats of endurance similar to those needed to survive the original event. *Gimme Shelter*, on the other hand, is a different story altogether: begun as a documentary of the Rolling Stones' "triumphal" 1969 American tour as the "undisputed" greatest rock 'n' roll band in the world (now that the Beatles were no longer touring), the harrowing footage of Altamont turns the movie into a tragedy. Both the cinematic accounts of Woodstock and Altamont emphasized certain elements of those events that downplayed the range of audience reactions.

still believing in the "reality of a new culture of opposition" that was basically antimaterialist.[2] J. R. Young's "fictional" review of the album *Woodstock*, released almost a year after the festival, brings out some of the self-delusion involved in the counterculture at the level of interpersonal relationships; in other words, even if the counterculture managed to resist the lures of materialism, status and prestige were still important, even when acquired nonmaterialistically. Many of Young's other fictional reviews address issues of conformity and the persistence of prehippie values within the counterculture.[3]

Review of Various Artists, *Woodstock*
J. R. Young

Bill hadn't been to Woodstock that August weekend the summer before, although Plattsburgh, his home, was less than 300 miles due north on the Northway. He'd gone drinking at Filion's Friday night, and when he awakened terribly hungover the next afternoon, as did most of his 18-year-old buddies, it was too late to make the trip down to Bethel. You couldn't have convinced anyone in the months that ensued, however, that not only was Bill not *at* the Music and Art Show in the alfalfa fields, but that he hadn't also played some integral part in the whole proceeding—a dope runner for the Airplane, perhaps ("Hey, Bill, you got a bomber?" Grace, resplendent in white, tits high and firm, asked him standing behind the giant platform as the Who finished up their set with the sun edging orange up the mountain from its resting place), or a candy bar for Jerry Garcia. Bill believed, too, and if pressed he had a whole Abbie Hoffman Rap about the "actuality" of being there not actually being the important thing, but only a minor side trip.

"I *live* in Woodstock nation," Bill told people when the topic came up, "If you can dig it. I mean how many were actually there. You don't know. We'll never know. But it doesn't make any difference. The Woodstock actuality has become a media trip. That's where it's at. More cameras, writers, and that kind of shit than at Kennedy's funeral. Like the people on the outside probably know more than those who were actually there. What it's come down to is Woodstock Nation, and Woodstock Nation, man, is in your head if you want it to be."

Probably. But Bill still knew a whole lot about the Music Show itself, and took great pains to seek out said information. He had clippings, articles, ads, the illustrious *Life* Magazine Special Edition, *Rolling Stone's Woodstock*, the *Village Voice* issue, and now in late spring had seen the movie three times at four bucks a throw, and also had the album committed to memory. His head, in fact, was a living monument to

---

2. See Andrew Kopkind, "Woodstock Nation," in *The Age of Rock 2: Sights and Sounds of the American Cultural Revolution*, ed. Jonathan Eisen, 312–18 (New York: Random House, 1970). Originally published in *Hard Times* in 1969.

3. See, for example, J. R. Young, review of the Grateful Dead, *Live Dead* (Warner Brothers 1830), *Rolling Stone*, February 7, 1970; and idem. review of Crosby, Stills, Nash, Young, Taylor, and Reeves, *Déjà Vu* (Atlantic SD 7200), *Rolling Stone*, April 30, 1970.

Source: "Review of Various Artists, Woodstock (Cotillion SD 3–500)" J.R. Young, "Review of Various Artists, Woodstock," *Rolling Stone*, 9 July 1970.

the whole Woodstock thing, even down to the little things. Somehow Bill had found someone who had some of the infamous "brown acid." He paid ten bucks for the tab so that he could find out "what was going down." True to form, he took it the second time he saw *Woodstock*.

"Man, that brown acid at Woodstock was a real bummer," he told assorted freaks at assorted gatherings. "A real bummer. Knocked me out for hours. Paranoia personified."

As time passed, Bill became more assertive in such situations. No one now bothered to question him directly as to whether he had been there, but merely what was it like. Bill went along with them because he felt he really knew what it was like.

"Cocker was crazy, man, beautiful. And Alvin Lee, wow."

"Were there really a lot of naked people," a far out chick asked handing him a joint, "like cunt and cock and everything?"

"Well," Bill would smile, "you saw the movie didn't you?"

"Yeh."

"What else do you want to know?"

"Far out."

Woodstock was now the new American Dream, a pipe dream, how it had been those three glorious days of sun and rain, mud and music, and the 500,000 patriots whose ranks were growing day by day, patriots of Woodstock "flying their freak flags high," Groupies, the Dope, and good ol' Rock & Roll, and the national anthem, understood for the first time by Hendrix and his buzz saw guitar. It was all coming home to rest now, and Bill, like many, was proud to stand up and be counted for his own People, for Life, Liberty, and the Pursuit of Happiness, for his Country. Woodstock Nation was a reality.

So it was, until one night at a party in West Chazy when the conversation once more found its way to Woodstock as it always did whenever Bill happened to show. Bill dropped facts and recollections amidst the circle of listeners who sat rapt about him like Leary dropped acid. They all shook their heads at the good dope being passed and at the general incredulity of the whole Woodstock affair. But they believed. That is, all but one believed, and this one hairy ragamuffin of hipdom lay back against a sofa, hitting on his own kief, and coolly taking in Bill's polished exposition. He listened for a long time. At some point, indiscernible to the rest of the gathering, he apparently had heard enough.

"Hey, man," he said, leaning his well-coiffed head into the circle. "Did you ever understand what happened down front just before the Band went on?"

Bill looked up and smiled.

"No, I wasn't there when that happened. I must have been somewhere else. What happened?"

"I don't know. I was sitting about 50 yards out." The kid leaned back out again.

Bill eyed him for a moment, and then continued on from the point where he had disengaged. He had his stuff down.

Seconds later however, the kid again poked his head inside the circle.

"What happened, man, when that weird rumor. . . ."

"About Dylan showing up?" Bill cut him off in stride.

"No, man, that was a media hype. No, the rumor just before Creedence Clearwater went on about the latrines?"

Bill looked at the kid again, and didn't answer for the longest time. And then it was only a reticent shrug.

"Well, where, man, did you take a dump after that? Where'd you spend most of your time?"

Everyone turned and looked at Bill, but Bill had nothing to say, no one to look at, nowhere to go.

"I mean," the kid went on, driving his point home, "when I arrived, the can situation, and that strange tale, well, it was weird. Right? You do remember that, don't you?"

"Sure, but. . . ."

"Did you fork out any bread to get in?"

"No," Bill answered, looking down at the flickering candle, "but. . . ."

"Did you get back to Leon's down the. . . ."

"Groovy Way?"

"Wrong direction, man, wrong direction."

There was a silence, a certain moment of embarrassment because now everyone knew. Bill didn't look up.

"You're right, though," the kid finally said, "the movie was pretty far out. But it wasn't like being there. Nothing was like being there." A second silence followed, and then the kid turned to the far out chick. "Hey, you got anything to drink or eat, man? This is your place, isn't it?"

"Yeh," someone echoed, and in seconds the crowd was on its feet, eager to be up and away. Everyone but Bill. He was still on the floor staring into the flame. The rest of the gang trooped to the kitchen.

"Look, man, it was clear he hadn't been there if you'd been there."

"And you'd been there," the girl said.

"Yeh. Anybody who had would have known immediately he was shucking us. It was obvious, if you knew."

"Sure, maybe, but dig where it's at. Two wrongs don't necessarily make a right, as my grandmother used to tell me, if there were even two wrongs. You know what I mean?"

"But, look. He'd been sold a bill of goods, man, a product that had little to do with anything but money, and that's what he was selling. What, I'm supposed to feel bad for coming down on him for fucking around with us? He's an asshole, it's that simple. I mean, like he really believes it, and that's weird."

"Apparently you believe it too. Perhaps more so than Bill. But then you *were* there. You are Woodstock Nation, and if it's come down to this, then that's sad. That's why there will never really be a Woodstock Nation. You won't let anybody live on your land. You were there. Bill wasn't. Bang, bang. Sad. It's too bad you didn't remember what Dylan said."

"What?"

"'Those dreams are only in your head.'" She turned and walked away. At the door she paused and looked back at the kid, and smiled. "'I'll let you be in my dreams, if I can be in yours.'"

The following account of Altamont by George Csicsery explores the cultural ramifications of the event. Many hip commentators of the time viewed Altamont as the symbolic and literal "end of the sixties" and a "loss of innocence," an interpretation that grew stronger in retrospect. In the following article, Csicsery discusses how Altamont revealed that the counterculture's emphasis on peace and love had not excised fear and violence but, rather, had displaced it so that it was perceived as existing only in the rest of society. The question forced to the surface here is how separate a subculture can really be.

Altamont, California, December 6, 1969
George Paul Csicsery

In the beginning there was rock 'n' roll. The Beatles came and made it good with love and the bluebird of Paradise. But even while the children lifted their faces to the sun, Mick Jagger coiled himself around the tree of flesh, offering a sweet bite of chaos. Saturday, the children swallowed that bite, after chewing and tasting their alliance with evil for nearly a decade.

Until Saturday, evil was value-free, something to dig for its own sake. A lot of people who thought they were children of chaos dropped out of their sugar-coated camp trips Saturday to see the core of their religion at work.

Altamont, like the massacre of Song My, exploded the myth of innocence for a section of America. As the country grows more sophisticated, it learns to confront its own guilt.

The media projected WOODSTOCK. A great people event put on by the younger generation to celebrate its freedom. Traffic jams creating technological time-space motion transcending normal blurb time events. Birth, death, dope, violence, groovy teenyboppers dancing—an instant consumer package of life. Look at all the hippies, America. They're grooving while the rest of you schmucks have to watch it on TV, because you're too uptight. The media needs hippies now more than ever, to show there is still someone in America who can dig on a scene.

But this time it didn't work. The helicopters could not feel that something more than a happening with three hundred thousand people was going on below. Altamont was America. Years of spreading dope, hair, music, and politics came together and reflected nothing less than the whole trip.

Those who expected the illusion of their own inherent goodness to last forever are still freaked. Others who pay less attention to the rhetoric of a cultural revolution say they had a good time. Putting it all together reads like America's pulse NOW. After all we not only make beautiful music, love, and beadwork; we pay our pigs to exterminate Black Panthers, we fry Vietnamese in their own homes, and we elect Spiro Agnew to govern our lives.

Altamont was a lesson in micro-society with no holds barred. Bringing a lot of people together used to be cool. Human Be-Ins, Woodstock, even a Hell's Angel funeral, were creative communal events because their center was everywhere. People would play together, performing, participating, sharing, and going home with a feeling that somehow the communal idea would replace the grim isolation wrought on us by a jealous competitive mother culture.

But at Altamont we were the mother culture. The locust generation come to consume crumbs from the hands of an entertainment industry we helped create. Our one-day micro-society was bound to the death-throes of capitalist greed. The freeway culture delivered the crowd, separate, self-contained in Methedrine isolation, to an event where they could not function as private individuals. The crowd came from a country where everything is done for you. Welfare state—relax, work, and pay your taxes. We'll take care of the war in Vietnam and the war at home.

Source: "Altamont, California, December 6, 1969" *The Age of Rock 2: Sights and Sounds of the American Cultural Revolution,* © George Paul Csicsery.

Yeah, but nobody made sure the machine would function at Altamont. Three hundred thousand people sucked on a dry nipple because it was free. Everyone tried to get to the same place all by himself, and since everyone made it there was no pie. The pie was watching yourself at the spectacle, watching the spectacle watching you at the spectacle doing your own thing watching.

America at Altamont could only muster one common response. Everybody grooved on fear. One communal terror of fascist repression. The rest was all separate, people helping, people walking, people eating, people standing in line to shit. The revolutionaries were there too. Everybody related to people freaking out as well as the mother culture relates to Yippies. Here they were running through the crowd naked, stoned, trampling on our thinning privacy.

They expressed our own lack of control, our desire for space, for the freedom to live out our own body lives. But the crowd reacted with blind hatred, paranoia pressing them forward to get a better look at their own private crush on his satanic majesty.

But it wasn't all a freakout. Back up the slopes of Altamont Speedway, as in the secluded suburbs and woods of America, people kept to the illusions of better dope and more space. The loners, couples, and communes saw nothing, heard nothing and cared less about the crowded valley of fear. Most of them say they had a good time, but few escaped the heavy vibes from below.

Around the stage, at the epi-center, the Angels lost control. Their violence united the crowd in fear. Even people who had no fear of the Angels grew tense from a repressed feeling of panic that swirled around the stage. Mostly it was a fear of being trampled that was intensified by fights and people who did freak out. Since the Angels were the only group there who were together enough to organize their violence they became a clear focus of crowd hatred. Thousands of times we've blamed pigs for less while holding the myth of right-wing Anarchist sacred. Marlon Brando, freewheelin' agent of chaos, another of Saturday's toppled camp heroes.

The Angels protected Mick, their diabolic prince, well. He escaped without serious injury. Later on KSAN they too defended their actions on the grounds that their private property was violated. ". . . ain't nobody going to kick an Angel's bike and get away with it . . ." The official cover-up came Ronald Reagan style from the Stones' Manager Sam Cutler. When asked about the Angels' violence he answered ". . . regrettable, but if you're asking for a condemnation of the Angels . . ."

It was over. No explanation was needed, only a feeble plea for someone in America to clean it up. The stirrings of a young but growing movement to salvage our environment. The job of cleaning up Altamont, or America, is still up for grabs. America wallows in the hope that someone, somewhere, can set it straight. Clearly nobody is in control. Not the Angels, not the people. Not Richard Nixon or his pigs. Nobody. America is up for grabs, as it sinks slowly into Methedrine suffocation with an occasional fascist kick to make her groan with satisfaction.

Further Reading

Bennett, Andy, ed. *Remembering Woodstock*. London: Ashgate, 2004.

Eisen, Jonathan, ed. *The Age of Rock 2: Sights and Sounds of the American Cultural Revolution*. New York: Random House, 1970.

Makower, Joel. *Woodstock: The Oral History*. New York: Doubleday, 1989.

Mayes, Elaine. *It Happened in Monterey: Modern Rock's Defining Moment*. London: Britannia Press, 2002.

Discography

Monterey International Pop Festival. Razor and Tie, 2007.
Woodstock: Music from the Original Soundtrack and More. WEA International, 1970.

Videography

The Complete Monterey Pop Festival. Criterion, 2002.
The Rolling Stones—Gimme Shelter. Criterion, 2000.
Woodstock—3 Days of Peace and Music. Warner Home Video, 1997.

PART 4

The 1970s

47. The Sound of Autobiography

SINGER-SONGWRITERS, CAROLE KING

From the ashes of the folk revival rose the singer-songwriter genre. While Bob Dylan's early work up through *Blonde on Blonde* forms the obvious prototype for this genre, one can look back further and find an even earlier model in Woody Guthrie, who wrote his own songs, accompanied himself on guitar, and presented a romantic image of poetic individualism, albeit without the strong autobiographical currents that run through Dylan's work. While Dylan acknowledged Guthrie as his major influence, we should not forget the blues and country musicians (especially a figure such as Hank Williams who wrote songs with strong autobiographical connotations) who also embodied many of the qualities just ascribed to Guthrie.

Among the many musicians influenced by Dylan, two in particular were important for setting the stage for the singer-songwriter movement: Joan Baez (b. 1941), who, while not known primarily as a songwriter, projected a strong image of personal sincerity as she accompanied herself on the guitar and was the most successful of the early 1960s folk singers; and Paul Simon (b. 1941), whose earnest, melodic anthems (which were not without a sense of humor), performed in partnership with Art Garfunkel, struck a strongly resonant note with collegiate audiences.

In the early work of Dylan and Simon, lyrics focused on personal issues in a realistic way, and songs therefore took on strong autobiographical associations. After hearing Simon sing "Kathy's Song" (on Simon and Garfunkel's *Sounds of Silence,* late 1965), one would not be surprised to learn later that Simon wrote the song about a young woman named Kathy with whom he was involved during a sojourn in England (as the story has emerged from the biographical literature on Simon). When Simon and Garfunkel were accompanied by a band, the

261

arrangements grew not out of riffs, as in the blues-rock or psychedelic rock of the mid- to late 1960s, but, rather, out of the accompaniment patterns played by Simon on the guitar. The same tendency was true of the singer-songwriter genre in general, since band arrangements were based on the guitar or piano part played by the singer-songwriter who was accompanying herself or himself. These patterns were rhythmic arpeggiations, known as "fingerpicking" on the guitar (the style has no specific designation when originating on the piano). In terms of politics, singer-songwriters might espouse antiwar and (especially) antimaterialist views, but they tended to eschew the affiliation with specific causes that was characteristic of the 1960s folk revival.

The most prominent musicians associated with the singer-songwriter genre came from diverse backgrounds. Carole King (b. 1940) had honed her songwriting craft in the Brill Building, writing for rhythm and blues artists such as the Drifters and the Shirelles in the early 1960s and bubblegum, rock, and soul artists like the Monkees, the Byrds, and Aretha Franklin in the late 1960s. Joni Mitchell (b. 1943) and James Taylor (b. 1948) wrote and performed music with clearer ties to the folk revival, while Carly Simon (b. 1945) betrayed more mainstream pop and Broadway show tune influences. Yet all these artists released influential albums between 1970 and 1972 that were recognized as introducing a new "introspective," "intimate" quality into rock music.[1] They were solo artists primarily, employing other musicians as necessary to amplify their own accompaniments. And their lyrics were heard as somehow referring to their own lives: critics frequently introduced biographical elements into articles and reviews as important information that might explain the meaning of the songs. Many writers also recognized that a relatively high number of women were involved in the singer-songwriter genre and frequently attributed this to the "gentler," "prettier" quality of the music.[2]

We already encountered Carole King as one of the creative forces behind the girl groups in Chapter 26. The following article recounts King's early career and transition from a behind-the-scenes songwriter to a popular performer in her own right in the wake of the massive

---

1. That these attributes have been widely accepted as exemplifying the genre can be seen from a recent blurb in the Spring 2002 *Time-Life* music catalogue:

> During the 1960s, thanks in large part to Bob Dylan, singers started believing they should write their own material. The singer-songwriter movement was born, and it has influenced rock ever since. This TIME-LIFE MUSIC series gathers hits from the Singer-Songwriter era: sincere, sensitive, deeply personal songs, performed by the artists who created them.

2. See, for example, Noel Coppage, "Troubadettes, Troubadoras, and Troubadines . . . or . . . What's a Nice Girl Like You Doing in a Business Like This?" *Stereo Review,* September 1972, 58–61. Two years later, *Time* featured an article on the same subject (with a focus on Joni Mitchell) as its cover story, "Rock 'n' Roll's Leading Lady," *Time,* December 16, 1974, 63–66 (the title on the cover is "Rock Women: Songs of Pride and Passion").

success of her album *Tapestry* (1971). All the major ideas that dominated writing about singer-songwriters in the music press may be
found here: the emphasis on autobiography, the "softer" sound, and
the "mature" tone of the music that positioned it as the antidote to
hard rock. The author, Robert Windeler, notes the new prominence of
female singers who wrote their own material as a preamble to discussing King's success, but then quickly moves to stress how she shuns
the accoutrements of fame; her love of privacy and dislike of interviews; and, of course, her domesticity—as her producer Lou Adler
states at the end of the article, "She's a Laurel Canyon housewife."[3]
All this highlights how neither the mainstream press (represented by
Stereo Review, the publication where this article originally appeared)
nor the publications most associated with rock criticism (there are
remarkably few articles from this period on female singer-songwriters)
could accommodate the new musical roles afforded to women by the
singer-songwriter genre.

Carole King: "You Can Get to Know Me through My Music"

Robert Windeler

The unquestioned queen of the singer/songwriter phenomenon that has already
led to some quieter sounds and more thoughtful lyrics in the music of the 1970's is
Carole King. (The question of kingship remains highly debatable and must be taken
up another day.) And where Carole has led, others have followed. In fact, the disc
jockeys and record buyers of the United States haven't had such an array of female
voices to choose from since the days when Patti Page, Jo Stafford, and Rosemary
Clooney were singing about sand dunes on Cape Cod, jambalaya and crawfish pie
in New Orleans, waltzes in Tennessee, and pyramids along the Nile, and that was
so long ago that it only cost a nickel a song to hear Teresa Brewer on the jukebox.
However, there is a crucial difference between now and those earlier times: most of
today's women write their own material.

Carole King was a successful songwriter for a dozen years before she released,
at the age of thirty-two, her second solo album as a performer. The record was called
"Tapestry," and the songs on it do weave a highly subjective view of life. They have
also kept Carole King and half a dozen other singers at the top of music surveys ever
since. "Tapestry" at last count had sold more than 5,500,000 copies in this country
alone and has long since surpassed the movie soundtrack of *The Sound of Music*, the
original Broadway-cast recording of *My Fair Lady*, and Simon & Garfunkel's "Bridge
over Troubled Water" as the best-selling record album of all time. Carole won three
Grammy Awards at the 1972 ceremonies of the Academy of Recording Arts and

---

3. This description is strangely reminiscent of the profile of Aretha Franklin given in Chapter 37.

Source: "Carole King: 'You Can Get to Know Me through My Music'" © Robert Windeler/*Stereo Music Review*/Wright's Media.

Sciences in Hollywood. Such artists as Peggy Lee, Barbra Streisand, and James Taylor sing Carole King songs, as do Blood, Sweat and Tears and Dionne Warwicke, but so far no one sings *You've Got a Friend, I Feel the Earth Move,* or *Where You Lead* as successfully as Carole herself does.

She is a near-recluse who is married for the second time and the mother of three. She didn't attend her triple-win Grammy ceremonies because she was still nursing her latest baby. When not rehearsing, performing, or recording, she keeps house in Laurel Canyon, West Hollywood, and still considers herself a writer rather than a performer.

Carole's long climb to the top has been dazzling, but she is most reluctant to talk about it. She likes her three dogs, her privacy, and most other musicians. She dislikes interviews, and even the very rare one she grants will have to take place after a whole long list of other more important things get done, such as taking empty soda bottles to the recycling center. The young woman who stuns audiences whenever she appears on tour, and sits at the piano nearly mesmerized by her own music, says simply "I want my music to speak for me. You can get to know me through my music." Music industry insiders have been doing just that since 1959 when she wrote (ironically, with her ex-husband) *Will You Still Love Me Tomorrow?*, a Shirelles hit then and a standard now.

She was born in New York, went to high school in Brooklyn, attended college in Manhattan (City) and Queens (Queens), married her high-school sweetheart, and had two children (her third was not born until November 1971). Carole and her husband-collaborator, Gerry Goffin, had a string of hits, including a song they wrote and produced for their maid, who billed herself as Little Eva when she performed her employers' *Loco-Motion.* Goffin and King survived rather than participated in the brasher sounds of the 1960's, and created songs in their own style for Aretha Franklin (*Natural Woman*), the Drifters (*Up on the Roof*), and others. The marriage did not survive, however, and in 1968 Carole left New York for Los Angeles. "I needed to get together a new identity," Carole says. "It's very hard to maintain a marriage writing together." But the Goffins found they were occasionally able to collaborate after their breakup.

As early as 1961, Carole had auditioned as a recording artist, doing a demonstration record of her own *It Might as Well Rain Until September,* which was eventually recorded by Bobby Vee. And Atlantic Records' president Ahmet Ertegun says he remembers "this little Jewish girl constantly hanging around begging me to let her make a record." But Carole didn't really get the chance to record until she joined with guitarist Danny Kootch and a drummer in a Los Angeles group called the City in 1968. James Taylor came to L.A., and Kootch, who had worked with him in New York, introduced Taylor to Carole. Taylor played guitar in jam sessions with the City, and they produced a nice, straightforward sound that was slightly ahead of its time.

Taylor asked Carole to play piano on his second album, "Sweet Baby James," which introduced the phenomenal *Fire and Rain.* Carole then approached Lou Adler, producer of "Tapestry" and founder/head of Ode Records, Carole's label, to help her do a solo record. She had known him in the late Fifties and early Sixties when she was under contract to Colgems Music Publishing and he was their West Coast manager. Although a fan of Carole's who had often tried to persuade her to record, Adler was still busy with the Mamas and the Papas, so he turned her over to a friend, John Fishback, who produced her first album. "Carole King: Writer," as it was called, contained twelve King songs and ten lyrics by Gerry Goffin, who also mixed the recording. "Writer" sold all of eight thousand copies, mostly to friends and fans in the business who had been collecting her old demos and tapes all those years anyway. But the album was critically acclaimed, and Adler, one of the boy wonders of the music business since his Dunhill days, took personal charge of Carole's second, third, and fourth albums.

Taylor, Kootch, and Charles Larkey (a bass player with a group called Jo Mama and Carole's current husband), played on her first album and all subsequent ones. Carole began touring with Taylor, at first just playing the piano for him, then doing an occasional solo, finally as second act on the bill (with Jo Mama opening the show). She electrified audiences, but the album remained a dud commercially. Adler, who speculates that it was because "Writer" was soft-sell and had more of a jazz feel than "Tapestry," which managed to be commercial without compromising Carole's basic musical integrity, said, "Nothing discouraged me. I'm a fan and in love with her."

Suddenly it was Carole King, performer, and she, for one, was scared. "As a writer it's very safe and womb-like," is Carole's view, "because somebody else gets the credit or the blame." She was nervous about performing live, and credits the laconic country-tinged singer/composer Taylor with teaching her how to relax. As for the singer/songwriter phenomenon she finds herself such an important part of, "It's a question of everything moving in cycles. In the Sixties, after President Kennedy's death, everything got very 'anti.' The Beatles in all their glorious insolence were the start of anti-heroism, anti-romanticism. Now the cycle has gone back to romanticism. People got sick of the psychedelic sound and wanted softer moods."

She counts herself fortunate to have "happened to be there at the right time." And Carole characterizes herself as not being success-motivated. "I want to play music, but I have no particular desire for the limelight itself."

"I have always written more in the direction of my friends and family," she says. "I like to touch them with my songs; touching a mass of people is a whole other trip—it is a high-energy trip and it's very exciting, but it's another trip. I don't want to be a Star with a capital S. The main reason I got into performing and recording on my own was to expose my songs to the public in the fastest way. I don't consider myself a singer."

Carole's husband Charles is several years her junior (Carole is quite hung up on being 34, an advanced age for a pop heroine, and wishes she were a good deal younger). She lives with him, her two daughters by Goffin, who are now eleven and thirteen, and the Larkeys' own child in her white frame house in Laurel Canyon.

When she writes a song (now often serving as her own lyricist), Carole has a general idea about what she wants, discusses it with Adler, and then sits down with the musicians selected, always including Taylor and her husband. "We play it a couple of times and we learn it just by listening because we are all so close," she says. "Then it's only a question of polishing and refining it, until it has a degree of spontaneity about it but is still tight."

Carole's third and fourth albums, "Music" and "Rhymes and Reasons," have come and gone. Although "Music" did not come close to the sales total for "Tapestry," it sold 1,200,000 copies, hardly an embarrassment in an industry in which $1,000,000 in sales is recognized by a gold record award. The acceptance she's received as a composer is what keeps her going as a performer. And it is in writing that she really expresses herself, as in her poignant *Child of Mine* (which Anne Murray and others have also recorded), a song written to and rejoicing in her daughter. If others like to listen—and today's increasingly sophisticated and honest audiences apparently do—that's fine too.

"But she's still basically a writer," says Lou Adler. "The performing part is amazing to her. All of those artist trips don't interest her at all. She's a Laurel Canyon housewife. She's always been writing and thinking in much the same way; the only difference is that now, with a different kind of music listener, she's being heard."

Further Reading

Browne, David. *Fire and Rain: The Beatles, Simon and Garfunkel, James Taylor, CSNY, and the Lost Story of 1970*. New York: Da Capo, 2011.

Emerson, Ken. *Always Magic in the Air: The Bomp and Brilliance of the Brill Building Era*. New York: Viking, 2005.

Hoskyns, Barney. *Hotel California: The True-Life Adventures of Crosby, Stills, Nash, Young, Mitchell, Taylor, Browne, Ronstadt, Geffen, the Eagles, and Their Many Friends*. Hoboken, N.J.: John Wiley & Sons, 2006.

Weller, Shelia. *Girls Like Us: Carole King, Joni Mitchell, Carly Simon—and the Journey of a Generation*. New York: Atria Books, 2008.

Discography

Browne, Jackson. *For Everyman*. Asylum, 1973.

King, Carole. *Tapestry*. Ode, 1971.

Simon, Carly. *Reflections: Carly Simon's Greatest Hits*. Arista, 2004.

Simon and Garfunkel. *The Best of Simon and Garfunkel*. Sony, 1999.

Taylor, James. *Sweet Baby James*. Warner Brothers, 1970.

48. Exclusive Joni Mitchell Interview
PENNY VALENTINE

Of all the early '70s singer-songwriters, Mitchell best exemplifies what might be called the "autobiographical effect": the impression that the songs are directly relaying events from her life (as well as conveying her psychologically acute reflections upon them). A quote from a review of her 1971 album *Blue* in *Rolling Stone* typifies this perception of Mitchell's work: "Her primary purpose is to create something meaningful out of the random moments of pain and pleasure in her life."[1] This is not to say that her lyrics are without humor; nevertheless, the main persona that emerges in her work from *Song to a Seagull* (1968, sometimes called

---

1. Timothy Crouse, review of *Blue*, *Rolling Stone*, August 5, 1971, 42.

Joni Mitchell) through *Don Juan's Reckless Daughter* (1977) is that of a restless romantic torn between adventurousness and stability. And, as noted in the interview in the piece that follows, the persona created by her songs is that of one "intent on having freedom even if it's a deceptive kind of freedom."

The following conversation with the British journalist Penny Valentine comes from 1972, in the period immediately after a string of concerts in London's Festival Hall and the release of Mitchell's fifth album, *For the Roses* (the "two-year hiatus" mentioned in the article refers to Mitchell's temporary cessation of performing activities in 1970). Mitchell touches on the autobiographical nature of her work and the importance of introspection and analysis to her creative activity. Other themes emerge as well: a search for remnants of a natural state unblemished by industrialized society (shared by many other popular musicians during this period) and the idea of creativity as catharsis.

Joni Mitchell: An Interview (part 1)
Penny Valentine

A lot of new songs have emerged from the two-year hiatus and in themselves are interesting insights into the change in Joni's outlook. The loving humor of "You Turn Me On (I'm a Radio)," the pain in "Cold Blue Steel and Sweet Fire," retrospective bitterness in "Lesson in Survival," but then there is that feeling—haven't all her songs been directly autobiographical, total personal emotions?

"Well, some of them are, yes, directly personal and others may seem to be because they're conglomerate feelings. Like, remember we were talking about before about that song for Beethoven and I was telling you that's written from the point of view of his Muse talking to him. But that comes from an understanding that I thought I perceived. By reading books about Beethoven I got a feeling which I felt was familiar, as I had felt about people that are friends of mine. So that's from my own experience, because it's my feeling for other people."

And yet one had stuck particularly in my mind—"Cactus Tree"—the song about a girl who everyone loved and yet who was "too busy being free" to concentrate on returning that feeling properly....

"I feel that's the song of *modern* woman. Yes, it has to do with my experiences, but I know a lot of girls like that...who find that the world is full of lovely men but they're driven by something else other than settling down to frau-duties."

But then, I say, there is this impression she gives out—someone on the move all the time, someone intent on having freedom even if it's a deceptive kind of freedom.

"Freedom is deceptive, though. It's like that line of [Kris] Kristofferson's: 'Freedom's just another way of nothing left to lose' [*sic*]. Freedom implies a lot of loneliness you know, a lot of unfulfillment. It implies always the search for fulfillment, which sometimes is more exciting than the fulfillment itself. I mean, so many times I've talked to friends of mine who are just searching for something and one day they come to you and they've FOUND IT! Then two weeks later you talk to them and they aren't satisfied. They won't allow themselves to think they've found it—because they've come to enjoy the quest so much. They've found it—then what?"

Source: "Joni Mitchell: An Interview (part 1)" by Penny Valentine, originally published in *Sounds*, 3 June 1972/ Back Pages Limited.

"I think that there's a new thing to discover in the development of fulfillment. I don't think it necessarily means trading the search, which is more exciting than the actual fulfillment. I still have this dream that you can come to a place where there's a different kind of medium—a more subtle kind of exploration to do of one thing or one place or one person. Like, drifting through lives quickly and cities quickly, you know, you never really get to understand a person or a place very deeply. Like, you can be in a place until you feel completely familiar with it, or stay with a person until you may feel very bored. You feel you've explored it all. Then all of a sudden, if you're there long enough, it'll just open up and flash you all over again. But so many people who are searching and traveling come to that point where it's stealing out on them and they just can't handle that and have to move on."

We talk about the time she spent traveling and how—although songs came out of it and so it was a productive experience—there was an innate disappointment. A sense—and this came out in her spoken intros at the Festival Hall—of disillusionment that what she had believed would be magical somehow never turned out that way. She was affected by that too, she admits, and yet after a thought she smiles at her own naivete in expecting places to be untouched, in expecting to be totally absorbed into them and accepted.

"You tailor make your dreams to 'it'll be this way' and when it isn't...like, if you have a preconceived idea of anything, then inevitably it can't live up to your hopes. Hawaii had so many really beautiful parts to it, and the island of Kuwaii is still agricultural. I guess I had thought of [Hawaii] from all those *Occa Occa* movies I had seen—sacrificing the maidens to the volcano, rivers running with blood and lava, guava trees and," she laughs, "Esther Williams, you know, swimming through the lagoon. And you get there and have to sort through the stucco and the pink hotels. Crete was for the most part pretty virgin, and if you walked to the market you'd find farmers with burros and oranges on the side; it was wonderful. Matela was full of kids from all over the world who were seeking the same kind of thing I was, but they couldn't get away from ummm—I mean they may as well have been in an apartment in Berkeley as in a cave there because the lifestyle continued the same wherever they were. And the odd thing to me was that after my initial plans to be accepted into the home of a Greek family fell apart, we came to this very scene—the very scene we were trying to escape from—and it seemed very attractive to us. There were so many contradictions, so much I noticed about life generally on those trips. Like, the kids couldn't get used to seeing all the slaughtered meat hanging in the shops—they'd only ever seen bits of meat wrapped in cellophane, and to see it there on it's frame turned their stomachs. Most people have that reaction—look at last night over dinner when we started to complain because people were talking about eating birds. We got so upset, and yet at the same time we were eating chicken by the mouthful without even thinking. I go on vegetarian things every so often—well, fruitarian really. In California it's easy because it's warm most of the time. I think you need meat in winter. I have this friend who's a vegetarian and helped me build my house in Canada. We lived on fruit all summer, and he was a fanatical vegetarian—sneering at me when I looked at sirloin—but as winter approached he got colder and colder and I said 'Look you've got to eat some meat if we're going to finish this house.' I had visions of him collapsing. He actually did break down finally and have a steak, and I felt really terrible corrupting, breaking down a man's principles like that."

I wonder if the house in Canada is a permanent move, whether she's had enough of the California scene and is moving back to her roots.

"Not really—moving back is like burning your bridges behind you. For one thing, I don't want to lose my alien registration card, because that enables me to work in the States. So I have a house in California—not the one in Laurel Canyon I used to have—for an address. The house in Canada is just a solitary station. I mean, it's by the sea and it has enough physical beauty and change of mood so that I can spend two or three weeks there alone.

"The land has a rich melancholy about it. Not in the summer, because it's usually very clear, but in the spring and winter it's very brooding and it's conducive to a certain kind of thinking. But I can't spend a lot of time up there. Socially I have old schoolfriends around Vancouver, Victoria and some of the islands, but I need the stimulation of the scene in Los Angeles. So I really find myself down there almost as much now as when I lived there—because then I was on the road most of the time anyway.

"I'm so transient now that even though I have the house in Canada I really don't feel like I have a home—well, it's home when I'm there, you know, but then so is the Holiday Inn in its own weird way."

We get on to the two-year break and I wonder how she'll take the intrusion into her reasons and her personal kick-back. But she's relaxed and forthright and somehow you feel it's a question she feels right in answering now that it's in the past and she hasn't spoken of it before publicly. . . .

Did it help her in that troubled time to get her feelings out on paper?

"Yes, it does, you know, it translates your mood. You can be in a really melancholic depressive mood, you're feeling downright bad and you want to know why. So you sit down and think 'why?' You ask yourself a lot of questions. I find if I just sit around and meditate and mope about it all, then there's no release at all, I just get deeper and deeper into it. Whereas in the act of creating—when the song is born and you've made something beautiful—it's a release valve. And I always try and look for some optimism, you know, no matter how cynical my mood may be. I always try to find that little crevice of light peeking through. Whatever I've made—whether it's a painting, a song, or even a sweater—it changes my mood. I'm pleased with myself that I've made something."

Further Reading

Luftig, Stacey, ed. *The Joni Mitchell Companion: Four Decades of Commentary*. New York: Schirmer Books, 2000.
O'Brien, Karen. *Joni Mitchell: Shadows and Light*. London: Virgin, 2001.
"Rock 'n' Roll's Leading Lady." *Time*, December 16, 1974, 63–66.
Whitesell, Lloyd. *The Music of Joni Mitchell*. New York: Oxford University Press, 2008.

Discography

Mitchell, Joni. *Song to a Seagull*. Warner Bros./WEA, 1968.
_____. *Blue*. Warner Bros./WEA, 1971.
_____. *Court and Spark*. Elektra/WEA, 1974.
_____. *Don Juan's Reckless Daughter*. Elektra/WEA, 1977.
_____. *Hits*. Warner Bros./WEA, 1996.
_____. *Both Sides Now*. Warner Bros./WEA, 2000.
The Very Best of Singers and Songwriters. Time Life Records, 2003.

49. Sly Stone

"THE MYTH OF STAGGERLEE"

The phenomenal popularity of Aretha Franklin, the ongoing success of James Brown along with the grittiest practitioners of Southern Soul, and the continued ubiquity of the pop-oriented productions of Motown attested to soul music's continued relevance to a broad cross-section of the U.S. audience in the late 1960s. However, the activity and popularity of many of the first wave of soul practitioners declined after 1968. Producer/songwriters Holland-Dozier-Holland, who had been responsible for the bulk of the hits for the Supremes and the Four Tops during the peak 1964–67 period, left Motown, while Stax, following the death of Otis Redding, underwent administrative reorganization and became increasingly inconsistent in both artistic and commercial terms (by 1975, the company had filed for bankruptcy).

Nevertheless, soul music was far from finished; instead, it split in two directions: a "sweet" soul style taking its cue from Motown and balladeers such as Curtis Mayfield, and a "funky" soul style taking its cue from James Brown, the "Southern Soul" practitioners, and Aretha Franklin. The discussion of funk rightfully began in Chapter 33 with the excerpts from James Brown's autobiography. Brown's innovations and their adoption by other artists in the late 1960s also had an explicit political component, since these musical innovations coincided with a shift in African American politics from the integrationist stance of the civil rights movement (associated with the rise of soul music) to the more radical stance of the black power movement, a shift heralded by Brown's recording "Say It Loud, I'm Black and I'm Proud" (1968).[1] These shifts were discussed in Part 3 in conjunction with artists like Aretha Franklin and songs such as "Respect."

Concurrent with the developments in Brown's band, other bands created their own forms of funky soul music, including Booker T. and the MGs, the Bar-Kays, the Meters, and Charles Wright and the Watts 103rd Street Rhythm Band. In an important contrast to earlier rhythm and blues and soul performers, these bands were self-contained, writing their own material and producing all vocal and instrumental parts. The first band to absorb Brown's rhythmic approach and extend it was

---

1. The fullest (and most entertaining) account of funk to date may be found in Rickey Vincent, *Funk: The Music, the People, and the Rhythm of the One* (New York: St. Martin's Griffin, 1996).

Sly and the Family Stone. The San Francisco Bay Area–based aggregation joined Brown's rhythmic and textural innovations with a fragmented doo-wop vocal style featuring rapidly alternating voices and with aspects of psychedelic rock, a fusion evident in their first successful single, "Dance to the Music" (1968). The psychedelic influence (particularly that of Jimi Hendrix) was felt by other funk bands as well, most notably Funkadelic ("Maggot Brain," 1971) and the Isley Brothers ("Who's That Lady," 1973).

Sly and the Family Stone played a significant role in another important development in funk: the role of the bass expanded as the band's Larry Graham created an innovative thumb-popping technique particularly evident in an early 1970 release, "Thank U Falettin Me Be Mice Elf Agin." Brown's new bass player, William "Bootsy" Collins, was another crucial influence on subsequent bassists in recordings such as "Sex Machine" and "Superbad" from 1970–71.

Greil Marcus's piece on Sly Stone (b. 1944) documents how Sly's stylistic blend satisfied a particular need within the white counterculture, as well as within the soul music audience. In Marcus's words, the music of Sly and the Family Stone "fill[ed] a vacuum" in which "the racial contradictions of the counterculture" were worked out.[2] Marcus's overriding concern, here as in the rest of *Mystery Train* (the book from which this essay was taken), is to illuminate how Sly articulates "shared unities in the American imagination" through the connections between his music and certain American myths.[3] In this case, Marcus relates Sly Stone's public persona to the myth of Staggerlee, the archetypal "bad man." Marcus spends much of the chapter discussing Sly's dystopian album *Riot* (1971), a recording that underscored the self-destructive nature of Sly's attachment to the Staggerlee character.

By the time of *Mystery Train,* Marcus was already well known to readers as a critic for *Rolling Stone* and its close competitor *Creem*. In addition to exemplifying Marcus's music criticism, which displays an unusual talent for making music come alive with prose, the essay that follows conveys vividly the history of an extraordinary wave of black popular music during the early 1970s. In providing a broader context for the understanding of Sly Stone's brand of funk and the reception of *Riot,* Marcus details the relationship of black popular music of the time to social changes, the emergent black cinema known as "blaxploitation," and political developments such as black nationalism as embodied by the Black Panther Party, all of which are tied together by their connection to the myth of Staggerlee.

---

2. Greil Marcus, *Mystery Train: Images of America in Rock 'n' Roll Music,* 3rd rev. ed. (New York: Plume, [1975] 1990), 69.

3. Ibid., xvii.

from Mystery Train: Images of America
in Rock 'n' Roll Music
Greil Marcus

Sly versus Superfly

The best pop music does not reflect events so much as it absorbs them. If the spirit of Sly's early music combined the promises of Martin Luther King's speeches and fire of a big city riot, *Riot* represented the end of those events and the attempt to create a new music appropriate to new realities. It was music that had as much to do with the Marin shootout and the death of George Jackson as the earlier sound had to do with the pride of the riot the title track of this album said was no longer going on.

"Frightened faces to the wall," Sly moans. "Can't you hear your mama call? The Brave and Strong—Survive! Survive!"

I think those faces up against the wall belonged to Black Panthers, forced to strip naked on the night streets of Philadelphia so Frank Rizzo and his cops could gawk and laugh and make jokes about big limp cocks while Panther women, lined up with the men, were psychologically raped.

A picture was widely published. Many have forgotten it; Sly probably had not. This again is why *Riot* was hard to take. If its spirit is that of the death of George Jackson it is not a celebration of Jackson, but music that traps what you feel when you are shoved back into the corners of loneliness where you really have to think about dead flesh and cannot play around with the satisfactions of myth.

The pessimism of *Riot* is not the romantic sort we usually get in rock 'n' roll. Optimistic almost by definition, pop culture is always pointing toward the next thing and sure it is worth going after; rock 'n' roll is linked to a youthful sense of time and a youthful disbelief in death. Pop culture pessimism is almost always self-indulgent; not without the power to move an audience, but always leaving the audience (and the artist) a way out. In retrospect, records made in this spirit often seem like reverse images of narcissism. *Riot* is the real thing: scary and immobile. It wears down other records, turning them into unintentional self-parodies. The negative of *Riot* is tough enough to make solutions seem trivial and alternatives false, in personal life, politics, or music.

Rock 'n' roll may matter because it is fun, unpredictable, anarchic, a neatly pack-aged and amazingly intense plurality of good times and good ideas, but none save the very youngest musicians and fans can still take their innocence for granted. Most have simply seen and done too much; as the Rolling Stones have been proving for ten years, you have to *work* for innocence. You have to win it, or you end up with nothing more than a strained naïveté.

Because this is so pop needs an anchor, a reality principle, especially when the old ideas—the joy of the Beatles, the simple toughness of the Stones—have run their course and the music has begun to repeat its messages without repeating their impact. Rock 'n' roll may escape conventional reality on a day-to-day level (or remake it, minute-to-minute), but it has to have an intuitive sense of the reality it means to escape; the audience and the artists have to be up against the wall before they can climb over it. When the Stones made "Gimmie Shelter," they had power because their toughness had taken on complexity: they admitted they had doubts about finding even something as simple as shelter, and fought for it anyway. But because the band connected with its audience when they got that across, and because the music that did it was the best they ever made, the song brought more than shelter; it brought life, provided a metaphor that allowed the Stones to thrive when Altamont proved toughness was not the point, and gave them the freedom to go on to sing about other things—soul survivors, suffocation, a trip down a moonlight mile.

Riot matters because it doesn't just define the wall; it makes the wall real. Its sensibility is hard enough to frame the mass of pop music, shuffle its impact, jar the listener, and put an edge on the easy way out that has not really been won. It is not casual music and its demands are not casual; it tended to force black musicians to reject it or live up to it. Some months after *Riot* was released—from the middle of 1972 through early 1973—the impulses of its music emerged on other records, and they took over the radio.

I don't know if I will be able to convey the impact of punching buttons day after day and night after night to be met by records as clear and strong as Curtis Mayfield's "Superfly" and "Freddie's Dead," the Staple Singers' "Respect Yourself" and the utopian "I'll Take You There," the O'Jays' "Back Stabbers," War's astonishing "Slipping into Darkness" and "The World Is a Ghetto," the Temptations' "Papa Was a Rolling Stone," Johnny Nash's "I Can See Clearly Now," Stevie Wonder's "Superstition," for that matter the Stones' *Exile on Main Street* (the white *Riot*)—records that were surrounded in memory and still on the air as recent hits, by Marvin Gaye's deadly "Inner City Blues," by the Undisputed Truth's "Smiling Faces Sometimes (Tell Lies)," by the Chi-Lites' falsetto melancholy, by *Riot* itself. Only a year before such discs would have been curiosities; now, they were all of a piece: one enormous answer record. Each song added something to the others, and as in a pop explosion, the country found itself listening to a new voice.

To me, the Temptations took the prize. Imagine—or simply remember—the chill of driving easily through the night, and then hearing, casually at first, then with interest, and then with compulsion, the three bass patterns, repeated endlessly, somewhere between the sound of the heart and a judge's gavel, that open "Papa Was a Rolling Stone." The toughest blues guitar you have heard in years cracks through the building music like a curse; the singer starts in.

More than one person I knew pulled off the road and sat waiting, shivering, as the song crept out of the box and filled up the night.

Four children have gathered around their mother to ask for the truth about their father, who has been buried that very day. They don't know him; he was just another street-corner Stagolee. So they ask. Was he one of those two-faced preachers, mama—"Stealing in the name of the Lord?"* A drunk? A hustler? A pimp? With another wife, more kids? They slam the questions into their mother, and all she can give them is one of the most withering epitaphs ever written, for them, as well as for him "When he died, all he left us was alone."

Some thought "Back Stabbers" hit even harder. It moved with a new urgency, heading into its chorus with an unforgettable thump; it was like hearing the Drifters again, but the Drifters robbed of pop optimism that let them find romance even in the hard luck of "On Broadway." The O'Jays sounded scared when they climaxed the song with an image that was even stronger than the music: "I wish somebody'd take/Some a' these *knives* outta my back!"

---

*A reference to Paul Kelly's single of the same name, which, along with Jerry Butler's "Only the Strong Survive," had opened up the new territory the Tempts were exploring.

Stevie Wonder reached number one with "Superstition"—his first time on top in ten years. It was the most ominous hard rock in a long while, a warning against a belief in myths that no one understood; Wonder made the old chicka-chicka-boom beat so potent it sounded like a syncopated version of Judgment Day.

All these records were nervous, trusting little if anything, taking *Riot's* spirit of black self-criticism as a new aesthetic, driven (unlike *Riot*) by great physical energy, determined to get across the idea of a world—downtown or uptown, it didn't matter—where nothing was as it seemed. These black musicians and singers were cutting lose from the white man's world to attend to their own business—and to do that, they had to tell the truth. And so they made music of worry and confinement that, in their very different way, the Chi-Lites took to even greater extremes.

The Chi-Lites—like all the artists discussed here—had been around for many years, but they broke into the Top 40 in the seventies, with a dark chant called "(For God's Sake) Give More Power to the People." Stylistically, this was an old kind of record, but it was a new kind of politics; instead of a demand, or an affirmation, it was a plea, and a desperate one at that. The Chi-Lites' persona was open and vulnerable, the antithesis of machismo (something they explicitly dismissed with the great "Oh, Girl"). Other hits—"A Lonely Man," "Have You Seen Her," and "The Coldest Day of My Life"—undercut the high-stepping burst of mastery on which Wilson Pickett and so many other black artists of the sixties had based their careers; the Chi-Lites made Pickett's old bragging music sound fake. Pickett had told his audience that ninety-nine and a half won't do and made them believe it, but the Chi-Lites seemed ready to settle for a lot less—or to beg for something else altogether. The key to any black singer is in that old catch phrase about the way you talk and the way you walk; the Chi-Lites spoke softly and moved with great care.

This new music was a step back for a new look at black America; it was a finger pointed at Staggerlee and an attempt to freeze his spirit out of black culture. On many levels—direct, symbolic, commercial, personal—this music was a vital, conservative reaction to the radical costs Sly had shown that Staggerlee must ultimately exact. And since Stack was roaming virtually unchallenged in the new black cinema, this musical stance amounted to a small-scale cultural war.

All the new black movies—from *Hit Man* to *Trouble Man* to *Detroit 9000* to *Cleopatra Jones*—were cued by the reality behind one very carefully thrown-away line from *The Godfather* (a movie, it is worth remembering, that attracted millions of black Americans, even though it had no black characters, let alone any black heroes).

"They're animals anyway," says an off-camera voice, as the Dons make the crucial decision to dump all their heroin into the ghettos. "Let them lose their souls."

The Mafia may have missed the contradiction in that line, but Francis Coppola certainly did not; neither did the black men and women in the theaters. They suffered it; in *Lady Sings the Blues*, Diana Ross was stalking screens all over the country showing just what it meant. The audience had a right to revenge.

And so the fantasy went to work again. If that line had opened up the abyss, the old black hero shot up from the bottom and pushed in the white man instead. Stack slipped through the hands of the white sheriff, won his fight, got his girl, and got away.

Superfly summed up the genre; perhaps its first scene did, more than it was meant to. The hero, cocaine dealer Priest (played by Ron O'Neal, who looked uncomfortably like a not-very-black Sean Connery) stirs in the bed of his rich white mistress. Some black fool has made off with his stash. Priest chases him through the alleys, up the side of a building, and traps him in a tiny apartment. There, in full view of the man's family, Priest beats him half to death.

Still, Priest is nervous. Hustling's all the Man has left us, he tells his partner, who thinks that's just fine; Priest wants out of the Life, but the invisible whites who run the show want him in—or dead. He bets everything on one last big deal. He turns on the pressure; one of his runners, Freddie, can't take it, and he panics and gets himself killed. Another man, a sort of father figure (who started Priest out peddling reefers when just a lad) is talked into the game, and he too loses his life to Priest's bid for freedom. Priest's partner weighs the odds and sells him out.

Moving fast, Priest penetrates the white coke hierarchy, takes out a first-class Mafia contract on Mr. Big to cover his bet, unmasks Mr. Big as a queer, and, with his money and his strong black woman, gets away clean. He turned up one movie later as a crusader for social justice in Africa, where life was simpler.

It was a fairy tale; but like most of the Staggerlee movies, *Superfly* had a sound-track by an established soul singer, and in this case Curtis Mayfield's songs were not background, but criticism. (Mayfield had appeared in the picture singing in a deal-ers' bar, grinding out an attempted parody of his audience—but they thought it was a celebration.) His music worked against the fantasy, because to him one incident in the movie counted for more than all its triumphs: Freddie's dead. "Pushin' dope for *the Man!*" he sang, incredulous and disgusted. The movie hadn't even slowed to give Freddie an epitaph, but Mayfield clearly aimed his song at the hero as well.*

Superfly had a black director, Gordon Parks, Jr.; there was a surface ghetto real-ism, and there were touches of ambiguity, but the movie had Hollywood in its heart, and that was enough to smother everything else. Most of the pictures that followed simply shuffled *Superfly* clichés, but they kept coming.

One movie was different, but it never found its audience, not among blacks, or whites either. *Across 110th Street* (directed by Barry Shear, who earlier made *Wild in the Streets*, the most paradoxical youth exploitation picture; written by Luther Davis) looked enough like all the others to make it easy for nearly all critics to dismiss it. The film was almost unbelievably violent, which gave reviewers license to attack it. It began with the same clichés everyone else used, but intensified them mercilessly. It pumped so much pressure into the world of the new black movies that it blew that world apart.

Three black men—Jamaica, Superflake, and Dry Clean—murder a pack of black and white Mafia bankers and make off with the week's take for all of Harlem. They don't steal because they hate the mob; they steal because they want the money. A Mafia lieutenant—played by Tony Franciosa—is sent out to bring back the money and execute the thieves, knowing full well he can forget his future if he fails. Anthony Quinn plays a bought cop caught in the middle. He has to take the case straight to make his pension, and a new black cop is keeping an eye on him, but he has to do it without losing his payoff—or his life—to the Mafia hirelings who control his district: a black man who runs a taxi company and looks like Fats Domino risen from the swamp of evil, and his bodyguard, a Staggerlee who watches over the entire film with the cold eyes of someone who sold his soul to the devil the day he was old enough to know he had one.

You paid for every bit of violence, perhaps because the film refused its audience the pleasures of telling the good guys from the bad guys, and because the violence was so ugly it exploded the violence of the genre. It wasn't gratuitous, but it wasn't "poetic" either. Every character seemed alive, with motives worth reaching for, no matter how twisted they might turn out to be; every character (save for Taxi Man and

---

*Interestingly, these lyrics were not in the movie, even though the backing track was. Mayfield held off until the film was in the theaters, then wrote the words, released the record, and so took on the picture on his own turf: the radio. You could say he chickened out, and you could also say he was very smart.

his gunman) fled through the story scared half out of his wits, desperate for space, for a little more time, for one more chance.

The thieves speed away from the litter of corpses, divide up the money, and go into hiding. Superflake is too proud of himself to stay holed up; good times are what it was all for, right? His best hustler's clothes—tasteless Sly Stone, but gaudy—have been hanging for this moment. Down at the best whorehouse in Harlem Superflake has a dozen women and he's bragging.

Franciosa picks up the scent, and with Taxi Man's Staggerlee at his side, his eyes glazing over with a sadism that masks his own terror, he rips Superflake out of the whorehouse bar. When Quinn finds Superflake crucified, castrated, and skinned alive, you realize that along with no heroes, this movie may offer no way out. It was made to take your sleep.

Jamaica and Dry Clean pass the word and panic; they know that Superflake had to finger them. Dry Clean shoves his money into a clothes bag from his shop and hails a cab for Jersey. The driver spots the markings on the bag, radios back to Taxi Man, and delivers Dry Clean straight to Franciosa at 110th Street—the border of Harlem and the one line the movie never crosses. Dry Clean breaks away; Franciosa traps him on a roof, ties a rope to his leg, and hangs him over a beam, dangling him into space. Staggerlee holds the rope; his eyes show nothing as he watches the white man torture the black. If Dry Clean talks, they say, they won't kill him; he is so scared he believes them. He talks, and the rope shoots over the side.

Jamaica and his girl meet in his wretched apartment (there is a little torn-out picture of Martin Luther King taped to the wall, a gray reminder of some other time) to plan an escape, or a better hideout. And in one of the most extraordinary scenes in any American movie, a death's-head reversal of every warm close-up you have ever seen, Jamaica begins to talk—about green hills and a blue sky; about quiet, rest, peace of mind; about going home. He has only killed nine men to get there. His face is scarred by smallpox; his eyes try hard to explain. Jamaica goes on; you don't hear him; the camera stays in tight. Every few seconds his whole face shudders, seems almost to shred, as a ghastly, obscenely complex twitch climbs from his jaw to his temple, breaks, and starts up again.

It is the visual equivalent of that last song on *Riot*, "Thank you for talkin' to me Africa," another reach for a home that isn't there. Like Sly's music, the scene is unbearably long, it makes you want to run, but each frame like each note deepens the impact, until everything else in the world has been excluded and only one artistic fact remains. Jamaica's twitch traces the fear of every character in the movie; it is a map of the ambiguities the other movies so easily shot away; and in this film, it is most of all the other side of Staggerlee's face, which never moves.

Finally, Franciosa, Quinn, and their troops converge on the abandoned tenement where Jamaica and his girl are hiding. Taxi Man gets word of the showdown. "Wanna watch," says Staggerlee. "No," says Taxi Man. "I know how it's gonna turn out."

A bullet cuts through the girl's forehead and pins her to the wall behind Jamaica. She stays on camera, standing up dead, a blank ugliness on her face. When Jamaica turns to see her you can feel the life go out of him, but he keeps shooting. Franciosa is killed; the cops take over. Jamaica flees to the roof with his gun and his bag of money, still firing. He kills more. Staggerlee, sent to cover for Taxi Man, watches from another rooftop. Jamaica falls, and in the only false moment in the picture, flings his money down to children in a playground. Staggerlee sets up a rifle, takes aim on Quinn, who has proved himself too weak to be worth the mob's time, and kills him.

In one way, then, this movie was like all the others: Staggerlee wins. But this time, the audience was not given the benefit of any masks; they had to take him as he came, and they were not about to pay money to see that.

Further Reading

Marcus, Greil. *Mystery Train: Images of America in Rock 'n' Roll Music*, 3rd rev. ed. New York: Plume, 1990.

_____. "Muzak with Its Finger on the Trigger: The New Music of Sly Stone." *Creem,* April 1972.

Selvin, Joel, and Dave Marsh, eds. *Sly and the Family Stone: An Oral History*. New York: Avon, 1998.

Vincent, Rickey. *Funk: The Music, the People, and the Rhythm of the One*. New York: St. Martin's Press, 1996.

Discography

Mayfield, Curtis. *Superfly*. Custom, 1972.

Sly and the Family Stone. *Anthology*. Sony, 1990.

_____. *Stand!* Sony, 2007.

_____. *There's a Riot Goin' On*. Sony, 2007.

_____. *Dance to the Music*. Sony, 2007.

Soul Hits of the 70s: Didn't It Blow Your Mind!, Vol. 10. Rhino/WEA, 1991.

50. Not-So-"Little" Stevie Wonder

Stevie Wonder (b. 1950) blended funk, jazz, reggae, rock, African and Latin rhythms, and electronic experimentation with old-fashioned songwriting craft to create a fusion that made him the most popular black musician of the early- to mid-1970s.

Wonder's career has superficial similarities to that of another Motown artist, Marvin Gaye. Like Gaye, Wonder's music became noticeably more eclectic and his lyrics more personal and political as his career progressed. Unlike Gaye, who came to Motown in his early 20s, Wonder's first success came at age 13: billed as "Little Stevie Wonder," his novelty instrumental hit, "Fingertips, Pt. 2" in 1963 hit the top of *Billboard's* pop chart. By the late 1960s, Wonder was recording jazz-influenced ballads like "My Cherie Amour" (1969) and uptempo songs with an almost manic vocal intensity, such as "I Was Made to Love Her" (1967). This variety only hinted at the transformation in style that would occur after his 21st birthday in 1971. In a development that paralleled the release of Gaye's creative breakthrough *What's Going On* (1971), Wonder signed a new contract with Motown that gave him vastly increased artistic autonomy. The albums that followed—*Where I'm Coming From* (1971), *Music of My Mind* and *Talking Book* (both 1972), *Innervisions* (1973), *Fulfillingness' First Finale* (1974), and *Songs in the Key of Life* (double album, 1976)—all displayed an increased social awareness and utopianism in his lyrics, as well as an adventurousness as a performer of both the synthesizer and conventional instruments (he played almost all the instruments on the albums just listed). Wonder's use of the synthesizer was particularly innovative, since he introduced many experimental timbres and techniques to popular music.

The following profile and interview by Ben Fong-Torres appeared early in 1973, when it became clear that *Talking Book* was becoming an unprecedented critical and commercial success for Wonder. This article, as did others from this period, addresses the notion that Wonder's audience had expanded to include a greater number of white, countercultural listeners without losing his core fan base of African Americans.[1] The publication of this interview in *Rolling Stone* is at least partly responsible for the focus on Wonder's "new audience." This article-interview also provides additional background on Motown in the 1960s (discussed in Chapter 32) from the perspective of Wonder's career with the company and again calls attention to the important role played by Motown's mostly unheralded studio musicians.

The Formerly Little Stevie Wonder
Ben Fong-Torres

[Stevie Wonder:] I had a dream about Benny Benjamin [Motown's first studio drummer, who died of a stroke in 1969]. I talked to him a few days before he died; he was in the hospital. But in my dream I talked to him, he said, "Look man, I'm . . . I'm not gonna make it." "What, you kiddin'!" The image . . . he was sitting on my knee, which means like he was very weak. And he said, "So, like I'm leavin' it up to you." That was like a Wednesday, and that following Sunday I went to church and then to the studio to do a session; we were gonna record "You Can't Judge a Book by Its Cover," and they said, "Hey, man, we're not gonna do it today. Benny just died."

---

1. For a lengthy profile of Wonder from two years later that rehabilitates this theme, albeit in a paternalistic manner, see Jack Slater, "A Sense of Wonder," *New York Times Magazine*, February 23, 1975, 18, 21–23, 26–32. In one telling passage, Slater compares the effect of Wonder's synthesis to that of Bob Dylan in the mid-1960s (pp. 30–32).

Source: "The Formerly Little Stevie Wonder" Ben Fong-Torres, "The Formerly Little Stevie Wonder," *Rolling Stone*, 26 April, 1973, pp 48–50.

He died without notice. I mean, nobody really knew who he was.
Man, he was one of the major forces in the Motown sound. Benny could've very well been the baddest—like [Bernard] Purdie. He was the Purdie of the Sixties. But unknown.

Why unknown?
Well, because for the most part these cats'd be in the studios all day and as musicians they weren't getting that recognition then, you know. People weren't really that interested in the musicians.

Couldn't they also have had jobs with performing groups?
They'd do clubs, but they all were basically . . . Benny would be messin' up all the time. Benny'd be late for sessions, Benny'd be drunk sometimes. I mean, he was a beautiful cat, but. . . . Benny would come up with these stories, like [in an excited, fearful voice] "Man, you'd never believe it man, but like a god-damn *elephant*, man, in the middle of the road, stopped me from comin' to the session so that's why I'm late, baby, so [clap of hands] it's cool!" But he was *ready* man. He could play drums, you wouldn't even need a bass, that's how bad he was. Just listen to all that Motown shit, like "Can't Help Myself" and "My World Is Empty Without You Babe" and "This Old Heart of Mine" and "Don't Mess with Bill." "Girl's All Right with Me," the drums would just *pop*!

Did Benny teach you a lot about drumming?
Yeah, you can hear it, you know, I learned from just listening to him.

Is it true that you put out a drum album once?
Well, I put out an album that I played drums on, called *The Jazz Soul of Little Stevie*. I did another album which was called *Eivets Rednow* about '68, an instrumental with "Alfie" and a few other things . . . "Eivets Rednow" being "Stevie Wonder" spelled backwards.

Everybody knew who it was right away. . . .
Some people did, some didn't. As a matter of fact there was a cat in the airport that came up and said, "Hey, man" [laughs], he said, "Man, these whites takin' over everything," he says, "Look, I heard a kid today, man, played 'Alfie' just *like* you, man!" "O yeah, this cat named Rednow?" "Yeah, that's it!" I said, "Ooooh, man, that cat is—well, don't worry about *him!*" [laughs]

You've said that the first song you ever wrote was "Uptight," but the credits were given to Sylvia Moy, Henry Cosby and a "S. Judkins." Was that you?
Well, Judkins is my father's name. But it's crazy to explain it. Morris was on my birth certificate and everything, but Judkins was the father. I took his name when I was in school. We just signed the song contract like that.

Why didn't you sign Stevie Wonder?
I don't know.

You signed "Wonder" on songs like "I'm Wondering" and "I Was Made to Love Her."
Well, that was later; I decided I wanted people to know that I wrote those songs.

How did you get the name Wonder?
It was given to me by Berry Gordy. They didn't like "Steve Morris" so they changed it.

Were there some alternatives?
"Little Wonder". . . "Wonder Steve. . . ." I think we should change it to Steveland Morris [laughs]. That would put a whole different light on everything.

You weren't an immediate hit, were you? You put out a record called "I Call It Pretty Music."

It was a thing that Clarence Paul wrote . . . an old blues thing . . . The first thing I recorded was a thing called "Mother Thank You." Originally it was called "You Made a Vow," but they thought that was too lovey for me, too adult.

How did the first records do?

They started after we did "Contract on Love." That made a little noise. "Fingertips" was after that. That was a biggie.

The first production credit you were given was on the "Signed Sealed and Delivered" album, but that wasn't the first producing you did.

Well, that was the first that was *released*. I also did a thing with the Spinners, "It's A Shame," and the follow-up, "We'll Have It Made." I wanted that tune to be big. I was so hurt when it didn't do it.

You also produced Martha once?

Yeah, they never released it. Called [sings, snapping fingers], "Hey, look at me, girl, can't you see. . . ."

And one on David Ruffin.

Yeah, [sings] "Lovin' you's been so wonder-ful. . . ." In the midst of all that, I was in the process of getting' my thing together and decidin' what I was gonna do with my life. This was like I was 20, goin' on 21, and so a lot of things were left somewhat un-followed-up by me. I would get the product there and nobody would listen and I'd say, "Fuckit." . . . I wouldn't worry about it.

This was around "Signed Sealed and Delivered." . . .

It was a little after that. "Signed Sealed and Delivered" was like the biggest thing I'd had.

Then you went into a lull.

Yeah, we did *Where I'm Coming From*—that was kinda premature to some extent, but I wanted to express myself. A lot of it now I'd probably re-mix. But "Never Dreamed You'd Leave in Summer" came from that album, and "If You Really Love Me" . . . but it's nothing like the things I write now. I love getting into just as much weird shit as possible. I'll tell you what's happening. Syreeta's album is better than my last two albums, man, shit! [laughs] No, but it's cool.

But the public Stevie Wonder is a lot of ideas and images that people have of you, regardless of what you actually are.

I know there are thousands of images of me. There was a guy one time, I heard: "Hey, uh, Stevie Wonder told me to come and get this grass from you, so where is it?" He said, "Stevie Wonder told you? He didn't man, 'cause I'm his guitar player, and he doesn't even smoke grass. He doesn't even get high." I guess people expect or figure me to be a lot of different things.

You've actually said that you considered your blindness to be a gift from God.

Being blind, you don't judge books by their covers; you go through things that are relatively insignificant, and you pick out things that are more important.

When did you discover that there was something missing, at least according to other people's standards?

I never really knew it. The only thing that was said in school, and this was my early part of school, was something that made me feel like because I was black I could never be or would never be.

So being black was considered to be more a weight. . . .

I guess so. [laughs] This cat said in an article one time, it was funny: "Damn! He's black! He's blind! What else?!" I said, "Bull*shit*, I don't wanna *hear* that shit, you know."

So you wouldn't even bother having people describe things to you. Colors and. . . .
Well, I have an idea of what colors are. I associate them with the ideas that've been told to me about certain colors. I get a certain feeling in my head when a person says "red" or "blue," "green," "black," "white," "yellow," "orange," "purple"—purple is a *crazy* color to me. . . .

Probably the sound of the word . . .
Yeah, yeah. To me brown is a little duller than green, isn't it?

In school, what subjects did you like best?
History, world history, but it got kind of boring. And science. The history of this country was relatively boring—I guess because of the way it was put to us in books. The most interesting to me was about civilizations before ours, how advanced people really were, how high they had brought themselves only to bring themselves down because of the missing links, the weak foundations. So the whole thing crumbled. And that's kind of sad. And it relates to today and what could possibly happen here, very soon. That's basically what "Big Brother" is all about.

I speak of the history, the heritage of the violence, or the negativeness of being able to see what's going on with minority people. Seemingly it's going to continue to be this way. Sometimes unfortunately violence is a way things get accomplished. "Big Brother" was something to make people aware of the fact that after all is said and done, that I don't have to do nothing to you, meaning the people are not power players. We don't have to do anything to them 'cause they're gonna cause their own country to fall.

"My name is Secluded; we live in a house the size of a matchbox." A person who lives there, really, his name *is* Secluded, and you never even know the person, and they can have so many things to say to help make it better, but it's like the voice that speaks is forever silenced.

I understand that when you don't hear anything and you hear this very high frequency, that's the sound of the universe.

Or a burglar alarm, which takes some of the mystery out of it. . . . Tell me about your experiments with electronic effects and music. First have you listened to Beaver and Krause, or Pink Floyd, Emerson Lake and Palmer, or Walter Carlos?
Walter Carlos, yes, but for the most part I've listened to just what's in my head, plus Bob Margoloff and Malcolm Cecil—they just built a new synthesizer you should see—they have their own company, Centaur, and they did an album, *Tonto's Expanding Headband.* They are responsible for programming and I just tell them the kind of sound I want.

I hadn't got tired of strings or horns or anything, it's just another dimension. I'd like to get into doing just acoustic things, drums, bass, no electronic things at all except for recording them.

What else are you checking out these days?
There's this string instrument made in Japan. You tune it like a harp to a certain chord scale. It takes you somewhere else that's sort of earthy and in the direction where my head is slanting—like going to Africa. Maybe I'll take a tape recorder over there and just sit out and write some stuff.

In concert, your opening number includes African scatting.
I got that from this thing called *The Monkey Chant* that we used in different rhythms, and we came up with [chop-chants, in speedtime} *ja-ja-ja-jajajajajaja.* . . .

And there are three pairs of drumsticks going.
It's like fighting. I'd love to go to Ghana, go to the different countries and see how I'd like to live there.

Do you know Sly Stone?

I've seen him a couple of times. I haven't heard too much about him lately, just rumors. . . .

He influenced you to a degree.

Ah . . . I think there's an influence in some of things I've done, like "Maybe Your Baby." But I can hear some of the old Little Stevie Wonder in a lot of his early things [Stevie sings a bit of "Sing a Simple Song"]. It used to tickle me. . . .

You've said that your writing was influenced by the Beatles.

I just dug more the effects they got, like echoes and the voice things, the writing, like "For the Benefit of Mr. Kite."

Did it make you feel that you could be more loose yourself?

Yeah, I just said, "Why can't I?" I wanted to do something else, go other places. Same thing abut keys. I don't want to stay in one key all the time.

I understand that in the old days at Motown, groups had to compete for tracks. Writers would come up with a song and a track, and artists would all sing over it, and the best would get a single released.

I could see why that would happen though. It's kind of crazy. But then again you think the writer, whoever the writer is—the music, the sound wasn't really Motown as much as the writer. I think for the most part they should listen in advance and know the artists. Holland-Dozier-Holland usually would sing the melodies themselves and say, "This is how I want you to do it."

What about you? Did you always have more independence?

I had the independence because I was somewhat distant, because I was in school, and I would just come back home sometime and do some singing.

"Blowing in the Wind" and "Alfie" were unusual songs for a Motown artist to be doing back when you did them.

Most of them came about from doing gigs and wanting certain kinds of tunes. Clarence Paul, who was my arranger and conductor when we had the big group—we would work out doing tunes, ridin' in cars like in England around '65. We'd think of different songs like "Funny How Time Flies Away" or "Blowin' in the Wind."

 Writers are so important. I think a lot of our artists could have been more sustained if they had other writers, besides Holland-Dozier-Holland, because then they would have found their identity—and that's what everybody needs.

So you can understand why groups like Gladys and the Pips, Martha and the Vandellas, the Tops, the Spinners, left.

I do, when you become just one of the others, it's difficult to be a sustaining power for a long period of time. It's like a person comes out with a beat, and you keep on doing it and doing it and driving it to the ground.

Further Reading

Lodder, Steve. *Stevie Wonder—A Musical Guide to the Classic Albums.* San Francisco: Backbeat, 2005.

Ribowski, Mark. *Signed, Sealed, and Delivered: The Soulful Journey of Stevie Wonder.* Hoboken, N.J.: John Wiley & Sons, 2010.

Rockwell, John. "Stevie Wonder." In *Calling Out around the World: A Motown Reader,* ed. Kingsley Abbott, 131–34. London: Helter Skelter, 2000.

Selvin, Joel. "Stevie Wonder." *Mojo*, April 2003.

Slater, Jack. "A Sense of Wonder." *New York Times Magazine*, February 23, 1975, 18, 21–23, 26–32.

Werner, Craig. *Higher Ground: Stevie Wonder, Aretha Franklin, Curtis Mayfield, and the Rise and Fall of American Soul*. New York: Crown, 2004.

Discography

Gaye, Marvin. *What's Going On*. Motown, 2003.

Wonder, Stevie. *Music of My Mind*. Motown, 1972.

_____. *Talking Book*. Motown, 1972.

_____. *Innervisions*. Motown, 1973.

_____. *Songs in the Key of Life*. Motown, 1976.

_____. *The Definitive Collection*. Motown, 2002.

51. Parliament Drops the Bomb

Funk as a genre really came into its own during the early 1970s. Bands as diverse as the Latin-influenced War; the jazz-influenced Tower of Power and Kool and the Gang; the earthy Ohio Players; the utopian, Afro-centric Earth, Wind, and Fire; and the adjective-defying Parliament-Funkadelic, all began to achieve success during this period. Parliament, with mastermind George Clinton (b. 1940), began a string of recordings with "Up for the Down Stroke" that succeeded on the R&B charts for the duration of the 1970s, including "Tear the Roof Off the Sucker" (1976), "Flash Light" (1977), "One Nation Under a Groove— Part 1" (by Parliament alter-ego, Funkadelic), and "Aqua Boogie (A Psychoalphadiscobeta-bioaquadoloop)" (both 1978). Clinton created a striking form of funk: emphasizing a clear backbeat (often reinforced with electronic hand claps), he thickened the texture with a wealth of contrasting, overlapping parts, featuring "Bootsy" Collins's (following his tenure with James Brown) extroverted bass lines, Bernie Worrell's innovative synthesizer work (including the use of the "synthesizer bass" on "Flashlight"), horn players from Brown's band, and gospel-rooted group vocals. Clinton expanded the Parliament stage show into a spectacle that set new standards for grandiosity in black popular music. Beginning with the album *Mothership Connection* (1975), Clinton developed a cosmological narrative that proselytized the redemptive power of funk. Concerts would enact the landing of the "Mothership" while Clinton and up to 50 performers would hold forth in outlandish garb. Clinton's utopian vision of a black "Nation [United] Under a Groove" and his commitment to undiluted funk have continued to influence numerous hip-hop musicians.

George Clinton's popularity and influence were at their peak in the late 1970s, the period from which the following interview comes. The epigraph by Sun Ra underscores the continuity between the science fiction–inspired visions of Sun Ra's interplanetary "Arkestra" and Clinton's various intergalactic projects; both point to a continuing African American fascination with the possibility of a society beyond the reach of racism, and one that can be imagined only in outer space. The article-interview also adopts the language of Clinton and of funk music in general and provides background on Clinton in a fanciful manner while outlining a basic history of funk. Clinton's empire of bands, which arose as a creative response to elude music industry control, is described here, as are Clinton's views on the relationship between his music and a socially responsible politics.

George Clinton: Ultimate Liberator of Constipated Notions
W. A. Brower

If you are not a reality whose myth are you?
    —*Sun Ra*

A concept can just be thrown in the air around the funk and before it hit the ground you got two albums. You know? What I am saying is that a mafunkah will shoot holes in that bad boy 'fore it hits the ground, like you do in the ghetto.
                                                                    —*George Clinton*

George Clinton (a.k.a. the Long Haired Freaky Sucker, Star Child, Dr. Funkenstein, just plain Dr. Funk, and now Mr. Wiggles the Worm—"ultrasonic, semi-bionic clone of Dr. Funkenstein," who was specially grafted for Clinton's latest on-stage extravaganza and recording *Motor Booty Affair*, Casablanca 7125) is no one's myth. Although the lineup from his newest production, which includes Queen Freakalene, Monkey

Source: "George Clinton: Ultimate Liberator of Constipated Notions," W. A. Brower. Courtesy of *Downbeat* Archives.

Sea and Monkey Woo, Minus Mouf, Howard Codsell, Octave Pussy, Rita Mermaid and P-Nut Booty Jellyfish sounds like a cast of renegade cartoon characters from a Motor Bugged Out Affixation, George Clinton is *fo' real, alllllll* the way, live and in 3-D, Dig—

Clinton walks around dressed like it's Halloween 365 days a year. He is Head Funkentelecktual-In-Charge of P-Funk Labs from which such uncontrolled substances as the Bomb, the P. Funk, the Uncut Funk, the Pee, Supergroovalisticprosifunkstication, Flash Lights, DooDoo Chasers and Liquid Sunshine originate. Dr. Clinton told me, in an unguarded moment, that his work is dedicated to ego reduction and the eradication of mental ghettos. Clinton is also Head Referee of the Funk-Mob, a voluntary association of barnstorming funkateers, who get their hard core jollies off funkin' with folks' heads. Through the Dr.'s own funkreative mitosis, the First Family of Funk has grown to include Parliament, Funkadelic, Bootsy's Rubber Band, Brides of Funkenstein, Parlet, the Horny Horns, and Bernie Worrell's Woo. George Clinton is the main purveyor of the funk which, along with rock and disco, dominates the popular music market.

Recently, George Clinton has also become a wizard of finance and a big reality in the record business. Everythang he touches turns funky. The P. Funk Earth Tour made 30 million funky dollar bills in two years. A few months ago, Funkadelic's album *One Nation Under A Groove* (Warner Bros. 3209) went platinum funk.

The success of *One Nation* put Clinton in a funkified dilemma. For sure, *One Nation* was the Pee, a monstrous hit, but it came right on the heels of three years of touring with such huge productions as the Mothership Connection. The Mothership, an Apollo 15 lookalike from which the Dr. disembarked on stage, cost a stankin' quarter of a million all by his lonesome.

Clinton's problem was mounting a stage show that could outfunk the last two. His response to the situation says a bunch about how his mind funktions. "We had just come off that [major tour] one month before *One Nation* came out, which meant we had to do somethang. We *had* to go back out on the road and we couldn't go back in them same places. And the Brides was comin' out so they had to have some place to play.

"So we said, 'We'll take a tour of small joints where we can play three or four hours and we'll call it the *anti-tour*, which will de-program our heads from that big 20,000 seats. Let all the young members see what it's really like to have to play a *gig*,' you know, where you have to play fo' real. And they could get off on it because they can play their shit. And best of all, in going to these cities under *One Nation*, playin' small places, we could get down with the people.

"The people that get in, the *real* fans, will say, 'Them mathahfunkahhhaas played three hours and turned that mathahfunkah out!' With no props, no nothing." In Washington, D.C. (which he has dubbed a Chocolate City encircled by a Vanilla Suburbia) Clinton took the anti-tour into the legendary Howard Theatre. Instead of three hours the show ran nearly five. At 1:30 a.m. 2000 militants of the funk were damn near tearin' the roof off the sucker, hyperventilating to *One Nation* for the umpteenth time.

P-Funk was mega-funk that night. The Dr. was decked out in red beret and fatigues, and looked more like Captain Zero, the Sandinista guerilla, than the Star Child, as he pumped the audience with stuff like, "Get funky . . . get loose . . . free your mind . . . let your ass follow . . . let your booty do its duty." The anti-tour was typical of Clinton's "anti-logic or expanded framework for logic." Instead of shooting for an even bigger production and possibly reaping a diminished return he did just the opposite and funked better.

The Dr. is big fun to talk to, being that he is an advanced student of mentalcourse—which is to say mindfunkin' and gamin' on ya as necessary. He studied signifying for ten years in a Plainfield, New Jersey barbershop which he ended up owning. In the process he specialized in conking heads. ". . . pre-Superfly . . . just scorchin' heads in the name of the cool."

When the bloods put the torch to Plainfield Ave. during the '67 riots, George Clinton's barbershop was the only thang left standing. By then Clinton had a Master's in street rhythms and consense, the highest form of game. He survived the '60s and went on to get his doctorate in poetic licentiousness from the Universal Corner . . . hanging out and eating reality sandwiches from Harvard Square to the Motor City. George Clinton is a deep dude. Dig.

The Dr. is from Cannapolis, North Carolina—if they've got olfactory glands strong enough to claim him. He spent his early years funkin' up in the Chocolate City and in Chase City, Virginia, before his family settled in Plainfield. That's where he started Parliament in '55, lifting their name from a still-popular oral fixation.

"It was ego," says Clinton. "I was a little Leo. If I couldn't have a baseball team I wanted a singing group. You know that was our only out . . . out of the ghetto . . . if you could sing, dance, or some shit." Ego is okay with the Dr. if it motorvates you to some goal beyond yourself. But, in itself, ego will "do-loop," that is to say, self-destruct. Self-destruction through dysfunktional ego rhythms is something Clinton manages to avoid by diggin' on the One.

He runs it down like so: "No one person can do it. No philosophy, no religion, no scientist, no state. This shit takes a *whole* mathahfunkin' band and singers and everythang. To actually get out there takes planets because they are all connected . . . magnetic . . . revolving around. All this shit is connected. So any one mafunker sayin', 'Hey, *I'm* going to do it myself.' You know? Let the *sun* stop shinin' on that mafunkah. He be a dull mathahfunkah and that's all it is to it. He'll need a dynamite Flash Light. . . . I'll put it that way. Ain't no one mafunkah can do this shit. And no one species . . . no one state . . . no one nothin'. 'Cause it's all on the One. I mean I am not one. I am *part* of one. We are all part of one.

"All this shit put together . . . all life . . . it takes it all. I mean anybody thinking that he is deep enough to be One is truly trippin'. You know what I mean? Truly trippin'. I mean, we ego trip on stage. We got a spaceship. But we park that mafunker when it's snowing cause it ain't got no snow tires."

Believe it. If you don't feel this funk one way *or* the other you better get your family physician to check your bottom inside out because it just may be false, phony as play money, devoidoffunk and other et ceterasses. This is dancing music, be it the Freak, the Rock or the Wiggle. The Dr.'s funk is, first of all, plenty of feet in the bass drums and thumping ostinatos in the bass guitars. The sock cymbal is steady against them bootin' feet. The Dr.'s idea of bottom is to find a groove, even it out, and hold it dead, as they say, in the pocket. At base the funk is rhythmic, and being in the pocket is a rhythmic concept analogous to the classical idea of swing. Once time is in the pocket, the funk is ready to roll.

Funk is the rawest rhythm and blues happening today. It is minimalist gutbucket in the space age. It descends from the jump band school that spawned r&b, with doses of sock hop doowop and street corner harmonizing. It asscends directly from the sound of Papa James Brown, Godfather of Soul and precursor of funk. It incorporates the innovations of Sly Stone and Jimi Hendrix, who between them foreshadowed the liberation of r&b from its song form limitations and introduced freer instrumental styles. The funk, to a large extent, represents the assimilation of Hendrix and Sly's influences into the r&b mainstream. Funk is the antithesis of its main contender in the r&b world, disco.

The Dr. has two basic brands of the funk. The number one selling funk is Parliament, which draws heavily from the James Brown style. The current edition of Parliament nods in JB's direction, featuring the Horny Horns, led by JB alumni, Fred Wesley and Maceo Parker, and their punching, brass-heavy riffs. The Funkadelic, on the other hand, is basically a guitar band bordering black rock with its own cult-like following. Funkgeetarists Gary Shider and Mike "Kid Funkadelic" Hampton lay down supercharged heavy metal in the tradition of Hendrix. Whichever way the funk is going, the Dr. calls upon two of the finest keyboard players in pop music—Bernie "DaVinci" Worrell, a Funk Mob veteran, and Walter "Junie" Morrison, formerly of the Ohio Players. Clinton is a master at layering each collaborator's contribution into a series of massive crescendos aimed at *Tearin' The Roof Off The Sucker.*

Like most all of what the Dr. knows, the concept of diversifunkation was born of cold realities. When Parliament ventured to Detroit in '67 it was basically a doo-wop group, aspiring to success in the Motown mold. They cut a mini-hit called *I Wanna Testify* and seemed on their way to plenty of that golden chicken scratch. Then came what the Dr. likes to call the "big blow."

"Dig," the Dr. says, "the label we was with, that had *I Wanna Testify* out, went out of business. And they had our name and we couldn't use it because the court wouldn't clear it. The problem was immediate. We had to survive. So the only thing to do was to take the musicians that we had and put them up front and the singers became backup. We just said that the musicians are the Funkadelic and the singers sing *with them* as opposed to *them* playing with the singers. They were friends of ours from Jersey; they came with us. The only shift we had to make was one of ego. Could we stand our brothers to be up front? It was just who's singing lead and who's not. That was easy to say because it was basically my group.

"So they couldn't stop us from doing that. In the meantime Parliament became free from that record thang. We had records out as Funkadelic by then. So we had two names because the Parliament was known. It made sense to me to get a separate deal on a separate label for them, not with any person's name on it, just the name Parliament. We had to do it for survival because a group gets shelved when it's only one group and they funk up or they don't get no hits. The companies just automatically think, 'Well, they thang ain't happenin'.' When you got two names you got a better chance. I have know that since '68. The only way to justify having two groups was to have different personalities."

With the emergence of funk as a real power in the market, Clinton began generating contracts for members of the Mob as solo acts or groups as the major labels bid for their piece of the funk. Thus there are five female singers playing various characters and popping in and out of a Parliament-Funkadelic show. Two of them open the evening as Brides of Funkenstein while the other three (who back them) are billed as the Bridesmaids. The Brides record for Atlantic while the Bridesmaids have become Parlet when recording for Casablanca. To manage his funky conglomerate Clinton employs Leber and Krebs, the people who handle Aerosmith, Ted Nugent and Beatlemania . . . all biggies. Yes, the Dr. and his family are a big reality in the record business.

The Dr. has it in his head to be even bigger. Parliament-Funkadelic returned stateside in December from three months in France, Holland and Germany, and now the Dr. talks about the possibility of "one planet under a groove." Moreover, Clinton claims, "We are negotiating higher—I mean *higher*—than any thang that's ever been done, black or white. We are negotiating from the point of view that we are the biggest thang ever happened. But we know we have to do it five times bigger than anybody, just to be equal."

Does the Dr. worry about the inherent personal vulnerabilities that come with that kind of power? Will he become a target? "Not really," he grins, "because again, it ain't me, you know, it's the funk, and I am careful not to let it get into *that* rhythm. It only self-destructs you when it's personality . . . dominant personality. Right now it's all flattery and amazement and shit. But that'll wear off and it'll just be the funk. I ain't gon' provoke it, is what I am saying. And that's not a dangerous position. It's a good position to be in as long as you don't do it really out of rhythm and you can back up what you say with some good funk.

"It's the same concept that Muhammad Ali used, 'I am the baddest mafunkah around.' You know what I am saying? When you knock out enough people you can even get knocked out yourself and people still say, 'Cool.' But you got to know when to back off, when you did a thing enough, 'cause the novelty wear offa anythang."

Clinton is way ahead of the game when it comes to keepin' the novelty from wearing offa *his* thang. Many of the major groups in pop music augment their performances with fantastic special effects and props. Players appear and disappear in large clouds of pastel colored smoke, or play their axes suspended in air. The Dr. takes multi-media dramatization to its logical conclusion, creating his own funky operettas. Every Parliament-Funkadelic recording is programmatic in concept. His themes include: *Standing On the Verge Of Gettin It On, Maggot Brain, America Eats Its Young, Funkenteleckty* vs. *The Placebo Syndrome, Chocolate City, the Mothership Connection, The Clones Of Dr. Funkenstein, Hard Core Jollies, One Nation Under A Groove,* and now, the *Motor Booty Affair*. On stage, the First Family perform these themes with the aide of rather graphic scatological and sexual imagery, special effects, costumes and scenarios.

The *Motor Booty Affair* takes the funk underwater. "It's basically the same themes that we have been doing for a while," he explained: "Two meanings. One is that Sir Nose and Dr. Funkenstein is rivalring. And the other is Psychoalphadiscobetabioaquadoloop, which is a rhythm that is compatible to dancing in the streets and not getting funked up. It's the same rhythm you can have under water and not get wet. That's about how deep you have to be in this world and not really get funked up."

On stage, Clinton leaves most of the singing to the five ladies, Gary Shider and the Funkateer of longest tenure, basso-profunkdo Ray Davis. Clinton's funktion is to run down the rap, the rhythm, the onomatopoeia. The Dr. cuttin' loose with the funk is poetic licentiousness on the bizarre side, and that aspect of his "rhythm and business" has caused consternation in some quarters of the black community. The Rev. Jesse Jackson, whose organization, People United to Save Humanity (PUSH) has launched a national self-improvement campaign, "Push for Excellence," among inner city youth, has raised questions about the impact of Clinton's lyrics on the impressionable, youthful segment of the audience. But the Dr. sees himself as a deprogrammer in a culture that is telling its youth, particularly black youth of the urban underclass, that they can't handle themselves, that they are dysfunktional, and that the system is their solution. Rather than exploiting sex, Clinton defetishizes, satirizing an already demeaned subject. He views his slogans (e.g., "Get off your ass and jam") as exhorting youth, in language they can clearly understand, to burn down the ghettos in their minds. Thus each production portrays blacks in an alternative reality—dealing in space, underwater, or whatever. Apparently the impetus to project alternative realities is an imperative in black culture. The analogies to be found in Sun Ra and the Nation of Islam are too uncanny to be coincidental.

"The language," Clinton says, "helps deprogram you, too—*and* it's marketable. It's really the rhythm. Actually, the only communication that can penetrate the semantics and the structure, the straightjacket of what's happening with the logic and language of today, is to do it the way we do it, which is the same language but with our own rhythm and a few words Xed out because certain words have emotional value. This other shit is cold and calculated and no emotion. So when you say 'shit'. . . no matter if you sayin' it to be funny, it penetrates."

It's the same attitude toward language that permits "nigger," which has its own odious history, to be a term of endearment when uttered by the proper party with the proper rhythm. The sense of double entendre which pervades Clinton's lyrics, like the various vocalisms with which they are delivered, are as old as the blues.

"So," Clinton reasons, "I try to give them something interesting, give them what they want. I just don't be up there, talkin' about, 'I'm into my music . . . I'm for peace and happiness and there is a message in my music and I hope the brothers and sisters . . .' That one has a patent on it and people don't even hear it. But when you say 'Promentalshitbackwashpsychosis Enema Squad (The Doodoo Chasers) comin' to tidy the bowl of your brain, giving you music to get your shit together by,' muthafunkahs have to say what the funk?—and just that *what* is cool. That's enough, 'cause then they have got to think about it. It's not telling you what to think. All we do is say, '*think.*' We don't preach and we don't guru, other than, 'Hang loose for the night.' It's that basic mother wit shit. It's a party tonight and if they don't get nothin' else out of it but the party, that's cool. And the rest of it they talk about until they get something else out of it. It's multi-sided."

George Clinton puts his money where his motor mouth is. Dig: "When you think about it, it's another thing when groups come in the community and take all the money and keep moving. And just to make sure we ain't gettin' absorbed into the *they*, we dedicate from now on, throughout the rest of our career, 25¢ on every ticket we sell to the United Negro College Fund. All our groups gonna do it and gonna challenge all the other groups to do it. Those people are the ones that buy our records and come to our concerts and *they* trying to phase out black colleges anyway—too much vibes and rhythm in it. We think we *should*, because the only people that's gonna be able to do anything about what is happening is the young people. And the *thang* for them to do is think. We can't tell them what to do. We don't know no answers. But giving them a chance to think is one thang that *we can* do.

"It's all relative, you know, 'cause I have found so much about the funk that I had no idea of. It's got such heavy meaning. In a German dictionary it's got the rhythm of life from the heartbeat, of amoebas coming out of the water. So that's a definition of the shit of the funk. 'Cause I had it as a good excuse after I did the best I could do. The next best thing to saying funk it. Now I done the best I could do and I ain't jumpin'. And to me that's a rhythm and I guess that's the rhythm of life. Cause if you got a funk, a good one, you ain't goin' commit suicide."

Further Reading

Vincent, Rickey. *Funk: The Music, the People, and the Rhythm of the One.* New York: St. Martin's Press, 1996.

Ward, Ed. "The Mothership Sails at Dawn! Roots It Ain't." *Creem,* 8, 1977.

Willhardt, Mark, and Joel Stein. "Dr. Funkenstein's Supergroovalisticprosifunkstication: George Clinton Signifies." In *Reading Rock and Roll: Authenticity, Appropriation, Aesthetics*, ed. Kevin J. H. Dettmar and William Richey, 145–72. New York: Columbia University Press, 1999.

Discography

Funkadelic. *Maggot Brain.* Westbound Records US, 2005.
_____. *Motor City Madness: The Ultimate Funkadelic Westbound Compilation.* Westbound Records US, 2006.
Parliament. *Funkentelechy vs. the Placebo Syndrome.* Island/Mercury, 1977.
_____. *Motor Booty Affair.* Island/Mercury, 1978.
Pure Funk. UTV Records, 1998.
_____. *20th Century Masters—The Millennium Collection: The Best of Parliament.* Island/Mercury, 2000.
_____. *Mothership Connection.* Island/Mercury, 2003.

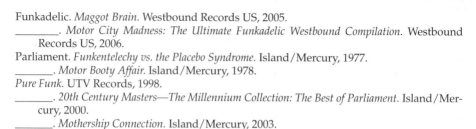

52. Heavy Metal Meets the Counterculture

The thriving London blues-rock scene; the riff-oriented songs of the Kinks, the Who, and the Yardbirds; and the improvisatory flights of psychedelic rock gradually coalesced into a genre forming the antithesis of the "soft rock" of the singer-songwriters. Jimi Hendrix, Cream, and the Jeff Beck Group stand as the main intermediaries and progenitors of the new genre, retrospectively named "heavy metal."[1] What separated bands such as Led Zeppelin, Black Sabbath, and Deep Purple from their blues revival antecedents was not a lesser reliance on the blues but, rather, a less reverent attitude toward the form. These new bands were not so interested in faithful re-creation as in taking certain elements—the tonality, riff orientation, sexual imagery, and sense of aggression—found in some blues songs and heightening or refashioning them for an audience

---

1. This genealogy is borne out by *Hit Parader's Top 100 Metal Albums* (Spring 1989) and *Hit Parader's* "Heavy Metal: The Hall of Fame" (December 1982), reprinted in Robert Walser, *Running with the Devil: Power, Gender, and Madness in Heavy Metal Music* (Hanover, N.H.: Wesleyan University Press and University Press of New England, 1993), 173–74. The account here is also indebted to Steve Waksman's in *Instruments of Desire: The Electric Guitar and the Shaping of Musical Experience* (Cambridge, Mass.: Harvard University Press, 1999), 263; and Walser's in *Running with the Devil.*

that was less interested in folklore and more interested in visceral power.[2] In metal, the peace-loving idealism of folk-rock and psychedelia also diminished in favor of darker visions and expressions of crude sexuality that spoke to another aspect of the countercultural experience.

The "power chord"—the root and fifth of a chord sounded without the third but magnified by distortion in a sonic emblem of transgressive masculinity—joined forces with riffs played in unison by guitar and bass and a heavy "bottom" (bass and bass drum mixed up front, memorialized by Spinal Tap in their anthem "Big Bottom") to create a genre of unparalleled volume, and one that found a large audience of working- and middle-class white youths. The initial rumblings from England were aided and abetted by sheets of noise from late 1960s American aggregations such as Blue Cheer and the highly political MC5.

The early 1970s witnessed a dispersion of a hard rock style, as writers of the time lumped bands like Alice Cooper, Grand Funk Railroad, and Iggy and the Stooges together with Black Sabbath and Led Zeppelin.[3] New attitudes toward showmanship emerged in the mid-1970s with Kiss, and hard rock reached a peak of pop stylization with one-word bands—Journey, Foreigner, Boston, and Toto. Of these bands, the crown for longevity goes to Aerosmith, a band whose hard rock (and lead singer's lips) owed more to the Stones than to anybody else (note: critics often used "hard rock" and "heavy metal" interchangeably at this time).

Heavy metal spoke to class and age divisions in the audience: lower and lower-middle class versus bourgeois, and college students versus high school students. The following entry features a record review of Led Zeppelin's first album that appeared in *Rolling Stone* and the response of some readers to this review. This exchange reveals early public recognition of divisions in the rock audience and a divide between part of the audience and the aesthetic of *Rolling Stone*'s rock critics. John Mendelsohn, the reviewer, compares Led Zeppelin's album unfavorably to the first album by the Jeff Beck Group, which had received positive reviews a short time before.

---

2. Walser, in fact, focuses on the concept of "power" as a defining feature of the heavy metal genre and traces this connection in the historical usage of the term dating back two hundred years; see *Running with the Devil*, 1–3.

3. Lester Bangs wrote several essays exploring these interconnections; see the following: "Heavy Metal," in *The Rolling Stone Illustrated History of Rock and Roll*, ed. Anthony DeCurtis and James Henke with Holly George Warren, 459–63 (New York: Random House, [1976] 1992); "Bring Your Mother to the Gas Chamber (Part 1)," *Creem*, June 1972, 40ff; "Bring Your Mother to the Gas Chamber: Black Sabbath and the Straight Dope on Blood-Lust Orgies, Part 2," *Creem*, July 1972, 47ff.

Review of Led Zeppelin
John Mendelsohn

Led Zeppelin

Led Zeppelin (Atlantic SD 8216)

The popular formula in England in this, the aftermath era of such successful British bluesmen as Cream and John Mayall, seems to be: add, to an excellent guitarist who, since leaving the Yardbirds and/or Mayall, has become a minor musical deity, a competent rhythm section and pretty soul-belter who can do a good spade imitation. The latest of the British blues groups so conceived offers little that its twin, the Jeff Beck Group, didn't say as well or better three months ago, and the excesses of the Beck group's *Truth* album (most notably, its self-indulgence and restrictedness), are fully in evidence on Led Zeppelin's debut album.

Jimmy Page, around whom the Zeppelin revolves, is, admittedly, an extraordinarily proficient blues guitarist and explorer of his instrument's electronic capabilities. Unfortunately, he is also a very limited producer and a writer of weak, unimaginative songs, and the Zeppelin album suffers from his having both produced it and written most of it (alone or in combination with his accomplices in the group).

The album opens with lots of guitar-rhythm section exchanges (in the fashion of Beck's "Shapes of Things" on "Good Times Bad Times," which might have been ideal for a Yardbirds' B-side). Here, as almost everywhere else on the album, it is Page's guitar that provides most of the excitement. "Babe I'm Gonna Leave You" alternates between prissy Robert Plant's howled vocals fronting an acoustic guitar and driving choruses of the band running down a four-chord progression while John Bonham smashes his cymbals on every beat. The song is very dull in places (especially on the vocal passages), very redundant, and certainly not worth the six-and-a-half minutes the Zeppelin gives it.

Two much-overdone Willie Dixon blues standards fail to be revivified by being turned into showcases for Page and Plant. "You Shook Me" is the more interesting of the two—at the end of each line Plant's echo-chambered voice drops into a small explosion of fuzz-tone guitar, with which it matches shrieks at the end.

The album's most representative cut is "How Many More Times." Here a jazzy introduction gives way to a driving (albeit monotonous) guitar-dominated background for Plant's strained and unconvincing shouting (he may be as foppish as Rod Stewart, but he's nowhere near so exciting, especially in the higher registers). A fine Page solo then leads the band into what sounds like a backwards version of the Page-composed "Beck's Bolero," hence to a little snatch of Albert King's "The Hunter," and finally to an avalanche of drums and shouting.

In their willingness to waste their considerable talent on unworthy material the Zeppelin has produced an album which is sadly reminiscent of *Truth*. Like the Beck group they are also perfectly willing to make themselves a two- (or, more accurately, one-and-a-half) man show. It would seem that, if they're to help fill the void created

Source: "Review of Led Zeppelin" John Mendelsohn, *Rolling Stone*, 15 March 1969.

by the demise of Cream, they will have to find a producer (and editor) and some material worthy of their collective attention.

JOHN MENDELSOHN

3-15-69

SIRS:

Mendelsohn's review of Led Zeppelin was a 100% lie. Pure bullshit. Never has there been such a great band since Winwood's departure from Traffic.

Eric Charles

Brooklyn, N.Y.

SIRS:

If I used your record reviews as a guide to my personal record purchases, I would have the worst pile of garbage in the history of record collecting.

A few issues back, your unbelievably fucked review of Led Zeppelin. This, plus past reviews of Creedence Clearwater, Cream, etc.

I don't know where the musical taste of San Francisco is at, but if your magazine is an indicator—perhaps you all ought to come east on your vacation this summer.

Charles Laquidara

WBCN-FM

Boston, Massachusetts

In discussions of heavy metal's genealogy, heated debates often rage over whether Led Zeppelin or Black Sabbath were the "first." The two bands share instrumentation (a trio of guitar, bass, and drums fronted by a noninstrumentalist singer), images featuring the occult and supernatural, and an unenthusiastic reception by rock critics. While it is true that Led Zeppelin sometimes used a textural approach strongly identified with heavy metal on songs such as "How Many More Times" and "Whole Lotta Love" (both from 1969), many of their songs also reveal ties to psychedelic rock and even folk-rock: "Babe I'm Gonna Leave You," from their first album, was a cover of an early 1960s recording by Joan Baez, and "Stairway to Heaven," perhaps their most famous song, evokes these earlier genres in its lyrics, elaborate instrumentation, and arrangement. In general, then, Led Zeppelin share certain aesthetic conceits with their 1960s forbears in a way that seems antithetical to Black Sabbath.

Black Sabbath's first two albums, *Black Sabbath* (released February, Friday the 13th, 1970) and *Paranoid* (1971), feature songs stripped down almost entirely to their riff-infused bones. Their gloomy, religious-tinged lyrics portending doom and offering moral advice are light years away from the alternately flowery, hedonistic, and sometimes conventionally romantic images of Led Zeppelin. Sabbath's tempos and textures ooze primordial sludge, lending their music a monolithic gravity. For example, the title song from their first album ("Black Sabbath" from the album *Black Sabbath*, as performed by Black Sabbath) begins with the sound of rain, thunder, and tolling church bells, followed by a riff played by guitar and bass at a dirgelike tempo consisting entirely of the pitches G, G an octave higher, and C-sharp, thereby outlining the tritone, or *diabolus in musica*, the interval symbolizing the "devil in music" in the middle ages. The band maintains this riff and tempo for the first 4'30" of the song, with only soft-loud dynamics used to provide contrast. The lyrics of "Black Sabbath" speak of the "chosen one," "Satan," and immolation, announcing the song's difference forcefully from the rock music that had preceded it.

Black Sabbath posed a riddle for rock critics similar to, but even more extreme than, Led Zeppelin: How could such apparent disdain for complexity and artfulness be reconciled with enormous popularity? In this respect, Black Sabbath presented a conundrum similar to that of the American hard rock group Grand Funk Railroad. Both bands came from regions far removed from the carnivalesque celebrations of the counter-culture in San Francisco and London or from the hipster scene of New York City: Black Sabbath from Birmingham (England), Grand Funk from Flint, Michigan. Critics like Greil Marcus and Richard Goldstein specu-lated that this phenomenon was related to the emergence of a younger audience that had not absorbed the aesthetic premises of 1960s rock.[4] The most sympathetic critic, however, was Lester Bangs, for whom Black Sabbath's rejection of artifice fit nicely into his "outline of a cure," con-tinuing a line established by the Velvet Underground and the Stooges; in the words of Bangs, "since when is monotony so taboo in rock and roll, anyway? . . . [Black Sabbath's music is] naïve, simplistic, repetitive, absolute doggerel—but in the tradition."[5]

Shunned by both critics and radio, where the playlists of "underground" rock stations usually aligned with critical taste, heavy metal had to wait until the development of the album-oriented rock for-mat in the late 1970s to acquire a true mass media outlet.

Black Sabbath Don't Scare Nobody
Ed Kelleher

Ozzy Osbourne talking:

"I was standing out at the back of the club between sets and this guy says, 'Is it true you've gone insane?' I said, 'what?' And he says, 'The word's out on you that you're mad, didn't you hear?' I just shook my head, 'I dunno.'"

4. See Steve Waksman's discussion of this critical debate in the context of the response to Grand Funk Railroad in "Grand Funk Live! Staging Rock in the Age of the Arena," in *Listen Again: A Momentary History of Pop Music*, ed. Eric Weisbard, 157–71 (Durham, N.C.: Duke University Press, 2007).

5. Lester Bangs, "Review of Black Sabbath, *Master of Reality*," in *The Rolling Stone Record Review Volume II* (New York: Pocket Books, 1974), 309, 310 (first published in *Rolling Stone*, November 25, 1971). See also Bangs's extended essay on Black Sabbath, "Bring Your Mother to the Gas Chamber (parts 1 and 2)," cited in the introduction to this chapter. For a history of heavy metal placing Black Sabbath unequivocally as its progenitor, see Ian Christe, *Sound of the Beast: The Com-plete Headbanging History of Heavy Metal* (New York: HarperEntertainment, 2003).

Source: "Black Sabbath Don't Scare Nobody," Ed Kelleher, *Creem*, Vol. 3, no. 7.

It's the morning after. Ozzy looks like the morning after. His expression says that if he was losing his mind he would probably be the last to know. Or care. He stares into a cup of hotel coffee which has turned cold. Ozzy is exhausted. He's been sick most of the night from the too many ups he took to get through the last show. Black Sabbath has just wound up their third American tour, a rigorous coast to coast excursion of one-nighters that's taken its toll in the bags under Ozzy Osbourne's eyes and in the similarly weary faces of fellow band members, guitarist Tony Iommi, drummer Bill Ward, and bass player Terry "Geezer" Butler.

"Any group from England that can do an American tour deserves credit," says Ozzy. "At home there's no great distances to travel, no time changes and no planes to catch. It's really very tiring here." Last time over, Ozzy had to enter a hospital with a bad case of nervous fatigue. Proof that Sabbath is beginning to adjust to the rigors of being a visiting supergroup: all four members managed to stagger through this tour relatively intact.

Even their instruments made it. Three and a half tons of equipment which was shipped and air freighted from city to city. During this trip there were no major hitches, but the group and road manager Michael Double remember nights like the one they spent in Paramus, New Jersey earlier this year. Their equipment had been stranded at the Chicago airport and they had to work with power supplied by the local Catholic church. The concert was a disaster. After half of the first number, Ozzy led the band off the stage. Some amateur engineers came out and toyed with the equipment. The audience sat for about an hour and didn't bitch. Finally, Sabbath returned, played an additional five songs in desultory fashion and split. Despite the disappointment of the set, they received a standing ovation. Black Sabbath fans may be a hard lot, but they're also understanding.

It wasn't always so. The early stages of the band's career were marked by incidents of performer-audience confrontations. Thinking back on it now, Ozzy can manage a smile as he recalls a gig Sabbath played in Northern Scotland. "It was one of those horrible little towns, you know the type: three shops and about ten boozers. To get there we had to drive for hours over these bumpy dirt roads. There were three people in the whole club for our entire first set. Then it got to be ten o'clock and that's the hour when the pubs close, so pretty soon all these farmers started coming in. They were all drunk out of their minds and started shouting things like, 'Play something we can dance to, you cunt!' Some of them had these pennies they would heat over a flame and throw at the stage. There we were trying to play music and they were pelting us with these horrible bloody hot coins that stick to your skin when they hit you. Then they started complaining about our volume. They sent up a note 'Turn down or . . .' and below that was a large bloodstain."

"What did you do?"

"We turned up!"

"We had to," adds Geezer. "After all, we're only in it for the volume."

Volume. Loudness. For some that is what Black Sabbath is all about. The lights come up. The group kicks into the opening bars of "War Pigs" with bass vying with drums vying with guitar in a heads-on battle for decibel supremacy—and over all comes the insistent voice of Ozzy, loud, louder, loudest! The true fans revel, smiling as their brains are bathed in it. The uninitiated are startled ("This is loud shit." "You mean I was supposed to play their records at high volume?"). Those whose job it is to be there even come prepared. One record company exec packs a pair of earplugs whenever he attends a Sabbath show.

"Louder than Led Zeppelin" was a line from the early promotion copy on Black Sabbath. It was only partly a put-on. Loudness, particularly when accompanied by intensity, is mighty marketable, just as softness blended with innocence can be. In the agora of the record business, extremities and aberrations turn a nice dollar. Ask Tiny Tim. If you can find her, ask Mrs. Miller.

Actually, Sabbath had something else going for them in the extremities department. Witchcraft. Age old, but new gold. In England witchcraft was already sacred. There was widespread interest in Satanism and magic. The time was right for a rock and roll band which personified all the cults and rituals of the day. Let them frown into the hearts of our children. Let their lyrics play upon infant fears. Dress them in sombre raiment, iron crosses gleaming on their breasts. Give them all the darkest crayons to draw with. Have them set a funereal beat to march to. And there was Black Sabbath, just hanging out, calling themselves Earth and wondering why they hadn't made it yet, even while they spent a good part of the time explaining that no, they weren't Rare Earth, they were not to be confused with Mother Earth and they sure weren't the Nitty Gritty Dirt Band.

The story of how they made their name change is splashed with the wash of press-agentry and gimmickry. After an unsuccessful tour of the Continent, the boys were coming back to England by boat and decided to chuck the Earth tag for something more mysterioso. Right after returning, they got word that one of the fellow's aunts had died. They took a trip to Holland. When they got back, you guessed it. Another relative had bit the dust. The pattern continued. The group got scared. Enter Ozzy Osbourne's father who fashioned for them iron crosses to wear around their necks. Presto! No more family funerals. And, for extras, the band starts to prosper. The tale is a natural. Does it matter if it's true? We're dealing with myth here just as surely as if we were skimming a page of Homeric verse.

For a time Sabbath were confused in many people's minds with Black Widow, a group whose main claim to fame was that they simulated a black mass ritual as part of their concert act. Some say that on special occasions Widow raped the girl serving as victim right on the stage. One ecstatic admirer of the group told me in all serious-ness that one night they murdered her! Confusing the bands was far less prevalent in England than here in the U.S. where neither was really known. While Sabbath's first LP, entitled simply *Black Sabbath*, established their identity for most American fans, mix-ups continued. The most striking appeared in the pages of *Rolling Stone*. In its April 15, 1971 issue, Sabbath's second album, *Paranoid* was reviewed. After the music had been written off as "bubblegum Satanism," the critic blew it. He launched into a put-down of "lead singer Kip Treavor." Kip, of course, had been the vocalist with Black Widow.

* * *

New York record producer talking:

"For a long time I was just vaguely aware of Black Sabbath. Then I heard a cou-ple of their things and I dismissed them. You know what happened? It's a year later and I'm an absolute Sabbath freak! My kid sister turned me on to them."

Black Sabbath got the predictable amount of bad press when they first came along. Predictable because the usual number of people weren't willing to give them a chance. "Witches and devils? What is this shit?" And another album went flying into the dustpile of the rock cognoscenti. "People say they didn't really hear what we were doing," Ozzy laughs. "How could they *not* hear us?"

What critics didn't figure on was word of mouth. Sabbath is the kind of band that a friend comes over, plunks the record on your turntable, hands you a thick joint, points you to your favorite easy chair, turns up the juice and says, "Hey listen." It's this variation on missionary zeal that has put the group over and helped them to succeed against really phenomenal odds. How phenomenal? Take the last two years. Make a list of the supergroups which have emerged during that period. Not your personal favorites, necessarily, just an objective list of the groups that sell records in the millions and fill concert halls wherever they go. Now cross out the names of all the bands which were formed as offshoots of already successful groups. Only a very few names will be left and among them will be Black Sabbath.

In the grand tradition of British groups, Sabbath came out of dead end streets. It's a downer just to drive through Birmingham; to actually live there must be mind-strangling. It's a factory town but with a difference — it's spread out in all directions, a big sprawling splotch in the center of England. "There are so many suburbs to it," says Ozzy, "that there is no such thing as a 'Birmingham sound.'" The boys were headed down the usual badass road until rock and roll bailed them out. "If I hadn't got with a band," says Ozzy soberly, "I really would be in prison right now."

Of the four only Geezer had any aspirations of escaping a boring workingclass life. And he was only studying for it. Yes, Geezer wanted to be an accountant. The others were more realistic. Bill Ward alternated between lorry driving and laboring in a rubber mill. Tony Iommi fixed typewriters ("I was also a part time bully."). Ozzy worked in a slaughterhouse.

"What did you do there?"

No reply. He makes a cutting motion with his fingers. He grins in what he must think is fiendish fashion. Yeah, Ozzy, you would have gone to the slam.

* * *

Lillian Roxon talking:

"If I was a little kid and I saw those four up on the stage looking like that and with those iron crucifixes, I'd be scared!"

Nobody is really scared of Black Sabbath but I know what Lillian means. There is a very delicious quality to fear, something that as children we understand completely but that we lose hold of as we get older. Sabbath, with their images of rat salad, iron men and bits of finger, get right through to the dark areas of our memory. It's Saturday matinee, the lights go out and the horror show begins. Slip into the weird world. A doctor brings corpses from the grave. Slip back and laugh. An actor is mugging outrageously. The same combination of the vivid and the comic works for Black Sabbath.

"We are serious about our music," declares Ozzy and he means it. "We write about things that are true." But the send-up is there too. A person doesn't have to look very deeply into the Black Sabbath songbook to come up grinning at some of the lyrics. "What is this that stands before me?" asks Ozzy in the opening verse of their very first song. You might well arsk, as John Lennon might well say. Sabbath is having their fun and why shouldn't they? What the hell is rock and roll if it isn't fun?

A closer look at their lyrics reveals that the boys have gotten their heads together and come up with some relevant ideas on topics of the day. Nothing intensely intellectual, you understand, just a few observations on the planet and mostly in their latest LP, *Master Of Reality*. The despair of their earlier songs has given way to a kind of cautious optimism. "Children Of The Grave," probably the most relentless rocket on the album, offers the hope that love can be a force for survival:

Show the world that love is still alive, you must be brave
Or you children of today are children of the grave.*

Another song, "After Forever," examines survival on a personal plane and is almost religious in tone:

Perhaps you'll think
    before you say that God is dead and gone
Open your eyes, just realize that he is the one
The only one who can save you now
    from all this sin and hate.
Or will you just jeer at all you hear?
Yes! I think it's too late.*

The last line is pure Sabbath. When they say "it's too late," it's a whole lot heavier than Carole King. It's *over*! Still, the idea of the verse isn't entirely negated by the tagline. Sabbath is asking you to believe in something.

Usually they don't ask much. They dish it out. Cruelty has been a common characteristic of their songs. Sometimes it takes the form of judgment and retribution in a manner which is almost Calvinistic— in "War Pigs" the generals who have perpetrated death and destruction on the world are stripped of their power and made to crawl on their knees for mercy. Other times it is just dismissal. "Finished with my woman 'cause she couldn't help me with my mind" is the matter-of-fact opener to "Paranoid."

Instrumentally, too, they are uncompromising, and often when they hit on a good hard riff they will bring it back over and over. On records this can be exciting or boring, depending on your mood, but in concert when you're primed for the Sabbath sound, it's exhilarating. Other bands might try to entice your mind. Sabbath drives a spike into it.

Instrumentally they are really just a three man band. Occasionally, Ozzy will pitch in with a bit of harmonica, but mostly it's a three way street as far as axes are concerned. Rarely mentioned too is the fact that Tony Iommi is fast becoming one of rock's most technically proficient guitarists. What he might lack in showbusiness-y flash he more than makes up for in ability. On the last album he also emerged as a talented composer—his surprisingly gentle, almost medieval songs give a nice balance to the record.

Now that they have achieved recognition, Sabbath seems interested in widening their spectrum. They're glad that their audience is becoming more diverse. "After we had a number one single in England," says Ozzy, "we started attracting very young kids and nothing else. So we never followed 'Paranoid' up with another single. We're not interested in just appealing to a lot of knickerwetters." More and more, older fans like the New York record producer quoted earlier are showing up at Sabbath gigs and this has got to have an effect on which way the group will go.

"When we play, we try to get off," explains Ozzy. "If we can get the audience off too, that's all the better 'cause then we get a good thing going back and forth between us and we play better."

The next album, their fourth, hasn't been worked out yet. "We've got a little cottage in the country," says Ozzy. "We'll stay there a few weeks, get loaded all the time and write some new songs." Look for some surprises. Sabbath worked hard to get where they're at and they're not about to let up. Next time you see Ozzy Osbourne, make a cutting motion with your fingers. He'll know what you mean.

---

*Copyright Tro/Essex Music International, Inc. (ASCAP)

Further Reading

Christe, Ian. *Sound of the Beast: The Complete Headbanging History of Heavy Metal*. New York: Harper Entertainment, 2003.

Cope, Andrew L. *Black Sabbath and the Rise of Heavy Metal Music*. Farnham, UK: Ashgate, 2010.

Waksman, Steve. *Instruments of Desire: The Electric Guitar and the Shaping of Musical Experience*. Cambridge, Mass.: Harvard University Press, 1999.

———. *This Ain't the Summer of Love: Conflict and Crossover in Heavy Metal and Punk*. Berkeley: University of California Press, 2009.

Walser, Robert. *Running with the Devil: Power, Gender, and Madness in Heavy Metal Music*. Hanover, N.H.: University Press of New England, 1993.

Weinstein, Deena. *Heavy Metal: The Music and Its Culture*. Rev. ed. New York: Da Capo Press, 2000.

Discography

Beck, Jeff. *Truth*. Sony, 1968.

Black Sabbath. *Black Sabbath*. Warner Bros./WEA, [1970] 1990.

———. *Paranoid*. Warner Bros./WEA, [1970] 1990.

———. *Master of Reality*. Warner Bros./WEA, [1971] 1990.

Blue Cheer. *The History of Blue Cheer: Good Times Are So Hard to Find*. Island Mercury, 1990.

British Rock, Vol. 1. Original Sound, 1988.

Cream. *Disraeli Gears*. Polydor/UMGD, 1967.

Deep Purple. *The Very Best of Deep Purple*. Rhino/WEA, 2000.

Heavy Metal. Rhino/WEA, 2007, esp. disc 1.

Heavy Metal: The First 20 Years. Time Life Records, 2006.

Led Zeppelin. *Led Zeppelin I*. Atlantic/WEA, 1969.

———. *Led Zeppelin II*. Atlantic/WEA, 1969.

53. Led Zeppelin Speaks!

The following interview of Jimmy Page by Dave Schulps originally appeared in *Trouser Press* over three successive issues in 1977. While several years had passed since the critical disdain that greeted Led Zeppelin's early albums, this interview is littered with references to the gap between their success with audiences and the negative response from critics. Numerous interviews with Led Zeppelin were published in the mid-1970s (usually with Robert Plant), but Schulps's piece is unusual in its focus on Zeppelin's music.[1] Other interviews tended to obsess about Plant and Page's mystical predilections or about other aspects of Zeppelin's image, such as their reputation for destroying hotel rooms and ravaging groupies. This interview covers the entirety of Page's career, including his background in art school and London-area blues bands, his experiences as a session guitarist, his stint with the Yardbirds, and his friendship with Jeff Beck. Page comes across as thoughtful and humble—a far cry from the public perception of heavy metal guitarists as craven wildmen. In passages that may be responding directly to Mendelsohn's review, Page answers charges about a lack of originality in relation to the Jeff Beck Group and discusses another somewhat controversial issue: Led Zeppelin's use of traditional blues lyrics and tunes on their early albums without attribution.[2]

The Crunge: Jimmy Page Gives a History Lesson
Dave Schulps

Were you into the blues as much as the Stones or was it more rock 'n' roll for you?
I was an all-arounder, thank God.

Do you think that's helped your career?
Immensely. I think if I was just labeled a blues guitarist I'd have never been able to lose the tag. When all the guitarists started to come through in America—like Clapton, Beck, and myself—Eric, being the blues guitarist, had the label. People

---

1. This interview was not alone in this approach, however; for an interview that goes to great lengths to convince readers of Page's seriousness as a musician from earlier in his career, see Chris Welch, "Jimmy Page, Part Three," *Melody Maker,* February 28, 1970, 10. For another interview that gives both Page and Plant space to talk about music, see Cameron Crowe, "Jimmy Page and Robert Plant Talk," *Rolling Stone,* March 13, 1975, 33–37. Perhaps the strangest interview, and one that does dwell on Page's interest in the occult, is his interview with William Burroughs (Beat-associated author of *Naked Lunch,* a hallucinatory chronicle of a junkie), "Rock Magic: Jimmy Page, Led Zeppelin, and a Search for the Elusive Stairway to Heaven," *Crawdaddy,* June 1975, 34–35, 39–40.

2. For a musicological defense of Led Zeppelin against charges of appropriation and plagiarism, see Dave Headlam, "Does the Song Remain the Same? Questions of Authorship and Identification in the Music of Led Zeppelin," in *Concert Music, Rock, and Jazz since 1945: Essays and Analytical Studies,* ed. Elizabeth West Marvin and Richard Hermann, 313–63 (Rochester, N.Y.: University of Rochester Press, 1995). For the most thorough and sophisticated scholarly study of Led Zeppelin to date, see Susan Fast, *In the Houses of the Holy: Led Zeppelin and the Power of Rock Music* (New York: Oxford University Press, 2001). See also "Heavy Music: Cock Rock, Colonialism, and Led Zeppelin," in Steve Waksman, *Instruments of Desire: The Electric Guitar and the Shaping of Musical Experience* (Cambridge, Mass.: Harvard University Press, 1999), 237–76.

Source: "The Crunge: Jimmy Page Gives a History Lesson," Dave Schulps/Trouser Press.

just wanted to hear him play blues. I saw the guitar as a multifaceted instrument and this has stayed with me throughout. When you listen to the various classical guitarists like Segovia and Julian Bream, brilliant classical players, and Manitas de Plata doing flamenco, it's two totally different approaches to acoustic. Then there's Django Reinhardt and that's another approach entirely.

In those early days I was very interested in Indian music, as were a lot of other people too. Most of the "textbook" of what I was forced to learn was while I was doing sessions, though. At that point you never knew what you were going to be doing when you got to the session. In America, you were a specialist. For example, you would never think of Steve Cropper to do a jazz session or film session or TV jingles, but in Britain you had to do everything. I had to do a hell of a lot of work in a short time. I still don't really read music, to be honest with you. I read it like a six-year-old reads a book, which was adequate for sessions, and I can write it down, which is important.

What got you into guitar playing? You listened to a lot of music being a collector, so was it just hearing it on record?

Exactly. I've read about many records which are supposed to have turned me on to want to play, but it was "Baby, Let's Play House" by Elvis Presley. You've got to understand that in those days "rock 'n' roll" was a dirty word. It wasn't even being played by the media. Maybe you'd hear one record a day during the period of Elvis, Little Richard, and Jerry Lee Lewis. That's why you were forced to be a record collector if you wanted to be part of it. I heard that record and I wanted to be part of it; I knew something was going on. I heard the acoustic guitar, slap bass, and electric guitar—three instruments and a voice—and they generated so much energy I had to be part of it. That's when I started. Mind you, it took a long time before I got anywhere, I mean any sort of dexterity. I used to listen to Ricky Nelson records and pinch the James Burton licks, learn them note for note perfect. I only did that for a while, though. I guess that after one writes one's first song you tend to depart from that. It's inevitable.

How old were you when you left Neil Christian[3] and started going heavily into sessions?

I left Neil Christian when I was about 17 and went to art college. During that period, I was jamming at night in a blues club. By that time the blues had started to happen, so I used to go out and jam with Cyril Davies's Interval Band. Then somebody asked me if I'd like to play on a record, and before I knew where I was I was doing all these studio dates at night, while still going to art college in the daytime. There was a crossroads and you know which one I took.

You mentioned you were good friends with Beck before the Yardbirds. How did your friendship come about? Did you see the Yardbirds often when Beck was with them?

When I was doing studio work I used to go see them often, whenever I wasn't working. I met Beck through a friend of mine who told me he knew this guitarist I had to meet who'd made his own guitar. Beck showed up with his homemade guitar one day and he was really quite good. He started playing this James Burton and Scotty Moore stuff; I joined in and we really hit it off well.

We used to hang out a hell of a lot when he was in the Yardbirds and I was doing studio work. I remember we both got very turned on to Rodrigo's Guitar Concerto by Segovia and all these sorts of music. He had the same sort of taste in music as I did. That's why you'll find on the early LPs we both did a song like "You Shook Me." It was the type of thing we'd both played in bands. Someone told me he'd already recorded it after we'd already put it down on the

3. "Neil Christian" is a reference to Page's first band, Neil Christian and the Crusaders.

first Zeppelin album. I thought, "Oh dear, it's going to be identical," but it was nothing like it, fortunately. I just had no idea he'd done it. It was on *Truth* but I first heard it when I was in Miami after we'd recorded our version. It's a classic example of coming from the same area musically, of having similar taste. It really pissed me off when people compared our first album to the Jeff Beck Group and said it was very close conceptually. It was nonsense, utter nonsense. The only similarity was that we'd both come out of the Yardbirds and we both had acquired certain riffs individually from the Yardbirds.

Under what circumstances did you finally join the Yardbirds when Paul Samwell-Smith quit in late summer of 1966?

It was at a gig at the Marquee Club in Oxford which I'd gone along to. They were playing in front of all these penguin-suited undergraduates and I think Samwell-Smith, whose family was a bit well to do, was embarrassed by the band's behavior. Apparently Keith Relf had gotten really drunk and he was falling into the drum kit, making farting noises into the mike, being generally anarchistic. I thought he'd done really well, actually, and the band had played really well that night. He just added all this extra feeling to it. When he came offstage, though, Paul Samwell-Smith said, "I'm leaving the band." Things used to be so final back then. There was no rethinking decisions like that. Then he said to Chris Dreja, "If I were you, I'd leave too." Which he didn't. They were sort of stuck.

Jeff had brought me to the gig in his car and on the way back I told him I'd sit in for a few months until they got things sorted out. Beck had often said to me, "It would be really great if you could join the band." But I just didn't think it was a possibility in any way. In addition, since I'd turned the offer down a couple of times already, I didn't know how the rest of them would feel about me joining. It was decided that we'd definitely have a go at it; I'd take on the bass, though I'd never played it before, but only until Dreja could learn it as he'd never played it before either. We figured it would be easier for me to pick it up quickly, then switch over to a dual guitar thing when Chris had time to become familiar enough with the bass.

What about your own desire for stardom, did that have any role in your quitting sessions to join the Yardbirds in the first place?

No. I never desired stardom, I just wanted to be respected as a musician.

Do you feel the extent of your stardom now has become a burden for you in any way?

Only in relation to a lot of misunderstandings that have been laid on us. A lot of negative and derogatory things have been said about us. I must say I enjoyed the anonymity that was part of being one fourth of a group. I liked being a name but not necessarily a face to go with it. The film, *The Song Remains the Same*, I think, has done a lot to put faces to names for the group.

And after Relf and McCarty said they were quitting the Yardbirds, you planned to keep the group going with Chris Dreja and bring in a new drummer and singer, is that right?

Well, we still had these dates we were supposed to fulfill. Around the time of the split John Paul Jones called me up and said he was interested in getting something together. Also, Chris was getting very into photography; he decided he wanted to open his own studio and by that time was no longer enamored with the thought of going on the road. Obviously, a lot of Keith and Jim's attitude of wanting to jack it in had rubbed off on him, so Jonesy was in.

I'd originally thought of getting Terry Reid in as lead singer and second guitarist but he had just signed with Mickie Most as a solo artist in a quirk of fate. He suggested I get in touch with Robert Plant, who was then in a band called Hobbstweedle. When I auditioned him and heard him sing, I immediately thought there must be something wrong with him personality-wise or that he had to be impossible to work with, because I just could not understand why, after he told me he'd been singing for a few years already, he hadn't become a big name yet. So I had him down to my place for a little while, just to sort of check him out, and we got along great. No problems. At this time a number of drummers had approached me and wanted to work with us. Robert suggested I go hear John Bonham, whom I'd heard of because he had a reputation, but had never seen. I asked Robert if he knew him and he told me they'd worked together in this group called Band of Joy.

So the four of you rehearsed for a short time and went on that Scandinavian tour as the New Yardbirds.

As I said, we had these dates that the Yardbirds were supposed to fulfill, so we went as the Yardbirds. They were already being advertised as the New Yardbirds featuring Jimmy Page, so there wasn't much we could do about it right then. We had every intention of changing the name of the group from the very beginning, though. The tour went fantastically for us, we left them stomping the floors after every show.

What were the original ideas behind Zeppelin when the band first got together? Was it immediately decided to be a high energy thing?

Obviously, it was geared that way from the start. When Robert came down to my place the first time, when I was trying to get an idea of what he was all about, we talked about the possibilities of various types of things, "Dazed and Confused," for example. Then I played him a version of "Babe I'm Gonna Leave You." It was the version by Joan Baez, the song is traditional, and I said, "Fancy doing this?" He sort of looked at me with wonder and I said, "Well, I've got an idea for an arrangement," and started playing it on acoustic guitar. That's indicative of the way I was thinking with regards to direction. It was very easy going.

There was a bit of a fuss made at one point because on the first couple of albums you were using a lot of traditional and blues lyrics and tunes and calling them your own.

The thing is they were traditional lyrics and they went back far before a lot of the people that one related them to. The riffs we did were totally different, also, from the ones that had come before, apart from something like "You Shook Me" and "I Can't Quit You," which we attributed to Willie Dixon. The thing with "Bring It on Home," Christ, there's only a tiny bit of that taken from Sonny Boy Williamson's version and we threw that in as a tribute to him. People say, "Oh, 'Bring It on Home' is stolen." Well, there's only a little bit in the song that relates to anything that had gone before it, just the end.

Your next album, Led Zeppelin III, presented a very different image of Led Zeppelin from the first two albums. Most importantly, it was predominantly acoustic. It was a very controversial album. How and why did the changes that brought about the third album take place?

After the intense touring that had been taking place through the first two albums, working almost 24 hours a day, basically, we managed to stop and have a proper break, a couple of months as opposed to a couple of weeks. We decided to go off and rent a cottage to provide a contrast to motel rooms. Obviously, it had quite an effect on the material that was written.

Did you write the whole album there?

Just certain sections of it. "That's the Way," "Bron-Y-Aur Stomp," quite a few things. It was the tranquility of the place that set the tone of the album. Obviously, we weren't crashing away at 100 watt Marshall stacks. Having played acoustic and being interested in classical guitar, anyway, being in a cottage without electricity, it was acoustic guitar time. It didn't occur to us not to include it on the album because it was relative to the changes within the band. We didn't expect we'd get thrashed in the media for doing it.

Was there a rethink by the band about the stage act, since you were faced with having to perform material from a predominantly acoustic LP?
It just meant that we were going to have to employ some of those numbers onstage without being frightened about it. They were received amazingly well.

Had you wanted to bring in more of the English folk roots to Zeppelin or was it just the influence of living in the cottage that gives the album a pastoral feeling?
It has that because that's how it was. After all the heavy, intense vibe of touring which is reflected in the raw energy on the second album, it was just a totally different feeling. I've always tried to capture an emotional quality in my songs. Transmitting that is what music seems to be about, really, as far as the instrumental side of it goes, anyway. It was in us, everything that came out on *Zeppelin III* can still be related to the essence of the first album when you think about it. It's just that the band had kept maturing.

Were you surprised when the critical reaction came out?
I just thought they hadn't understood it, hadn't listened to it. For instance, *Melody Maker* said we'd decided to don our acoustic guitars because Crosby, Stills and Nash had just been over here. It wasn't until the fourth LP that people began to understand that we weren't just messing around.

You did take a lot of stock in the criticism of the third record. Personally, you seemed to be hit hard by it at the time.
To pave the way for 18 months without doing any interviews, I must have. Silly, wasn't I? That was a lot of the reason for putting out the next LP with no information on it at all. After a year's absence from both records and touring, I remember one agent telling us it was professional suicide. We just happened to have a lot of faith in what we were doing.

Was the cover of the fourth album meant to bring out the whole city/country dichotomy that had surfaced on the third record?
Exactly. It represented the change in the balance which was going on. There was the old country man and the blocks of flats being knocked down. It was just a way of saying that we should look after the earth, not rape and pillage it.

Do you think the third record was good for the band, regardless of the critical reaction, because it showed people that the band was not just a heavy metal group, that you were more versatile than that?
It showed people that we weren't going to be a stagnant group. There were some people who knew that already and were interested to see what we'd come up with; there were others who thought we were just an outright hype and were still living back in the '60s. They just didn't take anything we did seriously. A lot of them have since come around. You should read that *Melody Maker* review, though, it's absolutely classic. I felt a lot better once we started performing it, because it was proving to be working for the people who came around to see us. There was always a big smile there in front of us. That was always more important than any proxy review. That's really how the following of the band has spread, by word of mouth. I mean, all this talk about a hype, spending thousands on publicity campaigns, we didn't do that at all. We didn't do television. Well, we did a pilot TV show and a pilot radio show, but that's all. We weren't hyping ourselves. It

wasn't as though we were thrashing about all over the media. It didn't matter, though, the word got out on the street.

Once a band is established it seems to me that bad reviews can't really do anything to a band.

No, you're right. But you've got to understand that I lived every second of the albums. Whereas the others hadn't. John Paul and Bonzo would do the tracks and they wouldn't come in until needed. And Robert would do the vocals. But I'd be there all the time and I'd live and cringe to every mistake. There were things that were right and wrong on a subjective level.

The fourth album was to my mind the first fully realized Zeppelin album. It just sounded like everything had come together on that album.

Yeah, we were really playing properly as a group and the different writing departures that we'd taken, like the cottage and the spontaneity aspects, had been worked out and came across in the most disciplined form.

"Rock and Roll" was a spontaneous combustion. We were doing something else at the time, but Bonzo played the beginning of Little Richard's "Good Golly Miss Molly" with the tape still running and I just started doing that part of the riff. It actually ground to a halt after about 12 bars, but it was enough to know that there was enough of a number there to keep working on it. Robert even came in singing on it straight away.

I do have the original tape that was running at the time we ran down "Stairway to Heaven" completely with the band. I'd worked it all out already the night before with John Paul Jones, written down the changes and things. All this time we were all living in a house and keeping pretty regular hours together, so the next day we started running it down. There was only one place where there was a slight rerun. For some unknown reason Bonzo couldn't get the timing right on the twelve-string part before the solo. Other than that it flowed very quickly. While we were doing it Robert was penciling down lyrics; he must have written three quarters of the lyrics on the spot. He didn't have to go away and think about them. Amazing, really.

"Black Dog" was a riff that John Paul Jones had brought with him. "Battle of Evermore" was made up on the spot by Robert and myself. I just picked up John Paul Jones's mandolin, never having played a mandolin before, and just wrote up the chords and the whole thing in one sitting. The same thing happened with the banjo on "Gallows Pole." I'd never played one before either. It was also John Paul Jones's instrument. I just picked it up and started moving my fingers around until the chords sounded right, which is the same way I work on compositions when the guitar's in different tunings.

When did Sandy Denny come in to sing on "Gallows Pole"?

Well, it sounded like an old English instrumental first off. Then it became a vocal and Robert did his bit. Finally we figured we'd bring Sandy by and do a question-and-answer-type thing.

"Misty Mountain Hop" we came up with on the spot. "Going to California" was a thing I'd written before on acoustic guitar. "When the Levee Breaks" was a riff that I'd been working on, but Bonzo's drum sound really makes the difference on that point.

You've said that when you heard Robert's lyrics to "Stairway to Heaven" you knew that he'd be the band's lyricist from then on.

I always knew he would be, but I knew at that point that he'd proved it to himself and could get into something a bit more profound than just subjective things.

Not that they can't be profound as well, but there's a lot of ambiguity implied in that number that wasn't present before. I was really relieved because it gave me the opportunity to just get on with the music.

Did you know you'd recorded a classic when you finished?
I knew it was good. I didn't know it was going to become like an anthem, but I did know it was the gem of the album, sure.

Was the idea of the symbols on the cover of the fourth album yours?
Yeah. After all this crap that we'd had with the critics, I put it to everybody else that it'd be a good idea to put out something totally anonymous. At first I wanted just one symbol on it, but then it was decided that since it was our fourth album and there were four of us, we could each choose our own symbol. I designed mine and everyone else had their own reasons for using the symbols that they used.

Do you envision a relationship between Zeppelin cover art and the music on the albums?
There is a relationship in a way, though not necessarily in a "concept album" fashion.

Does Robert usually come into sessions with the lyrics already written?
He has a lyric book and we try to fuse song to lyric where it can be done. Where it can't, he just writes new ones.

Is there a lot of lyric changing during a session?
Sometimes. Sometimes it's more cut and dried, like on "The Rain Song."

There are a few tracks on the fifth album that seemed to exhibit more of a sense of humor than Zeppelin had been known for. "The Crunge" was funny and "Dyer Mak'er" had a joke title which took some people a while to get.
I didn't expect people not to get it. I thought it was pretty obvious. The song itself was a cross between reggae and a '50s number, "Poor Little Fool," Ben E. King things, stuff like that. I'll tell you one thing, "The Song Remains the Same" was going to be an instrumental at first. We used to call it "The Overture."

You never performed it that way.
We couldn't. There were too many guitar parts to perform it.

But once you record anything with overdubs, you end up having to adapt it for the stage.
Sure. Then it becomes a challenge, a tough challenge in some cases. "Achilles" is the classic one. When Ronnie Wood and Keith Richard came to hear us play, Keith said, "You ought to get another guitarist; you're rapidly becoming known as the most overworked guitarist in the business." Quite amusing. There are times when I'd just love to get another guitarist on, but it just wouldn't look right to the audience.

Further Reading

Burroughs, William. "Rock Magic: Jimmy Page, Led Zeppelin, and a Search for the Elusive Stairway to Heaven." *Crawdaddy*, June 1975, 34–35, 39–40.
Crowe, Cameron. "Jimmy Page and Robert Plant Talk." *Rolling Stone*, March 13, 1975, 33–37.
Fast, Susan. *In the Houses of the Holy: Led Zeppelin and the Power of Rock Music*. New York: Oxford University Press, 2001.
Headlam, Dave. "Does the Song Remain the Same? Questions of Authorship and Identification in the Music of Led Zeppelin." In *Concert Music, Rock, and Jazz since 1945: Essays and*

Analytical Studies, ed. Elizabeth West Marvin and Richard Hermann, 313–63. Rochester, N.Y.: University of Rochester Press, 1995

Discography

Led Zeppelin. *Led Zeppelin III*. Atlantic/WEA, 1970.
_____. *Led Zeppelin IV (aka ZOSO)*. Atlantic/WEA, 1971.
_____. *Houses of the Holy*. Atlantic/WEA, 1973.
_____. *Physical Graffiti*. Atlantic/WEA, 1975.
_____. *Presence*. Atlantic/WEA, 1976.
The Yardbirds. *Little Games*. Capitol, 1996.
_____. *Roger the Engineer*. Warner Bros/WEA, 1966.

54. "I Have No Message Whatsoever"

The stars of glam (or glitter) rock in the early 1970s—David Bowie, T-Rex, Slade, Gary Glitter, and Sweet—all hailed from the United Kingdom, and all (with the eventual exception of Bowie) achieved greater success there than in the United States. Part of the resistance in the United States stemmed from how glam artists emphasized the artificial at the expense of the authentic passion so carefully cultivated by other genres of the era. However, campiness and androgyny gradually became hip in the United States in the mid- to late 1970s, as evidenced by the success of films such as the *Rocky Horror Picture Show* and some of the later new-wave bands like the B-52s. Not accidentally, this development coincided with the mass acceptance of Bowie in the United States.

In the early 1970s, however, when he first became a phenomenon in the United Kingdom, Bowie (David Jones, b. 1947), along with the other glitterati just mentioned, shared a style founded on a riff-based, hard rock with rather exaggeratedly stiff rhythms. While the actual heyday of glam was brief, its emphasis on androgyny and campy posing influenced many other rock stars of the time, such as Mick Jagger, Rod Stewart, Elton John, and Lou Reed. Although not necessarily glam, Alice Cooper emerged during the early 1970s with a sound that is sometimes described as the prototype for a kind of American heavy metal. In addition to a hard-rock sound, Cooper shared with glam an emphasis on the theatrical, at first with gender-bending androgyny and then with an act that relied on images gleaned from horror movies and pulp magazines.

The following interview with Bowie, conducted by teenage phenom reporter Cameron Crowe,[1] highlights Bowie's unabashed acknowledgment that his performances present him as an actor playing a part. This apparent distance from his persona places him at the opposite end of the authenticity spectrum from singer-songwriters, who had made self-revelation the cornerstone of their art. Within the flow of his exaggerated egocentricity, Bowie touches on different perceptions about gender and sexual identity on opposing sides of the Atlantic, glories in his superficiality and lack of depth, takes a jab at Elton John for allegedly ripping off aspects of his persona, and expresses pride in artistic theft and lack of originality. Calculated to offend the rock establishment of the day, Bowie presents an antidote to the pompousness and self-seriousness pervading other rock genres and anticipates the media machinations of later stars such as Madonna.

David Bowie Interview
Cameron Crowe

Playboy: Let's start with the one question you've always seemed to hedge: How much of your bisexuality is fact and how much is gimmick?

Bowie: It's true—I am a bisexual. But I can't deny that I've used that fact *very* well. I suppose it's the best thing that ever happened to me. Fun, too. We'll talk all about it.

Playboy: Why do you say it's the best thing that ever happened to you?

Bowie: Well, for one thing, girls are always presuming that I've kept my heterosexual virginity for some reason. So I've had all these girls try to get me over to the other side again: "C'mon, David, it isn't all that bad. I'll show you." Or, better yet, "We'll show you." I always play dumb.

On the other hand—I'm sure you want to know about the other hand as well—when I was 14, sex suddenly became all important to me. It didn't really matter who or what it was with, as long as it was a sexual experience. So it was

---

1. Crowe may be better known to readers as a writer and/or director of many films, including *Fast Times at Ridgemont High* (1982) and *Almost Famous* (2001), his semiautobiographical account of coming of age as a rock critic in the early to mid-1970s.

some very pretty boy in class in some school or other that I took home and neatly fucked on my bed upstairs. And that was it. My first thought was, Well, if I ever get sent to prison, I'll know how to keep happy.

Playboy: Which wouldn't give much slack to your straighter cellmates.

Bowie: I've always been very chauvinistic, even in my boy-obsessed days. But I was always a gentleman. I always treated my boys like real ladies. Always escorted them properly and, in fact, I suppose if I were a lot older—like 40 or 50—I'd be a wonderful sugar daddy to some little queen down in Kensington. I'd have a houseboy named Richard to order around.

Playboy: How much of that are we supposed to believe? Your former publicist, the celebrated ex-groupie Cherry Vanilla, says she's slept with you and that you're not gay at all. She says you just let people *think* you like guys.

Bowie: Oh, I'd love to meet this impostor she's talking about. It sure ain't me. That's actually a lovely quote. Cherry's almost as good as I am at using the media.

Playboy: Why, at a time when nobody else in rock would have dared allude to it, did you choose to exploit bisexuality?

Bowie: I would say that America forces me into it. Someone asked me in an interview once—I believe it was in '71—if I were gay. I said, "No, I'm bisexual." The guy, a writer for one of the English trades, had no idea what the term means. So I explained it to him. It was all printed—and that's where it started. It's so nostalgic now, isn't it? 'Seventy-one was a good American year. Sex was still shocking. Everybody wanted to see the freak. But they were so ignorant about what I was doing. There was very little talk of bisexuality or gay power before I came along. Unwittingly, I really brought that whole thing over. I never, ever said the word gay when I first got over here to America. It took a bit of exposure and a few heavy rumors about me before the gays said, "We disown David Bowie." And they did. Of course. They knew that I wasn't what they were fighting for.

Nobody understood the European way of dressing and adopting the asexual, androgynous everyman pose. People all went screaming, "He's got make-up on and he's wearing stuff that looks like dresses!" I wasn't the first one, though, to publicize bisexuality.

Playboy: Who was?

Bowie: Dean. James Dean did, very subtly and very well. I have some insight on it. Dean was probably very much like me. Elizabeth Taylor told me that once. Dean was calculating. He wasn't careless. He was not the rebel he portrayed so successfully. He didn't want to die. But he did believe in the premise of taking yourself to extremes, just to add a deeper cut to one's personality.

James Dean epitomized the very thing that is so campily respectable today—the male hustler. It was part of his incredible magnetism. You know, that he was . . . a whore. He used to stand in Times Square to earn money so he could go to Lee Strasberg and learn how to be Marlon Brando. He had quite a sordid little reputation. I admire him immensely—that should take care of any question you may have about whether or not I have any heroes.

Playboy: Thanks. Now what about you posing in drag for the cover of the English album of *The Man Who Sold The World*?

Bowie: Funnily enough, and you'll never believe me, it was a parody of Gabriel Rossetti. Slightly askew, obviously. So when they told me that a drag-queen cult was forming behind me, I said, "Fine, don't bother to explain it; nobody is going to bother to try to understand it." I'll play along, absolutely *anything* to bring me through. Because of everybody's thirst for scandal—look at how big *People* is—they gave me a big chance. All the papers wrote *volumes* about how sick I was, how I was helping to kill off true art. In the meantime, they used up all the space they could have given over to true artists. That really is pretty indicative of how compelling pretension is, that it commanded that amount of bloody writing about what color my hair was gonna be next week. I want to know why they wasted all that time and effort and paper on my clothes and my pose. *Why?* Because I was a dangerous statement.

The follow-up to that, now that I've decided to talk a little more—if only to you—was, "How dare he have such a strenuous ego?" That, in itself seemed a danger to some people. Am I, as a human being, worth talking about? I frankly think, Yes, I am. I've got to carry through with the conviction that I am also my own medium. The only way I can be effective as a person is to be this confoundedly arrogant and forthright with my point of view. That's the way I am. I believe myself with the utmost sincerity.

Playboy: But aren't you having trouble getting *other* people to believe you? Take, for example, your well-publicized farewells to showbiz. You've retired twice, swearing you'd never have another thing to do with rock 'n' roll. Yet you've just finished a six-month world concert tour, promoting your newest rock-'n'-roll album, *Station to Station.* How do you rationalize these contradictions?

Bowie: I lie. It's quite easy to do. Nothing matters except whatever it is I'm doing at the moment. I can't keep track of everything I say. I don't give a shit. I can't even remember how much I believe and how much I don't believe. The point is to grow into the person you grow into. I haven't a clue where I'm gonna be in a year. A raving nut, a flower child or a dictator, some kind of reverend—I don't know. That's what keeps me from getting bored.

Playboy: In the song *Station to Station*, though, you do refer to cocaine—

Bowie: Yes, yes. The line is, "It's not the side effects of the cocaine. . . . I'm thinking that it must be love." Do the radio stations bleep it out?

Playboy: None that we've heard. Did you have any reservations about using the line in the song?

Bowie: None whatsoever.

Playboy: One might easily construe it as advocating the use of cocaine. Or is that the message?

Bowie: I have no message whatsoever. I really have nothing to say, no suggestions or advice, nothing. All I do is suggest some ideas that will keep people listening a bit longer. And out of it all, maybe *they'll* come up with a message and save me the work. My career has kind of been like that. I get away with murder.

Playboy: Do you have trouble deciding which is the real you?

Bowie: I've learned to flow with myself. I honestly don't know where the real David Jones is. It's like playing the shell game. Except I've got so many shells I've forgotten what the pea looks like. I wouldn't know it if I found it. Being famous helps put off the problems of discovering myself. I mean that. That's the main reason I've always been so keen on being accepted, why I've striven so hard to put my brain to artistic use. I want to make a mark. In my early stuff, I made it through on sheer pretension. I consider myself responsible for a whole new school of pretensions—they know who they are. Don't you, Elton? Just kidding. No, I'm not. See what I mean? That was a thoroughly pretentious statement. True or not. I bet you'll print that. Show someone something where intellectual analysis or analytical thought has been applied and people will yawn. But something that's pretentious—that keeps you riveted. It's also the only thing that shocks anymore. It shocks as much as the Dylan thing did 14 years ago. As much as sex shocked many years ago.

Playboy: You're saying sex is no longer shocking?

Bowie: Oh, come on. Sorry, Hugh. Sex has never *really* been shocking, it was just the people who performed it who were. Shocking people, performing sex. Now nobody really cares. Everybody fucks everybody. The only thing that shocks now is an extreme. Like me running my mouth off, jacking myself off. Unless you do that, nobody will pay attention to you. Not for long. You have to hit them on the head.

Playboy: Is that the Bowie success formula?

Bowie: That's always been it. It's never really changed. For instance, what I did with my Ziggy Stardust was package a totally credible, plastic rock-'n'-roll singer— much better than the Monkees could ever fabricate. I mean, *my* plastic rock-'n'- roller was much more plastic than anybody's. And that was what was needed at the time. And it still is. Most people still want their idols and gods to be shallow, like cheap toys. Why do you think teenagers are the way they are? They run around like ants, chewing gum and flitting onto a certain style of dressing for a day; that's as deep as they wish to go. It's no surprise that Ziggy was a huge success.

Playboy: Is that why you said you became Ziggy at one point?

Bowie: Without even thinking about it. At first, I just assumed that character onstage. Then everybody started to treat me as they treated Ziggy, as though I were the Next Big Thing, as though I moved masses of people. I became convinced I was a messiah. Very scary. I woke up fairly quickly.

Playboy: Do you ever worry about your fans' giving up on you—not wanting to hear Bowie as a soul singer or whatever?

Bowie: Well, they must understand what my trip was in the beginning. I've never been a musician.

Playboy: What have you been?

Bowie: The unfortunate thing is that I've always wanted to be a film director. And the two media got unconsciously amalgamated, so I was doing films on record. That creates your basic concept album, which becomes a bit of a slow pack horse in the end. Now I know that if I'm going to make albums, I've got to make albums that I enjoy musically, or else just make the fucking film. A lot of my concept albums, like *Aladdin Sane, Ziggy* and *Diamond Dogs,* were only 50 percent there. They should have been visual as well. I think that some of the most talented actors around are in rock. I think a whole renaissance in film making is gonna come from rock. Not because of it, though, despite it.

Playboy: But you've said that you find rock depressing and sterile, even evil.

Bowie: It *is* depressing and sterile and, yes, ultimately evil. Anything that contributes to stagnation is evil. When it has familiarity, it's no longer rock 'n' roll. It's white noise. Dirge. Just look at *disco* music—the endless numb beat. It's really dangerous.

So, I've moved on. I've established the fact that I am an entertainer, David Bowie, not just another boring rock singer. I've got a film out, Nicolas Roeg's *The Man Who Fell to Earth.* And I'll be doing a lot more, taking a lot of chances. The minute you know you're on safe ground, you're dead. You're finished. It's over.

The last thing I want is to be established. I want to go to bed every night saying, "If I never wake again, I certainly will have *lived* while I was alive."

Playboy: Let's go back to *disco* music. You say it's a dirge, yet you had the biggest *disco* hit of last year in *Fame* and you scored again this year with *Golden Years.* How do you explain that?

Bowie: I love *disco.* It's a lovely escapist's way out. I quite like it, as long as it's not on the radio night and day—which it is so much these days. *Fame* was an incredible bluff that worked. Very flattering. I'll do *anything* until I fail. And when I succeed, I quit, too. I'm really knocked out that people actually dance to my records, though. But let's be honest: my rhythm and blues are thoroughly plastic. *Young Americans,* the album *Fame* is from, is, I would say, the definitive plastic soul record. It's the squashed remains of ethnic music as it survives in the age of Muzak rock, written and sung by a white limey. If you had played *Young Americans* to me five years ago and said, "This is an R&B album," I would have laughed. Hysterically.

Playboy: How about if we had said, "This is going to be *your* album five years from now"?

Bowie: I would have thrown you *and* the record out of my house.

Playboy: How did you become a rock-'n'-roller anyway?

Bowie: Truth? I was broke. I got into rock because it was an enjoyable way of making my money and taking four or five years to puzzle my next move out. I was a painter before that, studying commercial art at Bromley Technical High School. I tried advertising and that was *awful.* The *lowest.* But I was well into my little saxophone, so I left advertising and thought, Let's give rock a try. You can have a good time doing that and usually have at least enough money to live on. Especially then. It was the Mod days; nice clothes were half the battle.

Playboy: What do you believe in?
Bowie: Myself. Politics. Sex . . .

Playboy: Since you put yourself first, do you consider yourself an original thinker?

Bowie: Not by any means. More like a tasteful thief. The only art I'll ever study is stuff that I can steal from. I do think that my plagiarism is effective. Why does an artist create, anyway? The way I see it, if you're an inventor, you can invent something that you hope people can use. I want art to be just as practical. Art can be a political reference, a sexual force, any force that you want, but it should be usable. What the hell do artists want? Museum pieces? The more *I* get ripped off, the more *flattered* I get. But I've caused a lot of discontent because I've expressed my admiration for other artists by saying, "Yes, I'll use that," or, "Yes, I took this from him and this from her." Mick Jagger, for example, is scared to walk into the same room as me even *thinking* any new idea. He knows I'll snatch it.

Playboy: Is it true that Jagger once told you he was hiring the French artist Guy Peellaert for the jacket of a Rolling Stones album and you ran right off to hire Peellaert for your own album, *Diamond Dogs,* which was released first?

Bowie: Mick was silly. I mean, he should never have shown me anything new. I went over to his house and he had all these Guy Peellaert pictures around and said, "What do you think of this guy?" I told him I thought he was incredible. So I immediately phoned him up. Mick's learned now, as I've said. He will never do that again. You've got to be a bastard in this business.

Playboy: You stated in *Rolling Stone* that you'd like to use your music to "rule the world . . . subliminally." Would you care to elaborate?

Bowie: I think subliminal advertising is great. If it hadn't been outlawed, it would have gone out of advertising very quickly and straight into politics. I would have excelled at it. Think of it, an empty screen that people could stare at for an hour and a half and not actually see anything but leave with an entire experience in their heads.

Of course, *Rolling Stone* got hate mail. So did Dali in his day. He knew exactly what he was doing when he painted his paintings. He knew what all the objects meant. Should his work have been destroyed and he forced to paint a vase of flowers? The attitude that says the artist should paint only things that the proletarian can understand, I think is the most destructive thing possible. That sounds a little like Hitler's going around to museums and tearing modern paintings down, doesn't it?

You mustn't be scared of art. Rock 'n' roll is only rock 'n' roll. People hold it so sacred—mustn't tamper, in case you find out that it really does govern kids. Those old Fifties antirock movies were right. Rock-'n'-roll records are dangerous to the moral fiber. But then, records are a thing of the past now, so who knows?

Playboy: We're not quite sure how you made the leap from subliminal advertising to reporting the death of the record industry, but since you have, what do you propose will happen to music in the future?

Bowie: It will return to the sensitivities of the working class. That excites me. Sound as texture, rather than sound as music. Producing noise records seems pretty logical to me. My favorite group is a German band called Kraftwerk—it plays noise music to "increase productivity." I like that idea, if you have to play music.

Playboy: Do you feel *you've* been taken advantage of over the years?

Bowie: Not taken advantage of. Exploited.

Playboy: Are you suggesting you haven't made all that you should have?

Bowie: What, moneywise? Oh, Lord no—we made nothing. All I've made is an impact and a change, which of course, is worth a lot. I keep telling myself that. The best thing to say about it all is that it's archetypal rock-'n'-roll business. Read the reports of the Beatles, the Stones and a lot of other big entertainers and take some kind of amalgamation of all that; it's a pretty accurate picture of my business. John Lennon has been through it all. John told me, "Stick with it. Survive. You really go through the grind and they'll rip you off right and left. The key is to come out the other side." I said something cocky at the time like, "I've got a great manager. Everything is great. I'm a *Seventies* artist." The last time I spoke to John, I told him he was right. I'd been ripped off blind.

Playboy: You're not a rich man? After five gold albums?

Bowie: *Now*, yes, exceedingly. No! Wait, America! Not at all. Haven't got a penny to my name. I'm pleading poverty at the moment, but I'm *potentially* very rich. Theoretically rich but not wealthy.

Playboy: Are you as bitter about the music business as Lennon and Jagger have said they are?

Bowie: No, no, no. You see, I needed to learn about it. You've got to make mistakes. It's very important to make mistakes. Very, very important. If I glided through, I wouldn't be the man I'm not today.

Playboy: Last question. Do you believe and stand by everything you've said?

Bowie: Everything but the inflammatory remarks.

Further Reading

Geyrhalter, Thomas. "Effeminacy, Camp and Sexual Subversion in Rock: The Cure and Suede." *Popular Music* 15 (May 1996): 217–24.

Hoskyns, Barney. *Glam! Bowie, Bolan and the Glitter Rock Revolution*. New York: Pocket Books, 1998.

Sontag, Susan. "Notes on 'Camp.'" In *Against Interpretation*, 275–92. New York: Anchor Books, [1964] 1990.

Discography

Bowie, David. *Space Oddity*. RCA Victor, 1972.

_____. *The Rise and Fall of Ziggy Stardust*. RCA Victor, 1972.

_____. *Aladdin Sane*. RCA Victor, 1973.

_____. *Diamond Dogs*. RCA Victor, 1974.

_____. *Young Americans*. RCA Victor, 1975.

_____. *Station to Station*. RCA Victor, 1976.

_____. *Best of Bowie*. Virgin Records US, 2002.

Dynamite: Best of Glam Rock. Repertoire, 1998.

John, Elton. *Goodbye Yellow Brick Road*. Island, 1973.

55. Rock Me Amadeus[1]

The spawn of psychedelic rock and European art music ("classical" music), progressive rock (alternately known as "art rock," "prog rock," or simply "prog"), emerged from a complex of genres (including heavy metal and glam) that formed in the late 1960s–early 1970s. What distinguished prog from other contemporary genres with similar influences was the tendency to include overt references to classical music in terms

---

1. I stole the title of this section from the 1986 hit single of that name by Austrian pop star Falco. The song has nothing to do with the subject of the chapter, progressive rock, but my title of choice, "Rocking the Classics," was already taken by Edward Macan's book on prog rock, which is, by the way, the most systematic history of the genre; see Macan, *Rocking the Classics: English Progressive Rock and the Counterculture* (New York: Oxford University Press, 1997).

of form and texture. Occasionally, the melody and harmony of a particular piece of art music might influence a specific song.

Mostly a British phenomenon, several stages of classicizing influence can be observed in the genre as it developed.[2] The first of these influences was the incorporation of orchestral instruments, not in the manner of pre–rock 'n' roll background filler, but as active participants in the texture. The Beatles' use of a string quartet in "Yesterday" (1965) and the Baroque-influenced harpsichord break in "In My Life" (1965) may have initiated this phenomenon, which was echoed by other Baroque-influenced pop hits in the mid-1960s, like the Left Banke's "Walk Away Renee" (1966) and Procul Harum's "A Whiter Shade of Pale" (1967).[3] Another phase involves the use of complex forms: suites, multimovement works, and so forth. While the Beatles' *Sgt. Pepper's Lonely Hearts Club Band* (1967) arguably inaugurated this trend with its recapitulation of the title track and its overall framework of a "show," works such as King Crimson's *In the Court of the Crimson King* and side two of the Beatles' *Abbey Road* extended the idea to more complex notions of musical unity.[4] The Who also contributed to this direction, first with a mini-opera "A Quick One" (1966); then with a concept album, *The Who Sell Out* (1967); and, finally, with the first "rock opera," *Tommy* (1969).

Eventually, Emerson, Lake, and Palmer, as well as other bands, rearranged classical pieces, basing their new "works" on themes taken from the classical canon. Finally, in the apotheosis of the progressive rock style as realized by groups like Yes and Gentle Giant, one finds rock instrumentation and sections featuring improvisation embedded within complex multimovement forms alternating with carefully worked-out contrapuntal textures. Progressive rock bands also incorporated other influences, such as jazz, avant-garde electronic sounds, and musical processes borrowed from 1960s minimalism.

An interesting point of departure between progressive rock musicians and other rock or soul artists of the period is the emphasis on artifice. The "authentic" baring of the soul, so important to the aesthetics of other genres at this time, is avoided in favor of technical prowess that does not necessarily emphasize spontaneity. This is not to say that prog

---

2. John Rockwell, in an excellent overview of the genre, ascribes the British domination of prog rock to the more overt persistence and awareness of class difference in the United Kingdom versus the United States; see "The Emergence of Art Rock," in *The Rolling Stone Illustrated History of Rock and Roll*, ed. Anthony DeCurtis and James Henke with Holly George-Warren, 493 (New York: Random House, [1976] 1992). Greg Lake (the "Lake" of "Emerson, Lake and Palmer") explains it thusly: "I think it's a question of heritage. European musicians tend to come from a classical heritage. American bands tend to come from a blues-based heritage"; see Eric Gaer, "Emerson, Lake and Palmer: A Musical Force," *Down Beat*, May 9, 1974, 14.

3. The connection in these songs with European art music may be felt as much or more in the classically influenced voice leading and harmonic progressions as in the instrumentation.

4. And, as I stated in Part 3, *Freak Out!* by the Mothers of Invention and *Pet Sounds* by the Beach Boys (both 1966) are both sometimes put forward as the first concept album.

rock fans necessarily eschewed "authenticity" as an aesthetic criterion; rather, "authenticity" in prog is earned by the display of mastery over the materials and in lofty intellectual ambitions projected through formal manipulation and "deep," cosmic lyrics (another legacy from psychedelic rock).

The majority of articles and interviews with musicians associated with progressive rock took place in a new form of publication that began to prosper in the 1970s: magazines, such as *Guitar Player* and *Contemporary Keyboard*, that catered to the aspiring rock musician and were filled with articles about playing techniques, practice regimens, and equipment. The seriousness of the prog rockers made them obvious subjects for these magazines, which paid far more attention to them than did publications that were directed more toward the lay rock audience, such as *Rolling Stone* and *Creem*. Thus, the following interview with Keith Emerson (of Emerson, Lake, and Palmer) concentrates on the gigantism of his band's stage show, his equipment (not included here), and his approach to adapting classical music. I've also included a statement from Aaron Copland about the band's adaptation of his "Fanfare for the Common Man."

Keith Emerson
Domenic Milano

In late 1969, Keith met bassist/vocalist Greg Lake, then of King Crimson, in San Francisco where the two were playing on the same bill. Both were dissatisfied with the bands they were in, and each liked the other's playing. The two joined musical forces and began their search for the proper drummer. Carl Palmer of Atomic Rooster was their choice, and so was formed Emerson, Lake & Palmer—ELP for short.

Works, Vol. 1 [their most recent album] has been the subject of much talk among the followers of ELP, because of the extensive use of an orchestra throughout the album. Many feel that the band is smothered behind the lavish strings and brass, while others find those elements pleasant additions to the ELP sound. Another radical move on the album was Emerson's forsaking his Hammond organ and modular Moog synthesizer, the latter of which he had been the first to use in a live performance situation. Instead he chose to use Yamaha's mammoth $50,000 polyphonic synthesizer, the GX-1, and a Steinway grand piano.

In the early spring of 1977, the group mounted a tour which included a 59-piece orchestra, 6 vocalists, 19 technicians, 6 roadies, and others, for a total of 115 people. It was the largest touring production ever attempted in a rock context. However, by mid-summer the group was forced to drop the orchestra for financial reasons.

Source: "Keith Emerson," Domenic Milano/*Contemporary Keyboard*

How do you go about re-arranging tunes by classical composers?

I sit down with the score. As far as Aaron Copland's "Fanfare for the Common Man," on *Works*, goes, it needed transposing, so I did that first. I wanted to improvise in a key that was sort of bluesy. It ended up in *E*. The rest of it was straightforward, really. You know, in order to get the shuffle sound, the timing needed to be changed, but it was common sense.

What about earlier things like "The Barbarian"?

That was taken from Bartok's *Allegro Barbaro*. There were a few timing things that needed to be changed to fit what we were doing there. Ginastera's *First Piano Concerto*, fourth movement, which we called "Toccata" on *Brain Salad Surgery*, was about the most complicated piece we did. I had to go through the whole thing and condense it, to bring out the parts of it that I thought were the most important. Of course, we couldn't do it exactly the way Ginastera had written it because all of it uses the whole keyboard on the piano. So those bits I got the synthesizer to do. Ginastera loved it when I took it along to him. He made some comment that that was exactly how his music should always sound. And the same with Copland. In fact, I've got a tape of what Copland thinks of our version of "Fanfare for the Common Man." [*Ed. Note:* For a transcription of that tape see page 319.] This always pleases me, because I don't want to adulterate the music or anything.

How do you orchestrate your keyboard parts?

You mean what music is to be played on what instrument? I don't know. I invariably start with the piano. From there on it'll go out either to the organ or to another instrument. It depends on how it sounds and on what the original intention is for the piece. If I'm pretty convinced it is going to be, say, a piano concerto, or it's going to be for ELP, then that will determine what instruments I'll use. Sometimes I've got that in mind before I start. I swap around for variety. I may have been playing one line on the organ for a long time and just by way of a change I'll play it on the Yamaha.

Where did your interest in arranging other people's music come from?

Simple reason—I like the tunes. I want to play these tunes, but I want to play them in a way that's acceptable to our audience. And stimulate new interest in the original. You know I started doing this back in the Sixties, and that was my intention. But obviously since that time, audiences have become far more perceptive— intelligent. One doesn't really have to do that now. I think people are going for classical music as much as for any other form. You wouldn't have had your Chick Coreas five years ago. Chick Corea doesn't have to really dress up in blazer gear to get a wide following. It just goes to show you that it's not a question of image these days. It's more a question of the actual music. So I don't mean to be insulting the public's intelligence by saying the reason I'm playing "Fanfare for the Common Man" is because I want them to listen to the original. That may have been the case six years ago, but since then it's become part of what people expect of me. I still occasionally enjoy other people's music. If a piece comes out which lends itself to a particular situation, a particular meter, then I use it. If it doesn't, I don't force the issue. My music has been tagged with the label "classical rock," which I guess is okay. Broadly speaking, I guess that's true, but it's not a term that I want to really like.

What would you call it?

I guess it *is* classical rock [laughs], mainly because I can't think of anything else to call it. It's playing classical music with a definite meter behind it. That sounds nicer. It's like calling a guy who collects rubbish a waste disposal officer instead of a dustman. It sounds far more polite. Like, how would you term what you call your music? I call it playing classical music with the focus on the meter, a straight, rigid meter—one that's different from what the composer originally intended. Or, rudely speaking, dustman—classical rock.

What made you want to write a piano concerto?

I said, "Look, I'm gonna write a piano concerto. That's my biggest wish." And I went to John Mayer for technical advice. He said, "Fine. What form would you like it to be in?" And I said, "Sonata form." And we went from there. He'd tell me what I need here and there and this is what has to come next to make it work. It's all instinctive with me. Often there were times he'd say, "Well, look. It's stuck. We have to . . . *You* have to make a movement there that's fast." And I'd invariably come up with something on the spot. We always worked together, either at my house or at his. Then I'd be listening to it and it just seemed to work. And he'd say, "Well, of course it works, because. . . ." And then he'd reel off the formula for why it worked.

Can you play just about anything you can hear?

No. I mean the "Fugue" on the *Trilogy* album was literally written out on paper before I ever played it. I couldn't work a fugue any other way. Some people are very clever and can improvise them. It's great to be able to do that. But as for me, I have to write it down, look at it, and work it out. I don't write things that are easy for me. Everything that I write is a new step forward. Sometimes I hear it in the back of my mind and know the effect that I want, but I can't get it. I work at it for days and days and days.

Do you write out all of the music for the band to learn?

Now I do in order to get the orchestrations down, but the earlier stuff like *Tarkus* wasn't written out. I'm very aware of what Carl and Greg like to do, and in the case of *Tarkus* Carl was very struck by different time signatures. He told me that he'd like to do something in 5/4, so I said I'd keep that in mind and started writing *Tarkus* from there. Greg wasn't too sure about it at the beginning. It was too weird. But he agreed to try it, and afterwards he loved it. Listening back to those things, I think they just scratch the surface. It moves too quickly from one idea to another. One thing I manage to do now is expand more on an idea. I get more out of it than doing just little bits and pieces. I think if I did *Tarkus* again today, I'd orchestrate it and it would sound marvelous.

Aaron Copland on the ELP Version of "Fanfare for the Common Man"

"Of course it's very flattering to have one's music adapted by so popular a group as Emerson, Lake & Palmer. A lot depends on what they do with what they take. And naturally, since I have a copyright on the material, they're not able to take it without my permission. In each case where I have given my permission there was something that attracted me about the version that they perform which made me think I'd allow them to release it. Of course, I always prefer my own version, but what they do is really *around* the piece, I'd say, rather than a literal transposition of the piece. They're a gifted group. In that particular case I allowed it to go by because when they first play the 'Fanfare,' they play it fairly straight, and when they end the piece they play it fairly straight. What they do in the middle—I'm not sure how they connect that to my music, but they do it somehow, I suppose. But the fact that at the beginning and at the end it is 'Fanfare for the Common Man' gave me the feeling I ought to allow them to do with it as they please."

> These excerpts from interviews with the members of Yes discuss two of their best-known recordings: the single "Roundabout" (1971) and the album *Close to the Edge*. Of particular interest here is Yes's ad hoc process of assembling their most ambitious tracks, which turn out to result from an extensive trial-and-error method of collective composition, rather than from the master plan of a single composer (as in the writing of art music).[5]

from Yesstories: Yes in Their Own Words
Tim Morse

"Roundabout"

Steve [Howe, guitarist] (1987): When we recorded "Roundabout" we thought we had made one of the all-time epics. Jon Anderson and I wrote that in Scotland. It was originally a guitar instrumental suite. You see, I sort of write a song without a song. All the ingredients are there—all that's missing is the song. "Roundabout" was a bit like that; there was a structure, a melody and a few lines. When the Americans wanted us to edit it for a single we thought it was sacrilege. Here the song was so well-constructed and quite over the top—but in the end we did have to edit it. The song did very well. In fact Jon and I won an award for it in 1972.

Jon [Anderson, vocalist] (1989): We were traveling from Aberdeen through to Glasgow and we'd started this song . . . me and Steve were singing it in the back of the van on the way down. One of the things you'll drive through is a very winding small road that goes through this incredible valley and the mountains are sheer from both sides of the road—they just climb to the sky. And because it was a cloudy day, we couldn't see the top of the mountains. We could only see the clouds because it was sheer straight up. . . . I remember saying, "Oh, the mountains—look! They're coming out of the sky!" So we wrote that down: Mountains come out of the sky and they stand there. And we came to a roundabout right at the bottom of this road and within twenty-four hours we were back in London. We'd been on tour then for about a month. So it was sort of twenty-four hours before I'll be home with my loved one, Jennifer. So the idea as twenty-four before my love and I'll be there with you. In around the lake—just before you get to Glasgow there's a lake—a very famous one— the Loch Ness. So we were driving in around the lake—mountains come out of the sky—they stand there.

---

5. For more on *Close to the Edge*, see John Covach, "Progressive Rock, 'Close to the Edge,' and the Boundaries of Style," in *Understanding Rock: Essays in Musical Analysis*, ed. John Covach and Graeme M. Boone (New York: Oxford University Press, 1997) 3–32.

Source: from *Yesstories: Yes in Their Own Words* © Tim Morse/St. Martin's Press

Steve (1982): [The intro is] the easiest thing in the world to play. I could show any-body and they could play it. But because of sound and the intensity, so nice and strong . . . that in itself is a different kind of connection. It's not that the music or musical idea is that good. It's the come-on, the intensity. One of the secret ingredients of Yes wasn't only the sort of material we were using, it was the intensity of the color. Maybe the beginning of "Roundabout" without the backward piano wouldn't have been so dramatic. People don't even know it's a backward piano, all they hear is "mmmmmweeng!" But it really intensified that idea and I think that's a good side to the music that I have been involved in.

Chris [Squire, bassist] (1994): I overdubbed my entire part an octave higher on one of Steve's old Gibson hollow-body jazz guitars. We just miked it acoustically and mixed it in with the bass. That's what gave the part such a bright sound.

(1985): "Roundabout" was done in a series of edits. That was the time when we started getting into that idea. Although we'd already played the song in rehearsal, we'd go in the studio and get the first two verses really good.

Jon (1989): We always tried to make sure we had a lot of harmony. Me, Steve, and Chris singing together had a certain texture and we worked on that all the way through that period of time. And the strong melody [was] sometimes very, very sim-ple. On the end of "Roundabout" we sing "Da-da-da-da-duh-duh-da" a very simple melody repeated eight times. Over that there's another melody "Ba-ba-ba" . . . "Three Blind Mice!"

Close to the Edge

Released September 1972

This is considered by many to be the definitive Yes album. Everything the band was trying to do was uniquely realized on this recording, so that even now it sounds as fresh as the day it came out. It was a very successful and progressive release at the time, featuring just three songs: the celestial "And You and I," the fiery "Siberian Khatru," and their first masterpiece epic, "Close to the Edge."

The making of this record was not without the loss of some blood in the proc-ess. After the laborious rehearsals and endless late nights at Advision Studios, Bill Bruford decided to leave Yes when the album was completed, to join King Crim-son. His decision left his band mates in shock and desperate because an American tour was to start within a week. (Bruford did offer to do the tour, but the band decided to try to find someone else.) Luckily for the group, Alan White (of the Plastic Ono Band) agreed to climb up the drum riser and he has been with them ever since.

Bill [Bruford, drummer] (1989): *Close to the Edge* had a sense of discovery for us—and presumably for the people who bought it. I'm sure it sounds trite now, but in those days it was quite a big deal. Rock musicians hadn't been capable of an arrangement of any kind of complexity at all. But now I find it's fundamentally good music, its form, its shape are timeless.

Jon (1992): *Close to the Edge* is close to the edge of realization, of self-realization, that's what the theme was all about. It was based on a book I'd read called *Siddhartha* by Hermann Hesse. So there we were on the edge of learning about our potential as art-ists, as musicians, in order to jump into a new world of music. That's what *Close to the Edge* was all about and it did push us in a direct fashion into the limelight, one could say, of total progressive music. To the point where today, we can perform nearly twenty years later "And You and I" and it has more power now than it ever had. It's a remarkable piece of music, as though it was crafted by the heavens and we were just the vehicles to pull it together.

Bill (1992): If we'd known how horrible it was going to be, we would have never done it. But it's like five guys trying to write a novel at the same time. One guy has a good beginning and the second guy had quite a good middle and the third guy thinks he knows what the ending is, but the fourth guy doesn't like the way the middle goes towards the ending, and the second guy who used to like the third section has changed his mind and now likes the first section.

It was torture. None of these arrangements were written and they weren't really composed. We all sat in the rehearsal room and said, "Let's have the G after the G#." And every instrument was up for democratic election, you know and everyone had to run an election campaign on every issue. And it was horrible. I mean it was incredibly unpleasant and unbelievably hard work. And Squire was always late for every rehearsal. And after about two months of this unbelievable punishment, people still say to me, "Bill, why didn't you do another one?"

People always imagine that there was this carefully structured plan. Like they do with King Crimson, they always imagine Robert Fripp enters the room and scowls at everybody and lays out sheet music, which of course is the exact opposite. And they always think that Jon Anderson somehow knew how *Close to the Edge* was going to be right from the beginning to the end. [Which is] not true at all . . . it was kind of a shambles from beginning to end, the whole thing. It was a miracle that we managed to make anything of this stuff. If we'd actually find a rehearsal room, could we actually get to it? Would Squire turn up? Would we have enough equipment to do it with? Was anyone starving? Was the band about to run out of money?

We were well served in all of this by having the ability to tape-edit. And having Eddie Offord, who would slash a two-inch master tape without even thinking about it and just glue another bit onto it. Tape editing was fundamental to this band creating this music at all. Because we couldn't play any of it through until we'd learned it. We'd play a thirty-second segment and say, "What happens now?" We'd stop the tape and write another thirty-second segment. It would go on like that, [like] climbing Mount Everest.

Steve (1991): We had to hang on to our ideas and develop and arrange them and try not to forget them the next day. Because sometimes we would come in and say, "God, what did we do to this?" Many classic Yes bits of arranging have gone out the window. We actually forgot them. They were too intricate, too specialized, or one guy was the key to it and he was the guy who didn't remember it the next day. So obviously we taped things and started to have tapes of rehearsals going on all the time.

"Close to the Edge"

Chris (1995): I think it was Jon's idea to open the song with the sound effects. He got hold of a bunch of those environmental tapes and I think that's why it appeared there.

Jon (1976): The lyrical content became a kind of dream sequence in a way. The end verse is a dream that I had a long time ago about passing on from this world to another world, yet feeling so fantastic about it that death never frightened me ever since. I think in the early days when I was very small I used to be frightened of this idea of not being here—where else can there be if there isn't "here"? And it just seemed a matter of course that death being such a beautiful experience for a man physically to go through as being born is. That's what seemed to come out in this song, that it was a very pastoral kind of experience rather than a very frightening and "Oh gosh, I don't want to die" kind of thing.

(1973): There are several lines that relate to the church. Churchgoers are always fighting about who's better and who's richer and who's more hip. So at the end of the middle section there's a majestic church organ. We destroy the church organ through the Moog. This leads to another organ solo rejoicing in the fact that you can turn your back on churches and find it within yourself to be your own church.

Bill (1994): The thing about "Close to the Edge" is the form, I think. The shape of it is perfect. It's a real little part of history and it just fit on the side of an album perfectly. Again as we were making that I don't think anyone really knew how we were going to finish it. It felt like we were going on and on adding section after section. Lots of music in different meters and things without anybody really knowing what the conclusion to this piece of music would be. I don't think we had any idea of its length and I don't think we said, "Oh! Let's make this the side of an album." The other thing I remember was everybody saying that Simon and Garfunkel had spent three months on "Bridge Over Troubled Water" and that seemed like a record that needed to be smashed. (TMI)

Further Reading

Covach, John. "Progressive Rock, 'Close to the Edge,' and the Boundaries of Style." In *Understanding Rock: Essays in Musical Analysis*, ed. John Covach and Graeme M. Boone, 3–31. New York: Oxford University Press, 1997.
Gaer, Eric. "Emerson, Lake and Palmer: A Musical Force." *Down Beat*, May 9, 1974, 14.
Holm-Hudson, Kevin. *Progressive Rock Reconsidered*. New York: Routledge, 2001.
Macan, Edward. *Rocking the Classics: English Progressive Rock and the Counterculture.* New York: Oxford University Press, 1997.

Discography

E.L.O. *The Essential Electric Light Orchestra.* Sony, 2003.
Emerson, Lake and Palmer. *Trilogy.* Rhino/WEA, 1972.
_____. *Works, Vol. 1.* Rhino/WEA, 1977.
King Crimson. *In the Court of the Crimson King.* Discipline Us, 1969.
Pink Floyd. *Dark Side of the Moon.* Capitol, 1973.
Yes. *Close to the Edge.* Elektra/WEA, 2003.
_____. *Roundabout and Other Hits.* Rhino Flashback, 2007.

56. The Global Phenomenon of Reggae

Jamaica, first as an English colony beginning in 1655, and then as a former colony after 1962, possessed the status of being a part of the Western European–North American cultural nexus, yet simultaneously remaining separate. The development in the 1950s of the first indigenous music designed for mass production, ska, suggests this curious quality of not-quite-belonging, merging as it did the Jamaican traditional music of *mento* and Trinidadian *calypso* with rhythm and blues from the United States. The ease of this merger discloses the background of Afro-diasporic musical practices and Protestant hymn singing shared by Jamaicans and African Americans. The mode of presentation of ska was at least as influential as its musical-stylistic features, with recordings, "sound systems" (large playback systems consisting of powerful amplifiers and larger speakers), and DJs often supplanting live performances. The transformation of ska into the slower tempi and socially conscious lyrics of rock steady and then into reggae paralleled a boom in Jamaican-produced recordings and created international recognition by the late 1960s for recordings like Desmond Dekker's "Israelites" (although countrywoman Millie Small had preceded Dekker in 1964 with "My Boy Lollipop"). Reggae took the offbeat accents of ska and the slower tempi, more active basslines, and identification with the marginalized found in rock steady, and created a style with complex, neo-African-inspired drumming and a moral outlook influenced by the indigenous Jamaican Rastafari movement. The Rastafari movement advocates the repatriation of people of African descent to "Zion," located in Africa; recognizes Haile Selassie (emperor of Ethiopia from 1930 to 1974) as the son of Jesus; and treats the smoking of cannabis as a sacrament. Although very few people in Jamaica were (and are) adherents of the Rastafari movement, the philosophy as espoused in many reggae songs proved to be influential beyond the boundaries of that movement.

Bob Marley (1945–81) became the best-known exponent of Jamaican music in general and reggae in particular, and is sometimes referred to (presumably by people in the "first world") as the first "third world superstar." Marley began recording ska in 1962 and enjoyed local success in a series of recordings with his band, The Wailers. "Simmer Down" (1964) is an early example of a song with lyrics that feature social commentary, anticipating themes in both Marley's later work and the rock steady genre in general. After several years of fluctuating levels of success, Marley signed with Chris Blackwell's Island Records in 1972, which led to his breakthrough album, *Catch a Fire* (1973). Marley's access to audiences outside of Jamaica was aided by the almost-simultaneous release of the Jamaican movie *The Harder They Come* (featuring songs by Jimmy Cliff, the Wailers, Toots and the Maytals, and others) and the interest of several North American artists in reggae, such as Paul Simon ("Mother and Child Reunion," 1972) and Johnny Nash ("I Can See Clearly Now," 1972). Marley's career grew steadily, with artists such as Nash ("Stir It Up," 1973) and Eric Clapton ("I Shot the Sheriff," 1974) having hits with cover versions of his songs, and with the release of his albums *Burnin'* (1973) and *Natty Dread* (1974), which featured his first international hit, "No Woman, No Cry."

The following article by Robert Hilburn captures Marley at the moment of his breakthrough, following the release of the album *Rastaman Vibration* (1976). Hilburn sets the stage by comparing the breakthrough of reggae with *The Harder They Come* to rock 'n' roll in *Blackboard Jungle,* as well as with the most highly touted new star of the previous year (1975), Bruce Springsteen. He provides an excellent concise history of reggae, emphasizing its combination of musical accessibility and social critique, and of Marley, who reminds Hilburn of other pop cultural heroes of then-recent vintage, such as Bob Dylan and John Lennon. Although Hilburn was dubious that the coiffure associated with reggae would become popular, what he could not have known is that American teenagers, both black and white, would begin wearing their hair in the "long, uncombed Rasta strands" known as dreadlocks. He also could not have predicted that Marley's powerful charisma would continue to exert its force for over 30 years after his untimely death in 1981, sustaining his status as an international cultural hero.

Third-World Theme of Bob Marley
Robert Hilburn

Wouldn't it be ironic if it turns out we've been looking in the wrong place during the 1970s in our continuing, often intense search for the Next Big Thing in pop music?

There's no guarantee, in short, that the first signs of a major new musical style or direction has to come through the clubs or the often hopelessly stagnant radio. As in the 1950s, the catalyst for change could once again be a film. If so, "The Harder They Come" may turn out to be the "Blackboard Jungle" of the 1970s.

Just as it was difficult for any teenager who saw "Blackboard Jungle" in its early showings to forget the exciting emotional chill that came from hearing Bill Haley's

Source: "Third-World Theme of Bob Marley" Robert Hilburn, *Los Angeles Times* published May 16, 1976.

"Rock Around the Clock" over the film's opening credits, it's likely that many pop music fans who see "The Harder They Come" will be able to escape the spell of reggae—a highly infectious and distinctive blend of rhythm & blues, calypso and early rock influences.

And that spell ultimately leads to Bob Marley. In his triumphant U.S. tour last year, 31-year-old Marley displayed the kind of stunning musical stance and convincing persona that has made him the most important and acclaimed new arrival in rock since Bruce Springsteen.

If he can now stay free of the covers of Newsweek and Time (and the resultant backlash and suspicion which that kind of mass media attention often creates in pop music), Marley may well emerge as one of the most influential figures in all of pop in the 1970s. His following among rock musicians is already staggering.

Despite the hundreds of hit albums and singles each year in the multi-billion-dollar record industry, there are only a dozen or so artists of each generation (Elvis, Chuck Berry, Little Richard, Jerry Lee Lewis, among the most prominent in the 1950s; the Beatles, Stones, Dylan, Hendrix, among others, in the 1960s) who carry both the artistic vision and popular appeal to be truly influential.

Marley is an artist with enough impact, originality and purpose to join them. While it is unlikely that large numbers of American teen-agers will begin wearing their hair in long, uncombed Rasta strands or embrace other aspects of his specialized religious sect, the fact that Marley reflects such vitality and conviction in music should be some kind of inspiration during a period when so much of pop music is clearly vapid.

But Marley's problem (and reggae music's problem in general) has been the difficulty of attracting a mass audience in this country. Some of his songs—"I Shot the Sheriff," "Stir It Up"—have been hits here, but only through cover versions by Eric Clapton and Johnny Nash.

The crucial difference between "Blackboard Jungle"—a tale of juvenile delinquency set in a New York City high school—and "The Harder They Come"—a haunting, striking look at socio-economic oppression in both the slums and music industry in Jamaica—is that the former was a box-office smash while the latter was a low-budget effort that has received only spotty distribution in this country.

But the film, with its magnificent soundtrack album, has helped build something of an audience for reggae. Indeed, there are signs the music is on the verge of a breakthrough. The irony of the film, however, is that Jimmy Cliff, the man whose music was featured in the movie, has no more turned out to be the strongest artistic spokesman for reggae than Bill Haley proved to be rock's ultimate spokesman in the 1950s.

Just as Haley proved unacceptable to rock audiences two decades ago (for reasons ranging from the diluted nature of his music to his post-30s family-man image), Cliff—who portrays the struggling, victimized musician in the film and wrote many of its songs—has not lived up to the promise of his role.

Besides the highly infectious syncopation of the music itself, part of the appeal of "The Harder They Come" was the strong, convincing sense of socio-cultural purpose behind such songs as Cliff's "Many Rivers to Cross"—a masterfully crafted expression of one's burdens that Linda Ronstadt has included on her latest album—to the Slickers' "Johnny Too Bad," a look at the way crime is bred in the hopelessness and poverty of the slums.

Indeed, the soul of reggae music—despite the light, inviting, sing-along nature of such reggae-based hits as Johnny Nash's "I Can See Clearly Now" or Paul Simon's "Mother and Child Reunion"—is built in large part around a strict political dedication.

Many reggae songs, for instance, reflect aggressive Third World aspirations and/ or hostilities. Often using Biblical allegories in the lyrics, much of the music speaks out against racial, economic, political injustices in both Jamaica and elsewhere. Consider, for example, Marley's "Slave Driver": *Every time I hear the crack of a whip/My blood runs cold/I remember on the slave ship/How they brutalized my very soul/. . . The tables have turned . . ./You're gonna get burned."*

Several reggae artists, including Marley, adhere to the religious beliefs of the Rastafarian sect, which encourages its members to wear their hair in the long, uncombed strands and live in communes.

But Cliff fell outside this strict, independent stance. His post-"Harder" albums and concert appearances failed to capitalize on the momentum the film had built for him. He began diluting his reggae sounds in a way that was out of keeping with the convictions suggested in the heart of the film.

While Marley was much closer to the fierce, rebellious mood of the film, his first U.S. album (titled "Catch a Fire") lacked the appeal and variety of the film's music. He also seemed distant in his initial concerts here. Thus, he, too, was a disappointment. With neither Cliff nor Marley able to live up to expectations, the first wave of the reggae "invasion" fizzled.

While Marley's second and third U.S. albums ("Burnin'" and "Natty Dread") gained him increasing critical attention, the key factor in his approaching commercial breakthrough was a 1975 tour that proved him to be a compelling, even electrifying performer. He had replaced the old distance and uncertainty with bold, aggressive manner and sound.

In his best moments on stage, the vitality of his music erased the occasional sterility that marred some of his recordings. The combination of musical purpose and dynamic presence on stage led him to be labeled both the Bob Dylan (for Marley's social consciousness) and the Mick Jagger (for his sensualness) of reggae. He had, in short, the moves, music, charisma and image to excite. His albums began appearing on the lower rungs of the national album charts. His name began slowly filtering through the mass pop consciousness.

Sensing the building interest, Island Records mapped out a promotion/publicity campaign for Marley's new album that makes Columbia's controversial campaign for Springsteen (the campaign that stirred so many "hype" charges) seem downright paltry.

Though there is always the danger of a backlash in such a massive publicity push (especially in the case of an artist whose music is built, in part, on fiercely anticapitalist sentiments), the new Marley album—"Rastaman Vibration"—burst on the Billboard album charts this month at No. 40. It was a major breakthrough in the effort to establish reggae.

While a live album that is available only in English import copies remains perhaps the best introduction to Marley, "Rastaman Vibration" (Island ILPS 9838) is his most appealing and balanced studio album. Crucially, Marley has extended his basic reggae approach (by incorporating various U.S. soul music tendencies, from some of the Philadelphia slickness to the old Memphis funk) without invalidating his original stance. He has also broadened his themes.

But the album opens on two disastrous notes. "Positive Vibrations" and, especially, "Roots, Rock, Reggae"—a particularly absurd bit of reggae promotion that speaks about the music's status on the record charts—are just the kind of pointless fluff that caused many "The Harder They Come" enthusiasts to sour on Cliff.

Once those tracks are past, however, the album begins reflecting the power and punch that has characterized Marley's finest work. While the main thrust of the songs ("Want More," "Crazy Bald Head." "Who the Cap Fit," "War" and "Rat Race") continues to deal with sociopolitical matters, there is an increasing emphasis on melodic structure and a more flexible instrumental base.

In fact, "Cry to Me," one of the two songs on the album written by Marley, is as close to a pure rhythm & blues ballad style as Marley or his band, the Wailers, have yet offered. It's a rare, but particularly effective, excursion by Marley into the romantic as opposed to social arena:

You're gonna walk back through the heartaches
You're gonna walk back through the pain
You're gonna shed those lonely teardrops
The reaction of your cheating game.

While those lyrics fit easily and quite smoothly into the traditional pop mold, most of Marley's lyrics (either his own or those by other writers) are more effective in part than in whole. As with early rock and R&B, it's the performance that matters most. And it is in the area of performance that Marley excels.

Whether he is singing with defiance or tenderness, Marley has the rare ability to embellish the words without appearing false or self-conscious. When, for instance, he sings the title phrase in "Cry to Me," he treats the word "cry" differently each time. He divides it into three syllables the first time, keeps it as an extended single syllable later in the song and somehow merges the two approaches the final time.

Despite the bite and trigger-edge that seems such a basic part of Marley's music, there is a compassion in "Johnny Was"—a song about a mother's grief over the accidental death of her son by (apparently) a policeman's stray bullet—that keeps his music from being simply one-dimensional.

But Marley can still be fiercely combative. He has felt the sting and agony and anger of the socially oppressed. Born in Kingston, Jamaica, Marley is the son of a white British Army captain from Liverpool—"I only remember seeing him twice when I was small"—and a black Jamaican who wrote spirituals and sang in the local Apostolic church.

Marley sang in church, too, as a child, but he eventually found greater satisfaction in the rock records of such American artists as Ricky Nelson, Elvis Presley and Fats Domino. He studied welding in school, but longed for a career in music.

With an assist (ironically) from Jimmy Cliff, Marley made a record in 1964, but it flopped. A bit later he decided to form a group which came up with several hits, but received few if any royalties, Marley claims. Thus, Marley again ran into a web of social manipulation and economic mistreatment. Frustrated, he moved to the United States where he worked for several months in an auto assembly factory in Delaware. But that too left him dissatisfied.

So, he returned to Jamaica, where two things happened that would greatly affect his future: He met Island Records' Chris Blackwell, and he joined the Rastafarian sect.

While the latter gave him a purpose and direction in his music, Blackwell's guidance and resources gave Marley the chance to grow and experiment as an artist. "Rastaman Vibration" is the latest example of that growth. It should make him a major force in American pop. Marley will be at the Roxy on May 26 (sold out) and Shrine Auditorium May 27.

Further Reading

Bordowitz, Hank. *Every Little Thing Gonna Be Alright: The Bob Marley Reader.* Cambridge,
     Mass.: Da Capo Press, 2004.
Daynes, Sarah. *Time and Memory in Reggae Music: The Politics of Hope.* Manchester, UK: Man-
     chester University Press, 2010.
Grant, Colin. *I and I: The Natural Mystics: Marley, Tosh and Wailer.* London: Jonathan Cape,
     2011.
Katz, David. *Solid Foundation: An Oral History of Reggae.* New York: Bloomsbury, 2003.
Salewicz, Chris. *Bob Marley: The Untold Story.* New York: Faber & Faber, 2010.

Discography

Marley, Bob. *Catch a Fire.* Tuff Gong/Island, 1973.
_____. *Burnin'.* Tuff Gong/Island, 1973.
_____. *Natty Dread.* Tuff Gong/Island, 1974.
_____. *Rastaman Vibration.* Tuff Gong/Island, 1976.
_____. *Exodus.* Tuff Gong/Island, 1977.
_____. *Legend.* Tuff Gong/Island, 1984.
The Harder They Come. Island, 1972.
Tougher than Tough: The Story of Jamaican Music. Mango, 1993.

57. Get On Up Disco

From an underground phenomenon at the outset of the 1970s, disco
grew to dominate popular music by the end of the decade. In its heyday, "disco" referred to at least three distinct phenomena: a musical
style, a performance site, and a mode of participation and musical fandom. While the rock music embraced by the counterculture increasingly
made dancing difficult (if not impossible), clubs catering to gay, African
American, and Latino subcultures in New York City began relying on
music featuring a blend of Motown soul; Latin-inflected funk; and a new,
sophisticated type of uptown soul associated with Philadelphia-based
producers (discussed earlier in Greil Marcus's essay; see Chapter 49).
Artists such as Harold Melvin and the Blue Notes, Barry White, White's
Love Unlimited Orchestra, and Cameroonian jazz-pop artist Manu

Dibango, had national hits that "crossed over" from dance clubs to pop radio. The genre name "disco" was applied first to such "rockin'" dance hits as The Hues Corporations' "Rock the Boat" and George McCrae's "Rock Your Baby," both from 1974, while another important early disco recording, Van McCoy's "The Hustle" (early 1975), launched the most popular dance step of the era. Disco's impact extended beyond its musical style, challenging prevalent notions in popular music criticism about authorship and creativity.

The central figure in this challenge to the critical status quo was the disc jockey or "DJ." Because DJs were responsible for selecting and sequencing songs, it was their taste that dictated disco's sense of style, rather than the singers and instrumentalists of soul and rock musics, and successful DJs could acquire their own following in much the same way as a recording artist. DJs shared the creative locus of the disco scene with the audience itself, since the focus on dancing stressed social interaction (this is vividly portrayed in Andrew Kopkind's article, reprinted here).

During 1975–76, disco began to concentrate on three main tendencies. The first, "R&B disco," was derived more directly from previous styles of soul and funk, often retained gospel-oriented vocals and syncopated guitar and bass parts, and was sometimes recorded by self-contained bands associated with funk, such as the Ohio Players, Kool and the Gang, the Commodores, and KC and the Sunshine Band. A second trend, "Eurodisco," tended to feature simple, chanted vocals, less-syncopated bass parts, and thicker arrangements filled with orchestral instruments and synthesizers, and relied on a producer who directed anonymous studio musicians. Eurodisco recordings often filled entire album sides and attempted to usurp some of the DJ's creative role by sequencing a series of contrasting episodes over an unvarying tempo. The style could be said to have arrived with Donna Summer's "Love to Love You Baby," in which producers Pete Bellote and Giorgio Moroder embedded Summer's suggestive moaning in a 17-minute orchestrated epic. A third variant, "pop disco," was represented by mainstream pop artists such as the Bee Gees, an Australian trio who hopped on the disco bandwagon in 1975 to revive their dormant careers; pop disco's importance grew throughout the decade.[1]

The final transformation of disco from a genre associated with gays, blacks, and Latinos to one embraced by straight, white Americans occurred with the success of the film *Saturday Night Fever*, released late in 1977. The film's soundtrack featured new songs by the Bee Gees and an assortment of songs from the preceding two years by the Bee Gees, Kool and the Gang, Walter Murphy, and the Trammps. The soundtrack yielded four number one singles and became the best-selling album up

---

1. This typology-taxonomy is used by Stephen Holden in his article "The Evolution of a Dance Craze," *Rolling Stone,* April 19, 1979, 29. *Rolling Stone* dedicated its August 28, 1975, issue to disco, just as disco was becoming more than an underground phenomenon. Of special note in that issue is Vince Aletti's discussion of early disco's history, aesthetics, and musical influences; see Vince Aletti, "Dancing Madness: The Disco Sound," *Rolling Stone,* August 28, 1975, 43, 50, 56.

to that time. The most popular disco clubs, such as Studio 54 in New York City, became celebrity-studded hangouts where high society and a gay sense of style intertwined.[2] The Eurodisco and pop disco styles had clearly superseded R&B disco in the public notion of what constituted the genre, although a few artists on the borderline between funk and disco continued to succeed. The most important of these artists was Chic, whose last major hit, "Good Times" (1979), is notable for providing the musical basis for the first rap hit, "Rapper's Delight," by the Sugarhill Gang (1979).

Andrew Kopkind addresses the broader cultural significance of disco at the height of its popularity in the wake of *Saturday Night Fever*. Writing at the end of the 1970s, he uses disco as a way of discussing shifts in popular music, the music industry, and the relationship of popular music to politics and lifestyle. Most strikingly, he sees the rise of disco as representing the triumph of artifice over the authenticity so valued by the 1960s counterculture (a quality that underscored a not-so-obvious link among glam, disco, and some new wave). An important point in this article is how the popularity of disco marks the acceptance (albeit somewhat unconsciously) of a kind of gay sensibility into the mainstream. As Kopkind notes, however, the heightened visibility of gay subcultures also occasioned a backlash among rock fans.[3]

The Dialectic of Disco: Gay Music Goes Straight
Andrew Kopkind

Disco is the word. It is more than music, beyond a beat, deeper than the dancers and their dance. Disco names the sensibility of a generation, as jazz and rock— and silence—announced the sum of styles, attitudes, and intent of other ages. The mindless material of the new disco culture—its songs, steps, ballrooms, movies, drugs, and drag—are denounced and adored with equal exaggeration. But the consciousness that lies beneath the trendy tastes is a serious subject and can hardly be ignored: for it points precisely where popular culture is headed at the end of the American '70s.

Disco is *phenomenal*—unpredicted and unpredictable, contradictory and controversial. It has spawned a new $4 billion music industry, new genres in film and

---

2. For an account of Studio 54 that paints a portrait of corruption, celebrities, and Steve Rubell's obnoxious chutzpah during the club's high point from April 1977 to March 1978, see Henry Post, "Sour Notes at the Hottest Disco," *Esquire*, June 20, 1978, 79–86.

3. This led most infamously to a riot in Chicago's Comiskey Park during the intermission of a White Sox doubleheader; see Don McLeese, "Anatomy of an Anti-Disco Riot," *In These Times*, August 29–September 4, 1979, 23.

Source: "The Dialectic of Disco: Gay Music Goes Straight" © Andrew Kopkind/*Village Voice*

theatre, new radio stations, a new elite of promoters and producers, and a new attitude about the possibilities of party going. It has also sparked major conflicts: "Death to Disco" is written on SoHo walls and "Disco Sucks!" rises from the throats of beleaguered partisans of rock, punk, or jazz who find their cultural identity threatened by disco's enormous commercial power.

Scenes from disco wars erupt across the landscape. Gangs of rockers and hustlers (the dancing kind) fight furiously in the streets outside disco clubs in provincial cities. When Mick Jagger or Rod Stewart "goes disco" (with "Miss You" and "Do You Think I'm Sexy?" respectively), their cultural conversion is debated in hip salons as well as in the *New York Times*. The rock critical establishment still treats disco music as an adolescent aberration, at best; many cultural commentators look on the whole sensibility as a metaphor for the end of humanism and the decline of the West.

The sense of the '60s provided coherence, contest, and validity to rock, when the critics of an earlier era proclaimed such sounds to be junk. Rock was "our music": only "we"—whoever we were—knew that it was good and what parts of it were best. The music was riding an historical tide; it was the sound of the politics, the expectations, the explorations, and the institutions of an era. It was the background music as well as the marching melody for civil disobedience, sexual liberation, crunchy granola, and LSD. The Buffalo Springfield's "For What It's Worth" was perfect music-to-avoid-the-FBI-by. "Street Fighting Man" was made for trashing draft boards. "Mr. Tambourine Man" was for smoking dope. "Up the Country" was for dropping out of the city. "Let It Be" was for letting it be.

History hardly stops. Disco in the '70s is in revolt against rock in the '60s. It is the antithesis of the "natural" look, the real feelings, the seriousness, the confessions, the struggles, the sincerity, pretensions and pain of the last generation. Disco is "unreal," artificial, and exaggerated. It affirms the fantasies, fashions, gossip, frivolity, and fun of an evasive era. The '60s were braless, lumpy, heavy, rough, and romantic; disco is stylish, sleek, smooth, contrived, and controlled. Disco places surface over substance, mood over meaning, action over thought. The '60s were a mind trip (marijuana, acid); Disco is a body trip (Quaaludes, cocaine). The '60s were cheap; disco is expensive. On a '60s trip, you saw God in a grain of sand; on a disco trip, you see Jackie O. at Studio 54.

In describing "camp" in her influential essay 15 years ago, Susan Sontag remarked that "a sensibility (as distinct from an idea) is one of the hardest things to talk about." It is "not only the most decisive, but also [the age's] most perishable, aspect. To name a sensibility, to draw its contours and to recount its history, requires a deep sympathy modified by revulsion."

The performance and production of disco music creates a technical and economic foundation on which the intangible aspects of culture and sensibility develop. The ways in which the sounds are chosen, the records produced, the performers packaged, and the cultural artifacts marketed will profoundly influence the styles we see.

Disco, first of all, is not a natural phenomenon in any sense. It is part of a sophisticated, commercial, manipulated culture that is rooted exclusively in an urban environment. Disco music is produced in big cities and its fashions are formed in big cities, at considerable expense, by high-priced professionals. Almost as an afterthought is the product then disseminated to the provinces. All the sparkle, speed, cynicism, and jaded irony associated with metropolitan life is attached to disco. It is far from wholesome. Provincials may either envy or abhor it. But it belongs to the city.

"Disco is a New York thing. It happened here," says Kenn Friedman, the 26-year-old promotion wizard of Casablanca Records. "And it still happens here." Of a weekend evening in the city, Friedman may commandeer the label's limo—or slip out on his own—and make the rounds of the hottest New York clubs: Infinity, Flamingo, Les Mouches, Studio 54, 12 West. He holes up with the disc jockeys in their sound booths, then quickly moves out onto the dance floors, soaking up the spirit of the music and catching the response of the crowds. He and his crew are eminently successful (Casablanca is the new miracle mogul in the disco record business) because he can feel the hits.

"I *know* what will be number one, what the hottest record is going to be on the street this weekend," Friedman told me matter-of-factly. At the time we spoke he predicted it would be James Wells's "My Claim to Fame"; and sure enough, when I went round to the clubs the next Saturday, it was the song that provoked the peak excitement of the night. "I can't tell you exactly how I know, but it's because I'm part of the culture, I love to dance, I love the music."

Dancing is what does it. Last week at Casablanca's "Casbah"—the company's New York digs in an arabesque townhouse on 55th Street—I found Casablanca's top disco director, Marc Simon, boogying excitedly in Friedman's cramped office. Just back from the world record industry's annual congress in Cannes, Simon was effusive about the "completely new sound" his label will introduce as its 1979 line later this month. The first group making this as-yet unknown music is called Nightlife, and Simon says he's banking his business ($100 million last year) on his intuitions.

"I heard a different producer's sound every 15 minutes, five hours a day, all the time I was in Cannes," Simon said coolly, "and I picked the ones I felt were going to be the *dance* hits. While the sounds of disco are highly synthesized, the hits cannot be completely determined. Nobody dreamed up the whole disco promotion campaign in the first place. "In the beginning we used to dance to the best rhythms from Motown and other rhythm-and-blues records," Simon recalled. "There was nothing called 'disco' back in the '60s—just Diana Ross, Freda Payne, the Temptations." Then the producers in Philadelphia—Gamble and Huff—started making a specific disco sound, with the familiar heavy beat and the modified samba rhythm.

By reckonings, the first big disco hit—as *disco*—was Gloria Gaynor's 1974 top-of-the charts "Never Can Say Good-bye." Others pick "Love's Theme," by Love Unlimited Orchestra. But the record companies seemed bewildered by what they had, and promo people continued their quirky disregard of the disco category in their portfolios. Instead, they inflated passing fancies into seismic cultural events: Peter Frampton, reggae, and punk, for example. Not that some of those sounds or stars lacked merit; certainly Springsteen, Bob Marley, and the best of the New Wave deserve seats high in rock and roll heaven. But disco would soon swamp them all, and nobody was watching.

There are real differences in disco numbers that those who have learned to appreciate the music—and dance to it—can easily distinguish but may be missed by others. "All disco sounds alike" is commonly heard among rock fans; it is a bit like Caucasians saying, "All Chinese people look alike." Certain features of disco songs hardly vary from one tune to another (compare: flat noses or epicanthic folds). If you look for continuous changes in beat or for nuances of poetry in the lyrics, you will find few differences among disco songs. But the lengthy *construction* of a disco record (more than a "song") and its emotional *intensity* are highly changeable aspects, and may account for success or failure.

Or they may not. The fact is that while disco is racing to new levels of sophistication and elaboration at high speed, there is yet no reliable test for a hit. The reason is that the disco phenomenon has turned the pop industry upside-down, as no development has since the advent of '60s rock.

First, the disco wave crashed on unseen shores, catching producers and musicians without adequate cultural or commercial bearings. There were few critics to say what was good or bad—that is, what their readers or listeners should buy. There were no researchers to test the market; no one knew what questions to ask. The one or two music writers who dove into disco—notably the *Voice's* frequent contributor, Vince Aletti—often felt overwhelmed by the legitimacy and power wielded by the rock establishment, and they hid their opinions under barrels or in closets.[4]

Second, the primary sales medium of popular records changed, from radio for rock to dance clubs for disco. The shift entailed no small change: billions of dollars had come to rest on the "airplay" system of marketing music. Consumers heard their tunes on the air and rushed to their dealer for the vinyl version. Now, there were no stations, AM or FM, playing disco music as a regular feature of their format.

The third major change that disco wrought in the industry was the concentration of performance. For all its New York and L.A. stars, rock was a decentralized popular form. It carried provincial and suburban values with it as it came up the river from Mississippi, or down the slopes from Colorado, or down the pike from Greenwich. Any four young people with axes and amps could start a band in the hinterlands, playing local clubs with a repertoire of original songs and "covered" hits of national stars. Some groups would work their way up to regional fame (J. Geils in Boston, the Allman Brothers in Atlanta) and then make it big in the continental markets.

But disco must be produced in a few studios in the urban centers—here and abroad. If there is talent in the small towns it must travel to the big city *before* that process begins; and in so doing, the performers must shed their innocent attitudes and naïve notions before they open their mouths. Donna Summer began in Boston and in Germany and Austria (singing pop and folk opera, as well as other genres) before Casablanca launched her record career as a cosmopolitan sex siren.

"People don't want local bands anymore," says John "T.C." (for Top Cat) Luongo, an impresario in MK Promotions, one of the country's leading disco promotional companies (it is largely responsible for the success of the *C'est Chic* album). "They'd rather hear the stars on records over sensational sound systems than listen to the local rock band play third-rate versions of old hits."

Many of the disco "stars," of course, are nonpeople—interchangeable studio musicians who shuttle between group names, from one album to the next. MFSB, Love Unlimited, and many of the Philadelphia bands of the mid-'70s were composed of the same people, give or take the odd sideman. Salsoul, the Ritchie Family, and other current hot groups are wholes that add up to less than the sum of their parts. Only recently have genuine musicians broken through disco anonymity into stardom: Donna Summer and the Bee Gees, for better and worse, are the best example of the new personalized wave.

Fourth, disco facilitated the birth of a lucrative subcategory of record sales—the new 33 rpm 12-inch "disco mix" or "long version." The Salsoul group, originally an Hispanic manufacturer of ladies' lingerie, made a more substantial fortune by turning from *schmatas* to the sounds of the Latin Hustle; Salsoul brought out some of the first big disco-mix 12-inches six years ago. The industry yawned. Now a 12-inch disco single can sell 17,000 copies in New York City alone, and the companies carefully regulate the availability of the various versions of a hit song to maximize sales. For example, Atlantic put 200,000 copies of the "Le Freak" disco mix on sale to stimulate

---

4. Aletti, cited earlier for his insightful early article on disco, eventually became involved in running RFC Records, a label devoted to disco.

interest in the *C'est Chic album*—then withdrew the long 12-inch single to eliminate competition for the high-priced package and the mass-volume 45 rpm versions.

Finally, the music business has been jolted by the sudden prominence of the record *producer* which the technical requirements of disco now entails. The European producers of the suave, lush "Eurodisco" sounds are perhaps the brightest lights: Giorgio Moroder, Cerrone, Alex Costandinos, Roger Tekarz. Many of them use their own names instead of their performers' to identify albums; thus, the latest album produced by Cerrone is called, simply, "Cerrone IV." Moroder uses the name "Giorgio" both as an album title and also as an advertisement for his productions; a sticker slapped on the new Three Degrees album announces "Produced by Giorgio," as rock albums feature the most familiar cut.

Today, the disco record industry is a mammoth $4 billion enterprise—bigger than television, movies, or professional sports in America. "Disco accounts for about 40 percent of all the 'chart activity,'" Friedman estimated. By the end of the decade, half the top 100 songs on *Billboard's* lists will be disco numbers. Disco radio stations are sweeping the country. New York's WKTU is a story in itself: in nine months of disco programming (it used to send out "mellow rock") it has gone from the dregs of stations too low to rate to the number one broadcaster in the country, either AM or FM—beating out the gargantuan WABC. Boston's WBOS was miniscule before it went all-disco; it now tops the biggest FM rock stations in America's hottest "youth market." And there are 20,000 disco clubs in the U.S., earning $6 billion annually.

What all this means is that a sizable hunk of capital in the entertainment industry is now in the hands of the disco elite—a mixed breed of newcomers, switchovers and fast dancers who had the sense to accommodate themselves to the sensibility of the '70s.

The new disco elite has its own vocabulary and its own values, and they are quite different from those of the rock entrepreneur. For one thing, the disco people have to feel like dancing—not autistic, explosive fits of movement but the more controlled, stylized dancing of the disco clubs. And for another, they have to be able to mingle and mix in gay discos as well as straight ones, for the locus of the emerging disco culture is pointedly in urban male homosexual society.

"There *is* a big cultural difference between rock and disco," Kenn Friedman said firmly, "and it's gayness. Some people don't like to talk about it, but it's true. Disco began in gay clubs. At first, it was just a case of speeding up the gap between records on the juke box. But that's how the concept of continuous music began. The disco club was the first entertainment institution of gay life, and it started in New York, as you would expect."

Disco promoter John Luongo agrees. "In the beginning, there was the gay audience for disco. The 'primo' disc jockeys were gay. Gays couldn't find any rock bands to play in their clubs, so they had to make records their own form of entertainment."

Not long ago, Kenn Friedman took John Brody around to several clubs on his Saturday night rounds, and Brody gave me this report:

"The intensity was different at Infinity, which is predominantly straight, and at 12 West, which is mostly gay. At Infinity the energy was lower, there was less emphasis on dancing. At 12 West everybody was dancing, and it was a kind of sexual thing. It was very powerful. There was a strong smell of poppers—amyl nitrate—in the air, and I guess a lot of people were high on whatever. That must be part of the mood. But the gays seemed a lot less hung up in their environment than the heterosexuals seemed in theirs. At 12 West, I looked at these people dancing at four in the morning; it looked like the last night of their lives."

Even so, Friedman did not take Brody to Flamingo, the most intense and emotionally powerful gay disco in New York. "I didn't think he could handle it," Friedman joked.

What Brody would have seen was this:

Flamingo is an enormous loft on the edge of SoHo, undistinguished by signs or lights. Members (who pay $75 a year plus a substantial fee for each visit) start wandering in well after midnight on Saturday nights, the only day of the week the club is regularly open. By 3 A.M., several thousand people, almost entirely men, mostly shirtless and universally stoned, are dancing feverishly to the most imaginatively mixed, most persistently powerful music ever assembled in one continuous set. One wall of the danceroom is paneled with colored lights, which flicker and race at appropriate intervals in harmonious correlation to the music. Along another wall, a dozen or so men dance by themselves on a raised banquette, acting as erotic cheerleaders to the swirling crowd. The fume of poppers is overpowering.

Many Saturday night dances at Flamingo have a theme like a senior prom. Late last month there was a "Western/Tattoo" night, which featured a raised platform in the lobby where party-goers could be tattooed in their moments of relaxation from dancing. Another annual feature is the "Black Party"—named not for the race of the customers but for the suggested color of attire, the decorations, and the mood of the evening. Last spring's black party was one of the final Saturdays of the season—before Flamingo closes for the summer while its thousands of members repair to Fire Island for whatever adventures await them in dunes. Now this was some senior prom. In the entrance hall there were cages, platforms, and theatrical sets where various happenings were in progress, all in accordance with a vaguely S&M, "black," leather-gear theme. Some of the goings-on were semimentionable: people (actors?) were in chains, under the whip, groveling and groping, disheveled. Other attractions were unmentionable, and getting more so as the evening wore on. There were more people in the loft at 6 A.M. than there were at 1. When *do* these people sleep?

A strange fascination kept me at Flamingo past my bedtime, and I have returned many times in the months since then. Most often, the mood is lighter than on that black night (the "White Party" is coming up later this month), but the extravagant sense of theatricality is maintained. The throbbing lights, the engulfing sound, the heightened energy, and the hyperbolic heat of Flamingo gives me the sense (which I have heard that others share) that the world is enclosed in this hall, that there is only *now*, in this place and this time. It can be extraordinarily assaultive; I have felt trapped forever in a theater of sound, of flesh, like a character in Bunuel's *The Exterminating Angel,* unable to leave a party even after its positive appeal has fled. But what is worse is the prospect of a chill gray Manhattan dawn outside. Leaving is more depressing than staying: the disco beat is like a life rhythm, and to stop would be to create a killing thrombosis.

Danae—it's his *nom de disco*—is a well-known disc jockey on the New England and New York circuit. I asked him what he does to make the special blend of music that distinguishes the disco club sound from just "playing records":

"The mix starts at a certain place, builds, teases, builds again, and then picks up on the other side. The break is the high point. It's like asking a question, repeating and repeating it, waiting for an answer—and then giving the answer. That is the great, satisfying moment."

In practice, a "hot" disco mix in a dance club is a sexual metaphor; the deejay plays with the audience's emotions, pleasing and teasing in a crescendo of feeling. The break is the climax.

"That's the rush," Danae says. "The dancers cheer, they pump the air with their fists, they wave and shout. It's very exciting. I played at 12 West last Christmas, and it was one of the best nights I've ever had. After a while, someone came up to me, all excited, and said, 'You were fucking me with your music! Do me a favor, fuck me again with your music.' I took it as a great compliment."

"There's gay disco and straight disco, although there's overlap between the two," Danae continued. "Straight disco is heavy-duty funk, the driving sound, that has all the power without much of the emotion. Gays like to hear black women singers; they identify with the pain, the irony, the self-consciousness. We pick up on the emotional content, not just the physical power. The MFSB sound was gay; Barry White was a gay sound, so is Donna Summer, Gloria Gaynor. We knew the Trampp's 'Disco Inferno' was a great song years before it got into the *Saturday Night Fever* soundtrack. To me, the epitome of gay disco this year is Candi Staton. She's all emotion, you can feel it when she says, 'I'm a victim of the very song I sing.'"

There are contradictions within contradictions in the sexual implications of disco. Consider The Village People, the singing group that claims to hail from Greenwich Village and parodies the macho styles of its homosexual culture. One of the members is dressed as a leather biker, another as a construction worker, a third as an Indian, a fourth as a cowboy, and so on. They perform songs that extend the parody—notably "Macho Man" and "YMCA." For gays, the line "I want to be a macho man" from the mouths of these butch impersonators is a bit like "I want to be white" if it were sung by Stevie Wonder for a black audience.

Gays are amused by The Village People, but the group is finding its biggest fans among straights. "YMCA" is never heard at Flamingo. Kenn Friedman, whose Casablanca label produces the group (one of the most profitable in his stable) agrees:

"'Macho Man' did not happen in gay clubs but in straight ones. The Village People is the first gay-to-straight 'crossover' group, a group with an originally gay image and following that's made it in straight discos. The funny thing is that straights don't really believe the group is gay. They love 'em in Vegas and in tacky suburban dinner theaters in Midwestern shopping centers. Did straights ever catch on with Paul Lynde? With Liberace? People will protect their identity at all costs, they'll pretend to the last possible minute that it's all an act."

Gay activists have protested that Casablanca is deliberately closeting The Village People to make the act "safe" for straights. A Casablanca PR functionary says that producer Jacques Morali (who reportedly picked all the members except possibly the accomplished lead singer because of their tough good looks rather than their musical talent) became visibly upset when a *Newsweek* interviewer began probing into the gay issue. But the group is coming out, as it were, with ever more outrageous lyrics and postures. Their biggest hit to date is "YMCA," which concerns a young boy who comes into the big city, looks around for a place to hang out, and lands in a hostelry that is legendary in the gay community as a cruising spot. What did Middle America think it all meant when The Village People sang that number, with all the appropriate gestures, at the height of the Macy's Thanksgiving Day parade on national television?

There are two levels on which The Village People's campiness works: the first is with the "knowing" gay audience, the listeners who are in on the joke, the images, the allusions (Fire Island, the bushes, Castro Street, Key West, the Y). The other is with the "naive" straight audience, the listeners who either don't know (or mind) what's going on in the lyrics, or else think it is all theatrical drag.

In much the same way, disco music as a whole appeals to a "knowing" audience that sees what Friedman calls the "cultural gayness" in it, and a naive audience that simply likes the fashion and the beat.

"The straights don't see the gay culture, they've only seen what they've made—the styles," Friedman says. Just before Casablanca's disco movie, *Thank God It's Friday*, opened across the country last year, Friedman took a short segment of it to several cities and showed it on videotape to selected audiences. Casablanca boss Bogart was worried that straight Americans would be offended if they detected the goings-on in the background of one sequence on the tape: two men were dancing together and sniffing amyl nitrate.

"I interviewed hundreds of people, showed it to thousands, and as far as I know not one straight person ever saw the men dancing, even after I showed the segment to them two or three times," Friedman reported. "And yet the gay viewers saw it immediately."

One more example: Paul Jabara's song, "Disco Queen," on the TGIF soundtrack, concerns a "queen" who is "known from L.A. to San Francisco to the Fire Island shore." She "even sleeps with her tambourine." She flirts with a handsome young marine. The chorus asks: "Where does she get her energy? Where does she get her energy?" *Really.* The images in the song are all attached to male homosexual styles. This queen is certainly a queen. But I'll bet heterosexuals never even consider the possibility that the disco queen is not a woman. To them, it's just another nice dance tune; which it is.

Disco became the theme music of gay culture in the '70s (not only in America but in Europe and Latin America as well). Of course, the straight audience now far outnumbers the gay one, but the music still has a special meaning for gays: if '60s freaks could say that rock was "our music," gays now say the same for disco. It is the background music for the activities and institutions of the burgeoning urban gay culture—for the shops, the bars, the restaurants, and the offices where gays go about their business. It is music for sex, for dancing, and for looking at the straight world go by. It is reassuring and supportive; in an important way, it is the sensational glue that unites a community.

But disco has deep roots and strong attachments in other cultural groups as well. Disco is, after all, a mixture of certain black rhythm-and-blues sounds, Latin forms, and an African beat.

New York's first major disco station was WBLS, a "black" radio outlet. Many of the best disco performers are black—while rock is bleached and white. For years disco suffered several disadvantages to total acceptance: major disco artists were black or Latin, many were women, the principal white audience was gay, and the nongay white audience was located in the urban ethnic working class—all reasons for cultural disability.

Saturday Night Fever illustrated the class aspect of disco for urban whites. While rock was infused with middle-class attitudes (although often downwardly mobile in its aspirations), disco was originally proletarian. One clue: the "weekend" theme reappears in disco lyrics, as in "Thank God It's Friday," "I Just Can't Wait for Saturday," "Funky Weekend," and, of course, in the film title *Saturday Night Fever* itself. Working-class kids toil all week and wait for their one big shot at fun, escape, and dreams on the weekend; they dress up, get drunk, and play out sexual fantasies in a community context.

Quite the other way with the rock culture: hippies hang out all week and can't tell Saturday night from Tuesday afternoon. They don't do much dancing, and when they do, they do not care much for dressing up, spending money, having dates, and controlling their movements on the dance floor.

There are certain immutable characteristics of rock culture: it is white, straight, male, young, and middle class. The exceptions to those rules prove them. For example, female stars and their songs must conform to male sexual fantasies—Linda

Ronstadt, Christine McVie. Black musicians must be chlorinated to make it up the rock charts—Jimi Hendrix, Stevie Wonder, Chubby Checker. What may appear to be lower-class images in rock usually turn out to be middle-class myths and fantasies: punk violence, "Working Class Hero" radicalism, dropout dreams. And performers who tinker with sexual stereotypes must remain determinedly "ambiguous" or turn up with partners of the opposite sex from time to time, to beard their offensive nakedness: Bowie with Angie, Jagger with Bianca, Elton John, Alice Cooper, the Kinks. Jagger may French kiss Ron Wood on *Saturday Night Live,* but it's fortunate that he can lose a paternity suit with, figuratively, the same breath. Sexual deviation (like gender, class, and race aberrations from the norms) must be playful and let's pretend: it cannot seriously threaten straight identity.

For a time, it appeared that disco culture might change those rules to a degree, particularly in the case of sexual identity. It now looks as if the dominant demands of American society will prevail, to no one's great surprise. The past year has seen several disco stars or groups achieve the necessary "cross-over" effect, bringing the music out of the subcultural ghettoes into mainstream life. The Bee Gees were crucial to that passage; they made disco safe for white, straight, male, young, and middle-class America. What Elvis Presley did for black rhythm and blues, and Diana Ross did for soul, and Elvis Costello did for punk, the Brothers Gibb have done for disco. Now all Nassau County is lining up for disco lessons. '60s survivors who steadfastly resisted disco because it was apolitical, or dehumanized, or feminine, or homosexual, or too Bay Ridge, are suddenly skipping to the beat. They have found what Gladys Knight calls out, in one of the best songs of the season: "It's *better* than a good time."

The rise of disco music occurred alongside the decline of rock, but whether there is connection between these two aesthetic events is not at all clear.

"Rock and roll is at an all-time low in creativity," promoter John Luongo fretted. "It's all rehashed material, there's no freshness. I love rock," he insisted, "and it's where I started. But the music has let people down. There was a big hole, and disco filled it. There's no other form of music that offers the power, the excitement, the party atmosphere of disco."

Disco is the word, as grease was the word. It is a handle on the '70s, as the other was a metaphor for the '50s, for in the extraordinary cultural and commercial success of disco several of the new elements of this generation can be identified. Disco has many functions, but one of the most essential may be as a drug: it feeds artificial energy, communal good feelings, and high times into an era of competition, isolation, and alienation. As drugs go, it is not egregiously harmful, but it is easily abused, quickly tolerated, and naggingly addictive.

Sensibility is dialectical—which is to say that it grows from the material of history and the experience of society. It does not descend from the heavens of invention or corporealize out of thin air. The '70s sensibility emerged from the achievements and excesses, the defeats and triumphs of the years before. Our end is *always* in our beginning, and we are, as Candi Staton croons, the victims of the very songs we sing.

Further Reading

Aletti, Vince. "Dancing Madness: The Disco Sound." *Rolling Stone,* August 28, 1975, 43, 50, 56.

Echols, Alice. *Hot Stuff: Disco and the Remaking of American Culture.* New York: W.W. Norton, 2010.

Holden, Stephen. "The Evolution of a Dance Craze." *Rolling Stone,* April 19, 1979, 29.

Krasnow, Carolyn. "Fear and Loathing in the 70s: Race, Sexuality, and Disco." *Stanford Humanities Review* 3 (Fall 1993): 37–45.

Lawrence, Tim. *Love Saves the Day: A History of American Dance Music Culture, 1970–1979.* Durham, N.C.: Duke University Press, 2003.

McLeese, Don. "Anatomy of an Anti-Disco Riot." *In These Times,* August 29–September 4, 1979, 23.

Shapiro, Peter. *Turn the Beat Around: The Secret History of Disco.* London: Faber and Faber, 2006.

Discography

Chic. *Dance, Dance, Dance: The Best of Chic.* Atlantic/WEA, 1991.

Moroder, Giorgio. *From Here to Eternity.* Repertoire, 1977.

Saturday Night Fever: The Original Movie Sound Track. Polydor/UMGD, 1977.

Summer, Donna. *Love to Love You Baby.* MCA Special Products, 1975.

Ultimate Disco: 30th Anniversary Collection. Madacy Records, 2003.

Van McCoy. *The Hustle and the Best of Van McCoy.* Amherst Records, 1995.

Village People. *The Best of Village People.* Island/Mercury, 1994.

White, Barry. *Can't Get Enough.* Island/Mercury, 1974.

58. Punk

THE SOUND OF CRITICISM?

At the end of the preceding article, promoter John Luongo decried the creative stasis that had overcome rock music during the 1970s. Many musicians working in rock (and critics devoted to it) could not have agreed more. While Kopkind's essay mentions punk and new wave in passing, these genres arose as rock musicians' response to the same crisis that spurred the popularity of disco.

Punk, a favorite subject of rock critics,[1] is one of the few genres in the history of rock 'n' roll in which the people who read about it may have outnumbered the people who heard it (at least during its initial heyday

---

1. For an excellent discussion of rock criticism from this period, and one to which the following discussion is much indebted, see Bernard Gendron, *Between Montmartre and the Mudd Club* (Chicago: University of Chicago Press, 2002), chaps. 10–13.

in the late 1970s). The genre may also be the first to have followed the aesthetic imperatives of rock criticism, rather than the reverse. We need only think back to the impassioned manifestos of Lester Bangs and his colleagues at *Creem* magazine in the early 1970s, many of which antici-pated the style of mid-1970s punk as represented, in particular, by the Ramones. The self-consciousness of the participants (musicians and audience members alike) about style—in musical, sartorial, and politi-cal terms—made it a rich field for sociologists as well as critics.[2]

The critics and musicians who either identified with or took an interest in punk in the mid-1970s were also aware of the legacy of the Velvet Underground, the band established by Bangs as the sine qua non of punk in his early writings.[3] A genealogy gradually evolved that gained tacit acceptance by most other writers:

> (ca. 1966) Velvet Underground (+ 60s garage bands +
>   "rave-ups" of Yardbirds and Kinks) →
> (ca. 1969) Stooges/MC5 →
> (ca. 1973) Modern Lovers/New York Dolls →
> (ca. 1975) Ramones/Patti Smith/Talking Heads →
> (ca. 1976) Sex Pistols/Clash

In musical terms, this genealogy emphasizes a deliberately simplistic, "do-it-yourself" amateur aesthetic; many writers referred to this quality with the term "minimalism," by which they meant the stripping of rock music down to its most basic elements (not to be confused with the music of Terry Riley, Philip Glass, Steve Reich, et al.). By 1975, the term "punk" included a great diversity of musical styles under its rubric, held together by a common attitude toward the growing gentrification of rock and the common use of a performance venue in New York City, CBGB's. Writing in 1977, Robert Christgau provided a pithy summary of punk:

The underlying idea of this rock and roll will be to harness late industrial capitalism in a love hate relationship whose difficulties are acknowledged, and sometimes dis-armed, by means of ironic aesthetic strategies: formal rigidity, role-playing, humor.[4]

James Wolcott was one of the first critics to recognize the historical and potential theoretical importance of punk rock as it developed in New York City. The following article describes a festival presented at CBGB's in the summer of 1975 and gives an overview of the scene at that moment. Wolcott uses the term "underground" (i.e., unrecorded

---

2. For a classic academic study dating from this period, see Dick Hebdige, *Subculture: The Meaning of Style* (London: Methuen, 1979).

3. In addition to Bangs, the connection between the Velvet Underground and punk was explic-itly addressed by James Wolcott in "Lou Reed Rising" (entitled "The Rise of Punk Rock" on the inside), *Village Voice*, March 1, 1976, back page, 87–88.

4. Robert Christgau, "A Cult Explodes—and a Movement Is Born," *Village Voice*, October 24, 1977, 57, 68–74.

bands) to describe the music and calls the festival "the most important event in New York rock since the Velvet Underground played the Balloon Farm." Like other writers of the time, he views punk as opposed to the "baroque theatricality of rock" and observes the stagnant quality of rock music, sensing that dance music is where "the scenemakers" are.[5] Wolcott's usage of "conservative" here means "to carry on the rock tradition," and he approves of the manner in which the CBGB's bands are accomplishing it.

The article also mentions the use of past styles in punk, not as parody or homage, but as pastiche, somewhat in the manner of the camp sensibility found in Andy Warhol's "pop art."[6] This is particularly prominent in bands such as Television and the Talking Heads, and Wolcott captures well their affectless presentation with phrases like "banal façade" and "a sense of detachment." Tina Weymouth, bassist for the Talking Heads, sums up the attitude behind such self-presentation when she states: "Rock isn't a noble cause."[7]

A Conservative Impulse in the New Rock Underground
James Wolcott

Arabian swelter, and with the air-conditioning broken, CBGB resembled some abbatoir of a kitchen in which a bucket of ice is placed in front of a fan to cool the room off. To no avail of course, and the heat had perspiration glissading down the curve of one's back, yeah, and the cruel heat also burned away any sense of glamour. After all, CBGB's Bowery and Bleeker location is not the garden spot of lower Manhattan, and the bar itself is an uneasy oasis. On the left, where the couples are, tables; on the right, where the stragglers, drinkers and love-seekers are, a long bar; between the

---

5. For an earlier example that discusses the New York Dolls in these terms, see Lorraine O'Grady, "Dealing with the Dolls Mystique," *Village Voice*, October 4, 1973, 52.

6. Since the preceding article by Kopkind already referred to a camp sensibility as one of the aspects of disco's appeal, the mention of that term here may suggest an unsuspected affinity between disco and punk. Interested readers are encouraged to seek out Susan Sontag's influential essay on the subject, "Notes on 'Camp,'" in *Against Interpretation* (New York: Anchor Books, [1964] 1990), 275–92.

7. For a later discussion of the Talking Heads that further discusses their music and the impact of their art school background, see John Rockwell, "The Artistic Success of Talking Heads," *New York Times*, September 11, 1977, D14, 16. Rockwell, longtime music critic for the *New York Times*, is certainly as well positioned as anyone to discuss the artistic aspirations of rock music. His *All-American Music: Composition in the Late Twentieth Century* (New York: Vintage Books, 1984), in its inclusion of rock music, salsa, jazz, Broadway, and a wide range of classical music, presciently anticipates the crossing of musical categories that has since become more common for music critics and academics. *All-American Music* also contains an in-depth examination of the Talking Heads (pp. 234–45).

two, a high double-backed ladder which, when the room is really crowded, offers the best view. If your bladder sends a distress signal, write home to your mother, for you must make a perilous journey down the aisle between seating area and bar, not knock over any mike stands as you slide by the tiny stage, squeeze through the piles of amplifiers, duck the elbow thrust of a pool player leaning over to make a shot . . . and then you end up in an illustrated bathroom which looks like a page that didn't make *The Faith of Graffiti.*

Now consider the assembly-line presentation of bands, with resonant names like Movies, Tuff Darts, Blondie, Stagger Lee, the Heartbreakers, Mink de Ville, Dancer, the Shirts, Bananas, Talking Heads, Johnny's Dance Band and Television; consider that some nights as many as six bands perform, and it isn't hard to comprehend someone declining to sit through a long evening. When the air gets thick with noise and smoke, even the most committed of us long to slake our thirst in front of a Johnny Carson monologue, the quintessential experience of bourgeois cool.

So those who stayed away are not to be chastised, except for a lack of adventurousness. And yet they missed perhaps the most important event in New York rock since the Velvet Underground played the Balloon Farm: CBGB's three-week festival of the best underground (i.e. unrecorded) bands. The very unpretentiousness of the bands' style of musical attack represented a counter-thrust to the prevailing baroque theatricality of rock. In opposition to that theatricality, this was a music which suggested a resurgence of communal faith.

So this was an event of importance but not of flash. Hardly any groupies or bopperettes showed up, nor did platoons of rock writers with their sensibilities tuned into Radio Free Zeitgeist brave the near satanic humidity. When the room was packed, as it often was, it was packed with musicians and their girlfriends, couples on dates, friends and relatives of band members, and CBGB regulars, all dressed in denims and loose-fitting shirts sartorial-style courtesy of Canal Jeans. The scenemakers and chic-obsessed were elsewhere.

Understandable. Rock simply isn't the brightest light in the pleasure dome any longer (my guess is that dance is), and Don Kirschner's *Rock Awards* only verifies the obvious: rock is getting as arthritic, or at least as phlegmatic, as a rich old whore. It isn't only that the enthusiasm over the Stones tour seemed strained and synthetic, or that the Beach Boys can't seem able to release new material until Brian Wilson conquers his weight problem, or that the album of the year is a collection of basement tapes made in 1967. "The real truth as I see it," said the Who's Pete Townshend recently, "is that rock music as it was is not really contemporary to these times. It's really the music of yesteryear."

He's right and yet wrong. What's changed is the nature of the impulse to create rock. No longer is the impulse revolutionary—i.e., the transformation of oneself and society—but conservative: to carry on the rock tradition. To borrow from Eliot, a rocker now needs a historical sense; he performs "not merely with his own generation in his bones" but with the knowledge that all of pop culture forms a "simultaneous order." The landscape is no longer virginal—markers and tracks have been left by, among others, Elvis, Buddy Holly, Chuck Berry and the Beatles—and it exists not to be transformed but cultivated.

No, I'm not saying that everyone down at CBGB is a farmer. Must you take me so literally? But there is original vision there, and what the place itself is doing is quite extraordinary; putting on bands as if the stage were a cable TV station. Public access rock. Of course, not every band which auditions gets to play, but the proprietor, Hilly, must have a wide latitude of taste since the variety and quality of talent ranges from the great to the God-condemned. As with cable TV, what you get is not high-gloss professionalism but talent still working at the basics; the excitement (which borders on comedy) is watching a band with a unique approach try to articulate its vision and still remember the chords.

Television was once such a band; the first time I saw them everything was wrong—the vocals were too raw, the guitar work was relentlessly bad, the drummer wouldn't leave his cymbals alone. They were lousy all right but their lousiness had a forceful dissonance reminiscent of the Stones' *Exile on Main Street*, and clearly Tom Verlaine was a presence to be reckoned with.

He has frequently been compared to Lou Reed in the Velvet days, but he most reminds me of Keith Richard. The blood-drained bone-weary Keith on stage at Madison Square Garden is the perfect symbol for Rock '75, not playing at his best, sometimes not even playing competently, but rocking, swaying back and forth as if the night might be his last and it's better to stand than fall. Though Jagger is dangerously close to becoming Maria Callas, Keith, with his lanky grace and obsidian-eyed menace, is the perpetual outsider. I don't know any rock lover who doesn't love Keith; he's the star who's always at the edge and yet occupies the center.

Tom Verlaine occupies the same dreamy realm, like Keith he's pale and aloof. He seems lost in a forest of silence and he says about performing that "if I'm thinking up there, I'm not having a good night." Only recently has the band's technique been up to Verlaine's reveries and their set at the CBGB festival was the best I've ever seen; dramatic, tense, tender ("Hard On Love"), athletic ("Kingdom Come"), with Verlaine in solid voice and the band playing as a band and not as four individuals with instruments. Verlaine once told me that one of the best things about the Beatles was the way they could shout out harmonies and make them sound intimate, and that's what Television had that night: loud intimacy.

When Tom graduated from high school back in Delaware, he was voted "most unknown" by his senior class. As if in revenge, he chose the name Verlaine, much as Patti Smith often invokes the name Rimbaud. He came to New York, spent seven years writing fiction, formed a group called Neon Boys, then Television. The name suggests an aesthetic of accessibility and choice. It also suggests Tom's adapted initials: T.V.

"I left Delaware because no one wanted to form a band there," he says. "Then I came to New York and no one wanted to form a band here either." Verlaine came to New York for the same reason every street-smart artist comes to New York—because it's the big league—even though he realizes "New York is not a great rock & roll town."

Still, they continue to arrive: Martina Weymouth, bassist, born in California; Chris Frantz, drummer, in Kentucky; David Byrne, singer and guitarist, in Scotland. All attended the Rhode Island School of Design, and according to their bio, are "now launching careers in New York"—a sonorous announcement, yes?

These people call themselves Talking Heads. Seeing them for the first time is transfixing: Frantz is so far back on drums that it sounds as if he's playing in the next room; Weymouth, who could pass as Suzi Quatro's sorority sister, stands rooted to the floor, her head doing an oscillating-fan swivel; the object of her swivel is David Byrne, who has a little-boy-lost-at-the-zoo voice and the demeanor of someone who's spent the last half-hour whirling around in a spin-drier. When his eyes start ping-ponging in his head, he looks like a cartoon of a chipmunk from Mars. The song titles aren't tethered to conventionality either: "Psycho Killer" (which goes, "Psycho killer, qu'est-ce c'est? Fa-fa-fa-fa-fa-fa-fa"), "The Girls Want To Be With The Girls," "Love is Like A Building On Fire," plus a cover version of that schlock classic by ? and the Mysterians, "96 Tears."

Love at first sight it isn't.

But repeated viewings (precise word) reveal Talking Heads to be one of the most intriguingly off-the-wall bands in New York. Musically, they're minimalists: Byrne's guitar playing is like a charcoal pencil scratching a scene on a note pad. The songs are spined by Weymouth's bass playing which, in contrast to the glottal buzz of most rock bass work, is hard and articulate—the bass lines provide hook as well as bottom. Visually, the band is perfect for the cable-TV format at CBGB; they present a clean, flat image, devoid of fine shading and colour. They are consciously anti-mythic in stance. A line from their bio: "The image we present along with our songs is what we are really like."

Talking to them, it becomes apparent that though they deny antecedents—"We would rather advance a 'new' sound rather than be compared to bands of the past"— they are children of the communal rock ethic. They live together, melting the distinction between art and life, and went into rock because as art it is more "accessible." They have an astute sense of aesthetic consumerism, yet they're not entirely under the Warholian sway, for as one of them told me, "We don't want to be famous for the sake of being famous." Of all the groups I've seen at CBGB, Talking Heads is the closest to a neo-Velvet band, and they represent a distillation of that sensibility, what John Cale once called "controlled distortion." When the Velvets made their reputation at the Balloon Farm, they were navigating through a storm of multi-media effects; mirrors, blinking lights, strobes, projected film images. Talking Heads works without paraphernalia in a cavernous room projecting light like a television located at the end of a long dark hall. The difference between the Velvets and Talking Heads is the difference between phosphorescence and cold gray TV light. These people understand that an entire generation has grown up on the nourishment of television's accessible banality. What they're doing is presenting a banal façade under which run ripples of violence and squalls of frustration—the id of the vid.

David Byrne sings tonelessly but its effect is all the more ominous. The uneasy alliance between composure and breakdown—between outward acceptance and inward coming-apart—is what makes Talking Heads such a central seventies band. A quote from ex-Velvet John Cale: "What we try to get here [at the Balloon Farm] is a sense of total involvement." Nineteen sixty-six. But what bands like Television and Talking Heads are doing is ameliorating the post-'60s hangover by giving us a sense of detachment. We've passed through the Dionysian storm and now it's time to nurse private wounds. Says Tina Weymouth, quite simply: "Rock isn't a noble cause."

The Ramones recently opened at a Johnny Winter concert and had to dodge flying bottles. During one of their CBGB sets, they had equipment screw-ups and Dee Dee Ramone stopped singing and gripped his head as if he were going to explode and Tommy Ramone smashed the cymbal shouting, "What the FUCK'S wrong?" They went offstage steaming, then came back and ripped into "Judy Is A Punk." A killer band.

"Playing with a band is the greatest way of feeling alive," says Tom Verlaine. But the pressures in New York against such an effort—few places to play, media indifference, the compulsively upward pace of city life—are awesome. Moreover, the travails of a rock band are rooted in a deeper problem: the difficulty of collaborative art. Rock bands flourished in the sixties when there was a genuine faith in the efficacious beauty of communal activity, when the belief was that togetherness meant strength. It was more than a matter of "belonging"; it meant that one could create art with friends. Playing with a band meant art with sacrifice, but without suffering. Romantic intensity without Romantic solitude.

What CBGB is trying to do is nothing less than to restore that spirit as a force in rock & roll. One is left speculating about success: will any of the bands who play there ever amount to anything more than a cheap evening of rock & roll? Is public access merely an attitude to be discarded once stardom seems possible, or will it sustain itself beyond the first recording contract? I don't know, and in the deepest sense, don't care. These bands don't have to be the vanguard in order to satisfy. In a cheering Velvets song, Lou Reed sings: "A little wine in the morning, and some breakfast at night. Well, I'm beginning to see the light." And that's what rock gives: small unconventional pleasures which lead to moments of perception.

Further Reading

Christgau, Robert. "A Cult Explodes—and a Movement Is Born." *Village Voice*, October 24, 1977, 57, 68–74.

Frith, Simon, and Howard Horne. *Art into Pop*. London: Methuen, 1987.

Gendron, Bernard. *Between Montmartre and the Mudd Club*. Chicago: University of Chicago Press, 2002, chaps. 10–13.

Hebdige, Dick. *Subculture: The Meaning of Style*. London: Methuen, 1979.

Laing, Dave. *One Chord Wonders*. Philadelphia: Open University Press, 1985.

O'Grady, Lorraine. "Dealing with the Dolls Mystique." *Village Voice*, October 4, 1973, 52.

Savage, Jon. *England's Dreaming: Sex Pistols and Punk Rock*. London: Faber and Faber, 1991.

Waksman, Steve. *This Ain't the Summer of Love: Conflict and Crossover in Heavy Metal and Punk*. Berkeley: University of California Press, 2009.

Wolcott, James. "Lou Reed Rising" ("The Rise of Punk Rock"). *Village Voice*, March 1, 1976, back page, 87–88.

Discography

The Heartbreakers. *What Goes Around*. Bomp Records, 1991.

New York Dolls. *New York Dolls*. Island/Mercury, 1973.

No Thanks! The '70s Punk Rebellion. Rhino/WEA, 2003.

The Ramones. *Ramones*. Rhino/WEA, 2001.

_____. *Greatest Hits*. Rhino/WEA, 2006.

Smith, Patti. *Horses*. Arista, 1975.

59. Punk Crosses the Atlantic

Punk's musical style, do-it-yourself attitude, and disdain for the bourgeois hedonism of rock superstars resonated strongly among sectors of British youths. With pub-rock, older styles of rock 'n' roll, and the Ramones forming the immediate musical backdrop, the stage was set for a distinctive British punk to emerge. Punk in the United Kingdom was felt to have more social and political relevance than U.S. punk because of the identification of British working-class youths with punk's nihilism, an identification facilitated by rampant unemployment and a depressed economy.[1] While a band like the Sex Pistols emphasized the nihilist aspects of punk, the Clash pursued a more overt political agenda.

Another major difference between U.S. and U.K. punk was the amount and type of attention they received in the press. As early as 1976, near-hysterical reports surfaced in Britain, some of them appearing before any recordings had even been released. As a writer for the British publication *Melody Maker,* Caroline Coon was well positioned to observe the burgeoning punk scene from close range. Coon's sympathetic account focuses as much on what British punk was reacting against as it does on punk itself. While some might quibble with claims of British punk's autonomy from New York City punk, this belief was widespread at the time, and it is certainly true that the British punks were free of the "retro" influences favored by some of the New York bands. In addition to describing the music, Coon captures the distinctive sartorial approach and "subcultural style" of the British scene.[2] For Coon, the dynamic fulcrum of this scene revolves around the most notorious band of the era, the Sex Pistols, and its equally notorious lead singer, Johnny Rotten.

Rebels Against the System
Caroline Coon

Johnny Rotten looks bored. The emphasis is on the word "looks" rather than, as Johnny would have you believe, the word "bored." His clothes, held together by safety pins, fall around his slack body in calculated disarray. His face is an under-

---

1. Robert Christgau was drawn to British punk for its projection of a greater sense of political engagement; see his "A Cult Explodes—and a Movement Is Born," *Village Voice,* October 24, 1977, 57, 68–74. Simon Frith explores the political contradictions of British punk in "Beyond the Dole Queue: The Politics of Punk," *Village Voice,* October 24, 1977, 77–79. For the first in-depth portrait of the Sex Pistols to appear in *Rolling Stone,* and one that conveys some of the shock felt by certain sectors of the rock establishment, see Charles M. Young, "Rock Is Sick and Living in London: A Report on the Sex Pistols," *Rolling Stone,* October 20, 1977, 68–75.

2. From roughly the same period, see Caroline Coon, "Punk Alphabet," *Melody Maker,* November 27, 1976, 33, in which she gives more space to the interconnections between British and American punk and stresses the increased role of women in punk relative to other genres.

Source: "Rebels against the System" Caroline Coon © IPC Media

nourished grey. Not a muscle moves. His lips echo the downward slope of his wiry, coat-hanger shoulders. Only his eyes register the faintest trace of life.

This malevolent, third generation child of rock & roll is the Sex Pistols' lead singer. The band play exciting, hard, basic punk rock. But more than that, Johnny is the elected generalissimo of a new cultural movement scything through the grass-roots disenchantment with the present state of mainstream rock.

You need look no further than the letters pages of any *Melody Maker* to see that fans no longer silently accept the disdain with which their heroes, rock giants, treat them.

They feel deserted. Millionaire rock stars are no longer part of the brotherly rock fraternity which helped create them in the first place.

Rock was meant to be a joyous celebration; the inability to see the stars, or to play the music of those you can see, is making a whole generation of rock fans feel depressingly inadequate.

Enter Johnny Rotten. Not content to feel frustrated, bored and betrayed, he and the Sex Pistols, Glen Matlock (bass), Paul Cook (drums), and Steve Jones (guitar), have decided to ignore what they believe to be the elitist pretensions of their heroes who no longer play the music they want to hear. The Pistols are playing the music they want to hear. They are the tip of an iceberg.

Since January, when the Sex Pistols played their first gig, there has been a slow but steady increase in the number of musicians who feel the same way—bands like the Clash, the Jam, Buzzcocks, the Damned, the Subway Sect and Slaughter and the Dogs. The music they play is loud, raucous and beyond considerations of taste and finesse. As Mick Jones of the Clash says: "It's wonderfully vital."

These bands' punk music and stance is so outrageous that, like the Rolling Stones in the good old days, they have trouble getting gigs. But they play regularly at the 100 Club, which is rapidly becoming the venue at which these bands cut their teeth.

The musicians and their audience reflect each other's street-cheap, ripped-apart, pinned-together style of dress. Their attitude is classic punk: icy-cool with a permanent sneer. The kids are arrogant, aggressive, rebellious. The last thing any of these bands make their audience feel is inadequate.

Once again there is the feeling, the exhilarating buzz, that it's possible to be and play like the bands on stage.

We're back where we were in 1964. The Beatles, Stones, Kinks, Who, Them, Animals and the Yardbirds—in effect, a new wave—blasted out of the national charts the showbiz pop of Adam Faith, Bobby Vee, Cliff Richard and Paul Anka, which had replaced the initial vibrant explosion triggered by Bill Haley's "Rock Around The Clock" and Elvis's "Heartbreak Hotel" in 1956.

The last five years of rock can be compared to the early sixties when the rock stars of the fifties were wiped out. Buddy Holly's plane crashed. Elvis was drafted into the army, Chuck Berry was jailed. Car crashes killed Eddie Cochran and hospitalized Gene Vincent and Carl Perkins. The field was left open to the businessmen.

The parallels with today are uncanny.

What happened to the rock stars—the new wave—who revolutionized the scene from 1964–7? Jimi Hendrix, Jim Morrison, Brian Jones and Janis Joplin are dead. Clapton retired, and is only just returning, Dylan rested up for several years with a broken neck. Those who are left—the ex-Beatles, Stones, Who, Kinks, have become businessmen. OK, some are still playing rock & roll—but aren't they a little more motivated by making money than making music?

When these bands first shook the foundations of the established musical order they reveled in their image as *rebels:* misfits, outcasts. The Beatles played in Hamburg with toilet seats around their necks, the Who smashed expensive equipment they could ill afford every night, the Rolling Stones, with their long hair and tieless shirts, were chucked out of hotels and restaurants wherever they went.

These rock & rollers were the heroes of their generation because they rejected and broke through the restrictions which had kept teenagers bound to the outdated authority of their parents. Their music was loud, the clothes outrageous.

Most important of all, they were anti-elitist, voices from and of the people—or so we believed. They spoke our language. Every kid who sang along to "My Generation," "All Day And All Of The Night" and "Let's Spend The Night Together" felt that he was as involved with the music as the musicians.

And the bands tried to keep it that way. When the Beatles felt they were becoming the acceptable face of rock with songs like "Michelle," "Norwegian Wood" and "Yesterday," they zapped it back to the true believers with a mind-blowing concoction of backward tapes, multi-tracking and psychedelic weirdness that only youth could really understand.

The trouble is, in the last five years, the rock stars have become "adults"; they have forgotten that crucial to their appeal was their rebellious stance. Instead they are bending over backwards to become acceptable.

Mick Jagger, once the arch-deacon of iconoclasm, now couldn't be farther removed from his fans. It's no longer possible to imagine him as a man of the people, if he ever was—his yobbo accent doesn't wash any more. He's elitist, the aristocracy's court jester, royalty's toy. How long before his name appears on the Queen's honours list?[3]

The Who are becoming Pete Townshend's private nightmare—trotting out their musical history, the seventies' Chuck Berry.

The Beach Boys and the Byrds, America's initial reply to the British eruption, haven't been a vital force in rock for eight years.

The Beatles are the fastest-expanding nostalgia industry yet conceived. On an individual level Paul McCartney and Wings is the only one to have maintained the tradition of an artist consistently performing for an audience, and he speaks mainly to the generation he grew up with.

To his credit, although Lennon is now a quiet family man, he, with Yoko, was the only rock giant to attempt to bring the rebellious protest of his generation to a political level which transcended the rhetoric of rock.

With few exceptions, the interim bands, the ones who sprang up while the old wild men were moving from cellar to penthouse, never transcended their music to become cultural heroes. The psychedelic bands like Jefferson Airplane, Grateful Dead, Soft Machine and Pink Floyd were musically important until they disintegrated with the underground, or disappeared into their own insularity.

Basically middle class, affluent or university academics, they set the stage for bands like Genesis, Jethro Tull, ELP, Yes, Rick Wakeman, Roxy Music and Queen, whose "progressive rock" uses an increasing amount of technical apparatus, has become increasing quasi-orchestral and quotes liberally from the classics.

All these bands have been acclaimed by the critics, sometimes justifiably. But the crucial element is missing. These musicians have always been gentlemen rockers and their music can only be played by people with similar academic temperaments. The music, although inspired, is far beyond what the average teenager, without expensive equipment, can reproduce in his own front room.

---

3. Coon's worst fears were realized in December 2003 when Jagger was knighted.

David Bowie is the one person the growing wave of third-generation rock fans seem to identify with. Although a musical stylist rather than an innovator, he's captured their imagination with a film and stage persona creating him as a mutant alien from another planet.

Thus he has brilliantly detached himself from the conventional jet set, rock star establishment. Unlike other stars whose private lives are totally disparate with their rock stance, Bowie's private life seems freaky enough, weird and secret enough to get him elected the first Punk Space Cadet.

There was a time when it looked as though Led Zeppelin and Bad Company might have carried the torch for raw, raunchy rock & roll but they became multinational corporations, casualties of the business ethic.

The present state of rock came to a dramatic climax in May and June of this year, at the series of businessmen's conventions held at Wembley, Earls Court and Charlton.

The Who, the Stones, Elton John, David Essex, Steve Harley, David Bowie, Uriah Heep, all put on shows which, whatever they may have said and whatever attempts they may have made to overcome their self-imposed problems, had little to do with music and everything to do with the kind of gestures these stars think is all that's needed to keep their fans happy.

The fans, wanting to give their heroes the benefit of the doubt, weren't as angry as they had the right to be. But a great many were heartsick, disillusioned and bored rotten.

Of course, thousands of people, especially those who grew up with Rock Giants, were still loyal fans, still buying the albums and having a good time. But this is simply not the atmosphere in which the new generation of rock musicians can thrive or have any desire to carry on from where the old guard has left off.

There is a growing, almost desperate, feeling that rock music should be stripped down to its bare bones again. It needs to be taken by the scruff of its bloated neck and given a good shaking, bringing it back to its sources and traditions.

The time is right for an aggressive infusion of life-blood into rock.

It's no coincidence that the week the Stones were at Earls Court, the Sex Pistols were playing to their ever-increasing following at London's 100 Club. The Pistols are the personification of the emerging British punk rock scene, a positive reaction to the complex equipment, technological sophistication and jaded alienation which has formed a barrier between fans and stars.

Punk rock sounds simple and callow. It's meant to.

The equipment is minimal, usually cheap. It's played faster than the speed of light. If the musicians play a ballad, it's the fastest ballad on earth. The chords are basic, numbers rarely last longer than three minutes, in keeping with the clipped, biting cynicism of the lyrics.

There are no solos. No indulgent improvisations.

It's a fallacy to believe that punk rockers like the Sex Pistols can't play dynamic music. They power through sets. They are never less than hard, tough and edgy. They are the quintessence of a raging, primal rock-scream.

The atmosphere among the punk bands on the circuit at the moment is positively cutthroat. Not only are they vying with each other but they all secretly aspire to take Johnny Rotten down a peg or two. They use him as a pivot against which they can assess their own credibility.

It's the BSP/ASP Syndrome. The Before Or After Sex Pistols debate which wrangles thus: "We saw Johnny Rotten and he *changed* our attitude to music" (the Clash, Buzzcocks), or "We played like this *ages* before the Sex Pistols" (Slaughter and the Dogs), or "We are *miles* better than the Sex Pistols" (the Damned). They are very aware that they are part of a new movement and each one wants to feel that he played a part in starting it.

All doubt that the British punk scene is well under way was blitzed two weeks ago in Manchester, when the Sex Pistols headlined a triple, third-generation punk rock concert before an ecstatic capacity audience.

Participation is the operative word. The audiences are reveling in the idea that any one of them could get up on stage and do just as well, if not better, than the bands already up there. Which is, after all, what rock & roll is all about.

When for months, you've been feeling that it would take ten years to play as well as Hendrix, Clapton, Richard (insert favourite rock star's name), there's nothing more gratifying than the thought: Jesus, I could get a band together and blow this lot off the stage!

The growing punk rock audiences are seething with angry young dreamers who want to put the boot in and play music, regardless. And the more people feel "I can do that too," the more there is a rush on to that stage, the more cheap instruments are bought, fingered and played in front rooms, the more likely it is there will be the "rock revival" we've all been crying out for.

There's every chance (although it's early days yet) that out of the gloriously raucous, uninhibited melee of British punk rock, which even at its worst is more vital than most of the music perfected by the Platinum Disc Brigade, will emerge the musicians to inspire a fourth generation of rockers.

The arrogant, aggressive, rebellious stance that characterizes the musicians who have played the most vital rock and roll has always been glamorized. In the fifties it was the rebel without a cause exemplified by Elvis and Gene Vincent, the Marlon Brando and James Dean of rock. In the sixties it was the Rock & Roll Gypsy Outlaw image of Mick Jagger, Keith Richard and Jimi Hendrix. In the seventies the word "rebel" has been superseded by the word "punk." Although initially derogatory it now contains all the glamorous connotations once implied by the overused word— "rebel."

Punk rock was initially coined, about six years ago, to describe the American rock bands of 1965-8 who sprung up as a result of hearing the Yardbirds, Who, Them, Stones. Ability was not as important as mad enthusiasm, but the bands usually dissipated all their talent in one or two splendid singles which rarely transcended local hit status. Some of the songs, however, like "Wooly Bully," "96 Tears," "Psychotic Reaction," "Pushin' Too Hard," have become rock classics.[4]

In Britain, as "punk rock" has been increasingly used to categorize the livid, exciting energy of bands like the Sex Pistols, there has been an attempt to redefine the term.

The new British bands emerging have only the most tenuous connections with the New York punk rock scene which has flourished for the last four years. Bands like the New York Dolls, the Ramones, Patti Smith, Television and the Heartbreakers are much closer, musically, to the Shadows of Knight, the Leaves and other punk rock bands of the sixties.

And they dress almost exclusively in the classic punk uniform. Those not in Levis, sneakers, T-shirts and leather jackets are still pretending to be English rock stars circa 1965.

---

4. This description of punk is a reference to articles such as one by Lester Bangs ("Of Pop and Pies and Fun," in The Pop. Rock, and Soul Reader: Histories and Debates, second edition, ed. David Brackett [New York: Oxford University Press, 2009], 273–78), or to other early classics such as Greg Shaw's "Punk Rock: The Arrogant Underbelly of Sixties Pop," *Rolling Stone*, January 4, 1973, 68–70.

On the other hand, the British punk scene, far from glorifying, is disgusted by the past. Nostalgia is a dirty word. The music's only truck with yesterday's rock is an affection for one or two classics, "Substitute," "What'cha Gonna Do About It," "Help," "I Can't Control Myself," "Stepping Stone": all vitriolic outbursts mirroring the spirit of the bands' own songs, which have titles like "Pretty Vacant," "No Feelings," "Anarchy In The UK," "You're Shit!" or "I Love You, You Big Dummy."

While New York cultivates avant-garde and intellectual punks like Patti Smith and Television, the British teenager, needing and being that much more alienated from rock than America ever was, has little time for such aesthetic refinements.

British punk rock is emerging as a fierce, aggressive, self-destructive onslaught.

There's an age difference too. New York punks are mostly in their mid-twenties. The members of the new British punk band squirm if they have to tell you they are over eighteen. Johnny Rotten's favourite sneer is: "You're too old." He's twenty.

British punk rock garb is developing independently too. It's an ingenious hodgepodge of jumble sale cast-offs, safety-pinned around one of the choice, risqué T-shirts especially made for the King's Road shop, Sex.

Selling an intriguing line of arcane fifties cruise-ware, fantasy glamour-ware, and the odd rubber suit, this unique boutique is owned by Malcolm McLaren, exmanager of the New York Dolls, now the Sex Pistols' manager.

His shop has a mysterious atmosphere which made it the ideal meeting place for a loose crowd of truant, disaffected teenagers. Three of them were aspiring musicians who, last October, persuaded McLaren to take them on. They wanted to play rock & roll. They weren't to know what they were about to start and even now no one is sure where it will lead. All Steve, Glen and Paul needed then was a lead singer.

A few weeks later Johnny Rotten strayed into the same murky interior. He was first spotted leaning over the jukebox, looking bored. . . .

Further Reading

Coon, Caroline. "Punk Alphabet." *Melody Maker*, November 27, 1976, 33.

_____. *1988: The New Wave Punk Rock Explosion*. London: Orbach and Chambers Limited, 1977.

Frith, Simon. "Beyond the Dole Queue: The Politics of Punk." *Village Voice*, October 24, 1977, 77–79.

Young, Charles M. "Rock Is Sick and Living in London: A Report on the Sex Pistols." *Rolling Stone*, October 20, 1977, 68–75.

Discography

Buzzcocks. *Singles Going Steady*. EMI International, 2001.

The Clash. *The Clash*. Epic, 1977.

_____. *London Calling*. Epic, 1979.

No Thanks! The '70s Punk Rebellion. Rhino/WEA, 2003.

Sex Pistols. *Never Mind the Bollocks, Here's the Sex Pistols*. Warner Bros./WEA, 1977.

_____. *Kiss This: The Best of the Sex Pistols*. EMI/Virgin, 1992.

60. Punk to New Wave?

"New wave" began to be used as a complementary term to "punk" during 1976 and 1977. The term did not originate in order to supplant "punk" or to provide a competing category, but, rather, in the words of Bernard Gendron, "to capture in punk bands what the designator 'punk' left out—the arty, avant-gardish, studied, and ironic dimension that accompanied the streetwise, working-class and raucously 'vulgar' dimension."[1] Initially, the terms were used interchangeably or, when distinctions were attempted, confusingly. Gradually, by 1978, consistent usages developed whereby the "punk" label was affixed retroactively to bands that had fit the definition developed by Bangs: loud, fast, crude, and angry or pseudo-angry, while "new wave" began to be used exclusively for bands that tended toward the ironic, cool, and distant.[2] Of the original CBGB bands, the Talking Heads most clearly fit the "new wave" label.

By the time the punk–new wave labeling crisis began to subside, musicians and critics in New York City shared a growing sense that the scene was stagnating. Among rock critics, this sense was fueled by the fact that punk represented the first critically acclaimed genre not to find a large audience. Several new directions arose that constituted a "second" wave of new wave bands. One branch was represented by the decidedly noncommercial turn of "no wave," led by Lydia Lunch, the Contortions, and the D. N. A., which became a new underground and shared much with the downtown avant-garde art scene. Another aspect of this second wave was directed toward a wider audience, had more in common with the Talking Heads than the Ramones, and was best represented by bands such as Devo and the B-52s (from Ohio and Georgia, respectively).

---

1. Bernard Gendron, *Between Montmartre and the Mudd Club* (Chicago: University of Chicago Press, 2002), 270. Also see Gendron's chapter on "no wave" (pp. 275–97).

2. An article from early 1978 begins with a discussion of this dilemma of terminology: "One of the more interesting aspects of the current popular music scene is the discussion surrounding the admittedly hairsplitting distinction between punk and new wave. . . . Taken as two sides of a constantly fluctuating and dynamic equation, these terms help describe what is so fascinating about the current renaissance in rock 'n' roll. . . . What has distinguished the local scene, of course, are the ties that join the N.Y. art community with the rock 'n' roll world" —the implication here being that this is also what distinguishes new wave from punk; see Roy Trakin, "Avant Kindergarten (Sturm and Drone)," *Soho Weekly News,* January 26, 1978, 31.

Stephen Holden's article on the B-52s focuses on the "retrotrash" aesthetic of the band, one that was most clearly anticipated by a "first wave" new wave band like Blondie (who, curiously enough, belatedly achieved popularity around the same time as the B-52s). The "historicist" approach of the band has much in common with aspects of what cultural theorist Fredric Jameson later labeled "postmodernism," but perhaps more responsible for the B-52s' impact was their sense of fun and the danceability of the music.[3]

The B-52s' American Graffiti
Stephen Holden

Though they've arrived some 15 years after Andy Warhol made the cover of *Time*, the B-52s strike me as the ultimate pop art rock band. Urbane, funny, and sharp, they use *American Graffiti*–era trash with the precision and purpose of "serious" artists. Yet the actual content of their lyrics is defiantly nonserious. If 15 years ago the Velvet Underground-Fugs art/rock nexus nudged rock & roll along the road to literary respectability, the B-52s nudge it back toward silliness. I haven't seen them perform, but their first album is the most likable New Wave debut since Talking Heads. You can spend hours sifting through its trivia, but you can also frug to it. They may have a New York sensibility, but that sensibility is so ubiquitous in 1979 that they could develop their sound in southern Georgia, a locale which probably accounts for their funkwise rhythm section.

Through a scrupulous compilation of kitsch, the B-52s lovingly reconstruct the sounds and attitudes of post-Sputnik, pre-Vietnam pop America within a New Wave context. Their mining of the past is so thorough that it becomes the basis of a rock style—one that implies almost as much by what it omits (literary sense, adult emotion) as by what it enshrines (nonsense). If I got on my critical high horse, I could mount an argument about how their music consciously reflects a media-disintegrated environment, an electronically blitzed-out culture in which all values have been leveled. But I won't, because the B-52s' music is too much fun. It's not the slightest bit polemical, and they have a great time making it. Clearly, the group cherishes all the detritus—the cultural backdrop of their collective adolescence—that's gone into the album. At their best, they're awesomely convincing in their assertion of the positive side of culture shock, by pointing out the democracy of pop culture. Among dozens of references, some subliminal but most deliberate, they treat early Kinks, *Peter Gunn*, the Shangri-Las, *Star Trek*, early Motown, Duane Eddy, "Telstar," "Pipeline," Petula Clark, and *Beach Blanket Bingo* all with equal respect and humor. No rock group has made me so aware that pop culture, even its dregs, has had a lot more to do with shaping my fantasy life than the "high" culture I was brought up to revere.

---

3. The classic formulation of Jameson's theory may be found in "Postmodernism, or the Cultural Logic of Late Capitalism," *New Left Review* 146 (July–August 1984): 59–92; reprinted in *Postmodernism, or the Cultural Logic of Late Capitalism* (Durham, N.C.: Duke University Press, 1991), 1–54.

Source: "The B-52s' American Graffiti" © Stephen Holden/*Village Voice*.

Their song lyrics seem consciously McLuhanist in their post-literate allusiveness. The language is fractured, reduced to telegraphic popisms. "This is the Space Age/Just don't worry/This is the Space Age/Others like you," they proclaim in the robot chorus that winds up "There's a Moon in the Sky (Called the Moon)." The rest is a confused catalog of pseudo-sci-fi catch-phrases that jumble reality and fantasy so casually you begin to question not only if there's a difference between kiddie-show space travel and the real thing, but also if it matters whether there's a difference. Gamma rays and kryptonite—aren't they finally the same thing, catch words to the stars in a child's garden of TV trash? If the TV screen literally shrinks everything to the same size and degree of reality, don't the transistor radio and even the walkie-talkie do the same thing? In the B-52s' world, all these communications devices are operating at once. Mediums and styles are scrambled together, so that one's time sense finally collapses under the barrage, and all modern culture becomes as simultaneous as the rerun of an instant replay—20 years of trash compacted into a 40-minute docudrama.

At the very least, the B-52's is a superb exercise in camp nostalgia. But I think it's more than that. The best cuts burst with a spirit of real celebration. "Dance This Mess Around," in which they invent wonderful dance names like the Shy Tuna and the Aqua-velva, is an affectionate tribute to the Mashed Potato-Frug era and also a killer boogie cut that's eager to compete with "Stop! In the Name of Love," which it proudly quotes. The quintet's tense, post-primal vocals brim with excitement; Fred Schneider sounds like a Devo-ed Ringo Starr finally "getting back," while Kate Pierson, pleading that she "ain't no limburger," does Patti Smith doing Yoko Ono just about perfectly. "Lava" is a hot, funny, sexual anthem that gets hilarious mileage out of its lava-love-Mauna Loa alliteration. It's also a beautifully constructed call-and-response rock song—terse, catchy, with a knockout punchline (Schneider: "I'm gonna jump in a crater." Girls, gleefully: "See ya later."). "Planet Clare" is a deft exercise in '60s sci-fi kitsch with an absurdist satiric edge ("She drove a Plymouth Satellite/Faster than the speed of light"). "Rock Lobster" conjures up a surrealistic '60s beach party where bikini-clad mermen frug with warbling manta-rays and narwhales. The instrumentation is transcendently tacky, a rollicking farce of guitar and Farfisa.

Is it "great" rock? Maybe. The three major charges that could be leveled against the B-52s are that they're hopelessly arty, hopelessly New Yorky, and hopelessly silly. But for all its arty precision, their music is totally accessible. It may lack classic American roots, but in the endless garbage heap of modern pop culture, the band has found a tradition—and an American one at that. To me, their silliness shows considerable courage. They recapture rock & roll innocence—or at least this 38-year-old writer's idea of innocence—in the only way that seems possible nowadays, by reconstructing it. Their trash rock anthem squirming with animated sea creatures belongs squarely in the tradition of "Tutti Frutti."

Further Reading

Gendron, Bernard. *Between Montmartre and the Mudd Club.* Chicago: University of Chicago Press, 2002.

Jameson, Fredric. "Postmodernism, or the Cultural Logic of Late Capitalism." *New Left Review* 146 (July–August 1984): 59–92; reprinted in Fredric Jameson, *Postmodernism, or the Cultural Logic of Late Capitalism* (Durham, N.C.: Duke University Press, 1991), 1–54.

Rockwell, John. "The Artistic Success of Talking Heads." *New York Times*, September 11, 1977, D14, D16.

Trakin, Roy. "Avant Kindergarten (Sturm and Drone)." *Soho Weekly News,* January 26, 1978, 31, 37.

Discography

The B-52s. *The B-52s.* Reprise/WEA, 1979.
Blondie. *Greatest Hits.* Capitol, 2002.
Devo. *Q: Are We Not Men? A: We Are Devo!* Warner Bros./WEA, 1978.
The Knack. *Get the Knack.* Capitol, 2002.
Lydia Lunch. *Deviations on a Theme: Retrospective.* Provocateur Media, 2006.
Talking Heads. *The Best of Talking Heads.* Rhino/WEA, 2004.

61. UK New Wave

Emerging during the same period in the United Kingdom as the Sex Pistols were artists who bore roughly the same relationship to the Sex Pistols that the Talking Heads and the B-52s had to the Ramones. And while Elvis Costello, Graham Parker, and Joe Jackson all recycled models from pop music's past, they also all featured an angry edge that put them in accord with the "vulgar" side of punk. As described vividly by Caroline Coon, these musicians were all rebelling against the slick professionalism of contemporary rock superstars. Elvis Costello (b. 1954), in addition to employing musical pastiche, extended the notion of pastiche to his appearance (which resembled a nerdish yet defiant Buddy Holly) and, of course, to his name—born Declan MacManus, his first record was released, by a strange coincidence, almost simultaneously with the announcement of Elvis Presley's death on August 16, 1977.

The following interview-profile comes from early in Costello's career. The interviewer, Allan Jones, is clearly in Costello's camp, as he waxes enthusiastically about a solo performance and the two singles that Costello had released thus far, while eagerly anticipating the first album, which was due out shortly. While Jones seems a bit frustrated by Costello's reluctance to explain himself (a tendency decisively reversed in later interviews[1]), Jones observes (or succeeds in getting Costello to observe) Costello's originality and emotional range as a songwriter and his avoidance of clichés. Costello's comments clarify his links with punk: projecting an antiromantic persona, he presents what is virtually a manifesto advocating a return to a "core" ideal of rock that had been lost in the 1970s and rejecting the trappings of fame and celebrity, along with grandiose displays of musical virtuosity that rock stars had increasingly embraced. As he says toward the end of the interview, "The songs are the most important thing."

The Elvis (Costello, That Is) Interview
Allan Jones

Let's talk about the future now, we'll put the past away.
—Elvis Costello, "Less Than Zero"

Elvis Costello was emphatic: he would volunteer no information about his past. "I don't," he said, adjusting his shades impatiently, "really think that the past—my past—is all that interesting.

"I don't see any point in talking about the past. I don't want to get into that. I mean, I haven't just learned the guitar in the last ten minutes, but I'm not going to get talking about what I've done in the past.

"Nobody showed any interest in me then. If you weren't there, you missed it and that's it. It's gone. The people who were there then either appreciated it or they didn't. The past would only be relevant to them. As far as I'm concerned, it's pointless talking about the past. F_____it. I'd just rather talk about the future, you know."

There, I told you he was emphatic didn't I?

Elvis Costello and I are bickering this sundrenched Tuesday afternoon in an office above Stiff Records' London HQ because I had, accidentally, seen and been enthralled by his performance a week earlier at the Nashville Rooms.

Friday, May 27, it was: I'd tubed over to West Kensington to catch the Rumour that night. The presence at the bar of the Nashville, of Stiff executive Jake Riviera, accompanied by an assorted crew of Stiff hirelings and lackeys, seemed, initially, to be of no profound consequence.

---

1. See, for example, Bill Flanagan, "The Last Elvis Costello Interview," *Musician*, March 1986, 40, 42, 44. In this interview, Costello explains how he wanted to create a space free of either macho posturing (as in hard rock or heavy metal) or soul-baring autobiography (as in the singer-songwriter tradition) and reveals a rarely discussed connection between the discourse of music critics and musicians' own ideas about creativity.

Source: "The Elvis (Costello, That Is) Interview," Allan Jones © IPC Media.

There exist, after all, several connections between Stiff, Graham Parker and the Rumour; and, anyway, Jake ain't the kind of cat who'd miss out on a decent lig should one appear on the horizon as it had that evening.

Jake's appearance, however, was not on this occasion relegated to the pursuit of hedonistic adventures. He announced casually that one Elvis Costello, a recent Stiff protege, was to make a previously unscheduled debut as supporting attraction for the Rumour.

This information I received with considerable interest: Elvis Costello, though not yet a name on the lips of the nation, had released two singles ("Less Than Zero" and, more recently, "Alison") of rare distinction.

To see this enigmatic charmer in action was, unquestionably, a proposition not to be overlooked. Well, I dragged myself away from the bar as a brief whisper of applause signalled El's appearance. And there he stood, alone on the stage: black cropped hair swept back, the inevitable shades shielding his eyes, slickly cut Harry Fenton jacket, blue jeans and Fender guitar.

His attitude and performance were both characterised by an aggressive conviction and, as the applause between songs intensified, a clear and thrilling confidence.

Elvis Costello, let me tell you, bowled me out of my breeches that night.

Why, I even swore that if a platter containing such Costello meisterwerks as "(The Angels Wanna Wear) My Red Shoes," "Mystery Dance," "I'm Not Angry" and "Waiting For The End Of The World," was not in the vicinity of my Dansette turntable by the end of the month I'd be around to Stiff looking for the head of Jake Riviera.

The fact that Jake's head remains unsevered would suggest that the platter for which I yearned has been delivered: and so it has, to my immense delight. Trouble is that Stiff, after falling out with Island, are without a distribution organisation. El's album has been temporarily suspended—it was originally due for release this very week, actually. Fear not, however. It will be with you soon: in the meantime, I thought I'd bring you a despatch from the Elvis Costello front . . .

Here we go: Elvis Costello is 22. He's been writing songs for eight years. Since he first negotiated three juvenile chords on a battered guitar, in fact. He reluctantly admits to listening to the likes of the Beatles, Cliff Bennett and Georgie Fame as an adolescent; "Standard stuff. Whatever was on the radio."

Elvis, though he elsewhere proves to be refreshingly honest and forthright in the opinions he expresses, remains defiantly vague about the songs he was composing during this early period of his career: "I've written hundreds of songs," he says. "I write at least a song a week. That doesn't necessarily mean I keep them all.

"They're not all classics. I mean, I've discarded songs I wrote last month because I thought they were inept or didn't match up to the best of what I've written. I wouldn't talk about them, let alone songs I wrote eight years ago."

I had been interested in these earlier songs, I explain, simply because I wanted to form some idea of the pattern and evolution of his writing. The songs collected on his forthcoming album, "My Aim Is True," for instance, are marked by a precocious maturity.

Costello may deal principally with themes familiar in rock—the majority, in fact, are concerned with fiercely detailed accounts of romantic encounters and failures—but he introduces a ruthless honesty to these themes and invests his observations and scenarios with perceptive insights and astonishingly vivid images.

The insecurities and infidelities of relationships, adolescent attempts to attain a personal identity and independence, are examined with sensitive compassion and wit (often quite acerbic, but equally as often, as on the classic "Alison," with an exquisite tenderness).

Always, Costello retains his originality as a lyricist: he avoids conclusively the obvious and tiresome teendream preoccupations of comparative writers like Nils Lofgren (the midget Yank's recent work, at least), Elliott Murphy and Springsteen.

No, Elvis' songs possess the cutting clarity of the best of Graham Parker and Van Morrison: indeed, like this latter pair, Costello's music refers constantly to the classic pop/rock standards of the last decade, each song being sharply defined and full of irresistible hooks and delightful instrumental phrasing (for the verve and incisiveness of the album's sound, some considerable credit must be attributed to Nick Lowe, Elvis' producer).

"This influence stuff," says Costello, when several of the aforementioned musicians are mentioned, "is really irritating, 'cos people are always trying to pin you down to sounding like somebody else. I appreciate the comparison you drew with Graham Parker. I suppose that it's because he's currently maybe the only person that's doing anything like me.

"If there's a general musical area that he's working in, then I accept that I'm working in a similar area and the comparison is validly drawn. And I'd rather be compared to Graham Parker than Tom Jones. If someone came along and said that I sounded like John Denver then I'd f_____worry. It's better to be compared to somebody good; but it still doesn't mean that I sit at home trying to think of ways to re-write songs from 'Heat Treatment.'

"Anyway, if I'd had a record out before Graham Parker, it would all be reversed . . . 'cos, you know, the people who're saying that I sound like Graham Parker are the same people who said that Graham Parker sounded like Bruce Springsteen, who are the same people who said that Bruce Springsteen sounded like Van Morrison, who are the same people who said that Van Morrison sounded the same as Bobby Bland or whoever. You know, the people who NEVER listen to the f_____music."

The prospect of being compared to Springsteen, whose panavision scenarios—replete with so much obvious romantic, rock-mythology imagery of a kind quite antithetical to Costello's writing—fills Elvis with anguish and dread.

"Springsteen always romanticizing the f_____street," he complains, with no little justification. "I'm bored with people who romanticize the f_____street. The street isn't f_____attractive. I mean, I don't pretend to live in the heart of one of the worst areas of the world, right.

"I live near Hounslow. It's a very boring area. It's a terrible place. Awful, Nowhere, Nothing happens.

"There's nothing exciting or glamorous or romantic about it.

"There's nothing glamorous or romantic about the world at the moment. There is no place for glamour or romance. Romance, in the old pop song sense, has gone right out of the f_____window for the moment. Nobody's got the time or the money. It's gone beyond all that. But, please remember, I don't sit around wondering how people see the world, or how they feel about things.

"I don't attempt to express their feelings. I only write about the way I feel. I mean, I'm not arbitrator of public taste or opinion. I don't have a following of people who are waiting for my next word. I hope I never have that kind of following. People should be waiting for their own next word, not mine."

Elvis approached Stiff Records last August: he arrived at their office in West London with a tape of his songs and the response of Jake Riviera and Dave Robinson (also manager of Graham Parker) was immediate and enthusiastic.

They signed him to the label, in fact.

"There was no phenomenal advance," he laughs. "They've bought me an amp and a tape recorder. I'm glad that they're not subsidizing me to any greater extent.

I don't want to be put on a retainer and spend my time ligging around record company offices like a lot of other musicians.

"I don't want any charity. I want to be out gigging, earning money. I don't want anything for nothing. I'm not askin anybody for their f_____charity. I went to a lot of record companies before I came to Stiff. Major record companies. And I never asked them for charity. I didn't go in with any servile attitude.

"I didn't go in and say, 'Look, I've got these songs and, well, with a bit of patching up and a good producer I might make a good record.' I went in and said, 'I've got some great f_____songs, record them and release them.' Stiff were the only ones that showed that kind of faith in me.

"They let me do it. I'm still working, right. I'll only give up the job when I start working with a band."

Elvis mentions, mischievously, that none of the musicians that contributed their services to his album are credited on the sleeve (Nick Lowe gets a production credit on the label, though). It transpires that this was El's idea of a caustic comment upon the contemporary state of the music business—an industry for which Elvis has very little admiration or respect.

He had a caption, in fact, prepared for the sleeve of his album, which would have read: "No thanks to anybody." Unfortunately, the Damned got there first when they had printed on the sleeve of their album: "Thanks to no one." El didn't want anyone to think he'd copped the idea so it was abandoned.

"The people who were directly involved with the album know who they are," El explains, "and they're not the kind of people who'd be worried about credits and namechecks. Equally, the people who were instrumental in stopping me from recording before know who they were, and I wanted to remind them that I hadn't forgotten them.

"Like, I went around for nearly a year with demo tapes before I came to Stiff, and it was always the same response. 'We can't hear the words.' 'It isn't commercial enough.' 'There aren't any singles.' Idiots. Those tapes were just voice and guitar demos. I didn't have enough money to do any thing with a band. It was just a lack of imagination on the part of those people at the record companies. I felt as if I was bashing my head against a brick wall, those people just weren't prepared to listen to the songs.

"It's a terrible position to be in. You start thinking you're mad. You listen to the radio and you watch the TV and you hear a lot of f_____rubbish. You very rarely turn on the radio or TV and hear anything exciting, right? And, all the time, you know that you're capable of producing something infinitely better.

"But I never lost faith. I'm convinced in my own talent, yeah. Like I said, I wasn't going up to these people meekly and saying, 'Look, with your help and a bit of polishing up, and with all your expertise and knowledge of the world of music we might have a moderate success on our hands.'

"I was going in thinking. 'You're a bunch of f_____idiots who don't know what you're doing. I'm bringing you a lot of good songs, why don't you go ahead and f_____well record them.' They didn't seem to understand that kind of approach.

"No, it didn't make me bitter. I was already bitter. I knew what it would be like. I had no illusions. I have no illusions at all about the music business. It was no sudden shock to be confronted by these idiots. I didn't ever think that I was going to walk into a record company to meet all these fat guys smoking big cigars who'd say something like. 'Stick with me son, I'll make you a STAR.'

"I'm not starry-eyed in the slightest. You can tell what all these people are like instinctively. You just have to look at them to tell that they're f_____idiots. But, I don't want to come off sounding like I'm obsessed with the music business.

"I couldn't give a s_____ about the music business. They just don't know any-thing. That's all you've got to remember. They're irrelevant. I don't give any thought to any of those people. They're not worth my time."

Elvis, who by this time seems to be metamorphising before my very eyes into the superhuman guise of Captain Verbals, is telling me about his album. It was recorded, he says, on his days off from work (he is a computer analyst in Acton), over a very brief period.

He was fortunate, he readily admits, that Nick Lowe was so sympathetic a pro-ducer: their respective ideas were entirely compatible and there were few arguments about the sound and instrumentation employed. All the songs were written within weeks of the first session; "Less Than Zero," his first single, was written three days before it was recorded, for instance.

Elvis just says he felt inspired and excited. The hits just kept on coming ("My Aim Is True," incidentally, is the first album I've heard for ages that sounds as if it is essentially a collection of Top Ten singles), as it were.

"I just love the sound of the album," Elvis enthuses. "'Cos I love things that sound great on the radio. 'Less Than Zero,' I thought sounded great on the radio. The record isn't for people with f_____great hi-fis. I'm not interested in those people, or that kind of mentality. I don't want my records to be used to demonstrate f_____ stereos in Lasky's. I just want people to listen to the f_____music.

"I don't want to be successful so that I can get a lot of money and retire to a house in the f_____country. I don't want any of that rock and roll rubbish. I don't want to go cruising in Hollywood or hang out at all the star parties. I'm not interested in any of that. It's the arse end of rock and roll. I'm just interested in playing.

"I want to put a band together as soon as possible and get out on the f_____ road. We're auditioning people this week. We're looking for young people. People that want to get out and play. Putting a band together is the most important thing at the moment.

"I think it might be difficult getting the right kind of people and I can imagine us wading through a right bunch of idiots. The group sound I want will be a lot sparser than the album sound. I just want bass, drum, guitar—my guitar—and for keyboards we'll probably go for a Vox or Farfisa sound.

"I want to get away from the conventional group sound. I'd say that I want a kind of pop group line-up, but people might take that as something lightweight or trivial. But it will be a pop line-up in the sense that it won't be a rock band.

"I hate hard-rock bands. I hate anything with f_____extended solos or bands that are concerned with any kind of instrumental virtuosity. I can listen to maybe 15 seconds of someone like the Crusaders, say, before I get very bored. I know how good they are because everybody keeps telling me how f_____marvellous they are. But I get bored.

"There are going to be no f_____soloists in my band. The songs are the most important thing. I want the songs to mean something to people. I don't mean by that that I want them to be significant. It's just that too much rock has cut itself off from people. It's become like ballet or something. Ballet is only for people who can afford to go and see it. It's not for anybody else. You don't get ballet going on in your local pub.

"There's a lot of rock music that's become exclusive and it's of no use to anyone. Least of all me. Music has to get to people. In the heart, in the head. I don't care where, as long as it f_____gets them. So much music gets thrown away. It's such a f_____waste.

"That's why I like and write short songs. It's a discipline. There's no disguise. You can't cover up songs like that by dragging banks of f_____synthesizers and choirs of angels. They have to stand up on their own. With none of that nonsense. Songs are just so f_____effective. People seem to have forgotten that.

"Like, people used to live their lives by songs. They were like calendars or diaries. And they were pop songs. Not elaborate f_____pieces of music. You wouldn't say, like, 'Yeah, that's the time I went out with Janet, we went to see the LSO playing Mozart.' You'd remember you went out with Janet because they were playing 'Summer In The City' on the radio."

You will have gathered by now that Elvis is committed to success: he's not, however, altogether sure when that success will be achieved.

"There are a lot of people," he says, "who should be successful. If ability had anything to do with success then there would be a whole lot of obscure people who'd be famous and there would be a whole lot of famous people who'd be lingering in obscurity."

Was there anyone, I wondered, that he would like to see becoming famous?

"Yeah," he replied "Me."

Further Reading

Clayton-Lea, Tony. *Elvis Costello: A Biography.* New York: Fromm International, 1998.
Coon, Caroline. *1988: The New Wave Punk Rock Explosion.* London: Omnibus Press, 1977.
Flanagan, Bill. "The Last Elvis Costello Interview." *Musician,* March 1986, 40, 42, 44.

Discography

Costello, Elvis. *My Aim Is True.* Columbia, 1977.
_____. *This Year's Model.* Columbia, 1978.
_____. *The Best of Elvis Costello: The First 10 Years.* Hip-O Records, 2007.
Jackson, Joe. *Look Sharp!* A&M, 1979.
_____. *Greatest Hits.* A&M, 1996.
Parker, Graham. *Heat Treatment.* Polygram International, 1976.

PART 5

The 1980s

62. *Thriller* Begets the "King of Pop"

We were already introduced to Michael Jackson (1958–2009) briefly in Berry Gordy's account of Motown in the 1960s (see Chapter 32). Jackson was arguably the greatest child prodigy in the history of post-1955 popular music, and his early recordings with the Jackson Five intrigued adults as much for their maturity (and uncanny absorption of James Brown's vocal style) as they did teenagers and preteens with their visceral excitement.

Jackson's first records as a solo artist in 1971, like those of the Jackson Five, were remarkably successful. However, Jackson's solo career did not really take off until the late 1970s. In 1978, while starring in the film musical *The Wiz* as the Scarecrow, Jackson met producer Quincy Jones. The two collaborated on Jackson's next album, *Off the Wall,* which outsold his previous solo efforts and garnered favorable critical notices. Jones and Jackson successfully updated Jackson's sound, presenting Jackson as a mature artist capable of appealing to dancers and Top 40 radio programmers alike. *Off the Wall* only hinted at what was to come. *Thriller,* Jackson's next album (again produced by Jones), released late in 1982, became an international phenomenon, breaking all sales records and selling over 110 million copies to date. *Thriller* did not so much create a new style as it successfully synthesized aspects of preexisting ones: on it, one hears soulful, middle-of-the-road ballads ("The Girl Is Mine," sung with Paul McCartney), slick funk-disco ("Billie Jean"), and funky heavy metal ("Beat It"). This stylistic blending enabled Jackson to transcend boundaries between audiences that music industry experts believed were unassailable. Robert Christgau offered an alternate explanation when he argued that synth-pop had helped prepare and create an audience for the album through "its rapprochement between white rock and dance music."[1]

Videos provided another key to Jackson's success, since he began conceiving of his songs as soundtracks. The videos for "Billie Jean," "Beat It," and "Thriller" were more than mere promotional vehicles for the recordings—they were "minifilms," small narratives with budgets that dwarfed those of previous videos. Jackson's understanding of how to employ his singing and dancing skills within the rhetoric of video enabled him to exploit his abilities as a *performer,* rather than as a *musician* per se. Viewed in this way, the magnitude of his success is inextricable from the age of music video.

The years following *Thriller* were tumultuous ones for Jackson: he released "We Are the World" (1985, cowritten with Lionel Ritchie and coperformed with many other stars to benefit famine relief); another Jones-produced album, *Bad* (1987); and an autobiography, *Moonwalker* (1988), and he began to receive an increasing amount of media attention, much of it sensationalistic. *Bad* was a very successful recording by any standard other than that set by *Thriller* and, like its predecessor, was extremely eclectic, featuring funk, heavy metal–influenced songs, love ballads, and humanitarian anthems in the vein of "We Are the World." But the reception of the album betrayed a split between the rapturous adoration of Jackson's fans and the lukewarm reaction of critics, especially in the United States, a reaction fanned by negative media attention over changes in Jackson's appearance and rumors about other personal eccentricities.

For many listeners and viewers, Jackson's physical transformation gave a new inflection to the concept of "crossover," and these cosmetic changes constitute the focus of Greg Tate's review of *Bad.* Tate revisits the idea of Jackson's precocity and discusses the relationship of Jackson's 1980s recordings to the legacy of Berry Gordy and the Motown recordings of the 1960s. Tate considers the relationship of black identity to the process of middle-class acculturation, an approach that cautions against the easy dismissal of Motown or *Thriller* as a racial "sellout." Yet, at the same time, he implies some connection between the aesthetic disappointment of *Bad* and Jackson's ongoing physical repudiation of his racial heritage. Tate is not alone: many other cultural critics have taken up the subject of Jackson's fluctuating physical appearance, which generates so much attention that it threatens to obscure appreciation of his musical achievements.[2]

---

1. "Rock 'n' Roller Coaster," p. 40. For an account in a music trade publication, see Paul Grein, "Michael Jackson Cut Breaks AOR Barrier," *Billboard,* December 18, 1982, 1, 58.

2. See, for example, Michele Wallace, "Michael Jackson, Black Modernisms and 'The Ecstasy of Communication,'" in *Invisibility Blues: From Pop to Theory* (London: Verso, 1990), 77–90; Kobena Mercer, "Monster Metaphors: Notes on Michael Jackson's *Thriller,*" in *Sound and Vision: The Music Video Reader,* ed. Simon Frith, Andrew Goodwin, and Lawrence Grossberg, 93–108 (London and New York: Routledge, 1993); and Susan Willis, "I Want the Black One: Is There a Place for Afro-American Culture in Commodity Culture," in *A Primer for Daily Life* (London: Routledge, 1991), 108–32.

I'm White! What's Wrong with Michael Jackson
Greg Tate

There are other ways to read Michael Jackson's blanched skin and disfigured African features than as signs of black self-hatred become self-mutilation. Waxing fanciful, we can imagine the-boy-who-would-be-white as a William Gibson-ish work of science fiction: harbinger of a trans-racial tomorrow where genetic deconstruction has become the norm and Narcissism wears the face of all human Desire. Musing empathetic, we may put the question, who does Mikey want to be today? The Pied Piper, Peter Pan, Christopher Reeve, Skeletor, or Miss Diana Ross? Our Howard Hughes? Digging into our black nationalist bag, Jackson emerges a casualty of America's ongoing race war—another Negro gone mad because his mirror reports that his face does not conform to the Nordic ideal.

To fully appreciate the sickness of Jackson's savaging of his African physiognomy you have to recall that back when he wore the face he was born with, black folk thought he was the prettiest thing since sliced sushi. (My own mother called Michael pretty so many times I almost got a complex.) Jackson and I are the same age, damn near 30, and I've always had a love-hate thing going with the brother. When we were both moppets I envied him, the better dancer, for being able to arouse the virginal desires of my female schoolmates, shameless oglers of his (and Jermaine's) tenderoni beefcake in *16* magazine. Even so, no way in those say-it-loud-I'm-black-and-I'm-proud days could you not dig Jackson heir to the James Brown dance throne. At age 10, Jackson's footwork and vocal machismo seemed to scream volumes about the role of genetics in the cult of soul and the black sexuality of myth. The older folk might laugh when he sang shake it, shake it baby, ooh, ooh or teacher's gonna show you, all about loving. Yet part of the tyke's appeal was being able to simulate being lost in the hot sauce way before he was supposed to know what the hot sauce even smelt like. No denying he *sounded* like he knew the real deal.

In this respect, Jackson was the underweaned creation of two black working-class traditions: that of boys being forced to bypass childhood along the fast track to manhood, and that of rhythm and blues auctioning off the race's passion for song, dance, sex, and spectacle. Accelerated development became a life-imperative after slavery, and R&B remains the redemption of minstrelsy—at least it was until Jackson made crossover mean lightening your skin and whitening your nose.

Slavery, minstrelsy, and black bourgeoisie aspirations are responsible for three of the more pejorative notions about blacks in this country—blacks as property, as ethnographic commodities, and as imitation rich white people. Given this history, there's a fine line between a black entertainer who appeals to white people and one who sells out the race in pursuit of white appeal. Berry Gordy, Bürgermeister of crossover's Bauhaus, walked that line with such finesse that some black folk were shocked to discover via *The Big Chill* that many whites considered Motown *their* music. Needless to say, Michael Jackson has crossed so way far over the line that there ain't no coming back—assuming through surgical transformation of his face a singular infamy in the annals of tomming.

The difference between Gordy's crossover dream world and Jackson's is that Gordy's didn't preclude the notion that black is beautiful. For him the problem was his pupils not being ready for prime time. Motown has raised brows for its grooming of Detroit ghetto kids in colored genteel manners, so maybe there were people

Source: "I'm White! What's Wrong with Michael Jackson" *Village Voice*, September 22, 1987. Reprinted in *Flyboy in the Buttermilk*, 1992, Simon & Schuster.

who thought Gordy was trying to make his charges over into pseudo-Caucasoids. Certainly this insinuation isn't foreign to the work of rhythm and blues historians Charles Keil and Peter Guralnick, both of whom write of Motown as if it weren't hot and black enough to suit their blood, or at least their conception of bloods. But the intermingling of working-class origins and middle-class acculturation are too mixed up in black music's evolution to allow for simpleminded purist demands for a black music free of European influence, or of the black desire for a higher standard of living and more cultural mobility. As an expression of '60s black consciousness, Motown symbolized the desire of blacks to get their foot in the bank door of the American dream. In the history of affirmative action Motown warrants more than a footnote beneath the riot accounts and NAACP legal maneuvers.

As a black American success story, the Michael Jackson of *Thriller* is an extension of the Motown integrationist legacy. But the Michael Jackson as skin job represents the carpetbagging side of black advancement in the affirmative action era. The fact that we are now producing young black men and women who conceive of their African inheritance as little more than a means to cold-crash mainstream America and then cold-dis—if not merely put considerable distance between—the brothers and sisters left behind. In this sense Jackson's decolorized flesh reads as the buppy version of Dorian Gray, a blaxploitation nightmare that offers this moral: Stop, the face you save may be your own.

In 1985 black people cherished *Thriller's* breakthrough as if it were their own battering ram against the barricades of American apartheid. Never mind how many of those kerzillon LPs we bought, forget how much Jackson product we had bought all those years before that—even with his deconstructed head, we wanted this cat to tear the roof off the all-time-greatest-sales sucker bad as he did. It's like *Thriller* was this generation's answer to the Louis-Schmeling fight or something. Oh, the Pyrrhic victories of the disenfranchised. Who would've thought this culture hero would be cut down to culture heel, with a scalpel? Or maybe it's just the times. To those living in New York City and currently witnessing a rebirth of black consciousness in protest politics, advocacy journalism (read *The City Sun!* read *The City Sun!*) and the arts, Jackson seems dangerously absurd.

Proof that God don't like ugly, the title of Michael's new LP, *Bad* (Epic), accurately describes the contents in standard English. (Jackson apparently believes that *bad* can apply to both him and L.L. Cool J.) No need to get stuck on making comparisons with *Thriller*, *Bad* sounds like home demos Michael cut over a long weekend. There's not one song here that any urban contemporary hack couldn't have laid in a week, let alone two years. Several of the up-tempo numbers wobble in with hokey bass lines out of the Lalo Schifrin fakebook, and an inordinate number begin with ominous science fiction synthnoise—invariably preceding an anti-climax. *Bad* has hooks, sure, and most are searching for a song, none more pitifully than the flyweight title track, which throws its chorus around like a three-year-old brat.

The only thing *Bad* has going for it is that it was made by the same artist who made *Thriller*. No amount of disgust for Jackson's even newer face (cleft in the chin) takes anything away from *Thriller*. Everything on that record manages a savvy balance between machine language and human intervention, between palpitating heart and precision tuning. *Thriller* is a record that doesn't know how to stop giving pleasure. Every note on the mutha sings and breathes masterful pop instincts: the drumbeats, the bass lines, the guitar chicken scratches, the aleatoric elements. The weaving of discrete details into fine polyphonic mesh reminds me of those African field recordings where simultaneity and participatory democracy, not European harmony, serve as the ordering principle.

Bad, as songless as *Thriller* is songful, finds Jackson performing material that he has absolutely no emotional commitment to—with the exception of spitefully named

"Dirty Diana," a groupie fantasy. The passion and compassion of "Beat It," "Billie Jean," and "Wanna Be Startin' Somethin'" seemed genuine, generated by Jackson's perverse attraction to the ills of teen violence and teen pregnancy. There was something frightful and compelling about this mollycoddled mama's boy delivering lapidary pronouncements from his Xanadu like "If you can't feed your baby, then don't have a baby." While the world will hold its breath and turn blue in the face awaiting the first successful Michael Jackson paternity suit, he had the nerve to sing, "This kid is not my son." Not even David Bowie could create a subtext that coy and rakish on the surface and grotesque at its depths.

Only in its twisted aspects does *Bad*, mostly via the "Bad" video, outdo *Thriller*. After becoming an artificial white man, now he wants to trade on his ethnicity. Here's Jackson's sickest fantasy yet: playing the role of a black preppie returning to the ghetto, he not only offers himself as a role model he literally screams at the brothers "You ain't nothin'!" Translation: Niggers ain't shit. In Jackson's loathsome conception of the black experience, you're either a criminal stereotype or one of the Beautiful People. Having sold the world pure pop pleasure on *Thriller*, Jackson returns on *Bad* to see his own race hatred. If there's 35 million sales in that, be ready to head for the hills ya'll.

After the record-setting *Bad* tour, Jackson released *Dangerous* late in 1991. With the assistance of producer Terry Riley, Jackson updated his sound to incorporate elements of hip-hop and new jack swing. Like *Bad*, the album was hugely successful in commercial terms (with worldwide sales eventually surpassing 40 million) but drew mixed critical notices. The release of the album was preceded by a single, "Black or White," the video of which premiered simultaneously on television channels around the world. The 14-minute video attracted attention for a famous "morphing" sequence toward the end of the song in which people of various races, ages, and genders blurred into one another, and for a long musicless coda in which Jackson dances, destroys property in a rage, and grabs his crotch.[3]

In 1993, negative media attention came to a head when Jackson became involved in a court case on charges of child molestation that were eventually settled out of court. The firestorm of publicity led to cancellation of Jackson's ongoing *Dangerous* tour and the withdrawal of tour sponsorship by Pepsi. Although he had devoted much effort to humanitarian causes throughout the eighties and early nineties— donating huge sums to charities for children, AIDS research, and scholarship funds for African Americans—by the mid-nineties his career was in danger of being overshadowed by scandals. His brief marriage to Lisa Marie Presley (daughter of Elvis) from 1994 to 1996 only seemed to add to the aura of strangeness that increasingly engulfed him.

Despite these personal setbacks, throughout the rest of the 1990s and into the early years of the new millennium Jackson remained quite active artistically, producing *HIStory: Past, Present and Future, Book I* (1995), a double CD that combined a greatest hits collection with 15 new tracks; *Ghosts* (1996), a mini-film with Stephen King described as the longest music video ever (it ran 38 minutes); *Blood on the Dance Floor:*

---

3. For more on "Black or White," see Eric Lott, "The Aesthetic Ante: Pleasure, Pop Culture, and the Middle Passage," *Callaloo* 17, no. 2 (Spring 1994): 545–55; and David Brackett, "Black or White? Michael Jackson and the Idea of Crossover," *Popular Music and Society* 35, no. 1 (2012): 1–17.

HIStory in the Mix (1997), a CD combining remixes of tracks from *HIStory* with five new songs; and, finally, *Invincible* (2001), the last album of new material released during his life. While the music and the videos all featured new touches (e.g., the increase of "industrial" timbres and other sounds associated with techno, sampling, collaborations with rappers), the dominant themes in his lyrics of paranoia, predatory women, and the need to address various humanitarian crises could all be traced back to his work in the 1980s, as could the seamless musical blend of genres that he pioneered in *Thriller*.

At the time of his death in 2009, Jackson had established himself as the most successful individual popular musician of all time, surpassing the sales records and global reach of Elvis Presley. To understand the international reach of his popularity, one need consider the fact that only 10 percent of the sales of his last three albums came from the United States, and that his record-setting tours after 1989 avoided the United States except for Hawaii. He virtually redefined the stylistic basis of the popular music mainstream in the early 1980s and established the music video as both a central feature of popular music promotion and an art form. Even as he experienced unprecedented celebrity, his physical transformations, androgynous appearance, and reclusive lifestyle provoked public debates on the nature of identity. When he died on June 25, 2009, Jackson was in the midst of preparations for a series of 50 concerts planned for the O2 arena in London. These preparations were edited into a film, *This Is It* (2009), which showed Jackson in top form working with musicians and dancers. *Michael*, a CD released in 2010, began what promises to be a long string of posthumous releases.

The following article is one of numerous career retrospectives on Jackson released in the wake of his death. This profile of Bruce Swedien, engineer on Jackson's most successful recordings, reveals a different side of the singer's personality, as Swedien focuses on Jackson's professionalism and musicality. That said, this article does not ignore Jackson's peccadillos, but rather presents them within the milieu responsible for producing the work through which he will be remembered.

Don't Stop 'Til You Get Enough: Bruce Swedien Remembers the Times with Michael Jackson
Daryl Easlea

Here's irony for you: there were several things timed for the release of Michael Jackson's London shows that were to provide testimony to the man's craft and heritage rather than focus on the walking *National Enquirer* story he had become. At the end

Source: Don't Stop 'Til You Get Enough: Bruce Swedien Remembers the Times with Michael Jackson, © Daryll Easlea 2009 With kind permission from Record Collector.

of July, the superlative Hip-O Select box set, *Hello World*, put all of his solo Motown recordings in one place. The other, Bruce Swedien's touching, technical book *In The Studio With Michael Jackson* gave a vital insight to Jackson the performer and craftsman.

Something he has been working on for the best part of three years, it's definitely a book for the aficionado, detailing the methods (and frequently, the microphones) that the pair used in the studio. These records are so perfectly formed; I'd rather like to think they were beamed in from Pluto than ascertaining what Shure™ high performance microphone they used. But find out, in a good way, we do. Swedien is an engaging raconteur and makes the occasionally dry text in his book come along with his joyous American Scandinavian.

There is a brilliant picture on the cover of Quincy Jones, Michael Jackson and Swedien in the studio from the mid-'80s that goes a long way to defining their relationship: Jones is looking to the left, his eye on the bigger picture, Jackson looking straight ahead, his afro growing out; and Swedien looking at them both with the air of a concerned relative. This care permeates his work. Can you think of a snare so crisp as on Billie Jean or a gospel choir so contained as that on another of his works, Donna Summer's on "Love Is In Control (Finger On The Trigger)."

Like the best work Jackson produced, "Love Is In Control" is one of those records that if you have a problem with, you have a problem with life itself. There must have been something in the water, Jones and Swedien created this bright otherworldly pop-funk that sounds like tomorrow, even thirty years later. And let us not forget that one of the records that they made together, *Thriller*, sold 104 million copies worldwide, which is why the global outpouring of grief for its maker has been so spectacular. . . .

Jones and Swedien first worked with Jackson on *The Wiz* in 1977, but their first true collaboration was Jackson's grown-up debut album, *Off The Wall*, released in August 1979. It remains Jackson's most exuberant statement. Keen to celebrate his maturity, Jackson stepped outside of the family cocoon and made a record that sounded at once futuristic and adventurous, bending and shaping the genre of pop. "The real transition was *Off The Wall*—he wanted that to be his coming of age musical statement, and if you really listen to that and compare it to the stuff before, that is exactly what it is."

The years of Motown schooling had paid off: "Michael was the complete professional," Swedien recalls. "Always prepared. When we did a vocal with Michael, I don't ever remember him ever having the lyrics on the music stand in front of him. He'd been up the night before and committed them all to memory. This is the mark of a true professional. Punch-ins weren't even an issue. They were the exception rather than the rule."

The opening track and lead single, "Don't Stop 'Til You Get Enough" is one of the best singles of all-time. Take away the contemporaneous references to "the force," and you have something that is timeless; from its itching bass synth intro and Jackson's vocal explosion, it is one of the greatest side one, track one records ever. The detail in the track is astonishing, yet this is hardly a clinical exercise in studio trickery. It even involves a lot of glass being tapped with sticks. "At the beginning of 'Don't Stop,' that's Michael, his brothers and even Janet playing soda bottles. I got out all my classic ribbon microphones to capture it." From rattling bottles to the smooth disco of "Rock With You" and the emotion of "She's Out Of My Life," *Off The Wall* was an enormous seller, and bridged the '70s and '80s effortlessly, seeing off the death of disco and founding the sort of pop-dance that no-one in the world could escape.

Recorded between April and November 1982, *Thriller* will be the album for which Jackson is remembered. Swedien remembers with great affection the ease of it all. "The main part of *Thriller* only took three months to record. That's the result of their musical understanding—talk about prepared, holy cow. Everything was written before it came to the studio. Most people would have been delighted to have material the strength of Michael's demos!"

Jackson, as he did for his entire career, did not just drop by for his vocals and leave. "Michael hung through the whole process. He was so different from anybody else I every worked with. A lot of people would be very late to a session. Michael was always early, always. And he was totally prepared. He'd have his lyrics, have a little briefcase. He used to carry a lot of stuff in a grocery bag, but always prepared, no exceptions."

It was a time of magic, experiment—from Rod Temperton writing the rap for Vincent Price on Thriller in a back of cab on the way to the session, to Paul McCartney dropping by and being the consummate professional to Eddie Van Halen popping in and rocking out to the undisputed pop masterpiece of Billie Jean,[4] the album was the height of the A team's collaborative work. And that was before the four foot by three piece of plywood with Masonite (*the all-purpose hardwood best used in wobble board—carpentry Ed.*) known as the "bathroom stomp board" on the album's opener, "Wanna Be Startin' Somethin.'" "The bathroom stomp board was Michael's idea—we brought it in the studio, we had to mic it up and he played it. Michael had drum cases set up that he would use as musical instruments that he always played those things himself." The effect is used for all of three seconds half way through the record. Such was the detail.

The final collaboration with Quincy Jones, *Bad* saw the whole Michael Jackson zoo in full effect. And, in this instance, it *was* an actual zoo. "Bubbles was in the studio with us," Swedien chuckles. "He was a juvenile delinquent though. When he'd get out of line, Michael would take off his black loafer and whap him on the head to shape him up a little. He would be up in the control room with us with his trainer Bob Hughes. After a while when we'd all had enough of Bubbles, Michael would send him home." And if the chimp wasn't enough, the snake would be there too. "The boa, Muscles, was with us during *Bad* as well. Quincy was absolutely terrified of snakes. Rod [Temperton] loved Muscles, though. We let him crawl all over the control console and he could not bump a button. He liked it because it was warm. He was everywhere." The chimp and the snake did Jackson's work rate or the hit rate, and *Bad* was one of the most eagerly anticipated album releases of all time when it appeared at the end of August 1987. Although chock-full of pop nuts, it was no *Thriller*, and *only* sold around 30 million. That said, it remains the only album in US history to contain five No. 1 singles.

By the time of the recording of the near 80 minute-long *Dangerous*, between June 1990 and October 1991, the mania really had kicked in; Jackson was self-producing; everything had become exaggerated. He was listening to the street, getting collaborators like new jack swing pioneer Teddy Riley to assist him. The album needed a grand statement to kick it off. Swedien co-wrote the album's opener, Jam. "It was no accident that Jam was such a huge song. I wrote it with René Moore; we had this idea of looping hi-energy drum tracks. Michael got really involved and we took it to the sky. It gives me chills thinking about those sessions. Michael and I had a saying when we were recording *Dangerous*—'the quality goes in before the name goes on,' and we believed that."

HIStory was recorded in the mid 90s, after Jackson's first court case; "I noticed a difference as the albums we worked together on progressed but his musicality never wavered. With Michael the musical boundaries were always very wide no matter how you looked at it." The studio became a place for Michael to escape, to retreat to what he knew. "I set up a room for him in the studio, where he had all his stuff in there and he could go in there and keep everybody out. He used to take a nap every day for 45 minutes and he'd lock the damn door! I used to worry that there would be a fire, but he told me repeatedly not to worry. He was a little out there."

For Swedien, he has been able to make his hobby his job for the best part of 50 years, and shows few signs of flagging. "It's been rather interesting, you could say.

---

4. Eddie Van Halen played on "Beat It" rather than "Billie Jean."

It kept me off the street. When anybody needs some high-class mixing here I am." And what next for the avuncular engineer? "I'm going to be messing around with Michael's stuff. I have been involved with some of the new material, but I have no idea of what they are intending to do with it. There is some wonderful stuff there." Swedien, ever the gentleman, would not divulge any more. His favourite artist has gone, and everything is rightfully a little raw.

Considering that Swedien worked with Jackson from "Ease On Down The Road" from 1977's *The Wiz* to his most recent work; to finish, what would be the one track if he had to distil it all down, that would encapsulate Michael's work? Swedien takes another long and considered pause. "I'd have to say one that isn't his, but it is Michael Jackson unique. It's his version of Smile, the Charlie Chaplin thing. That was his favourite song. And we'd long talked about recording it. We recorded it at the Hit Factory and Jeremy Lubbock did the orchestration, David Foster is on it. Michael sang that vocal live with the orchestra. Not many singers full stop could do that quality of vocal performance with the orchestra. Granted, we did some little fixes in it but not very much. That's the way he sang it. When we got to the end of it, it gets real quiet and Michael says to me, 'Bruce can I talk to the orchestra?' I held them in place and Michael comes out and thanked each and every one of them. They applauded him by tapping their bows on their music stands. I saw tears in his eyes." For those of you not familiar with his version, it's at the end of the second disc of *HIStory*. It's good, but it'll never be "Don't Stop 'Til You Get Enough."

As we say our goodbyes, Swedien says in a low, sombre voice. "Michael Jackson was the best. Not just as a vocalist but as musician. He took it to the sky. He could play piano a little but he wasn't that kind of a musician. Michael's instrument was his voice and his ideas. Quincy's instrument, and mine I guess, was the studio. It was such a great thing working with Michael; we just kept pushing the musical boundaries. Was I lucky or what?"

Further Reading

Brown, Geoff. *The Complete Guide to the Music of Michael Jackson and the Jackson Family.* New York: Omnibus Press, 1996.

George, Nelson. *The Michael Jackson Story.* London: Dell, 1984.

Hidalgo, Susan, and Robert G. Weiner. "'Wanna Be Startin' Somethin': MJ in the Scholarly Literature: A Selected Bibliographic Guide." *Journal of Pan African Studies* 3, no. 7 (March 2010): 14–28.

Jackson, Michael. *Moonwalk.* New York: Doubleday, 1988.

Mercer, Kobena. "Monster Metaphors: Notes on Michael Jackson's 'Thriller.'" In *Sound and Vision: The Music Video Reader*, ed. Simon Frith, Andrew Goodwin, and Lawrence Grossberg, 93–108. London and New York: Routledge, 1993.

Special Issue on Michael Jackson. *Journal of Popular Music Studies* 23, no. 1 (2011).

Special Issue on Michael Jackson. *Popular Music and Society* 35, no. 1 (2012).

Taraborrelli, Randy J. *Michael Jackson—The Magic, the Madness, the Whole Story, 1958–2009.* New York: Grand Central Publishing, 2009.

Wallace, Michelle. *Invisibility Blues: From Pop to Theory.* London: Verso, 1990.

Willis, Susan. *A Primer for Daily Life.* New York: Routledge, 1991.

Discography

Jackson, Michael. *Off the Wall.* Epic, 1979.

_____. *One Day in Your Life.* Motown, 1981.

_____. *Thriller*. Epic, 1982.
_____. *Bad*. Epic, 1987.
_____. *Dangerous*. Epic, 1991.
_____. *HIStory: Past, Present and Future, Book I*. Epic, 1995.
_____. *Blood on the Dance Floor: HIStory in the Mix*. MJJ Music, 1997.
_____. *Invincible*. MJJ Music, 2001.

63. Madonna and the Performance of Identity

Along with Michael Jackson, Madonna (b. 1958) was one of the first stars to truly understand and exploit the potential of music video and MTV. Even more than Jackson, she relied less on conventional musical chops than on creative visual self-presentation, choreography, and dancing. Both Michael Jackson's hits from his *Thriller* album and Madonna's early hits proved that a significant audience existed for dance-oriented recordings. In fact, Madonna's early recordings found success in dance clubs before they were played on mainstream pop radio and before she ever made a video. Her early videos projected a kind of ironic pastiche, playing off well-known cinematic sequences; this occurred most strikingly in her video for "Material Girl" (1985), in which Madonna presented herself as a Marilyn Monroe–type character in a scene based on the performance of the song "Diamonds Are a Girl's Best Friend" (from *Gentlemen Prefer Blondes*, the 1954 film featuring Monroe).[1] Madonna's early image also made much of her thrift-store attire, a look that had a lot in common with another female star from this period who figured prominently on MTV: Cyndi Lauper.

Madonna subsequently proved herself adept at manipulating her image and in maintaining media interest in her career—Jon Pareles memorably described her as a "virtuoso of the superficial."[2] Her flaunting of her sexuality while presenting herself as being "in control" (i.e., consciously choosing to flaunt her sexuality) provided a particularly potent model for young female fans (dubbed "wannabes") and fueled debate about whether the Madonna persona represented a new form of feminism or the repudiation of it. Because of her obvious

---

1. See E. Ann Kaplan's analysis in *Rocking around the Clock: Music Television, Postmodernism and Consumer Culture* (London: Methuen, 1987), 117–27.

2. Jon Pareles, "Madonna's Return to Innocence," *New York Times*, October 23, 1994, sec. 2, 1, 38.

delight and skill in publicly manipulating this persona, Madonna has become a favorite of cultural critics.[3]

The following essay by Camille Paglia presents a good overview of Madonna's career up through the early 1990s, with a particularly strong focus on her videos. While Paglia's views on feminism provoked a storm of controversy in the early 1990s, her enthusiasm for Madonna is related to her ideas about the importance of instinctual sexuality, which, in turn, formed part of her critique of feminism. Since Madonna's presentation of her sexuality constituted an undeniable part of her fascination, Paglia's account illuminates Madonna's enormous impact in ways that a more conventional, "distanced" academic account could not.

Venus of the Radio Waves
Camille Paglia

I'm a dyed-in-the-wool, true-blue Madonna fan.

It all started in 1984, when Madonna exploded onto MTV with a brazen, insolent, in-your-face American street style, which she had taken from urban blacks, Hispanics, and her own middle-class but turbulent and charismatic Italian American family. From the start, there was a flamboyant and parodistic element to her sexuality, a hard glamour she had learned from Hollywood cinema and from its devotees, gay men and drag queens.

Madonna is a dancer. She thinks and expresses herself through dance, which exists in the eternal Dionysian realm of music. Dance, which she studied with a gay man in her home state of Michigan, was her avenue of escape from the conventions of religion and bourgeois society. The sensual language of her body allowed her to transcend the over-verbalized codes of her class and time.

Madonna's great instinctive intelligence was evident to me from her earliest videos. My first fights about her had to do with whether she was a good dancer or merely a well-coached one. As year by year she built up the remarkable body of her video work, with its dazzling number of dance styles, I have had to fight about that less and less. However, I am still at war about her with feminists and religious conservatives (an illuminating alliance of contemporary puritans).

Most people who denigrate Madonna do so out of ignorance. The postwar baby-boom generation in America, to which I belong, has been deeply immersed in popular culture for thirty-five years. Our minds were formed by rock music, which has

---

3. For an examination of Madonna as feminist and a musicological analysis of how her recordings encode empowering messages for women, see Susan McClary, "Living to Tell: Madonna's Resurrection of the Fleshy," in *Feminine Endings* (Minneapolis: University of Minnesota Press, 1991), 148–66. For a contrasting view, see bell hooks, "Madonna: Plantation Mistress or Soul Sister?" in *Black Looks: Race and Representation* (Boston: South End Press, 1992), 157–64. For collections of essays by cultural studies scholars, see Paul Smith, ed., *Madonnarama: Essays on Sex and Popular Culture* (Pittsburgh, Penn.: Cleis Press, 1993); and Cathy Schwichtenberg, *The Madonna Connection: Representational Politics, Subcultural Identities, and Cultural Theory* (Boulder, Colo.: Westview Press, 1993).

Source: "Venus of the Radio Waves" © Camille Paglia/Sex, Art, and American Culture (Vintage Books).

poured for twenty-four hours a day from hundreds of noisy, competitive independent radio stations around the country.

Madonna, like Venus stepping from the radio waves, emerged from this giant river of music. Her artistic imagination ripples and eddies with the inner currents in American music. She is at her best when she follows her intuition and speaks to the world in the universal language of music and dance. She is at her worst when she tries to define and defend herself in words, which she borrows from louche, cynical pals and shallow, single-issue political activists.

Madonna consolidates and fuses several traditions of pop music, but the major one she typifies is disco, which emerged in the Seventies and, under the bland commercial rubric "dance music," is still going strong. It has a terrible reputation: when you say the word *disco,* people think "Bee Gees." But I view disco, at its serious best, as a dark, grand Dionysian music with roots in African earth-cult.

Madonna's command of massive, resonant bass lines, which she heard in the funky dance clubs of Detroit and New York, has always impressed me. As an Italian Catholic, she uses them liturgically. Like me, she sensed the buried pagan religiosity in disco. I recall my stunned admiration as I sat in the theater in 1987 and first experienced the crashing, descending chords of Madonna's "Causing a Commotion," which opened her dreadful movie *Who's That Girl?* If you want to hear the essence of modernity, listen to those chords, infernal, apocalyptic, and grossly sensual. This is the authentic voice of the *fin de siècle.*

Madonna's first video, for her superb, drivingly lascivious disco hit "Burnin' Up," did not make much of an impression. The platinum-blonde girl kneeling and emoting in the middle of a midnight highway just seemed to be a band member's floozie. In retrospect, the video, with its rapid, cryptic surrealism, prefigures Madonna's signature themes and contains moments of eerie erotic poetry.

"Lucky Star" was Madonna's breakthrough video. Against a luminous, white abstract background, she and two impassive dancers perform a synchronized series of jagged, modern kicks and steps. Wearing the ragtag outfit of all-black bows, see-through netting, fingerless lace gloves, bangle bracelets, dangle earrings, chains, crucifixes, and punk booties that would set off a gigantic fashion craze among American adolescent girls, Madonna flaunts her belly button and vamps the camera with a smoky, piercing, come-hither-but-keep-your-distance stare. Here she first suggests her striking talent for improvisational floor work, which she would spectacularly demonstrate at the first MTV awards show, when, wrapped in a white-lace wedding dress, she campily rolled and undulated snakelike on the stage, to the baffled consternation of the first rows of spectators.

I remember sitting in a bar when "Lucky Star," just out, appeared on TV. The stranger perched next to me, a heavyset, middle-aged working-class woman, watched the writhing Madonna and, wide-eyed and slightly frowning, blankly said, her beer held motionless halfway to her lips, "Will you look at this?" There was a sense that Madonna was doing something so new and so strange that one didn't know whether to call it beautiful or grotesque. Through MTV, Madonna was transmitting an avant-garde downtown New York sensibility to the American masses.

In "Lucky Star," Madonna is raffish, gamine, still full of the street-urchin mischief that she would portray in her first and best film, Susan Seidelman's *Desperately Seeking Susan* (1984). In "Borderline," she shows her burgeoning star quality. As the girlfriend of Hispanic toughs who is picked up by a British photographer and makes her first magazine cover, she presents the new dualities of her life: the gritty, multiracial street and club scene that she had haunted in obscurity and poverty, and her new slick, fast world of popularity and success.

In one shot of "Borderline," as she chummily chews gum with kidding girlfriends on the corner, you can see the nondescript plainness of Madonna's real face, which she again exposes, with admirable candor, in *Truth or Dare* when, slurping soup and sporting a shower cap over hair rollers, she fences with her conservative Italian father over the phone. Posing for the photographer in "Borderline," Madonna in full cry fixes the camera lens with challenging, molten eyes, in a bold ritual display of sex and aggression. This early video impressed me with Madonna's sophisticated view of the fabrications of femininity, that exquisite theater which feminism condemns as oppression but which I see as a supreme artifact of civilization. I sensed then, and now know for certain, that Madonna, like me, is drawn to drag queens for their daring, flamboyant insight into sex roles, which they see far more clearly and historically than do our endlessly complaining feminists.

Madonna's first major video, in artistic terms, was "Like a Virgin," where she began to release her flood of inner sexual personae, which appear and disappear like the painted creatures of masque. Madonna is an orchid-heavy Veronese duchess in white, a febrile Fassbinder courtesan in black, a slutty nun-turned-harlequin flapping a gold cross and posturing, bum in air, like a demonic phantom in the nose of a gondola. This video alone, with its coruscating polarities of evil and innocence, would be enough to establish Madonna's artistic distinction for the next century.

In "Material Girl," where she sashays around in Marilyn Monroe's strapless red gown and archly flashes her fan at a pack of men in tuxedos, Madonna first showed her flair for comedy. Despite popular opinion, there are no important parallels between Madonna and Monroe, who was a virtuoso comedienne but who was insecure, depressive, passive-aggressive, and infuriatingly obstructionist in her career habits. Madonna is manic, perfectionist, workaholic. Monroe abused alcohol and drugs, while Madonna shuns them. Monroe had a tentative, melting, dreamy solipsism; Madonna has Judy Holliday's wisecracking smart mouth and Joan Crawford's steel will and bossy, circus-master managerial competence.

In 1985 the cultural resistance to Madonna became overt. Despite the fact that her "Into the Groove," the mesmerizing theme song of *Desperately Seeking Susan,* had saturated our lives for nearly a year, the Grammy Awards outrageously ignored her. The feminist and moralist sniping began in earnest. Madonna "degraded" womanhood; she was vulgar, sacrilegious, stupid, shallow, opportunistic. A nasty mass quarrel broke out in one of my classes between the dancers, who adored Madonna, and the actresses, who scorned her.

I knew the quality of what I was seeing: "Open Your Heart," with its risqué peep-show format, remains for me not only Madonna's greatest video but one of the three or four best videos ever made. In the black bustier she made famous (transforming the American lingerie industry overnight), Madonna, bathed in blue-white light, plays Marlene Dietrich straddling a chair. Her eyes are cold, distant, all-seeing. She is ringed, as if in a sea-green aquarium, by windows of lewd or longing voyeurs: sad sacks, brooding misfits, rowdy studs, dreamy gay twins, a melancholy lesbian.

"Open Your Heart" is a brilliant mimed psychodrama of the interconnections between art and pornography, love and lust. Madonna won my undying loyalty by reviving and re-creating the hard glamour of the studio-era Hollywood movie queens, figures of mythological grandeur. Contemporary feminism cut itself off from history and bankrupted itself when it spun its puerile, paranoid fantasy of male oppressors and female sex-object victims. Woman is the dominant sex. Woman's sexual glamour has bewitched and destroyed men since Delilah and Helen of Troy. Madonna, role model to millions of girls worldwide, has cured the ills of feminism by reasserting woman's command of the sexual realm.

Responding to the spiritual tensions within Italian Catholicism, Madonna discovered the buried paganism within the church. The torture of Christ and the martyrdom of the saints, represented in lurid polychrome images, dramatize the passions of the body, repressed in art-fearing puritan Protestantism of the kind that still lingers in America. Playing with the outlaw personae of prostitute and domi-natrix, Madonna has made a major contribution to the history of women. She has rejoined and healed the split halves of woman: Mary, the Blessed Virgin and holy mother, and Mary Magdalene, the harlot.

Madonna's inner emotional life can be heard in the smooth, transparent "La Isla Bonita," one of her most perfect songs, with its haunting memory of paradise lost. No one ever mentions it. Publicity has tended to focus instead on the more blatantly message-heavy videos, like "Papa Don't Preach," with its teen pregnancy, or "Express Yourself," where feminist cheerleading lyrics hammer on over crisp, glossy images of bedroom bondage, dungeon torture, and epicene, crotch-grabbing Weimar elegance.

"Like a Prayer" gave Pepsi-Cola dyspepsia: Madonna receives the stigmata, makes love with the animated statue of a black saint, and dances in a rumpled silk slip in front of a field of burning crosses. This last item, with its uncontrolled racial allusions, shocked even me. But Madonna has a strange ability to remake symbol-ism in her own image. Kitsch and trash are transformed by her high-energy dancer's touch, her earnest yet over-the-top drag-queen satire.

Madonna has evolved physically. In a charming early live video, "Dress You Up," she is warm, plump, and flirty under pink and powder-blue light. Her voice is enthusias-tic but thin and breathy. She began to train both voice and body, so that her present sil-houette, with some erotic loss, is wiry and muscular, hyperkinetic for acrobatic dance routines based on the martial arts. Madonna is notorious for monthly or even weekly changes of hair color and style, by which she embodies the restless individualism of Western personality. Children love her. As with the Beatles, this is always the sign of a monumental pop phenomenon.

Madonna has her weak moments: for example, I have no tolerance for the giggling baby talk that she periodically hauls out of the closet, as over the final credits of *Truth or Dare*. She is a complex modern woman. Indeed, that is the main theme of her extraor-dinary achievement. She is exploring the problems and tensions of being an ambitious woman today. Like the potent Barbra Streisand, whose maverick female style had a great impact on American girls in the Sixties, Madonna is confronting the romantic dilemma of the strong woman looking for a man but uncertain whether she wants a tyrant or slave. The tigress in heat is drawn to surrender but may kill her conqueror.

In "Open Your Heart," Madonna is woman superbly alone, master of her own fate. Offstage at the end, she mutates into an androgynous boy-self and runs off. "What a Tramp!" thundered the *New York Post* in a recent full-page headline. Yes, Madonna has restored the Whore of Babylon, the pagan goddess banned by the last book of the Bible. With an instinct for world-domination gained from Italian Catholicism, she has rolled like a juggernaut over the multitude of her carping critics. This is a kalei-doscopic career still in progress. But Madonna's most enduring cultural contribution may be that she has introduced ravishing visual beauty and a lush Mediterranean sensuality into parched, pinched, word-drunk Anglo-Saxon feminism.

Further Reading

Fouz-Hernández, Santiago, and Freya Jarman-Ivens. *Madonna's Drowned Worlds: New Approaches to Her Cultural Transformations, 1983–2003.* Burlington, Vt.: Ashgate, 2004.
McClary, Susan. *Feminine Endings.* Minneapolis: University of Minnesota Press, 1991.
Metz, Allan, and Carol Benson. *The Madonna Companion: Two Decades of Commentary.* New York: Schirmer, 1999.
Vernallis, Carol. "The Aesthetics of Music Video: An Analysis of Madonna's 'Cherish.'" *Popular Music* 17 (1998): 153–85.

Discography

Madonna. *Madonna*. Sire, 1983.
_____. *Like a Virgin*. Sire, 1984.
_____. *True Blue*. Sire, 1986.
_____. *Who's That Girl*. Sire, 1987.
_____. *Like a Prayer*. Sire, 1989.
_____. *The Immaculate Collection*. Sire, 1990.
_____. *Ray of Light*. Warner Bros./WEA, 1998.

64. Bruce Springsteen

REBORN IN THE USA

Hailed as the latest in a series of "New Dylans" upon the release of his first albums in 1973 and 1975, lauded by critic Jon Landau (who later became his manager and producer) in a review that exclaimed, "I saw rock & roll's future and its name is Bruce Springsteen,"[1] Bruce Springsteen (b. 1949) had to wait for the beginning of the video era in the early 1980s to achieve superstar status. Springsteen's early success relied as much as on his epic-length performances as on his early recordings, which ranged from the Spector-esque "Born to Run" (1975), to early rock 'n' roll à la Gary "U.S." Bonds and Roy Orbison, to bleak acoustic ballads of resignation. The subjects of his songs vacillated between sensitive portraits of working-class people stuck in dead-end lives and rousing, celebratory rockers.

A yearning for a return to rock's roots (that may have been related to the critical manifestos leading to punk) ran through the ecstatic responses to Springsteen in the mid- to late 1970s. References to rock 'n' roll's past also figure in Springsteen's aesthetic, and it is this nostalgic, or "retro," aesthetic, in which pastiche as a strategy is never far away, that links successful early 1980s artists that may be as stylistically disparate as Springsteen and Madonna. Can it be a coincidence that Springsteen's first two albums, *Greetings from Asbury Park, N.J.*, and *The Wild, the Innocent and the E Street Shuffle* both appeared in 1973,

---

1. Jon Landau, "I Saw Rock and Roll's Future . . . ," *The Real Paper,* May 23, 1974; reprinted in Clinton Heylin, ed., *The Da Capo Book of Rock and Roll Writing* (New York: Da Capo Press, [1992] 2000), 227–28.

the same year as that cinematic evocation of the innocence of the pre-1964 era, *American Graffiti*?

David Marsh came to prominence as a rock critic in the early 1970s on the staff of *Creem*. He wrote the first biography of Springsteen, *Born to Run: The Bruce Springsteen Story* (1979), which he followed with a second volume in 1987, *Glory Days: Bruce Springsteen in the 1980s*. The following may be Marsh's first article on Springsteen—it appeared in 1975 immediately prior to the release of Springsteen's album *Born to Run*—and it represents well the enthusiasm expressed by critics over Springsteen's early efforts. Marsh's predictions of breakthrough success proved to be on the money, since *Born to Run* and the single bearing the same title became Springsteen's first hits.

Little Egypt from Asbury Park—and Bruce Springsteen Don't Crawl on His Belly, Neither
David Marsh

Bruce Springsteen sits cross-legged on his half-made bed, and surveys the scene. Records are strewn across the room, singles mostly, intermixed with empty Pepsi bottles, a motley of underwear, socks and jeans, half-read and half-written letters, an assortment of tapes, and a copy of Richard Williams's *Out of His Head*, the biography of Phil Spector.

"Here," he says, "I'll play ya something else." He puts on a tape of he and the E Street Band at the Main Point in Philadelphia. Suddenly, out of the speakers booms his own voice, cracking up at what he's singing. ("That song has some of the best lines," he says shaking his head, "and some of the *dumbest*.") "Stan-din' on a moun-tain lookin' down at the city, the way I feel t'nite is a dawgawn pity." When the band comes in, the room is charged. The playing and the singing is rough, even ragged, but it is alive, sparked with the discovery of something vital in an old, trashy song. It has been a long time since I heard anyone get this interested in rock and roll, even classic old rock and roll. It has been a lot longer since anyone has gotten me so interested.

Song done, Springsteen snaps the tape recorder off. "There," he says, with the characteristic delinquent twinkle in his eye, "If that don't get a club goin', *nothin'* will."

Bruce Springsteen is determined to get 'em going. The magic is that he doesn't have to be so determined to get himself going. Without being constantly "on," like a performer, Springsteen is constantly on, like someone who knows how good he is. He is full of himself, confident without being arrogant, almost serene in his awareness of what he is doing with his songs, his singing, his band. . . . Unlike say, Roxy Music, which makes very exciting music out of a nearly desperate sense of boredom, Springsteen makes mesmerizing rock out of an inner conviction that almost everything is interesting, even fascinating.

Take the three songs which, at this point, form the focus of the long awaited third Springsteen album. "Born to Run" is almost a rock opera. But, rather than building his concept piece around a derivative European anti-funk motif, Springsteen has built his masterwork around a guitar line ripped straight from the heart of "Telstar." It may be too long (4:30) and too dense (layer upon layer of glockenspiel, voice, band, strings) to be a hit, but it does capture the imagination with its evocation of Springsteen's usual characters—kids on the streets and 'tween the sheets—and its immortal catch-line: "Tramps like us, baby we was born to run."

The sense that he is special has begun to pervade even Springsteen's semi-private life. When he showed up at a party for label mates Blue Oyster Cult, Springsteen completely dominated the room. So much so that Rod Stewart and a couple of the Faces, no slouches at scene-stealing themselves, were all but ignored when they made a brief appearance. Yet he has yet to lose his innocence. Going to visit the Faces later that night, at the ostentatiously elegant Plaza Hotel, Springsteen feigned awe—although you wondered if it were entirely feigned—at the mirrored, plushly carpeted lobby.

Fragments of a legend have begun to build. There are the stories about school—in high school, the time when he was sent to first grade by a nun, and, continuing to act the wise-ass, was put in the embarrassing position of having the first grade nun suggest to a smaller child: "Johnny, show Bruce how we treat people who act like that down here." Johnny slapped Springsteen's face. Or in college, the story of how the student body petitioned the administration for his expulsion, "because I was just too weird for 'em, I guess." The news that his father was a bus driver, which gives added poignancy to "Does This Bus Stop at 82nd Street?" (Which begins, "Hey, bus driver, keep the change.") Aphorisms are not beyond him: On Led Zeppelin: "They're like a lot of those groups. Not only aren't they doing anything new, they don't do the old stuff so good, either." On marriage: "I lived with someone once for two years. But I decided that to be married, you had to write married music. And I'm not ready for that." On the radio: "I don't see how anyone listens to [the local progressive rock station]. Everything's so damn long. At least if you listen to [the local oldies station] you know you're gonna hit three out of five. And the stuff you don't like doesn't last long."

All of this goes only so far, of course. A record, a *hit* record, is a crucial necessity. Sales of the first two albums are over 100,000 but that's nothing in America. There are still large areas of the country where Springsteen hasn't played—even important large cities such as Detroit have been left out—and though the word travels fast, and frequently, articles like this ultimately seem like just the usual rhetoric without something to back them up. As one Californian put it, "I've heard enough. It's like having everyone tell me I'm really missing something by not seeing Egypt. When's he going to come out here?"

Presuming he has the hit he deserves, Springsteen should be hitting most of America over the rest of the year. After an abortive arena journey with Chicago, he is, he says, reluctant to play large halls ever again. But he is one of the few rockers who would have any idea of what to do—except blast—in a room the size of a hockey rink. (Mick Jagger is about the only example who comes to mind, though Rod Stewart and Elvis do pretty well now that I think of it.)

Suppose that he does hit the big time. Even, suppose that he really is, as the ads have it, "rock and roll future." What happens then?

Since I believe that all of the above is true, and is going to happen, I have been at some pains to try to figure it out. Certainly, not a new explosion, à la Beatles and Elvis. Those phenomena were predicated upon an element of surprise, of catching an audience unaware, that is simply no longer operative. Not with rock on nationwide

TV too many times a week. And not the kind of quiet, in-crowd build-up that pro-pelled Dylan into the national eye. What Springsteen is after—nothing less than everything—has to be bigger than that, in mass terms, though it obviously cannot exceed Dylan in influence, his biggest achievement.

Springsteen's impact may very well be most fully felt as a springboard, a device to get people to do more than just pay attention. He can, potentially, polarize people in the way that Elvis, the Beatles, the Stones, Dylan—all the great ones—initially did. (Already, some early Springsteen fans feel alienated by his ever more forceful occu-pation with his soul influences.) The key to the success of those four is that as many hated them as loved them—but everyone had to take a position. God knows who he'll drag into the spotlight with him—it might have been the N.Y. Dolls, whose pas-sion for soul oldies was equal to his, or Loudon Wainwright, whose cool, humorous vision parallels Bruce's in a more adult (sort of) way—but that ought to be something like what will happen. Sort of the way Carl Perkins, Jerry Lee Lewis and the other rockabilly crazies followed Elvis.

He's smart though. He said it all, one night, introducing "Wear My Ring Around Your Neck," the Presley oldie. "There have been contenders. There have been pre-tenders. But there is still only one King."

But no king reigns forever.

> Springsteen's second album of the 1980s, the introspective *Nebraska*
> (1982), was recorded at home on a four-track tape recorder, after which
> he radically reversed directions with *Born in the U.S.A.* (1984). On that
> album Springsteen retooled the populist themes of his earlier work in
> anthemic settings, while placing an American flag on the album cover
> and using the flag on his stage sets. The inherent political ambiguity of
> populism meant that Springsteen's message could be appropriated by
> people with whose political stance he was not necessarily sympathetic:
> Ronald Reagan cited the title song approvingly during his presidential
> reelection campaign in 1984. The singles taken from *Born in the U.S.A.*
> also marked Springsteen's successful entry into the video arena with his
> newly buffed-up bod. No fewer than seven Top 10 singles were released
> from the album in 1984–85, attesting to new legions of fans, and his
> videos were constant features on MTV.

> Simon Frith's 1987 article followed the release of Springsteen's
> immensely successful box set, *Live/1975–85*. Frith documents well
> the contradictions of mass-market populism and analyzes several of
> the myths attached to the Springsteen image, one of which asserts that
> his disdain for commerce renders him impervious to charges of commer-
> cialism. Frith uses the discussion of these myths to take up the issue
> of authenticity, an issue that he has addressed many times in other
> writings (and an issue that, as we have seen, has been central to rock
> criticism since it began in the mid-1960s).[2] Springsteen's authenticity

---

2. Frith's most thorough explorations of this issue may be found in *Sound Effects* (New York: Pantheon Books, 1981); and *Performing Rites: On the Value of Popular Music* (Cambridge, Mass.: Harvard University Press).

springs from both his image and his storytelling technique: a "refusal to sentimentalize social conditions, a compulsion to sentimentalize human nature," a celebration "of the ordinary, not the special." Frith is not necessarily insisting that Springsteen is a sham, but rather that "music can not *be* true or false, it can only refer to *conventions* of truth and falsity." Frith voices a European counterweight to the celebratory tones of many American critics, remaining skeptical about divisions between "democratic populism" and "market populism."[3]

The Real Thing—Bruce Springsteen
Simon Frith

Introduction

My guess is that by Christmas 1986 Bruce Springsteen was making more money per day than any other pop star—more than Madonna, more than Phil Collins or Mark Knopfler, more than Paul McCartney even; *Time* calculated that he had earned $7.5 million in the first *week* of his *Live* LP release. This five-record boxed set went straight to the top of the American LP sales charts (it reputedly sold a million copies on its first day, grossing $50 million "out of the gate") and stayed there throughout the Christmas season. It was the nation's best-seller in November and December, when more records are sold than in all the other months of the year put together. Even in Britain, where the winter charts are dominated by TV-advertised anthologies, the Springsteen set at £25 brought in more money than the tight-margin single-album compilations. (And CBS reckon they get 42% of their annual sales at Christmas time.) Walking through London from Tottenham Court Road down Oxford Street to Piccadilly in early December, passing the three symbols of corporate rock—the Virgin, HMV and Tower superstores—each claiming to be the biggest record shop in the world, I could only see Springsteen boxes, piled high by the cash desks, the *safest* stock of the season.

Whatever the final sales figures turn out to be (and after Christmas the returns of the boxes from the retailers to CBS were as startling as the original sales), it is already obvious that *Bruce Springsteen and the E Street Band Live* is a phenomenal record, a money-making achievement to be discussed on the same scale as *Saturday Night Fever* or Michael Jackson's *Thriller*. Remember, too, that a live record is cheaper to produce than a new studio sound (and Springsteen has already been well rewarded for these songs from the sales of previous discs and proceeds of sell-out tours). Nor did CBS need the expensive trappings or promo videos and press and TV advertising to make this record sell. Because the Springsteen box was an event in itself (the only pop precedent I can think of is the Beatles' 1968 *White Album*), it generated its own publicity as "news"—radio stations competed to play the most tracks for the longest times, shops competed to give Bruce the most window space, newspapers competed

---

3. Daniel Cavicchi noted in a book on Springsteen fandom how arguments about the constructedness of Springsteen's authenticity are bound to have little weight for fans of the Boss; for them, "authenticity is about Springsteen as a real person." See *Tramps Like Us: Music and Meaning among Springsteen Fans* (New York: Oxford University Press, 1998), 65.

Source: "The Real Thing—Bruce Springsteen," Simon Frith, *Music for Pleasure: Essays in the Sociology of Pop* (Routledge).

in speculations about how much money he was really making. The Springsteen box became, in other words, that ultimate object of capitalist fantasy, a commodity which sold more and more because it had sold so well already, a product which had to be *owned* (rather than necessarily used).

In the end, though, what is peculiar about the Springsteen story is not its marks of a brilliant commercial campaign, but their invisibility. Other superstars put out live sets for Christmas (Queen, for example) and the critics sneer at their opportunism; other stars resell their old hits (Bryan Ferry, for example) and their fans worry about their lack of current inspiration. And in these sorry tales of greed and pride it is Bruce Springsteen more often that not who is the measure of musical integrity, the model of a rock performer who cannot be discussed in terms of financial calculation. In short, the most successful pop commodity of the moment, the Springsteen Live Set, stands for the principle that music should not be a commodity; it is his very disdain for success that makes Springsteen so successful. It is as if his presence on every fashionable turntable, tape deck and disc machine, his box on every up-market living-room floor, are what enables an aging, affluent rock generation to feel in touch with its "roots." And what matters in this post-modern era is not whether Bruce Springsteen *is* the real thing, but how he sustains the belief that there are somehow, somewhere, real things to be.

False

Consider the following:

Bruce Springsteen is a millionaire who dresses as a worker. Worn jeans, singlets, a head band to keep his hair from his eyes—these are working clothes and it is an important part of Springsteen's appeal that we do see him, as an entertainer, working for his living. His popularity is based on his live shows and, more particularly, on their spectacular energy: Springsteen works *hard*, and his exhaustion—on our behalf—is visible. He makes music physically, as a *manual* worker. His clothes are straightforwardly practical, sensible (like sports people's clothes)—comfortable jeans (worn in) for easy movement, a singlet to let the sweat flow free, the mechanic's cloth to wipe his brow.

But there is more to these clothes than this. *Springsteen wears work clothes even when he is not working*. His off-stage image, his LP sleeves and interview poses, even the candid "off duty" paparazzi shots, involve the same down-to-earth practicality (the only time Springsteen was seen to dress up "in private" was for his wedding). Springsteen doesn't wear the clothes appropriate to his real economic status and resources (as compared with other pop stars), but neither does he dress up for special occasions like real workers do—he's never seen flashily attired for a sharp night out. It's as if he can't be seen to be excessive or indulgent except on our behalf, as a performer for an audience. For him there is no division between work and play, between the ordinary and the extraordinary. Because the constructed "Springsteen," the star, is presented plain, there can never be a suggestion that this is just an act (as Elvis was an act, as Madonna is). There are no other Springsteens, whether more real or more artificial, to be seen.

Springsteen is employer-as-employee. It has always surprised me that he should be nicknamed "the Boss," but the implication is that this is an affectionate label, a brotherly way in which the E Street Band honor his sheer drive. In fact "boss" is an accurate description of their economic relationship—Springsteen *employs* his band; he has the recording contracts, controls the LP and concert material, writes the songs and chooses the oldies. And whatever his musicians' contributions to his success (fulsomely recognized), he gets the composing/performing royalties, could, in principle, sack people, and, like any other good employer, rewards his team with generous bonuses after each sell-out show or disc. And, of course, he employs a stage crew too, and a manager, a publicist, a secretary/assistant; he has an annual turnover now of millions. He may express the feelings of "little" men and women buffeted by distant company boards but he is himself a corporation.

Springsteen is a 37-year-old teenager. He is 20 years into a hugely successful career, he's a professional, a married man old enough to be the father of adolescent children of his own, but he still presents himself as a young man, waiting to see what life will bring, made tense by clashes with adult authority. He introduces his songs with memories— his life as a boy, arguments with his father (his mother is rarely mentioned)—but as a performer he is clearly *present* in these emotions. Springsteen doesn't regret or vilify his past; as a grown man he's still living it.

Springsteen is a shy exhibitionist. He is, indeed, one of the sexiest performers rock and roll has ever had—there's a good part of his concert audience who simply fancy him, can't take their eyes off his body, and he's mesmerizing on stage because of the confidence with which he displays himself. But, for all this, his persona is still that of a nervy, gauche youth on an early date.

Springsteen is superstar-as-friend. He comes into our lives as a recording star, a radio sound, a video presence and, these days, as an item of magazine gossip. Even in his live shows he seems more accessible in the close-ups on the mammoth screens around the stage than as the "real" dim figure in the distance. And yet he is still the rock performer whose act most convincingly creates (and depends on) a sense of community.

Springsteen's most successful "record" is "live." What the boxed set is meant to do is reproduce a concert, an *event*, and if for other artists five records would be excessive, for Springsteen it is a further sign of his album's truth-to-life—it lasts about the same length of time as a show. There's an interesting question of trust raised here. I don't doubt that these performances were once live, that the applause did happen, but this is nevertheless a false event, a concert put together from different shows (and alternative mixes), edited and balanced to sound like a live LP (which has quite different aural conventions than an actual show). Springsteen fans know that, of course. The pleasure of this set is not that it takes us back to somewhere we've been, but that it lays out something ideal. It describes what we *mean* by "Springsteen live," and what makes him "real" in this context is not his transparency, the idea that he is who he pretends to be, but his art, his ability to articulate the right *idea* of reality.

True

The recurring term used in discussions of Springsteen, by fans, by critics, by fans-as-critics is "authenticity." What is meant by this is not that Springsteen is authentic in a direct way—is simply expressing himself—but that he represents "authenticity." This is why he has become so important: he stands for the core values of rock and roll even as those values become harder and harder to sustain. At a time when rock is the soundtrack for TV commercials, when tours depend on sponsorship deals, when video promotion has blurred the line between music-making and music-selling, Springsteen suggests that, despite everything, it still gives people a way to define themselves against corporate logic, a language in which everyday hopes and fears can be expressed.

If Bruce Springsteen didn't exist, American rock critics would have had to invent him. In a sense, they did, whether directly (Jon Landau, *Rolling Stone*'s most significant critical theorist in the late sixties, is now his manager) or indirectly (Dave Marsh, Springsteen's official biographer, is the most passionate and widely read rock critic of the eighties). There are, indeed, few American rock critics who haven't celebrated Springsteen, but their task has been less to explain him to his potential fans, to sustain the momentum that carried him from cult to mass stardom, than to explain him to himself. They've placed him, that is, in a particular reading of rock history, not as the "new Dylan" (his original sales label) but as the "voice of the people." His task is to carry the baton passed on from Woody Guthrie, and the purpose of his carefully placed oldies (Guthrie's "This Land Is Your Land," Presley and Berry hits, British beat classics, Edwin Starr's "War") isn't just to situate him as a fellow fan but also to identify him with a particular musical project. Springsteen himself claims on stage to represent an authentic popular tradition (as against the spurious commercial sentiments of an Irving Berlin).

To be so "authentic" involves a number of moves. Firstly, authenticity must be defined against artifice; the terms only make sense in opposition to each other. This is the importance of Springsteen's image—to represent the "raw" as against the "cooked." His plain stage appearance, his dressing down, has to be understood with reference to showbiz dressing up, to the elaborate spectacle of cabaret pop and soul (and routine stadium rock and roll)—Springsteen is real *by contrast*. In lyrical terms too he is plain-speaking; his songwriting craft is marked not by "poetic" or obscure or personal language, as in the singer/ songwriter tradition following Dylan, folk-rock (and his own early material) but by the vivid images and metaphors he builds from common words.

What's at stake here is not the authenticity of experience, but authenticity of feeling; what matters is not whether Springsteen has been through these things himself (boredom, aggression, ecstasy, despair) but that he knows how they work. The point of his autobiographical anecdotes is not to reveal himself but to root his music in material conditions. Like artists in other media (fiction, film) Springsteen is concerned to give emotions (the essential data of rock and roll) a narrative setting, to situate them in time and place, to relate them to the situations they explain or confuse. He's not interested in abstract emotions, in vague sensation or even in moralizing. He is, to put it simply, a story-teller, and in straining to make his stories credible he uses classic techniques. Reality is registered by conventions first formulated by the nineteenth-century naturalists—a refusal to sentimentalize social conditions, a compulsion to sentimentalize human nature. Springsteen's songs (like Zola's fictions) are almost exclusively concerned with the working-class, with the effects of poverty and uncertainty, the consequences of weakness and crime; they trawl through the murky reality of the American dream; they contrast utopian impulses with people's lack of opportunity to do much more than get by; they find in sex the only opportunity for passion (and betrayal). Springsteen's protagonists, victims and criminals, defeated and enraged, are treated tenderly, their hopes honoured, their failure determined by circumstance.

It is his realism that makes Springsteen's populism politically ambiguous. His message is certainly anti-capitalist, or, at least, critical of the effects of capitalism—as both citizen and star Springsteen has refused to submit to market forces, has shown consistent and generous support for the system's losers, for striking trade union-ists and the unemployed, for battered wives and children. But at the same time, his focus on individuals' fate, the very power with which he describes the dreams they can't realize (but which he has) offers an opening for his appropriation, appropri-ation not just by politicians like Reagan but, more importantly, by hucksters and advertisers, who use him to sell their goods as some sort of *solution* to the problem he outlines. This is the paradox of mass-marketed populism: Springsteen's songs suggest there is something missing in our lives, the CBS message is that we can fill the gap *with a Bruce Springsteen record.* And for all Springsteen's support of current causes, what comes from his music is a whiff of nostalgia and an air of fatalism. His stories describe hopes-about-to-be dashed, convey a sense of time passing beyond our control, suggest that our dreams can only be dreams. The formal conservatism of the music reinforces the emotional conservatism of the lyrics. This is the way the world is, he sings, and nothing really changes.

But there's another way of describing Springsteen's realism. It means celebrat-ing the ordinary not the special. Again the point is not that Springsteen is ordinary or even pretends to be, but that he honors ordinariness, making something intense out of experiences that are usually seen as mundane. It has always been pop's func-tion to transform the banal, but this purpose was to some extent undermined by the rise of rock in the sixties, with its claims to art and poetry, its cult-building, its heavy metal mysticism. Springsteen himself started out with a couple of wordy, worthy LPs, but since then he has been in important ways committed to common sense. Springsteen's greatest skill is his ability to dramatize everyday events—even his stage act is a pub rock show writ large. The E Street Band, high-class professionals, play with a sort of amateurish enthusiasm, an affection for each other which is in sharp contrast to the bohemian contempt for their work (and their audience) which has been a strand of "arty" rock shows since the Rolling Stones and the Doors. Springsteen's musicians stand for every bar and garage group that ever got together in fond hope of stardom.

His sense of the commonplace also explains Springsteen's physical appeal. His sexuality is not displayed as something remarkable, a kind of power, but is coded into his "natural" movements, determined by what he has to do to sing and play. His body becomes "sexy"—a source of excitement and anxiety—in its routine activity; his appeal is not defined in terms of glamour or fantasy. The basic sign of Springsteen's authenticity, to put it another way, is his sweat, his display of *energy*. His body is not posed, an object of consumption, but active, an object of exhaustion. When the E Street Band gather at the end of a show for the final bow, arms around each other's shoulders, drained and relieved, the sporting analogy is clear: this is a team which has won its latest bout. What matters is that every such bout is seen to be real, that there are no backing tapes, no "fake" instruments, that the musicians really have played until they can play no more. There is a moment in every Springsteen show I've seen when Clarence Clemons takes center-stage. For that moment he is the real star—he's bigger than Springsteen, louder, more richly dressed. And he's the saxophonist, giving us the clearest account all evening of the relationship between human effort and human music.

To be authentic and to sound authentic is in the rock context the same thing. Music can not *be* true or false, it can only refer to *conventions* of truth and falsity. Consider the following.

Thundering drums in Springsteen's songs give his stories their sense of unstop-pable momentum, they map out the spaces within which things happen. The equation of time and space is the secret of great rock and roll and Springsteen uses other classic devices to achieve it—a piano/organ combination, for example (as used by The Band and many soul groups), so that melodic-descriptive and rhythmic-atmospheric sounds are continually swapped about.

The E Street Band makes music as a group, but a group in which we can hear every instrumentalist. Our attention is drawn, that is, not to a finished sound but to music-in-the-making. This is partly done by the refusal to make any instrument the "lead" (which is why Nils Lofgren, a "lead" guitarist, sounded out of place in the last E Street touring band). And partly by a specific musical busy-ness—the group is "tight," everyone is aiming for the same rhythmic end, but "loose," each player makes their own decision as to how to get there (which is one reason why electronic instruments would not fit—they're too smooth, too determined). All Springsteen's musicians, even the added back-up singers and percussionists, have individual voices; it would be unthinkable for him to appear with, say, an anonymous string section.

The textures and, more significantly, the melodic structures of Springsteen's music make self-conscious reference to rock and roll itself, to its conventional line-up, its cliched chord changes, its time-honoured ways of registering joys and sadness. Springsteen himself is a rock and roll star, not a crooner or singer/songwriter. His voice *strains* to be heard, he has to shout against the instruments that both support and compete with him. However many times he's rehearsed his lines they always sound as if they're being forged on the spot.

Many of Springsteen's most anthemic songs have no addresses (no "you") but (like many Beatles songs) concern a third person (tales told about someone else) or involve an "I" brooding aloud, explaining his situation impersonally, in a kind of individualised epic. Listening to such epics is a public activity (rather than a private fantasy), which is why Springsteen concerts still feel like collective occasions.

Conclusion

In one of his monologues Springsteen remembers that his parents were never very keen on his musical ambitions—they wanted him to train for something safe, like law or accountancy: "they wanted me to get a little something for myself; what they did not understand was that I wanted *everything*!"

This is a line that could only be delivered by an American, and to explain Springsteen's importance and success we have to go back to the problem he is really facing: the fate of the individual artist under capitalism. In Europe, the artistic critique of the commercialization of everything has generally been conducted in terms of Romanticism, in a state of Bohemian disgust with the masses and the bourgeoisie alike, in the name of the superiority of the *avant-garde*. In the USA there's a populist anti-capitalism available, a tradition of the artist as the common man (rarely woman), pitching rural truth against urban deceit, pioneer values against bureaucratic routines. This tradition (Mark Twain to Woody Guthrie, Kerouac to Credence Clearwater Revival) lies behind Springsteen's message and his image. It's this tradition that enables him to take such well-worn iconography as the road, the river, rock and roll itself, as a mark of sincerity. No British musician, not even someone with such a profound love of American musical forms as Elvis Costello, could deal with these themes without some sense of irony.

Still, Springsteen's populism can appeal to everyone's experience of capitalism. He makes music out of desire aroused and desire thwarted, he offers a sense of personal worth that is not determined by either market forces (and wealth) or aesthetic standards (and cultural capital). It is the USA's particular account of equality that allows him to transcend the differences in class and status which remain ingrained in European culture. The problem is that the line between democratic populism (the argument that all people's experiences and emotions are equally important, equally worthy to be dramatized and made into art) and market populism (the argument that the consumer is always right, that the market defines cultural value) is very thin. Those piles of Bruce Springsteen boxes in European department stores seem less a tribute to rock authenticity than to corporate might.

"We are the world!" sang USA for Africa, and what was intended as a statement of global community came across as a threat of global domination. "Born in the USA!" sang Bruce Springsteen, on his last great tour, with the Stars and Stripes fluttering over the stage, and what was meant as an opposition anthem to the Reaganite colonization of the American dream was taken by large sections of his American audiences as pat patriotism (in Europe the flag had to come down). Springsteen is, whether he or we like it or not, an American artist—his "community" will always have the Stars and Stripes fluttering over it. But then rock and roll is American music, and Springsteen's *Live—1975–85* is a monument. Like all monuments it celebrates (and mourns) the dead, in this case the idea of authenticity itself.

Further Reading

Bruce Springsteen, the Rolling Stone File: The Ultimate Compendium of Interviews, Articles, Facts and Opinions from the Files of Rolling Stone. New York: Hyperion Books, 1996.

Carman, Bryan K. *A Race of Singers: Whitman's Working-Class Hero from Guthrie to Springsteen.* Chapel Hill: University of North Carolina Press, 2000.

Cavicchi, Daniel. *Tramps Like Us: Music and Meaning among Springsteen Fans.* New York: Oxford University Press, 1998.

Guterman, Jimmy. *Runaway American Dream: Listening to Bruce Springsteen.* Cambridge, Mass.: Da Capo Press, 2005.

Marsh, Dave. *Bruce Springsteen: Two Hearts, the Story.* New York: Routledge, 2003.

Discography

Springsteen, Bruce. *Greetings from Asbury Park, N.J.* Columbia, 1973.

_____. *Born to Run.* Columbia, 1975.

_____. *Born in the USA.* Columbia, 1984.

_____. *Live 1975–85.* Columbia, 1986.

_____. *Tunnel of Love.* Columbia, 1987.

_____. *The Essential Bruce Springsteen.* Sony, 2003.

65. R&B in the 1980s

TO CROSS OVER OR NOT TO CROSS OVER?

Thriller opened the door to blockbuster, "crossover" hits by black artists. In addition to Jackson's album, the increasingly visible mainstream successes of Prince and Lionel Richie in the mid-1980s owed something to the end of apartheid policies on MTV. Changes in the music industry and in the number of small, black-owned record stores, however, raised the question of whether these crossover artists, in the process of reaching a large audience, had somehow forsaken the black community or were "selling out" to white commercial dictates in some other fashion (we already read Greg Tate's criticism of Michael Jackson along those lines in Chapter 62).

During the 1980s, Nelson George was one of the music critics who was the most consistently devoted to articulating the links between African American popular music and arguments about black economic self-sufficiency. George advanced his views in a column on black music from a perch on *Billboard*'s staff throughout much of the decade.[1] His 1988 book *The Death of Rhythm and Blues* presented the most cogent version of a recurring argument in his writing: looking at the history of African American popular music through the prism of the opposition between early 20th-century views advanced by W. E. B. DuBois on economic self-determination and those advanced by Booker T. Washington on assimilation, George contended that R&B in the 1980s had lost much of its expressive power because of its separation from the black community. In this excerpt, George looks at the well-known crossover artists just mentioned, as well as artists such as Anita Baker (b. 1957) and Frankie Beverly (b. 1946), whom he terms "retronuevo": musicians who celebrate the history of rhythm and blues by remaining true to previous standards of musicianship and soulfulness.

---

1. For a more in-depth discussion and analysis of George's *Billboard* articles and of the issues involved in crossover in the early 1980s, see David Brackett, "(In Search of) Musical Meaning: Genres, Categories, and Crossover," in *Popular Music Studies*, ed. David Hesmondhalgh and Keith Negus, 65–82 (London: Arnold, 2002).

from The Death of Rhythm and Blues
Nelson George

Sometimes it seems really funny, but it's also quite sad that in surveying black America through its music in the eighties, much of the discussion revolves not around music but skin color, cosmetic surgery, and the rejection of Negroid features. Case in point: Compare current photographs of George Benson with pictures from early in his career. You will be confronted with facial alterations that have nothing to do with age. Surgery has reshaped him into a commercial product for mass consumption. It's as simple and, I think, as frightening as that. Change your face to sell a hundred thousand more units, to do the movies, to make more money. Stop looking like your mother and father, in the name of commerce. Maybe, like Whoopi Goldberg, Oprah Winfrey, and the otherwise sweet Janet Jackson, wear blue or green contact lenses. After all, it might help you achieve that most tempting symbol of eighties assimilation: an MTV video.

The two greatest black stars of the decade, Michael Jackson and Prince, ran fast and far both from blackness and conventional images of male sexuality (and their videos got on MTV). Michael Jackson's nose job, often ill-conceived makeup, and artificially curled hair is, in the eyes of many blacks, a denial of his color that constitutes an act of racial treason. Add to that a disquieting androgyny and you have an alarmingly un-black, unmasculine figure as the most popular black man in America.

Prince is similarly troublesome. Where Jackson's androgyny was like that of an innocently unaware baby, Prince preached sex as salvation in explicit and often clumsy terms. "Head" (oral sex), "When You Were Mine" (sexual ambiguity), and "1999" (sex as resignation in the face of nuclear war) were just a few of the songs in which Prince expressed his funky yet fanciful fascination with physical engagement. Onstage, he went from wearing black bikini, g-strings, and leg warmers to taking seductive pseudobaths and dry-humping his piano, all with a wink and shimmy that suggested his lover could be of any sexual persuasion. No black performer since Little Richard had toyed with the heterosexual sensibilities of black America so brazenly.

Prince's more irksome trait was that, like Jackson, he aided those who saw blackness as a hindrance in the commercial marketplace by running from it. Unlike the many black stars who altered their face to please "the mass market," Prince didn't have to; his features suggested he was a product of the interracial marriages so popular in Minneapolis. But he really wasn't. Both his parents were black. Yet in the quasi-autobiographical film *Purple Rain*, Prince presented his mother as white, a "crossover" marketing strategy as unnecessary as Jackson's tiresome claims to "universality." In fact, it can be argued that Prince's consistent use of mulatto and white leading ladies convinced many black male (and some female) artists to use romantic interests of similar shading in their videos, hoping to emulate Prince's success. The resulting videos seem to reinforce the stereotypic idea that dark-skinned black women are not as attractive as their lighter sisters. As icons of style, Jackson and Prince were assimilation symbols as powerful as Bill Cosby. But thankfully, there was more to them than image. There was music, but we'll deal with that a bit later. . . .

On November 18, 1982, I wrote a story for the front page of *Billboard*, "Times Tough for Black Retailers," that revealed the social schism found between the assimilated and unassimilated in the R&B world and in the larger black society. "Black-oriented mom-and-pop retailers are going out of business in increasing numbers, and are

Source: The Death of Rhythm and Blues, Nelson George/Pantheon Books.

not being replaced by new enterprises. At the same time, black music is holding its own in the depressed sales environment and is generating a slew of popular new performers. This dichotomy emerges from a *Billboard* survey of black retailers, label executives, and other industryites. As reasons for the problems of the small operator, they cite unemployment, poor management, locations in declining inner-city neighborhoods, and competition from stores in active city centers. General market retail chains are said to be increasing their awareness and sales of black music."

Counting the Losses

The Commodores' black manager, Benny Ashburn—"the sixth Commodore"—who died of a heart attack in 1982, was one of the few black managers to build and hold on to a mainstream rhythm & blues group capable of million-selling albums. It was not unexpected that after Ashburn's death, Richie split from the Commodores and signed with Kenny Rogers's manager, Ken Kragen. But it was surely disheartening to those who hoped he'd give a brother or sister a shot at managing one of the industry's most promising careers.

Richie went for a manager who had turned a country singer, for a time, into America's most popular male vocalist. Richie wanted the same thing, and Kragen, if not for the incredible ascendence of Michael Jackson into pop heaven, would have accomplished it. However, Richie's acceptance by Middle America didn't mean he had escaped the turmoil of the rhythm & blues world. Richie, like Jackson, Prince, and other crossover stars, was a target of verbal abuse and boycott threats from black concert promoters, as the bitterness revealed at the 1979 BMA conference continued into the next decade.

[The lack of talented songwriter-producers in R&B] played a role in the growing difficulty black artists found reaching the pop charts. Musically the songs weren't as good as in the sixties and early seventies. As dance records, the grooves were still inventive, but they were hampered by a disco backlash at pop radio. As a cultural force, the term "disco" went out as quickly as it had come in. Unfortunately, all black dance music was for a time labeled "disco." It was stupid. It was racist. It revealed again how powerful a force semantics can be in the reception of pop music. Just as rock & roll came to mean white music, disco came to represent some ugly amalgam of black and gay music. The Bee Gees went straight down the tubes because of such labeling. They were, after all, disco's biggest white group.

As for the decline in black crossover, you can look it up.[2] Of the fourteen records to reach number one on the black chart in 1983, only one reached the pop top-ten. "She Works Hard for the Money" by Donna Summer, the only disco-bred artist to escape the genre's career-deflating stigma. In contrast, some of that year's great number one black singles—Mtume's sensual "Juicy Fruit," the hard-core funk of Rick James's "Cold-Blooded" and George Clinton's "Atomic Dog," the melodic and danceable "Candy Girl" by New Edition, the soulful boogie songs "Get It Right" by Aretha Franklin and "Save the Overtime for Me" by Gladys Knight and the Pips—only went to number forty or lower on the pop chart. That of course was the same year that Michael Jackson's *Thriller* sold 20 million copies in the U.S. and Lionel Richie's singles "All Night Long" and "Can't Slow Down" sold over 10 million, only confirming the

---

2. Perhaps George meant to precede this sentence with "Excluding recordings by Michael Jackson and Lionel Richie . . . ," since recordings by Jackson and Richie released during 1983 made both the pop and R&B Top 10, in several cases going to number one. George implies as much in his comments later in this paragraph.

feast-or-famine cycle in popular music. A black who crossed over could sell a humongous number of records. And the fact that so few succeeded didn't stifle the dream.

For many black entertainers, chasing that dream was a fixation, and one that could destroy a career. Peabo Bryson, a smooth, soulful vocalist and distinctive, if limited, songwriter, began his career in the early seventies as a songwriter-vocalist with a number of bands on independent labels. In 1977, he signed with Capitol and immediately became one of the best-loved singers in black America. Deep in the heart of disco he recorded ballads like "Reaching for the Sky," "I'm So Into You," and one of the rare soul classics to be written and recorded in the 1975–85 period, "Feel the Fire." With its devotional lyrics, dramatic piano chords, and wonderful arrangement by coproducer Johnny Pate, a former Curtis Mayfield collaborator, "Feel the Fire" was one of the most respected and covered R&B compositions of the period.

From 1977 to 1983, every new album released by Bryson sold at least half a million copies, and he became a major concert attraction. However, in the age of crossover, Bryson wanted what Lionel Richie and Michael Jackson had, a white audience, and he attempted to get it. A duet with Roberta Flack on the Barry Manilow-like ballad "Tonight I Celebrate My Love" in 1984 gave him his first taste of pop success. In 1985, he jumped to Elektra and had another top-ten hit with "Whenever You're in My Arms Again," another mushy mainstream ballad. Bryson did not see the drop-off in his album sales during this transition as a bad omen. Sure that a pop audience awaited him, Bryson changed his image: gone were the white suits and modest Afro of his Capitol years. He draped himself in ultratrendy English threads and had his low Afro styled into a "fade" cut, high on top, low on the sides. His Elektra debut was synthesized, uptempo, and contemporary, and it was received with all the enthusiasm of a broken computer chip. His old audience hated it, and without a breakthrough single, whites paid no attention. It was clear that the whites who had bought his hit singles had liked the record but didn't know who Bryson, the artist, was. As a result, this album sold a meager 200,000 copies and his concert bookings dwindled. Peabo Bryson, once a staple of what was left of the old R&B world, had tried to leap the barrier and stumbled. It remains to be seen whether he can pick himself back up.

Retronuevo

It was in studying the history of rhythm & blues that I came to admire those in the eighties who have been able to break away from, ignore, or battle the crossover consciousness and remain true to the strength of R&B, while not conceding that that approach left them unacceptable to white America. Inspired by that attitude and the music it produced, I created in 1986 the term "retronuevo," which can be defined as an embrace of the past to create passionate, fresh expressions and institutions. It doesn't refer just to music. The willingness of broadcaster Percy Sutton to revive the Apollo Theater in New York and of black haircare kingpin Robert Gardner to do the same in Chicago for the Regal Theater showed that some black businesspeople possessed the heart and moxie to understand how much symbolic importance and economic potential these once grand R&B showcases hold for now downtrodden inner city neighborhoods. With *She's Gotta Have It* and *Hollywood Shuffle*, Spike Lee and Robert Townsend used hustle and comedy to create non-Hollywood, profoundly black films that partially realized the ambitious dreams of Booker T. Washington in the 1920s and Melvin Van Peebles in the 1970s.

But mostly retronuevo means black music that appreciates its heritage. Until the eighties, R&B never emphasized looking back—one reason for its ongoing creativity, as I've said in earlier chapters. But as too much of the music became as enticing as a ripped diaphragm and not nearly as dangerous, artists emerged to bring back some of the soul and subtlety its audience deserves.

Maze, featuring Frankie Beverly, had been retronuevo from record one. From 1977 to 1985, this Bay Area band released five albums on Capitol, each selling half a million but never breaking the million mark. Many a black artist would have been frustrated by this inability to crack the magical million mark, and Beverly often complained about Capitol's inability to cross him over. But, crucially, Beverly wasn't willing to sell his soul to cross over. He just continued with an idiosyncratic sound that balanced the street feel of his native Philadelphia with the relaxed mood of his Bay Area home. He'd been signed by Larkin Arnold after touring as an opening act for Marvin Gaye. Arnold was a black attorney who'd been brought in to mastermind the expansion of Capitol's black music. Coming on the heels of the jazzy Earth, Wind and Fire and the raunchy Parliament-Funkadelic, Beverly's Maze established itself as a less frantic, less abrasive alternative. Moreover, Maze had the kind of cross-generational appeal that eluded most other young black acts of the time. The 1981 *Live in New Orleans* double album was classic Beverly, with all but one of the twelve songs featuring slow to medium tempos with arrangements rich in glowing electric pianos, humming organs, and tasteful synthesizer figures. The rhythm section—drummer Billy Johnson, bassist Robin Duhe, and percussionists McKinnley William and Roame Lowery—interlocked as smoothly as the keyboards, never pushing the beat, a discipline vital to the aura of Beverly's soothing compositions.

With these sultry grooves as the frame, Beverly paints his wholesome pictures on top with voice and pen. In his phrasing, I hear echoes of his benefactor, Marvin Gaye, and his idol, Sam Cooke. But Beverly's voice has an understated, more working-class quality that differentiates him from those love men. Instead, he sounds like a dedicated husband still madly in love with his wife after all these years. His love songs exist in a world where one-night stands are spurned and real affection is sought, appreciated, returned.

Beverly also has a real gift for nonspecific protest songs in the tradition of the Isley Brothers' "Fight the Power"—songs that refer to the troubles of black America without the nuts-and-bolts rhetoric of an overtly political songwriter like Gil Scott-Heron. In addition to "We Need to Live," a tribute to Atlanta's murdered children, *Live* includes two inspirational numbers with the upbeat sixties flavor of Mayfield's "People Get Ready" and Cooke's eloquent "A Change Is Gonna Come." "Changing Times" assures us, "We'll get through these changing times," while "Running Away" preaches, like Booker T. Washington, that "the things you want are the things you have to earn."

Just as Beverly grew stronger by swimming against the tide, so did the radio format originated by WHUR in 1976 called "the Quiet Storm." Ten years later, stations in every major market and in many of the secondary markets made three- to five-hour blocks of mellow music a crucial part of their programming day. Some stations, like Los Angeles' KUTE went totally Quiet Storm, while others utilized the format, if not the title, from late evening into the morning. The program gave new life to the title of one of Smokey Robinson's last great compositions and proved a comfortable home, not just for Beverly, but for singers more interested in ballads than boogie. My favorite example is the woman who originally inspired the retronuevo idea: Anita Baker.

Baker's brilliant *Rapture* album, one of the surprise hits of 1986, was an album of contemporary intelligence and old-fashioned pipes. The intelligence was primarily Baker's. As executive producer, Baker made an eight-cut album with no uptempo songs, a complete reversal of the norm for black female vocalists in the post-disco era. In making that decision she displayed an understanding of her voice as instrument and demonstrated why more women should demand control of their recordings.

The pipes were Baker's, too. Wrapping her voice in supportive arrangements and using real live bass players and drummers, Baker shone with the maturity of a Dinah Washington. It is unashamedly adult music that, as did her 1982 Beverly Glen hit "Angel," sounds progressive despite its old-fashioned values.

Baker's impact was profound because it exposed how superficially so many vocal divas had pursued their crossover dreams, diluting the power of their voices in the process, and because in *Rapture*'s wake the industry allowed some of its most gifted young voices (Miki Howard, Regina Belle) to record with a minimum of production overkill.

Yes, Baker made music for assimilated black Americans, though unlike that of crossover artists, her work tapped into the traditions of jazz and blues with a feeling that suggested being middle class didn't make your taste the musical equivalent of a Big Mac.

Considering my earlier comments, the following conclusion may be a surprise, but the two most important retronuevo artists have been Michael Jackson and Prince. Despite the unfortunate impact of their imagery, this dynamic duo proved to be the decade's finest music historians, consistently using techniques that echoed the past as the base for their superstardom.

During his epochal 1983 performance on *Motown 25*, Jackson suggested Jack Wilson's athleticism, James Brown's camel walk, the intensity of the Apollo amateur night, and the glitter of Diana Ross. In *Purple Rain*, Prince with the sensitivity of a poet, made historical allusions to Hendrix, Little Richard, Patti LaBelle, and Brown, while his employee, the Time's Morris Day, was molded into a modern-day Louis Jordan. Both Jackson (on "Beat It") and Prince (on "Let's Go Crazy" and "Purple Rain") made rock & roll for black folks while injecting their own idiosyncratic perspective into black dance music. Jackson's "Billie Jean" and "Wanna Be Startin' Something" raise superstar paranoia to a high art over grooves just as technologically assured as they were funky. "Don't Stop Til You Get Enough" is an incredible dance record, an anthem of spiritual and physical liberation in a wonderful synthesis of disco, the Philly sound, and Quincy Jones's own understanding of the drama in musical arrangement.

Prince, the auteur of the Minneapolis sound and himself a major talent scout, created the only competition to hip hop in the eighties, injecting fresh musical ideals into black music. Vanity, Morris Day, Jesse Johnson, the production team of Jimmy Jam Harris and Terry Lewis, Alexander O'Neal, Monte Moir, Andre Cymone, Sheila E., and quite a few others were ripples that came to our attention when Prince hit the shore. Not all these folks have great affection for Prince, but either their image or their music owes a debt to his fertile, cunning mind. Prince says that when he was a kid he didn't hear much black radio or music, but if his Brownesque 1986 *Parade* tour and the dancing in the film, *Sign "O" the Times*, is any indication, this retronuevo innovator had done a lot of catching up.

More, if we look at Jackson and Prince from the perspective of economic self-sufficiency, there is no question that this duo exercise a control over their careers and business that neither James Brown nor Sam Cooke, as ambitious as they were, could have envisioned. All major decisions, and even a great many minor ones, involving their money and artistic direction are determined personally by these performers. In Jackson's case this has meant, most significantly, the multimillion-dollar acquisition of the song catalogues of Sly Stone and the Beatles, two of his major influences, and the willingness to pay major directors like John Landis and Martin Scorsese big-budget money to expand the scope of music videos.

Where most of Jackson's business activities have been designed to promote and perpetuate his larger-than-life persona (much as with James Brown), Prince has used his energy to build and direct a multi-media empire that has spawned a slew of

artists, launched a record label (Paisley Park), and led to the production of three feature films (*Purple Rain, Under the Cherry Moon,* and *Sign "O" the Times*), two of which
he's directed himself.

Also as with James Brown, of course, there are disagreeable elements in the way
that they each manifest their power and in the images of themselves they choose to
project to both black and white audiences. However, to ignore their power, artistically and within their own organizations, solely because of their cosmetics would
be ignorant. By using star clout to further their own interests (and, yes, whims) in
unprecedented directions, Michael Jackson and Prince have set new standards of
autonomy for black musicians—and for black-music businesspeople, too.

Further Reading

Brackett, David. "(In Search of) Musical Meaning: Genres, Categories, and Crossover." In
    Popular Music Studies, ed. David Hesmondhalgh and Keith Negus, 65–82. London:
    Arnold, 2002.
Garofalo, Reebee. "Crossing Over: 1939–1989." In *Split Image: African-Americans in the Mass
    Media,* ed. Jannette L. Dates and William Barlow, 57–121. Washington, D.C.: Howard
    University Press, 1990.
_____. "Black Popular Music: Crossing Over or Going Under?" In *Rock and Popular Music:
    Politics, Policies, Institutions,* ed. Tony Bennett, Simon Frith, Lawrence Grossberg, John
    Shepherd, and Graeme Turner, 231–48. New York: Routledge, 1993.
George, Nelson. *The Death of Rhythm and Blues.* New York: Pantheon Books, 1988.
Harper, Philip Brian. "Synesthesia, 'Crossover,' and Blacks in Popular Music." *Social Text* 23
    (Fall–Winter 1989): 102–21.
Perry, Steve. "Ain't No Mountain High Enough: The Politics of Crossover." In *Facing the
    Music,* ed. Simon Frith, 51–87. New York: Pantheon Books, 1988.

Discography

Baker, Anita. *Rapture.* Elektra, 1986.
Benson, George. *Twice the Love.* Warner Bros., 1988.
Bryson, Peabo. *Straight From the Heart/Take No Prisoners.* Collectables, 2003.
The Commodores. *Night Shift.* Motown, 1985.
Houston, Whitney. *Whitney Houston.* Arista, 1985.
Prince. *Ultimate Prince.* Rhino/WEA, 2006.
Prince and the Revolution. *Purple Rain.* Warner Bros., 1984.
_____. *Parade: Music from the Motion Picture* Under The Cherry Moon. Warner Bros., 1986.
Richie, Lionel. *Dancing on the Ceiling.* Motown, 1986.
Ross, Diana. *Swept Away.* RCA, 1984.
Turner, Tina. *Private Dancer.* Capitol, 1984.

66. Heavy Metal Thunders On!

Chapter 52 discussed the dispersion of heavy metal approaches in genres such as hard rock, glam, and punk. Heavy metal persisted in its own right, however, becoming more stylized, with bands like Judas Priest, Iron Maiden, and AC/DC focusing on a riff-oriented approach while emphasizing guitar heroics and high-pitched vocals. A uniquely American form of metal developed in the United States in the late 1970s, with bands such as Van Halen recording catchy, hook-laden material that eschewed the more arcane lyrics of their British counterparts. The guitarist for the band, Eddie Van Halen, developed the most significant addition to rock guitar playing since Hendrix with his mastery of the two-handed "tapping" technique, enabling him to slur rapid-fire arpeggios that would have been physically impossible using conventional guitar technique.[1] "Tapping" would soon become standard practice among metal guitarists.

If during the mid- to late 1970s heavy metal had been a very popular "underground" phenomenon (in terms of media attention and radio play), the early 1980s saw the genre emerge into the bright light of the mass media. During the time that mainstream outlets were ignoring heavy metal, metal bands were nonetheless filling arenas and selling millions of records. As the sound of metal became associated with lower- and lower-middle-class white youths and suburban ennui, bands from both sides of the Atlantic began to build on Van Halen's blend of pop hooks with guitar virtuosity. The result? "Glam metal" or "hair metal" bands, such as Def Leppard and Mötley Crüe, began to cross over to the pop charts, inflecting the legacy of Foreigner-Boston et al. with a harder edge and a fashion sense derived from glam via Queen.

The following article by J. D. Considine was published in 1984 at a time when media attention documenting the widespread appeal of heavy metal was growing more common. The two bands discussed in

---

1. See Robert Walser's chapter analyzing Eddie Van Halen's solo guitar *tour de force*, "Eruption," and its influence on subsequent heavy metal guitarists (Walser, *Running with the Devil: Power, Gender, and Madness in Heavy Metal Music* [Hanover, N.H.: Wesleyan University Press and University Press of New England, 1993], 67–107).

the article, Judas Priest and the Scorpions (the section on the Scorpions is largely deleted), do not hail as much from the pop end of the heavy metal spectrum, although both bands nudged their way onto MTV during the early to mid-1980s. Instead, what this article captures is the emphasis on visceral power and excitement and on an unironic seriousness about technique that Priest's lead singer, Rob Halford, compares to that of Western classical music (much to the amusement of Considine).[2] We also hear a description of why heavy metal caught on in Britain from Priest guitarist K. K. Downing and a few ideas about the appeal of metal to its audience.

Purity and Power—Total, Unswerving Devotion to Heavy Metal Form: Judas Priest and the Scorpions

J. D. Considine

No doubt about it, heavy metal is the Music Which Gets No Respect. Oh, sure, the fans like it. For some of them, metal is the very marrow of their cultural existence. And there are even a few broad-minded critics who are willing to let the music, like any other dog, have its day, even if their appreciation is more sociological than musical.

But for most folks, heavy metal is a musical moron joke, fodder for frustrated teens and dominion of dim-witted devil-worshippers. At best, the phrase conjures up the likable lunkheads of Rob Reiner's satiric *This is Spinal Tap;* at worst, the mind turns to Ozzy Osbourne, biting the heads off dead bats in Des Moines or pissing on the Alamo. In all, not exactly what you'd call positive images.

"You get narrow-minded critics reviewing the shows, and all they think about heavy metal is that it is just total ear-splitting, blood-curdling noise without any definition or point," complained Judas Priest's Rob Halford. "This is a very, *very* professional style of music. It means a great deal to many millions of people. We treat heavy metal music with respect."

Halford paused to gaze out the window at the passing Texas countryside. It was a bright Saturday afternoon. Judas Priest were en route from Houston to San Antonio, smack in the middle of a nine-month American tour which had found the band playing to both narrow-minded critics and adoring heavy metal fans, the latter being in the distinct majority. Nevertheless, the question of heavy metal's aesthetic worth is one which Halford takes very much to heart. Heavy metal, he insisted, was genuine *art.*

"This might sound like a bizarre statement," he said, leaping back into the fray, "but I don't think playing heavy metal is that far removed from classical music. To do either, you have to spend many years developing your style and your art,

---

2. This connection is not as ridiculous as it seemed to some critics, and it is the focus of the chapter cited in note 1 from Walser's Running with the Devil.

whether you're a violinist or a guitarist, it still takes the same belief in your form of music to achieve and create. It is very much a matter of dedication."

As a herd of cattle receded in the distance, I tried to imagine Halford, in white tie and tails, standing center-stage in a New York recital hall to sing the celebrated art song "Eat Me Alive," while somewhere in the Midwest, a leather-clad Robert Mann of the Julliard String Quartet is screaming into a microphone, asking a rowdy coliseum crowd if they're "ready for some Beethoven?" Somehow the image refused to come.

No, heavy metal isn't exactly serial composition, but then again, art isn't always a matter of complexity. Sometimes, getting and keeping things simple takes as much or more skill.

"A funny story," said Judas Priest's Glenn Tipton, backstage one night, "When we were recording *Defenders Of The Faith* in Spain, this guy from South America came up, a friend of mine. He plays guitar—amazing things, rhythms, phrases, strange South American-type beats, stuff I couldn't begin to play, much more complex than those Police things. Real sambas and stuff, and difficult as hell. All he wanted off me was to learn how to play things with rock accents.

"He couldn't play 'em," Tipton laughs. "An entirely different feeling."

It's that bone-headed simplicity, the art of knowing what *not* to play, that Tipton feels makes heavy metal so ultimately British.

"To me, and I can say this honestly, there are not very many American heavy metal bands. There are some great rock bands, the best rock bands in the world. But it's not heavy metal. The American bands are too sophisticated. And I think that's it—English bands, like ourselves, have that lack of sophistication which, I suppose, has to do with upbringing, the fact that we were born and raised poverty-struck. I think you can lose that out of your music, if you're not careful."

In other words, great heavy metal turns its limitations into assets, its insularity into a sense of community, and ends up doing everything art is expected to do. True, heavy metal is often musically limited, culturally reactionary and too damned loud, but at its best, it is *transcendently* so. Which is why, ludicrous as it may seem, Rob Halford's analogy between heavy metal and classical music contains a grain of truth: both disciplines ultimately aim for the triumph of emotion over form.

It's Saturday night in San Antonio, the last night of the city's annual Easter Fiesta. There's a buzz of excitement throughout the city and a roar inside the Civic Arena. When the lights go down for Judas Priest's set, 12,000 kids are on their feet, fists in the air, screaming. As a taped synthesizer growl drones ominously, the curtains part to reveal "the Metallian," a twenty-foot high aluminum gargoyle who holds the drum kit in its left claw. Fog wafts across the stage as the Metallian's vari-light eyes scan the audience: then, in a blinding burst of flashpots, the members of Priest materialize, leaping headlong into the hyper-adrenal pulse of "Love Bites."

As spectacle, it's pretty impressive. With the Metallian looming above like a malevolent building, Halford's macho strut and the rest of the band's leather-clad choreography seem less a matter of vainglorious posturing than an assertion of will, a dance against the demons of the city. Even at the end of the set, as the Metallian breathes fire through the final, crashing chords to "The Green Manalishi (With The Two-Pronged Crown)," it wields its menace almost in defeat, a vanquished dragon.

Granted, that's a lot of meaning to read into an elaborate prop, but it would be foolish to overlook the resonances of such devices. As Halford puts it, "When we use those props, people see them and they say, 'Oh, what is *this?*' But when they suddenly connect with the props, it's a total unification, music and material object working together."

The night before, in Houston, guitarist K. K. Downing had begun to explain his theory of heavy metal. "In certain parts of Great Britain, some bands started taking progressive blues and playing them in their own way. Heavy metal is our own blues, actually."

This "white man's blues," as Downing is fond of calling it, worked because it translated the emotional impact of American blues into a form that young musicians in Britain's industrial heartland could more easily understand. "It was more aggressive," Downing said. "It's a way of getting rid of your blues by expending energy. And it's a way for the audience to expend energy as well."

This makes sense if you look at the music's structure. "All the licks that we play," explained Glenn Tipton, who shares the lead guitar role with Downing, "form around the blues. You get something like the lead break in 'Another Thing Comin',' it's all blues stuff, all the same runs. Even the fast stuff." Grabbing a guitar and practice amp, he plugged in. "Something like this," he said, spinning off a fast splatter of notes, "is just from cadences like this." He began to play a typical blues riff—up from the 7th to the tonic, up again to the minor 3rd, and back down to the tonic—and slowly sped it up, letting the syncopation bleed out as the figure turned into insistent eighth-notes, moving the pattern up the neck by half-steps. Pure metal, "and it's all blues stuff."

Except, of course, that the rhythm is completely different. Where American blues, whether country acoustic or urban electric, maintain an easy rhythmic bounce, heavy metal surges with almost mechanical regularity, pushing the downbeat instead of laying behind the backbeat. It's not a party energy, certainly not dance music; it's more like a football cheer, group aggression focused through rhythm and sheer volume.

Of course, no football crowd could ever hope to muster a sound like Judas Priest's (much to the relief of Pete Rozelle). Despite the volume, Priest's sound isn't noisy or brittle, but sits comfortably in the midrange with a presence so great you could immerse yourself in it. "A total wallow," Halford cheerfully admitted. And during the three Priest shows I attended, the fans did almost seem to be floating, reacting to shifts in dynamics like toy boats in a bathtub.

"A lot of the access and understanding of our music for so many people is that they're able to relate to what we're singing about," Halford continued. "Beyond the vocals, it's the way a guitar makes you feel when someone hits a particular chord, the way a snare drum is cracked."

Flashing back to Halford's classical analogy, I suddenly realized that the difference between the kid playing air guitar in his bedroom to "Rock Hard, Ride Free" and his father in the family room, conducting the last movement of the *Symphonie Fantastique* along with Herr von Karajan, is not much more than a matter of props. That's not to say that classical music and heavy metal are necessarily equivalents, just that the listener's experience can be, because for both father and son, it's a matter of release through pure sound. So it wasn't hard to nod appreciatively when Halford concluded by remarking, "I just hope that, after seeing us for the first time, people go away from a show fulfilled by what they've experienced."

I'll bet Herr von Karajan feels the same way.

Call it another side-effect to adolescent glandular mayhem, or just call it zit cream for the soul. In any case, both Priest and the Scorps agree that the key to the heavy metal's popularity is the power transfer between performer and audience. "We have a high energy level," says Scorpion Matthias Jabs, "and when the audience is great, they feel that and give it back to you."

"You can't analyze it much beyond the fact that there are 11,000 separate individual human beings getting off on what you're doing," concludes Priest's Halford, "each of them experiencing an emotional vibe and throwing it back at you. I mean, that's what art is all about. We all need each other."

Further Reading

Bennett, Andy, and Kevin Dawe, eds. *Guitar Cultures*. New York: Berg, 2001.
Christe, Ian. *Sound of the Beast: The Complete Headbanging History of Heavy Metal*. New York: Harper Entertainment, 2004.
Laing, Dave. "'Sadeness,' Scorpions and Single Markets: National and Transnational Trends in European Popular Music." *Popular Music* 11 (1992): 127–40.
Walser, Robert. *Running with the Devil: Power, Gender, and Madness in Heavy Metal Music*. Hanover, N.H.: University Press of New England, 1993.

Discography

AC/DC. *Back in Black*. Atlantic, 1980.
Def Leppard. *Pyromania*. Mercury, 1983.
Iron Maiden. *Powerslave*. EMI, 1984.
Judas Priest. *Sad Wings of Destiny*. Janus, 1976.
_____. *Screaming for Vengeance*. Columbia, 1982.
Racer X. *Street Lethal*. Shrapnel Records, 1986.
Ratt. *Out of the Cellar*. Atlantic, 1984.
Scorpions. *Blackout*. EMI, 1982.
Van Halen. *Van Halen*. Warner Bros., 1978.
_____. *Fair Warning*. Warner Bros., 1981.

67. Metal in the Late Eighties

GLAM OR THRASH?

Many of the bands of the "hard" heavy metal school were influenced not only by earlier metal bands, but by hardcore punk, and they developed new subgenres of metal, dubbed "speed metal," "thrash metal," and "death metal." Within the heavy metal subculture, these latter bands represented the "purer," "non-commercial" strains of metal in contrast to the "glam metal" bands. If one of the best examples of a pop metal band in the late 1980s was Bon Jovi, then the clearest example of a band that seemed to follow its own inclinations and respond to a core audience of metal fanatics was Metallica (which, by the way, went on to become wildly popular themselves).[1]

In the following piece, Richard Gehr portrays Metallica on the verge of moving from an extremely popular cult band to a band with mass popularity, a topic that comes to the fore in the band's comments about their "outsider" status. Particularly fascinating is the description of Metallica's songwriting process, one of the factors responsible for song structures that were unusually complex within the context of other metal of the time. Gehr also describes how the content of Metallica's lyrics was one of the factors separating their brand of "thrash" from "pop metal." The highpoint of heavy metal's popularity in the late 1980s and early 1990s created a situation in which bands like Metallica could simultaneously maintain "underground" status and experience mass popularity, a balancing act taken over by grunge after 1991. Gehr begins the article writing in the voice of the two members of Metallica who are profiled in this piece, James Hetfield and Lars Ulrich.

Metallica
Richard Gehr

Ulrich has recently risen from the sleep, dreamless or otherwise, of the very successful. His band, billed fourth (between Led Zep wannaboys Kingdom Come and metal morons Dokken) on the Monsters of Rock tour—a.k.a. the "Fucking Monsters of Fucking Rock" tour, a.k.a. the "weekend" tour—has garnered *at least* as much critical oom-pah as their co-"Monsters," even Van Fucking Halen.

During their non-touring weekdays, Metallica was ensconced in the bucolic environs of Woodstock, New York, feverishly mixing tracks for their fourth LP, . . . *And Justice for All!* Ulrich doesn't remember that the studio where they're working is named Bearsville; he only knows that it's several miles from the nearest watering hole. But when bleary-eyed singer/guitarist James Hetfield joins us a little later, he'll helpfully add, "It's out in the middle of the forest up there. I heard something about The Band."

Ulrich and Hetfield formed Metallica in Los Angeles in 1981 as a hard-edged response to late-Seventies mainstream rock. Inspired in equal parts by the so-called "new wave of British heavy metal" and by the Southern California hardcore scene, Metallica stripped away the gothic excesses of the former and expanded the short-form song structures of the latter to produce five- to eight-minute mini-epics of

---

1. For a profile of Metallica on the cusp of mass popularity as they struggle with the contradictions engendered by their shifting status, see David Fricke, "Heavy Metal Justice," *Rolling Stone*, January 12, 1989, 42–49.

Source: "Metallica" © Richard Gehr/*Music Sound and Output*/Rock's Backpages.

ear-shattering volume and mind-boggling speed. They compounded multiple riffs within single tunes, linking them with subject matter that rejected "gonna-rock-ya-all-night-long" HM cliches (not to be confused with "gonna-love-ya-all-nite-long" HM cliches) in favor of darker meditations on power, violence, aggression and death.

Young and hungry, Metallica evinces absolutely no influence prior to, say, 1976. For example: an AOR "oldies" station plays quietly in the background as we talk. At one point, a strange expression passes across Hetfield's face. He looks at the radio and, almost complaining, asks, "What's this?!" The scrap that caught his attention was Leigh Stevens's guitar solo on "Help Me Doctor" from Blue Cheer's first LP, *Vincebus Eruptum*—arguably the finest heavy metal album ever recorded.

Rather than subsisting as just another metal band from L.A., the group, which included lead guitarist Kirk Hammett and bassist Cliff Burton, moved to New York in 1983. After signing with Megaforce, they released their first LP, *Kill 'Em All*, whose leather-roots popularity kept them on the road in the United States and Europe for the next nine months. The band's second Megaforce LP, a post-adolescent death trip titled *Ride the Lightning*, was quickly snatched up by Elektra and went on to sell more than half a million copies. As to the record's morbid theme, Ulrich says, "around then we were talking about capital punishment and had a lot of fucking thoughts about dying and death."

"We were putting ourselves in various situations," adds Hetfield, "like the electric chair and cryonics."

Both make a big deal about how none of their records, including *Lightning*, is a concept album. "I think records reflect whatever shit you're going through at that point in time," noted Ulrich sagely.

With the success of *Lightning*, Metallica's stock quickly ascended. They were still a cult band, but they were a cult band like Pee-Wee Herman is a cult comedian. By the time Elektra released *Master of Puppets* in 1986, Metallica had welded shut their position in the metal pantheon, despite the fact that virtually no radio station dared to air their savagely sophisticated megawattage and they made no music videos.

Collectively, Metallica's members thrive on their independence and outsider status, scorning anything short of total musical and personal autonomy. Ulrich describes *Puppets*, for example, as being about the dangers of "drugs, manipulation, anything that takes you over." The lyrics' syntax may scan in the most bizarre of fashions—just try and parse lines like "Not dead which eternal lie/Stranger eons death may die"—but the impact and emotion is unmistakable. What do you expect from a metal band, after all. Cole Porter?

An American tour with Ozzy Osbourne following the release of *Puppets* nailed their appeal. The album has since sold more than 750,000 copies domestically and penetrated *Billboard's* Top 30.

Sadly, bassist Cliff Burton was killed in Scandinavia when the band's tour bus crashed that summer. Rather than fade into oblivion, however, the band resuscitated itself in his honor and added bass player Jason Newsted (of Flotsam & Jetsam fame). After touring Japan, they even returned to Europe and made up the dates they'd missed.

For Metallica, writing and recording an album is an extremely piecemeal, even abstract process. Their songwriting begins literally in a garage, where Ulrich and Hetfield sift through riff tapes compiled by the four band members.

"We've got riffs from years and years," explains Hetfield. "On the road we constantly riff and write it down."

"The riffs have *feels*," says Ulrich. "First we start separating the riffs into . . . "

". . . Categories. . . ." says Hetfield.

"Like, some shit is strong enough to be the main idea of a tune. Then we go through the tapes and try to find possible bridges, choruses, middle bits or whatever. After we have the skeleton of a song, we start getting a feel for what the song's really like. Then we search for a title from a list of titles that fits with the riffing's mood."

After assembling the song, the group works it out on a demo.

Hetfield: "Then Lars and I sit with the demos and go, Well, this is a little too fast here, and this is a little too slow. We'll play it live and see if it really grooves. If not, we'll try it a little faster."

Ulrich and Hetfield next assemble a click track that schematizes the song's various tempos.

Hetfield: "First I'll lay down a scratch rhythm, then he'll go in and do his drums. I think our click track situation is something unique from what other bands do because some songs have between 10 and 15 click-track samples, which really freaks people out. They can't understand it. Usually clicks keep the time steady, but we have many moods and grooves within each eight- or nine-minute song. So for every riff we figure out what tempo it sounds best at, to make it fit better with the whole thing's overall feel.

"Putting down the clicks for a couple of songs on *Justice!* took two days each. But when I tell that to other people they think I mean two hours or something."

After completing the click track, the group is ready to record. Here again Metallica differ from standard procedure by going after a full, "live" sound in the most roundabout of ways.

"We record about as nonlive as possible," says Ulrich. "There's never more than one guy in the studio at any one point in time."

Building the click track, says Hetfield, takes "a lot longer, probably, than it would to actually do it live." The recording procedure goes something like this: Hetfield lays down his scratch rhythm, Ulrich records his drum tracks, Hetfield returns and completes his final rhythm-guitar parts, Newsted adds the bass, then Hetfield and Hammett alternate leads and vocals, "so we don't burn ourselves out."

Metallica's last two LPs were recorded in Copenhagen's Sweet Silence Studios. One of the differences between most studios in Los Angeles and their European equivalents, says Ulrich, is how "all that shit's included. You don't have to fucking *rent* anything." Another difference is the tendency of European studios to employ an in-house engineer, which is how the group discovered Flemming Rasmussen.

During their '84 European tour, the band decided to concentrate their energies on an extended stay on the continent, where they could tour, record an album, blitz the press and "really spread a lot of shit around."

They met the man with whom they would record their next three albums during their first day in Sweet Silence Studios. "Flemming had done some Rainbow stuff that sounded pretty good and he was supposedly a really happening engineer," recalls Ulrich. "At that point in time we had had a really bad experience with an I-use-the-term-loosely 'producer' on the first album [Paul Curcio on *Kill 'Em All*], and we were glad to have two more weeks of studio time instead of spending $10 or $15 thousand on someone who really didn't know anything about the band. So we went in and did it with Flemming, and instantly there was some sort of happening vibe there. There still is, and it's been growing stronger, really. He's like the fifth member when it comes to recording."

Unfortunately, Rasmussen wasn't immediately available after Metallica began recording . . . *And Justice for All!*, so the band hooked up with Guns N' Roses producer Mike Clink for their first sessions at One on One. On *Master of Puppets,* according to Ulrich, "we booked studio time and fucking got all the decisions together way too early in the songwriting. But when it came time to go into the studio, we weren't really ready." With *Justice!*, however, the situation was exactly the opposite.

"This time around we didn't want to make any recording decisions until we had all the songs written. So we started writing in October and it only took eight or nine weeks to write the songs. It went a lot quicker than we thought it would." By January, they were ready to record, but Rasmussen wasn't, having been unavoidably detained by a prior commitment to a band amusingly called Danish Pregnant Woman. But Metallica wanted him bad, and did everything in their power to snare him, but to no avail.

"We fucking tried everything, but there was no fucking way to get this fucking Danish Pregnant Woman to fucking give Flemming up. We offered to fucking fly engineers in at our expense, pay for studio time, anything, right? No. See ya.

"So basically we were faced with the situation of whether we wanted to sit around and *dwell* for fucking three months, let the fuckin' songs get burned out, and kind of fuckin' start hating things. We're all sitting around on our couch going flump, we've gotta fuckin' start doing something with our time."

The decision was made to go into the studio with Mike Clink, get comfortable by wailing on a couple of Diamondhead and Budgie chestnuts, work out some B-sides and prepare for Rasmussen's availability. But, according to Ulrich, "The Clink situation emphasized that we really can't work, or at least record, with anyone other than Flemming."

"Well, we can." Adds Hetfield, "but it's a slow process."

"We'd still be in there right now doing drum tracks," moans Ulrich.

Rasmussen finally came to the rescue, and the drummer and guitarist acknowledge that their time with Clink wasn't totally wasted. Rather, it was just enough to loosen the group up and enable them to start recording within a couple of days of Rasmussen's arrival six weeks into their studio block. "If we'd started from scratch it probably would have taken us three weeks," says Ulrich.

Metallica mixed . . . *And Justice for All!* with Michael Barbiero and Steve Thompson, whose credits include Whitney Houston, Madonna, the Rolling Stones, Prince, Cinderella, Tesla and Guns N' Roses. Ulrich and Hetfield are optimistic about the collaboration.

"Looking back," opines Ulrich, "I don't think we've been too comfortable with any of the mixes we've ever done."

Hetfield agrees, adding, "I think the problem with a lot of people who specialize in mixing is they set up the mix the way they're used to mixing bands, and everyone ends up sounding like those mixes. What's great about these guys is they go out of their way to keep the band's identity completely together."

How does *Justice* differ from *Puppets*?

"It's a lot . . ." begins Ulrich.

"Drier," continues Hetfield.

"A lot drier, and a lot more . . ."

"In your face," Hetfield pipes in again. "Everything's way up front and there's not a lot of 'verb or echo. We really went out of our way to make sure that what we put on the tape was what we wanted, so the mixing procedure would be as easy as possible and not like the old saying, 'We'll save it in the mix.'"

"*Puppets* was very well recorded," says Ulrich, "and had a very huge sort of sound, but didn't really fuckin' come out of the speakers and hit you in the face."

"Compared to *Ride the Lightning* it did," Hetfield reminds him.

"I don't want to listen to *Ride the Lightning*," groans Ulrich.

"Flemming was in a reverb daze," explains Hetfield.

Did the experience of recording *The $5.98 EP* affect *Justice's* sound?

"I think we were pretty pleased with the way it was so upfront and raw," reckons Hetfield.

"We learned something from that mix," says Ulrich.

"We learned that the bass is too loud," says Hetfield.

"And when is the bass too loud?" chants Ulrich.

Together: "When you can hear it!"

Upon completion, . . . *And Justice for All!* will be another Metallica mouthful of supercharged riffs and vaguely upsetting lyrics just this side of deeply disturbing. Although they joke flippantly about its content, Ulrich and Hetfield obviously place much greater existential stock in their work than your typical metal numbskulls.

What's it about? I inquire.

"Walking your dog in the park," quips Ulrich.

"And not wanting to clean up after it," continues Hetfield, as usual. "But there's a law, so you have to. It's basically about independence and freedom, and how they are stopped in certain ways."

"How they're very surfacey things," adds Ulrich. "At a certain point they really start shoving those words in your face, but when you really start thinking about a lot of shit . . ."

". . . how free is it?" concludes Hetfield.

Ulrich goes on. "You have freedom of choice, but how many choices do you have? It's easy to say you can make up your own mind, but you can only make up your mind about two or three different things."

Like, for example, between Dokken, the Scorpions, Kingdom Come, Poison, Venom, Van Fucking Halen, and a skidillion other munsters of rock. Metallica prove it that Sunday afternoon in Foxboro, where they play an abbreviated, probably even mediocre set for several thousand curious complexions. No matter. It's clear that Metallica embody an electrically overamped power and passion that rings a hundred times truer than their monster mates. Like free jazz, New York noise or even composer Krystof Penderecki, Metallica are original dynamos, weekend warriors outstanding in a very loud field of their own. And that's the fucking truth.

Further Reading

Christe, Ian. *Sound of the Beast: The Complete Headbanging History of Heavy Metal.* New York: Harper Entertainment, 2004.

Fricke, David. "Heavy Metal Justice," *Rolling Stone,* January 12, 1989, 42–49.

Garofalo, Reebee. "Setting the Record Straight: Censorship and Social Responsibility in Popular Music." *Journal of Popular Music Studies* 6 (1994): 1–37.

Irwin, William, ed. *Metallica and Philosophy: A Crash Course in Brain Surgery.* Oxford, UK: Blackwell, 2007.

Pillsbury, Glenn T. *Damage Incorporated: Metallica and the Production of Musical Identity.* New York: Routledge, 2006.

Discography

Guns N' Roses. *Appetite for Destruction.* Geffen, 1987.

Metallica. *Master of Puppets.* Elektra, 1986.

_____. . . . *And Justice for All.* Elektra, 1988.
Poison. *Look What the Cat Dragged In.* Capitol, 1986.
Quiet Riot. *Mental Health.* Pasha, 1983.
W.A.S.P. *W.A.S.P.* Capitol, 1984.

68. Parents Want to Know: Heavy Metal, the PMRC, and the Public Debate over Decency

The popularity of heavy metal could not remain underground forever: Top 40 hits by Def Leppard, Quiet Riot, Ratt, Mötley Crüe, and the Scorpions and the growing ubiquity of metal-influenced guitar solos in the early to mid-1980s presaged the genre's full-scale breakthrough. A clear sign of this change of status was the addition to MTV's schedule in 1985 of a show devoted entirely to metal, *Heavy Metal Mania*, which was renamed *Headbanger's Ball* in 1987. This reflected a change in MTV's format as the video channel moved away from continuous 24-hour video flow into a schedule broken down into specialized time slots, as well as the recognition that heavy metal was now acceptable to the demographic represented by MTV's audience.

This development in the realm of music video was paralleled by increased radio play for metal bands, not only for the ever-expanding progeny of "glam" or "lite" metal bands such as Poison and Warrant, but also for bands that followed the "harder" Judas Priest/Iron Maiden approach. Earlier distinctions between British and American metal began to erode, and a band like Guns N' Roses (probably the most popular metal band of the late eighties) successfully combined several of the different strands of the genre.

The rise in popularity of heavy metal in the guise of glam metal occasioned an increase in media attention by the mid-1980s. As these artists' songs, public personae, and images (from music videos and album covers) became more widely known, they disturbed the sensibilities of those outside their main fan base. The look (long, frequently-blond hair, "glam" makeup, black leather with spiked gauntlets), music (high-pitched, semi-screamed male vocals, power chords, distortion), and imagery of male domination were all perceived as shocking by people who had previously had little exposure to the genre. The fact that selected song lyrics and video and album images contained explicitly sexual and/or violent content was enough to set off mass-mediated alarm bells. At the same time, more mainstream artists such as Prince and Sheena Easton were also featuring explicit sexual details in their lyrics, a coincidence sufficient to ignite a full-blown moral panic. Contrary to what its subsequent history might suggest, rap sailed beneath the radar of moral righteousness at this time, perhaps because its public profile was too low, or perhaps because prior to the large-scale emergence of gangsta rap around 1987, the frequency of explicit lyrics in rap songs was lower than that in the other genres that became the focus of public debate.

At any rate, greater public awareness of these now-controversial artists and their attendant lyrics and images led to a response from the national Parent Teacher Association (PTA) and the founding of the Parent Music Resource Center (PMRC) by the wives of several prominent Washington politicians. The PMRC was led by Tipper Gore (wife of then–U.S. Senator Al Gore, a Democrat) and Susan Baker (wife of then–U.S. Secretary of the Treasury James Baker, a Republican). In a rare display of bipartisanship, the founders of the PMRC focused on several examples of what they called "porn rock": the namesake of Prince's "Darling Nikki," who masturbates in a hotel lobby; the video of Mötley Crüe's "Looks That Kill," which features "scantily clad women being captured and imprisoned in cages by a studded-leather-clad male band"; and the lyrics of Judas Priest's "Eat Me Alive," which describe "oral sex at gunpoint."[1] During the period of these media campaigns by the PTA and PMRC, the subjects of the newly dubbed "porn rock" received a wave of attention from journalists in op-ed pieces.[2]

Public concern with the level of sexual and violent images in this music (and in entertainment in general) came to a head when Congress opened hearings on the subject in September 1985. Neither the positions for nor the positions against were as simple as have sometimes been portrayed. The PMRC voiced the concerns of parents of all political stripes about the desire to control the kind of material to which their kids had access (a concern that continues to the present day in issues such as how to control children's access to Internet and cable TV). The

---

1. Quotes are drawn from the book that most fully explains the PMRC's position: Tipper Gore, *Raising PG Kids in an X-Rated Society* (New York: Bantam, 1988), 3, xi.

2. For a sample, see the following: Patrick Goldstein, "Parents Warn Take the Sex and Shock out of Rock," *Los Angeles Times*, August 25, 1985; George F. Will, "No One Blushes Anymore," *Washington Post*, September 15, 1985; and Barbara Jaeger, "Sex, Violence, and Rock n' Roll, Young Fans Can See It All," *Denver Post*, April 28, 1985. An article from the same period by Deborah Frost ("White Noise—How Heavy Metal Rules," *Village Voice*, June 18, 1985) stands out for its thoughtful social analysis rather than the moral proselytizing featured by the other articles cited here. These articles and several others were produced as evidence and included in the published proceedings of the congressional hearings that form the focus of this chapter.

aspect of the PMRC's campaign that most troubled critics, however, concerned the slippage between a request for greater information and the promotion of a "cause and effect," or "hypodermic," cultural model.[3] Social ills, according to the PMRC's point of view, were caused by music and other forms of entertainment, rather than the social inequities and negative social interactions supported by powerful institutions; according to this outlook, a song with violent, misogynistic lyrics creates young men who are violent and misogynistic, a song about suicide causes a teenager to commit suicide, and so on. Surfacing frequently in these critiques was the nostalgic view that these forms of entertainment were making it impossible for the nuclear family to act as the positive foundation that it once had, or, alternately, that these songs reflected the decay of the nuclear family. Furthermore, the PMRC and its supporters did not account for variations in reception of cultural texts, that is, why everyone who hears a song that mentions suicide does not commit suicide, and they overstated the frequency of the most extreme lyrics and images and the centrality of lyrics to the listening experience, thereby exaggerating the seriousness of the threat. Opponents of the PMRC, for their part, often expressed sympathy with the stated aims of the group to control children's access to the relevant materials while criticizing the cause-and-effect model and voicing concern about the implications for future censorship.

The following proceedings from the 1985 congressional hearings give voice to these different positions. On one side, we meet Senator Ernest F. Hollings from South Carolina and Susan Baker, whose concern with the effect of popular music on society leads them to consider (or advocate) censorship; representing a somewhat different point of view, Tipper and Al Gore lean more toward the "voluntary" approach, which would have the record industry of its own volition label its products with warning stickers. Among critics, the most famous response came from Frank Zappa. Perhaps the most surprising aspect of Zappa's statement is his concession that parents are justified to request that some type of additional information accompany albums; in this case, Zappa suggests adding a lyric sheet, a request for which Senator Gore (in a passage not reproduced here) subsequently voiced his support. A recurring theme in the statements of many of the participants is confusion over

---

3. For a discussion of the PMRC that highlights this slippage, see Robert Walser, *Running with the Devil: Power, Gender, and Madness in Heavy Metal Music* (Hanover: Wesleyan University Press, 1993), 137–60; for more on censorship and the PMRC, see Reebee Garofalo, "Setting the Record Straight: Censorship and Social Responsibility in Popular Music," *Journal of Popular Music Studies* 6 (1994): 1–37. The moral panic over popular music resurfaced later in the decade in a more academic, yet still populist, form in Allan Bloom's *Closing of the American Mind* (New York: Simon & Schuster, 1987). Like Gore and the PMRC, Bloom anchors his argument in the defense of supposed universal humanist ideals.

the purpose of the hearing: was it simply a discussion about some kind of system to warn parents about content, or were they gathered in order to advocate for legislation that would actively censor the music industry? Not included here is testimony by several senators and scholars, as well as musicians Dee Snider of Twisted Sister (one of the targets of the PMRC) and John Denver (not one of the targets of the PMRC), both of whom argue against the PMRC's proposals. Although parental advisory stickers were recommended in November 1985 and have accompanied selected new recordings since 1988, they did not create the sea change that was predicted (though they did limit access to products thus labeled in certain large chain stores such as Walmart). The true disaster for the music industry had to wait until the advent of improvements in digital file-sharing technology.

Record Labeling: Hearing before the Committee on Commerce, Science, and Transportation, United States Senate, 99th Congress, September 19, 1985

Opening Statement by the Chairman

The Chairman: Ladies and gentlemen, this hearing is on the subject of the content of some, and I want to underscore the word "some," not all rock music, which it has been pointed out by a number of people as having really broken new ground as to the content of music and the lyrics that are used in music.

There have, I suppose, always been cases of songs that are suggestive in one way or another. However, certain rock music that is now being sold deals very explicitly with sexual subjects. Some music glorifies violence in various forms, sexual violence. Some music advocates the use of drugs, drug abuse, and so on.

And so, the reason for this hearing is not to promote any legislation. Indeed, I do not know of any suggestion that any legislation be passed. But to simply provide a forum for airing the issue itself, for ventilating the issue, for bringing it out into the public domain.

The concern is that the public at large should be aware of the existence of this kind of music, and the fact that it is now available to kids, and that kids of all ages are able to buy it.

It is my understanding that various private groups have been holding discussions with people who are in the music publishing and music industry to try to achieve

Source: RECORD LABELING: HEARING BEFORE THE COMMITTEE ON COMMERCE, SCIENCE, AND TRANSPORTATION. UNITED STATES SENATE, NINETY-NINTH CONGRESS. FIRST SESSION ON CONTENTS OF MUSIC AND THE LYRICS OF RECORDS. SEPTEMBER 19, 1985. Printed for the use of the Committee on Commerce, Science, and Transportation. U.S. GOVERNMENT PRINTING OFFICE, WASHINGTON : 1985. Accessed at http://www.joesapt. net/superlink/shrg99-529/index.html, January 7, 2012.

some sort of understanding with respect to the labeling of records so that at least the whole family knows what is in them, and not just the child who buys the record.

That seems to me to be a reasonable suggestion, but the point of this hearing is not for me to make any particular suggestions, but to simply provide [a] forum so that the whole issue can be brought to the attention of the American people. . . .

Opening Statement by Senator Hollings

Senator Hollings: Mr. Chairman, I first want to commend the Parents Music Resource Center for bringing this to the Nation's attention. I have had the opportunity to attend a showing, you might say, or presentation of this porn rock, as they call it. In the test of pornography, one of the things to look at is whether or not it has any redeeming social value. There could be an exception here, because having attended that presentation, the redeeming social value that I find is inaudible. . . .

In all candor, I would tell you it is outrageous filth, and we have got to do something about it. I take the tempered approach, of our distinguished chairman, and commend it. Yet, I would make the statement that if I could find some way constitutionally to do away with it, I would. . . .

I want everyone to know I am keeping that foremost in mind, and I am asking the best of constitutional minds, if there is some way in the world to try to limit it as we go along with the voluntary labeling. I commend those who are now beginning to label. That is what we would like to have, truth in labeling. I do not think we can outlaw pornography. I do not have that in mind at all. But take 6 to 7 hours daily—the average listening time, Senator, as I understand, by the youngsters of this particular porn rock and rock music and everything else of that kind. Well, let us say rock music and intersperse it with pornography. This is a matter of national concern, and it is something that we have got to give some kind of attention to within the constrictions of free speech.

So, I will be looking from the Senator's standpoint, not just to bring pressures to try to see if there is some constitutional provisions to tax, but an approach that can be used by the Congress to limit this outrageous filth, suggestive violence, suicide, and everything else in the Lord's world that you would not think of. Certainly the writers and framers of our first amendment never perhaps heard this music in their time, never considered the broadcast airwaves and certainly that being piped into people's homes willy nilly over the air. I will be listening closely. . . .

Opening Statement by Senator Gore

Senator Gore: Thank you very much, Mr. Chairman. I would like to thank you and commend you for calling this hearing. Because my wife has been heavily involved in the evolution of this issue, I have gained quite a bit of familiarity with it, and I have really gained an education in what is involved.

The two most important things I have learned which have changed my initial attitude to this whole concern are, No. 1, the proposals made by those concerned about this problem do not involve a Government role of any kind whatsoever. They are not asking for any form of censorship or regulation of speech in any manner, shape, or form.

What they are asking for is whether or not the music industry can show some self-restraint and working together in a manner similar to that used by the movie industry, whether or not they can come up with a voluntary guide system for parents who wish to exercise what they believe to be their responsibilities to their children, to try to prevent their children from being exposed to material that is not appropriate for them. . . .

Mrs. Baker: Before I begin, I would like to introduce the president of the PMRC, Pam Howar, and our treasurer, Sally Nevius.

The Parents Music Resource Center was organized in May of this year by mothers of young children who are very concerned by the growing trend in music toward lyrics that are sexually explicit, excessively violent, or glorify the use of drugs and alcohol.

Our primary purpose is to educate and inform parents about this alarming trend as well as to ask the industry to exercise self-restraint.

It is no secret that today's rock music is a very important part of adolescence and teenagers' lives. It always has been, and we don't question their right to have their own music. We think that is important. They use it to identify and give expression to their feelings, their problems, their joys, sorrows, loves, and values. It wakes them up in the morning and it is in the background as they get dressed for school. It is played on the bus. It is listened to in the cafeteria during lunch. It is played as they do their homework. They even watch it on MTV now. It is danced to at parties, and puts them to sleep at night.

Because anything that we are exposed to that much has some influence on us, we believe that the music industry has a special responsibility as the message of songs goes from the suggestive to the blatantly explicit.

As Ellen Goodman stated in a recent column, rock ratings: "The outrageous edge of rock and roll has shifted its focus from Elvis's pelvis to the saw protruding from Blackie Lawless's codpiece on a WASP album. Rock lyrics have turned from 'I can't get no satisfaction' to 'I am going to force you at gunpoint to eat me alive.'"

The material we are concerned about cannot be compared with Louie Louie, Cole Porter, Billie Holliday, et cetera. Cole Porter's "the birds do it, the bees do it," can hardly be compared with WASP, "I f-u-c-k like a beast." There is a new element of vulgarity and violence toward women that is unprecedented.

While a few outrageous recordings have always existed in the past, the proliferation of songs glorifying rape, sadomasochism, incest, the occult, and suicide by a growing number of bands illustrates this escalating trend that is alarming.

Some have suggested that the records in question are only a minute element in this music. However, these records are not few, and have sold millions of copies, like Prince's "Darling Nikki," about masturbation, sold over 10 million copies. Judas Priest, the one about forced oral sex at gunpoint, has sold over 2 million copies. Quiet Riot, "Metal Health," has songs about explicit sex, over 5 million copies. Motley Crue, "Shout at the Devil," which contains violence and brutality to women, over 2 million copies.

Some say there is no cause for concern. We believe there is. Teen pregnancies and teenage suicide rates are at epidemic proportions today. The Noedecker Report states that in the United States of America we have the highest teen pregnancy rate of any developed country: 96 out of 1,000 teenage girls become pregnant.

Rape is up 7 percent in the latest statistics, and the suicide rates of youth between 16 and 24 has gone up 300 percent in the last three decades while the adult level has remained the same.

There certainly are many causes for these ills in our society, but it is our contention that the pervasive messages aimed at children which promote and glorify suicide, rape, sadomasochism, and so on, have to be numbered among the contributing factors.

Some rock artists actually seem to encourage teen suicide. Ozzie [sic] Osbourne sings "Suicide Solution." Blue Oyster Cult sings "Don't Fear the Reaper." AC/DC sings "Shoot to Thrill." Just last week in Centerpoint, a small Texas town, a young man took his life while listening to the music of AC/DC. He was not the first.

Now that more and more elementary school children are becoming consumers of rock music, we think it is imperative to discuss this question. What can be done to help parents who want to protect their children from these messages if they want to?

Today parents have no way of knowing the content of music products that their children are buying. While some album covers are sexually explicit or depict violence, many others give no clue as to the content. One of the top 10 today is Morris Day and the Time, "Jungle Love." If you go to buy the album "Ice Cream Castles" to get "Jungle Love," you also get, "If the Kid Can't Make You Come, Nobody Can," a sexually explicit song.

The pleasant cover picture of the members of the band gives no hint that it contains material that is not appropriate for young consumers. . . .

We believe something can be done, and Tipper Gore will discuss the possible solution. Thank you.

Mrs. Gore: Thank you, Mr. Chairman.

We are asking the recording industry to voluntarily assist parents who are concerned by placing a warning label on music products inappropriate for younger children due to explicit sexual or violent lyrics.

The Parents Music Resource Center originally proposed a categorical rating system for explicit material. After many discussions with the record industry, we recognize some of the logistical and economic problems, and have adjusted our original suggestions accordingly. We now propose one generic warning label to inform consumers in the marketplace about lyric content. The labels would apply to all music.

We have asked the record companies to voluntarily label their own products and assume responsibility for making those judgments. We ask the record industry to appoint a one-time panel to recommend a uniform set of criteria which could serve as a policy guide for the individual companies. Those individual recording companies would then in good faith agree to adhere to this standard, and make decisions internally about which records should be labeled according to the industry criteria.

We have also asked that lyrics for labeled music products be available to the consumer before purchase in the marketplace. Now, it is important to clearly state what our proposal is not.

A voluntary labeling is not censorship. Censorship implies restricting access or suppressing content. This proposal does neither. Moreover, it involves no Government action. Voluntary labeling in no way infringes upon first amendment rights. Labeling is little more than truth in packaging, by now, a time honored principle in our free enterprise system, and without labeling, parental guidance is virtually impossible.

Most importantly, the committee should understand the Parents Music Resource Center is not advocating any Federal intervention or legislation whatsoever. The excesses that we are discussing were allowed to develop in the marketplace, and we believe the solutions to these excesses should come from the industry who has allowed them to develop and not from the Government.

The issue here is larger than violent and sexually explicit lyrics. It is one of ideas and ideal freedoms and responsibility in our society. Clearly, there is a tension here, and in a free society there always will be. We are simply asking that these corporate and artistic rights be exercised with responsibility, with sensitivity, and some measure of self-restraint, especially since young minds are at stake. We are talking about preteenagers and young teenagers having access to this material. That is our point of departure and our concern. . . .

Senator Rockefeller: Is there any serious doubt with serious people to whom you have talked that there is a direct relationship between violence and disturbing tendencies and occurrences among young people and the proliferation of this type of material that we have seen this morning. Is there any serious doubt that there is not a direct relationship between those two?

Or are there some who would argue that you are simply trying to suppress first amendment rights?

Mrs. Baker: Well, some make the point—and it is certainly true—that sex and violence pervade every level of our society today. So we would just say that music, which is a very important part of young people, young people who are forming their characters and developing their value systems, learning how to relate to the opposite sex—even what they think about sex is not defined in their minds yet.

We think that it does have an influence on these young minds. But we certainly do not blame music for the ills, all the ills that exist in the teenage population, the younger children.

Senator Rockefeller: Is the relationship between the escalation of the so-called MTV phenomenon and the things that we have seen this morning, and the problems that exist in the teenage population is incontrovertible in your mind?

Mrs. Baker: Absolutely. . . .

Mr. Zappa: These are my personal observations and opinions. I speak on behalf of no group or professional organization.

The PMRC proposal is an ill-conceived piece of nonsense which fails to deliver any real benefits to children, infringes the civil liberties of people who are not children, and promises to keep the courts busy for years dealing with the interpretational and enforcemental problems inherent in the proposal's design.

It is my understanding that in law First Amendment issues are decided with a preference for the least restrictive alternative. In this context, the PMRC demands are the equivalent of treating dandruff by decapitation.

No one has forced Mrs. Baker or Mrs. Gore to bring Prince or Sheena Easton into their homes. Thanks to the Constitution, they are free to buy other forms of music for their children. Apparently, they insist on purchasing the works of contemporary recording artists in order to support a personal illusion of aerobic sophistication. Ladies, please be advised: The $8.98 purchase price does not entitle you to a kiss on the foot from the composer or performer in exchange for a spin on the family Victrola.

Taken as a whole, the complete list of PMRC demands reads like an instruction manual for some sinister kind of toilet training program to house-break all composers and performers because of the lyrics of a few. Ladies, how dare you? ...

Is the basic issue morality? Is it mental health? Is it an issue at all? The PMRC has created a lot of confusion with improper comparisons between song lyrics, videos, record packaging, radio broadcasting, and live performances. These are all different mediums and the people who work in them have the right to conduct their business without trade-restraining legislation, whipped up like an instant pudding by "The wives of Big Brother." ...

Children in the vulnerable age bracket have a natural love for music. If as a parent you believe they should be exposed to something more uplifting than "Sugar Walls," support music appreciation programs in schools. Why have you not considered your child's need for consumer information? Music appreciation costs very little compared to sports expenditures. Your children have a right to know that something besides pop music exists.

It is unfortunate that the PMRC would rather dispense governmentally sanitized heavy metal music than something more uplifting. Is this an indication of PMRC's personal taste or just another manifestation of the low priority this administration has placed on education for the arts in America?

The establishment of a rating system, voluntary or otherwise, opens the door to an endless parade of moral quality control programs based on things certain Christians do not like. What if the next bunch of Washington wives demands a large yellow "J" on all material written or performed by Jews, in order to save helpless children from exposure to concealed Zionist doctrine?

Record ratings are frequently compared to film ratings. Apart from the quantitative difference, there is another that is more important: People who act in films are hired to pretend. No matter how the film is rated, it will not hurt them personally.

Since many musicians write and perform their own material and stand by it as their art, whether you like it or not, an imposed rating will stigmatize them as individuals. How long before composers and performers are told to wear a festive little PMRC arm band with their scarlet letter on it?

Bad facts make bad law, and people who write bad laws are in my opinion more dangerous than songwriters who celebrate sexuality. Freedom of speech, freedom of religious thought, and the right to due process for composers, performers and retailers are imperiled if the PMRC and the major labels consummate this nasty bargain. ...

Now, I have done a number of interviews on television. People keep saying, can you not take a few steps in their direction, can you not sympathize, can you not empathize? I do more than that at this point. I have got an idea for a way to stop all this stuff and a way to give parents what they really want, which is information, accurate information as to what is inside the album, without providing a stigma for the musicians who have played on the album or the people who sing it or the people who wrote it. And I think that if you listen carefully to this idea that it might just get by all of the constitutional problems and everything else.

As far as I am concerned, I have no objection to having all of the lyrics placed on the album routinely, all the time. But there is a little problem. Record companies do not own the right automatically to take these lyrics, because they are owned by a publishing company. . . .

If you consider that the public needs to be warned about the contents of the records, what better way than to let them see exactly what the songs say? That way you do not have to put any kind of subjective rating on the record. You do not have to call it R, X, D/A, anything. You can read it for yourself.

But in order for it to work properly, the lyrics should be on a uniform kind of a sheet. Maybe even the Government could print those sheets. Maybe it should even be paid for by the Government, if the Government is interested in making sure that people have consumer information in this regard.

And you also have to realize that if a person buys the record and takes it out of the store, once it is out of the store you can't return it if you read the lyrics at home and decide that little Johnny is not supposed to have it.

I think that that should at least be considered, and the idea of imposing these ratings on live concerts, on the albums, asking record companies to reevaluate or drop or violate contracts that they already have with artists should be thrown out.

That is all I have to say.

The Chairman: Thank you very much, Mr. Zappa. You understand that the previous witnesses were not asking for legislation. And I do not know, I cannot speak for Senator Hollings, but I think the prevailing view here is that nobody is asking for legislation.

The question is just focusing on what a lot of people perceive to be a problem, and you have indicated that you at least understand that there is another point of view. But there are people that think that parents should have some knowledge of what goes into their home.

Mr. Zappa: All along my objection has been with the tactics used by these people in order to achieve the goal. I just think the tactics have been really bad, and the whole premise of their proposal—they were badly advised in terms of record business law, they were badly advised in terms of practicality, or they would have known that certain things do not work mechanically with what they suggest.

69. Postpunk Goes Indie

As stated earlier, the critical attention given to the initial wave of New York and British punk in the late 1970s surpassed its popular appeal. Punk, as both musical and subcultural style, nevertheless continued to spread, branching out into a variety of subgenres. As we have already seen, the most commercial of these branches resulted in the synth-pop "New Romantic" movement. A variety of underground genres, based on different regional scenes and supported by a loose network of fanzines, independent record labels, college radio stations, and clubs in urban areas and college towns, gradually earned the label "indie rock." The many "scenes" that developed were one of the ways that college-age, post–baby boomers created a distinction between themselves and the long shadow cast by the musical dispositions of their boomer parents and older siblings.[1] Indie scenes sprang up in college towns as far flung as Athens, Georgia; Austin, Texas; and Champaign, Illinois.[2]

The liveliest scene most directly descended from Ramones-style punk was the Los Angeles–based hardcore movement. Memorialized in Penelope Spheeris's documentary, *The Decline of Western Civilization*, this scene featured bands such as X, Black Flag, and the Minutemen, who gloried in life on the margins while their songs focused on speed, anger, and aggression. That being said, the Los Angeles bands were hardly of a piece; X combined the quasi-folk harmonizing of husband-wife team John Doe and Exene Cervenka with the rockabilly-flavored antics of guitarist Billy Zoom; Black Flag could be humorous ("TV Party"), as well as scabrous ("Fuck the Police"); and the Minutemen showed what could be done in a rock song lasting 60 seconds or less. In Minneapolis, an active club scene developed around bands like

---

1. This is one of the conclusions drawn by Holly Kruse in "Subcultural Identity in Alternative Music Culture," *Popular Music* 12, no. 1 (January 1993): 33–41.

2. For an in-depth examination of the scene in Austin, see Barry Shanks, *Dissonant Identities: The Rock 'n' Roll Scene in Austin, Texas* (Hanover, N.H.: Wesleyan University Press and University Press of New England, 1994). The Holly Kruse article cited in note 1 focuses on the scene in Champaign. On the scene in Athens, see Anthony DeCurtis, "The Athens Scene," in *Rocking My Life Away: Writing about Music and Other Matters* (Durham, N.C.: Duke University Press, [1981] 1998), 21–27.

the Replacements and Hüsker Dü, who added a melodic edge to their distorted guitars and up-tempo songs.

The following article by Al Flipside (copublisher of the fanzine *Flipside*) presents a brief history of punk's transformation into hardcore. Flipside makes an important connection between the policies of then-president Ronald Reagan and the emergence of hardcore, and he observes how in some ways the new political realities of the early 1980s parallel those in the United Kingdom five years earlier. The latter part of the article presents a survey of hardcore scenes around the United States, but I include here only the section on Los Angeles, because that is the area that developed the most widely known scene; this section provides a taste of the thorough cataloguing provided by Flipside in the rest of the article.

What Is This Thing Called Hardcore?
Al Flipside

What is this "hardcore" movement anyway? Doesn't it mean slam dancing like there's no tomorrow? Is it beating people violently on the dance floor and doing a back flip off the p.a. column? Is it loud as you can go, fast as you can play? Is it beach punks, surf punks or skate punks? An excuse for excessive drug and alcohol imbibition? Does it mean you hate your parents, teachers and the police? Is it kids too young to know any better or too frustrated to want anything else? Is it the youth of the nation speaking up for what they believe in and what they see is wrong with today's world? Is it just another fad? Is it another name for "punk rock"?

Hardcore is all of the above, in various combinations and proportions. To some of us it is simply punk by another name. The term "punk" is still acceptable in England, and the English rallying cry, "punk's not dead" refers to the same music as the American expression "hardcore." The recent explosion of hardcore punk comes after years of development. It is the work of many dedicated people and was inspired (directly and indirectly) by America's decaying social, political and economic situation.

Let's start by looking where "punk" came from in the first place. Cities have always had their own music scenes. In the late '60s and early '70s, local activity dwindled as "stadium rock" reigned. By the mid-'70s, though, rock musicmaking again became a more personal concern. Local groups emerged playing original music and clubs emerged to showcase them.

Around 1976 punk rock sprang up simultaneously in New York, London and Los Angeles. Each area developed an individual style while being influenced by the others. London borrowed the Ramones' guitar style and leather jackets, but developed the pogo dance, safety pin look and political grounding. Los Angeles sped up the basic sound, adding its own dress, dances, political twists, etc. This exciting and energetic new punk scene was alive and kicking by 1977. However, with the breakup of the Sex Pistols in 1978 the media declared punk rock dead. Disco became the next fad, and for the most part that's what teenage America

---

Source: "What Is This Thing Called Hardcore?" © Al Flipside/*Trouser Press.*

was all about. But the media were wrong about punk. It hadn't died, it just went underground.

Most of the London punk bands put out great first albums and then sold out with shitty second releases; many disbanded. New York's so-called punk rockers turned out to be just plain flakes. The Los Angeles punk bands (those of San Francisco too) never got anything going, and most disappeared or were incorporated into other projects. The original attitude, however, was firmly established. Punk would not die; the seeds were sown.

All was not lost as the pioneering punk bands disappeared. "New wave" came along to gloss over any remaining sore spots, but the scars were too deep to heal. Out of this new music rage came many important independent record labels and distributors, in America as well as England.

Where does hardcore fit into this ancient history? I first saw the word used as a noun on a poster announcing a new tour by Vancouver band D.O.A. The term signified dedication and defiance, and at the same time named the new breed.

This new breed developed on a foundation that the early punks had no idea they had set up. In 1977 there were almost no independent record labels in the US willing to sign a new act, let alone a network to distribute such a record. Today there are literally hundreds of labels willing to take the chance and a handful of distributors eagerly awaiting any new releases. The pattern has repeated itself all over the country: One band forms a label as its only means to release its own material. That label then offers the opportunity for other bands to be heard. A distribution network set up once can work again and again. Where there was one single, now there are EPs, LPs and compilation albums. Although new labels spring up all the time, the older labels find themselves with growing catalogues.

The machinery, then, is waiting. But I would have to think an entire scene could develop out of sheer opportunity—and this wasn't the case.

London's punk scene re-emerged in a big way with bands like Crass, Discharge and Exploited. They had a new look (mohawk haircuts) and new seriousness to their pro-anarchy, anti-war stance. In America the remaining hardcore bands, in an amazing act of faith, were making cross-country tours. Their records were out there, but the record-buying public still wasn't aware of them and radio stations (except for a few) were hopeless. Black Flag, D.O.A., the Dead Kennedys and others screamed their messages to anyone who would listen and inspired more than they could imagine.

Who was inspiring the bands themselves? Time now to pay tribute to hardcore's chief impetus: President Ronald Reagan.

Listen to any hardcore band's lyrics: recession, depression, WWIII, nuclear war, the arms race, unemployment—Reagan brainstorms every one. There are probably more "I hate Reagan" songs around than on any other topic. As federal aid cutbacks hit close to home, political theories become frighteningly real, just as they did for English punks five years ago. Most hardcore bands are dead serious.

On the other hand, there are opportunists and hordes of hardcore recruits who are into the scene only because it's cool to be a punk in their high school. As with any movement, these imbeciles can only ruin hardcore for its sincere fans. There's always hope the new punks will listen to what the bands are saying and be enlightened. They're obvious at every gig, with their mindless fighting, drug abuse and peer pressure that punk never stood for.

The hardcore scene is full of people with ideals who have healthy things to say (like the Washington, DC bands). There are also people—sometimes I think in the majority—who are just plain assholes out to exploit punk's reckless reputation. Everyone and every place has to be judged individually. The second half of this article is a rundown on the American hardcore punk scene based on reading and talking to fanzine editors and bands themselves.

Los Angeles

We'll start on the west coast, just as American hardcore did. Los Angeles, of course, is at the heart of the movement. The LA punk scene has remained strong, although underground at times, since its beginnings. Clubs open and close but there's always somewhere to play. The vast suburbs, stretching for at least 100 miles from one end of the San Fernando valley to the edge of Orange County, supply new faces and room for individual development. There are undoubtedly more hardcore bands and gigs here than in any city in the US.

The LA hardcore scene started around 1980 with the beach punks and the Fleetwood club at Redondo Beach. But not everyone lives at the beach. Today's hardcore bands come from all over the giant suburb that is Los Angeles.

Black Flag is probably America's best and best known hardcore band. They've been around for quite a while in many forms, and are admired for their hardcore stance in both music and lifestyle. Few LA groups come close to matching Black Flag's dedication.

Los Angeles has many hardcore bands who have been around for several years, among them Fear, Circle Jerks, Social Distortion, Red Cross—even the Dickies. The Fleetwood/beach punk era saw bands rise to prominence like TSOL, Adolescents, Bad Religion, Channel 3, China White and Saccharine Trust. Most of these bands have released records and now headline at smaller clubs. The hardcore club Godzillas has hosted a new crop, including Circle One, Sin 34, Symbol Six, Suicidal Tendencies, Public Nuisance, Social Dismay, Modern Protest, Moral Decay and Lost Cause.

Other bands, like Wasted Youth, the Dischords and RE7, have just begun gaining popularity from gigs and records. There's also a "horror band" contingent that some consider hardcore. TSOL used to be among them: these bands have names like Christian Death, Super Heroines, Voodoo Church and 45 Grave. The Sins are a hardcore band from Riverside, not far from LA although it might as well be another country.

Further Reading

DeCurtis, Anthony. "The Athens Scene," in *Rocking My Life Away: Writing about Music and Other Matters* (Durham, N.C.: Duke University Press, [1981] 1998), 21–27.

Kruse, Holly. "Subcultural Identity in Alternative Music Culture." *Popular Music* 12 (January 1993): 33–41.

Shanks, Barry. *Dissonant Identities: The Rock 'n' Roll Scene in Austin, Texas* (Hanover, N.H.: University Press of New England, 1994).

Discography

Black Flag. *My War*. SST, 1984.

Circle Jerks. *VI*. Combat, 1987.

Hüsker Dü. *Flip Your Wig*. SST, 1986.

The Minutemen. *Double Nickels on the Dime*. SST, 1984.

R.E.M. *And I Feel Fine . . . : The Best of the I.R.S. Years 1982–1987*. Capitol/IRS, 2006.

The Replacements. *Let It Be*. Twin/Tone, 1984.

Social Distortion. *Prison Bound*. Restless Records, 1988.

X. *Los Angeles*. Slash, 1980.

70. Hip-Hop, Don't Stop

"Rap" had been around for years in African American neighborhoods in the New York City area before the first hit recording appeared in 1979 with "Rapper's Delight" by the Sugarhill Gang. Rap music existed as part of a larger complex of cultural practices known as "hip-hop," which, in addition to rap, included breakdancing, graffiti writing, and a distinct fashion sense. However, rap, like rhythm and blues in the 1950s, did not initially elicit much public disapproval because it was (in the words of the 1955 *Variety* editorial included in Chapter 20) "restricted to special places" and "off in a corner by itself . . . [as part of] the music underworld—not the main stream."

The history of hip-hop has been voluminously detailed since its debut in the South Bronx during the 1970s, and the story gives new meaning to the idea of "making the best of a bad situation." On the one hand, the South Bronx post-1970 qualifies as one of the most disastrous examples of "urban renewal" in recent U.S. history: a combination of declining manufacturing jobs and affordable housing, along with decreased funding for public education, left a whole generation without the resources that had sustained decades of optimism about upward mobility. On the other hand, rap arose from the combination of people thrown together by adversity and the happy collusion of DJ'ing practices from disco; the sound systems and "toasting" of recent Jamaican émigrés, such as the legendary Kool DJ Herc; and centuries of African American rhyming, which lends credence to the notion of rap as the product of an overarching "Afrodiasporic" cultural background.[1]

The following two articles on hip-hop may have been the first to appear in print. In the first article, published in the summer of 1978, *Billboard* writer Robert Ford, Jr., reported on an unusual phenomenon in the Bronx: young DJs, led by Kool Herc (Clive Campbell, b. 1955), were seeking out

---

1. My account is most indebted to Tricia Rose's in *Black Noise: Rap Music and Black Culture in Contemporary America* (Hanover, N.H.: Wesleyan University Press and University Press of New England, 1994). For another excellent history of rap up to 1991, see David Toop, *Rap Attack 2: African Rap to Global Hip Hop* (London: Serpent's Tail, 1991).

obscure records with hot rhythm breaks. Herc describes the emergence of a new aesthetic, one more attuned to rhythm than to singing or lush textural enhancements such as string tracks. The second article, also by Ford from a year later, documents the rise of rapping as a popular practice that was being joined to spinning records in black clubs in the Bronx and Manhattan. This article also attests to the circulation of self-produced rap tapes before the release of "Rapper's Delight" and, as a point of curiosity, points to how the roles of DJ and MC were not yet defined as separate entities.

B-Beats Bombarding Bronx: Mobile DJ Starts Something with Oldie R&B Disks
Robert Ford, Jr.

NEW YORK—A funny thing has been happening at Downstairs Records here.

The store, which is the city's leading disco product retailer, has been getting calls for obscure R&B cutouts, such as Dennis Coffy's "Son Of Scorpio," on Sussex, Jeannie Reynolds' "Fruit Song" on Casablanca, and the Incredible Bongo Band's "Bongo Rock" on Pride.

The requests, for the most part, come from young black disco DJs from the Bronx who are buying the records just to play the 30 seconds or so of rhythm breaks that each disk contains.

The demand for these records, which the kids call B-beats, has gotten so great that Downstairs has had to hire a young Bronxite, Elroy Meighan, to handle it.

According to Meighan the man responsible for this strange phenomenon is a 26-year old mobile DJ who is known in the Bronx as Cool Herc. It seems Herc rose to popularity by playing long sets of assorted rhythm breaks strung together.

Other Bronx DJs have picked up the practice and now B-beats are the rage all over the borough and the practice is spreading rapidly.

Herc, who has been spinning for five years, says that his unique playing style grew from his fascination with one record, "Bongo Rock." "The tune has a really great rhythm break but it was too short so I had to look for other things to put with it," Herc relates.

Since Herc was not completely satisfied with the new disco product coming out at the time, he started looking in cutout bins for tunes with good rhythm breaks.

Herc's intensive searching for tunes has now even come up with a new remake of "Bongo Rock." The '73 tune has been covered by a group called the Arawak All-Stars on an apparently Jamaican-based label, Arawal records.

Herc has also found that some of the rhythm breaks get better response when they are played at a faster speed. Herc plays tunes such as the Jeannie Reynolds record at 45 rather than the 33 1/3 at which it was recorded.

Herc thinks the popularity of B-beats stems from the kids' dissatisfaction with much of today's disco product. "On most records, people have to wait through a lot

Source: "B-Beats Bombarding Bronx: Mobile DJ Starts Something with Oldie R&B Disks" / Robert Ford Jr. / *Billboard* / Wright's Media, Published July 1, 1978, pg 65.

of strings and singing to get to the good part of the record," Herc believes. "But I give it to them all up front."

Herc hopes that someday he will be able to produce an entire B-beat album featuring "Bongo Rock" and other obscure numbers. Till then he plans to keep packing them in at the clubs and dances he works in the Bronx.

Jive Talking N.Y. DJs Rapping Away in Black Discos
Robert Ford, Jr.

NEW YORK—Rapping DJs reminiscent of early R&B radio jocks such as Jocko and Dr. Jive are making an impressive comeback here—not in radio but in black discos where a jivey rap commands as much attention these days as the hottest new disk.

Young DJs like Eddie Cheeba, DJ Hollywood, DJ Starski and Kurtis Blow are attracting followings with their slick raps. All promote themselves with these snappy show business names.

Many black disco promoters now use the rapping DJs to attract young fans to one-shot promotions and a combination of the more popular names have filled the city's largest hotel ballrooms.

The young man credited with reviving the rapping habit in this area is DJ Hollywood, who started gabbing along with records a few years ago while working his way through school as a disco DJ.

Hollywood is now so popular that he has played the Apollo with billing as a support act. It is not uncommon to hear Hollywood's voice coming from one of the countless portable tape players carried through the city's streets. Tapes of Hollywood's raps are considered valuable commodities by young blacks, here.

A close friend and disciple of Hollywood's, Eddie Cheeba, has been working as a mobile jock for five years and talking over the records for the last two. He now travels with an entire show, which includes seven female dancers and another DJ, Easy Gee, who does most of the actual spinning. Cheeba and his Cheeba Crew are now booked two months in advance.

Cheeba says the rapping craze grew out of a need for something more than records.

"These people go to discos every week and they need more than music to motivate them," Cheeba observes. "I not only play records, but I rap to them and they answer me."

Though they often work before crowds in the thousands, Cheeba and most of the popular rapping DJs do not get records from labels or from pools. Most of them buy their own product and do so without complaining.

As DJ Starski puts it, "Most of the records the labels send us won't go up here anyway, so I'd rather buy what I want."

Starski is one of the most popular DJs with high school and college age blacks in the Bronx and Manhattan. He has played almost every major black club and ballroom in the area. He generally works with Cool DJ AJ, who does not rap but is a

Source: "Jive-Talking N.Y. DJs Rapping Away in Black Discos" Robert Ford Jr./*Billboard*/Wright's Media, published May 5, 1979, pg 3.

master of B-beats. B-beats are series of short rhythm breaks strung together to sound like one song.

Starski is proud of his ability to excite a crowd with his rapping. "It's a beautiful thing to see a dance floor full of people dancing to your music and answering your rap," Starski says.

Kurtis Blow, the most popular rapping DJ in Queens, hopes disco will be a springboard into broadcasting for him. Blow, a student at CCNY, has been working about a year and got his first break at the now defunct Small's Paradise. Blow built a following at Small's and is now booked solid for weeks.

Cheeba already had a shot at radio during a fill-in run last summer at Fordham's WFUV-FM.

Further Reading

Chang, Jeff. *Can't Stop Won't Stop: A History of the Hip-Hop Generation*. New York: St. Martin's Press, 2005.

Forman, Murray, and Mark Anthony Neal. *That's the Joint! The Hip-Hop Studies Reader*. London: Taylor and Francis, 2007.

Greenwald, Jeff. "Hip-Hop Drumming: The Rhyme May Define, but the Groove Makes You Move." *Black Music Research Journal* 22 (2002): 259–71.

Hager, Steven. *Hip Hop: The Illustrated History of Break Dancing, Rap Music, and Graffiti*. New York: St. Martin's Press, 1984.

Rose, Tricia. *Black Noise: Rap Music and Black Culture in Contemporary America*. Hanover, N.H.: University Press of New England, 1994.

Tate, Greg. *Flyboy in the Buttermilk: Essays on Contemporary America*. New York: Simon and Schuster, 1992.

Toop, David. *Rap Attack 2: African Rap to Global Hip Hop*. London: Serpent's Tail, 1991.

The Vibe History of Hip-Hop. New York: Three Rivers Press, 1999.

Discography

Bambaataa, Afrika. *Planet Rock: The Album*. Tommy Boy Records, 1986.

Grandmaster Flash and the Furious Five. *The Message*. DBK Works, [1982] 2005.

The Hip-Hop Box. Hip-O Records, 2004.

Kurtis Blow Presents the History of Rap: Vols. 1–2. Rhino, 1997.

Run-D.M.C. *Run-D.M.C.* Profile, 1984.

———. *Run-D.M.C. Greatest Hits*. Arista, 2002.

Sugarhill Gang. *Sugarhill Gang*. Sugarhill Records, 1980.

71. "The Music Is a Mirror"

Following the commercial success of "Rapper's Delight," rap continued to transform rapidly, albeit still as a largely underground phenomenon. In the wake of Kool Herc came the further exploitation of "break beats" (i.e., the repeating of a drum break taken from the middle of a recording), led by virtuosi of the turntable such as Grandmaster Flash (Joseph Saddler, b. 1958), who developed those staples of hip-hop craft—scratching (moving the needle rapidly back and forth across the grooves of a record) and backspinning. Breakdancers, many of them Puerto Rican residents of the South Bronx, also formed an integral part of the scene, as nearly every early account attested.[1]

Subsequent developments included the electro-funk and social activism of Afrika Bambaataa (Kevin Donovan, b. 1960), especially in his "Planet Rock" (1982); the political protest and social realism of Grandmaster Flash and the Furious Five featuring Melle Mel in "The Message" (1982); and the emergence of commercially savvy Def Jam Records with stars like Run-DMC. Instrumental tracks were largely collages, built up from fragments of previous recordings, synthesizer riffs, drum machines, and the efforts of skilled studio funk musicians.

Run-DMC developed the first successful crossover strategy for rap by explicitly incorporating rock elements into their music. Videos for recordings like "The King of Rock" (1985) presented the group entering a "Rock and Roll Hall of Fame" (only two years before the actual Rock and Roll Hall of Fame opened) and commenting on the racial politics involved in the construction of conventional rock histories. The recording itself uses a heavy metal guitar riff throughout, backed by a thunderous drum machine track. "Walk This Way" (1986) adopted an even bolder strategy, using the 1970s hit by the rock band Aerosmith as the backing track, newly rerecorded by members of Aerosmith with Run-DMC for the occasion. The video also included members of both bands; the narrative climaxes with Run-DMC breaking through the barriers that separate them from Aerosmith and, by implication, from the larger record-buying public of white consumers of rock music.

In another sense, however, the use of rock music had been a part of hip-hop from the beginning. Many rap DJs discuss how they

---

1. For an example, see Tim Carr, "Talk That Talk, Walk That Walk," *Rolling Stone*, May 26, 1983, 20–25.

delighted in getting a crowd of hip-hop fans to get down to the drum break from the Monkees' "Mary, Mary," and heavy metal riffs had long formed a staple of the DJ's repertoire.[2] Def Jam records was also home to the first successful white rap act, the Beastie Boys, who projected jokey-punky personas while taking a few pages out of Run-DMC's musical playbook.

The invention and commercial accessibility in the mid-1980s of the digital sampler was quickly exploited by hip-hop musicians. Samplers, which make possible the manipulation of recorded sounds (or "samples"), played right into the collage aesthetic of hip-hop, greatly easing the looping of grooves previously accomplished through backspinning. Sampling also made it easier to use fragments of previous recordings as historical references or homages that could place a recording within a lineage of African American popular music. This greater control over sonic sources and the enhanced ability to manipulate them also led to new possibilities for the musical use of what might have previously been considered "noise."[3] Eric Sadler of the Bomb Squad, the production team responsible for the instrumental tracks of Public Enemy's recordings, put it this way:

Turn it all the way up so it's totally distorted and pan it over to the right so you really can't even hear it. Pan it over to the right means put the sound only in the right side speaker, and turn it so you can't barely even hear it—it's just like a noise in the side. Now, engineers . . . they live by certain rules. They're like, "You can't do that. You don't want a distorted sound, it's not right, it's not correct." With Hank (Shocklee) and Chuck (D) it's like, "Fuck that it's not correct, just do this shit." And engineers won't do it. So if you start engineering yourself and learning these things yourself— [get] the meter goin' like this [he moves his hand into an imaginary red zone] and you hear the shit cracklin,' that's the sound we're lookin' for.[4]

Indeed, Public Enemy's "Bring the Noise" (1988), with its densely layered, noisy backing track, sounds almost like a credo for this aesthetic, calling into question received notions of both music and musicianship (with lines like "Run-DMC first said a deejay could be a band"). On this and other recordings, the band's frequent use of samples of James Brown's recordings emphasized the linkage between the grooves of rap and those of the Godfather.

While bands like Public Enemy extended the use of political content pioneered in "The Message," women began to take a greater role in the genre, with Salt 'n' Pepa becoming the first female hip-hop superstars.

---

2. For an account of this playful approach to source material, see the interviews with Grandmaster Flash and Afrika Bambaataa in *The History of Rock and Roll* (PBS/BBC video series), "The Perfect Beat."

3. For more on the use of "noise" in rap, see David Brackett, "Music, " in *Key Terms in Popular Music and Culture*, ed. Bruce Horner and Thomas Swiss, 124–40 (Malden, Mass.: Blackwell, 1999); and Robert Walser, "Rhythm, Rhyme, and Rhetoric in the Music of Public Enemy," *Ethnomusicology* 39 (1995): 193–217. See Part 6 of this volume for more on the media debates about whether rap was "noise" or "music."

4. Tricia Rose, *Black Noise: Rap Music and Black Culture in Contemporary America* (Hanover, N.H.: University Press of New England, 1994), 74–75.

These developments were part of the increasing inclusion of rap in the mainstream initiated by Run-DMC. By 1989, recordings such as "Wild Thing" by Tone Loc had entered heavy rotation on MTV, and the cable channel had made the ultimate concession to hip-hop by creating a show devoted entirely to the genre, "Yo! MTV Raps."

The growth of rap's popularity forms the immediate backdrop for the following article by Harry Allen, which appeared in *Essence*, the "preeminent lifestyle magazine for today's African-American woman." Allen's article provides a history of hip-hop, placing it within other African American cultural practices, and raises such issues as the relationship of rap to black identity, the appropriate terms for the criticism of rap, and the growing commentary about misogyny. Allen started writing about hip-hop in 1983 and has continued to be involved with hip-hop since the publication of this article, acting as the "Media Assassin" for Public Enemy and even uttering the title line in the group's recording "Don't Believe the Hype." More recently, Allen created the newsletter *rap dot com* and is developing a Larry King Live–style talk show with Chuck D under the aegis of their multimedia production company, Scramjet.

Hip Hop Madness: From Def Jams to Cold Lampin', Rap Is Our Music
Harry Allen

The young, brown-skinned woman stood in the middle of the group, patting out a beat on the ground with her feet, at the same time beating out a rhythm on her chest and legs with her hands. People crowded closer, caught by the quiet, distinct, funky sound. Suddenly she began to rhyme, fast and furiously. As people listened, swayed and swung to the beat, she shot poetic insults at friends nearby, to their chagrin and the crowd's delight. She rhymed about her experiences, things that both she and her audience had seen and experienced. She kept that same funky rhythm as the dancing crowd went crazy with loud screams and shouts.

Basement party beat-box in the Bronx? L.A. street-corner performer? Neither. A description of "pattin' juba," circa 1850, from historian Eileen Southern's revelatory work *The Music of Black Americans.*

Nearly 140 years later, over the sound of a drum machine and one eerily repeating, mournful, four-note horn riff, 20-year-old Mike G matter-of-factly drops science on the Jungle Brothers's recording "In Time": *"In time this rhyme will be more than just a fantasy/A Black man will be the man to claim presidency/Is it hard to see? So try to see as I see/In time I see a better Black reality/It took one man to open the door/He let in one million more/And I don't think/That this country knows/What the hell that it's in for. . . ."*

You won't hear lyrics like that from 50,000 of today's R&B artists. Such frank talk will only be found in hip-hop music, or "rap," to use a term that we invented

---

and whites coopted to rename, defame or claim the music. If sales, influence and visibility are any indication, hip-hop is now runnin' thangs; it's the dominant African-American music. It's about time. Hip-hop is youthful, strong. It exhibits none of the creative listlessness with which much of R&B is currently burdened. Nor does it have the hands-off, gloves-on reverence with which jazz often finds itself draped. Rather than pretending to bourgeois standards of style, or attempting musically to evoke a time dead and gone, as many jazz and R&B artists are wont to do, rappers instead sling the rawest, most realistic insights at your ear. Deejays take your favorite records, cut 'em up, mix 'em around and serve 'em to you on a record platter. Meanwhile their crowds move and shake their bodies in ways that Grandmother once said would definitely get you pregnant or arrested. It all comes together in a whole: funky. Youknowhumsayin?

"Rats in the front room, roaches in the back/Junkies in the alley with the baseball bat/I tried to get away, but I couldn't get far/ 'Cause a man with a tow truck repossessed my car. . . ."

"To me, hip-hop's always been around," says Melvin Glover, aka Melle-Mel, lead vocalist for Grandmaster Flash & the Furious Five, who gave us "The Message," above, and are no doubt the most important crew in the music's short history. "It's the same shit that Black people was chantin' on the chain gang, and that they was sayin' when they was slaves. 'Hi-de-ho!'—all that shit is rap. Pigmeat Markham and 'Heah Comes De Judge'. . . . That's rap! Rap always been out there. It was just waitin' for somebody to claim it."

Pigmeat Markham, Muhammad Ali, Cab Calloway, Isaac Hayes, Moms Mabley, Millie Jackson, Joe Tex, Malcolm X. As Mel says, "That's always been *our* essence—just to talk, you know what I'm sayin'?"

"Now what you hear is not a test/I'm rappin' to the beat/And me, the groove, and my friends/Are gonna try to move your feet. . . ."

When many people think of the beginnings of hip-hop, they head back to the Sugarhill Gang's "Rapper's Delight," a 15-minute jam quoted above whose "Ho-tel, mo-tel, Holiday Inn" refrain drove dancers wild back in September 1979. That wasn't the first "rap" record, however. The honor goes to Fatback Band's "King Tim III," which was released earlier that same year. Says Pebbles Riley, aka Pebblee-Poo, one of hip-hop's first female vocalists, "I started in '78, and I was definitely hearing people rapping at block parties in '76, '77." And, according to Ralph Blandshaw, aka Van Silk, who was one of the music's earliest, most ardent party promoters, you could hear mobile deejays, the rhythmic founders of hip-hop, in New York City parks as early as 1974. Hmm. Trying to pin down a start time for hip-hop is, as RUN-D.M.C. would say, tricky.

Andrei L. Strobert, a Brooklyn-based scholar, musician and artist, says that to get to the real roots of hip-hop, you have to go back even farther than "King Tim III," mobile deejays, Pigmeat Markham, or slavery—say, to the Yoruba people of Nigeria, or the Nago of Dahomey (now Benin). "The scratch that you hear in hip-hop is similar to the African *sekere*," says Strobert, "A *sekere* is a big gourd with beads around it. If you think about scratching, you see how it connects. 'Cause, see, the scratch is *shk shk-shk shk-shk*. The *sekere* sound is basically the same thing. Rappers come to my studio to record rhythms that they want to use to their rhymes. A lot of the rhythms that they use are Ibo rhythms, from the Ibo tribe of Nigeria."

For all African music, including African-American music, rhythm is the key, the point of entry. The only way you could get us to pay attention to and love something as fundamentally antimusical as a turntable scratch was to make it funky, and in this is hip-hop's genius. I believe that this concept of "funky" is the dividing line between people of African descent, people of non-African descent, and our respective traditions. That is to say, Picasso copied West African art, but couldn't make his painting "guitar" *nowhere* near as funky as a Dogon mask. The difference between the late Jimi Hendrix and an acre of white rock guitarists was funk. Elvis was loud, but he was never funky. Little Richard's "Rip It Up" still does. Knowhumsayin?

"Cause the 'D' is for 'dangerous'/You can come and get some of this/I teach and speak so when it's spoke it's no joke/The Voice of Choice; the place shakes with the bass/Go one for the treble/The rhythm is the rebel!"

To get from the Yoruba Nation to Public Enemy's "Louder Than a Bomb," quoted above, you have to jet through 400 not-so-hot years in America. Stop just long enough to hear early forms of rapping from Douglas "Jocko" Henderson, the Last Poets and Parliament/Funkadelic. Eventually you'll wind up in a place where three Black guys called RUN-D.M.C. sell more than 3 million copies of *Raising Hell* . . . and four white guys called the Beastie Boys, after being coached by those three Black guys, sell 4 million copies of *Licensed to Ill.* You've entered . . . the twilight zone, the point where this very African art "is being accepted by middle America," in the words of Hurby Azor, producer of million-selling crew Salt-n-Pepa. "That's one of the biggest developments. The white people are gettin' into it now. Which is funny. The music business is always interested in the white people."

And vice versa. White music critics and cultural historians are talking about hip-hop and find themselves tossing long, funny words into the air to describe it. Words like *deconstruction, appropriation, iconography* and *recontextualization.* But those words have little to do with the way African-American people live or make music, and hip-hop is no more or less than Black life on black vinyl. Whatever one finds in the community, they'll find in the records. This has a lot to do with why it's so attractive to some people and repulsive to others.

For African-Americans, especially young people, the music is a mirror. "These aren't cheap records," says Nat Robinson, president of MC Lyte's label, First Priority Music. "These are natural records." Hip-hop talks like us; it's rooted in African-American wordplay, like "snapping" or "the dozens." It moves like us. It homes in like radar on our "musicultural" values. Rhythm. Call and response. Repetition. Reinterpretation of original ideas via improvisation. The voice as instrument, and as rhythmic and tonal ideal. And other values . . .

"Rappers take a step back or you will soon regret that you ever had to confront me and you can bet that I come correct perfect in full effect/Disconnect dissect eject as I wreck/Shop/Stand in command with the clan/Caravan or band/We go man for man. . . ."

Hip-hop speaks to a view of life that is expressly communal in nature. In Africa, there are cultures with musical categories solely for *the praise of friends,* for instance. When Big Daddy Kane ends the elastic "Set It Off," quoted above, by naming more than 30 friends one at a time, when Kool Moe Dee turns the names of his neighborhood crew into exultant, defiant poetry on "Wild Wild West," when Public Enemy thanks 240-plus people and groups on the crew's liner notes, that's African. That's "posse," "brotherhood," "community" being expressed on the terms of African-American young people. "I say the names of my posse to look out for 'em, to acknowledge that they do exist," admits 19-year-old Dana Owens, aka Latifah, who thanks the R.E. (Ram Enterprise) Posse on her fluid, funky single, "Wrath of My Madness/Princess of the Posse," quoted below. "Had it not been for them, I probably wouldn't have even started in this. You know what I'm saying?"

"I-ray/The lesson of today/You have to listen to each and every single word I have to say because/The Ruler Lord Ramsey is on my side/And I'm the Princess of the Posse so, yo . . . take it light. . . ."

So, yo. Why is hip-hop so hype? What are those millions of rappers and record buyers really getting out of it? Fab 5 Freddy, cohost of MTV's (Ooh! Now it's hip) hip-hop video show *Yo! MTV Raps!*, puts it like this: "There's sum'n in hip-hop that makes it good, that you can't even really *record*, because a lot o' hip-hop is about attitude, feeling and style, as opposed to musical virtuosity as we know it, dealing with Western forms of music. Like L. L. Cool J said, when you hear a good hip-hop record, you make that *face*, youknowhumsayin'? You hear a regular record, you just go, 'Yeah, that's pretty good.' But when you hear a good hip-hop record, you make that face like, '*Yeeeah!*'"

"Flowin' in file with the new style/Barrels are cleaned then loaded for salute/Chanters with the choice standing steady like my mouthpiece/Paragraph preacher is now introduced/ Drums are heard sounding off in each and every person/Vocal confetti is thrown at top stage/ Roses and violets aren't proper for throwing for showing in appreciation (why?)/This is the D.A.I.S.Y age!"

Listen to "Plug Tunin'," above, by the trio De La Soul, or to almost any cut from their *3 Feet High and Rising*. You'll make that face all album long. But some think that when people hear a good hip-hop record, they do other things. Like stick chemicals up their noses, snatch gold chains, rampage and even kill, if you're talking about the murder of Julio Fuentes at Long Island's Nassau Coliseum on September 10, 1988. Ask the usually serene Latifah what the most common misconception about hip-hop is, and you touch a nerve. "Definitely that it's violent, that it's a bunch of hoodlums and nondescripts making records about bullshit. That we can't put out a goddamn positive message. If they took a second to listen to the words, then they would know that wasn't the case."

Word. The fact is that drugs and crime live in our communities. Their habitation there predates the music called hip-hop. These ills have less to do with Schoolly D calling his album *Smoke Some Kill* than they do with the government drug-jogging with Manuel Noriega. They have less to do with beeper-carrying brothers than they do with the U.S. banks and other multinationals for which we work. These corporations know that drug money is the only thing that'll keep a flow of American dollars going into the debt-ridden Latin American countries they lend to.

To say that hip-hop is surrounded by violence and drug use sounds like a captive African blaming work songs and field hollers for the perpetuation of slavery, don't you think? Hip-hop is descriptive and often attempts to be prescriptive. African-American people are, again, using music to make sense of and mediation for our circumstances.

However, there is certainly one real problem. Hip-hop has taken a rap for being sexist. It is. When Ice-T releases a record called "Girls, Let's Get Butt Naked and Fuck" ("Girls, L.G.B.N.A.F." on the album cover), when 2 Live Crew on a cut called "S & M" calls to women to bring their "d- -k-sucking friends," when Ultramagnetic M.C.'s Kool Keith on "Give the Drummer Some" talks about smacking up his bitch in the manner of a pimp, sisters understandably scream. Hip-hop is sexist. It is also frank.

As I once told a sister, hip-hop lyrics are, among other things, what a lot of Black men say about Black women when Black women aren't around. In this sense, the music is no more or less sexist than your fathers, brothers, husbands, friends and lovers, and, in many cases, more up-front. As an unerringly precise reflection of the community, hip-hop's sexist thinking will change when the community changes. Because women are the ones best able to define sexism, they will have to challenge the music—tell it how to change and make it change—if change is to come. Only then will record companies cease the release of cuts that call for bitch-smacking.

"How could I keep my composure/When all sorts of thoughts fought for exposure?"

Hip-hop is here to stay. As Eric B. & Rakim note in their "Musical Massacre" above, the music is bursting with ideas. It is, says Kay Gee The All from the seminal crew Cold Crush Brothers, "up-to-date music," and it speaks to a change in the way we socialize and get our music. When *Billboard,* the bible of the music industry, began its charts in the 1940's, they tallied sales of sheet music. Today they tally records-by-ethnicity, compact discs and videos. That reflects a huge change in the way we get music and think about it. So do cassettes, almost nonexistent 20 years ago. So does a Walkman, non-existent ten years ago. Music we choose goes where we do. Says master percussionist and composer Max Roach in *New York Newsday* music used to go where we did in another way. "When I was growing up in Bedford-Stuyvesant [Brooklyn], there was always an instrument a student could take home from school; if a student wanted to study rhetoric, he could. That's all been wiped out; our urban centers are in shambles."

How are you going to get kids to read music if they can't read? "These kids were never exposed to poets or playwrights in school," continues Roach. "They had all this talent, and they had no instruments. So they started rap music. They rhymed on their own. They made their own sounds and their own movements."

I couldn't have said it any better. Why hasn't this hip-hop "fad" died out? The same reason we haven't. If nothing else, hip-hop speaks most directly to African-American pride and sense of self, failures of the American mess, our history, the things we lack and, ultimately, hope. Hope that people without the benefit of a common musical language, articulated by bars, staffs and bass clefs, will come up with one on their own, made from the stuff of their lives. Hope that, for at least a moment, an average Joe-Ski from around the way will have his place in the spotlight. Hope that we survive and prosper as a people into the twenty-first century and beyond. We will. It promises to be a ferocious, funky future.

> In the same issue of *Essence* that published Harry Allen's article, Carol Cooper looks at the gender-specific obstacles faced by female rappers and at the progress made by them in the late 1980s. By detailing the institutional obstacles to women's access to creative roles in rap recordings, she offers an implicit riposte to Allen's assertion that it is up to female rappers to challenge misogyny in rap. Like Allen, Cooper had already been active writing about hip-hop for several years before this article appeared. She has continued since that time writing for a wide range of publications, as well as occasionally working for the music industry in positions like East Coast director of black music artists and repertoire for A&M Records.

Girls Ain't Nothin' but Trouble
Carol Cooper

For all its immense popularity, rap music is still very much a man's world. Women are buying the records, but by and large they aren't on them nor are they producing them—though as the music progresses, that's beginning to change. Women rap artists such as Princess (Criminal/WTG), Salt-n-Pepa (Next Plateau) and The Real Roxanne (Select) are excited about getting on the mike and on vinyl; for the moment, issues of creative and financial autonomy are taking a backseat. Don't expect these women to address sexism directly. Much as we might like them to, that's not happening—yet.

As a popular art form that, like standup comedy, draws inspiration from "out-law" oral traditions such as pimp toasts, prison doggerel and urban childhood's "dirty dozens," rap is accepted by its practitioners—male and female—as the most brutally honest form of self-expression possible.

"Rap is cultural," says Princess, whose first records came out on Arthur Baker's Criminal/WGT label only this winter, despite the fact that she has been writing and producing her own raps for three years. "I grew up with it, and it's here to stay. But when I started making and shopping my own tapes as a teen, because I thought the things other people wanted to produce on me were too commercial, the male label owners were very unreceptive. I spoke to people at Uptown Enterprises, at Next Plateau, Sleeping Bag, Reality . . . I made the rounds. Only when I led them to believe that a man had written or produced my stuff did they show interest."

Along the same lines, when Roxanne Shante defended the skeezer's (groupie's) low-slung lifestyle on Rick James's "Loosey's Rap," she was just doing a job. Female rappers are often invited to participate in a statement devised by a male artist and expected to contribute "something appropriate." As professionals, these girls deliver what is asked, get paid and get credit—relatively oblivious to how that participation might be perceived by others.

"There are a lot of rhymes we write on our album, but we don't go for the credit," admits Cheryl James (Salt), of platinum rap duo Salt-n-Pepa. "And I guess we should, because people are on this kick about why we don't write. It doesn't bother *us*, but it bothers us that it bothers other people. Most singers don't write all their own lyrics, either, and nobody cares about that. I guess because Hurby Azor is our producer, manager and one of our songwriters, it gives the impression that he has total control. But we all got into this business together, it's like a family. And if he ever came up with a song or a video concept we didn't want to do, we wouldn't do it."

Most contemporary rap women (coming along in a time when rap is so much more profitable than it was for their sister pioneers of five or six years back) are philosophical about the internecine name-calling and cross-gender "dissing" that sometimes make it into the grooves. None of them seem to think that "explicit" or sexist lyrics are harmful in and of themselves, and all of them are aware that there is a definite cash-money fandom out there for dirty talk. The Puerto Rican rapper, The Real Roxanne, co-wrote her single "Respect" around that very dilemma. The Real Roxanne has felt pressure toward "propriety" both from within and as the young mother of an articulate first-grader: "Girls disrespecting each other on stage is just not me; not the image I want to promote. But at the beginning, with all the Roxanne answer records and all these girls coming onstage to challenge me and each other, my production company back then who'd had the original 'Roxanne' concept had to show them what time it was!" Roxanne laughs.

"Now, with my first album out, I hear that [fellow rapper] MC Lyte has started in on me. I hear that she has a girl dressed like me in one of her videos and has some-thing to say. Oh boy," she grins wryly, "sounds like fun."

Because rap prides itself on staying thematically true to the African-American experience in America today, it stands to reason that every issue—good or bad—that manifests itself in our communities will eventually be exposed in a rap forum. In the case of normally touchy subjects such as sex, sexism, racism, crime, VD, homophobia and light-skin privilege, a rap dialogue may be the only discussion certain youngsters ever have on these subjects. If so, perhaps we ought to take advantage of rap's daring to start the discussion, so that we, as knowledgeable adults, can finish it.

Further Reading

Chuck D (with Yusuf Jah). *Fight the Power: Rap, Race, and Reality*. New York: Delacorte Press, 1997.

Gaunt, Kyra. *The Games Black Girls Play: Learning the Ropes from Double Dutch to Hip-Hop*. New York: NYU Press, 2006.

Hess, Mickey. *Icons of Hip Hop: An Encyclopedia of the Movement, Music, and Culture*. Westport, Conn.: Greenwood Press, 2007.

Walser, Robert. "Rhythm, Rhyme, and Rhetoric in the Music of Public Enemy." *Ethnomusicology* 39 (1995): 193–217.

Discography

Classics—Fat Beats and Brastraps: Women of Hip-Hop. Rhino/WEA, 1998.
Public Enemy. *Yo! Bum Rush the Show*. Def Jam, 1987.
_____. *It Takes a Nation of Millions to Hold Us Back*. Def Jam, 1988.
_____. *Fear of a Black Planet*. Def Jam, 1990.
Salt-n-Pepa. *Hot, Cool and Vicious*. Next Plateau, 1986.
_____. *Blacks' Magic*. London, 1990.

72. Where Rap and Heavy Metal Converge

The sense of panic over rap in the mass media grew in proportion to its increased visibility on outlets such as MTV and its increased audibility on the radio. This reaction was further exacerbated by the fact that MTV was widely watched in the suburban hinterlands, previously believed to be hostile to rap, and by the emergence of an angrier, more militant style spearheaded by Public Enemy and N.W.A. (Niggas with Attitude). The following article by Jon Pareles makes clear, however, that it was public statements made by Public Enemy's "minister of information" Professor Griff that attracted attention, rather than the political statements in Public Enemy's songs.[1] Yet, as Pareles notes, while they may have received more attention than other entertainers, rap artists were not alone in projecting volatile messages via mass cultural products. And Pareles also raises interesting points about the *amount* of attention received by Public Enemy for controversial statements in relation to bigoted statements made by white heavy metal band Guns N' Roses and white comedian Andrew Dice Clay. Pareles has been the main pop music critic at the *New York Times* since the late 1980s and was one of the first critics at a major daily to write sympathetically about hip-hop (much to the chagrin of many stodgy readers of the *Times*).[2]

There's a New Sound in Pop Music: Bigotry
Jon Pareles

Has hatred become hip? From isolated spots in pop culture, racial and sexual prejudice have slithered back into view. Andrew Dice Clay, a comedian whose Nassau Coliseum performance on Saturday sold out immediately, mixes dirty-word jokes with vicious put-downs of women, homosexuals, blacks and Japanese. During a sketch on "The Tonight Show" Aug. 11, Johnny Carson, as his yokel character Floyd R. Turbo, invoked "baseball the way it was meant to be played, on real grass, with no designated hitter and all white guys"; the studio audience gasped, then tittered nervously.

In a recent *Rolling Stone* magazine cover story, Axl Rose of the heavy metal band Guns N' Roses, whose debut album sold nine million copies, defends his song "One in a Million," which includes the verse: "Immigrants and faggots/They make no sense to me/They come to our country/And think they'll do as they please/Like start some mini-Iran or spread some [expletive] disease." He also savors the word "niggers" in a verse that continues, "Get outta my way/Don't need to buy none/Of your gold chains today."

Across the color line, the rap group Public Enemy fired, then rehired Richard (Professor Griff) Griffin, who as its "minister of information" said in a May interview with the *Washington Times:* "The Jews are wicked. And we can prove this." He went on to say that Jews are responsible for "the majority of wickedness that goes on across

---

1. Public Enemy continued to attract attention both for its militant messages critiquing racism and advocating African American economic self-determination, and for its anti-Semitic references, which they have never fully retracted. For more on the debate, fueled in particular by the release of "Welcome to the Terrordome" shortly after the Pareles article reprinted here, see Robert Christgau, "Jesus, Jews, and the Jackass Theory," *Village Voice*, January 16, 1990, 83–86. Chuck D's fullest account may be found in his autobiography; see Chuck D (with Yusuf Jah), "Black and Jewish Relationships," in *Fight the Power: Rap, Race, and Reality* (New York: Delacorte Press, 1997), 205–39.

2. Some of these other articles by Pareles, and readers' responses to them, are discussed at the beginning of Part 6.

the globe." Mr. Griffin was made the group's liaison to the black community and local youth programs, but no longer gives interviews. In a statement announcing the rehiring, Public Enemy's leader, Carlton (Chuck D.) Ridenhour, said, "Please direct any further questions to Axl Rose."

Meanwhile, numerous rappers include homophobic asides in the course of an album. For example, Heavy D. and the Boyz, whose album "Big Tyme" recently reached No. 1 on Billboard's black-music chart, boast that with their rhymes, "you'll be happy as a faggot in jail."

It's ugly stuff, and, as the sticker on Mr. Clay's album package puts it, "offensive." While those examples are vastly outnumbered by nonracist, nonhomophobic cultural messages, they are like cockroaches in a clean kitchen, signaling more trouble to come.

Ethnic stereotyping runs deep in American popular culture. Blacks have been caricatured since the days of slavery; during World War II, the Japanese were portrayed as evil incarnate. Ethnic jokes have always been comedians' staples. But the triumphs of the civil rights movement of the 1960's, and the feminist and homosexual-rights movements that followed, made prejudicial statements less tolerable in mainstream society, almost taboo. Now, that taboo is cracking.

"On the one hand, it seems like a new openness," said Alvin Poussaint, associate professor of psychiatry at Harvard Medical School and a consultant to "The Cosby Show." "But on the other, it shows a new acceptance, a license to say derogatory things about other people. The argument is that the people making these statements are being for real and not covering anything up, and they have a point. Young kids, particularly kids from working-class backgrounds, have had these racist attitudes for a long time. But until recently, it was not publicly acceptable to say so."

Popular culture, like the regulator that jiggles atop a pressure cooker, vents tensions in the society it addresses. "One in a Million" and Mr. Clay's comedy suggest not only deep resentment but an attempt to reassert white male heterosexual power over others. Whether it is a last gasp backlash or a new majoritarianism remains unclear. Meanwhile, minorities battle one another.

Prejudice against and among minorities isn't confined to popular culture, where it is still relatively rare. But culture shifts with politics. Surveys have shown renewed prejudice in the United States across all income levels and classes in recent years, not least among young people—who, experts in race relations point out, face competition for entry-level jobs and may resent newly franchised, visibly distinguishable minorities. Another factor they cite has been the Reagan Administration's opposition to affirmative-action programs, a signal that minority rights were vulnerable.

Joel Kovel, a social science professor at Bard College who teaches a course on ideology in mass culture, said, "The need in our society to express identity by excluding others has always been very, very strong. With the decline of the cold war, demonizing the Soviets doesn't carry the symbolic weight it used to, and there's a resurgence of more old-fashioned nativism and racism."

Racial divisions have made headlines in recent politics. This week's mayoral primary in New York takes place under the shadow of a racial killing in Bensonhurst. David Duke, a former Ku Klux Klan official, was elected to the Louisiana Legislature; George Bush's Presidential campaign was accused of stirring racial fears with its Willie Horton commercial about a black convicted murderer who raped a white woman while on furlough from prison.

"That commercial legitimized prejudicial speech, and the Bernhard Goetz case legitimized it," Dr. Poussaint said, "And the Reagan Administration set the tone. They were openly militant against affirmative action and for giving Federal money to segregated, church-related schools. Reagan didn't even make any symbolic gestures toward the black community. He set a tone that you can keep blacks shut out and they can't do anything about it."

Increasing Prejudice in the Age of AIDS

Another longstanding prejudice, homophobia, has been rekindled by fear of AIDS, which was at first stigmatized as the "gay disease." The offhand virulence of homophobia in music with a largely teen-aged audience is particularly telling. "Male teenagers generally go through a period of fear that they're going to be homosexual," Dr. Poussaint said. "Some teenagers, especially those with a lot of conflict, go through a very homophobic stage to reinforce their heterosexuality." Heavy D.'s rap, Guns N' Roses's heavy metal and Mr. Clay's comic universe are all overwhelmingly male clubhouses; they flaunt homophobia.

Randy Shilts, author of "And the Band Played On," a book about the AIDS epidemic, sees resurgent homophobia as a political backlash. "Whenever you have a group that begins to assert itself, you're going to have a reaction. Something like Guns N' Roses is obviously emblematic of the alienation that some younger people feel from what they presume to be a reigning liberal morality—it's a way of rebelling against authority. But to me, it's an incredibly unsophisticated analysis that sees gay people as part of the power structure. Nobody can look at what's gone on around AIDS and gay people in the United States and think that gay people are in power."

As power relationships are re-drawn and an us-against-them mentality sets in, sexual and ethnic lines make convenient divisions. "For young men growing up," said Peggy R. Sanday, an anthropologist at the University of Pennsylvania, "their manhood seems to be based on expressing their rights, but with those rights phrased in terms of power over others."

Prejudicial statements have slipped through the mass media. Many radio stations, especially in the South and Middle West, broadcast "One in a Million," with its four-letter word bleeped out; rappers, however, generally save their homophobic lines for album tracks rather than more widely broadcast singles. Mr. Clay had his own Home Box Office special, and he serves up his milder material on talk shows. Mr. Carson's line came out of the mouth of a comic character, and in that context was approved for broadcast after discussion between programming and network standards executives, said Pat Schultz, an NBC spokeswoman. In context, she added, the line, "clearly did not represent the opinion of Johnny Carson or of 'The Tonight Show.'"

Record companies' main concerns are commercial. Although they regularly work with performers on everything from packaging to song choices, they obviously didn't expect Heavy D.'s homophobia or Mr. Rose's scapegoating to hurt their prospects. Most popular music steers away from divisiveness in order to garner larger audiences; rock has a tradition of embracing (or exploiting) the contributions of racial and sexual outsiders. Yet in an increasingly fragmented pop market, it is also possible to succeed by rallying a single constituency against outsiders.

Mr. Rose in his interview indicated that to him, racial epithets represent artistic freedom, a position echoed by his recording company, Geffen Records. According to Bryn Bridenthal, Geffen Records' director of media and artist relations, "There were a lot of discussions about 'One in a Million,' and if it were totally a label decision, the decision would probably have been not to release it. But if you're going to start censoring your artists, it's going to damage your relationship. There's always somebody who's going to release it, and if you've got an artist like Guns N' Roses, you want to keep the relationship with the company. In the end, Geffen Records just does not support censorship of the artist's creative desires.

"Guns N' Roses have a lot of power because they've sold a lot of records," she added. "But if they hadn't sold a lot of records, no one would have paid any attention to that song." Interestingly, Geffen also released Mr. Clay's album, "Dice," produced by its Def American subsidiary—but the album was deemed so controversial that no Geffen information appears on the package. Mr. Clay's next album is tentatively titled "No Tolerance."

Censorship of popular culture would not eliminate prejudice, although censorship efforts are rising. Universities are trying to regulate prejudicial statements published by students; pressure groups are battling what they see as permissiveness on television; the United States Senate recently moved to restrict public support of controversial art. (The Parents' Music Resource Center in Washington, which monitors rock lyrics, has concerned itself with violence, sexual explicitness, drug references and blasphemy, not bigotry.)

Racist and sexist statements are a byproduct of societal tensions, and they belong well within constitutionally defined free speech. They're worth allowing because the alternative, the imposition of governmental regulations—like Senator Jesse Helms's guidelines for government financed arts programs—could hobble virtually all controversial expression. Politically correct art, under any definition of political correctness, tends to be strangulated art.

Free Speech Allows Denunciation of Bigotry

But legal tolerance need not mean acceptance. Free speech allows those who are disgusted by prejudicial conduct to denounce it, as Jewish groups did after Public Enemy's actions; the Anti-Defamation League of B'nai Brith called Mr. Griffin's firing and rehiring a "repugnant charade." Yet Guns N' Roses, 10 times as commercially successful as Public Enemy, have generated hardly a peep. According to Ms. Bridenthal, Mr. Rose's comments to *Rolling Stone* brought not protests but requests for more interviews, which he has refused.

"Axl does not believe that what he said was a horrible racist thing," she said. "I think he's reflecting a whole stratum of our society that feels the same way. That may be a scary thing, but part of what art is supposed to do is to make people look at things, and that's how it changes the world."

There are differences between Public Enemy and Guns N' Roses. The rap group's overall message is one of self-determination for blacks. Mr. Ridenhour's lyrics are angry—one song describes Public Enemy as "prophets of rage"—and on stage he performs surrounded by what the group calls a "security force," young men in uniform who hold plastic Uzis. (Mr. Griffin used to lead them through quasi-military maneuvers; now his successor does.) The stance is militant, confrontational.

But Mr. Ridenhour kept racism out of Public Enemy's songs. While he calls himself a "follower of Farrakhan," referring to the Nation of Islam leader Louis Farrakhan, who has made inflammatory, anti-Semitic statements, he does not include such sentiments in his songs. His adversaries are the likes of "the media" and "the government," not targeted groups. In "Party for Your Right to Fight," mostly about the history of the Black Panther Party, he uses the phrase, "grafted devils," alluding to black-supremacist Nation of Islam theories that consider whites the end result of a diabolical genetic bleaching process. But the lyrics charge the "devils" with specific offenses.

Yet Public Enemy's actions outside its music send a different message. When Mr. Griffin's statements led to a public outcry, Mr. Ridenhour fired him and issued public apologies. But he effectively annulled those apologies when he rehired Mr. Griffin. Although Mr. Ridenhour has said Mr. Griffin apologized to him for his statements, Mr. Griffin has made no public apology, and in his final interview on Aug. 3, with the *Kansas City Jewish Chronicle*, he called his statements "100 percent pure."

Caving in to Pressure

Public Enemy is clearly torn privately (Mr. Griffin and Mr. Ridenhour are longtime friends) and publicly; Mr. Ridenhour does not want to be seen within the black community as caving in to pressure from whites. But in his actions self-contradiction reigns. A group that intends to fight racism should distance itself decisively from all forms of bigotry, including anti-Semitism. Public Enemy may already have been penalized for its actions; it was negotiating a new recording contract with MCA Records, but the deal collapsed during the controversy.

Guns N' Roses, meanwhile, addresses a white majority and remains unrepentant. While 1980's rock has had an obscure fringe of white-supremacist "skinhead" and, in Britain, "oi" bands, none has had major-label support or concert and radio exposure like Guns N' Roses, although standard heavy-metal boasting and sexism, not racism, is the band's main message. (On stage, Guns N' Roses goes through the motions of strutting narcissism and macho camaraderie.) Mr. Rose spewed his racism in a song on a Top 10 recording, the two-million-selling "G N' R Lies," and he considers himself brave and forthright.

"Why can black people go up to each other and say, 'nigger,' but when a white guy does it all of a sudden it's a big put-down?" Mr. Rose complains in the *Rolling Stone* interview. "I used the word 'nigger' to describe somebody that is basically a pain in your life, a problem. The word 'nigger' doesn't necessarily mean black."

Mr. Rose ascribed the "immigrants" verse to his being harassed at a convenience store run by immigrants, and to "very bad experiences with homosexuals"— inadvertently supplying classic examples of bigoted illogic, which extrapolates from individuals to demonize whole groups. Although the Gay Men's Health Crisis dropped Guns N' Roses from a June benefit concert for AIDS research, the band has been otherwise unscathed. Its record company is still solicitous about their "relationship."

In popular culture's market system, it is up to listeners to repudiate messages they dislike, passively or actively—and to disabuse bigots of any claim to the mainstream. Rock and comedy have a mandate to probe taboos, and they should be expected to go too far now and then. But what's pitiable about the current outbursts is how timid they are. They don't break new artistic ground—or, as Public Enemy chant, "fight the powers that be"—they scapegoat groups perceived as weaker. While the promise of American popular culture is its willingness to defy conventional wisdom and established hierarchies, performers who spew prejudice offer only their own ignorance and cowardice.

Further Reading

Asim, Jabari. *The N Word: Who Can Say It, Who Shouldn't, and Why.* Boston: Houghton Mifflin, 2007.

Forman, Murray. *The 'Hood Comes First: Race, Space, and Place in Rap and Hip-Hop.* Middletown, Conn.: Wesleyan University Press, 2002.

Discography

Clay, Andrew Dice. *The Day the Laughter Died*. American Recordings, 1990.
Guns N' Roses. *G N' R Lies*. Geffen, 1988.
Heavy D and the Boyz. *Big Tyme*. Uptown Records, 1989.
N.W.A. *Straight Outta Compton*. Ruthless, 1988.
_____. *100 Miles and Runnin'*. Priority, 1990s.

PART 6

The 1990s and Beyond

73. Hip-Hop into the 1990s

GANGSTAS, FLY GIRLS, AND THE BIG BLING-BLING

hip-hop without wit is like sushi without wasabi
—Greg Tate[1]

The surge of mainstream popularity experienced by rap at the close of the 1980s continued into the 1990s. One of the most curious aspects of this, because it was so unexpected at the time, was the commercial ascendance of "gangsta rap." Gangsta rap, although pioneered by northeast rappers, such as Schoolly D and Boogie Down Productions, achieved its broadest early circulation as a product of South Central Los Angeles and the nearby black communities of Long Beach and Compton. With lyrics featuring raw language in an unprecedented description of graphic violence, sex, and anger, N.W.A. (or Niggas with Attitude—mentioned briefly at the start of Chapter 72) brought a new sense of urban, quasi-cinematic realism to popular music. The majority of mass media reportage focused on the sensationalistic aspects of the recordings, thereby missing two important components of N.W.A.'s approach: the driving, noisy, hard-edged, and funk-inflected grooves of the instrumental tracks produced by Dr. Dre (Andre Young, b. 1965), accentuated by the rhythmic declamations of the group's rappers (especially Ice Cube and Easy-E), and the way in which N.W.A.'s depictions of violence criticized how social institutions (especially law enforcement) perpetuated systemic racism.[2]

---

1. "Above and Beyond Rap's Decibels," *New York Times*, March 6, 1994, sec. 2, 36.

2. Robin D. G. Kelley presents a thorough and sympathetic scholarly account of gangsta rap in "Kickin' Reality, Kickin' Ballistics: 'Gangsta Rap' and Postindustrial Los Angeles," in *Race Rebels: Culture, Politics, and the Black Working Class* (New York: Free Press, 1994), 183–227.

While the "hardcore" aspects of gangsta rappers and some other flamboyantly *outré* groups, such as 2 Live Crew, seized media attention for flaunting public taboos, the late 1980s and early 1990s witnessed some other, less controversial developments in rap that were every bit as notable. Prominent among them was what the music press later dubbed "alternative" or "progressive" hip-hop, represented by groups like De La Soul and A Tribe Called Quest. Greg Tate defined progressive hip-hop as "hiphop praxis wherein lyric content and raising the art form to the next level outweighs the profit margin."[3] Albums such as De La Soul's *Three Feet High and Rising* used the flow of radio variety shows from the pre-TV era to reinvent the album format (an innovation that was soon widely adopted), but with material that could only come from growing up in the post-TV era.[4] Combining skits that were takeoffs on TV game shows and witty, insightful, and (above all) nonviolent lyrics with samples taken from all over the pop music spectrum, De La Soul and other progressive hip-hop groups became critical darlings. Another development, the politically oriented rap initiated by Public Enemy, was extended by female artists such as Queen Latifah, who also received much favorable critical attention at the time.[5]

Nevertheless, mainstream media coverage of hip-hop almost single-mindedly conveyed a sense of moral outrage and panic, focused on the most lurid examples of hardcore rap. Articles in not-so-new publications ranging from *Newsweek* to the *New Republic* deplored what the authors viewed as the mindless glorification of violence and misogyny. Many of the writers directed their attention toward the "anger" that such writers heard in the music, although these accounts rarely seemed aware of how this anger was often politically motivated by a critique of white privilege (especially in recordings by Public Enemy and Boogie Down Productions/KRS-One). The growing appeal of gangsta rap to young, white listeners caused the writer of a 1991 article in the *New Republic* to claim that rap music was neither "music" nor "black."[6] In contrast, Jon Pareles wrote a series of sympathetic articles in the *New York Times*, which, however, invariably elicited a round of letters to the editor protesting that hip-hop should not be included

---

3. Greg Tate, "Diatribe," *Village Voice,* September 3, 1996, 46.

4. Jon Pareles explores the TV–hip-hop connection in "How Rap Moves to Television's Beat," *New York Times,* January 14, 1990, sec. 2, 1–2.

5. See, for example, Michelle Wallace, "When Black Feminism Faces the Music, and the Music Is Rap," *New York Times,* July 29, 1990.

6. The title says it all: David Samuels, "The Rap on Rap: The 'Black Music' that Isn't Either," *New Republic,* November 11, 1991, 24–29. The articles referred to in *Newsweek* were David Gates et al., "The Rap Attitude," *Newsweek,* March 19, 1990, 56–63; and John Leland, "Rap and Race," *Newsweek,* June 29, 1992, 47–52. Although this type of criticism has lessened in recent years, it has not disappeared entirely, as evidenced by the following statement: "Rap consists, in large part, of people ranting and cursing to a monotonous beat. It is now America's most popular music"; see Peter Carlson, "Uncivil Discourse: The Breathless Harangue Is All the Rage," *Binghamton Press and Sun Bulletin,* March 2, 2003, 9A. Originally published in the *Washington Post.*

in the music section of Arts and Leisure, since rap, after all, was not really music.[7]

We already heard from J. D. Considine in Chapter 66 in the article on Judas Priest and the Scorpions. Displaying impressive critical range, Considine turns his attention to many of the issues (described earlier) that dominated media discussions about hip-hop in the early 1990s. Considine uses interviews with Chuck D (Carlton Ridenhour, b. 1960) and Ice Cube (O'Shea Jackson, b. 1969, who left N.W.A. to embark on a successful solo career in 1990) to rebut many of the criticisms directed toward hip-hop, while paying particular attention to the "is it music?" question (posed here by nonrap musicians Al DiMeola, Lita Ford, and Ozzy Osbourne) and the social context for the violent imagery found in much rap.

Fear of a Rap Planet
J. D. Considine

In the 12 years since "Rapper's Delight" bum-rushed the Top 40, it would seem that rap has developed an unshakeable grip on popular culture. It's heard everywhere—on MTV, in movies, in advertising, even in Saturday morning cartoons, where Hammerman just replaced Kid 'N Play as the networks' favorite animated rapper.

Granted, a lot of people don't particularly *like* rap. They aren't down with "O.P.P.," have no memories of bliss concerning P.M. Dawn, and don't want to talk about sex—or anything else with Salt-N-Pepa.[8] These are the folks for whom rap is just noise with a beat, and they feel the same things their parents felt about rock 'n' roll: disinterest, distaste and disgust.

But fear? Who could possibly be afraid of rap?

Well, Bob Greene, for one. In his Chicago *Tribune* column last month, he wrote about a mugging in New York which happened to have been videotaped by the perpetrators themselves. Although he reports that police, who eventually arrested two teens, were "puzzled" by the event, what sparked this not-ready-for-prime-time crime was no mystery to Greene—rap music made them do it. Or, to be specific, rap videos, which, writes Greene, "are purposely glorifying armed violence and criminality. Most Americans probably have not seen these rap videos. But they are broadcast day and night by various cable channels, and they are frightening."

But not as frightening as the rap audience itself. Just ask all those radio stations that not only refuse to play rap records, but actually boast about it, courting listeners with

---

7. See Pareles, "How Rap Moves to Television's Beat"; letters to the editor, *New York Times*, February 4, 1990; Pareles, "Rap: Slick, Violent, Nasty and, Maybe, Hopeful," *New York Times*, June 17, 1990; idem, "On Rap, Symbolism and Fear," *New York Times*, February 2, 1992, sec. 2, 1, 23; letters to the editor, *New York Times*, February 16, 1992.

8. This sentence refers to then-recent hits by those artists.

Source: "Fear of a Rap Planet" © J. D. Considine/*Musician.*

slogans like "All the Best Music—And No Rap." Some are so petrified that they'll even excise rap-like passages from recordings by non-rap acts, as WLLZ-FM in Detroit did recently when it cut a few bars of unsung rhyming from "Roll the Bones" by Rush.

If you really want a sense of how deep this fear of a rap planet goes, however, check out the mass media, for whom rap seems to be a never-ending source of scare stories. When a white New York investment banker was beaten, raped and left for dead in the celebrated Central Park "wilding" incident, it was widely (and, apparently, erroneously) reported that the suspects after their arrest were happily chanting Tone-Loc's "Wild Thing"—the implication being that the rap had somehow inspired the rampage. Indeed, when *Newsweek* published its 1990 cover story lambasting rap culture, the magazine made sure it was Tone-Loc's face that was framed by the "Rap Rage" headline.

Then, after N.W.A.'s *Efil4zaggin* entered the *Billboard* album charts at number one (the first rap album ever to do so), the *New Republic* ran a cover story suggesting that rap, described in a subhead as "The 'black music' that isn't either," isn't even listened to by blacks. According to the *TNR* story, rap's primary audience is suburban white kids, and N.W.A.'s sex-and-violence posturing is little more than minstrelsy, cartoonish blacks doing their best to entertain thrill-seeking Caucasians.

And now there's the controversy over Ice Cube's *Death Certificate*, which has been denounced by anti-defamation activists, Korean citizen groups, syndicated columnists and even the editors of *Billboard*. Granted, Ice Cube has provided his critics with plenty of ammunition, what with lyrics that characterize Korean store owners as "Oriental one-penny-countin' motherfuckers," that insist "true niggas ain't gay," and that suggest his former bandmates in N.W.A. dispose of manager Jerry Heller:

> *Get rid of that devil real simple*
> *Put a bullet in his temple*
> *Because you can't be a Niggaz 4 Life crew*
> *With a white Jew telling you what to do.*

It's ugly, sure. Angry, too. But Ice Cube refuses to consider the quatrain quoted above to be anti-Jewish. "I'm really surprised that people would take that record so out of proportion," he says. "The record is not geared towards Jerry Heller or the Jewish community; the record is geared towards the group who attacked me. In most cases I felt that Jerry Heller attacked me—in the *Rolling Stone* interview, and the *Spin* articles.

"They even attacked me on the record, and said that when they caught me, they was going to cut my hair and fuck me with a broomstick. Now, I've seen them a couple of times after that record—they haven't cut my hair, and they definitely haven't fucked me with a broomstick." In other words, it's all just "woofing," with both sides making outrageous verbal threats they have no intention of following through on.

"So why are you taking rap music literally?" he asks, rhetorically. "It's stupid to take anything that literally, other than news. This is a form of *entertainment*. People keep forgetting that. I'm not a schoolteacher or a professor at any university. I'm a rapper. I entertain."

The question is, are you amused? Or are you afraid?

It's a Black Thing, You Wouldn't Understand

Ask Public Enemy's Chuck D why people are afraid of rap, and at first he just shakes his head. "That's ridiculous," he says, "Because we don't tear up hotels, we don't tear up arenas." It isn't, after all, as if he and his fellow rappers are inciting youths to riot on a nightly basis.

Chuck D's no dummy, though, and it doesn't take him long to come up with a real answer. "Anything that comes from a black point of view that the establishment doesn't have full control over or understanding of, they view as being offensive," he says. "And now even more so, since that point of view is coming across to white kids."

That's not to say Public Enemy's audience is entirely white, mind you. The crowd of young Baltimoreans he plays to this evening, for example, is almost 95 percent black (don't they read the *New Republic*?) But overall, the audience P.E. attracts is as broad as it is big, and that, as the establishment sees it, makes the group doubly dangerous.

"I look at this country as being a predominantly white male-dominated society," Chuck says. "It has never even given a black male his chance or his due, because we are seen as being not even part of that whole structure. It's a white male structure versus everything else.

"Now, some of the frustration is coming across. This stuff is coming out from all different angles, but the media have been built by white men, and the first maneuver when you can't control the play is to attack it."

If that seems a little paranoid from where you're sitting, it makes perfect sense from Public Enemy's perspective. After all, this group has spent much of its recording career articulating the black community's anger and taking flak for its efforts. First it was lambasted for endorsing Louis Farrakhan in "Bring the Noise," then for anti-Jewish remarks Professor Griff, its former Minister of Information, made in an interview with the Washington *Times*. The current controversy, for those keeping score at home, stems from a gay-bashing rhyme uttered by Flavor Flav in "A Letter to the New York Post"—"ask James Cagney/He beat up on a guy when he found he was a fagney."

Chuck shrugs off the "Letter" controversy. "I mean, you really can't take it that serious on Flavor," he says, "because he just found something that rhymes." Beyond that, though, he says he's more concerned with the motives behind these attacks than with what his attackers have to say. "I don't judge criticism, I judge the critic," he says, adding that as far as he can see, the only thing these anti-rap diatribes are meant to do is maintain the status quo.

"You have certain defense mechanisms up to keep things the way they are supposed to be and maintain order in this structure," he says. "That's because you have a lot of people who are paranoid, with no really full grasp of what they believe in, and they feel that they have something to lose. They lose belief in themselves and in their structure. They feel like they'll lose a grip on their future.

"In our view, that's not necessarily so. The black race is just trying to get a grip on itself to survive. I mean, the thing with black people in this country is they're real beat-down people. And it's really more serious than a lot of white people take to heart, because we have everything to lose—and we lost a lot. I try to tell our people, 'There's no time for making excuses, we've got to make the best of it.' But many of them are damaged goods, you know what I'm saying?

"To make a long story short, white people have to understand that black people already have respect for [them], because we've been trained to do so. We just don't have respect for ourselves. When a level of self-respect comes, then you'll see that it gets better. But self-respect has never been taught, so right now, black people are still slaves to that."

Unfortunately, what some rappers see as their efforts to uplift the race, their critics take as attacks on others. Ice Cube, for instance, explains in the liner notes to

Death Certificate that the album is divided into two parts, with the "Death Side" being "a mirrored image of where we are today," while the "Life Side" pictures "where we need to go." But it's disturbingly easy to translate that message as "Let's stop destroying ourselves, and start destroying others."

Which, Cube says, is dead wrong. "They figure when you're pro-black, you've got to be anti-whatever," he says. "But see, that's guilt from the pain that they inflicted on blacks. We aren't pro-black to be anti-white or anti-Korean, anti-Jewish. We're pro-black so we can look back at history and make sure that it doesn't repeat itself."

Being pro-black doesn't necessarily mean articulating your ideas as violently as Ice Cube does. Take the Afrocentric movement. Although the Allan Blooms of the world consider it a threat to the very foundations of Western Civilization, Afrocentricity as expressed by the likes of Queen Latifah is simply a means for young blacks to learn who they are, and have some pride in that knowledge.[9]

"It's very hard, because we're brainwashed in this country in a lot of ways," she says. "It's like when a little black kid grows up, what do they see on TV? They see so much white. What are they supposed to connect to? They connect to what this white thing is. So they think their hair is supposed to be long and their eyes are supposed to be light and their skin is supposed to be light and it's not, and they feel low about it. When they go out with the girls, all the guys want to talk to the light ones, or the one with long hair.

"We have a lot of stereotypes to fight, a lot of barriers to break down. And it's hard, because nobody's perfect. Nobody can just change all this stuff in one day. It's going to take years and years of barrier-breaking for things like this to change."

Rap Isn't Music

"I have a problem with rap," admits Guitarist Al Di Meola. "It's not music. It's not like I'm hearing an instrumentalist play, with some harmony and a good vocalist. Where are the people who've learned to play their instrument?"

"I'm really bored with this rap music," says fellow fretboarder Lita Ford. "I think it's about time that it was on its way out. It sounds like gang music to me."

"I'm a believer in melody," says singer Ozzy Osbourne. "Rap I can appreciate, but it drives me nuts after about an hour. I mean, if you haven't got a melody. . . ."

When musicians talk about what they don't like about rap, the points that come up rarely concern racial politics; instead, it's the rap musical value they question. *It hasn't got a melody. They don't play instruments, they don't have any ideas, they steal everything. It's just not music.*

Rappers, naturally, counter that such talk is just so much sour grapes. "It's not *their* instrument [on the record], so it's not music," laughs Russell Simmons, president of Def Jam Records. "Drummers are the same—they say there's no live drummers on it, so it's not real, it's not a record. 'Course, now that live drums are back, drummers think those same records are fine. I think they're ridiculous."

"A lot of people don't like that we could take a song that's been done before and probably sold 300,000, and do 1.3 million with it," adds Ice Cube. "Like Hammer took 'Super Freak,' and made it into a bigger hit than Rick James did. That's why I think people get mad at us. They've got to understand that we took something and

---

9. Allan Bloom, author of conservative diatribe against late 20th-century mass culture *The Closing of the American Mind* (New York: Simon and Schuster, 1987), which was widely discussed during this period.

just made it better. The talent we put on top of it was better than the talent that was on it originally."

Not that it takes a sampler to steal a groove. A decade ago, the pioneering rappers at Sugar Hill all recorded with a live rhythm section. But as Matt Dike, whose production credits include Tune-Loc's "Wild Thing," points out, "What they were doing was playing grooves from other records, that they had stolen. Like the bass in 'White Lines' was from a song by Liquid Liquid, this underground New York band. They were ballsier than anybody! They just replayed the whole thing, and acted like they wrote it."

Besides, if it takes no talent to make rap records, Ice Cube has a simple question: "I say, 'Why don't *you* try to do a hit rap record?'

"They'd be lost, in most cases."

Maybe so, but rap's critics do raise some valid questions. For instance, given that rap vocals rarely change pitch (and certainly aren't "sung" in any conventional understanding of the term), is it fair to say that rap records don't have any melody?

No way, answers producer Bill Laswell. "That's just people who have been conditioned into thinking a certain chord sequence ending on middle C is the absolute concept of melody," he argues. "If you're familiar with Asian or African music, you realize that a lot of the melody is inherent in the drumming. In African drumming, you hear all kinds of melodies and phrases, and there's as much melody in hip-hop and rap as in African drumming—and that's a lot of melody. You just have to listen."

True enough. Even a seemingly simple rap record, like Naughty By Nature's "O.P.P.," reveals unexpected complexity if you know where to look. Sure, it has the "ABC" piano hook, looped right off the original, which is probably the only "melodic" element anyone noticed when it first came up on the radio. But there's also a reggae-style bassline churning up a nice rhythmic cross-current with the syncopated kick drum, a fair amount of percussive interplay (check out the parallelism between the two-note piano part that sets up each two-bar phrase and the two-beat cowbell accent that leads into three each measure), and, of course, the raps themselves, which spin clever variations on the bassline's cadence—sometimes stretching across the bar, sometimes double-timing the beat, sometimes pulling up short to add to the track's rhythmic tension.

Even though they use samplers, sequencers and drum machines instead of guitars, bass and drums, rap acts orchestrate their rhythm frameworks as thoughtfully as any rock act would. Take Public Enemy, for example. "They're the only rap group I know of that can take five or six snippets of a record, put it together and make it sound like one band," said Branford Marsalis after contributing a tenor solo to "Fight the Power."

"They're not musicians, and don't claim to be—which makes it easier to be around them. Like, the song's in A minor or something, then it goes to D7, and I think, if I remember, they put some of the A minor solo on the D7, or some of the D7 stuff on the A minor chord at the end. So it sounds really different. And the more unconventional it sounds, the more they like it."

On the latest Public Enemy album, *Apocalypse 91 . . . The Enemy Strikes Black*, the group extends that approach. "We've taken a lot of instruments and processed them through computers," says Chuck D, who explains that the P.E. approach often relies on playing the samples on a keyboard to lend more of a live feel to the tracks. "The only difference between sampling and live sound is change," he says. "When a bass player plays bass, he makes mistakes sometimes. But he fixes the mistake so quick that it's just a change in the pattern, an ad-lib. But your programming is not going to program a mistake. So what we try to do is, we don't program it so much. We play the keys. Like 'Homey Don't Play That' from the *Terminator X* record. I played the bass on keys."

Then there's the rap itself. Those who don't rap often assume that rap lyrics are little more than simply metered rhyming doggerel—which, to be honest, a certain amount of them are. But the best rappers take as much care with their cadences as they do with the rhythm beds, so that the words flow along with the music instead of just hammering home the beat.

Chuck D, for instance, won't even start writing until he has a groove to work from, and often sketches out his rhythmic ideas with nonsense syllables before filling out his raps. "I'll have a groove that inspires me, do my vocals in a certain way and then fill it with words," he says. "And if it doesn't fit the groove, I'm not going to fuck with it."

Ironically, once he's finished recording, Chuck then has to go through the laborious process of relearning what he has written. "I have a bad memory for remembering words," he laughs. "People say, 'Didn't you write it?' I say, 'Yeah, I wrote it, and it's on a piece of paper. Is it in my head? It came out of my head, but now I have to relearn it.' A lot of people don't understand that.

"You know who's got a crystal-clear memory? Ice-T. Ice-T recites records from back in 1981, line for line. He can recite every single one of his records line for line, word for word. Ice Cube is the same thing. They're like Michael Jordan or Magic Johnson. I guess I'm like [Charles] Barkley—I gotta work for everything I got.

"The only thing that might be natural about me is my voice. But a voice doesn't mean nothing if you don't know how to use it."

"It all comes with style," explains Ice Cube. "A lot of raps that come straight on the beat were written without a beat, know what I'm saying? They put a beat in their head and just write from that. Then they get the music and the music isn't exactly what they had in their head, but they can come down on every beat and make it work. I choose to have my music first. I'll write a rap that fits it like a glove, or at least try to. I can take breaths here, I can slow down here, I can speed up here, and just try to throw some style and flavor on it without sounding so robotic."

As for material, Ice Cube says there's never any shortage of things for him to write about. "Living just gives me records to do," he says. "I just finished *Death Certificate*, and I've thought of three topics that I might want to write on for my new album.

"I just live life, man, however it comes. When things come up that I think need to be talked about, then I do it. I just start writing."

Further Reading

Chang, Jeff. "Word Power: A Brief, Highly Opinionated History of Hip-Hop Journalism." In *Pop Music and the Press*, ed. Steve Jones, 65–71. Philadelphia: Temple University Press, 2002.

Chuck D (with Yusuf Jah). *Fight the Power: Rap, Race, and Reality*. New York: Delacorte Press, 1997.

McLeod, Kembrew. "The Politics and History of Hip-Hop Journalism." In *Pop Music and the Press*, ed. Steve Jones, 156–67. Philadelphia: Temple University Press, 2002.

Rose, Tricia. *Black Noise: Rap Music and Black Culture in Contemporary America*. Hanover, N.H.: University Press of New England, 1994.

Walser, Robert. "Rhythm, Rhyme, and Rhetoric in the Music of Public Enemy." *Ethnomusicology* 39 (1995): 193–217.

Discography

De La Soul. *Three Feet High and Rising*. Tommy, 2001.

Ice Cube. *AmeriKKKa's Most Wanted*. Priority, 1990.

_____. *Death Certificate*. Priority Records, 1991.

N.W.A. *Straight Outta Compton*. Priority Records, 1989.

Public Enemy. *Apocalypse 91 . . . The Enemy Strikes Black*. Def Jam, 1991.

Queen Latifah. *Black Reign*. Motown, 1993.

Schoolly D. *The Best of Schoolly D*. Jive, 2003.

74. Nuthin' but a "G" Thang

In the wake of the successes of N.W.A. and Ice Cube, gangsta rap became the dominant form of hip-hop in the early 1990s. The level of censorship and political attention that rap received rose correspondingly. Political militancy assumed heightened levels of confrontational violence in tracks such as N.W.A.'s "Fuck tha Police" (1988), Public Enemy's "Arizona" (1991, criticizing Arizona's failure to recognize Dr. Martin Luther King's birthday), Ice-T with Body Count's "Cop Killer" (1992), and Dr. Dre's (now recording on his own) "Deep Cover" (1992). Many of the songs emanating from Southern California seemed eerily to anticipate or comment upon the May 1992 uprising following the exoneration of Los Angeles police officers in the beating of Rodney King. With the PMRC's rating system already in place (and with the recordings just mentioned all receiving "parental advisory" stickers), pressures mounted on recording companies to limit such confrontational recordings. Time-Warner, in response to the pressure, first dropped "Cop Killer" from the *Body Count* album and then released Ice-T (a Los Angeles rapper who had recorded an album called *O.G. Original Gangster* in 1991) from his contract.

Dr. Dre's *The Chronic* became the best-selling hip-hop album of 1992 (the title is a reference to test-grade marijuana). Dre had modified his sound from N.W.A., producing a smoother form of funk that featured high-pitched, whiny synthesizers and (frequently) sung choruses. Now recording with soon-to-be-notorious Death Row Records, Dre introduced rapper Snoop Doggy Dogg (Calvin Broadus, b. 1972) on *The Chronic* and "Deep Cover," the single that preceded it. Dre and Snoop shared rapping duties on about half the tracks on *The Chronic*, the lyrics of which were written mainly by Snoop. The critique of racist institutional policies that had featured prominently in early N.W.A. recordings became increasingly implicit in *The Chronic*'s detailed depictions of sex and violence, which fans appreciated because of their humorous language and apparent fidelity to experience. The notion of "keeping it real" thus assumed greater importance in the evaluation of hip-hop.

Snoop Doggy Dogg's solo album *Doggystyle*, repeatedly described in the press of the time as the "most anticipated rap album of all time," was released in late 1993 and quickly became the best-selling rap album ever. As described in the following article by Touré, the notion of "keeping it real" took on a macabre cast when Snoop was arrested in conjunction with a shooting while finishing the album. Yet, as he notes here (echoing the words of Ice Cube in Chapter 73), the words of his songs should not be taken literally, but rather as entertainment. Clearly, the line was blurring between the way in which the words "should be taken," and how rappers and listeners were actually taking them. Also of interest here are Snoop's comments on his delivery and approach to rhythm, which, again, confirm the statements by Chuck D and Ice Cube in the previous article.[1]

Snoop Dogg's Gentle Hip Hop Growl
Touré

It's past midnight on a cool Friday in September, and a photo shoot for a beer ad is breaking up. The photographer's lights still illuminate a small parking lot in West Hollywood, Calif., which is empty save for a few Mercedes-Benzes, Jeeps and low-riders and a handful of young black men.

At the center of the group, looming over all, is the shoot's subject, a thin, dark-skinned 6-foot-4 rapper with sunken cheeks and a razor-sharp nose. He leans at what appears a 45-degree angle, surveying the scene around him out of the corners of his eyes. Hours ago he had turned himself in to the police on the charge of murder and was released on $1 million bail; in minutes he will return to the studio to work on his

---

1. For a more in-depth portrait of Snoop around this time, see dream hampton, "Snoop Doggy Dogg: G-Down," *The Source* 48 (September 1993): 64–70. Particularly interesting in this article are Snoop's comments about the early stages of the West Coast–East Coast rivalry and his connections with the Crips and Bloods—rival African American gangs in Southern California.

debut album, "Doggystyle," the most anticipated hip-hop album ever. His name is Snoop Doggy Dogg.

Over this past year the 22-year-old rapper has been the most ubiquitous man in hip-hop. His voice has flowed from Walkmans, DJ turntables and Jeep stereos as his face graced MTV and the cover of Rolling Stone, all thanks to his featured role on Dr. Dre's album, "The Chronic," which has sold more than three million copies, becoming the fifth-biggest-selling rap album.

On Tuesday, Death Row Records will release "Doggystyle," from the man born Calvin Broadus in Long Beach, Calif., and nicknamed Snoop by his mother. The album follows the first single and video, "What's My Name?" and is expected to enter Billboard's pop album chart at No. 1, a first for a debut album. "This is the biggest buzz I've ever seen," says Chris Lighty, president of Rush Management, which handles many of the top rappers. "The last time there was anything close was probably Jimi Hendrix, no, N.W.A.'s *Niggaz4Life*. People are going to the store asking, 'Is it in yet? Is it in yet?'"

Snoop's music is gangster rap, a genre marked by rhymes that describe the violent challenges of urban living. Gangster rap is probably hip-hop's best-known subset, but it is no more the definitive expression of hip-hop than fusion is of jazz. Like jazz, all hip-hop may sound the same to the inexperienced ear, but beneath the posturing and booming beat lies one of pop's most complex forms. With its collagist ethic, hip-hop pulls from all of popular culture, from old television shows to up-to-the-minute slang, to inform the rapper's often autobiographical presentation. But just as jazz celebrates mastery, hip-hop prizes originality; in (now dated) hip-hop parlance, the word fresh meant excellent. At the moment, "dope" means great.

There are rappers with greater rhythmic flexibility and tonal dynamism than Snoop, but where newness is the virtue, Snoop matters, because his vocal approach is, in every sense, fresh. "Snoop ain't the dopest," says Jermaine Dupri, the producer of the platinum-selling rap group Kris Kross, "but he's king right now."

Snoop's vocal style is part of what distinguishes him: where many rappers scream, figuratively and literally, he speaks softly. Compare the treatment of the murder of a police officer in the song "Deep Cover," from the soundtrack of the 1992 movie of that name, with that of Ice-T's "Cop Killer." Both songs gained popularity in the summer of 1992, but "Deep Cover" did not provoke the controversy "Cop Killer" did because of Snoop's subtlety: to understand "Deep Cover"'s refrain—"'cuz it's one eight seven on a undercover cop"—one has to know that in Los Angeles police terminology the number 1-8-7 means homicide.

"It's the way you put it down," Snoop explains. "I put it down with a twist. Everybody in the whole world knew 'Cop Killer' meant kill a cop. And every policeman knows the municipal code is 187, but everybody in the whole world didn't know that."

Soft tones mark Snoop as vocal descendent of the soul vocalists Al Green and Curtis Mayfield. His voice is a nasal tenor, especially distinct because of his Southernish twang (derived from his Mississippi-born parents and grandparents) and the considerable restraint of his delivery. It all projects the aura of a man who is ultra-cool.

"It's a basic conversation," Snoop says of his style. "I don't rap, I just talk. I don't like to get all pumped up and rap fast 'cause that ain't me. I want to be able to relax and conversate with my people. It's a distinction between Steven Seagal and Clint Eastwood. Seagal ain't laid back. Eastwood is."

Laid-back cool places Snoop in the African-American tradition of making light of personal horror. From the same emotional source from which bluesmen found the grace to understate the weight of their pain comes Snoop's nonchalance in the middle of warring gangs and the police.

Snoop Doggy Dog sounds even cooler when that conversation is juxtaposed against the ominous, sinister, funk-inspired music of his producer, Dr. Dre, an innovator as important in hip-hop as Quincy Jones has been in jazz. Unlike most hip-hop producers who create tracks by sampling from original sources, Dr. Dre uses a band. It's led by T-Green, a one-time George Clinton collaborator and a longtime member of the funk band the Dramatics.

"You know how you would be real sensitive and delicate with a newborn baby," Snoop asks. "That's how I treat the beat when I'm rapping: like a newborn baby. Even if it's a hard track, what I'm saying will move you, because I'm delicately putting it down."

Rage, a female rapper who appears on "The Chronic" and "Doggystyle," says Dr. Dre has contributed much to Snoop's success. "I don't know if Snoop would be as big, because Dre's production plays a big part," she says. "If you don't have good beats, then you might not get as much recognition."

While Snoop delivers rhymes delicately, the content is anything but. Growing up poor, often surrounded by violence, and having served six months in the Wayside County jail outside of Los Angeles (for cocaine possession) gave Snoop experiences upon which he draws: "My raps are incidents where either I saw it happen to one of my close homies or I know about it from just being in the ghetto," he says. "I can't rap about something I don't know. You'll never hear me rapping about no bachelor's degree. It's only what I know and that's the street life. It's all everyday life, reality."

It's all reality is the most-repeated refrain in hip-hop, a proclamation of integrity in a world where it's cool to be from the inner city with a checkered past and many lie about their background. Hip-hop fans prefer artists who are honest, but, in fact, the argument over "realness" may be pointless: they are entertainers. As Rakim, widely considered one of the best rappers, puts it: "You got groups that come out saying they're killing, but in all reality, they're just rappers."

It is important that the rapper's voice and stories be realistic, but must they be the author's own? To thoughtful fans, what's important is how credible the lyrics sound. Here again Snoop stands out: his attention to detail makes him sound extremely credible. According to Mr. Dupri, the producer, "The details in Snoop's writing makes people think, 'Damn, he must've really seen that.'"

For example, in Snoop's favorite song on "The Chronic"—whose title is laden with obscenities—he describes a hot day, when, minutes after completing six months in prison, the protagonist is driven to his girlfriend's house, bursts in brandishing a Glock pistol and finds her having sex with his cousin. He considers shooting her but does not, deeming women not worth killing.

Snoop may sound—and be—more honest than most, but that does not mean he is as tough as his gangster posture or his handlers would suggest. Snoop began rapping in the sixth grade, sang in the choir of Golgotha Trinity Baptist Church in Long Beach and graduated from Long Beach Polytechnic High School. He maintains that he never joined a gang, though he hung out with gang members. Watching them gave Snoop his subject matter; imprisonment focused him.

"I started thinking about my life," he says. "Do I want to keep coming back to this place, or do I want to elevate myself and make my mother proud of me? At Wayside I listened to all the stories people told, wrote them down on my note pad and turned them into raps. That's the first time I really started getting serious about rapping. The older inmates would take me aside and say, 'Youngster, you don't need to be inside this place. God gave you some talent, and you ought to use it.'"

The assertion that lyrics are drawn from reality is also hip-hop's biggest excuse for not passing judgment on what it describes. Rappers routinely discuss violent and obscene situations without taking responsibility for the implications, like reporters from the street willfully lacking a worldview.

Snoop contends he does take a stand against what he describes. "I feel like it's my job to play the backup role for parents who can't get it across to their kids," he says. "For little kids growing up in the ghettos, it's easy to get into the wrong types of things, especially gangbanging and selling drugs. I've seen what that was like, and I don't glorify it, but I don't preach. When my momma would whoop me and tell me, 'You can't do this,' it made me want to go do that; I bring it to them rather than have them go find out about it for themselves."

It takes very critical listening to hear Snoop's implicit message. Far easier is losing oneself in his accounts of renegade days and nights. He may not intend to, or want to admit it, but Snoop adds epic gloss to his life with the skill of a Hollywood movie star.

Yet soon, all of Snoop's talent may be overshadowed. On Aug. 25, Snoop's bodyguard, Malik (McKinley Lee), shot a man named Philip Woldermariam twice—once in the back—from the passenger seat of the Jeep that Snoop was driving. Other details surrounding the event are in dispute. Snoop says the shooting was in self-defense and pleaded not guilty at his arraignment on Oct. 1; his next hearing is set for Nov. 30.

Back in the parking lot, Snoop speaks of his dream. "After I take care of my album," he says, "I'm going to try to eliminate the gang violence. I'll be on a mission for peace." If the trial is on his mind, it does not appear so as he speaks of the future, neglecting to note that on Aug. 25 he could not prevent the 187 that may destroy his life. "I know I have a lot of power," Snoop says. "I know if I say, 'Don't kill,' niggers won't kill."

Further Reading

Garofalo, Reebee. "Setting the Record Straight: Censorship and Social Responsibility in Popular Music." *Journal of Popular Music Studies* 6 (1994): 1–37.

hampton, dream. "Snoop Doggy Dogg: G-Down." *The Source* 48 (September 1993): 64–70.

Kelley, Robin D. G. "Kickin' Reality, Kickin' Ballistics: 'Gangsta Rap' and Postindustrial Los Angeles." In *Race Rebels: Culture, Politics, and the Black Working Class*, 183–227. New York: Free Press, 1994.

Discography

Body Count. *Body Count*. Sire/London/Rhino, 1992.

DeVaughn, William. *Be Thankful for What You Got*. Roxbury, 1974.

Dr. Dre. *The Chronic*. Death Row Koch, 1992.

N.W.A. *Niggaz4Life*. Priority Records, 1991.

Snoop Doggy Dogg. *Doggystyle*. Death Row Records, 1993.

_____. *The Doggfather*. Interscope Records, 1996.

75. Keeping It a Little Too Real

Gangsta rap and the notion of "keeping it real" continued to dominate hip-hop music following *Doggystyle*. New rappers emerged in the New York City area who modified elements of the West Coast style, either by emphasizing partying and material acquisitions, as in the recordings of Biggie Smalls (Christopher Wallace, a.k.a. the Notorious B.I.G., 1972–97), or through heightened obscurantism and bizarrely imaginative humor and music, as in the Wu Tang Clan. Wu Tang Clan, which boasted up to nine members, illustrated the tendency toward increasingly large posses or crews among rap artists. Touré, writing in 1995, describes the development as a move from the late 1980s–early 1990s emphasis on Afro-centrism to "blockism," this being

the idea that your neighborhood block is the center of the world, the people there the most important audience to impress. It's also the directive that if you get off the block, your peeps come too. . . . It's led to the family-like structure behind the three biggest entities in hiphop today: the Wu-Tang Clan, Death Row, and the Biggie Smalls clique.[1]

The contradictions and ambiguity embedded in notions of "keeping it real" and rap as "only entertainment," which the arrest of Snoop in 1993 had begun to expose, intensified with the arrest of 2Pac (Tupac Shakur, 1971–96) late in 1994 on sexual assault charges, followed by the shooting of Shakur (from which he recovered) under mysterious circumstances before the trial began. Tensions began to build between West Coast rappers, centered on Death Row Records, and East Coast rappers, many of whom recorded for Bad Boy Records (the "Biggie Smalls clique" referred to earlier, which included Sean "Puff Daddy" Combs). A crisis point was reached in the murders, first of 2Pac in September 1996, and then of Biggie Smalls in March 1997. The following articles provide background on the West Coast–East Coast feud and show a range of reactions to the murders. While many decried how mass media accounts misrepresented the victims by implying that everyone involved with hip-hop was a criminal, even committed fans could not

---

1. Touré, "The Family Way: The Hiphop Crew as Center of the World," *Village Voice*, October 10, 1995, 49.

ignore the relationship between the deaths of two of hip-hop's biggest stars and the increasing rate of black-on-black violence.[2]

Rap Sheet
Sam Gideon Anso and Charles Rappleye

The murder of Brooklyn rapper Notorious B.I.G. early Sunday morning in Los Angeles cast a pall over a rap industry that had for weeks basked in the glow of a declared truce in the so-called East Coast/West Coast wars—an outbreak of peace that infused the festivities of the annual Soul Train Awards the night before.

Instead, the shooting recalled the scene at the 1996 Soul Train Awards, an event marred by a guns-drawn confrontation between delegations including Tupac Shakur of L.A.'s Death Row Records, and Biggie Smalls, who'd sold platinum for New York's Bad Boy Entertainment. Shakur was gunned down in September in Las Vegas; now B.I.G., whose real name was Christopher Wallace, is dead as well.

Kevin Kim, who was on the scene providing security for Faith Evans, Wallace's estranged wife, said he believes the shooting was a planned attack on Wallace. "They knew who they were shooting at," Kim said in an interview Sunday afternoon. "Look at the shot pattern—tight shots, not like a regular West Coast drive-by where gang members are spraying bullets all over the place."

However, Kim cautioned against speculation that Wallace's murder was linked to the much publicized rivalry between Wallace, Shakur, and the respective companies. "The East Coast/West Coast thing is all blown up," Kim said. "At the party that night, everybody was dancing together, artists hugging each other. . . . They squashed that beef, and it is still squashed."

Kim is referring in part to the truce, memorialized last month in an episode of the sitcom *The Steve Harvey Show*, in which Death Row's Snoop Doggy Dogg and Sean "Puffy" Combs, CEO of Bad Boy Entertainment, publicly laid aside the dispute that has been simmering between rap's leading labels for more than two years.

In the twisted logic of the rap game, even the coziness between Snoop and Puffy, who had been seen together in recent weeks in New York, raised eyebrows and fueled talk that Puffy—and by extension B.I.G.—was disrespecting Death Row and its chief Marion "Suge" Knight, who'd been sentenced to nine years in state prison the week before. "Puffy and Biggie thought with Suge put away it was all good," said one West Coast rap insider. "But it's not all good. There is still a lot of tension out there. And Snoop and Puffy hanging out like they are best friends—that shit ain't right."

The chronology of the feud begins with gunfire in the building lobby of a Manhattan recording studio, where Tupac Shakur, then on trial for the rape of a fan, was shot five times and robbed of $40,000 worth of jewelry. In a jailhouse interview with *Vibe* following his conviction, Shakur left no doubt that he suspected Wallace, who was upstairs in the studio at the time of the shooting, had set him up. Wallace and Combs denied any involvement in the shooting.

From there the events unfold in rapid succession. In August 1995, Knight "disrespected" Combs from the podium of The Source Awards at Manhattan's

---

2. Particularly moving in this account was Touré's eulogy for hip-hop in the form of a letter to a cousin, "It Was a Wonderful World," *Village Voice*, March 18, 1997, 41.

Source: "Rap Sheet" © Sam Gideon Anso and Charles Rappleye/*Village Voice*

Paramount Theater. A month later, Knight accused Combs of having a hand in the shooting death of Death Row employee (and reputed member of a Compton Blood set) Jason "Big Jake" Robles at an industry party in Atlanta. Combs again denied involvement, but Knight was sufficiently suspicious that he allegedly assaulted an independent record promoter named Mark Anthony Bell at yet another party—this one following an MTV awards show in Los Angeles in December 1995—in an effort to get information about Combs, including his home address.

While Knight and Combs issued repeated denials that a beef existed at all, their albums and videos were peppered with incendiary remarks directed coast to coast, most notoriously Shakur's boast, "I fucked your bitch, you fat motherfucker," on last year's "Hit 'Em Up." All of which helped sell millions of records and magazines, and all of which made fertile ground for speculation when Shakur was slain in Las Vegas.

Las Vegas police have named a suspect in Shakur's murder—a Compton resident and reputed member of the Southside Crips gang named Orlando Anderson, who fought with Shakur and his entourage in the lobby of the MGM hours before the shooting. According to a search warrant affidavit made public last month, the fight at the MGM grew out of an earlier incident in which Anderson and a group of seven or eight Southside Crips stole a Death Row Records medallion from Travon Lane, a Death Row associate and reputed member of the MOB Piru Blood set, at a Foot Locker store in the Lakewood Mall. Anderson denies any involvement in the Shakur killing. Police detained him for questioning in September, but have made no arrests.

While this would seem to lay to rest any East Coast connection in Shakur's killing, the affidavit also suggests a link between Wallace's label and Anderson's Southside Crip set. Bad Boy Entertainment, according to the affidavit, "employed Southside Crips gang members as security."

The Compton connection figures prominently in some informed speculations on the killing. According to one source, the hit on Wallace was pulled off by Compton Bloods, who came to the party in the entourage of a well-known Compton rap artist, and coordinated the shooting over cell phones. Another report put an individual dressed in red standing outside the party with a cell phone saying "Biggie is here now."

"This was a hit, something pre-planned," said one Blood from Compton. "And there's going to be a few more hits."

The killing is harder to swallow coming in the midst of a reduction of hostilities in the hip hop nation. At last year's Soul Train Awards, says one source, "Biggie had half a dozen or so bodyguards and they were very conscious of looking over their shoulders." With the exception of a smattering of boos from the balcony as Wallace and Combs came onstage to present an award, this year's festivities were marked by positive vibes. Which may have something to do with the fact that Suge Knight was cooling his heels in the L.A. County jail.

"For the next six months no one is going to feel comfortable," says Kevin Kim. "Can I trust this person? Or is he setting me up?"

Party Over

Selwyn Seyfu Hinds

As with Tupac, much has been made of the self-prophetic element in Big's passing. *Ready To Die*, his classic debut, was an organic mesh of Brooklyn bad boy narratives and the flossy party aesthetic, all tinged by no meager dose of suicidal musings—a

Source: "Party Over" © Selwyn Seyfu Hinds/*Village Voice*

phenomenon encapsulated by a frighteningly realistic video that featured a scream-ing Puff, a depressed Biggie dying from a self-inflicted gunshot wound, and the pound of a reverberating, eventually stilling heartbeat.

Big's pending album, *Life After Death . . . 'Til Death Do Us Part*, is very different, although certain elements remain consistent. Part cinematic (and calculated) tie-in to the debut, it is the creation of a once desperate, now well-paid baller negotiating the pitfalls endemic to rap success—jealousy, envy, and the like. It is celebratory and triumphant at some junctures, remorseful and contemplative in others.

Life After Death also possesses no small degree of tragic irony—the intro, which picks up where *Ready to Die* left off, with a morose Puffy mourning the passing of his man: "Damn/We was supposed to rule the world baby/We was unstoppable/The shit can't be over"; the enthusiastic "Going Back to Cali": "Y'all niggas is a mess/Thinkin' I'm gon stop/Giving L.A. Props"; an interlude where an anonymous caller threatens to kill Big and urges him to "watch his fucking back"; and "You're Nobody 'Til . . ." ("somebody kills you"), a piece of metaphoric tough talk that now packs a heartbreak.

Big's gone and this album is his last artistic testament. An MC who felt that he'd never received his due props *Life After Death* would have allowed Big to witness the 'cross-the-board affirmation he so desired. And although it's too late to pour this sen-timent out, maybe Christopher Wallace can still feel it somewhere and rest satisfied: you were the best, baby baby.

Town Criers
Natasha Stovall

Radio station Hot 97 acted as town crier and community center, just as they did after Tupac. In one of the most painful moments of the day's broadcast, Biggie protégé Delvico, from Junior M.A.F.I.A., called in from Brooklyn, in tears and waiting for the call to go to the West Coast. "I don't believe it, yo. I just don't believe it's real." The DJs let him know, "Y'all are our family, on the air, off the air, we're here for you. Ain't nothing fake going on here."

"I'm turning on the news and that's really what's getting me upset," the Fugees' Wyclef told 97 DJ Dr. Dre. "Let's get one thing straight. Biggie Smalls was an inspira-tion to us MCs and the whole hip hop community. Every time it's hip hop they're try-ing to bring us down." "I look at it this way," said Public Enemy's Chuck D, also on Hot 97. "When the magazines and the newspapers and the radio shows all come out and go 'Whoop! Whoop! East Coast/West Coast,' it becomes a big story. It becomes a hysteria. If you add hype and hysteria to a situation, it can bring craziness from any direction."

Chuck D spoke at length about the larger picture, in which Biggie Smalls's death is only a puzzle piece. "It's bigger than rap. Until black people control our reality, not only will art imitate life, but life will start to imitate art." The fact that Biggie's and Tupac's deaths were just larger manifestations of the staggering number of black men under 30 who are murdered each year loomed large in the minds of Brooklyn residents. Back in front of Baker's, Janice's friend Tasha sighed, "It was just a murder, not a West Coast/East Coast thing."

Source: "Town Criers" © Natasha Stovall/*Village Voice*

Ultimately, the most numbing thing about Biggie's death is its proximity to Tupac's. "I feel like I just hung up with you about Tupac," Roxanne Shante told Hot 97. Brooklyn lost another son way too early, but next week another death will eclipse his. "I loved the brother. He was a good brother, a righteous young man," a man selling pictures of Biggie for $2 outside KFC put it. "Now I'm a capitalist, and I've got two of these left. Do you want to buy one?"

Further Reading

Dyson, Michael Eric. *Between God and Gangsta Rap: Bearing Witness to Black Culture.* New York: Oxford University Press, 1997.

Touré. "It Was a Wonderful World." *Village Voice,* March 18, 1997, 41.

_____. "The Family Way: The Hiphop Crew as Center of the World." *Village Voice,* October 10, 1995, 49.

Discography

Jay-Z. *Reasonable Doubt.* Roc-A-Fella, 1996.

Nas. *Illimatic.* Columbia, 1994.

Notorious B.I.G. *Ready to Die: The Re-master.* Bad Boy, 2006.

_____. *Life after Death.* Bad Boy, 1997.

Puff Daddy. *No Way Out.* Bad Boy, 1997.

2Pac. *Greatest Hits.* Interscope Records, 1998.

Wu-Tang Clan. *Legend of the Wu-Tang Clan: Wu-Tang Clan's Greatest Hits.* RCA, 2004.

76. Women in Rap

It may be that the death of gangsta rap's stars hastened its demise, or that the genre had simply run its course; whatever the reasons, gangsta rap seemed to fade from view following the shootings of Biggie and 2Pac. As mentioned earlier, the recordings and videos of Biggie Smalls, while depicting gang life and violence, had also featured grandiose displays of wealth. Biggie's producer, Sean "Puff Daddy" (later "P-Diddy") Combs, heightened this trend in many of the songs and videos for his first solo album, **No Way Out**, which followed closely on the heels of

Biggie's *Life after Death* (both 1997). Combs, while a weak rapper, was a great judge of talent and an astute reader of the audience. His image, in both his appearances in *Life after Death* and his own album, attempted to project hipness via association with material success, rather than with the "hardness" associated with gangsta rap, and, as such, demonstrated the increasing importance of "image" relative to the MC'ing skills that defined "old-school" artists of the 1980s.

Another aspect of some of the songs on *No Way Out and Life after Death* was the use of large sections of previous songs, which inaugurated a new era in sampling and quotation. Fans and critics debated whether this new development in sampling differed from the types of creative reuse of materials that have characterized previous forms of African American music. Writers such as Neil Strauss highlighted the connections between Puff Daddy's work and the recordings of earlier rappers such as MC Hammer and Vanilla Ice, who were often ridiculed in their day.[1] Such critiques did not explain, however, the difference between these recordings and those that were already forming part of the hip-hop canon, such as Sugarhill Gang's "Rapper's Delight" and Run-DMC's "Walk This Way," which were also constructed almost entirely around preexisting recordings.

The increased use of sampling was only one aspect of the new pluralism in hip-hop in the mid-1990s, which also expanded the role of women. Rappers such as Foxy Brown and L'il Kim emerged who used their sexuality aggressively, often presenting men in their songs as important only for how they might satisfy their (the rappers') needs.[2] This development might be viewed as resurrecting the classic blues singer's persona: a strong woman who knows what she wants and isn't afraid to demand it, while refusing to be defined by her relationship with a man. In another vein, Lauryn Hill (b. 1975) broke through with the Fugees in *The Score,* which became the hip-hop smash of 1996—an album viewed as "progressive hip-hop" and a critical favorite by some, while being dismissed as inauthentic fluff by others. Hill impressed with her verbal skills and rapping dexterity, as well as with her R&B singing chops: the biggest hit on the album, a remake of Roberta Flack's "Killing Me Softly," featured Hill's alto in a faithful re-creation of Flack's vocal.

The following year Missy "Misdemeanor" Elliot (Melissa Elliot, b. 1971) released her first solo album after writing songs for and performing on many other people's recordings. Her wacky, surreal, and decidedly nonglamorous (in the conventional sense) persona/image has proved remarkably durable, and her subsequent releases, aided and abetted by the innovative production of Timbaland, resulted in a string of successful albums.

---

1. Neil Strauss, "Sampling Is (a) Creative or (b) Theft?" *New York Times*, September 14, 1997.

2. See "Nuthin' but a G String," a forum featuring two articles: Robert Marriot, "Starring Lil' Kim as the Posthiphop Hussy," and Kweli I. Wright, ". . . and Foxy Brown as the Moschino Macktress," *Village Voice*, December 24, 1996, 63.

Although the careers of many female rappers thrived in the late 1990s, it was Lauryn Hill who became the first big crossover female superstar in hip-hop. Her solo album *The Miseducation of Lauryn Hill* received five Grammy awards in 1999, and her photo appeared on the February 8, 1999, cover of *Time* next to the caption, "Hip-Hop Nation: After 20 Years—How It's Changed America." Hill's crossover (and the largely favorable *Time* article) signaled a new level of acceptance of hip-hop by the mainstream audience, and it was safe to say that, in terms of recording sales at any rate, hip-hop had *become* the mainstream. Hill seemed to be the perfect figure to accomplish this: multitalented, a philosophy major at Columbia, attractive, articulate, and adamantly religious, she was a far cry from the denizens of Death Row. The rest of the *Time* article and the portrait of Hill, which are reprinted here, discuss the turn in hip-hop toward the glorification of materialism and the withering of political content. In discussing figures such as Hill and Puff Daddy, it becomes clear that the popularity of hip-hop had largely transcended racial boundaries and that the influence of hip-hop had spread to other genres. Whether this symbolized a breakthrough in race relations or new opportunities for white voyeurism of African Americans remained an open question. Although this change in status raised worries about whether hip-hop could maintain its creativity and "underground" credibility, changes in recording technology meant that an increasing number of people who were not successful enough to worry about such issues could create their own high-quality demos. The contrast between the generally favorable tone of this article and a number of articles that appeared in mass circulation publications in the 1980s and early 1990s (cited in Chapters 70 and 73) reveals how rapidly the social position of hip-hop had changed. Of course, a lot of this change may have been due to hip-hop's increasing slice of the music industry pie, as noted in the beginning of the article that follows.

Hip-Hop Nation
Christopher John Farley

Now tell me your philosophy
On exactly what an artist should be.
—Lauryn Hill, "Superstar"

It's a Friday night, early December 1998, and you're backstage at *Saturday Night Live.* You're hanging out in the dressing room with Lauryn Hill, who is sitting on the couch, flipping through a script. The 23-year-old rapper-singer-actress is the musical guest on this week's show. It's her coming-out party, the first live TV performance she's done since releasing her critically acclaimed and best-selling album *The Miseducation*

Source: "Hip-Hop Nation," Christopher John Farley © Time, Inc.

of Lauryn Hill. She might also do a little acting on the show—*SNL* staff members have asked her to appear in a skit. But as Hill reads, her small rose-blossom lips wilt into a frown. She hands you the script. It's titled *Pimp Chat*—it's a sketch about a street hustler with a talk show. Hill's role: a 'ho. Or if she's uncomfortable with that, she can play a *female pimp*. Hmmm. Now, being in an *SNL* sketch is a big opportunity—but this one might chip away at her image as a socially conscious artist. What's it going to be?

> It's all about the Benjamins, baby.
> —Sean ("Puffy") Combs, "It's
>   All About the Benjamins"

You are in a recording studio in midtown Manhattan, hanging out with hip-hop superproducer Sean ("Puffy") Combs. It's 1997, and Puffy is keeping a low profile, working on his new album, his first as a solo performer. This album will be his coming-out party. He's eager to play a few tracks for you. People have him all wrong, he says. He majored in business management at Howard. He's not just about gangsta rap. Sounds from his new album fill the room. One song is based on a bit from the score to *Rocky*. Another, a sweeping, elegiac number, uses a portion of *Do You Know Where You're Going To?* That's what he's about, Combs says. Classic pop. "I'm living my life right," he says. "So when it comes time for me to be judged, I can be judged by God."

> You're mad
> because my style
> you're admiring
> Don't be mad—UPS is hiring.
> —The Notorious B.I.G., "Flava in Your Ear (Remix)"

Hip-hop is perhaps the only art form that celebrates capitalism openly. To be sure, filmmakers pore over weekend grosses, but it would be surprising for a character in a Spielberg film to suddenly turn toward the camera and shout, "This picture's grossed $100 million, y'all! Shout out to DreamWorks!" Rap's unabashed materialism distinguishes it sharply from some of the dominant musical genres of the past century. For example, nobody expects bluesmen to be moneymakers—that's why they're singing the blues. It's not called the greens, after all. As for alternative rockers, they have the same relationship toward success that one imagines Ally McBeal has toward food; even a small slice of the pie leaves waves of guilt. Rappers make money without remorse. "These guys are so real, they brag about money," says Def Jam's Simmons. "They don't regret getting a Coca-Cola deal. They brag about a Coca-Cola deal."

Major labels, a bit confused by the rhythms of the time, have relied on smaller, closer-to-the-street labels to help them find fresh rap talent. Lauryn Hill is signed to Ruffhouse, which has a distribution deal with the larger Columbia. Similar arrangements have made tens of millions of dollars for the heads of these smaller labels, such as Combs (Bad Boy), Master P (No Limit), Jermaine Dupri (So So Def), and Ronald and Bryan Williams (Co-CEOs of Cash Money, home to rising rapper Juvenile).

"I'm not a role model," rapper-mogul-aspiring-NBA-player Master P says. "But I see myself as a resource for kids. They can say, 'Master P has been through a lot, but he changed his life, and look at him. I can do the same thing.' I think anyone who's a success is an inspiration."

Master P introduced something new to contemporary pop: shameless, relentless and canny cross-promotion. Each of the releases on his New Orleans-based No Limit label contains promotional materials for his other releases. His established artists (like Snoop Dogg) make guest appearances on CDs released by his newer acts, helping to launch their debuts. And his performers are given to shouting out catchphrases like "No Limit soldiers!" in the middle of their songs—good advertising for the label when the song is being played on the radio.

Madison Avenue has taken notice of rap's entrepreneurial spirit. Tommy Hilfiger has positioned his apparel company as the clothier of the hip-hop set, and he now does a billion dollars a year in oversize shirts, loose jeans and so on. "There are no boundaries," says Hilfiger. "Hip-hop has created a style that is embraced by an array of people from all backgrounds and races." However, fans are wary of profiteers looking to sell them back their own culture. Says Michael Sewell, 23, a white congressional staff member and rap fan: "I've heard rap used in advertising, and I think it's kind of hokey—kind of a goofy version of the way old white men perceive rap."

But the ads are becoming stealthier and streetier. Five years ago, Sprite recast its ads to rely heavily on hip-hop themes. Its newest series features several up-and-coming rap stars (Common, Fat Joe, Goodie Mob) in fast-moving animated clips that are intelligible only to viewers raised on Bone-Thugs-N-Harmony and Playstation. According to Sprite brand manager Pina Sciarra, the rap campaign has quadrupled the number of people who say that Sprite is their favorite soda. . . .

Corporate America's infatuation with rap has increased as the genre's political content has withered. Ice Cube's early songs attacked white racism; Ice-T sang about a *Cop Killer;* Public Enemy challenged listeners to "fight the power." But many newer acts such as DMX and Master P are focused almost entirely on pathologies within the black community. They rap about shooting other blacks but almost never about challenging governmental authority or encouraging social activism. "The stuff today is not revolutionary," says Bob Law, vice president of programming at WWRL, a black talk-radio station in New York City. "It's just, 'Give me a piece of the action.'"

Hip-hop is getting a new push toward activism from an unlikely source—Beastie Boys. The white rap trio began as a Dionysian semiparody of hip-hop, rapping about parties, girls and beer. Today they are the founders and headliners of the Tibetan Freedom Concert, an annual concert that raises money for and awareness about human-rights issues in Tibet. Last week Beastie Boys, along with the hip-hop-charged hard-rock band Rage Against the Machine and the progressive rap duo Black Star, staged a controversial concert in New Jersey to raise money for the legal fees of Mumia Abu-Jamal, a black inmate on death row for killing a police officer. Says Beastie Boy Adam Yauch: "There's a tremendous amount of evidence that he didn't do it and he was a scapegoat."

Yauch says rap's verbal texture makes it an ideal vessel to communicate ideas, whether satirical, personal or political. That isn't always a good thing. "We've put out songs with lyrics in them that we thought people would think were funny, but they ended up having a lot of really negative effects on people. [Performers] need to be aware that when you're creating music it has a tremendous influence on society." . . .

Wu-Tang Clan producer-rapper RZA is also concerned about maintaining standards. He believes many performers are embracing the genre's style—rapping—but missing its essence, the culture of hip-hop. "I don't think the creativity has been big. I think the sales have been big, and the exposure has been big," says RZA. "Will Smith is *rap*. That's not hip-hop. It's been a big year for rap. It's been a poor year for hip-hop." . . .

Other groups, signed to major labels, are trying to perpetuate rap's original spirit of creativity. The rapper Nas's forthcoming album *I Am . . . the Autobiography* promises to be tough, smart and personal. And the Atlanta-based duo OutKast's Bib Boi: "We're not scared to experiment."

One of the most ambitious new CDs is the Roots' *Things Fall Apart* (named after the book by the Nigerian Nobel laureate Chinua Achebe). The CD features live instrumentation, lyrics suitable for a poetry slam and a cameo from Erykah Badu. Roots drummer Ahmir hopes, in the future, the more creative wing of performers in hip-hop will form a support network. "There are some people in hip-hop that care about leaving a mark," he says. "There are some of us that look at *Innervisions* as a benchmark, or *Blood on the Tracks* or *Blue* or *Purple Rain*. Leaving a mark is more important than getting a dollar. I think Lauryn's album is one of the first gunshots of hip-hop art the world is gonna get."

> *You could get the money*
> *You could get the power*
> *But keep your eyes on the final hour.*
> —Lauryn Hill, "Final Hour"

It's Puffy's 29th birthday party, and the celebration is being held on Wall Street. Inside the party, women in thongs dance in glass cages. Above the door a huge purple spotlight projects some of Puffy's corporate logos: Bad Boy (his record company) and Sean John (his new clothing label). But where's Puffy?

The music stops. The crowd parts. Muhammad Ali arrives. He's only the appetizer. The score to *Rocky* booms over the speakers. Only then does Puffy enter, in a light-colored three-piece suit. Forget being street. He's Wall Street, he's Madison Avenue, he's le Champs Elysées. Donald Trump is at his side. It's Puffy's moment. His album *No Way Out* played on some familiar gangsta themes, but it's a smash hit. Puffy is a household name, a brand name. In fact his name comes up again and again, in gossip columns and other people's rap songs. He has transformed himself into a human sample. He is swallowed by the crowd.

You are at the Emporio Armani store on Fifth Avenue in downtown Manhattan. There's a benefit here tonight for the Refugee Project, a nonprofit organization Lauryn Hill founded to encourage social activism among urban youth. Hill is here, and the cameras are flashing. Her musical performance on *Saturday Night Live* has boosted her album back to the upper reaches of the charts. In a few days she will receive 10 Grammy nominations, the most ever by a female artist.

She never did do that *SNL* skit about the hooker. She says she feels too connected to hip-hop to do a movie or TV role that compromises the message in her music. She addresses the crowd. "I'm just a vehicle through which this thing moves," she says. "It's not about me at all." You think back to some of the rappers you've talked to—Jay-Z, Nas, the Roots, Grandmaster Flash. A record cues up in your mind: "Ain't no stopping us now . . ."

Lauryn Hill

Strange that something so alive now could have begun in a museum. In late 1997, Lauryn Hill was visiting Detroit to produce a song that she wrote for her childhood hero, Aretha Franklin. On the way to the airport, she stopped at the Motown Museum. The Supremes, Stevie Wonder, the Jackson 5—these were the performers she was reared on. She could picture their 45s scattered across her bed. "It was incredible to me and really inspiring," says Hill. Now she was ready to push forward on her own solo album.

Looking back, looking back, Hill grew up in South Orange, N.J.; her father was a management consultant, her mother a grade-school English teacher. From an early age, Lauryn (she has an elder brother Malaney) was into singing and performing. When she was in middle school, she was invited to sing the national anthem at a high school basketball game. "People went wild," says LuElle Walker-Peniston, Hill's guidance counselor at Columbia High School. "I don't think we had a winning team, but *she* was inspiring." Fans liked her rendition so much that recordings of it were played at subsequent games.

While still in high school, Hill landed a recurring role as the troubled runaway, Kira, on the TV soap *As The World Turns*. In 1993 she was cast as a difficult teen in *Sister Act 2*. There's a scene in that film in which Hill's character reels off a rap as her classmates look on. "None of that was scripted," says director Bill Duke. "That was all Lauryn. She was amazing." While in high school, she formed the rap trio the Fugees (short for refugees) with classmate Prakazrel ("Pras") Michel and Wyclef Jean, who went to a nearby school. The group's debut album, *Blunted on Reality*, sold poorly. Hill spent about a year at Columbia University but left school when the Fugees' second album, *The Score*, took off. It has sold more than 17 million copies worldwide.

But Hill wasn't satisfied. In the studio, she and Jean were "innocently competitive," gently sparring to see who could spin off the wittiest rhymes. Hill was eager to see what she could do solo. She booked a recording studio in New York City and gathered up every instrument she could think of—a harpsichord, a timpani, a trombone, a Hammond B-3 organ. She wanted to create hip-hop with live instruments.

She still needed another spark. So she flew to Jamaica. Hill is engaged to Rohan Marley, the son of reggae superstar Bob Marley and the father of her two children, one-year-old Zion and three-month-old Selah. ("We haven't been in front of a minister yet, but we will be soon," says Hill. "Our marriage right now is more a spiritual one.") As part of the extended Marley clan, she was allowed to record in the studio in the Bob Marley Museum. She says she could feel Marley's spirit as soon as she arrived. The first day there she wrote *Lost Ones*. As she began to rap, the various young Marley grandchildren who happened to be wandering around that day joined in, chanting the last word of every line. Everyone could feel the energy.

Hill says that before Rohan, she had "dysfunctional" relationships. She tried to channel the pain of those experiences into her music. "It wasn't someone writing for me; it wasn't someone telling me what I felt," says Hill, who wrote and produced the songs on *Miseducation*. "It was exactly how I felt the moment I felt it." Her maverick vision hasn't been without controversy. Late last year a group of four musicians who worked on *Miseducation* filed a suit claiming they deserved additional songwriting credits. Hill denies the allegations. Gordon Williams, who worked as the sound engineer on every song says, "Definitely the driving force behind that record was [Hill]."

Her colleagues worry about Hill's frantic pace. "She's a workaholic," says Williams. "She doesn't stop. To be a mother, two times, and then have all this stuff going on is crazy. Sometimes I just look at her and go, 'Lauryn, take it easy.'"

But Hill plans to push ahead. She says the Fugees "definitely aren't broken up," though the members have to "sit down and see where all our heads are at." She has her own production company, and she might steer it in a unique direction: "I'm looking to produce black science-fiction films." Then there's her tour. She'll perform her first solo show in the U.S. on Feb. 18 in Detroit. But she'll take time out to attend the Grammys in Los Angeles on Feb. 24, for which she has received 10 nominations. "There are kids in the audiences now who weren't born when there wasn't hip-hop," says Hill. "They grew up on it; it's part of the culture. It's a huge thing. It's not segregated anymore. It's not just in the Bronx; it's all over the world. That's why I think it's more crucial now that we, as artists, take advantage of our platform."

Further Reading

Berry, Venise. "Feminine or Masculine: The Conflicting Nature of Female Images in Rap Music." In *Cecilia Reclaimed: Feminist Perspectives on Gender and Music*, ed. Susan Cook and Judy Tsou, 183–201. Urbana: University of Illinois Press, 1994.

Demers, Joanna. *Steal This Music: How Intellectual Property Law Affects Musical Creativity.* Athens: University of Georgia Press, 2006.

Gaunt, Kyra. *The Games Black Girls Play: Learning the Ropes from Double Dutch to Hip-Hop.* New York: NYU Press, 2006.

Goodwin, Andrew. "Sample and Hold: Pop Music in the Digital Age of Reproduction." In *On Record: Rock, Pop and the Written Word*, ed. Simon Frith and Andrew Goodwin, 258–73. New York: Pantheon Books, 1990.

Lysloff, René T. A., and Leslie C. Gay, Jr. *Music and Technoculture.* Hanover, N.H.: Wesleyan University Press, 2003.

Peterson-Lewis, Sonja. "A Feminist Analysis of the Defenses of Obscene Rap Lyrics." *Black Sacred Music: A Journal of TheoMusicology* 5 (Spring 1991): 68–79.

Schloss, Joseph G. *Making Beats: The Art of Sample-Based Hip-Hop.* Middletown, Conn.: Wesleyan University Press, 2004.

Shelton, Marla L. "Can't Touch This! Representations of the African American Female Body in Urban Rap Videos." *Popular Music and Society* 21 (Fall 1997): 107–16.

Volgsten, Ulrik. "Copyright, Music, and Morals: Artistic Expression and the Public Sphere." In *Music and Manipulation: On the Social Uses and Social Control of Music*, ed. Steven Brown and Ulrik Volgsten, 336–64. New York: Berghahn Books, 2006.

Wallace, Michelle. "When Black Feminism Faces the Music, and the Music is Rap." *New York Times,* July 29, 1990.

Discography

Brown, Foxy. *Ill Na Na.* Def Jam, 1996.

DJ Shadow. *Entroducing . . .* Fontana Island, 1996.

Fugees. *The Score.* Sony, 1996.

Hill, Lauryn. *The Miseducation of Lauryn Hill.* Sony, 1998.

Jackson, Janet. *The Velvet Rope.* Virgin Records US, 1997.

Jean, Wyclef. *Greatest Hits.* Sony, 2003.

Lil' Kim. *Hard Core.* Big Beat/WEA, 1996.

———. *Not Tonight.* Atlantic/WEA, 1997.

Marley Marl. *In Control, Vol. 1.* Warner Bros./WEA, 1988.

MC Hammer. *U Can't Touch This.* Capitol Records, 1990.

Men In Black: The Album. Sony, 1997.

Missy Elliot. *Supa Dupa Fly.* East/West Records, 1997.

New MCs—Fat Beats and Brastraps: Women of Hip-Hop. Rhino/WEA, 1998.

Notorious B.I.G. *Life after Death.* Bad Boy Records, 1997.

Puff Daddy. *No Way Out.* Bad Boy Records, 1997.

Sugarhill Gang. *The Best of Sugarhill Gang: Rapper's Delight.* Rhino/WEA, 1996.

Vanilla Ice. *Ice Ice Baby.* SBK Records, 1990.

77. The Beat Goes On

The late 1990s and early 2000s witnessed an increased pluralism in hip-hop. While artists such as Ja Rule and P-Diddy continued to rap about diamonds, cars, and women's physical features, the bar for achieving "real" gangsta-hood floated ever higher and the utility of thug life stories for promotional purposes remained strong, as witnessed by the emergence of 50 Cent. A *Rolling Stone* article titled "No. 1 with a Bullet" described 50 with the following anecdotes: "After being shot nine times, Eminem protégé 50 Cent wisely decided to invest in protection," and "When 50 signed his contract, his first purchase was crack."[1] In other developments, the most significant hip-hop artists to emerge during this time were Jay-Z, who presented a fusion of the materialist rapper with the gangsta bravado of a slightly earlier era, accompanied by music that relied frequently on lush, old-school r&b samples; and Outkast, who updated the zany psychedelia of P-Funk and added a new sophistication to "progressive" rap.

The most successful and controversial turn-of-the-millennium rapper was, however, also the first white rapper to earn some measure of respect from the "hip-hop community." Mentioned in the preceding paragraph as the mentor of 50 Cent, Eminem's career took off when Dr. Dre took him on as *his* protégé (with Dre reviving his own moribund career in the process). Despite possessing undeniable originality and verbal skills, Eminem (Marshall Mathers, b. 1972) was the focus of (and has also probably benefited from) some of the most intense media scrutiny in years, and not only because of his race. Many of his songs feature virulent homophobia and a macabre form of misogyny.[2] He has been involved repeatedly in conflicts with other pop stars, public fights and confrontations, and ongoing suits involving his mother and ex-wife.

---

1. Mark Binelli, "No. 1 With a Bullet," *Rolling Stone*, February 6, 2003, 31–32. Perhaps even more chilling is the continuation of actual violence, as in the murder of Jam Master Jay (or Run-DMC) in October 2002. Rumor has it that Jay was murdered because of his association with 50 Cent.

2. For a well-measured critique, see Elizabeth Keathley, "Eminem's Murder Ballads," *Echo*, 4, no. 2 (Fall 2002), http://www.humnet.ucla.edu/echo/volume4-issue2/keathley/index.html. Loren Kajikawa, in " 'My Name Is': Signifying Whiteness, Rearticulating Race," *Journal of the Society for American Music* 3, no. 3 (2009): 341–63, examines Eminem's popularity and musical style in the context of millennial racial politics.

Renee Graham's brief article appeared near the end of 2003 and addressed the latest controversy to confront Eminem. Unlike previous controversies embroiling the rapper, this one centered on an event with implications that were more difficult for Eminem to dismiss: the discovery of a tape made (probably) in 1993 in which he made racist comments about African Americans. While, in spite of their offensiveness to many, his homophobic and misogynist lyrics had actually strengthened the connections between his work and some of his hip-hop contemporaries, Eminem had foresworn use of the "N-word" because of sensitivity about his position as a white rapper. The potential revelatory force of the new tape was weakened, however, by the vehemence with which it was pushed by the hip-hop magazine, the *Source*. The motivations of this publication, long notable for the way in which it eschewed conventional notions of reportorial distance, were suspect in this case and were quite possibly driven by the *Source*'s own questionable agenda.

Eminem's Old Words Aren't Hip-Hop's Biggest Problem
Renee Graham

When his Grammy-winning, multimillion-selling CD, "The Marshall Mathers LP," was vilified by some as homophobic and misogynistic, Eminem responded by abusing an inflatable doll (in the guise of his then-wife, Kim) in concert and flipping off the audience after performing a duet with Elton John at the 2001 Grammy Awards.

Defiant and unapologetic, Eminem racked up sales and awards. Accusations of hatred toward women and gays only enhanced his reputation as a rebel who, as he claimed on "The Real Slim Shady," was "only giving you things you joke about with your friends inside your living room, the only difference is I got the [expletive] to say it in front of y'all, and I don't gotta be false or sugarcoat it at all."

Yet Eminem's reaction has been markedly different since being branded a racist by the hip-hop magazine the *Source*.

Last week, a federal judge granted Eminem's request for an injunction against the magazine, preventing its editors from releasing with its February issue a CD featuring an old recording of the then-unknown rapper making derogatory remarks about black women. Monday, however, the judge authorized the *Source* to publish as much as 20 seconds of the recording on a CD. The tape was aired at a November news conference with the *Source's* owners, David Mays and Ray "Benzino" Scott. On an untitled song, Eminem drops N-bombs and disses black women.

Eminem quickly admitted that he had made the tape, but in a statement added the song was "made out of anger, stupidity and frustration when I was a teenager," after breaking up with a black girlfriend. Then the rapper did something he never did when he was called a homophobe and misogynist—he apologized.

"So while I think common sense tells you not to judge a man by what he might have said when he was a boy, I will say it straight up: I'm sorry I said those things when I was 16." (The *Source's* editors maintain the tape was made in 1993, when Eminem was 21.)

If Eminem never showed an ounce of remorse for his anti-woman, anti-gay rhymes, that's because he knew such vitriol was so commonplace in hip-hop lyrics that it would have no effect on his seemingly bulletproof career. But as a white rapper accused of racism, Eminem, probably for the first time in his career, is worried about negative public perceptions.

Without question, Eminem, 31, is one of the best rappers in hip-hop history. With a nasal Midwestern flow as outrageous as his lyrics, Eminem's considerable talent as a rapper cannot be denied, even if his lyrics are sometimes bullying and hateful.

But being called a racist in a musical culture that remains overwhelmingly African American could shake Eminem's career. Since his 1999 major-label debut, "The Slim Shady LP," put him on the hip-hop map, he has studiously avoided racial epithets that could alienate black fans. When asked several years ago why he never used the N-word, a staple of many mainstream hip-hop recordings, in his songs, Eminem told *Rolling Stone's* Anthony DeCurtis, "That word is not even in my vocabulary. And I do black music, so out of respect, why would I put that word in my vocabulary?" Eminem has always understood that making it in hip-hop meant more than clever lyrics and juicy beats—without the acceptance of black fans, he would be as dissed and dismissed as Vanilla Ice.

In the hip-hop industry, so far only Irv Gotti, head of the Inc. (formerly Murder Inc., label home of Ja Rule and Ashanti), has publicly criticized Eminem. But hip-hop entrepreneur and patriarch Russell Simmons defended the rapper, calling his apology "sincere and forthright." And the accusations haven't hurt Eminem with the Grammy folks; he received several nominations this month for his song "Lose Yourself."

The hip-hop community's apparent reluctance to address the tape is due to the fact that the *Source's* motives are suspect. Everyone knows Benzino is an Eminem archnemesis and seems spurred only by the notion that having a white rapper gain widespread success is somehow bad for hip-hop. (He has called Eminem "the rap Hitler" and a "culture stealer.") Benzino and Mays claim to be concerned with exposing "influences corrupting hip-hop," but there are far more serious issues—such as a lack of creativity, obsessions with wealth, and yes, anti-woman, anti-gay rhetoric—facing the community than the contents of a scratchy old tape.

Eminem has acknowledged the tape's veracity and has apologized. It's time to move on. Perhaps when the *Source* becomes as concerned with the state of rap music as with playing out a strange, personal vendetta with its own racist undertones, then the magazine may be more successful in exposing and ridding hip-hop of its corrupting influences.

Further Reading

Binelli, Mark. "No. 1 with a Bullet." *Rolling Stone,* February 6, 2003, 31–32.

Clarke, David. "Eminem: Difficult Dialogics." In *Words and Music,* ed. John Williamson, 73–102. Liverpool: Liverpool University Press, 2005.

Doggett, Peter. *Eminem: The Complete Guide to His Music.* London: Omnibus, 2005.

Nielsen, Steen Kaargaard. "Wife Murder as Child's Game: Analytical Reflections on Eminem's Performative Self-Dramatization." *Danish Yearbook of Musicology* 34 (2006): 31–46.

Discography

50 Cent. *Get Rich or Die Tryin'*. Interscope, 2003.
Eminem. *The Slim Shady LP.* Aftermath, 1999.
_____. *The Marshall Mathers LP.* Interscope Records, 2000.
Jay-Z. *The Blueprint.* Roc-A-Fella, 2001.
_____. *The Black Album.* Def Jam, 2003.
Nelly. *Country Grammar.* UMVD Labels, 2000.
Outkast. *Speakerboxxx/The Love Below.* La Face, 2003.

78. From Indie to Alternative to . . . Seattle?

At the close of the 1980s, no earth-shattering developments appeared to be on the horizon for indie rock. The "indie" genre label was proving increasingly capacious, including everything from the "goth" of the Cure to the "dream pop" of My Bloody Valentine to bands bearing a more obvious allegiance to punk. In fact, articles attempting to explain and identify the almost bewildering multiplication of subgenres appeared frequently throughout the 1990s.[1] Yet, in the late 1980s and early 1990s, an indie scene that had been developing in Seattle around the local label Sub Pop displayed a new fusion of musical styles and a new alliance of social groups and subcultural symbols that would ultimately remap and reorient the entire idea of indie rock. Around this time, a new term, "alternative," was increasingly substituted for "indie," indicating a turn toward populism and a rapprochement with non-indie rock practices, both musically (through more

---

1. See, for example, Jim Sullivan, "The Age of Hyphen-Rock," *Chicago Tribune,* October 13, 1991, sec. 13, 26–27 (a good overview of the splintering of rock genres); David Browne, "Turn that @#!% Down," *Entertainment Weekly,* August 21, 1992, 16–25 (describes the many varieties/subgenres of alternative); Neil Strauss, "Forget Pearl Jam: Alternative Rock Lives," *New York Times,* March 2, 1997 (a brief introduction to the many subcategories that function as alternatives to alternative); and Ben Ratliff, "A New Heavy-Metal Underground Emerges," *New York Times,* February 15, 1998 (a taxonomy of metal subgenres).

obvious "pop" music influences) and institutionally (through bands moving from indie record labels to majors).

The caption under the title of a 1990 report on Seattle by Dave DiMartino—"Record companies are flocking to the Great Northwest, signing bands like crazy and hoping to find the Next Big Thing"—sums up the article fairly well. While addressing the questions, "Why here? Why now?" DiMartino captures a moment of transition in the Seattle scene, as bands formerly affiliated with Sub Pop began to sign with major record companies. This article reveals that the term "grunge" had already entered circulation, describing both the overdriven guitar sound characteristic of Seattle postpunk bands and the dress style of faded flannel and torn jeans. Amusing in retrospect are the passages that ponder whether local bands like Nirvana will "make it." In the course of such ponderings, DiMartino introduces his readers to Soundgarden, Alice in Chains, and Mother Love Bone (which contained two members who would later form part of Pearl Jam)—groups that would achieve national prominence in less than two years—as well as bands such as the Young Fresh Fellows, who have now been swallowed by the sands of time.[2]

A Seattle Slew

Dave DiMartino

San Francisco moved to Oregon and Washington," says Bob Pfeifer, director of A&R of Epic Records. "The whole thing is psychedelic. You can see it in the T-shirts and the tie-dye. It's all hippies. These are the hippies' kids or something."

That's just one of several theories making the rounds these days about Seattle, a city that until recently was famous for its rainy weather and inexpensive real estate. But in the past two years, Seattle has become a regular music mecca—a haven for record-company executives who regularly fly in from Los Angeles and New York to compete for the privilege of signing such bands as Soundgarden, the Posies, Alice in Chains, Mother Love Bone and the Screaming Trees. And the labels are coming because amid the city's lush greenery, they smell money.

"I talked to somebody at CBS in New York last October," says one woman who works for a Seattle artist-management firm, "And he said, 'You're from Seattle. Just find me *any* Seattle band. I'm *dying* to sign a Seattle band—I'm so mad I didn't sign Alice in Chains.'"

It's a situation that is hardly unprecedented in rock's trend-ridden history—remember San Francisco, Detroit, Boston, New York, Cleveland, Athens,

---

2. For views of the Seattle scene after grunge broke nationally, see Michael Azzerad, "Grunge City," *Rolling Stone*, April 16, 1992, 43–48; and John Book, "Seattle Heavy," *Goldmine*, April 17, 1992, 46–54.

Source: "A Seattle Slew" Dave Dimartino, *Rolling Stone*, 20 September 1990, pp 23-24, 112.

Austin, Minneapolis. But the big question in Seattle at the moment is: *Why here? Why now?*

Producer Terry Date—who has had a hand in the careers of most of Seattle's better-known bands, starting with Metal Church in 1984 and continuing to the most recent albums by Soundgarden and Mother Love Bone—believes one reason local groups are attracting so much attention is that they are unique. "They're not in a major music market, so they don't follow any sort of formula at all," Date says. "They don't look at something on MTV and say, 'We're gonna look like that.' They pretty much find their style from the records they listen to—which are typically very underground.

"On top of that" Date adds, "the weather isn't always that great, and they sit in their garages a lot."

For such a hotbed of talent, Seattle doesn't offer its artists much choice. Aside from garage-land, only a handful of small clubs—the Vogue, the Central and the Backstage—are options open to bands itching to play live. "The funny thing is," says Charles Cross, editor and publisher of the local music paper *The Rocket*, "if you go to New Orleans, you go to Tipitina's. If you go to New York, I guess you have CBGB. And in Los Angeles there's Club Lingerie. There isn't that kind of club in Seattle. Our club scene has been horrible for years."

Instead, the driving force behind the Seattle scene has been a record label, Sub Pop. With a roster that includes Mudhoney, Nirvana and Tad, Sub Pop has defined the Seattle sound—loud, fast, grungy rock & roll. "And all these people were friends," Sub Pop co-owner Jonathan Poneman says of the bands on his label. "This is a small community of people, and when one person got into Scratch Acid, everybody got into Scratch Acid. When one person got into Big Black, everybody got into Big Black."

Two former Sub Pop bands, Soundgarden and Screaming Trees, have been snapped up by major labels (A&M and Epic, respectively), and CBS Records has reportedly been negotiating a pressing-and-distribution deal that would put Sub Pop acts Mudhoney and Tad in the same Sam Goody racks holding the latest by Fleetwood Mac and New Kids on the Block. "We want it to happen," says Poneman. "We're trying to make it happen, because we want to be able to get the records out there." But, he adds, "whether or not there will be full cooperation in terms of our agenda, and whether or not we will be able to acquiesce to the things they're asking for are still things that remain to be seen."

Indeed, one has to wonder whether such key label artists as Mudhoney or Nirvana could cross over into the Nineties mainstream without seriously compromising their sound. "I don't think we're really easy enough for a lot of people to swallow," says Mudhoney's Mark Arm, a former member of Seattle's legendary (and now defunct) Green River. "Motorhead never made it beyond a certain point, and they're one of the greatest bands on Earth."

But Bob Pfeifer, who signed both Metal Church and Screaming Trees to Epic Records, thinks some Seattle bands have long-term potential. "Screaming Trees are capable of selling 100,000 records," says Pfeifer. "Whether they will or not is another question. Three albums from now, I don't know *how* many albums they'll be able to sell—maybe a million. That's not the pressure I put on the band or the way I structured the deal. Everybody will be happy at a certain level, which allows the band to have the freedom and time to grow."

But major-label interest in Seattle hasn't been limited to one very hip record label that has so far seen great press coverage but less-than-great overall sales. Nastymix Records, the local label that features the best-selling rapper Sir Mix-a-Lot, has been approached by all the majors regarding a potential buy-in, according to

Ramon Wells, the label's national promotion director. "Even [Island Records chairman] Chris Blackwell flew in to talk with us," Wells says. But with one platinum and one gold album already, Wells adds, "we're perfectly content with where we are now."

Then there's PopLlama Products, a label helmed by Conrad Uno that has released the work of Seattle's Young Fresh Fellows and the Posies, among others. Both bands are now on different labels, both are miles away from the grunge that Sub Pop has glorified, and both are essential components of the Seattle scene.

The Fellows, as they're called, are enormously talented and extremely unfocused. Together, the two attributes are likely to confuse any market-conscious A&R person. The Fellows' most recent records for Frontier are now getting major-label distribution, thanks to a deal the California label signed with RCA Records last year. But so far, that linkup has been of little benefit to the Fellows, and they are pursuing other options.

"I guess we're finally making an effort to get signed to a major label," says vocalist Scott McCaughey. "I hate to say that, because it's always been totally anti-everything the Fellows were about. But I guess it's gotten to the point where we've been doing it for six or seven years, I've got a kid now, and we're thinking a little bit more about how rough it is to make a living. We're trying to figure out a way that we can be musicians and make a little bit more money, so we can live comfortably, because for the last three years we've just been musicians. We quit our jobs because we went on tour too much."

The Fellows recently hired former Concrete Blonde manager Frank Volpe to help them firm up a deal with a major and are now ready to "seriously try to step up" their career.

At the same time, the Fellows' former manager, Terry Morgan, recently inked a lucrative deal with Geffen Records' new label DGC for the Seattle popsters the Posies. And in the end, the city's more accessible bands—like the Posies, Alice in Chains and Mother Love Bone—may prove to be more attractive to the major labels than Sub Pop's unique brand of metallic grunge. All three of those bands have recently released their major-label debuts, and you don't have to be an A&R man to imagine their music getting played on the radio.

Meanwhile, one of the best-selling albums in Seattle's hipper record stores these days is a compilation called *Here Ain't the Sonics*. The album tells the story of the first wave of great Northwest rock—the Sonics, the Kingsmen, "Louie Louie." But the artists who perform on the album—the Young Fresh Fellows, Screaming Trees, the Mono Men—are part of the city's new generation.

Terry Date sees many parallels between the Seattle of 1990 and the one to which *Here Ain't the Sonics* pays tribute. "These bands are coming from all over the state," Date says, "and they're all playing a fairly similar type of music, attitude-wise. Especially the Sub Pop stuff. It's all real *garagey*, just like 'Louie Louie,' the perfect example of that era.

"It's really cool," continues Date, "because these guys do whatever they want—and the labels don't really know what they're trying to get, they just know people are buying it. And it leaves it wide open for us."

Further Reading

Arnold, Gina. *Route 666: On the Road to Nirvana*. New York: St. Martin's Press, 1993.
Azzerad, Michael. "Grunge City." *Rolling Stone,* April 16, 1992, 43–48.
Book, John. "Seattle Heavy." *Goldmine,* April 17, 1992, 46–54.

Browne, David. "Turn that @#!% Down." *Entertainment Weekly,* August 21, 1992, 16–25.
Ratliff, Ben. "A New Heavy-Metal Underground Emerges." *New York Times*, February 15, 1998.
Strauss, Neil. "Forget Pearl Jam: Alternative Rock Lives." *New York Times*, March 2, 1997.
Sullivan, Jim. "The Age of Hyphen-Rock." *Chicago Tribune*, October 13, 1991, sec. 13, 26–27.

Discography

Alice in Chains. *The Essential Alice in Chains.* Sony, 2004.
The Grunge Years: A Sub Pop Compilation. Sub Pop, 1991.
Here Ain't the Sonics. PopLlama, 1993.
Mother Love Bone. *Mother Love Bone.* Island/Mercury, 1992.
Nirvana. *Nevermind.* Geffen Records, 1991.
Pearl Jam. *rearviewmirror (Greatest Hits 1991–2003).* Sony, 2004.
Soundgarden. *Badmotorfinger.* A&M, 1991.

79. Grunge Turns to *Scrunge*

While the move of postpunk music toward mainstream popularity excited rock fans who longed for an "oppositional" quality in their music, as well as music critics who welcomed music that highlighted interesting sociological issues, it also occasioned a crisis within the remnants of the indie scene itself. This mainstreaming of bohemianism threatened the indie-punk notion that certain kinds of consumerism might somehow resist commodification. If this reaction of indie fans sounds suspiciously reminiscent of that old modernist credo "if it's popular, it must be bad," then that's because the arguments about authenticity versus commerce that developed in the wake of Dylan's "going the rock and roll route" were never fully vanquished. As Eric Weisbard states in the article that follows (in a section not reprinted here),

On some basic level, the fundamental unresolved issue here—one that artists and fans alike have to work out individually—is not major labels versus indies, but the extent to which rock gains in glory by seeking or attaining popularity.[1]

---

1. Eric Weisbard, "Over and Out: Indie Rock Values in the Age of Alternative Million Sellers," *Village Voice Rock and Roll Quarterly* (Summer 1994): 19.

The signs in the transformation of indie include (as was indicated earlier) the signing of an increasing number of bands by major record companies, the airing of indie-alternative videos on MTV, and the emergence of *scrunge*—music by bands that took elements of grunge-alternative's sound but left its indie values behind.[2]

Eric Weisbard was for many years a critic with *Spin*, the *Village Voice*, and other publications. The article of his that is reprinted here describes a moment three years after the release of *Nevermind* by Nirvana during which time numerous alternative acts reached a large audience of rock fans. The question "alternative to what?" arises (both for Weisbard and other critics) when the idea of a style's marginality (and oppositionality) remains central to its appeal even as the style has been accepted by the mainstream. The strength of this essay lies in the historical perspective and broad view that Weisbard brings to his discussion of alternative rock and the specificity provided by several anecdotes of what happens when bands move (or contemplate moving) from indie to major record labels. Weisbard clarifies the links to prior bohemian movements while not being uncritical, noting the privileged place within alternative music of what he calls "white guy angst," even though many critics (and fans) included certain types of hip-hop within the category. This article also captures a moment when major record companies had begun to grant alternative acts the same type of creative freedom allowed to rock bands in the late 1960s, hiring young experts in much the same fashion that companies in the 1960s hired "house hippies." In other ways, though, 1990s alternative represents the inverse of 1960s rock: as Weisbard notes, "Alternative strives clunkily for the massification of hip, as boomer rock was the hipification of mass."[3] This moment was doomed to be short-lived: in a year-end report for *Spin* magazine reflecting on developments in popular music for 1995 (only a year later), Weisbard echoed the sentiments of many critics when he pronounced the "indie" part of the "indie-alternative" movement all but dead.[4]

---

2. Eric Weisbard, "The Year in Music: The Great Pretenders," *Spin,* January 1996, 50.

3. Weisbard, "Over and Out," 17.

4. Weisbard, "The Year in Music," 48–54. By late 1997, Weisbard could offer a more definite eulogy: "Ultimately American postpunk insisted on rock at a human scale; that's why it dissolved when major-label muscle was put behind it" (Eric Weisbard, "The Me, Myself, and I Decade," *Spin,* December 1997, 157). Of course, the physical demise of grunge-alternative's biggest star Kurt Cobain (1967–94) did nothing to slow the dissolution of the indie ethos. For an exploration of the relationship between Cobain's suicide and indie ideology, see Dave Marsh, "Live through This," *Rock 'n' Roll Confidential,* May 1994.

Over and Out: Indie Rock Values in the Age of Alternative Million Sellers

Eric Weisbard

Indier Than Thou, a New Jersey zine is called, and it's an attitude I can tell you all about. Where'd I learn to care and sneer at the same time? From [Alex] Chilton, Lou Reed, the Feelies, Paul Westerberg, and dozens more, some brimming with energy and hope like Hüsker Dü and the Pixies, others prematurely jaded, like Dinosaur Jr. and Sonic Youth. Indie rock, it was called, though some of the heroes, like R.E.M. and X, had major-label deals or distribution from very near the beginning, and many of the ancestors, like the Velvet Underground and the Stooges, were never on small or "independent" record labels at all. Then too, these were the '80s, rock's postpunk interregnum. Smart, nonmetal guitar bands were a corporate taboo, at best signed, pressured to "broaden" their sound with an outside producer for that crucial mainstream appeal, then left to flop with no promo budget. In retrospect, the independence of a Big Black was about as coveted as the Gaza Strip.

But for those who were part of the indie rock network in those years—the musicians, label staffs, college radio DJs, zine writers, club workers, Drunks With Guns collectors—both pride and scars remain. Pride in creating a form of rock that could thrive on voluntarism, subsistence, and obscurity, where the distance between fanship and participation was no distance at all, so one could be a consumer without the traditional associations of gross commodification, audience passivity, and massness. Indie rockers essentially formed a cultural community, people whose attitudes toward consumption give them an oppositional identity similar (if weaker and less widely recognized) to that provided for others by race, gender, class, or sexuality.

In many ways indie resembled '80s radical movements, especially in its ingrained conviction that real power over the mainstream was unattainable, so the only workable model for resistance had to be small-scale change and self-transformation—the personal as political. Putting out a record by a friend's band that you loved but knew ordinary people would never like was indie's neighborhood recycling project. And such attitudes changed the nature of rock. Punk still required major labels so the Sex Pistols could at least spit in EMI's face. But indie rockers were content to discover a garage obscurity like "The Hunch" by Mad Mike & the Maniacs, or feud with Gerard Cosloy in the college-radio trade magazine *CMJ*, or yell out a request for a b-side at a hipster shrine like Maxwell's and briefly convince the band struggling onstage it was legendary.

The best account of these years to date is Gina Arnold's *Route 666: On the Road to Nirvana*, a book whose subtitle explains what happened next. R.E.M.'s rise had convinced indie to believe in itself; Nirvana's explosion onto the charts convinced the rest of the world to believe in indie. Artists who've never made any pretense of accessibility, from Daniel Johnston to the Boredoms, get signed by Atlantic and Warner Bros., who, reversing the assumptions of the postpunk interregnum, presume that fanzine followings indicate a basis for wider popularity, not hopeless obscurantism. The same labels hire A&R people with indie label and college radio backgrounds. MTV proves enormously willing to give "Buzz Clip" exposure to artists like the Breeders or Green Day, who would previously have been dismissed as too subtle or obnoxiously adolescent.

Source: "Over and Out: Indie Rock Values in the Age of Alternative Million Sellers" Eric Weisbard, *Village Voice Rock & Roll Quarterly*, Summer 1994, 15–19. Used by permission of Eric Weisbard.

Rock, these last couple of years, has in effect been revised. A new canon now gives marginal bohemians like Big Star equal status with long popular favorites. Rock stars no longer make a pageant of their power, as modesty and constant allusions to little-known underground bands become required decorum. At the level of *ideology* as much as music, today's alternative marketplace now offers a large-scale, corporate-sponsored version of indie rock. Green Day appears on Letterman the night Belly does Leno; Lollapalooza's the only sure money-making ticket in the business, apart from boomer nostalgia tours like the Eagles, who sold out five nights in San Francisco the week Big Star played. The word *mainstream* has virtually disappeared, even if the mainstream hasn't.

But as a result, the scars of the indie-only years have started to manifest themselves. In a recent issue of Chicago's indier-than-thou zine *The Baffler* headlined "Alternative To What?" Tom Frank writes: "Now we watch with interest as high-powered executives offer contracts to bands they have seen only once, college radio playlists become the objects of intense corporate scrutiny, and longstanding independent labels are swallowed whole in a colossal belch of dollars and receptions. Now *Rolling Stone* magazine makes pious reference to the pioneering influence of bands like Big Black and Mission of Burma whose records they ignored when new." Can the indie values of smallness, marginality, antipop as a basis for community formation and everything else, really serve as a blueprint for '90s mainstream rock? Isn't that a contradiction in terms, or something even worse—a betrayal of values?

Such questions are starting to seem inescapable. Kurt Cobain kills himself in a manner that indicts his own celebrity. *Maximumrocknroll*, bible to the hardcore punk scene that's always been indie's dumber big brother, runs a cover with an image of a man putting a gun in his mouth and the caption "Major Labels: Some Of Your Friends Are Already This Fucked." *Sassy*, which has been giving glossy coverage to the riot grrrl movement since practically before riot grrrl existed, gets an angry letter from Bratmobile's Molly Neuman. "Did you actually think the majority of your readers would know many indie labels or zines? . . . I think I speak for many girl bands (I'm in one) and punks when I say we don't want your attention or support. Stick to exploiting models." And [in] the next issue, Jenny Toomey of Tsunami responds to Neuman with a letter denouncing "an alternative community that claims to be inclusive and yet remains so enamored of the 'fringes' . . . that its main concern is not communication or accessibility but, ultimately cliquishness."

To give Frank credit as more than a subcultural purist, his *Baffler* piece recognizes a crucial dialectic at work. "Consumerism's traditional claim to be the spokesman for our inchoate disgust with consumerism was hemorrhaging credibility, and independent rock, with its Jacobin 'authenticity' obsession, had just the things capital required." Is this brave new alternative world creepy, even for those of us who understand that we're all better off that Elvis Presley got signed to a major from Sun Records after a few promising indie singles? (Today RCA would have Sam Phillips keep producing Elvis, then publicize his refusal to compromise.) Of course. I think the indie credo of fatalistic marginality is badly outdated in a Clintonian era where power is there for the taking. I was rooting for Big Star to seize the day on Leno. And I still resented having to share the live reunion with a crowd of neophytes. Was I being elitist?

Alternative Nation

Trent Reznor of Nine Inch Nails is bored with the grunge look. "I guess the statement was, 'Look this is honest; we don't need to pretend we're rock stars and all this shit,'" he told Moon Unit Zappa in a recent issue of *Raygun*. "I think that mindset is a good one . . . it killed off the Bon Jovis and those type of bands with our new earnest attitude. But that's become contrived now. . . . [W]hen I see a show, I want to be entertained. I'd rather see David Bowie/Ziggy Stardust on stage than that guy that just pumped gas for me."

Reznor is reenacting an almost hallowed argument, the sort of thing Depeche Mode might have said about R.E.M. clones 10 years ago; that is, the rock/pop split that drove primarily English bands in the New Wave era in the direction of dance rhythms, polished production, and visual style, while American outfits by and large clung belligerently to their street clothes and guitars. It went without saying, throughout the 1980s, that bands who went the former route would sign to major labels and, escaping the postpunk media ghettoes, be seen on MTV and heard on radio stations that called the music "modern rock." Indie bands on SST or Homestead, on the other hand, mostly got to claim the mantle of rock integrity; opposition to mass culture and unbridled experimentalism if you bought into the rhetoric; a space for privileged white guy angst to reign unchecked if you didn't.

In truth, a variety of stylish outfits found idiosyncratic ways to flourish during the postpunk interregnum with one foot in indie's door—New Order, Joan Jett, Violent Femmes, the Beastie Boys, R.E.M., and the Smiths, to name a few. By the time of 1991's first Lollapalooza, conceived by the leader of one such band, Jane's Addiction, and a breakthrough moment for another, Nine Inch Nails, such artists were cementing a new genre, "alternative," that seemed destined to heal the rock/pop split. (At the same time, a generation of former speed metal bands on indie labels, led by Metallica, staged a coup in the metal world, dooming the big hair and spandex crowd.) Even today, the indie guitar bands in pop abundance are only one musical subculture among many, especially if you set aside groups like Green Day, Bad Religion, and the Offspring, whose allegiances are to the separate hardcore set. Kurt Cobain, Sub Pop, K, and the appropriation of the indie aesthetic are hardly the only story in alternative 1994.

Nevertheless, it's Henry Rollins, once of Black Flag, and Sonic Youth's Thurston Moore who are MTV's favorite alternative faces. U2 act more like Negativland and less like Springsteen with every new album, realizing that the essence of rock's moral leadership has shifted. Lollapalooza '94, looking to regain its credibility, first begs Nirvana to appear, then in their absence features an indie-identified lineup including Smashing Pumpkins, the Breeders, L7, Nick Cave, and the Boredoms. *Sassy* would rather write about Fugazi than the Cure. Kurt Cobain is deemed the John Lennon of his generation. Why? Because of indie's status as the emblem of integrity, its ownership of rock's new yardstick: resistance to mass culture. Thus, it wasn't until "Smells Like Teen Spirit," when (mostly former) indie rockers started receiving media exposure without being pressured to revise their sound or stance, and the walls of the post-punk ghetto came down, that the interregnum ended and alternative came to be fully accepted as the new rock.

In trying to fuse modern rock's cynicism about traditional rock sounds and imagery with indie rock's commitment to modesty and a notion of the underground, alternative has discovered that you can't get by without that most traditional and immodest of animals: the rock star. Only given that selling records, exerting power, and reveling in stardom are all etiquette no-no's now, celebrity can only be seen as an aesthetic embarrassment—when the Pet Shop Boys sang "How Can You Expect To Be Taken Seriously?" did they have any idea how much further the kill rock star creed would take it? The role of the rock star is one of many crucial questions that alternative's emergence has left unanswered. What does the indie onslaught of new guitar bands do to modern rock's perfectly valid efforts to push the music away from sounding like the umpteenth version of AOR? Why are seemingly all the new gods of alternative white men? Must our integrity heroes be so cartoonish?

As an oppositional movement grounded in the tension between small-scale consumption and mass culture, indie has proven unable to articulate a cause that goes beyond remaining pure of outside influence—a nearly impossible position for a megastar to maintain. Yet, without megastars able to translate indie values into something socially meaningful, alternative loses whatever shred of justification it had left. All that remains is to wince as the process turns indie rhetoric into the worst possible parody of itself. Like the Bud Dry "reach for an alternative—Bud Dry" radio commercials, heard on modern rock stations, where an alternative musician spouts "some bands strive for artistic integrity and expressing their free creative identities. Us, hey, we just want free beer."

Eddie Vedder, Rollins, Perry Farrell, Cobain, Michael Stipe, and yes, Trent Reznor if he'd like, ultimately became sacrificial lambs for alternative's failure of self-definition. Their ability to hold up the tent allows dozens of other bands to flourish within, but what sort of a movement can survive by so thoroughly ripping apart its leaders? Mike Dirnt of Green Day said of Cobain: "To some extent he's like Jesus to me. He died for my sins, so I could get signed to a major label?"

Still, alternagods can't help seeming desperately ridiculous. They've become mass men. Vedder ostentatiously refuses to shoot a video for the new Pearl Jam album. Rollins is invited to *The Tonight Show*, not to perform "Liar" but to sit on the couch and talk with Jay. Hardly the sort to chicken out like Alex Chilton, he shows and the two cover Black Flag, Rollins's free-jazz fanship and poetry readings (is the guy a beatnik or what?) and then the big question: "So you haven't compromised at all?" "Zero."

Major or Minor?

Back in Indieland, Steve Albini starts another *Baffler* essay imagining major labels as a big long trench "filled with runny, decaying shit" that bands desiring contracts have to swim across. Then back. Mac, from Superchunk, is a little more reasonable, though his conclusion is exactly the same. "It just makes you feel that the bands are there to be used by someone else. Their bottom line is not the music." On Merge, his own label, of late grown large enough to employ full-time staff, "you're totally in control of everything. You know where your money's going, because it's you and not some far-reaching department of a company you don't know how big it really is." Why should he take an advance that's a loan, not a gift, spend more money to record than he needs to, and ultimately face the prospect of being dropped? Even the traditional reason for signing to a major—better distribution—makes less sense now that the chain stores have started to stock product from independent distributors like Merge's Touch and Go.

Major labels could supply the promotional capital to help Superchunk sell five or 10 times what they do already—a more than respectable 30,000 copies of the new *Foolish* in its first two months out. But then, to Mac, "the popular bands have usually been the crappiest bands." I wonder, though: let's say Mac did sign, took the advance, burned his bridges to the indie world, recorded with an outside producer, worried about getting dropped, thought about how to make Superchunk translate to the people outside his secure constituency. Isn't it possible that after five nearly identical albums he'd start making the best music of his life? Worked for Green Day.

A few days later, I'm talking all this over with Kim Deal, who made a similar jump between the first and second Breeders albums. She explodes into laughter at Mac's reticence. "Fucking turn up your vocals, please! I hate it when people make things so difficult that they actually don't work 'cause they're being so *indie*. That was one of the things recording *Last Splash*. I had to constantly remind myself, turn up the fucking vocals. I tried to do that so I wouldn't sound like this wimp indie band. Really, I thought it was cowardly not to." For Deal, a gold album has changed little in her life. "We're not that big." She contrasts herself to Hammer, whose album marketing plans once included Saturday cartoons and ads for Kentucky Fried Chicken. "With the Breeders it's like, 'Here's an article in *Spin*, do you want to do it?'"

Eddie Roeser of Urge Overkill, a band that started tweaking the indie rock staidness Trent Reznor hates, then caused serious bad feelings when it left Touch and Go for Geffen, basically concurs that signing to a major isn't necessarily stepping in shit. "At this stage of the game, if you have something that has some merit, the record company is not going to say well, we're not releasing it, it's not polished enough. You have to go back and record it again. They're not stupid. They're not going to fuck with us. And they haven't, at all. The real worrying starts when you've sold a million records, and they want you to sell a million records again, and maybe the band doesn't." Roeser knows what he's talking about—Urge Overkill spent time touring with Pearl Jam.

The Breeders and Urge Overkill are in the closest thing to an ideal position the alternative age has to offer. They've met the artistic challenge of reaching outside the hipoisie, while avoiding the point where artists are forced into the role of public figures. With their indie backgrounds, neither Deal nor Roeser, it's clear, feels comfortable aspiring to more. It's as if Grand Funk Railroad, instead of hoping to supplant the Rolling Stones, expressed a desire to remain cool like the New York Dolls. Roeser may play the star onstage and in videos, but he's careful to mention that he was just talking to Spiral Stairs of Pavement about how embarrassing it is to meet "these kids who really think you're a rock star. And in your own mind you're definitely not one. And you don't know how to treat someone who thinks that about you." "Who wants to wear spandex?" says Deal. "To communicate in a festival setting, you've got to do those moves and things. You just feel dumb. 'All right everybody, let's rock and roll!' No way. I'll do something if I think it makes sense musically."

Power? Pop?

Indie rock's cultural community most closely resembles two earlier eras when even smaller groups of musicians and consumer cultists developed subcultures that would eventually be diverted away from them. The hot jazz fans of the 1930s and 1940s maintained a rigorous distinction between "true" and "commercial" jazz, favoring small combo jams and Dixieland arrangements, even after their comrade Benny Goodman brought the mainstream a lot closer to the real thing by ushering in swing. The beat generation, who emerged in the later 1940s and early 1950s, later found themselves unexpectedly spawning beatniks—the six years *On the Road* waited to be published (to enormous media onslaught, from which Kerouac never recovered) is not unlike the gap between *New Day Rising* and *Nevermind*.

The fate of these predecessors offers interesting lessons. Jazz cultists, mostly white, would eventually be challenged by beboppers who could supplement their consumption-based ethic of oppositionality with the politics of race—much as women and queers seem to be doing within indie rock today. The beats, demoralized and fragmented by commercialization, watched hippies willingly use the media to gain social influence. Will a new wave of alternative, sufficiently distanced from its indie rock sources, eventually achieve the same mediated flamboyance?

It would be specious to argue that the last few years have shown that indie rock's qualities cannot survive on major labels. Even a cursory list of emergent artists—Nirvana, P.M. Dawn, My Bloody Valentine, A Tribe Called Quest, P. J. Harvey,

Pavement—shows how, if anything, "alternative" has opened up possibilities within rock to women, blacks, the English, and others mostly left out of the Homestead/ SST years, without in the least penalizing bands of determinedly indie sensibilities. Ironically, many of the more close-minded indie types, like former Amphetamine Reptile acts Helmet and Surgery, have proven the most irresistible to the majors, since as arrogant metallic white boys they're hardly a huge divergence.

But the clash between indie values and the realities of an alternative-rock obsessed pop world are real—and almost impossible to resolve. Why should Mac risk mutilating his fan base so I can hear a better record? How do we want our Eddie Vedders to behave, anyway? (For what it's worth, I think he's a terrible musician but a great star—for initiating antitrust inquiries against Ticketmaster he deserves the thanks of everyone.) And anyway, why should alternative fans be expected to work out questions of politics, art, consumption, and commodification that the left in general falls over itself trying to deal with? The only commentary on Cobain's death as pigheadedly determined to blame major labels as *Maximumrocknroll* ran in, no surprise, *The Nation*.

The tragedy here is that rock has lost its cultural populism, a sense that the most popular *can* be the best. Without that, rock will produce challenging and sophisticated works, some of them again on major labels. It will unite groups of people who aren't anybody's Generation X but share symbolic hipster affiliations. But it won't upset the applecarts of cultural hierarchy the same way it did with Presley or the Stones. It won't be the king of the popular arts. It won't be as powerful.

Power. That's what this [is] all about, isn't it? Indie, a genre bred out of powerlessness over mainstream rock, nevertheless, through the triumph of alternative, ended up reinscribing a certain notion of power back into rock. By prefiguring, at the level of cliques and individuals, the kind of unbridled rock culture that wasn't being tolerated at a corporate level, indie set a standard for how seriously rock needed to be taken. It provided a necessary counterbalance to modern rock's rejection of "rockism," the Depeche Mode/Cure argument that spins on fashion and style matter just as much as the frontier individualism of a distorted guitar. In pop art terms, Depeche Mode were right. But socially, they always seemed like market accomodationists, further proof that, as a legacy of their class system, the English inevitably rend popular culture trivial and ineffective.

Indie rock gave the notion that rock should speak truth to power, or at least offer the powerless a way to speak, a safe hiding place during the postpunk interregnum. (Go back and listen to songs like Hüsker Dü's "It's Not Funny Anymore" and "In a Free Land" and you'll see exactly what I mean.) Yet, interregnums end. The reshuffling of rock's elite has more than commenced. (To make one last Fillmore reference, when the place reopened this April, Smashing Pumpkins, not a '60s holdover, headlined the first night.) And it's time to see whether alternative can find enough power within itself to push rock's new momentum back into the culture at large. Because there, the positive aspects of alternative's bohemian-hipster legacy—a love for the diverse and eclectic, hostility to established sexual and gender norms, and a politics that, like MTV, is always at least liberal—are thoroughly needed. But the conditioned reflexes—toward smallness, away from the popular, in love with power as an ideal, not a reality—that indie culture instilled in so many of us are starting to stand in the way.

My head tells me all this, then my heart sends me off to the Thread Waxing Space in lower Manhattan to see Guided By Voices, indie's latest best hope. I'm compelled to point out that they were much better when, during a previous visit, I saw them in this same location over the winter. Was the summer heat to blame? Maybe it was a crowd at least three times as large. Or a guy onstage the whole time with a camera, filming for MTV.

Further Reading

Arnold, Gina. *Route 666: On the Road to Nirvana*. New York: St. Martin's Press, 1993.
Azerrad, Michael. *Come as You Are: The Story of Nirvana*. New York: Main Street Books, 1993.
Marsh, Dave. "Live through This." *Rock and Rap Confidential,* June 1995.
True, Everett. *Live through This: American Rock Music in the Nineties.* Virgin, 2002.

Discography

The Breeders. *Last Splash.* Elektra/WEA, 1993.
Green Day. *Insomniac.* Reprise/WEA, 1995.
Hüsker Dü. *Warehouse: Songs and Stories.* Warner Bros./Ada, 1987.
Nine Inch Nails. *The Downward Spiral.* Nothing, 1994.
R.E.M. *In Time: The Best of R.E.M. 1988–2003.* Warner Bros./WEA, 2003.
Smashing Pumpkins. *Mellon Collie and the Infinite Sadness.* Virgin Records US, 1995.
Sonic Youth. *Daydream Nation.* Geffen Records, 1988.
X. *The Best: Make the Music Go Bang.* Elektra/WEA, 2004.

80. "We Are the World"?

Going back to at least the 1950s, a category has existed for recordings produced outside of the U.S.–U.K. axis of mainstream popular music. This category, initially dubbed "international" in the 1950s, brought the sounds of Parisian cafés and Polynesian luau orchestras into the living rooms of North American and British listeners, who might find, upon careful perusal of the liner notes, that the polka recording they had just purchased was actually recorded not too far down the road from them.[1] As noted in Chapter 28, an audience hankering for

---

1. Keir Keightley, "Around the World: Musical Tourism and the Globalization of the Record Industry, 1946–66," unpublished manuscript, 1998.

popular music with the allure of the noncommercial might have been tempted in the 1950s to plunk down their hard-earned cash for a Harry Belafonte "calypso" record or a "folk" recording by the Kingston Trio. During the 1960s, other sounds began emerging from beyond the Western metropole. In addition to such one-off novelties as Kyu Sakamoto's "Sukyaki," the influence of "ska" (or "bluebeat" as it was known in Britain) began to be felt outside the Jamaican sound-system parties where it had developed, both in hits by West Indian artists like Millie Small and Desmond Dekker and in the incorporation of ska rhythms in recordings by the Beatles (1964's "I Call Your Name").

However, in the early 1970s, the success of the soundtrack from *The Harder They Come*, featuring reggae star Jimmy Cliff (James Chambers, b. 1948), followed by the international triumph of Bob Marley (1945–81), brought a new level of attention to Jamaican popular music and, in particular, to reggae. Jamaica subsequently had an impact on global popular music far out of proportion to its tiny population. The rise of what is sometimes called "second-wave ska" in Great Britain in the late 1970s, with its politically conscious "two-tone" bands, is but one example. Another example is the continuation of ska-punk hybrids throughout the 1980s and 1990s (in what could be called "third-wave ska"), and the fusions of hip-hop and reggae that continue to flourish in recordings of Jamaican dance-hall artists and U.S. hip-hop stars.

With Bob Marley's death in 1981, record companies sought to fill the void in a variety of ways. The first move by Marley's former company (Island) was to promote Nigerian jùjú star King Sunny Adé as the next Marley, an attempt that failed woefully. However, a type of sub-Saharan African music was destined to make an impact in the world of Western pop, but in a way that could not have been foreseen. Paul Simon, whose career had more or less stalled in the late 1970s, happened across some recordings of South African pop music. Simon subsequently traveled to Johannesburg to record with the musicians he heard on those recordings, and the rest, as they say, is history.[2] The resultant album, *Graceland* (1986), revived Simon's dormant career and succeeded in exposing millions of listeners to African popular music where Island's campaign had failed. Thus was born "World Music" as we now know it.

Simon's recording tapped into an urge felt by consumers of Western pop music for something new, yet familiar. Sales of other recordings from Africa and the Caribbean grew, but no one category yet existed in which to place the music (and thus no easy-to-find location in record stores), no *Billboard* chart, and no radio format. Aware of this dilemma,

---

2. This history includes a debate sparked by the album among music critics and academics; for a sample, see Steven Feld, "Notes on World Beat," in *Music Grooves: Essays and Dialogues*, ed. Charles Keil and Steven Feld, 238–46 (Chicago: University of Chicago Press, 1994); Veit Erlmann, "The Aesthetics of the Global Imagination: Reflections on World Music in the 1990s," *Public Culture* 8 (1996): 467–87; Charles Hamm, "Graceland Revisited," *Popular Music* 8 (October 1989): 299–304; and Louise Meintjes, "Paul Simon's *Graceland*, South Africa, and the Mediation of Musical Meaning," *Ethnomusicology* 34, no. 1 (1990): 37–73.

some 25 record industry executives met in a pub in London in 1987 and invented the name "World Music." The term has shifted since the late 1980s; from its initial emphasis on music from sub-Saharan Africa and the Caribbean (also known at the time as "World Beat"), it has increasingly included European "ethnic" musics and various new age, dance, and ambient fusions (which subsequently became the most successful varieties of "World Music").[3]

Much writing on the subject has focused on questions of power and economics. When Western pop stars and Western corporations record and produce recordings with non-Western musicians, who benefits? Are these Western entities exploiting Western consumers' naive fascination with the exotic for profit? If the answer to the last question is yes, is a nonexploitative involvement with non-Western music possible? How we respond to these questions will be affected by which musical projects we consider, some of which function more obviously to the advantage of the Western musicians and corporations involved than do others.[4]

In contrast to the notion of World Music, the emphasis in the following essay by George Lipsitz is on what may be termed "global music." Rather than focus on how Western-based multinational music corporations are profiting from the "raw material" of non-Western music or on famous Western musicians' interactions with non-Western musicians, Lipsitz focuses on how global flows of people, music, and technology have resulted in new fusions reflecting the experience of immigrants who fashion intriguing blends of tradition with sounds from the metropolis. By emphasizing creative responses to marginalization, this account performs an important disruption of what may otherwise seem like a unified narrative told from the perspective of dominant groups in the West (as in many accounts of World Music). At the same time, Lipsitz is careful to emphasize that the resourcefulness of Algerians in France, West and East Indians in the United Kingdom, and Mexican Americans in the United States does not negate the effects of racial domination and economic exploitation. Lipsitz's work here on the "poetics of place" builds upon previous work he has done on working-class and subaltern cultural practices and struggles in books such as *Time Passages* and *Class and Culture in Cold War America*.[5] One of the few overtly "academic" entries in this book, Lipsitz's clear prose and the timeliness

---

3. A useful overview and analysis of these developments may be found in Timothy D. Taylor, *Global Pop: World Music, World Markets* (New York: Routledge, 1997), 1–37.

4. For a particularly tendentious critique of the World Music phenomenon, see Herbert Mattelart, "Life as Style: Putting the 'World' in the Music," *Baffler* (1993): 103–09.

5. George Lipsitz, *Time Passages: Collective Memory and American Popular Culture* (Minneapolis: University of Minnesota Press, 1990); idem., *Class and Culture in Cold War America: A Rainbow at Midnight* (South Hadley, Mass.: Bergin and Garvey, 1982).

of the issues he discusses blur the line between academic and well-researched nonacademic criticism.

Immigration and Assimilation: Rai, Reggae, and Bhangramuffin

George Lipsitz

During the 1980s, popular-music listeners and enthusiasts throughout Europe began to notice new musical forms that captured their fancy. In London, the band Alaap blended bhangra music from the Indian state of Punjab with Greek, Middle Eastern, Spanish, and Anglo-American pop styles. At the same time, Joi Bangla, made up of immigrants from Bangladesh, mixed African-American funk sounds with traditional Bengali folk songs.[*] For their part, listeners in Paris expressed enthusiasm for a techno-pop album displaying "a faintly Moorish" sound underneath English, French, and Arabic lyrics by a Mauritanian singer recording under the name Tahra.[†]

Soaring to popularity at the same time that immigrant populations in London and Paris faced increasing hostility and even attacks from anti-foreign thugs, these recordings demonstrate the complicated connections and contradictions that characterize the links between popular music and social life. Audiences and artists in these cities carried the cultural collisions of everyday life into music, at one and the same time calling attention to ethnic differences and demonstrating how they might be transcended. Sophisticated fusions of seemingly incompatible cultures in music made sense to artists and audiences in part because these fusions reflected their lived experiences in an inter-cultural society.

Of course, inter-cultural communication and creativity does not preclude political or even physical confrontations between members of groups fighting for a share of increasingly scarce resources. But the very existence of music demonstrating the interconnectedness between the culture of immigrants and the culture of their host country helps us understand how the actual lived experiences of immigrants are much more dynamic and complex than most existing models of immigration and assimilation admit.

Government control over the production and distribution of popular music and the peculiarities of French culture have left French citizens with far less connection to international rock 'n' roll than their neighbors in Germany, Spain, or the Netherlands. In fact, the cultural fit over the years between rock 'n' roll and French culture has been so bad that it gave rise to a saying that *"le rock français, c'est comme la cuisine anglaise"* ("French rock is to rock as English cooking is to cooking"). But with the rise of rap, French musicians of African descent have become more involved with the currents of international popular music. Members of the rap group I.A.M. come from North African neighborhoods in the southern city of Marseilles. They titled their album *From the Planet Mars*, as a pun about Marseilles, but also as a statement about how different their experiences are from those of cosmopolitan and metropolitan

---

[*] Sabita Banerji, "Ghazals to Bhangra in Great Britain," *Popular Music* vol. 7, no. 2 (May) 1988, 208, 213.

[†] Philip Sweeney, *The Virgin Directory of World Music* (New York: Henry Holt, 1991), 17.

Source: "Immigration and Assimilation: Rai, Reggae, and Bhangramuffin" © 1994 George Lipsitz, *Dangerous Crossroads: Popular Music, Postmodernism, and the Poetics of Place* (Verso).

French citizens. I.A.M. stands for "Imperial Asiatic Men," but their music and lyrics deal mostly with Egypt, Algeria, and America.[††] The African-born Parisian rapper M. C. Solaar has immersed himself in the French hip hop subculture which he describes as "the cult of the sneaker," and "pretty much a U.S. branch office."[*]

The complicated culture mixing that has given rise to new forms of inter-cultural communication within French popular music has also had important political implications. Salif Keita of Mali recorded a powerful and popular French-language song, "Nous Pas Bouger," which championed the cause of immigrants resisting deportation.[†] Similarly, the men and women in the anti-racist folk/punk/new wave band Les Négresses Vertes base their music on French multi-culturalism. Their name means green black women, and the band's members are male and female, European and African, white and black. "It's music from the street today," explains Mathias, who plays accordion. "We all grew up with a large variety of different people who might have different roots but who are, nevertheless, French. Our musical hybrid wasn't a deliberate policy, it's the way we are. It mirrors the reality of France today."[‡]

Clearly the most important and most complicated expression of musical multiculturalism in France comes from the popularity of Algerian "rai" music. During the 1980s, political and cultural mobilizations by young people of North African origin competed with intense anti-Arab and anti-foreign organizing by French right wingers for the power to define "French" culture and citizenship.[§] Rai music took on extra-musical importance as a visible weapon in that struggle.

Referenced by many artists including Les Négresses Vertes and I.A.M., rai music blends Arabic lyrics and instruments with synthesizers, disco arrangements, blues chord progressions, and Jamaican reggae and Moroccan gnawa rhythms. Rai originated as women's music in the Algerian port city of Oran where *meddahas* sang to other women at weddings and other private occasions and by *chiekhas* who sang for men in taverns and brothels. In a city where French, Spanish and Arabic are all spoken, the music known as "Oran Modern" emerged from interactions among Spanish, French, and North African musicians.[¶] Now sung by both female Chebas and male Chebs, the term "rai" comes from the Arabic phrase "Ya Rai" ("It's my opinion").[||] Reed flutes and terracotta drums provided the original instrumentation for rai, but over the years musicians added violin, accordion, saxophone, and trumpet. Bellemou Messaoud played a particularly important role in the emergence of modern rai when he added guitars, trumpets, and synthesizers to rai ensembles.[**] Disco-influenced arrangements and blues chord progressions came later to bring rai closer to the Anglo-American international style.

A product of cultural collision between Europe and North Africa, rai music has its defenders and its detractors in both places. Some factions in Algeria see rai as too French, too Western, too modern, too obscene. At the same time, there are those

---

[††]John Rockwell, "Felicitous Rhymes and Local Roots," *New York Times*, August 23, 1992, section 2, 23.

[*] Jay Cocks, "Rap Around the Globe," *Time* (October 19, 1992), 70.

[†] Banning Eyre, "Routes: The Parallel Paths of Baaba Maal and Salif Keita," *Option* no. 53 (November–December, 1993), 45.

[‡]Jo Shinner, "Zzzzzobie!," *Folk Roots* vol. 74 (August) 1989, 35.

[§] Azouz Begag, "The 'Beurs,' Children of North-African Immigrants in France: The Issue of Integration," *Journal of Ethnic Studies* vol. 18, no. 1, 2–4.

[¶]Philip Sweeney, *The Virgin Directory of World Music*, 9.

[||] Miriam Rosen, "On Rai," *Artforum* vol. 29, no. 1 (September) 1990, 22; David McMurray and Ted Swedenburg, "Rai Tide Rising," *Middle East Report* (March–April) 1991, 39.

[**] Miriam Rosen, "On Rai," 22; Philip Sweeney, *The Virgin Directory of World Music*, 9.

in France who dismiss rai as too foreign, too primitive, too exotic, too strange. It is not easy to tell if a North African immigrant to France is being assimilationist or separatist by listening to rai music. Cheb Khaled spends more time in Marseilles than in Algiers, and uses rai music to comment on "racism in France, about what's happening in Algeria, and of course, I always sing about love."[*] Cheba Fadela created a sensation as a mini-skirted seventeen-year-old on French television in the late 1970s and helped start modern "pop rai" with her 1983 song "N'sel fik" ("You are Mine").[†] Cheb Sid Ahmed is openly homosexual and performs with a troupe of traditional female wedding singers.[‡] At the other extreme, Cheba Zahouania performs mainly at women's events, does not allow herself to be photographed, and does not appear on television, reportedly because her husband threatened to take her children from her if she sang in public for men.[§]

Not surprisingly, rai has been embroiled in repeated political controversies. "The history of rai is like the history of rock and roll," explains Cheb Khaled, one of the genre's premier performers.

> Fundamentalists don't want our concerts to happen. They come and break things up. They say rai is street music and that it's debauched. But that's not true. I don't sing pornography. I sing about love and social life. We say what we think, just like singers all over the world.[¶]

The Algerian government has sporadically looked with favor on rai as a source of revenue and as a cultural voice capable of competing with Islamic fundamentalism. Its popularity in France persuaded the authorities in Algiers to sponsor international youth festivals featuring rai performers in Algiers and Oran in 1985.[||] In France, racist attacks on Arabs led to the formation of SOS-Racisme, a massive anti-racist organization affiliated with the Socialist Party. It embraced rai as an expression of faith in France's inter-cultural future.[**] They helped persuade the French government to sponsor a rai festival in a Paris suburb in 1986, which seemed to mark the emergence of rai as a permanent force in French popular music.[††] In fact, rai may have become more secure in France than it is in Algeria. When anti-government rioters in Algiers adopted Cheb Khaled's "El Harba Wine" ("Where to Flee?") as their unofficial anthem in what became known as the "rai rebellion," many rai artists hastened to disassociate themselves from the violence.[‡‡]

Yet, the popularity of rai music among French and "world beat" audiences may mean little for children of immigrants facing massive unemployment and racist attacks. In Lyons, for example, seventy percent of the children of immigrants between the ages of 16 and 25 have no jobs and no vocational training. Even the success of an assimilationist group like France-Plus which has managed to elect close to 400 people of North African lineage to municipal offices throughout France may increase rather

---

[*] Banning Eyre, "A King in Exile: The Royal Rai of Cheb Khaled," *Option* vol. 39 (July–August) 1991, 45.

[†] Miriam Rosen, "On Rai," 23.

[‡] Philip Sweeney, *The Virgin Directory of World Music,* 12.

[§] Miriam Rosen, "On Rai," 23.

[¶] Banning Eyre, "A King in Exile," 45.

[||] Miriam Rosen, "On Rai," 23; Philip Sweeney, *The Virgin Directory of World Music,* 10.

[**] David McMurray and Ted Swedenburg, "Rai Tide Rising," *Middle East Report* (March–April) 1991, 42.

[††] Philip Sweeney, *The Virgin Directory of World Music,* 10.

[‡‡] David McMurray and Ted Swedenburg, "Rai Tide Rising," 42; Miriam Rosen, "On Rai," 23.

than decrease the pressures on those immigrants and their children who seem less assimilated.[§§]

Traditional arguments about immigration, assimilation, and acculturation assume that immigrants choose between two equally accessible cultures that are clearly differentiated and distinct from one another. But what if immigrants leave a country that has been shaped by its colonizers and enter one that has been shaped by those it colonized? What if immigrants leave a modernizing country that turns anti-modern and fundamentalist while they are gone? What happens if the host country becomes deeply divided between anti-foreign nativists and anti-racist pluralists? Which culture do the immigrants carry with them? Into which culture do they assimilate? Rai music might be defended as either Algerian or French music, but a more exact interpretation would establish it as a register for the changing dimensions and boundaries of Algerian, French, and Beur (a popular term for Arab mostly used in Paris) identities.

Afro-Caribbean and Southwest Asian immigrants to Britain experience many of the same dynamic changes facing North African immigrants to France. Here again, musical syncretisms disclose the dynamics of cultural syncretisms basic to the processes of immigration, assimilation, and acculturation in contemporary societies. Immigrants leaving the Caribbean and Asia took on new identities in Britain. If nothing else, they became "West Indian" or "East Indian" in England instead of Jamaican or Bahamian, Bengali, or Hindi as they had been at home. But they also became "Black" in Britain, an identity that they generally do not have in their home countries, but which becomes salient to them in England as a consequence of racism directed at them from outside their communities as well as from its utility to them as a device for building unity within and across aggrieved populations. Of course, the influx of immigrants changes England too. Once immigrants from the Indian subcontinent or the Caribbean arrive in the U.K., they transform the nature of British society and culture in many ways, changing the nature of the "inside" into which newer immigrants are expected to assimilate.

Mass migration from the West Indies to Britain began shortly after World War II. The expanding English economy offered jobs to immigrants, but the nation's cultural institutions rarely acknowledged their presence. According to Anthony Marks, as late as 1963, when some 15,000 records from Jamaica entered England every month, the British Broadcasting Corporation studiously ignored West Indian music and record shops rarely carried products from the Caribbean.[*] Denied the dignity of representation in the mainstream media, Afro-Caribbeans in England created spaces for themselves with neighborhood sound systems and record collections that enabled them to express their own culture and share it with others. At the heart of these new spaces was music from Jamaica.

While immigration flows included residents of all Caribbean islands, Jamaicans accounted for more than sixty percent of England's Caribbean population by the 1960s. Because of the size of the Jamaican-British community and because of the ways in which the politically-charged doctrines of Rastafarianism helped all diasporic Blacks in Britain understand and endure their treatment, Jamaican culture became the crucial unifying component in the composite Caribbean culture created

---

[§§] Azouz Begag, "The 'Beurs,'" 9.

[*] Anthony Marks, "Young, Gifted and Black: Afro-American and Afro-Caribbean Music in Britain 1963–88," in Paul Oliver, ed., *Black Music in Britain: Essays on the Afro-Asian Contribution to Popular Music* (Milton Keynes and Philadelphia: Open University Press, 1990), 106.

in England. Differences between island identities that might be deeply felt in the West Indies, and even in England, receded in importance because of the unifying force of Jamaican music, but even more because of the uniformity of British racism against *all* West Indians. "When you're in school you all get harassed together," explained one immigrant.[*] Another adds, "I think most of my friends feel Jamaican, the English helped us do it."[†]

Popular music affirms the positive qualities of the unity forged in part by negative experiences with British racism. Through shared experiences with music, carnival celebrations, and the political activism that sometimes grows out of them, primary groups dispersed over a broad territory find themselves united by elements of a Jamaican culture that many of them had never known first hand.[‡] Jazzie B of the British group Soul II Soul remembers the prominence of Jamaican "sound systems"—record players and amplified speakers—in his neighborhood as he grew up, and what they meant to him as the British-born son of immigrants from Antigua. "By the time I was 15 or 16, there was a sound system on every single street in the community. I'd guess that eight out of every 10 black kids would be involved in one way or another in a sound system."[§] These devices offered a focal point for social gatherings, allowed disc jockeys opportunities to display their skills, and provided a soundtrack to mark the experiences and aspirations of inner-city life. But they also served as one of those sites where people made new identities for themselves as West Indians and as Black Britons.

Just as the Paris described by Simon Njami functions as an African city offering opportunities found nowhere in Africa, London and other British cities became important centers of West Indian and Jamaican cultural forms found nowhere in the Caribbean. But these forms have important uses and implications for Southwest Asians in Britain as well. The pervasive practices of British racism and occasional self-defense strategies by immigrants lead West Indians and East Indians to a shared identity as "Black" in England. Interactions between Afro-Caribbeans and Southwest Asians have a long if not completely comfortable history in the Caribbean, especially in Trinidad, but in Britain the antagonisms can be even sharper. For members of both groups, the things that divide them often seem more salient than those bringing them together. One survey showed that more than eighty percent of West Indians and more than forty percent of East Indians felt they had more in common with British whites than with each other. Almost a third of Indians and Pakistanis stated that they had nothing in common with either white Britons or West Indian Blacks. Only eight percent of West Indians and twenty percent of Pakistanis and Indians felt they had more in common with each other than they had in common with the English.[¶] In a few extremely significant cases, Afro-Asians and Afro-Caribbeans have successfully repressed their differences to defend themselves and each other from white racist attacks or judicial frame-ups, but sustained political and cultural alliances have been elusive.[‖]

---

[*] Winston James, "Migration, Racism, and Identity: The Caribbean Experience in Britain," *New Left Review*, no. 193 (May–June 1992), 32.

[†] Winston James, "Migration, Racism, and Identity," 28.

[‡] Abner Cohen, *Masquerade Politics*, 36.

[§] Robert Hillburn, "Tracing the Caribbean Roots of the New British Pop Invasion," *Los Angeles Times*, September 24, 1989, Calendar section, 6.

[¶] Winston James, "Migration, Racism, and Identity," 45.

[‖] Ibid., 34, 46.

Yet, alliances between Southwest Asians and other groups that might appear unlikely in political life already exist within popular culture. Bhangra musicians fuse folk songs from the Indian state of Punjab with disco, pop, hip hop, and house music for appreciative audiences made up of people from many different groups. Like Algerian rai, bhangra originated in a part of the world characterized by extensive inter-cultural communication, but remained largely a music played for private parties, weddings, and harvest festivals before its emergence as a syncretic popular form. Bhangra brings together Punjabis of many religions (Hindu, Sikh, Muslim, Jain, and Christian) and from many countries (India, Pakistan, and Bangladesh), but in the past decade has started to speak powerfully to new audiences and interests.[*]

Like West Indians, East Indians came to England in the years after World War II, and like West Indians they found that their labor was more welcome than their culture in their new nation. As Sabita Banerji notes in an apt phrase, "South Asian communities in Britain have remained invisible, and their music inaudible, for a surprisingly long time."[†] In the early 1980s, South Asian youths following the Jamaican example set up sound systems to play reggae, soul, jazz, and funk records during "daytimer" discos in dance halls and community centers. At first the disc jockeys and sound systems took Caribbean-sounding names, but when they started to mix bhangra with the other musical styles they used Punjabi names like "Gidian de Shingar" and "Pa Giddha Pa."[‡] Almost a decade after Jamaican reggae established itself as a popular form capable of attracting audiences from every ethnic background, bhangra broke on the British scene as a viable commercial force. Alaap's 1984 album, *Teri chunni di sitare* drew an enthusiastic response from listeners for its blend of disco, pop, and Caribbean styles with bhangra. Holle Holle and Heera drew large crowds to mainstream venues including the Hammersmith Palais by adding digital sampling to the mix in their music, while bhangra groups in the Midlands blended bhangra with house music.[§] But the ultimate fusion awaited—the mixture of Jamaican "ragamuffin" and African-American hip hop with "bhangra" to create the "bhangramuffin" sound of Apache Indian.

Steve Kapur took the name Apache Indian as a reference to his Punjabi ancestry and as a tribute to the Jamaican ragamuffin star "Super Cat," sometimes known as "the wild Apache."[¶] But he took his art from the cultural crossroads he negotiated every day. He told a reporter,

> As a young Asian in Britain, you constantly lead a double life. At home, everything is as it was—very traditional, very strict. But when you close the front door and move onto the streets everything changes. I've had so many relatives disown my family because of my love for reggae. Now, after hearing my music, and hearing the Indian influences in it, it appeals to them. But my music is first and foremost street music.[||]

---

[*] Sabita Banerji and Gerd Bauman, "Bhangra 1984–8: Fusion and Professionalization in a Genre of South Asian Dance Music," in Paul Oliver, ed., *Black Music in Britain*, 137–8.

[†] Ibid., 138.

[‡] Ibid., 146.

[§] Ibid., 142.

[¶] Thom Duffy, "Apache Indian's Asian-Indian Pop Scores U.K. Hit," *Billboard*, February 20, 1993, 82.

[||] Brooke Wentz, "Apache Indian," *Vibe* (November) 1993, 9.

For Apache Indian, the "street" is a place where Afro-Caribbean and South Asian youths learn from each other. As a teenager he wore his hair in dreadlocks, danced to the blues, and spent hours shopping for reggae records.** His first recording, "Move Over India," paid tribute to the India that he had only visited once but knew well from the Indian films that his parents watched "every time I went home."* Apache Indian knew that his music was a success when his West Indian neighbors began saying hello to him in Punjabi. His song "Come Follow Me" offers a hip hop history and travelogue of India for the edification of a West Indian friend who closes the number by telling Apache Indian that his country sounds "lovely, and next time you go send a ticket for me."†

Standing at the crossroads of Punjabi and Jamaican cultures, Apache Indian shows that Afro-Asian and Afro-Caribbean Britons share more than a common designation as Black people, that they share a common history of using culture to strengthen their communities from the inside and to attract support from the outside. Punjabis and Jamaicans both come from regions that contain diverse cultures and beliefs, and they both belong to populations that transnational capital has dispersed all over the globe. From their historical experiences at home no less from what they have learned in order to survive abroad, Punjabis and Jamaicans draw upon long-standing and rich traditions when they create cultural coalitions that transcend ethnic and political differences.

The music made by Apache Indian uses performance to call into being a community composed of Punjabis and Jamaicans, South Asians and West Indians, reggae fans and bhangra enthusiasts. But it also demonstrates the potential for all of Britain to learn a lesson from the extraordinary adaptability and creativity of its immigrant cultures. Apache Indian reads "British" culture selectively, by venerating Mahatma Gandhi and Bob Marley rather than Winston Churchill or George Frederick Handel. He assimilates into the culture of the country where he was born by proudly displaying the diverse identities that he has learned in its schools and streets. He creates problems for nation states with their narratives of discrete, homogeneous, and autonomous culture, but he solves problems for people who want cultural expressions as complex as the lives they live every day.

Yet, we should not let the brilliance and skill of Jamaican or Punjabi musicians in securing space for themselves within popular culture blind us to the harsh realities facing immigrants all over the world. Despised and degraded, they face unremitting racism and exploitation with few opportunities to communicate their condition to others. People making popular music for communities like these must address immediate issues of survival and self-respect within their group before they can think about reaching a larger audience.

For example, on the west coast of North America Los Tigres del Norte (the Tigers of the North) sing for and about migrant communities shuttling back and forth between the U.S.A. and Mexico. The five musicians in the band grew up poor in a rural family with eleven children and a disabled father. They have lived the lives they sing about in their songs, and constantly receive suggestions for new stories from farm workers who tell them about their troubles. With expressly political lyrics, they turn their listeners' lives into poignant and powerful songs. "We talk a lot about immigration," explained group leader Jorge Hernandez to a reporter, "because it has given problems to a lot of people. We talk about families who come from different

---

** Paul Bradshaw, "Handsworth Revolutionary," *Straight No Chaser*, no. 23 (Autumn) 1993, 13, 26.
* Ibid., 29.
† Brooke Wentz, "Apache Indian," 86; Apache Indian, *No Reservations*, Mango 162–539, 932–3.

countries to learn a different language and lose where they came from. We tell them it's important not to lose where you are from."[‡]

Los Tigres del Norte have appeared in ten Mexican films, sold millions of albums, and regularly draw huge crowds to their live performances. Yet they have secured almost no "mainstream" commercial recognition in the U.S.A., perhaps because they sing in Spanish in a country dominated by Anglophone markets, but also perhaps because their lyrics contain values that threaten vested interests too much. In "La Jaula de Oro" ('The Gilded Cage"), an undocumented worker laments his decade of labor in the U.S.A., claiming that "even if the cage is made of gold it does not cease being a prison."[*]

The mechanisms of commercial culture that deprive Los Tigres del Norte of exposure to a broader audience also deprive Anglo listeners of needed knowledge about their country. As Jose Cuellar, Chairman of San Francisco State's La Raza Studies Department observes, "Those of us who are English-dominant would learn a great deal of the needs and aspirations of our immigrant population, of their frustrated hopes, their frustrated dreams. In these songs, it's all there."[†]

Anti-immigrant and anti-foreign sentiment plagues de-industrialized nations in the West as well as de-Stalinized countries in the East. During times of economic decline and social disintegration, it is tempting for people to blame their problems on others, and to seek succor and certainty from racist and nationalist myths. But the desire to seek certainty and stability by depicting the world solely as one story told from one point of view is more dangerous than ever before. As technology and trade inevitably provide diverse populations with common (although not egalitarian) experiences, the ability to adapt, to switch codes, and to see things from more than one perspective becomes more valuable. In the last analysis, nation states may be best served by those who refuse to believe in their unified narratives, and who insist instead on cultural and political practices that delight in difference, diversity, and dialogue. These do not need to be conjured up by political theorists, or wished into existence by mystics and visionaries. They already exist (albeit in embryonic form) in the communities called into existence by rai, ragamuffin, bhangra, and many other unauthorized and unexpected forms that people have for understanding and changing the world in which they live.

Further Reading

Banerji, Sabita. "Ghazals to Bhangra in Great Britain." *Popular Music* 7 (May 1988): 207–13.

Erlmann, Veit. "The Aesthetics of the Global Imagination: Reflections on World Music in the 1990s." *Public Culture* 8 (1996): 467–87.

Feld, Steven, and Charles Keil, eds. *Music Grooves: Essays and Dialogues.* Chicago: University of Chicago Press, 1994.

Jatta, Sidia. "Born Musicians: Traditional Music from the Gambia." In *Repercussions: A Celebration of African-American Music*, ed. Geoffrey Haydon and Dennis Marks, 14–29. London: Century, 1985.

Manuel, Peter. *Caribbean Currents: Caribbean Music from Rumba to Reggae.* Philadelphia: Temple University Press, 1995.

Meintjes, Louise. "Paul Simon's *Graceland*, South Africa, and the Mediation of Musical Meaning." *Ethnomusicology* 34 (1990): 37–73.

Taylor, Timothy D. *Global Pop: World Music, World Markets.* New York: Routledge, 1997.

[‡]Carolyn Jung, "S.J. Band's Rhythms Transcend Borders," *San Jose Mercury News*, March 5, 1994, 10.

[*] Ibid., 10.

[†] Ibid., 10.

Discography

Best of Ska. Disky Records, 2002.

Cliff, Jimmy, and Various Artists. *The Harder They Come.* Island, 1972.

Cooder, Ry, and the Buena Vista Social Club. *The Buena Vista Social Club.* Nonesuch, 1997.

King Sunny Ade. *E Dide.* Atlantic/WEA, 1995.

Marley, Bob. *Legend—The Best of Bob Marley and the Wailers.* Def Jam, 2002.

Rough Guide to Bhangra Dance. World Music Network, 2006.

Rough Guide to Raï. World Music Network, 2002.

Simon, Paul. *Graceland.* Rhino/WEA, 2004.

Tougher than Tough: The Story of Jamaican Music. Mango, 1993.

81. Genre or Gender?

THE RESURGENCE OF THE SINGER-SONGWRITER

As almost any woman (and many men) who are interested in popular music will attest, a category or genre that is determined primarily by the gender of its participants is rather odd (though not necessarily any odder than one that is determined by race, a linkage that is largely taken for granted). Despite the inconsistencies of such a category, throughout the 1990s (and into the 2000s), publications could not resist special issues with titles such as "The Girl Issue" and "The Women of Rock," or articles with titles like "When Women Venture Forth" or "The Angry Young Woman."[1] While the female artists discussed in these articles were by no means consistent in terms of musical style, the surge of publisher and reader interest in the topic did derive from a general shift in how young women were conceiving their identities; this was reflected not only in an increased number of prominent female artists, but in the emergence of a different kind of

---

1. See "The Girl Issue," *Spin,* November 1997; "The Women of Rock," *Rolling Stone,* November 13, 1997 (*Rolling Stone* publishes a special issue with a title like this every few years); Ann Powers, "When Women Venture Forth," *New York Times,* October 9, 1994, sec. 2, 32, 39; Jon Pareles, "The Angry Young Women: The Labels Take Notice," *New York Times,* January 28, 1996, sec. 2, 24.

female artist. These musicians incorporated frank sexuality and some of the conventional signs of feminine attractiveness into a rebelliousness that was more aggressive than the second-wave feminism of the 1970s. Seemingly in tune with the critical perspective of books like Susan Faludi's *Backlash: The Undeclared War against Women*,[2] many of these women merged the confessional stance of the singer-songwriter with the confrontational attitude of punk, emphasizing the importance of female desires that did not revolve around the need for male approval. A number of these musicians—"alternative" artists such as Polly Jean Harvey, Liz Phair, and Björk—received a relatively large amount of critical acclaim and commercial success in the mid-1990s.

The release of Alanis Morissette's *Jagged Little Pill* (1995), the biggest-selling album of the 1990s, seemed to signify the triumph of a new sensibility—a successor to male-dominated alternative of the early 1990s. Morissette's success quickly occasioned its own backlash: despite the grunge-influenced first single, the vitriolic "You Oughta Know," those who listened to the whole album quickly realized that it had stronger links to the confessional singer-songwriter genre than to grunge. Despite this backlash, the years 1996–97 witnessed the success of numerous female artists. Sarah McLachlan (b. 1968), a singer-songwriter who had been overshadowed by Tori Amos (b. 1963) in the early 1990s, organized an all-female summer tour beginning in 1997, entitled "Lilith Fair," that presented female pop musicians in their own forum and appeared at the time to champion the triumph of a new kind of "girl culture."[3]

No one singer captured a more devoted following in the 1990s than Tori Amos, who released her first solo recording in 1991. A classically trained pianist and dynamic performer, Amos (according to Ann Powers) "cultivates a forthright sexuality that is more concerned with capturing what women feel than turning men on."[4] This 1996 interview with Amos finds her revisiting the issues of self-confession and autobiography that seem to appear whenever singer-songwriters are asked to talk about their music. The interview also reinvokes the ever-powerful opposition of formulaic commercialism versus authentic self-expression, an

---

2. And, I might add, with a scholarly counterpart such as Tania Modleski's *Feminism Without Women: Culture and Criticism in a "Postfeminist Age"* (New York: Routledge, 1991). Both Faludi and Modleski discuss the "backlash" against the gains made by feminism in the 1970s and the subsequent incorporation of feminist ideas and imagery into patriarchal narratives during the 1980s.

3. Lilith Fair was seen by the press as a symbol of the triumph of female musicians; see Christopher John Farley, "Galapalooza," *Time*, July 21, 1997, 60–64; Neal Karlen, "On Top of Pop, But Not with One Voice," *New York Times*, June 29, 1997; and Ann Powers, "Wannabes: Lilith Fair," *Village Voice*, August 5, 1997, 63–64.

4. Ann Powers, "When Women Venture Forth," *New York Times*, October 9, 1994, 39.

opposition with particular force in this genre, but one that Amos herself seems to call into question in her reverent discussion of the Beatles. The interview concludes with a humorous critique of one type of emotional expression that circulated widely in the 1990s: the angry despair of white, male rockers.

Tori Amos: Pain for Sale
Robert L. Doerschuk

Why do you write songs?

[Long thoughtful silence.] I remember walking down the hallways of the Peabody Conservatory and hearing the same piece being played in ten rooms, pretty much all the same. I knew that I couldn't play this piece better than any of these people. It would probably be very different: You'd know where the redhead was, you'd figure out which practice room I was in. But I'd never win any competitions, ever, because nobody was interested in my take on Debussy. I never won anything. I always got marked down. Always. I had big arguments with these people, that these guys were pushing the limits of music in their time, just like John Lennon in his time. To understand their music, you have to understand the time. You have to know what's going on around them, especially when there's no lyric, when it's all music. Nobody, I thought, ever got the feel right. So I knew that if I was just gonna be playing some dead guy's music for the rest of my life, I'd probably never get a hearing, because their impression of what the dead guy should sound like was not mine at all.

But going even further back, was there ever a time when something in you said, "I want to make my own notes and words"?

I was seven [at Peabody]. I already knew what I was going to do. It was over when I was seven, a done deal. I was already writing. I didn't know how good or not good I could be. I knew that I could probably figure it out musically, but word-wise I was writing "The Jackass and the Toad Song." But I've always been a bit of a romantic. I'd be five years old, lying on my bed, with the afghan over me, squeezing my legs together and thinking, "Something should go here one day." I wanted to run away with all those guys, with Zeppelin and Jim Morrison and John Lennon. I [recently] told Robert Plant that I really wanted to pack my peanut butter and jelly and my teddy and my trolls and come find him.

So even then the power of the songs being done by the people who wrote them was something you could feel.

Yeah, I was totally conscious of that at five. It's funny, because I think I'm more affected by those writers than the ones who were happening when I was in high school. I wasn't really affected by what was going on in 1979. I had checked out; I was listening to my old records. Somebody played me the Sex Pistols after they had come and gone, and I wee'd in my pants. I said, "Shit, my father never showed me that this existed." I felt absolutely inadequate when I heard the Sex Pistols and the Clash, going, "Where was I?" I mean, I made Zeppelin and the Beatles and all those people when I was five. . . . Actually, Zeppelin didn't hap-

---

Source: "Tori Amos: Pain for Sale" by Robert Doerschuk, November 1994, Keyboard Magazine/ New Bay Media.

pen until I was nine or ten, when I started to bleed, so it was totally perfect; I was all ready for Robert.

How did those sorts of influences affect your growth as a songwriter?

First of all, I cannot contrive a song. I'm not nailing people who can. I know some very good writers who I respect a lot. They're called to do something for a movie, and they come up with it in two weeks. They're not schlock writers; I'm talking about people who don't do hack jobs. They've got two weeks, and they're watching the film, and they're getting inspired. And I'm like, "How do you do that?" I don't care what you offer me right now. If the fairies don't sprinkle their little wee on my head, it's not gonna happen. I can't make it happen. Now, say I'm walking down the street, eating a banana, and something happens—four bars, with a sketchy lyric. If you gave me two weeks, maybe I could develop it, just on my skills and craft alone. I'm not telling you it would be great. It might be passable. But there are certain songs I look at and say, "I would not change a breath."

Those who can produce songs on demand tend to rely on certain formulas. Are you saying that it's best to avoid formulas in order to write more personal material?

Well, we have to remember that hit records and good songs are not synonymous. Maybe in the old days, a little bit. But now most hit records are not great songs. I'm not saying that those formula writers cannot stumble on something. But at a certain point, it's not about formula writing. I know I'm going back to the Beatles, just because that's a big point of reference, but how consistent can you get? "Eleanor Rigby"? "Norwegian Wood"? How many great songs and hit songs do you get? I remember John Lennon talking about listening to songs that he loved, then changing them to make his own versions. He would say, "God, I love this song. I wish I'd written this song." Then it would come out totally different. You might not even know what song it is that inspired you to do something, but there is that ingredient. Sometimes I do think that we're really just rewriting songs. There are only twelve bloody notes, you know. So I'll listen to some song and say, "Why didn't I write that?"

Because it speaks to you . . .

. . . as if I would have written it. I could name five songs, right off the top of my head, that I would have given my right arm to write. [Joni Mitchell's] "Case of You": You don't get it any better. A better song hasn't been written. I don't care what female singer/songwriter you throw up in my face: None has done anything in the league of "Case of You," me included. For a woman to be able to say what that says, with that kind of addiction and yet that kind of grace, is just not done. Even Zeppelin and those guys listened to Joni. It kills me when the metal guys or the hard-rocking guys who are more poseurs than anything will show up and say, "You know, all the guys in my band are embarrassed to like you, because they're into Zeppelin." And I'll say, "That's kind of funny, 'cause I just did a duet with Robert." I don't think people understand that with songwriters, it's not about volume, you know?

Commercial songwriters can be like caricaturists who scale complex emotions and issues down to bite size. You and other more personal writers are more like abstract painters.

You're right, but my intentions for writing have changed. There's a time when you want people to sing your songs with you. If you didn't, you'd keep them in your living room. Let's not lie to ourselves; that's the truth. Even though I could tell you I'm writing because it's my form of expression, there is a need—that is a fair word, I think—to have them shared. Sometimes I'll listen to work that I've done, and I'll go, "I'm not in that place anymore. I couldn't write like that if my life depended on it. But I do understand an element of it that I would like to have in, say, this next piece." I do like that approach of, like, peeling your skin off. Although the whole concept of *Under the Pink* is about peeling the skin off, that's more of an abstract work, whereas *Little Earthquakes* is more like a diary.

There must be a limit to how far you want to open that diary in your work.
Funny you should say that. Since before I wrote *Little Earthquakes* I've had a pact with myself of no censorship. See, if you're a songwriter and people don't really know who you are, that's one thing. But if you're singing your own songs, it's a little different in this respect: I've found that the more known a writer gets, the less powerful and exposing their work gets, because the more they get known, the less they want to expose. I've caught myself trying to censor recently, going, "Oh, my God, they're gonna know who that is." But this is not about putting names next to things. That's irrelevant. If people want to speculate, they've missed the point.

The paradox in this kind of writing is that the more you personalize, or Tori Amosize, your songs, the more universal they become to those who work to get inside them.
But I don't think that these are Tori Amos songs. I translate them in such a way because of Tori's experiences that would be different from so-and-so's experiences. Emotions are very simple. I don't find them complex at all, to be quite honest. Everybody understands basic emotions: feeling like a coward, wanting to kill some cunt and having no remorse about it. It's like, "No, I don't feel guilty about this. What I feel bad about is that I don't feel bad about this." That's what I have to look at. I try and crawl into my unconscious, and it's not that different from what's inside any of us. All of us have a bit of the vampire and a bit of the nightingale. But don't tell me that the hardest cats rockin' out there right now aren't afraid of pain. I'm just saying that, whatever your lifestyle, they're all bummed out that Mom's gone.

In his last work, John Lennon even turned domesticity into art.
Well, who says that just because you fall in love and you open your heart to somebody that you're not gonna have more passion, more angst, more to look at than you ever had? The more you expose yourself to different feelings, the more you have to draw on. Obviously, if you're in a complacent relationship, your work might sound that way. But why does growing have to be synonymous with complacency? There's so much self-destruction on the artist's side. Not necessarily on the hack's side. Hacks aren't self-destructive, because they've got a business to run. But the artist will do anything to keep the machine going. We're so afraid to write things that won't be accepted. Well, I believe that audiences get bored very quickly.

Bored with someone's output over a period of years?
Yeah, at a certain point. Maybe you know it even before they do, because you feel it.

How do you keep in touch with real life from within the cocoon of fame?
Look, if my whole life was . . .

Not your whole life.
Wait. If most of my life was about going into the studio, making the record, doing the video, doing the tour, living and breathing only that, at a certain point, what would I fucking write about? I know that. Now, there are some very good ones out there whose work is still about one kind of energy. Say it's anger: That's all it is. Well, guys, hello? Can we have maybe a different angle on your anger today? All the angry boys out there talk about how they can't have this stuff. Now, I adore angry boys. I'd make 'em all apple pie with cinnamon ice cream. But they all talk

about how they can't have this and they can't have that. They've got this whole movement based on what they can't have. And I say to them, wrong. It's a choice. They've chosen not to have certain things. And none of them takes any responsibility for that. Those boys are gonna get interesting when they start to go, "I chose not to have love." Come on, boys. Let's say something interesting for a change, instead of, "I can never have this or that." That's your choice, because you think you're shit. There's very little responsibility for their part in it. They don't own up to, "The reason I can't have love is because I think I'm gonna shrivel when I'm with this woman, because I don't think I deserve her." Let's go into the why. To go into that, you have to live. You're not gonna get to those answers by I-IV-V-fucking-I.

And it's not just the boys. Some of the girls do it too. Ay-yi-yi, can we stop blaming the guys here? We can blame them for what they've done, but then we have to balance in what we've done. The work isn't interesting when people aren't constantly discovering. We're stopping our lives as writers because we think we won't make great art. Who has put this thought out there? It's like a virus.

You're saying that there's a loss with respect to talented writers who could have said so much more before getting stuck on a single riff.

Totally that's what I'm saying. It is such a sense of loss. I'm not gonna mention names, but I'll watch something and go, "I know that this is very calculated." Once you've been on the other side, you know what it is and what it isn't. You just smell it. You're like, "This person has so much. They could go further than they ever thought they could go in their pain and their darkness." I've always said that Lucifer understands love better than anybody. You know he's done a mean tango with Greta Garbo a few times. Really understanding love is the only way you get to that side of things. Otherwise, you're just renting videos. It's HBO. These guys and girls who write about one more torture device over and over again? That doesn't scare them. That's not a challenge. And that's not challenging those kids who really are screaming. Talk about pain: If they want to experience pain, they should go hold hands with the Little Mermaid. Then they'll get scared shitless because they'll have to be real.

The pain industry that you're describing . . .

That's a great term for it. I guess I'm part of it too, in a sense.

. . . strips real pain of its validity. When people tire of hearing songs that tell them how miserable they should be, they're robbed of the opportunity to feel real misery.

And they become parodies of themselves. It's so theatrical. Where's the real experience, so that when you take it to theatrics the foundation is still strong? But when it's just about anger for anger's sake . . .

. . . you're describing the fashion rather than the guts.

It is a fashion, and it isn't really that deep. We can all be a bit seduced by it. There's a masochist in me too, but my masochist is getting a little bit bored. It's not getting satisfied by those guys anymore. It's like, "You think that's painful?" My God, Baudelaire and Rimbaud were talking about and experiencing the heart. But it's so easy to contrive something. You know, "We're marketing dismemberment this week. That seems to be what kids want, so we'll do it. No problem." The whole point is that dismemberment isn't darkness, is it? It's just dismemberment. It's like, that's why God created video, so that you don't have to do any work on yourself. It's just a good distraction, an alternative to getting to what darkness is. The music business is packaging darkness, but for the most part I think it's just a parody of darkness.

Look, I'm just saying that the writers' community has been given a drug. "Tori takes another step in her life, so she won't be able to write songs like 'Silent All These Years' anymore." Guess what? You're right. She'll never be able to write that again. So why is that a bad thing?

Further Reading

Farley, Christopher John. "Galapalooza." *Time,* July 21, 1997, 60–64.

Karlen, Neal. "On Top of Pop, But Not with One Voice." *New York Times,* June 29, 1997.

Pareles, Jon. "The Angry Young Women: The Labels Take Notice." *New York Times,* January 28, 1996, sec. 2, 24.

Powers, Ann. "Wannabes: Lilith Fair." *Village Voice,* August 5, 1997, 63–64.

_____. Tori Amos. *Piece by Piece.* New York: Random House, 2006.

Woodworth, Marc. *Solo: Women Singer-Songwriters in Their Own Words.* New York: Delta, 1998.

Discography

Amos, Tori. *Little Earthquakes.* Atlantic/WEA, 1992.

_____. *Tales of a Librarian: A Tori Amos Collection.* Atlantic/WEA, 2003.

Bush, Kate. *The Dreaming.* Capitol, 1982.

_____. *The Whole Story.* Capitol, 1986.

Chapman, Tracy. *Collection.* WEA International, 2001.

Harvey, P. J. *To Bring You My Love.* Island, 1995.

McLachlan, Sarah. *Surfacing.* BMG, 1997.

Morissette, Alanis. *Jagged Little Pill.* Maverick, 1995.

Vega, Suzanne. *Solitude Standing.* A&M, 1987.

_____. *Retrospective: The Best of Suzanne Vega.* Interscope, 2003.

Wilson, Cassandra. *Blue Light Til' Dawn.* Blue Note Records, 1993.

82. Public Policy and Pop Music History Collide

Although public policy in the United States has affected the radio and recording industries since their inception—most spectacularly in the 1940s with laws that first eased restrictions on playing recorded music on the radio and then encouraged the spread of nonnetwork radio broadcasting—one development in the 1990s had particularly dramatic consequences. For those who wondered what the homogeneity of U.S. radio in the late 1990s and the dominance of teen pop had in common, one need look no further than the 1996 Telecommunications Act. A law that loosened restrictions on how many radio stations could be owned by a single company led to an unprecedented concentration of programming and, hence, to the sense that all radio broadcasts were emanating from an amorphous, all-American nowhere land. After 1996, as corporate entities such as Clear Channel bought as many as 1,200 radio stations throughout the country, one could hear the same classic rock/modern rock/adult contemporary, etc. playlists whether driving through Maine or Montana.

The oligopolistic nature of these companies gave them enormous clout: if a new recording gained access to their playlist, it was guaranteed a huge audience; on the other hand, the lack of access created sizable barriers to large-scale success. The teen pop being produced in Orlando, Florida, with consummate skill (N'Sync, Britney Spears, Backstreet Boys, and the like) was eminently well suited to the conservative aesthetic and social vision of the programmers at media behemoths such as Clear Channel. While teen pop had long been an important component of popular music, it had never achieved success on such a grand scale. The appearance of teen pop stars on the cover of *Rolling Stone* (a sure sign that the by-now venerable publication was experiencing an identity crisis), on college students' lists of favorite artists, and on MTV's "Total Request Live" countdown showed teen pop boldly going into audiences and media where it had rarely gone before. This development spoke to the symbiosis between changes in consumption and the way media (especially radio) were operating.

Jenny Toomey's involvement with music is remarkably diverse: as a solo singer-guitarist and member of many bands, including Edith Frost, Tsunami, and Liquorice; as cochair of Simple Machines Records; and as director of the Future of Music Coalition, a political organization that works for the improvement of conditions for musicians. In the following article, she analyzes the impact of the 1996 Telecommunications Act, mentioning the ominous spectre of ever further deregulation and its impact.[1]

---

1. For another view of the 1996 Telecommunications Act that details its potentially disastrous impact on the loss of local broadcasting in alerting the public in the event of emergencies (as well as on the decrease in protest music on the radio), see Brent Staples, "The Trouble with Corporate Radio: The Day the Protest Music Died," *New York Times,* February 20, 2003. Jenny Eliscu also addresses the issue in "Why Radio Sucks," *Rolling Stone,* April 3, 2003, 22. In another nearly contemporary editorial, Paul Krugman reveals the close links of Clear Channel to the George W. Bush administration and the role of the network in organizing prowar rallies before and during the 2003 invasion of Iraq even as Clear Channel lobbied for further deregulation; see Paul Krugman, "Channels of Influence," *New York Times,* March 25, 2003.

Empire of the Air
Jenny Toomey

For too long, musicians have had too little voice in the manufacture, distribution and promotion of their music and too little means to extract fair support and compensation for their work. The Future of Music Coalition was formed in June 2000 as a not-for-profit think tank to tackle this problem, advocating new business models, technologies and policies that would advance the cause of both musicians and citizens. Much of the work the FMC has done in the past two years has focused on documenting the structures of imbalance and inequity that impede the development of an American musicians' middle class, and translating legislative-speak into language the musicians and citizens can understand. Our most challenging work, however, and the project of which we are most proud, is our analysis of the effects of radio deregulation on musicians and citizens since the passage of the 1996 Telecommunications Act.

Radio is a public resource managed on citizens' behalf by the federal government. This was established in 1934 through the passage of the Communications Act, which created a regulatory body, the Federal Communications Commission, and laid the ground rules for the regulation of radio. The act also determined that the spectrum would be managed according to a "trusteeship" model. Broadcasters received fixed-term, renewable licenses that gave them exclusive use of a slice of the spectrum for free. In exchange, they were required to serve the "public interest, convenience and necessity." Though they laid their trust in the mechanics of the marketplace, legislators did not turn the entire spectrum over to commercial broadcasters. The 1934 act included some key provisions that were designed to foster localism and encourage diversity in programming.

Although changes were made to limits on ownership and FCC regulatory control in years hence, the Communications Act of 1934 remained essentially intact until it was thoroughly overhauled in 1996 with the passage of the Telecommunications Act. But even before President Clinton signed the act into law in February 1996, numerous predictions were made regarding its effect on the radio industry:

- The number of individual radio-station owners would decrease. Those in the industry with enough capital would begin to snatch up valuable but underperforming stations in many markets—big and small.
- Station owners—given the ability to purchase more stations both locally and nationally—would benefit from economies of scale. Radio runs on many fixed costs: Equipment, operations and staffing costs are the same whether broadcasting to one person or 1 million. Owners knew that if they could control more than one station in a local market, they could consolidate operations and reduce fixed expenses. Lower costs would mean increased profit potential. This would, in turn, make for more financially sound radio stations, which would be able to compete more effectively against new media competitors: cable TV and the Internet.
- There was a prediction based on a theory posited by a 1950s economist named Peter Steiner that increased ownership consolidation on the local

Source: "Empire of the Air," Jenny Toomey Reprinted with permission from the January 13, 2002 issue of *The Nation.*

level would lead to a subsequent increase in the number of radio format choices available to the listening public. (Steiner, writing in 1952, was not talking about oligopolistic control of the market by a few firms, as we have in the United States; rather, he was basing his predictions on an analysis of BBC radio, which is a nationally owned radio monopoly, not an oligopoly.) According to Steiner's theory, a single owner with multiple stations in a local market wouldn't want to compete against himself. Instead, he would program each station differently to meet the tastes of a variety of listeners.

But what really happened?

Well, one prediction certainly came true: The 1996 act opened the floodgates for ownership consolidation. Ten parent companies now dominate the radio spectrum, radio listenership and radio revenues, controlling two-thirds of both listeners and revenue nationwide. Two parent companies in particular—Clear Channel and Viacom—together control 42 percent of listeners and 45 percent of industry revenues.

Consolidation is particularly extreme in the case of Clear Channel. Since passage of the Telecommunications Act, Clear Channel has grown from forty stations to 1,240 stations—thirty times more than Congressional regulation previously allowed. No potential competitor owns even one-quarter the number of Clear Channel stations. With more than 100 million listeners, Clear Channel reaches more than one-third of the US population.

Even more bleak is the picture at the local level, where oligopolies control almost every market. Virtually every local market is dominated by four firms controlling 70 percent of market share or greater. In smaller markets, consolidation is more extreme. The largest four firms in most small markets control 90 percent of market share or more. These companies are sometimes regional or national station groups and not locally owned.

Only the few radio-station owners with enough capital to buy additional stations have benefited from deregulation. Station owners have consolidated their operations on a local level, frequently running a number of stations out of a single building, sharing a single advertising staff, technicians and on-air talent. In some cases, radio-station groups have further reduced costs by eliminating the local component almost entirely. Local deejays and program directors are being replaced by regional directors or even by voice-tracked or syndicated programming, which explains a marked decrease in the number of people employed in the radio industry.

Prior to 1996, radio was among the least concentrated and most economically competitive of the media industries. In 1990 no company owned more than fourteen of the more than 10,000 stations nationwide, with no more than two in a single local market. But we found that local markets have now consolidated to the point that just four major radio groups control about 50 percent of the total listener audience and revenue. Clearly, deregulation has reduced competition within the radio industry.

As a result, listeners are losing. With an emphasis on cost-cutting and an effort to move decision-making out of the hands of local station staff, much of radio has become bland and formulaic. Recall Steiner's hopeful theory that an owner would not want to compete against his own company and would therefore operate stations with different programming. We found evidence to the contrary: Radio companies regularly operate two or more stations with the same format—for example, rock, country, adult contemporary, top 40—in the same local market. In a recent *New York Times* article, "Fewer Media Owners, More Media Choices," FCC chairman Michael Powell denied this, propping up Steiner's theory by saying things like, "Common ownership can lead to more diversity—what does the owner get for having duplicative products?" But we found 561 instances of format redundancy nationwide—a parent company operating two or more stations in the same market, with the same format—amounting to massive missed opportunities for variety.

Still, from 1996 to 2000, format variety—the average number of formats available in each local market—actually increased in both large and small markets. But format variety is not equivalent to true diversity in programming, since formats with different names have similar playlists. For example, alternative, top 40, rock and hot adult contemporary are all likely to play songs by the band Creed, even though their formats are not the same. In fact, an analysis of data from charts in *Radio and Records* and *Billboard's Airplay Monitor* revealed considerable playlist overlap—as much as 76 percent—between supposedly distinct formats. If the FCC or the National Association of Broadcasters is sincerely trying to measure programming "diversity," doing so on the basis of the number of formats in a given market is a flawed methodology.

This final point may be the most critical one as we face an FCC that is poised to deregulate media even further in the next few months. (In September, the commissioners voted unanimously to open review of the FCC's media ownership rules.) It is time to put to bed the commonly held yet fundamentally flawed notion that consolidation promotes diversity—that radio-station owners who own two stations within a marketplace will not be tempted to program both stations with the same songs. There's a clear corporate benefit in "self-competition," and it's time we made regulatory agencies admit that fact.

Even in the beginning, radio was regulated to cultivate a commercial broadcast industry that could grow to serve the greatest number of Americans possible. As the decades have passed, most calls for deregulation have come from incumbent broadcasters interested in lifting local and national ownership caps that protect against the competitive pressures in other media.

While the effects of deregulation have been widely studied and discussed, scrutiny is focused on the profitability of the radio industry. But the effect of increased corporate profitability on citizens is rarely, if ever, discussed. Radical deregulation of the radio industry allowed by the Telecommunications Act of 1996 has not benefited the public. Instead, it has led to less competition, fewer viewpoints and less diversity in programming. Substantial ethnic, regional and economic populations are not provided the services to which they are entitled. The public is not satisfied, and possible economic efficiencies of industry consolidation are not being passed on to the public in the form of improved local service. Deregulation has damaged radio as a public resource.

Musicians are also suffering because of deregulation. Independent artists have found it increasingly difficult to get airplay; in payola-like schemes, the "Big Five" music companies, through third-party promoters, shell out thousands of dollars per song to the companies that rule the airwaves. That's part of why the Future of Music Coalition undertook this research. We at the FMC firmly believe that the music industry as it exists today is fundamentally anti-artist. In addition to our radio study, our projects—including a critique of standard major-label contract clauses, a study of musicians and health insurance, and a translation of the complicated Copyright Arbitration Royalty Panel proceedings that determined the webcasting royalty rates—were conceived as tools for people who are curious about the structures that impede musicians' ability to both live and make a living. Understanding radio deregulation is another tool for criticizing such structures. We have detailed the connections between concentrated media ownership, homogenous radio programming and restricted radio access for musicians. Given that knowledge, we hope artists will join with other activists and work to restore radio as a public resource for all people.

Further Reading

Eliscu, Jenny. "Why Radio Sucks." *Rolling Stone,* April 3, 2003, 22.
Krugman, Paul. "Channels of Influence." *New York Times*, March 25, 2003.
Staples, Brent. "The Trouble with Corporate Radio: The Day the Protest Music Died." *New York Times*, February 20, 2003.

Discography

Backstreet Boys. *The Hits—Chapter One.* Jive, 2001.
'N Sync. *'N Sync.* RCA, 1998.
Spears, Britney. *Greatest Hits: My Prerogative.* Jive, 2004.
_____. *Oops! . . . I Did It Again.* Jive, 2000.

83. Electronica Is in the House

After its tremendous efflorescence in the late 1970s, disco assumed a lower profile during the 1980s. Yet electronically based dance music maintained a lively existence in clubs, and DJs and studio producers never ceased producing variations on grooves that would prompt listeners to shake their booties. While many pop stars, most notably Madonna, brought some of these developments to the wider pop music audience, during the 1980s many of the changes in dance music remained out of the view of the mainstream. Frankie Knuckles in Chicago at the Warehouse Club and Larry Levan in New York City extended the embrace of purely synthesized sound initiated by Giorgio Moroder in Eurodisco. The new recordings produced for clubs like the Warehouse (largely black and mostly gay) emphasized those aspects of disco that the "disco sucks" crowd had found the most alienating, further "dehumanizing" their dance music with "tracks" that were often no more than rhythm patterns realized on drum machines. The new producers and DJs then superimposed simple synthesizer patterns and maybe a few chanted phrases sung by an African American woman onto these rhythm tracks.

Concurrently during the early and mid-1980s, DJs and record producers in Detroit, including Derrick May, Juan Atkins, and Kevin Saunderson, began producing recordings that sought to extend the futuristic techno sound of European groups such as Kraftwerk (at around the same time as Afrika Bambaataa used Kraftwerk as the basis for electro-funk). The resultant dance genre, "techno," moved at a slightly faster tempo than house and emphasized experimental "noisy" timbres rather than the remnants of disco elegance still prominent in house. According to Jon Savage, "Derrick May once described techno as 'just like Detroit, a complete mistake. It's like George Clinton and Kraftwerk stuck in an elevator.'"[1]

Beginning in 1986–87, both techno and house (and its psychedelicized descendant, acid house) began to catch on in the United Kingdom and Europe. "Techno," the umbrella term used in the United Kingdom for electronic dance music, rapidly split off in numerous directions. One of these, "hardcore," emerged around 1990 in the context of "raves": huge, all-night dance parties in which a large number of the participants ingested psychedelic drugs, especially MDMA, or Ecstasy. DJs achieved their reputations through their ability to produce sounds that were appealing to listeners in this particular altered state. Hardcore specialized in industrial "noise" and industrial-strength beats, joining the relentless four-to-the-bar bass drum of techno with syncopated patterns derived from the breakbeats beloved by hip-hop DJs. Another development, "ambient" or "intelligent" techno, relied on slightly slower tempos and softer, "spacier" sounds and was designed either for listening or for "chilling out" at the end of a night-long bacchanal. Ambient techno also drew on the latent avant-garde aspect of electronic music, tracing the interest back both to Kraftwerk's interest in futurism and to Brian Eno's percussionless "ambient" music.

Raves reached the United States in the early 1990s, but the development from the United Kingdom that really attracted the attention of the music press in the States was "jungle." Developing out of hardcore, jungle speeded up the tempo to ca. 160 bpm ("beats per minute"—the typical house track is around 125 bpm) and sampled dance-hall reggae drum patterns, often further scrambling them with a computer once they were sampled. The most rhythmically complex form of electronic dance music, jungle joins these fast, dauntingly syncopated drum patterns with slow-moving bass lines and ethereal, sustained synthesizer parts. An important sociological factor of jungle was its connection to the black British community, leading some commentators to view

---

1. Jon Savage, "Machine Soul: A History of Techno," *Village Voice Rock and Roll Quarterly* (Summer 1993): 19.

it as the British corollary to gangsta rap.[2] The origins of the term "jungle" were debated, but by the end of 1995, the term "drum 'n' bass" seemed to have replaced "jungle," presumably because of its less-racist connotations.

Another term, "electronica," began to come into play during 1996–97 as part of a larger campaign to promote electronic music as the next big thing in American popular music. Drum 'n' bass, trip hop, and big beat were all subgenres that featured prominently. While electronica never really became the next grunge, it has established itself as part of the larger field of North American popular music. Some artists, such as the Chemical Brothers (exemplars of "big beat") and Moby, have achieved mainstream recognition and success, while "ill-beint" and "trip hop" artists (like DJ Spooky, Tricky, and DJ Shadow) have pushed the artsy envelope. Electronic music's subgenres continue to proliferate at an amazing rate, making electronica the successor to indie-rock in terms of what it requires from its fans for insider status.[3]

The preceding passages offer only the barest sketch of electronic dance music in the 1980s and 1990s. For a fuller discussion, readers should turn to Simon Reynolds, *Generation Ecstasy: Into the World of Techno and Rave Culture*, the fullest treatment of the history presented here.[4] In the next entry, Reynolds discusses many of the factors that separate electronica from other forms of post–rock 'n' roll popular music, factors that are central to the enjoyment of its fans and the revulsion felt by its detractors. Not surprisingly, the issues that emerge bear more than a passing resemblance to those discussed in Chapter 57 in reference to disco.

As with discussions of the value of disco, dismissals of electronic dance music (EDM) can be related to the role of EDM in gay and lesbian identification. Thus, the overt artificiality of EDM may constitute a threat to the sincerity and substance found (or heard) in other, more critically sanctioned genres.[5]

---

2. Simon Reynolds, "Will Jungle Be the Next Craze from Britain?" *New York Times*, August 6, 1995, sec. 2, 28.

3. This aspect of electronic dance music is the focus of Sarah Thornton's *Club Cultures: Music, Media and Subcultural Capital* (Hanover, N.H.: Wesleyan University Press and University Press of New England, 1996).

4. Simon Reynolds, *Generation Ecstasy: Into the World of Techno and Rave Culture* (New York: Routledge, [1998] 1999). An excellent earlier overview is provided by Jon Savage, "Machine Soul," 18–21. A more recent overview may be found in Bill Werde, "Talking Music: Sounds from the Dance Floor," *New York Times*, March 24, 2000.

5. For more on the social context of rave culture, see Matthew Collins, *Altered State: The Story of Ecstasy Culture and Acid House* (London: Serpent's Tail, 1997); for an account of the role of raves in the "gay circuit" of dance parties, see Mireille Silcott, *Rave America: New School Dancescapes* (Toronto: ECW Press, 1999).

Historia Electronica Preface
Simon Reynolds

Every so often, people ask me: "Why are you so into electronic music and this whole dance culture thing? What's it all about? What makes it different?" Some add a slightly combative edge to the question, pointing out that there's always been "dance music," and that anyway people will dance to any music if they like it, even a group as overtly non-funky as The Smiths or REM. If they're really sharp, these people also point out that almost all pop today is "electronic," using synthesizers, sequencers, sampling, and digital editing software like Pro Tools, or processing "natural" acoustic sounds like the human voice or drums through effects, filters, and studio sorcery of all kinds. And after all, what's an electric guitar if not an electronic instrument?

These are all good points, but the fact remains that electronic dance culture is a distinct entity. What follows here is my attempt to sketch the broad foundational principles that give electronic dance music its coherence as a defined cultural field. Not every exponent of this music, not every scene or genre, fits each single criteria, and some actively flout "the rules." But taken en masse, these parameters define a kind of "field of possibility" within which the vast, variegated sprawl of electronic dance exists. For sure, it's a terrain with porous boundaries, through which seep influences from neighbouring areas of music. Sonically, the most influential of these neighbours are hip hop, avant-garde electronic experimentalism, industrial, and dub reggae. In terms of attitudes and values, rock in all its various forms, from psychedelia to punk, has had the most impact on electronic dance culture. From full-on rave madness to self-consciously avant-garde experimentalism, electronica has become the inheritor of rock's seriousness: its belief that music can change the world (or at least an individual's consciousness), rock notions of "progression" or "subversion," the conviction that music needs to be more than entertainment. Yet at the same time, the founding principles I sketch below frequently challenge and dismantle rock ideas of how creativity works, what defines art, and where the meaning and power of music is located.

1. Machine Music

Dance music isn't unique in being obsessed with technology: rock has its share of songs hymning cars, while guitars are fetishized as noise-weapons. But electronica goes further by defining itself as machine-music. This is upfront in the genre name "techno," and it comes through in the reverence for specific pieces of equipment: drum machines like the Roland 808 and Roland 909 to antique synths like the Moog and Wasp. You even have artists naming themselves in homage to gear: House of 909, 808 State, Q-Bass (a pun on the Cubase programming software). And you can see the cult of machinery in names that sound hyper-technical, robotic, or like models of cars or computers: Electribe 101, LFO, Nexus 21. Electronic musicians also love to describe what they do as scientific research, imagining the studio as a sound-laboratory.

Electronic music is driven by a quest to find the most radical or futuristic-sounding potential in brand-new technology. And that involves essentially (re)inventing the machines: producers are always claiming the first thing they do after

Source: "Historia Electronica Preface" © Simon Reynolds, *Loops: Una Historia de la Musica Electronica* (Reservoir Books).

acquiring new gear is to throw away the instruction manual and start messing around. Often creativity entails abusing the machines, employing them incorrectly. Mistakes—sometimes genuinely accidental, sometimes "deliberate errors"—become aestheticized. This is a pop echo of the 20th-Century classical avant-garde's project of pushing the envelope of what is conventionally regarded as "music," via the incorporation of noise-sound and environmental sonorities.

You can hear this in the contemporary genre of "glitch," where artists like Oval and Fennesz make radically beautiful music using the snaps, crackles and pops emitted by damaged CDs, malfunctioning software, etc. In dancefloor genres like speed garage and jungle, you can hear the same approach in the deliberate misuse of timestretching, a digital effect that allows a sample to be compressed or prolonged in duration without its pitch going up or down. Previously when producers speeded up a vocal sample to fit the ever-faster tempos of dance music, the effect was squeaky and cartoon-absurd, like the vocalist had inhaled helium. Timestretch was invented to enable producers to achieve pleasanter, more "musical" results, but ironically it's been seized on for the opposite effect: stretching out a vocal until the sample cracks up, creating a terrifying metallic rattle like a stuttering robot.

Even when machines aren't being used in ways never intended by the manufacturer, electronic dance music aestheticizes the mechanistic and industrial-sounding—sonic attributes opposite to the traditional musicianly premium on hands on "feel" and nimble dexterity. In electronic music, the cold precision and uninflected regularity of drum-machine beats and sequenced basslines aren't considered unmusical or lacking in "swing." Riffs tend to be angular rather than curvaceous; timbres are blatantly synthetic and artificial-sounding (unlike in pop music, where synthesisers are mostly used to inexpensively simulate acoustic instruments like horns or strings). The very inhuman aura of electronic music is part of the culture's obsession with the future, whether that is conceived as a utopia of streamlined pleasure-tech, or a dystopia of control and automation.

A lot of electronica is not "played" in any traditional instrumental sense, but is assembled using computers. Riffs are "step-written" one note at a time on a sequencer (sometimes resulting in note-patterns that would be unplayable by human hands). With the ever-more complex "virtual studio technology" software that's available, you can "draw" the music on a computer screen as a visually represented waveform; sonic material can be endlessly edited and recombined, layered and subjected to all kinds of treatments and effects. As a result, what you hear rarely correlates with physical human actions in the way that the sounds in rock music (even heavily studio-manipulated and overdubbed rock) still correlate to recognisable manual gestures. So you rarely visualize a person or band when you hear electronic music. Some find this unnerving, an erasure of humanity, but for others it frees up the imagination: the music becomes an intricate, maze-like environment, or an abstract machine taking the listener on a journey through a soundscape.

2. Texture/Rhythm Versus Melody/Harmony

Another aspect of electronica's break with traditional musicality is the way that processing is more important than playing; the vivid, ear-catching textures matter more than the actual notes played. For conventionally trained musicians, the chord progressions and harmonic intervals used in electronic music can seem obvious and trite. But this misses the point, for the real function of the simple vamps and melody-lines is as a device to display timbre, texture, tone-colour, chromatics. That's why so much electronica uses naive child-like melodies that sound like a music-box's chimes. Complicated melodies would distract from the sheer lustrous materiality of sound-in-itself; the pigment is more important than the line. Recent technology like DSP (digital signal processing) and "plug-ins" (the computer age equivalent to guitar effects pedals) allow for a fantastical palette of timbral colours.

In electronic dance, every element works as both texture and rhythm. Beats are filtered to sound metallic, crunchy, spongy, shiny, wet. Melodic units are mostly simple, little vamps and riffs that work as rhythmic cogs interlocking to form a groove. And rhythm usurps the place of melody. In much of this music, it's the drum patterns—off-kilter breakbeat arrangements in drum 'n' bass, intricate hi-hat figures in house and garage—that are the hooks, the most memorable element of a track. Each year the rhythmic subdivision of time gets ever more fantastically complex: micro-syncopations, assymetrical patterns riddled with hesitations, multiple tiers of polyrhythm. Factor in DSP treatment of the beats and the spatial distribution of drums across the stereo-mix, and the result is a kind of rhythmic psychedelia.

3. You're So Physical

With almost everything in the music working as rhythm, electronic dance is supremely physical music, engaging the body's psychomotor reflexes and tugging at your limbs. But this doesn't make the music "mindless." Rather, electronic dance music dissolves the old dichotomy between head and body, between "serious" music for home-listening and "stupid" music for the dancefloor. As British critic Kodwo Eshun argues, at its most sophisticated electronica makes your mind dance and your body think. There is a kinaesthetic intelligence in this music that involves your muscles and nerves, and which is seen at its utmost in the extraordinary grace and fractal fluidity of the dancing style, "liquid," that's popular at American raves. Yet still you get people who uphold a dichotomy between music for listening and music for dancing. Actually, a good dancer is "listening" with every sinew and tendon in her body.

Electronic dance is intensely physical in another sense: it's designed to be heard over massive club sound systems. Sound becomes a fluid immersive medium enfolding the body in an intimate pressure of beat and bass. The low-end frequencies permeate your flesh, make your body vibrate and tremble. The entire body becomes an ear.

4. Against Interpretation

Electronic music appeals to the mind in a quite particular way, however. Not by engaging the listener's interpretative mechanism (the traditional rock mode of treating songs as stories or statements), but rather through heightening perception through the sheer intricacy of the music: its rhythmic detail, otherworldly textures, and spatial depth. Most of this music is devoid of lyrics, and when it does have them, they tend to be simple catchphrases or cliched evocations of celebration, hope, intensity, mystical feelings. Ultimately, this music is not really about communication but about communion: a sensory unity experienced by everybody on the dancefloor. Hence the slogan "House is a feeling," used in countless dance tracks. The word "feeling" refers both to an emotional mood (elation tinged with a hint of blues, the sense of the club space as a blissful sanctuary circumscribed by a hostile, unstable outside world) and to a physical sensation: the waves of sound caressing your body, the collective feeling of being locked in a groove, every body in the house synchronized, entrained to the same rhythmic cycle, on the same track. Dance tracks are like vehicles, taking you on a journey, a pleasure-ride; there's a reason DJs use the term "train wreck" to describe when they do a bad mix between records.

The vagueness of the saying "house is a feeling" contains its own eloquence: this sensational sensation is hard to verbalize, almost impossible to explain to those who've never felt it. It bypasses "meaning" in the rock sense but is intensely meaningful. Hence dance music's recurrent use of religious imagery, its references to a knowledge that is privy only to initiates: slogans like "you know the score," "this is for those who know." Crucial distinction: this secret knowledge isn't elitist, but it is tribal, working through a powerful inclusion/exclusion effect.

5. Surface Versus Depth

People coming to this music from "outside"—that's to say with no direct club experience—often complain about an "emptiness" to the music: the sense that it is superficial, lacking in real-world referents, mere escapism. One of the most radical aspects of the music, though, is the way that electronica abolishes the depth model used by most criticism (in which some art is profound, some shallow) because all its pleasures are out there on the surface. The music is a flat plane of sensuous bliss.

You can see this in the way dance music uses the human voice. House divas have always been somewhat anonymous and depersonalized, rarely being the star focus of a song but more like a technically skilled artisan playing a role in a team effort. As the music evolved, producers increasingly used vocals in a non-expressive way, treating the singer as a source of raw material, a plastic substance to be folded, snipped, recombined, processed. From the simple voice-riffs in early house music (vocal samples distributed across a sampling keyboard and played, so that the voice becomes just an instrumental color) this has evolved into the complicated "vocal science" in today's 2step garage. Here samples from R&B songs are chopped up, resequenced, and turned into percussive elements of the groove, effectively transforming the singer into an adjunct to the drum kit. "Soul" is emptied out, and the human voice becomes two-dimensional, just one of an array of special effects and sonic pyrotechnics.

This depersonalising of the voice connects to a general anxiety that many people feel about electronic music: because it is not "saying" anything, its pleasures seem vicarious, indulgent, mere empty hedonism devoid of spiritual nourishment. Often detractors use metaphors like "ear-candy" to convey this sense of something that isn't good for you but just offers an empty sugar-rush.

6. Drug Me

Talking of getting a rush, electronic dance music is intimately bound up with drug culture. Even when it isn't designed explicitly to enhance drugs like Ecstasy, the way the music works on the listener is drug-like, and seems to demand drug metaphors. People use the music as a mood-modifier, something that swiftly transports them into a different emotional state with no necessary connection to their life-situation.

Drugs have played a crucial role in dance music's evolution. Specific music-technology innovations have synergized with particular drugs at different points: for instance, Ecstasy meshed with the trippy bass-patterns of the Roland 303 bass-synthesiser to catalyze the acid house revolution of the late Eighties. Changing drug use patterns also propel the music's evolution: escalating Ecstasy and amphetamine use in the early Nineties caused techno to get faster and faster, leading to hyperkinetic styles like jungle and gabba. Ultimately, what has happened is that the drug-sensations get encoded into the music, abstracted. By itself, the music trips you out, stones you, gives you a speed-rush.

This drug-tech interface syndrome is not unique to dance music, of course. You can see it with psychedelic rock (LSD coincided with the arrival of 24 track studios), and even late Seventies soft rock (the endlessly overdubbed guitar lines and excessively shiny sound of The Eagles or Fleetwood Mac reflect superstar cocaine abuse—the cocaine ear likes bright treble frequencies and tiny detailed sounds, while stimulant abuse makes people obsessive-compulsive, fussy, perfectionist). Electronic dance music is unique, however, in the way it has developed an entire musical language of sounds, riffs, and effects that are explicitly designed to trigger Ecstasy rushes or accompany the aural hallucinations induced by LSD, the coma-like dissassocation caused by ketamine, etc. Moreover, because drug-states are essentially excursions outside normal consciousness, a lot of this music can be seen as involving temporary trips into insanity and schizophrenia: the paranoid rhythmic delirium of jungle, the catatonic trance of minimal techno DJs like Richie Hawtin, the psychotic fury of gabba.

7. This Is a Journey into Sound

Electronic dance music is all about being lost in music, whether it's being engulfed by the sonic tsunami streaming out of a gigantic rave sound system, or being meditatively absorbed by the microscopic sonic events that pervade more experimental forms of electronica. These states of ego loss and oceanic connection, of being overwhelmed or entranced, are the reason why drug imagery is central to electronic imagination. And they also explain the recourse to religious language, whether taken from the Christian mystical tradition of surrender and Gnostic grace, or Eastern spiritual notions of nirvana and kundalini.

In some Eastern religions, the universe is sounded into being; hearing is the primary sense. Electronic dance culture likewise overthrows sight in the Western hierarchy of the senses, which privileges the eye. There's a good reason why clubs take place in the dark, why some warehouse raves are almost pitch black: diminishing the visual makes sound more vivid. Retinal perception is eclipsed by the audio-tactile, a vibrational continuum in which sound is so massively amplified it's visceral. This orientation toward sound can be seen in the way that ravers will literally hug speakers stacks, sometimes even climbing inside the bass-woofer's cavity and curling up like a foetus.

Beyond this worship of sound, electronic dance culture resists the tyranny of the visual in pop culture. The electronica revolution will not be televised (at least, not without being hugely compromised). Video channels like MTV are looking for stellar faces and heavenly bodies, but electronica promos tend not to feature either (indeed the video signature of some artists—The Chemical Brothers, Fatboy Slim—is only appearing in their own promos for a few seconds!). Success in pop depends on videogenic charisma, dance moves, even acting skill (with videos increasingly like mini-movies). All this is irrevelant to electronic dance music, which is simply not in the business of selling personalities. Moreover, electronic dance music simply sounds terrible through a television's mono speakers and non-existent bass: it is mixed for big club sound systems, with panoramic stereo and seismic sub-bass. A large proportion of this record's auditory content is inaudible on a television set.

Part of electronica's "underground"-ness relates to precisely this refusal of our contemporary culture of the icon. Video is about spectatorship, whereas dance culture is about participation. And so the more underground a club is, the less there will be in terms of visual distractions: the more hardcore the scene, the less there is to be seen. Clubs will always skimp on visuals and decor before cutting back on the sound-system. Many rock fans who go to see a DJ spin or a dance outfit play "live" find it dull because there's nothing to look at: no theatrics, no performance vocabulary of flamboyant gestures as there is with rock—just a few unglamorous looking guys twiddling knobs on machines. But that misses the point, because you're not supposed to focus on the artist. The crowd is the star.

8. Faceless Techno Bollocks

When rave culture first took off in the UK, some diehard rock fans started to rail against "faceless techno bollocks." Soon the slogan started appearing on T-shirts, but worn by techno fans who'd flipped it around into a badge of pride. In its purest forms, electronic dance music is a revolt against celebrity culture and the cult of personality. Artists deliberately seek anonymity by adopting an array of alter-egos. Marc Acardipane, the German hardcore techno pioneer, may have the world record, having used over twenty different pseudonyms. Richard D. James illustrates how contact with the record business can conventionalize someone's career: early on, he used multiple aliases, but as he became an iconic figure with a long-term album deal, he started to release his output via only one identity, Aphex Twin.

Sometimes there are pragmatic reasons for having multiple names. The artist's primary identity may be signed to one label, but they allow him to release stuff on different labels using other names. Some artists actually have discernibly different sonic characters in their different names. But the main effect of all this is to create an effect of distancing, a break with the traditional pop impulse to connect the music to an actual human being. Along with the use of depersonalized, technical-sounding or numeric names, this intensifies the music's posthuman aura, its abstract, disembodied quality. Unlike with rock or rap, you don't identify with the music-maker, you "intensify" with the music's energy. Facelessness also has the effect of disrupting the mechanism of band or brand loyalty, the rock fan's habit of following artists through their careers. Some connoisseurs of electronic music do this, priding themselves on collecting every last item of their favorite artist's oeuvre, under all the different alter-egos. But for hardcore dance fans, producers are only as good as their latest track.

The group Underground Resistance use anonymity as part of their anti-corporate, we-are-guerrillas-of-techno aura: they are literally faceless, refusing to be photographed except wearing masks. This militant stance is all the more resonant given the rise of a dance music industry in which DJs are sold as pseudo-personalities and magazines conduct interviews that ignore the only things interesting about them (their taste in music and mixing skills) and instead talk about the DJ's career struggles, drug intake, sex lives, and VIP lifestyles.

9. Death of the Auteur

We look at rock music in terms of innovators: the individual artists who revolutionized music and influenced others (or, if they failed in the marketplace of their day, who were "ahead of their time"). We look always to trace things back to the trailblazing originators, and deplore the swarm of copyists following in their wake. One of the worst insults that can be directed at a rock group is "generic." In electronic dance music, things work quite differently. It is often difficult, and pointless, to strive to identify who first came up with a breakthrough in rhythm or sound. Ideas mostly emerge through anonymous processes of collective creativity. Look at the genesis of acid house in mid-Eighties Chicago or the emergence of jungle in early Nineties England, and you'll see the cultural equivalent of an ecosystem. Maybe one individual happens to stumble upon an untapped potential in a piece of music-making technology, like the weird "acid" noises inside the Roland 303 bass synthesiser. But almost immediately this idea was seized upon by other producers and instead of being diluted in the process (as usually happens with rock) the new sound was intensified. Over the course of a year, the acid tracks got weirder, fiercer, more deranging, thanks to the intense competition between producers to drive dancefloor crowds wilder, until the new effect was taken as far as it could go and became exhausted.

With jungle's chopped-up, sped-up breakbeats, it's impossible to work out who came up with the idea first, or when exactly the style crystallized. Dozens, maybe scores, of rave producers started to experiment with the idea of using sampled breakbeats instead of programmed rhythms. Through a collective musical conversation stretched across 1990–1993, "breakbeat science" (digital techniques of micro-editing and resequencing beats) emerged in an incremental process: weekly instalments of small-scale innovation, a ping-pong match of ideas going back and forth between people who never met.

Brian Eno has dubbed this syndrome "scenius," punning on the words "scene" and "genius." He argues that our old Romantic notions of the auteur as an autonomous, endlessly fertile individual were precisely that: overly romanticized, out-of-date. And he called for a more depersonalized notion of creativity influenced by cybernetic theory, ideas of self-organizing systems and feedback loops. Another way of conceptualizing "scenius" is in terms of biogenetics or virology, metaphors of mutation or cultural viruses (memes). Like a successful gene characteristic, electronic dance innovations achieve their highest success by becoming clichés: sounds so good that nobody can resist using them. (At least until they're all used up, at which point the underground abandons them to mainstream pop, and dismisses the sounds as "corny" and "cheesy." Some sounds do enjoy an afterlife, though, coming back under the sign of camp ironic nostalgia).

Ideas in dance music sometimes seem to evolve according to an immanent non-human logic of their own. It's tempting to talk mystically of machines like the 303 having their own agenda. In reality, the creativity is entirely human, it's just collective rather than auteur-driven. Because dance cultures have a very fast turnover, a track can come out and within a week another producer has picked up the baton. The life-cycles of sonic evolution are incredibly rapid. Unlike with rock music, even the rip-off artists, the clone merchants and copyists, play a role, because each replication of a sound unavoidably warps it. Indeed, in dance music, "bastardisation" is positive, productive, progressive.

Another reason "generic" isn't an insult in electronic dance discourse is that tracks exist in a context. A "generic" track is a functional track: it has the right elements to enable the DJ to mix the tune in with a bunch of similar tracks, thereby creating a flow. This play of sameness and difference is something that electronic dance music has in common with black music, where what initially seems homogenous reveals subtle inflections and shifts through concentrated immersion by the listener. From the Motown sound in the Sixties through James Brown-style funk to the stop-start rhythms in modern R&B, black American music goes through different Beat-Geists (i.e. rhythmic Zeitgeists). These innovations may originate with specific labels (Motown) or producers (like Timbaland with contemporary R&B), but they become the rhythmic template used by everybody. Jamaican music culture goes even further, being based not just on generic sounds but rhythms that are literally identical: different singers and MCs do new vocals over the same currently hot, endlessly reused riddim track.

One side effect of all this is that dance music has a different distribution of brilliance than other kinds of music. Rock's aesthetic hierarchy divides everything between the handful of visionary geniuses and a vast mass of mediocre non-originals. But in electronic dance music, there's a huge number of good (meaning useful-to-DJs) tracks, and a much smaller number of true landmark records. In a word, dance music is democratic.

10. We Bring You the Future

Another aspect to all this is that genres and scenes take the place of stars and artists—this is the level on which it's most productive to talk about the music. In dance culture, a huge amount of energy goes into cultural taxonomy: identifying genres and subgenres like species. This profusion of new sounds, scenes and genre names is also what is off-putting to some newcomers to the music, who understandably find it confusing, and suspect that hype or willful obscurantism is involved. Actually, the endless generic splintering is simply a result of dance culture's 20 years of existence, the huge number and diversity of people involved, and the global span of the culture. Anything that big is going to fracture, and many of the fractures are going to be worth talking about.

Mostly the names emerge for practical reasons. In the beginning (meaning the mid-Eighties) people talked about "house" and that was pretty much it. Later, different flavors of the music were distinguished, using prefix terms: deep house, hard house, tribal house. Why? More and more records were being made, and the stylistic parameters were starting to drift apart. Clubs found it useful to specify what their sound was, and people working in record stores started to get terminologically precise, to help customers find exactly what they wanted. Some of the terms achieved currency and became established throughout the culture. Eventually, stylistic dispersal increased to the point where the primacy of "house" was overthrown, and brand new words—jungle, trance, gabba—came into use (often after an intermediary phase where people talked of jungle house or gabba house).

Confusing to the uninitiated and offensive to genrephobes this may be, but these definitions become urgent and crucial once you get involved in the culture. It becomes a way of talking about the music, arguing about where it should go next. It's an expression of enthusiasm and excitement, not hairsplitting or an attempt to baffle and exclude by talking in code. Above all, the hunger for the next big thing or new sound is an expression of electronic dance culture's neophilia, its impatience for the future to arrive.

11. Let's Submerge

Along with "living for the future," electronic dance culture is united by a vague, open-ended ideology of "underground-ism," in which grass-roots scenes are positioned against the pop mainstream and the corporate record industry. "Underground" as a concept doesn't have a huge amount of political content, though; it's not attached to any specific revolutionary aspirations, ideas about a utopian form of social organization, or even counter-cultural ideals (beyond a libertarian attitude towards drug-taking). Anti-corporate without being anti-capitalist, "undergroundism" expresses the struggle of micro-capitalist units (independent record labels, small clubs) against macro-capitalism (the mainstream leisure-and-entertainment industry).

Electronic indie labels can be as small as a single individual making music in his bedroom and putting out the tracks himself. More often, it'll be a small gang or crew that is tightly loyal, almost communistic, and typically clustered around a central figure—an engineer/producer who owns the equipment and enables DJs to realise their ideas and become producers. Another common syndrome is independent labels that start off based around a record store. The people who work in the store, who are often aspiring DJs, develop a good sense of what is selling and what works in the clubs; they also get to know more established DJs and aspiring producers who come in to check the latest releases. The obvious next step is to take this developing A&R instinct and start releasing records by new talent. And so, to give just one example, the East London record store Boogie Times gave birth to the influential jungle label Suburban Base.

This sort of small independent tends to be unstable, though, and often doesn't survive the high turnover of dancefloor trends. Inevitably the indies that do endure are those who adopt sound business plans and managerial structures—in other words, start to behave like small corporations. Warp Records started from a record store in Sheffield, England, but watching other labels of the early rave era fall by the wayside, they developed long-term album based deals with their artists (like Aphex Twin), and evolved into a successful company specializing in "electronic listening music" (also know as IDM, short for "intelligent dance music"). For many in the hardcore underground, Warp now represents the new establishment, catering to an audience of ex-clubbers and lapsed ravers with sounds that are basically dance music for the home environment.

Electronic dance music's antagonism towards the corporate music industry isn't based on political principles but aesthetic ones: the idea that the mainstream dilutes the underground's music, blunts the music's edge, tones down its harsh futurism, turns it into mere pop. In a crucial paradox, dance scenes are populist but opposed to pop culture in the "weak," universal sense of the word. Their populism takes the form of tribal unity against what they perceive as a homogenous, blandly uninvolving mass culture. Subcultural initiates are felt to have a more committed, active, participatory relationship with the music than the desultory, passive pop consumer. Often people who believe in underground music use military rhetoric, and talk of being a "soldier" or crusader, fighting for the cause, staying hardcore.

12. Site-Specific

Part of the inclusive/exclusive aura of these subcultures is that the music is site-specific. You have to go to clubs to get the full experience. This doesn't apply to home-oriented IDM, obviously, but there is a vast swathe of this music that simply doesn't really make sense outside the club context. Often I'll buy a house or 2-step 12 inch single and play it at home, and it'll sound weak, the beat monotonous and numbing. Hear the same song through a huge sound system, though, and the unrelenting pump and pound of the groove becomes the whole point. Massively amplified, the kick drum becomes so thick and wide, it's a cocooning environmental pulse: you feel like you're actually inside the beat. Similarly, there are numerous genres of dance music based around floor-quaking sub-bass frequencies that are barely audible on a domestic hi-fi, let alone a boom box. And there's an entire vein of "big room" dance tracks designed for superclubs, whose dancefloors hold a thousand plus people and are surrounded by towering speaker stacks. Often these "big room" tracks contain hardly any music in the traditional sense—only the most rudimentary two-note bass-pulses, barely any melody-lines. They don't sound good at home but they work in the superclub context because they're full of effects and whooshing noises that swoop and pan across the stereo-field, sounds that are literally spectacular, designed to astonish your ears.

The more functionalist kinds of dance music can sound "flat" at home because the tracks are essentially unfinished work. They are raw material for the DJs to transform into music by mixing very minimal tracks together: superimposing or cutting back and forth, creating dynamics by using EQing effects to boost certain frequencies, and all manner of turntable tricks. These records are often described as "DJ tools." With other genres, particularly those—jungle, 2step—that have a strong influence from dancehall reggae and hip hop—the tracks really come alive through the combination of the DJ's mixing and the MC chanting over the music: hyping the crowd, ordering the DJ to do a "rewind" (i.e., stop the track mid-song and go back to the start).

Beyond this, there's a sense in which the music is like the screenplay to a movie, and is completed by "the cast"—the crowd on the dancefloor. Styles like jungle and trance are full of behavioral cues encoded in the music—breakdowns, drum builds, bass drops, climaxes—all of which trigger certain mass responses: ritualized gestures of abandonment, like hands shooting up in the air at the entrance of a certain kind of riff or noise. The music sounds diminished in the absence of such tableaux of crowd frenzy. Ultimately, most dance tracks are components in a subcultural engine—heard decontextualized and isolated, they can seem as perplexing and functionless as a carburettor outside the car. And while it might have a certain surreal appeal to keep an engine part in the middle of your living room, you'd definitely not be getting full use of that component.

"Context" can be really specific. There are some tracks that are associated with just one specific club, like the song "Twilo Thunder," made in homage to the now-defunct New York club Twilo. Its sound was tailored to the immense Twilo sound system and designed to fuel the special atmosphere generated by the crowd who religiously attended Sasha & Digweed's eight-hour DJ sets. For a culture that typically boasts of its global reach and its transcendence of geography, electronica can be disconcertingly fixated on a sense of place. What these privileged sites, these temples of sound, create is a form of postmodern tribalism: people from different backgrounds and locations gather together to experience the same "tribe-vibe."

Part of the conditions of existence for these transient communities is that people check their ideologies at the door with their coats. This isn't apolitical so much as anti-political, or perhaps pre-political: an attempt to cut through all the divisions and rediscover some primal basis of connection, even if that unity is as simple as sharing the same sonic (and often drug) sensations, occupying the same space ("Everybody In the Place," as the Prodigy titled one of their early rave anthems). Which helps explain electronic dance culture's suspicion of words, its urge to dispense with language. Because words divide. And this music is about the urge to merge, about becoming part of something larger than yourself, whether it's the dancing crowd, a sublime vastness of sound, or the cosmos.

13. Only Connect

One of the key words in dance culture is "mix," a term with multiple applications and resonances. Mixed crowds: most dance scenes at least pay lip service to the idea that all are welcome and that clubs with a good social/racial/gender mix are the ones with the best vibe. Mix-and-blend: the musical ethos shared by most genres of electronic dance is a belief in stylistic border-crossing—a notion of hybridity similar to mesticagem, the national ideology of Brazil which takes pride in that country's miscegenated culture and music. (Which may explain why a lot of house producers have an almost utopian vision of Brazil and are infatuated with samba and bossa nova rhythms.) Remixes: rather than a definitively complete and inviolate work of

art, a dance track is treated as a provisional collection of sonic resources to be rearranged—hence the vogue for multiple remixes (sometimes as many as 10 different
versions), and for remix albums where DJ/producers pay tribute to an admired artist by reworking, sometimes to the point of obliteration, their music. Mix: the art
of DJing involves taking disparate tracks and connecting them into a meta-track,
a potentially interminable flow. Repetition and interconnection evoke a feeling of
boundless pleasure. Time is abolished ("3-AM Eternal," as one track title put it), and
so is lack. The music insists "go with the flow" and "be here now," lose yourself in a
never-ending present of pure sensation.

As you can see, my list of foundational principles is just a partial blueprint: culture
is always messy, evading our attempts at definition.[6] The aspects I've highlighted,
though, represent this music's claims to radicalism. They are the "emergent" elements, to use a concept from cultural studies referring to tendencies that point toward
future aesthetic and social formations. Any cultural phenomenon that has real impact
in the present, however, must inevitably be a mixture of "emergent" and "residual"
(meaning traditional). Generally speaking, music that is totally avant-garde and
ahead-of-its-time subsists in the academic ghetto, depending on state subsidies or
institutional support. You can see this with the most advanced forms of "sound art" or
"sound design": they can't survive in the rough-and-tumble of the pop marketplace,
but inhabit the world of art galleries, museums, seminars and symposiums and festivals. Which is fine, but for me the most exciting thing about electronic dance music is
that you get avant-garde ideas working in a popular context, carried by groove and
catchy hooks, and enlivened by a context of fun and collective celebration. One example is jungle's vibrant blend of "roots 'n' phuture" (as one early jungle track put it).
The "emergent," avant-garde elements in jungle wouldn't have worked without the
"residual" stuff: to have "breakbeat science," you need to have breakbeats (sweaty,
human musicians playing hot funky percussive breaks) in the first place, providing
the raw material to be sampled and digitally recombined.

Ultimately, electronic dance music is at its most enjoyable when it's impure:
rhythm/texture colliding with songcraft, soul-less machinery fighting it out with
traditional ideas of sonic beauty, avant-garde auteur impulses checked by the crowd's
demand for danceable grooves. These tensions are what keep the music vital.

Further Reading

Bradby, Barbara. "Sampling Technology: Gender, Technology and the Body in Dance Music."
    Popular Music 12/2 (1993): 155–76.
Brewster, Bill, and Frank Broughton. *Last Night a DJ Saved My Life*. New York: Grove Press,
    2000.
Collin, Matthew. *Altered State: The Story of Ecstasy Culture and Acid House*. London: Serpent's
    Tail, 1998.
Moorefield, Virgil. *The Producer as Composer: Shaping the Sounds of Popular Music*. Cambridge,
    Mass.: MIT Press, 2005.
Redhead, Steve, with Derek Wynne and Justin O'Connor, eds. *The Clubcultures Reader: Read-
    ings in Popular Cultural Studies*. Oxford, UK: Blackwell, 1997.
Scott, Mireille. *Rave American: New School Dancescapes*. Toronto: ECW Press, 1999.
Sicko, Dan. *Techno Rebels: The Renegades of Electronic Funk*. New York: Billboard Books, 1999.
Thornton, Sarah. *Club Cultures: Music, Media and Subcultural Capital*. Middletown, Conn.:
    Wesleyan University Press, 1995.

---

6. I omitted a section in which Reynolds discusses exceptions to his "foundational principles."

Discography

The Chemical Brothers. *Singles 93-03*. Astralwerks, 2003.
Classic Acid. Moonshine Music, 1998.
Classic House Mastercuts, Vol. 2. Mastercuts, 1995.
House Sound of Chicago. Vibe, 1996.
Jungle Massive, Vol. 1. Payday, 1995.
Kraftwerk. *Minimum-Maximum*. Astralwerks, 2005.
May, Derrick. *Innovator*. Transmat Records, 1997.
Moby. *Go: The Very Best of Moby*. V2, 2006.
Model 500. *Classics*. R&S, 1995.
The Orb's Adventures beyond the Ultraworld. Island, 1991.
Tricky. *Maxinquaye*. Island, 1995.

84. R&B Divas Go Retro

As Nelson George indicated in Chapter 65, old-school soul singing and R&B remained alive in the late 1970s and 1980s alongside the development of funk and disco. In addition to artists such as Chaka Khan (b. 1954) and Aretha Franklin, younger singers like Frankie Beverly (of Maze) and Anita Baker continued the tradition of impassioned gospel-schooled vocals that addressed romantic and social concerns. Another generation of R&B "divas," typified by Whitney Houston (b. 1963) and Mariah Carey (b. 1970), emerged in the late 1980s–early 1990s and merged superb vocal technique with well-crafted (some might say "slick") productions that were unusually attuned to the current tastes of the pop marketplace.

Ann Powers (at the time a pop music critic for the *New York Times*) describes another trend that became evident in the mid- to late 1990s as younger African American singers sought to merge the rhythms and tough attitude of hip-hop with some of the vocal technique and lyric subject matter of 1970s soul. These artists, led by Mary J. Blige's early 1990s recordings and D'Angelo's 1995 release *Brown Sugar*, were predominantly female, adding a different inflection to the subject of "women in pop music" discussed earlier in chapter 81. The year 1999 represented the crest of a wave that began in 1997 with releases by Erykah Badu (b. 1972) and Missy Elliot and surged in 1998 with the *Miseducation of Lauryn Hill*. While this trend represents continuity with earlier soul music, the nostalgic or "retro" element is new and links the late 1990s soul revival with other forms of musical recycling going on concurrently in popular music.[1]

The New Conscience of Pop Music
Ann Powers

During "Not Lookin,'" a new duet with her former beau, the urban love man K-Ci Hailey, Mary J. Blige demonstrates how to stop a man cold. The song, from Ms. Blige's new album, "Mary," pits a woman seeking true affection against a man out for pure pleasure. The two vocalists trade diatribes over a steady rocking rhythm, their wails building as the impossibility of resolution grows clear.

Mr. Hailey soothes and cajoles in his sexy baritone. Ms. Blige cries to any women listening to stand up with her and fight such "player" nonsense. "I hear you," moans Mr. Hailey, though he obviously doesn't. Finally, Ms. Blige just snaps. "I know you're sorry!" she exclaims. The track ends, without another sound.

This abrupt dismissal is a conveniently dramatic way for Ms. Blige to win a musical cutting contest. But it also captures the mood of the rhythm-and-blues being made by young artists eager to create something more than slick background for the well-appointed bedroom. This new style has been building for a few years, but only now is it reaching full flower. And although its pioneers include men like Mr. Hailey and D'Angelo, there is no question that the fragrance of this blossom is boldly feminine.

Throughout the 1990's, most discussions of women's increased power in pop have focused on alternative-rock transgressors like Tori Amos and Courtney Love or the songbirds of Sarah McLachlan's Lilith Fair. Rhythm-and-blues artists sold albums but were rarely viewed as culture shapers. Now, though, with mainstream rock again becoming a male bastion, it is clear whose music matters within the continuing emergence of women as equal players in contemporary music.

Ms. Blige, the standard-bearer for hip-hop-inflected soul, has reached a peak in her career. She has evolved from a passionate but erratic inner-city princess to a mature artist tackling the same complexities expressed by her idols, Aretha Franklin and Chaka Khan. Lauryn Hill, a professed Blige fan who wrote and produced "All That I Can Say," the first single from "Mary" (MCA), herself exceeded all expecta-

---

1. Almost two years later, Powers examined the continuing pressures and contradictions faced by women in popular music, focusing on the then-current success of R&B "girl group" Destiny's Child; see Ann Powers, "In Tune with the New Feminism," *New York Times,* April 29, 2001.

tions with her solo debut, "The Miseducation of Lauryn Hill." The girl group TLC is at its apex, ruling the charts with two singles, "No Scrubs" and "Unpretty," that have sparked spirited public conversations about sex, money and self-respect.

These are only the most visible forces in a renaissance that includes girl groups like Destiny's Child, answering TLC's challenge with its own fresh summer single, "Bills, Bills, Bills"; Missy Elliott, an artist growing ever more influential behind the scenes as a producer; seasoned songwriters now in the spotlight, like Faith Evans, Kelly Price and Angie Stone, and left-field contenders like Macy Gray and Melky Sedeck. These artists are as carefully packaged as the elegant stars they join in the spotlight, from Whitney Houston to Toni Braxton. But they are selling a very different sensibility.

They are more individualistic, more confrontational. They grew up loving hip-hop, and in their songs they tangle with that genre's cold-blooded male pronouncements instead of merely floating past them on a cushion of strings and strummed guitars. Some find allies in brash rappers like Lil' Kim. But while the female rapper's role remains mostly that of the sexual warrior, contesting masculine power with the easily available weapon of her own body, these singers also confront the emotional costs of such battles.

The new soul queens take advantage of nostalgia's ability to conjure authenticity. Their songs invoke forebears like Ms. Khan in music thick with funk and flecked with jazz, but the mix is salted with gritty hip-hop beats. These artists' lyrics, too, resurrect old-school domestic protests within a strikingly contemporary context, as they debate proper behavior within today's seeming sexual free-for-all.

The rising stars of female soul demand attention with audacity rather than coaxing it out through prettiness. Undoubtedly sexy, they are also unapologetically human. They embody not merely the dream girls of glossy magazines but also the "unpretty" women reading those magazines. And they are earning respect, so much so that pop angels like Ms. Houston, Mariah Carey and Janet Jackson have made themselves over to look rougher and tougher in their midst—and, in the process, have made some of the best music of their careers.

This current cycle is just the latest in the rebirth of soul. Two larger commercial trends have spurred it on: the triumph of hip-hop and the return of rhythm-and-blues as the basic form of teen-age pop. After briefly being displaced by punk-flavored rock in the mid-1990's, black music is again the essence of American pop music. But the new soul queens consciously invoke a side of that music that others have avoided.

Virtually all popular music centers on romance, and historically, black music has frankly celebrated love's sexual side. But, as the historian Brian Ward points out in "Just My Soul Responding: Rhythm-and-Blues, Black Consciousness and Race Relations" (University of California, 1998), black styles from the blues to disco have not just glorified bodily pleasures.

They have given artists a way of confronting the sexual stereotypes that racism has created—what Michelle Wallace famously called "black macho and the myth of the superwoman." Through songs ranging from Wynonie Harris's "Adam, Come and Get Your Rib" to Gwen Guthrie's "Ain't Nothin' Goin' On but the Rent," rhythm-and-blues artists have encapsulated the struggles waged in every room of the black household, from the bedroom to the kitchen.

In times of political pessimism, this debate has grown more vicious. The blues painted a bleak image of love, grounded in paranoia and murderous lusts. At the height of the civil rights movement, when integration seemed possible both in public spaces and on the pop charts, romantics like Aretha Franklin gained popularity. Then, in the early 1970's, when the radical Black Power movement arose in response to social setbacks, female artists once again found themselves metaphorically embattled.

"The women of soul rejected the role of helpless victims, not by articulating a discernibly feminist program, but by giving as good as they got in the male-defined sex wars of the late 1960's and early 1970's," Mr. Ward writes. "It was the equivalent of women in the Panthers earning the respect of their male colleagues by picking up the gun—the ultimate symbol of phallocentric power—and behaving as much like men as possible."

The rhetoric of hip-hop is firmly linked to this era. Its stars constantly mimic the styles seen in blaxploitation movies of the early 1970's, and when they do venture into political speech, they most often invoke radicals like Malcolm X and the Black Panthers. Rappers like Jay-Z and Master P take an outlaw stance with overtones of social revolt, if not genuine political rebellion. Today's most successful female rappers have adopted the image of the "ho" as a feminine counterpart in criminality.

The new soul queens are taking on the often vicious representations of women in hip-hop, assessing what real strength those images may offer and when they need to be defused. They are speaking to female hip-hop fans about the contradictions facing young women in a culture that craves female power but remains deeply suspicious of it. And they are confronting the men who, in rap and in contemporary rhythm-and-blues, so often describe seduction as a theft and love as a game.

Mary J. Blige has been working on gaining equality with her male counterparts since she released her debut album, "What's the 411?" in 1992. That album posited Ms. Blige as a fingernail-flaring, Kangol cap-wearing little sister whom B-boys could dream of and ghetto girls could identify with. (The future hip-hop kingpin Sean [Puffy] Combs is listed as "stylist" on the album's credits.)

Singing with passion if not technical mastery, Ms. Blige immediately distinguished herself from stars like Ms. Carey, who possessed better instruments but little of her street credibility. With her second album, "My Life," she began writing more of her material and showed herself to be given to dark pronouncements, like her magnificent version of the Norman Whitfield–Joel Schumacher ballad "I'm Goin' Down" from the movie "Car Wash" as well as optimistic hits like "Real Love." For many fans, she became a Lady of the Sorrows, expressing their anxieties and regrets in a powerful but always vulnerable voice.

The moody Ms. Blige wore her own troubles on her sleeve. She had adversarial encounters with the press and publicly indulged in drugs and alcohol. Gradually, she grew up, and her track record of hits has turned her into a soul matriarch by age 28. Her new album is not as obviously commercial as her previous studio efforts, nor is it as closely linked to hip-hop. With "Mary," Ms. Blige is making her case for really deserving the regal title hip-hop fans have given her from the beginning.

It is a crossover effort, with appearances by the distinctly non-ghettocentric guests Sir Elton John and Eric Clapton. Only one rapper, Jadakiss, appears; a cut featuring DMX and Nas was ultimately reserved for the B-side of "All That I Can Say." But if "Mary" gestures toward an older, non-hip-hop audience, it also makes the claim for Ms. Blige's canonization within the rhythm-and-blues hall of fame. The album's two duets enforce her status: her reunion with Mr. Hailey, who is also outrunning his bad-boy past via increasingly sophisticated recordings, and the spirited "Don't Waste Your Time," in which she receives a mentor's advice from that other queen of soul, Aretha Franklin.

The time is right for Ms. Blige to assert herself because her dramatic, direct vocal style is again soul's paradigm. Once, even the voices of Ms. Blige's imitators were heavily obscured within mixes where the producer's signature mattered more than the singer's. It was hard to find the real woman inside the work of vocally gifted artists like Ms. Braxton or Ms. Houston. The individual quirks that distinguished greats like Ms. Franklin, Ms. Khan and Patti LaBelle were processed out of most radio-ready mixes.

Gradually, though, outsiders began making commercial breakthroughs. Not only Ms. Blige, but Erykah Badu and Missy Elliott, neither of whom looked or sounded like the standard-model soul babe, became stars. Faith Evans and Kelly Price, writers who have collaborated with Ms. Blige, had hits that emphasized their unvarnished voices and dramatic range. The multiplatinum, multi-Grammy triumph of Ms. Hill, a boisterous singer and rapper whose most striking talent is for spacious vocal arrangements, cemented the change.

A shift was visible, too, among the often seemingly interchangeable girl groups of contemporary rhythm-and-blues. The trio that made the difference has progressed in much the same way Ms. Blige has. Tionne (T-Boz) Watkins, Rozonda (Chilli) Thomas and Lisa (Left Eye) Lopes, collectively known as TLC, started out as perky but artistically unremarkable teens. "Crazysexycool," the group's 1994 sophomore effort, solidified its sound by emphasizing the internal, almost conversational singing of T-Boz and Chilli and using Left Eye's sassy raps as zest. "Crazysexycool" sold upwards of eight million copies, guaranteeing that its formula would be endlessly imitated.

Before TLC's triumph, the most successful girl group was En Vogue, a quartet with stellar vocal prowess and a taste for glamour. Like Ms. Blige, the women of TLC seemed more accessible, partly because of their connections to streetwise hip-hop. "Fanmail," this year's long-awaited follow-up to "Crazysexycool," does not totally diverge from the tried and true, but its best tracks take on soul's classic conversation about gender in adventurous ways.

The album's monster hit, "No Scrubs," is a vintage dressing-down of a financially shifty man, while the group's current single, "Unpretty," bravely considers the downside of the beauty myth most women in pop eagerly cultivate. But the most daring song on "Fanmail" is "I'm Good at Being Bad," a musical re-enactment of the conflicting stereotypes that envelop black women.

The track begins as a silky ballad, like a bubble bath with a beat, but it gives way to a huge hip-hop beat and a snarling, obscenity-laced vocal. Here is the "ho" taking on the dream girl, the woman using sex as a weapon versus the one too dependent on love. The scenario remains unresolved, and the more powerful for it.

TLC's inside view of a sexual woman's split psyche is hardly the only song to confront hip-hop's ever-present ho. Ms. Hill cautioned young girls to preserve themselves in "Lost Ones," a song that has earned her accusations of self-righteousness. Because she is openly religious, Ms. Hill is blunt about her distaste for the mercenary sexual stance of some female artists.

For all the backlash it has caused, Ms. Hill's critique of hip-hop's skewed value system reflects another element of soul's artistic revitalization. Her challenge, "How you gonna win when you ain't right within?" echoes through this new music.

New artists like Angie Stone, Melky Sedeck and Macy Gray make such questions of conscience part of their metier. These new soul queens are not moralistic; their songs toast sensuality more often than they dissect social ills. But they also consider the consequences of the hunger for sex, drugs and money, especially in the context of racism. Doing so, they invoke not only past soul queens but progenitors like Sly Stone and Marvin Gaye.

The history of rhythm-and-blues is full of unruly divas like the ones currently stealing the microphone. They are lucky that popular taste is shifting their way, saving them from the outsider status that has long afflicted soul singers who push against the stereotypes of urban style. These women are determined to give voice to their own views on the matters that shape the intimate lives of their listeners, and they are artists enough to render those perspectives in tones as vibrant as the heritage they mine. Whether tackling emotional profundities or sticking to the plain facts of woman versus man, black women are the conscience of today's pop scene.

Further Reading

Gardner, Elysa. "Hip Hop Soul." In *The Vibe History of Hip Hop*, ed. Alan Light, 307–17. New York: Three Rivers Press, 1999.
McIver, Joe. *Erykah Badu: The First Lady of Neo-Soul*. London: Sanctuary Publishing, 2002.
Powers, Ann. "In Tune with the New Feminism." *New York Times*, April 29, 2001.

Discography

Badu, Erykah. *Baduizm*. UMVD Labels, 1997.
Blige, Mary J. *My Life*. MCA, 1994.
Carey, Mariah. *Greatest Hits*. Sony, 2001.
Gray, Macy. *On How Life Is*. Sony, 1999.
Hill, Lauryn. *The Miseducation of Lauryn Hill*. Sony, 1998.
Houston, Whitney. *The Greatest Hits*. Arista, 2000.

85. Country in the Post–Urban Cowboy Era

We last left country music in the early 1950s; this may create the mistaken impression that country music existed only insofar as it could contribute to the formation of rock 'n' roll and that it quietly faded away once that purpose was served. Of course, nothing could be further from the truth: Country music has its own rich history and has continued to thrive up to the present, although one could argue that its interactions with "race music" and "popular music" were more vigorous in the decades before 1955 than after. However, for the purposes of this book (which cannot possibly give due justice to country's semiautonomous history), it is important to note that country music has had numerous points of contact with the popular music mainstream in the past 50-odd years. Rockabilly, mentioned in the context of Elvis Presley's early career, displayed the clearest relationship to country music of all the varieties of early rock 'n' roll; almost concurrently, Nashville produced the lush "countrypolitan" sound that enjoyed crossover success with performers such as Jim Reeves, Johnny Cash, Patsy Cline, Faron Young, and Skeeter Davis, although, strangely enough, at the height of the countrypolitan crossover trend in 1962, the biggest country hit of the year was "Don't Let Me Cross Over" by Carl Butler and Pearl.

In the late 1960s, former session guitarist Glen Campbell presented an urbane updating of the countrypolitan sound and was given the bully pulpit of his own network television variety show in which to expose himself to the masses. Another strand of crossover country song was the "novelty" number, represented by Jeannie C. Riley's "Harper Valley P.T.A" (1968) or Jerry Reed's "Amos Moses" (1970). Kris Kristofferson wrote numerous songs during the early seventies, the appeal of which transcended music industry categories, whether they were recorded by country artists such as Johnny Cash ("Sunday Morning Comin' Down," 1970), Sammi Smith ("Help Me Make It through the Night," 1970), and Ray Price ("For the Good Times," 1970), or by rock musicians like Janis Joplin ("Me and Bobby McGee," 1971). The "urban cowboy" trend beginning in the late 1970s (and derived from the film of the same name) provides yet another example of a country crossover boomlet, and during this period country artists such as Dolly Parton and Kenny Rogers had numerous crossover hits.[1]

Yet the strongest indicator of the pervasive popularity of country music came not from an individual artist or a cross-marketing trend, but from a change in the way that the music industry calculated popularity itself. On May 25, 1991, the readers of *Billboard* magazine awoke to find that there were almost twice as many country albums in the "Hot 200" album chart than there had been the week before. The explanation? *Billboard* had replaced reports from individual retailers, which were previously used to compile their charts, with *SoundScan*, an automated system that recorded sales at the point of purchase at stores, most of which belonged to large chain networks. The results threw the purported objectivity of the previous charts into question and revealed that country artists, such as Garth Brooks, whose album *Ropin' the Wind* was the first album to debut at number one on both pop and country album charts on September 10, 1991, commanded a heretofore-unsuspected large appeal.

The following article captures Brooks at the height of his fame in early 1992, immediately after the success of *Ropin' the Wind* (1991) and its predecessor, *No Fences* (1990). It becomes clear that Brooks's popularity is due both to elements of personal style—a fusion of the autobiographical voice of 1970s singer-songwriters and the theatrics

---

1. Aaron Latham, "The Ballad of the Urban Cowboy: America's Search for True Grit," *Esquire,* September 12, 1978, 21–30.

and sonic density of arena rock with country new traditionalism—and to institutional factors such as the rise of cable channels devoted to country music and the growth of country radio. The author calls attention to what appeared to be a change in the audience demographics for country music: not only people living in the southern United States, but those throughout North America, both urban and rural. Brooks's musical values may have been conservative and his loyalty to core country music fans unquestioned, but his approach to marketing, live performance, and video cannily employed techniques from other types of music that gave his music a contemporary edge that is still pervasive in country music today.

Garth Brooks: Meet Nashville's New Breed Of Generously Stetsoned Crooner
Mark Cooper

Bandy-legged and pigeon-toed, Garth Brooks has finally taken off his stetson and is staggering around the stage of Atlanta's Omni like a man who's just won a particularly gruelling marathon.

Fists whirling at an invisible punchbag suspended just above his head, Brooks paces up and down in front of his band, chuckling maniacally. Suddenly he sprints up a ramp, leans backwards over his drummer with paper cups poised and douses him with water. Country singers simply aren't supposed to carry on like this but Brooks is no ordinary country singer and is clearly having too much fun to care.

Earlier, Brooks had sat alone on a stool with an acoustic guitar and had the 19,000-strong Omni crowd singing along with the homespun philosophising of a folksy ballad entitled "Unanswered Prayers." Now the lighters have been pocketed and the stoic fatalism of Brooks's tenderer moments have been replaced by a man intent on raising hell.

"You've taken 1991, wrapped it up and put it under my tree," he tells the crowd, before shimmying up a rope ladder handily suspended from a lurching lighting rig. As Brooks himself remarked earlier this year, "Not bad for a fat boy from Oklahoma . . . "

Garth Brooks is undoubtedly a country singer but his success is an American pop phenomenon that has placed him alongside the likes of U2 and Michael Jackson at the top of the charts proper. His third album, *Ropin' The Wind*, entered the *Billboard* pop album chart at Number 1 in the last week of September and proceeded to keep the likes of Michael Bolton, Metallica and Hammer at bay for an incredible seven weeks. *Ropin' The Wind* has sold over five million copies to date and still hasn't overtaken the six million sales of its predecessor, *No Fences*, which, at one point, rejoined *Ropin' The Wind* in the Top 10. Since his debut in '89, Brooks has sold over 14 million albums in the US without even attempting to release a single to pop radio

Source: "Garth Brooks: Meet Nashville's New Breed of Generously Stetsoned Crooner" © Mark Cooper

and "crossover." *Ropin' The Wind* was the first country album to top the American pop charts since *Johnny Cash At San Quentin* in '69 but Brooks has taken country into the mainstream on his own terms.

Country has been gaining ground since the mid-'80s, thanks to the rise of cable channels such as Nashville Network, the growth of country radio (2,400 radio stations now programme country, making it the third-biggest radio format in America—behind Adult Contemporary and News but ahead of Top 40) and the emergence of a bunch of handsome young crooners spearheaded by Randy Travis and including the likes of Clint Black and Alan Jackson. Television hasn't been slow to spot country's new audience with NBC launching *Hot Country Nights*—the first live music show on network TV in 15 years—last November. Brooks got his own 1-hour concert special on NBC in January. Country audiences now spread from the American South to the urban centres of the West and East and, judging from Brooks's crowd at the Omni, include as many tots and teenagers as good ole boys and gals.

This Omni show sold out in a mere 19 minutes back in November and seats were being scalped for as much as 500 dollars. There's a predominance of denim and silk and plenty of young Garth clones in hats and shirts buying their "You've Gotta Believe!" T-shirts. Brooks is not a conventional sex symbol but he makes plenty of knees tremble. "He has a voice like no other," one teenage female fan explains. "I'm just here to hear him sing 'Shameless' and I won't be responsible for my reaction."

Surprisingly, this young crowd reserves its most spontaneous applause for the most traditional country moments—a fiddle break, a fill from the pedal steel, a sudden curl in Garth's voice. The kids may also be into Turtles and New Kids but they've taken to Garth's style of country like a kind of Nintendo.

Brooks's own rise has undoubtedly been aided by country's recovery from the recession that succeeded the Urban Cowboy fad of the early '80s. When the *Billboard* charts were revamped this summer to rely more accurately on actual sales, Brooks was ready with *Ropin' The Wind* to prove that country couldn't be dismissed as a minority music. But Brooks's phenomenal success is ultimately more than the crest of a wave.

A marketing and advertising graduate, Brooks has succeeded by remaining remarkably faithful to the retro musical values pioneered by his hero George Strait while taking country's conservative and often lazy approach to video and live performance by the scruff of the neck. Brooks's main stream success was ensured by the video for "The Dance," a single from *No Fences* which employed footage of the likes of JFK, Martin Luther King and the Challenger crew. The song affirms Brooks's faith in American dreamers in the face of doubt, the video captured the imagination of an America besieged by recession and the tremblings of the Gulf War. Brooks emerged as a downhome boy-next-door, reaffirming traditional American values at a time of doubt.

Another single, the rowdy "Friends In Low Places," became a Gulf anthem and proved that Brooks could also be something of a yahoo. When he followed up these releases by "The Thunder Rolls," a tale of marital infidelity complete with a video which portrayed Brooks as a wife abuser who eventually gets smoked by his spouse, Nashville threw up its hands and temporarily banned the clip. Brooks was publicly hurt by the rejection but he had already proved that he had more of a finger on the public pulse than his critics; the "Thunder Rolls" promo duly won Video Of The Year at the '91 Country Music Association Awards.

Brooks proved he is his own man once again by releasing a cover of Billy Joel's "Shameless" as the second single from *Ropin' The Wind* and by gradually transforming his stage shows from the usual tight-lipped country outing into the rock-derived extravaganza on display at the Omni.

He may not be as good-looking as most of his country peers but he oozes an approachable charisma that his more wooden rivals must envy. In addition he is blessed with an almost unhealthy intensity, while his ambition knows no bounds: more than a hint of steel glints behind his pale blue eyes and painstaking country manners.

Prior to the Omni show, Brooks wanders affably around backstage, clad in sweatpants and without a hat anywhere in sight. Only 29, his hair is already thinning and he clearly has to work to keep his weight in check. Without his trademark stetson and striped shirts, Brooks is an unlikely superstar—more aging college jock than national pin-up. But then country artists traditionally have little time for the vanities that beset your average rock'n'roller, treating their fans with humility rather than contempt. Brooks is no exception and spends three or four hours after every show signing autographs into the wee small hours. Yet John Wayne is still his greatest idol and, as his rise has continued unhindered and unchecked, Brooks's modesty has begun to blend into a sense of manifest destiny befitting an all-American boy with a unquenchable thirst for conquest.

"The only way we can rationalise what's happening is to say that Garth Brooks isn't at the controls of this thing," Brooks observes with a scratch of his head, referring to himself as a third-person phenomenon. "We like to think that that seat is reserved for the Good Lord and the people. And the Good Lord and the people, when they want to move mountains—they can. I don't want to cop out or be modest but that's the only way I can explain what's going on. I'm more or less a passenger on this train . . . "

The Good Lord helps those who help themselves, however, and Brooks sheepishly admits that success has turned him into a workaholic who now has to think about the business side of music constantly. "This thing has gotten so competitive within myself that I don't sleep any more. The rush of this kind of success is addictive. It's 24 hours a day trying to make the last wave you made look small. It's moving and I want it to go bigger, I want it to go faster. I just want to be part of the biggest machine there ever was, just eatin' 'em up. I'll kill myself but it's something that I can't stop. When I eat something that tastes good, I just want more and more of it. This thing here—once you get a taste of the rush, you want—that feeling every second of the day."

Brooks wasn't always so driven. The sixth son of an Oklahoman oil engineer and a mother who was a country recording artist herself in the '50s, Brooks grew up in the small town of Yukon. He sailed through school, went to Oklahoma State on an athletics scholarship and is now profoundly critical of what he regards as his mis-spent youth. "I took everything for granted when I was growing up and wasted every opportunity," he remembers with a sigh. "Everything came so easy for me but I was a drifter and couldn't make any commitments to work or to women."

Just before he went to Oklahoma State, Brooks heard George Strait's debut single, "Unwound," on the radio and was immediately hooked. Previously he'd divided his musical loyalties between the stadium rock of Journey and Kansas and the sensitive introspection of Dan Fogelberg and James Taylor but when Brooks heard Strait, his fate was sealed. "I sat there and that fiddle kicked off and I just fell in love with it. All that time I'd been screaming at the top of my lungs to Journey and ELO, I'd never felt comfortable singing along because I couldn't sound like those guys, suddenly there was George Strait. Throughout the whole '80s, I became a George wannabe."

When Brooks failed to make it as a jock, he began to take the notion of a career in country more seriously. His degree in advertising was almost complete when he met his future wife Sandy in the ladies room of a club called Tumbleweeds. Brooks was working as a bouncer and Sandy had put her fist through the wall in a brawl. The couple are now expecting their first baby and Brooks is taking the first few months of this year off the road to get re-acquainted with the wife who supported him when he was nobody. It was Sandy who taught Brooks the value of commitment, a value that he has most conspicuously applied to his career.

"It never seemed logical to me that you could reach higher if you were tied down. Well, I got married to Sandy and I realised that you can sit on someone's shoulders or you can sleep while the other one is driving. All of a sudden, I could reach 10 times higher than I could on my own."

Brooks first ventured to Nashville in '85 but left 23 hours later with his tail between his legs. He'd failed to take the town by storm, and the streets weren't exactly paved with gold. Finally, the recently married couple gambled their last $1,500 on another stab in '87. Eventually, Garth was spotted by a Capitol talent scout at a showcase. His career took off when producer and industry veteran Jimmy Bowen took over at Capitol Nashville and began to put serious promotional muscle behind that debut album.

Once Brooks started scoring country hits with his one-two punch of explorations of mortality and hellraising hoedowns, his shows gradually began to take on a distinctly rock'n'roll edge. "There have been times when I've had a crowd and I've looked around at the band and the band were scared and I was scared and we knew we had the gas to push them over the cliff. You're holding a sword in your hands and you have to use it responsibly. We never know what's going to happen but we know we're not going to go over the edge. We stay in that little zone; it's a little strip, a warning track that I like to live my life upon on stage."

Brooks has even been known to surprise himself when the joint is really jumping. "I do some crazy things. I had this beautiful guitar that I just loved. But this one night I just couldn't help it. I had to. You could just feel it. Everything went into that slow-motion mode. And the crowd is screaming, you can actually see the veins in their throats, they're screaming so loud but you can't hear nothing and you just start spinning in that silence. I just remember the guitar coming up, I had the crown of it in the palm of my hand and I just took it and started smashing it into the stage. The whole time I'm smashing it, I'm thinking, What in the hell are you *doing*?"

Such moments have turned Brooks into a concert attraction to rival his own early heroes, heroes like Billy Joel. Brooks has already borrowed Joel's "Shameless" and encores every night with a stirring version of "You May Be Right, I May Be Crazy." Joel now seems equally smitten and recently joined Brooks on stage. When the pair first talked on the telephone, Joel said he couldn't wait to see Brooks live. "Don't bother," Brooks responded. "Just take a look at all your old videos—I stole it all from you!"

Certainly Brooks's insistence that country can be a rip-roaring live music relies heavily on his teenage grounding in the rock shows of the '70s. "I'm not here to mess with the tradition of country music but I would like to mess with the traditional way that country is portrayed on stage. I don't know how to say this without sounding contradictory but country music *rocks*! It hurts when I go to a country concert and I'm sitting in my seat going, Wow, man, what a tune, what a tune! but the band is just standing there like statues. Journey was one of the bands that totally spun my head around. In the late '70s you would go to one of those arena rock shows and those guys went after it. They didn't have lasers back then but they had lights upon lights: when they'd throw 'em, the city outside would just go dim because they had the power. Their sound was so thick and the crowd was allowed to participate in the shows."

Brooks's approach to video has proved similarly visionary in country circles. "Video is the future of all musics. It's plain and simple to me that soon a 10-cut CD will have 10 videos on it too. You'll be able to play it in the car without the visuals or at home with the TV. People in country are starting to realise that video is a hell of a marketing tool. It's a three-minute advert and if all you're going to do is stand there and lip-synch, cash it in, because the viewers are going to go get the potato chips or flip to another channel. In the past six months, country music television has come a million miles but still people will go to pick up a phone in a video and the phone will be from 1930. Wake up! Country is 1991, 1992. Country is not a way of life as much as it was any more, country is more a way of thinking. Why make people feel, Well, if I'm going to be a country fan, I've gotta be ignorant, I've gotta be behind the times?"

Brooks's eyes have taken on an almost messianic gleam as he delivers this speech. Here is a man from Oklahoma who likes to dress in sweatpants, who's reportedly uneasy around a horse but who is absolutely at ease wearing a cowboy hat and singing songs about rodeos. He clearly understands country's metaphorical appeal to the American nation.

"For me, country is morals," explains Brooks. "It's tough to draw a line somewhere but it's funny how freedom of speech or freedom of the press might have been the thing that liberated this country and becomes the thing that kills it. Or, I don't want to work or pay my way—I think the government owes me this or that. That's all overshot. To me, country is a frame of mind; it's about what's right. There's a balance between what's right and what's wrong and I'm just worried that people are losing the little man inside, the conscience."

It is country caution as much as country morality that has caused Brooks to keep his music away from pop radio even while he sits astride the pop album charts. He isn't about to go the way of Kenny Rogers, currently obliged to slog his way round radio stations trying to win back their support. "I'm a huge fan of Kenny Rogers the man," observes Brooks. "What happened to him, he was playing country music, this Urban Cowboy thing came along and he got some crossover success and went for it. When you're over there, country says, Well, he's gone to pop, and closes the door. Pop rapes you, uses everything you have, usually for about two months, then you're stuck in no man's land. I'd rather stay with country radio so people know where they can find me. As far as crossovering goes, if right now is as good as it gets, that's OK with me. This way, we don't have to kiss anybody's ass."

> The music industry reorganized in order to take the increased popularity of country music into account, and the 1990s thus provided a more receptive context for the mainstream acceptance of country acts.[2] On the heels of Brooks, Canadian Shania Twain appealed to both country and pop audiences, benefiting from the music industry acumen of her manager-producer-husband Mutt Lange, who formerly provided these services to pop-metal band Def Leppard. The Dixie Chicks first appeared as the heirs to both Twain, because of their genre, gender, and catchy tunes, and the Spice Girls, owing to their gender and the way in which their exhortation to "Chicks" in the audience seemed to echo the feel-good message of "Girl Power" promulgated by the Spice Girls. However, the "Chicks" confounded easy categorization because of the instrumental prowess of former child-prodigy sisters Emily Robison (née Erwin) and Martie Maguire (née Erwin) and rock-influenced lead singer Natalie Maines. Even listeners to their first album, *Wide Open Spaces* (1998), might have noticed the presence of older country styles (especially bluegrass) that played only a small role in the music of Shania Twain and Garth Brooks.

2. For more on this change within the music industry, see Keith Negus, *Music Genres and Corporate Cultures* (London and New York: Routledge, 1999), 103–30.

As early as 2000 with "Goodbye Earl," the Chicks showed an interest in the topical in a song that told the story of the murder of an abusive husband by his former wife and her best friend in an almost giddy fashion. "Goodbye Earl" and subsequent songs that highlighted social issues, such as "Long Time Gone," which criticized the historical amnesia of country radio, could hardly have prepared listeners for what was to ensue. At a concert in London on March 10, 2003, shortly before the beginning of the U.S.-led attack on Iraq, Maines told the audience, "Just so you know, we're on the good side with y'all. We do not want this war, this violence, and we're ashamed that the President of the United States is from Texas."[3]

The article included here returns us to those feverish moments in the wake of September 11, 2001, when tolerance for dissent in the United States declined, a sentiment that was only amplified by the invasion of Iraq in spring 2003. Both the reactions of country music fans, which included death threats and bulldozing Chicks' CDs, and the mainstream news media, which had asked few hard questions of the Bush administration in the run-up to war, had difficulty assimilating Maines's statement into an atmosphere in which there was no official public voice of opposition. The article begins with the first televised interview of the Chicks after "the statement" in April 2003 on ABC's "Primetime" show hosted by Diane Sawyer. The article implies that the indignity greeting the Chicks' statement was exacerbated by their gender—nice girls, after all, are not supposed to know about politics, let alone make controversial remarks. The author, Charles Taylor, makes clear, though, that the virulence of the reaction to the Chicks cannot be credited solely to their political views or their gender, but must take into account widely shared ideas among their massive audience about how a country musician should act. Taylor, in recognizing the affinity of spirit that the Chicks have with female punks associated with the riot-grrrl movement, reminds us that the homogeneity of country music performers and their audience has long been a myth. As a case in point, Merle Haggard, to whom the Chicks paid tribute in "Long Time Gone," came to their defense in words and conveyed his own opinion about the war when he released a song critical of U.S. media coverage.

Chicks Against the Machine
Charles Taylor

April 28, 2003 | Scandal in American public life follows a script as predictable as pornography. First come the initial scanty press reports. Then the "He/she/they said/did what?" reaction from the disbelieving public. After that the backlash, both

---

3. This is the full quote; it is often, as in the article that follows, printed as "Just so you know, [. . .] we're ashamed that the President of the United States is from Texas."

Source: "Chicks Against the Machine," Charles Taylor "This article first appeared in Salon.com, at http://www.salon.com An online version remains in the Salon archives. Reprinted with permission."

condemnation and defense. And ultimately, in a carefully selected media forum, the public mea culpa.

This final act is what was supposed to have played out last week on ABC's "Primetime Thursday" during Diane Sawyer's hour-long interview with the Dixie Chicks. Except for one thing: The Chicks weren't following anybody's script but their own. Over the course of the interview, filmed in band member Martie Maguire's Austin, Texas, home, Maguire, her sister Emily Robison and Natalie Maines, whose March 10 comment from the stage of London's Shepherd's Bush Empire—"Just so you know, we're ashamed that the president of the United States is from Texas"—started the controversy that continues to engulf the trio, the three refused to back down.

Forget the apology Maines issued to Bush a few days after the Associated Press first reported her words, or the stories that her comments had brought the band to the point of dissolution. Offered the chance to take it all back and make nice, the Dixie Chicks instead chose to turn the interview around. Sawyer wanted answers; the Chicks offered questions, hard questions. Sawyer wanted to talk about the damage they may have done to their career; the Chicks talked about the damage being done to America in an era where Vice President Dick Cheney has proclaimed "You're either with us or against us."

The band may have gotten more attention posing nude for the cover of the current *Entertainment Weekly*, with phrases like "Dixie Sluts," "Saddam's Angels" and "Traitors" stamped on their bodies. But it was the stubborn refusal they showed Sawyer that cut deepest. Yes, Maines, as she did in her apology, said that her statement was "disrespectful" and "the wrong wording with genuine emotion and question and concern behind it." But she didn't apologize for those questions. "I ask questions. That's smart, that's intelligent, to find out facts," she said.

The sisters, Emily and particularly Martie, not only defended Maines but amplified her comments. Given an hour for prime-time damage control, the Dixie Chicks instead stopped the network cheerleading for the war dead in its tracks and expressed the honest confusion many people are feeling far more effectively than any of the strident rhetoric that has emanated from the left as well as the right.

With the Chicks not following the preset P.R. script for smoothing over a public brouhaha, it was up to Sawyer to provide the pornography. You couldn't find it in her connecting narration, which was simply the typical pap that passes for writing in television journalism—"Freewheeling . . . high-spirits . . . the famously untamed lead singer . . . the rebel daughter of a renowned steel-guitar player . . . the refined sisters . . . in that friendly, country way, we know all about their lives. . . . There would be frightening threats, towering rage, in the words of another of their hit songs, a landslide." The pornography came from the way Sawyer, frustrated in her attempt to offer the band up for ritual sacrifice, chose to stand in for the bullies.

Since Maines' comment, the band has received death threats and had round-the-clock security posted at their homes. The people who attend their upcoming concert tour will have to pass through metal detectors. The threats haven't just come from yahoos, like the caller to a radio show heard during the "Primetime" interview who said, "I think they should send Natalie over to Eye-rack, strap 'er to a bomb, and just drop 'er over Baghdad." A San Antonio DJ claimed to know where Maines lived and said a posse should go over to her house and straighten her out. And in South Carolina, where the band will open its tour later this week, a legislator rose in the state assembly and said, "Anyone who thinks about going to that concert ought to be ready, ready, ready to run away from it."

Sawyer didn't descend to this level of bullying. And she didn't adopt the strategies of the higher thugs like Bill O'Reilly, who simply talk their opponents into submission. Sawyer's tactics were subtler, more insidious. Instead of journalist, the role Sawyer chose to play was the junior high school principal who aims to shame you into jelly with a combination of starch and steel.

From the beginning, Sawyer aimed to put the Dixie Chicks in their place. She began the show by saying, "They're not exactly the people your civics teacher would expect to find at the center of a raging debate over free speech in America." These are just country singers, after all, she was saying. Who would expect thought from them? And then, at every turn, the Dixie Chicks simply outthought Diane Sawyer.

Instead of playing a plea for forgiveness, the interview played out as a drama between two sharply different views of what it means to be an American citizen. There was Sawyer's view, in which only certain people are qualified to speak their minds, and the view of the Dixie Chicks, a vision shot through with contingencies and uncertainties far more complex than Sawyer could process. "I guess on some level I feel like me speaking out, not only that particular statement, but here today, is the most patriotic thing I can do," Maines said. . . .

One of the remarkable things about the interview was the Chicks' lack of invective—toward the troops, toward people who supported the war and even toward Bush. What they expressed about the president was honest disappointment. At one point, Maines imagined what she would have liked to have heard Bush say about the protesters. "You know," she imagined the president saying, "I saw them. I appreciate the sentiment that they're coming from. I appreciate that these are passionate citizens of the United States. But I feel, I really feel, that this is the right thing to do." Sawyer attempted to counter by saying the president had affirmed the right to protest.

But the clip that followed, of Bush on March 6 following worldwide antiwar protests, told a different story. Dripping contempt, Bush said, "First of all, size of protests, it's like deciding, well I'm going to decide policy based on a focus group." It's the perfect distillation of the arrogance of the Bush administration, reducing the fears and concerns of people all over the world to "a focus group." It's exactly what Maguire meant when she said, "I felt like there was a lack of compassion every time I saw Bush talking about this . . . for people questioning this, for people about to die for this on both sides."

At one point in the interview, Maines said, "People have died to give you this right. That's what I'm doing. I'm using that right." But she is speaking at a particularly ugly time in American history, when using that right is enough to get you branded a traitor. As Dick Cheney has said, "You're either with us or against us."

"That's not true—it's not true," Maines said of Cheney's comment. Though to many Americans, it is true. This weekend, I was walking through the central New York town of Clinton and came upon a flier in a store window for a rally in support of the troops. The legend on the top of the flier read "Loyalty Day." The meaning was clear: If you don't support the war, you're a disloyal American.

This is what public discourse has come down to in America right now. The litany is depressing and familiar, from Ari Fleischer's admonition to Bill Maher after 9/11 that Americans have to watch what they say, to the suspension of habeas corpus for thousands of people who've been arrested, to the even more onerous dissolution of civil liberties that would come under the PATRIOT II act. In the *New York Times* on April 27, Thomas Friedman wrote, "It feels as if some people want to use this war to create a multiparty democracy in Iraq and a one-party state in America."

And it cuts both ways. The left in no way holds power in America at this moment, but its vision of what politics should be often seems to partake of the same either/or dogmatism. In the current issue of *Dissent,* Michael Wreszin writes in response to an article by Michael Kazin, which he feels exemplifies the dangers of the magazine's belief that the left should speak "patriotically to our fellow citizens."

Wreszin writes, "Anyone seriously engaged in activist politics wants to develop a constituency and see it grow. But did Kazin expect [Martin Luther] King to communicate with the average white citizen in racist Mississippi and Cicero, Illinois?" The vision of politics that this statement reveals is remarkable. Wreszin apparently believes that Martin Luther King was preaching only to the choir, that he didn't try to communicate to the people who disagreed with him. (How then, you wonder, did he expect to change anything?) It's the opposite of the belief that politics is about engagement, and an affirmation of a politics that speaks only to true believers. In other words, it's a rejection of everything that it reasonably means to be political.

As much as I loathe the determination of the Bush administration to use the threat of terrorism to abolish civil liberties and create a government that feels it has no obligation to disclose the reasons for the decisions it takes, you can understand why people buy into that when you see protesters holding signs equating Bush with Saddam, or the placard shown in footage during "Primetime" that read "Bombing Is Terrorism." Real politics are not possible when people abdicate the responsibility to think in favor of ideology, because ideology is always the enemy of thought.

This is the atmosphere in which Natalie Maines chose to speak out. And it's the atmosphere in which she and Martie Maguire and Emily Robison maintain that their questioning of the government and of Bush's willingness to respect the opinions of others marks them as good patriots.

It's not just the clarity and persistence of what they've said that marks their bravery, but who they are. As "Primetime" pointed out, they are hardly the only celebrities to have spoken out against the war. The show noted that Susan Sarandon had been disinvited from a United Way fundraiser, and that her partner, Tim Robbins, had been barred from a celebration of "Bull Durham" at the Baseball Hall of Fame in Cooperstown, N.Y. But nobody is bulldozing cassettes of Sarandon and Robbins' movies, or Sean Penn's, who took a trip to Iraq a few months back. Nobody is boycotting "The West Wing," although Martin Sheen is a longtime activist. And nobody is burning Michael Moore's book *Stupid White Men*. Not to suggest that those celebrities haven't taken grief, but it's no surprise when Sarandon or Robbins or Sheen or Moore speak out against the war. That's a logical action, given their very public politics.

But none of these people reach as wide an audience as the Dixie Chicks, who are the biggest-selling female recording artists of all time. When my Salon colleague Stephanie Zacharek wrote a few weeks back that the backlash against the Chicks was certainly due in part to the traditional conservatism of country music, she got letters accusing her of painting country fans as a bunch of ignorant hicks. Those responses fail to take into account the simple fact of the disapproval that has traditionally been leveled at country stars who don't toe the line.

In the '60s, after saying he was a fan of the Beatles and recording versions of Chuck Berry's "Memphis" and "Johnny B. Goode," Buck Owens took out an ad in a Nashville fan magazine called "Pledge to Country Music" where, among other things, he said, "I Shall Sing No Song That Is Not a Country Song." Johnny Cash alienated many country fans with songs like "The Ballad of Ira Hayes" and later protest numbers like "Man in Black" and "Singin' in Vietnam Talkin' Blues" (an amazing song that has much to say about how you can be against a war and care about the safety of the troops). That didn't fit in with a format where a song like Merle Haggard's "Okie From Muskogee" (reactionary as hell and still a great song) could be a huge hit, or where, at the height of Watergate, Nixon was welcomed by Roy Acuff onto the stage of the Grand Ole Opry.

The simple fact is that country plays to a huge demographic, and often an older one, and the majority of Americans support the war. It was inevitable that the Dixie

Chicks were bound to have, among their fans, people who would be upset by any antiwar statements. In the "Primetime" interview, Maguire talked about trying to convert friends to country music, people who said, "That's redneck music, those people are so backward and conservative." It was obvious how that attitude pained her. But it's hardly painting a large segment of the country audience as rednecks to acknowledge the conservatism of country music.

"It's all about being country-music artists," Maguire told *Entertainment Weekly*. "And [country radio not playing our music] is proving that it is about country music." Maguire told Sawyer of their colleagues in country music, "I was surprised at how many would come forward but didn't want to come forward publicly." Among the things reported in the *Entertainment Weekly* cover story was the fact that Vince Gill has had his patriotism questioned for saying it was time to lay off the Dixie Chicks. EW also reported that Toby Keith projects a doctored image of Maines with Saddam Hussein during his stage show, and that Travis Tritt, that mullet that passes for a man, has called the band "cowardly."

On March 20, RCA Nashville publicity sent out an e-mail headed "Sara Evans Voices Her Views in Glamour Magazine," in which the country singer is quoted as saying, "I trust [President Bush] to do whatever is necessary to protect our nation from al-Qaeda, Saddam Hussein and other terrorists. It's disheartening to me to hear negativity about our President during this highly critical time—and it is especially disheartening to hear comments made outside the United States. Republican or Democrat, we have an immediate duty as Americans to rally around our President and troops." Wonder who she was talking about?

For all the talk about how the Dixie Chicks have destroyed their career, people haven't pointed out (or pointed out tangentially, as Sawyer did) that "Home" is still No. 3 on the country charts and selling about 33,000 copies a week, and that most of the shows on their upcoming tour have sold out. It makes no business sense for country radio to ban the band, but I think that the boycott was just the excuse that country radio was looking for to stick it back to the Dixie Chicks. The trio had already challenged the format with "Long Time Gone," the first single from "Home." One of the verses went "We listen to the radio to hear what's cookin'/But the music ain't got no soul/Now they sound tired but they don't sound haggard/They got money but they don't have cash/They got Junior but they don't have Hank."

Since the Chicks were the biggest stars in country, country radio had no choice but to play a single that slammed most of the music it played as prefab and anonymous. "Country music doesn't need the Dixie Chicks," said one caller to a radio show heard on "Primetime." But since the band has proved a huge crossover success, and did it with an album more "country" than their previous two, country music may find that it needs the Chicks more than they need it.

Given their huge success—which shows no signs of dissipating—you have to be a special kind of ass to claim, as some have done, that all this has been a bid for publicity. The biggest stars in country music didn't need publicity, especially coming off an album that debuted at No. 1 on the pop charts and stayed there for weeks. You would have to be very cynical or very stupid to believe that anyone would choose the kind of publicity that would bring them death threats.

Still, it seems to me that the Dixie Chicks are operating now less in the realm of country music than they are in the realm of punk, which, in his book *Ranters & Crowd Pleasers*, Greil Marcus called "infinitely more than a musical style, period . . . an event in a cultural time [that was] an earthquake . . . throwing all sorts of once-hidden phenomena into stark relief." The *Entertainment Weekly* cover, another example of how the band has refused to affect the demure pose that would prove they are backing down, appropriates the tactic used initially by the Riot Grrrl bands, who appeared onstage with words like "Bitch" and "Slut" scrawled on their midriffs. Again, it is impossible to divorce the courage of the Dixie Chicks' stance from the place they occupy in mainstream pop.

I don't mean to lessen the determination to find their own voice that characterized riot-grrrl bands like Bikini Kill, and Heavens to Betsy, Excuse 17, and that still characterizes Sleater-Kinney. But the fringe offers a safer place for people to pursue that voice. As the Dixie Chicks have seen, there is more at stake for mainstream performers who decide not to play by the rules. Implicitly, they call everything around them into question. And so it seems a harbinger when you go back and listen to "Home" and hear Natalie Maines sing "You don't like the sound of the truth/Coming from my mouth . . . I don't think that I'm afraid anymore to say that I would rather die trying," or see the roadside sign on the back of the CD booklet "We Are Changing the Way We Do Business."

But it's not just the terms of their own success, or even the terms of pop music, in which the Dixie Chicks are causing tremors. It's the very terms in which public discourse is conducted—or not conducted—in America at the moment. "The people who are calling for a boycott are also exercising their right to free speech," some are bound to write to me. Of course they are. But I question anyone's dedication to free speech when they express it by trying to shut down other voices—not by engaging them or debating them or making a case why they're wrong, but just trying to shut them down. "In wartime only the clandestine press can be truly free," Marcus wrote in an earlier essay about punk. For all the willingness of the mainstream press to roll over and frolic at the feet of the Bush administration, for all the ways in which Bush and Ashcroft are using the Constitution as a piece of toilet paper, I do not believe that a fascist takeover is imminent in America. That is an excuse to shy away from the work that needs to be done to defeat Bush and restore the civil liberties he has trashed.

What I do believe is that for all the fear in the air, fear of the terror without and the repression within, there is also open to us at this moment the chance of exhilaration. Freedom may never seem so alluring as when it is most threatened, when the Republic reaches a moment where, as Norman Mailer wrote in 1968, it can bring forth "the most fearsome totalitarianism the world has ever known . . . or a babe of a new world brave and tender, artful and wild." There's exhilaration in any moment when the country has the choice of living up to either the best or the worst version of itself. I'm grateful to the Dixie Chicks for reminding us of that exhilaration, for carrying on, aware of the social limits that have been placed on doubt and dissent, and still insisting that questioning and digging for facts are the mark of patriotism.

That was the freedom offered by the civil rights movement, and it's one of those voices I hear now, the voice of Fannie Lou Hamer, delegate of the Mississippi Freedom Democratic Party, addressing a committee at the 1964 Democratic Convention in Atlantic City, N.J., to challenge the seating of the state delegation elected under the system that prohibited many blacks from voting. "Is this America?" Hamer asked. "The land of the free and the home of the brave? Where we have to sleep with our telephones off the hook, because our lives be threatened daily?"

The comparison only goes so far. As rich pop stars, the Dixie Chicks have security options open to them that were not open to Hamer and the other people working for voters rights in Mississippi. But when people fantasize about strapping Natalie Maines to a missile headed for Baghdad, when a state legislator suggests that anyone who thinks about going to a Dixie Chicks' concert better be "ready to run" (from what—a lynch mob?), when it's held that you cannot question a war and still desire the safety of the troops, when you're told that it's OK to question policy but not the president, Hamer's question remains. Is this America? The thrill, and maybe the sorrow, of the months to come will be finding out.

Further Reading

Gumbel, Andrew. "Country Fans Spurn the Anti-war Dixie Chicks." *The Independent*, August 9, 2006. Accessed July 2007 at www.news. independent.co.uk/world/middle_east/Article1217824.ece.

Latham, Aaron. "The Ballad of the Urban Cowboy: America's Search for True Grit." *Esquire*, September 12, 1978, 21–30.

Malone, Bill C. *Country Music U.S.A.* Rev. ed. Austin: University of Texas Press, 1985.

Peterson, Richard A. *Creating Country Music: Fabricating Authenticity*. Chicago: University of Chicago Press, 1997.

Tosches, Nick. *Country: Living Legends and Dying Metaphors in America's Biggest Music*. New York: Charles Scribner's Sons, 1985.

Tyrangiel, Josh. "Chicks in the Line of Fire." *Time*, May 21, 2006. Accessed July 2007 at www.time.com/time/magazine/article/0,9171,1196419-1,00.html.

Discography

Dixie Chicks. *Taking the Long Way*. Sony, 2006.

_____. *Home*. Sony, 2002.

_____. *Wide Open Spaces*. Sony, 1998.

Brooks, Garth. *Ropin' the Wind*. Capitol, 2001.

Cash, Johnny. *The Essential Johnny Cash*. Sony, 2002.

Cline, Patsy. *The Definitive Collection*. MCA Nashville, 2004.

Parton, Dolly. *Ultimate Dolly Parton*. RCA, 2003.

Rogers, Kenny. *42 Ultimate Hits*. Capitol, 2004.

The Smithsonian Collection of Classic Country Music. PS 15640, 1981.

Twain, Shania. *Come on Over*. Mercury Nashville, 1997.

86. Performance as Simulacrum, Boy Bands, and Other 21st-Century Epiphanies

Chapter 82 mentioned the proliferation of teen pop in the late 1990s amid the increased concentration of radio formats in the United States. Teen pop and, in particular, the popularity of boy bands during this period represented the cresting of a trend that had long been part of mainstream popular music. The tradition of four or five men singing together in harmony can be found in the barbershop quartets and African American gospel quartets that thrived at the turn of the last century, which then transformed into 1940s-era groups like the Ink Spots and then into doowop in the 1950s. Add to this musical tradition the pursuit of a young teen or "tween," predominantly female audience established by the marketing of first the girl groups and then the Beatles and the Monkees in the mid-1960s, and all the elements were in place for the blossoming of the millennial boy bands. The Jackson five established the clearest prototype for the genre in the late 1960s: five young men, some of whose voices had not yet changed, sang and danced in a pop-inflected soul (or R&B) style. In a pattern that continues to the present day, the Jackson five begat a white version of themselves, the Osmonds, a musical family of seasoned professionals who shot to fame following a change to a style closely approximating that of the Jacksons.

New variations on this theme were produced in the early 1980s by the Puerto Rican group Menudo and Boston-area producer Maurice Starr, who formed first an African American group, New Edition, and then, shortly thereafter, a white group, New Kids on the Block. Starr subtly updated the Jackson five sound, adding elements of hip-hop and electro-funk. Early nineties groups such as Boyz II Men (African American) experienced great success in the format, but that only dimly presaged the explosion of popularity that greeted the Backstreet Boys and 'NSync (both white) at the end of the decade.

The late 1990s were also notable for two other cultural phenomena: the growth of "reality TV," and the "dot-com" bubble. Reality TV, like the boy band genre, could boast a long history preceding the late 1990s, dating back to the beginning of TV in the form of shows like *Candid Camera*, in which unsuspecting people were caught in the act of responding to pranks. However, not until the international success of *Big Brother* (Netherlands, 1997; U.S., 2000) and *Survivor* (Sweden, 1997; U.S., 2000) did these shows dominate programming and elicit their own genre name. The dot-com bubble was created by the belief that Internet-based companies that neither produced anything nor made a profit were nevertheless worth something—namely, whatever people thought they were worth, which from 1997 to 2000 was quite a lot. However, the effect of "reality" created by reality TV resembled the effect of market value created by dot-com stocks: what media theorist Jean Baudrillard termed a "simulacrum"—that is, a copy of an object for which there exists no original.[1]

Joshua Clover's article on the boy band phenomena came at the craze's height in the summer of 2000 and discusses the show that combined the boy band and reality TV manias, *Making the Band*, in which teen pop Svengali Lou Pearlman chose five contestants to form a new boy band, subsequently christened O-Town. "O-Town" stands for "Orlando," home of Disney World, and Clover makes plain that boy bands stand in the same relation to more "authentic" genres of popular music as Disney World stands to the world outside its gates. In other words, and to paraphrase Baudrillard, Disney World exists to convince us that the world outside of Disney World is real.[2] In a circle that comes close to being complete, turn-of-the-century pop stars Britney Spears, Christina Aguilera, and Justin Timberlake were cast members on the *Mickey Mouse Club* (broadcast on the Disney Channel), forming a (harmonized) echo to the barbershop quartet singing of the Osmond Brothers in Disneyland (ancestor of Disney World) almost 40 years earlier. Clover clarifies that the connection between these phenomena might lie in the heady delirium prompted by the gravity-free ascent of the dot-com stocks. Middle-class tweens, flush with their parents' excess cash, could buy boy band CDs while their parents' fantasies of instant wealth that they hoped to achieve through IPOs (initial public offerings) of dot-com stocks were fed by hybrid reality TV-game shows such as *Who Wants to Be a Millionaire* (the most-watched show in the United States during the 1999–2000 season).

Jukebox Culture:
How I Learned to Stop Worrying and Love the Boy Band
Joshua Clover

"The tortured misunderstandings between elitist taste and popular culture are to agonize the coming century: The potentially sublime is criticized for being cheap and unreal." So said architect-theorist Rem Koolhaas about Coney Island amusement

---

1. Baudrillard's fullest exposition of his notion of the simulacrum may be found in *Simulacra and Simulation*, trans. Sheila Faria Glaser (Ann Arbor: University of Michigan Press, [1981] 1994), 1–42.

2. Baudrillard, *Simulacra and Simulation*, 12–13.

Source: "Jukebox Culture: How I Learned to Stop Worrying and Love the Boy Band," Joshua Glover. Reprinted with permission from *SPIN* magazine.

parks circa 1900, but that goes double circa right about now for the gazillion-selling 'N Sync. And Backstreet Boys. And Britney and Christina. And LFO. And a thousand more waiting in the wings. They are the new world economy, they are the most brilliant dance pop ever made, and if you're still worried about how unreal they are, you are made to be faded.

Fakeness simply isn't a problem anymore (just ask pro wrestling, formerly an absurd sport and now a fab soap opera). What's mysterious is why it ever was. Consider it this way: Recorded music bears the same relationship to live music that movies do to plays. They are synthesized, technologized phantasmagorias that sacrifice realism for unalloyed pleasure. (Pssst…when the Death Star blows up, it doesn't really blow up.)

Hence the potentially sublime genius of *Making the Band*, the television series that synthesizes a new boy band from an ocean of auditioning wanna-be-a-millionaires. The products of the dream-making machinery will go on to live their lives on the charts as well as the airwaves. Nobody cares that the real artist here is no musician but grotesque Svengali Lou Pearlman, businessman behind 'N Sync and Backstreet Boys. And even the "boys" who make it know this isn't about Art: Finalist Trevor Penick notes that the selections were about "what five they thought looked best together." The kids can now admit what Milli Vanilli, fatally, could not: They are finely-tooled spokesmodels for a concept called O-Town. That's the band's name, as in their home base, Orlando, Florida, teen-pop's Emerald City.

Bryan Chan, who reached the final eight, says "The thing being based out of Orlando was very apropos. It's Theme Park City; everything that surrounds you is surreal." Sure, the local soundstages of Disney (which just happens to own ABC, which just happens to air *Making the Band*) gave you Mesdemoiselles Spears and Aguilera and any number of boy-bandits. But this town isn't about music any more than Space Mountain is about space or mountains. It's about contrived pleasure in its purest forms, as divorced from reality as possible.

The famous argument about the original Disneyland was that, in being such a fantasy, it made the bizarre world outside its gates—Beverly Hills, Compton, Hollywood—seem normal, acceptable. Teen pop does the same job with music, insuring that the formulaic and stylized performances of "real" rock and rap seem authentic by comparison. Blink-182 should lick the Backstreet Boys' boots in return for whatever shred of credibility they have.

But boy bands shouldn't be seen as simple unreal versions of actual musicians; they're complex versions of, say, Pokémon figures. If you like Pikachu, you'll go for Justin Timberlake; if you like Gengar, you're bound for A.J. If you don't know who these are, get out of the way. There are 27.6 million "tweens" (eight- to 14-year-olds) who do.

Beneficiaries of a bizarrely blossoming economy, tweens have pocket green and they know how to use it, feeding off the imperial power of their own market share. And just as wandering the mall is a kid's first taste of what it means to be part of a diversified multinational, committing to your first favorite boy band at the turn of the millennium is practice for owning the perfect tech stock. Call it "adventure capital"; the thrill that goes with owning a scrap of a massive winner and checking the Top 40 every week like it's the Nasdaq. The tween population will expand through 2010. And after that? When I asked Trevor Penick what he expected to be doing in 35 years, he paused for only a second and suggested, "A 35-year reunion tour?"

> The boom in reality TV led to a great variety of hybrid shows that applied aspects of the reality format to other genres. The most successful of these, *American Idol*, combined aspects of the *Star Search* type of talent

show with the ongoing narrative of the *Big Brother* type of reality show. *Idol* topped the U.S. television ratings for seven years in a row, while also confirming a new sort of vocal *lingua franca*, since reinforced in another top-rated TV drama, *Glee*: a breathy yet powerful melisma-infused style derived both from post-1980 R&B singers like Whitney Houston and Mariah Carey and from contemporary musical theater, which could be applied willy nilly to almost any sort of material. In what could be termed the "karaoke" approach to popular music, both *Idol* and *Glee* provided further evidence that the ability to provide a good performance of a well-known song had supplanted the notion of 60s-era authenticity based on the notion that the singer was also the songwriter and was thus expressing his or her own feelings. The emphasis thus shifts in discussions of value from a performance of the self to the evaluation of craft. An interesting aspect of this change in pop music aesthetics is the presence of judges on *American Idol* who attempt to produce a critical discourse that will be intelligible to a lay audience.

Nina Ayoub's interview of Katherine Meizel highlights many aspects of *Idol* that are arguably responsible for its appeal: the breakdown of production and consumption, so that the audience is perceived as creating the commodity that they will eventually purchase; the use of "American Dream" narratives as a thread to create interest and sympathy for the contestants; and what Meizel calls the "postmodern collapsing of boundaries." One of the most interesting collapsing or blurring of boundaries occurs in the distinction between politics and entertainment: the period in which audience participation in the form of "voting" has exploded has also witnessed growing apathy and shrinking participation in the realm of electoral politics in North America.

Idol Pursuits
Nina C. Ayoub

American Idol has long topped the ratings on television. In scholarly publishing, however, it has been more of a blip. This month, in what appears to be the first university-press book on *Idol*, Katherine Meizel's *Idolized: Music, Media, and Identity in American Idol* (Indiana University Press) hits the stage.

The author, a visiting assistant professor at the Oberlin Conservatory of Music, brings an intriguing background to all things Idolatrous. The new book derives from her Ph.D. work in ethnomusicology at the University of California at Santa Barbara. Meizel has also written extensively about the show for Slate, a site she thanks for allowing her to "work out my ideas without using words like 'postmodern' and 'teleological.'" However, with a nod to Fredric Jameson and Claude Lévi-Strauss on page one, the new book is firmly in the academic realm. Along with analyzing TV footage, commercial recordings, and discourse on Idol, Meizel conducted interviews with contestants as well as with an Idol music director and a vocal coach. She attended broadcast rehearsals and accompanied some of her former singing students to auditions. (Meizel has a second doctorate, in musical arts, also from UCSB.) Her next project will be on the crossover genre of "popera."

One is curious: Did the scholar audition for Idol? Alas, she was past the cutoff age, 28. "I absolutely would have," Meizel says, "but only for research. I know I would never have made it past the first round!"

Via e-mail, the author answered some questions on her work.

Q. American Idol is an unusual subject for an ethnomusicologist. You've suggested that the field is changing. How so?

A. I began as a graduate student, when ethnomusicology was seeing an intense broadening of approach and topics of study, and an increase in cross-disciplinary work. And there has been much more interest in popular music in general over the past decade. The Popular Music section at the Society for Ethnomusicology has grown exponentially every year that I've been a member—since 2003, I think.

Most importantly for my own work, there is a burgeoning interest in mainstream, commercial pop music—though to be honest, I think in certain ways that other kinds of popular music (rock, metal, jazz, hip-hop) that are understood as bastions of "art" or valued as musics of resistance are still privileged as research material. People will tell you that this is a battle that's already been won in academe, but though I've had lots of support, I'm also aware from experience that there is still some real resistance to acknowledging mainstream culture-industry phenomena like Idol as significant and legitimate for study. I hope that my book will join the work of my "poptimist" colleagues in solidifying the understanding of mainstream pop as socially meaningful.

Q. What do you see as the "serious cultural work" done by Idol?

A. American Idol was born nine months to the day after 9/11. That's a bit coincidental, since while it was conceived as an American show, it ended up being initially developed in the U.K. the year before—but its success has been anything but accidental. At this historical moment when everything was suddenly called into question—America's place in the world, who is American, and what that means—how could a show about exactly those things, embedded in a framework of American music, fail? American Idol at once reaffirms old ideas and ideologies of American culture, and helps to reshape it for the new 21st century. There is the constant, careful reiteration of particular American Dream narratives (crystallized during an earlier time of national crisis) and an associated centrality of movement (geographical and class) in the imagining of Americanness. There are clearly delineated, packaged-for-sale American identities, while at the same time Idol capitalizes on the tension between multiculturalist and assimilationist goals, and on the postmodern collapsing of boundaries—between music genres, between producer and consumer, and between politics and entertainment. The incorporation of audience voting is key here.

Q. What is the wider significance of the voting?

A. The voting process is one of the most important things about Idol, the way the show plays with the idea of consumer choice dressed up as the quintessential act of democracy. The process is basically deciding what you are going to buy, but it's made to look like an election. It's a very compelling feeling, that you have this choice ("you decide"), and it's also very smart business because it provides a guaranteed consumer market for a product (in Idol's case, albums or concert tickets, etc.). If people vote for something and believe that they have a part in creating it as a commodity, they'll be invested in it and more likely to buy it. And voting is an idea that's caught on like wildfire throughout popular culture and the media over the past 10 years—everything is about voting now, about making consumers feel like they have this cultural agency.

In the widest sense, Idol voting has gotten tangled up in discourse about democracy. Every year there are murmurs in the press asking why, if Idol got 500 million votes, a presidential election doesn't draw equivalent participation among American citizens. Of course, it isn't the same thing at all; Idol viewers can vote multiple times, or when they're 12 years old. But the fact that we draw this contrast is important. It points to our concerns about the conflation of enter-tainment and politics, about a perceived loss of boundaries (see "reality TV") in our 21st-century lives.

Q. One of your subjects is William "She Bangs" Hung, a rejected contestant in the audition phase who drew much ridicule but went on to become a celebrity. You link his winning by losing to the American Dream. How so?

A. We tend to focus on the idea of success as the ultimate and only possible out-come of the American Dream, but failure is an important part of Dream dis-course, too. We have to fall down if we're going to move on up, and being cut down to size is part of the process of making it big. In Dream terms, initial failure keeps us humble, makes us stronger, gives us something to overcome, and ultimately becomes a steppingstone on the way to success. William Hung's story (while there is certainly more to it) as presented on Idol exempli-fies this.

Q. Singers on Idol, you note, have been alternately praised and rebuked for melisma, a kind of ornamentation in singing also known as riffing or runs. What are the politics of melisma?

A. This is how I got into Idol in the first place, when I read some journalism criti-cizing Idol singers for an "overuse" of melisma in comparison to older singers like Aretha Franklin. At first, I actually went and measured melisma use in some older singers and in Idol singers (that part didn't make it into the book, because I didn't feel like my process was controlled enough), and didn't find an increase in occurrence so much as changes in practice—so I started to won-der, what are the real issues at stake here? Just aesthetics? The more I talked to people, the more I found that there's a history of critical and public resistance to melisma, linked to ideas about race and religion and nation, and the dif-ficult balance that is required in covering famous repertoire, to acknowledge pop history but at the same time establish individuality as a singer.

Q. The new season is still in its audition stage, but do you have first impressions of Jennifer Lopez and Aerosmith's Steven Tyler as Idol's new judges? What's your take on Tyler's "appreciation" of female contestants?

A. They haven't had much of a chance to shine yet, but there's a lot that's familiar so far. I think I said in my first Slate post this season that Steven Tyler is like the judging love child of Simon Cowell's wandering eye and Paula Abdul's wander-ing mind.

Further Reading

Levy, Frederick. *The Ultimate Boy Band Book*. New York: Pocket, 2000.

Meizel, Katherine. *Idolized: Music, Media, and Identity in American Idol*. Bloomington: Indiana
    University Press, 2011.

Rushfield, Richard. *American Idol: The Untold Story*. New York: Hyperion, 2011.

Discography

98 Degrees. *98 Degrees and Rising*. Motown, 1998.

Backstreet Boys. *Millenium*. Jive, 1999.

N'Sync. *No Strings Attached*. Jive, 2000.

87. Lady Gaga and the Triumph of Camp

Lady Gaga (Stefani Joanne Angelina Germanotta, b. 1986) appeared like a
meteor, a comet, or perhaps even an asteroid. Signaling the ascendance
and then utter domination of contemporary electronic dance music in its
pop form, as well as the primacy of video over audio, Gaga became the
first artist to go over 1 billion views on YouTube. A portent of post-post-
modern artists to come, the idea that a norm no longer exists with which
to compare a parody was so passé by the time she recorded her debut
album (*The Fame*, 2008) that the pastiches of the 1980s had become the
new material from which artists like Gaga could create *their* pastiches.
Further confirmation that the authenticity/artificiality debate has become
ever less relevant, Gaga takes irony and artificiality as a given and goes
from there. The descendant of Warhol and Bowie as much as Madonna
and Michael Jackson, her public life in the mass media is as significant
to her persona as are her musical productions. Her activities in all these
realms are animated by a camp aesthetic, which emphasizes artifice,
frivolity, and absurdity through the exaggeration of societal norms.[1]

---

1. The classic essay on the subject is "Notes on Camp" by Susan Sontag in *Against Interpretation and Other Essays* (New York: Farrar, Straus and Giroux, 1966), 275–92.

However, her supporters will hasten to add that she is a "real musician," proving nothing else, perhaps, than that the ghost of some aspect of authenticity continues to haunt us.

Sasha Frere-Jones begins his profile of Lady Gaga with a meditation on the nature of the ephemeral, which in this case includes the one-hit wonders that form such a significant part of pop music history. Some of these figures turn out to have a long-term significance that is impossible to sense in the moment of their initial popularity. In early 2009, when this piece first appeared, it was unclear whether Gaga would be a one- or two-hit wonder or an artist with a longer public presence. What Frere-Jones finds unusual about her is how she calls attention to herself as an artist, which is the basis for his comparison of Gaga to indie rockers. At the same time, he pinpoints a paradox: How weird can Gaga be, after all, when she is achieving such a high level of mass popularity? Presciently reading her ascendance as a sign of the shift from hip-hop to "electro-pop/disco," Frere-Jones draws parallels between Gaga and Madonna that have now become commonplace. The question he closes with is how the tension between indie quirkiness and mainstream grooves can be sustained. Three years later, the answer to this has become somewhat clearer.

Ladies Wild: How Not Dumb Is Gaga?
Sasha Frere-Jones

Dedicated fans of popular music have a certain conversation at least once a year. Call it The Question of Endurance. You and your friends are talking about music, and the conversation turns to a popular band. You express support. A friend voices her opinion, maybe as favorable as yours, but appends a qualifier: "I like them, but will they be around in ten years?" You may feel compelled to defend whomever it is you're talking about, covering the present moment and the future with your positive take. After trying this approach, though, you realize that pop music has no Constitution and doesn't operate like a de-facto Supreme Court: precedent is not always established, and isn't even necessary. Pop rarely accretes in a tidy, serial manner—it zigs, zags, eats itself, and falls over its shoelaces. Some pop successes go head to head with Blake and Bach; others win their blue ribbons by doing everything upside down and out of tune.

Exceptional pop creates a precedent precisely by abrogating the presumptive rules. How did that grouchy Bob Dylan become a critical favorite by spitting back at interviewers with silence and riddles? (Didn't being cute and funny help the Beatles? Why would the opposite behavior work just as well, and at exactly the same time?) How did the Jamaican shantytown hero Bob Marley become an American Ivy

League dorm-room staple? How did the tiny, androgynous Prince become a hero to alpha-male guitar-solo fiends? Pop acts become classic when they reveal the contingent nature of "classic."

So it goes with one-hit (or two-hit) wonders, who can also become classics—or not. The nature of pop recycling makes it hard to measure, or define, endurance. In 1980, Gary Numan's synthesizer pop song "Cars" was a reliable presence on broadcast radio here and in the United Kingdom. By 1985, though, you'd have been hard pressed to find a trace of Numan in the mainstream of pop. Today, he's ubiquitous—"Cars" has been referenced in television shows and pop songs steadily throughout the past decade, and Numan's synthesizer sounds are audible in the work of tiny Brooklyn bands and enormous stars alike. Just because the anonymous Euro-techno group Eiffel 65 was on the charts for only one stretch in 2000 does not mean that its mission was not accomplished. Eiffel 65's one known song—its nonsense hit "Blue"—is the basis for a new Top Forty hit by Flo Rida called "Sugar," and has inspired many user-generated videos on YouTube that are all better than the official video, a C.G.I. monstrosity. The artist who stays on the charts for years without interruption sometimes does it by virtue of professional acuity and inoffensive predictability. Some of pop's most delightful figures endure exactly because we can't figure out what they are up to.

Stefani Joanne Angelina Germanotta would have you believe that she's not just beating the system—in her version, she's stormed the castle walls, spirited away the Dauphin, and changed the national language to semaphore. Better known as Lady Gaga, Germanotta was born twenty-three years ago in Yonkers and has had two verifiable worldwide No. 1 hits, which are definitely dance music: "Just Dance" and "Poker Face." (The kids say electro-pop, I say disco, and I suppose we're both right.) Less verifiable is her theorizing about her work. She cites Andy Warhol, claims to be a "fame Robin Hood" who has lost her mind, opines in public about whether a certain shade of red is "Communist," and has dropped Rilke's name more than once. Don't take this skepticism for distaste—Lady Gaga and I share preferences, especially as far as well-written pop music goes, and I am thrilled to see Communism and Rilke getting ink. I am also happy that her album, "The Fame," will be with us all year, even if you can't find Marx or Rilke anywhere in the music. What is most amusing is watching a trained pro like Lady Gaga try to sell herself as the Flying Lizards. Who were they? A colorfully deadpan British art-school unit of brainy, primitive one-hit wonders ("Money") who did business in the early eighties and are resurrected in spirit every seven years or so. They were really odd.

Gaga is not odd, give or take some warbles and that one time during a session for AOL when she pounded on her keyboard with her high heel, but she is as smart as she repeatedly claims to be. Germanotta went to Convent of the Sacred Heart High School and grew up on the Upper West Side. (Her parents call her Joanne.) After a stint at N.Y.U.'s Tisch School, she dropped out and, while still a teen, went to Los Angeles, where she got a contract with Def Jam. That gig ended in three months, so Germanotta came home—not yet calling herself Lady Gaga—and began performing songs and burlesque routines in New York clubs with a friend, the d.j. Lady Starlight. Eventually, she returned to Los Angeles, and signed with Interscope Records. She wrote songs for the Pussycat Dolls and one for Britney Spears (a strange, compelling love song disguised as a dance number, called "Quicksand," which is available only on the European version of Spears's "Circus") and worked with Akon, the certified pop star with an ornately embellished criminal past, who signed Gaga to his label.

This is not as weird as it might sound. Gaga can really sing and really write. That said, she embellished when she says, of "The Fame," that she "did the whole goddamn thing." In reality, her collaborators on her début album are a wisely picked cast of new and old pros who know how to make pop records sound like pop records. Rob Fusari, who dubbed Germanotta Lady Gaga, after the Queen song "Radio Ga Ga," co-wrote some of Destiny's Child's best work. RedOne is a Moroccan producer whose song "Bamboo" was named the Official Melody of soccer's 2006 FIFA World Cup. More to the point, RedOne's longtime residence in Sweden means that he has access to the enormous ice pool of Nordic hooks that Americans never seem to match. It makes sense that RedOne and Germanotta received a Grammy nomination for "Just Dance," the song that presumably inspired Spears to enlist Ms. Gaga's help for "Circus."

How not dumb is Lady Gaga? Released exactly one year ago, "Just Dance" was one of the first big records to ride the sea change in pop, away from hip-hop and back toward disco, the music that has been in charge of the charts in Europe for a long time. (One current acknowledgment of this shift is a single by a rapper named Kid Cudi, who is currently jostling with Lady Gaga on the iTunes charts with his song "Day 'n' Nite," which re-imagines hip-hop as mumbling over disco rather than yelling over funk.)

With RedOne's help, Gaga summons generations of dance music. "Just Dance" is built around the brawny, slightly overbearing synthesizers of Gary Numan and his British peers like the Human League. (Those keyboards are also the foundation for Euro-techno like Eiffel 65 and for dozens of Continental hits that Americans rarely hear.) Gaga's hard vocal delivery lets her tone bounce off the walls, in the manner of Sharon Brown and Shannon and other eighties dance-floor workhorses. "Just Dance" is about being drunk in a club, which is a great idea, because songs for drunk people in clubs are rarely sharp enough to be so obvious: a lot gets lost in the quest for the clever. The Lady's had too much red wine, turned her shirt inside out, and has a Play-boy mouth, whatever that is. Her night could end up on the gossip blogs if she's not careful—she "can't see straight," and can't remember what club she's in, but sings to herself that it's "gonna be O.K.," which will reassure anybody with a liquor license doing business while the song is on. Later in the song, Lady Gaga semi-raps and recalls the weirdo she's borrowed a few moves from, Peaches, a Canadian musician who, like Germanotta, presented herself as a sexually ambiguous performance artist, though Peaches did it a decade ago. It was actually a plausible claim when Peaches made it—she has no worldwide No. 1s. (Yet.)

This is how "The Fame" works. Lady Gaga's current, very big hit, "Poker Face," will likely please the frat boys whom her pull quotes are designed to scare. As the punning title suggests, it's a song about rough sex. (Another song is entitled "I Like It Rough.") "Eh, Eh" echoes Madonna's lighter work, like "La Isla Bonita," and there's even a ballad, to be released as a single when the people who don't like dance music need to be pulled in, called "Brown Eyes."

If you want melody and a cheerful embrace of the moment as it happens, Lady Gaga is a wise bet. Her recent client Britney is currently sleepwalking through her own tour. Not so Ms. Germanotta. On "American Idol," Lady Gaga tore up "Poker Face" and short-circuited the conventions of the show by splitting the song into a drunken solo-piano ballad and an up-tempo truncated version of itself. Germanotta knows that the one-hit wonders are weirder and cooler than the well-paid musicians who stretch their careers over seven years on the stage and twenty more behind it. Can she have it both ways?

Further Reading

Christgau, Robert. "Monster Anthems." *Barnesandnoblereview.com*, June 22, 2011. http://bnreview.barnesandnoble.com/t5/Rock-Roll/Monster-Anthems/ba-p/5087 (accessed September 13, 2012).

Herbert, Emily. *Lady Gaga: Behind the Fame*. New York: Overlook Press, 2010.

Discography

Lady Gaga. *The Fame*. Interscope, 2008.
_____. *The Fame Monster*. Interscope, 2009.
_____. *Born This Way*. Interscope, 2011.

88. The End of History, the Mass-Marketing of Trivia, and a World of Copies without Originals

Finally, how can one sum up the complexity of popular music in the early 21st century? Several scholars of popular music have alluded to changes in the way young listeners consume popular music.[1] For those who grew up with the continuous broadcasting of music videos, linking music with visual media has become commonplace. Changes in the way multinational entertainment corporations operate, along with mergers between what were once companies devoted to separate media, have resulted in ever-new alliances between music and a range of other media forms, including music video, video games, and cinema. Reports that DVD sales outstripped sales of CDs in 2002 may come as a surprise, but with the advent of MP3 computer files that allow virtually unlimited downloading and storage of music, combined with the continuing inflated price of retail CDs, such a shift may have been predicted.

Accompanying this shift in the role of music as the privileged form of entertainment for the under-25 crowd has been a new kind of eclecticism among younger listeners of pop music. The claim "I listen to everything," familiar as a response to those who ask a student about

---

1. See Lawrence Grossberg, "Same As It Ever Was? Rock Culture. Same As It Ever Was! Rock Theory," in *Stars Don't Stand Still in the Sky: Music and Myth*, ed. Karen Kelly and Evelyn McDonnell, 99–121 (New York: New York University Press, 1999); Jason Middleton and Roger Beebe, "The Racial Politics of Hybridity and 'Neo-Eclecticism' Contemporary Popular Music," *Popular Music* 21, no. 2 (May 2002): 159–72.

his or her preference in music, is becoming more and more accurate. Connected to the decline in sales of the now-almost-extinct "single," compilations of recent hits, such as *NOW That's What I Call Music* and *Totally Hits,* have enjoyed runs at the top of the best-selling album charts. During the heyday of the single, such collections appeared only years after the fact and then were marketed on late-night TV, resulting in sales figures that were unlikely to earn a spot on *Billboard*. All these developments suggest a shift in the type and level of involvement with particular genres experienced by a significant part of the audience for popular music.

Yet another facet of the changing relationship between the youth of today and popular music is a new view of the history of popular music. Formerly the terrain of collectors and obsessives, historical trivia is now mass-marketed in the form of CD reissues, DVDs, websites, documentaries, VHI *Behind the Music* episodes, and trade books about every well-known genre and artist. One can note several factors in this transformation dating back to the 1980s: the rise of the "classic rock" radio format, which demonstrated that the popularity of music from the mid-1960s to the mid-1970s was not only a baby-boomer nostalgia trip, but also a genre that provided a viable listening choice for Generation X'ers; the reissue of long out-of-print CDs, often in compilations and box sets containing "rarities" that were previously unavailable commercially; the multiplication of specialized 'zines; and finally (somewhat later in the 1990s), the blossoming of the Internet as a source of information (in the form of websites) and as a marketplace where seemingly any recording (sonic and visual) ever released could be tracked down. As examples of the mass-marketing of former collectibles, one can point to the release of Bob Dylan's *The Bootleg Series—Volumes 1–3 [Rare and Unreleased] 1961–1991* in 1991 as a key moment—"bootlegs" had previously been defined by their scarcity and unavailability through official channels. This collection of Dylan's studio outtakes and live performances, which had circulated through unmarked albums in used record stores or on tapes passed from fan to fan, could now be consumed with considerably less effort. Offering proof that box sets make great stocking stuffers, all three of the Beatles *Anthology* CDs—a series of two-CD sets released in 1995 and 1996—sold millions of copies and made number one on *Billboard's* best-selling album charts, marking the definitive massification of musical marginalia.

The following article details the impact of this sea change on the material culture of popular music, described here in the music of numerous new, young bands that seem to evoke the music of 20-plus years ago without a self-consciously "retro" attitude. Babcock's references to how these young groups reproduce "good music" also testifies to how the aesthetics of classic rock have been successfully transmitted, a phenomenon that he attributes to a "critical consensus" and the development of a canon. Babcock reveals how critical and commercial canons often invert the sense of which music was significant at the time by bringing music from the margins into the center of a historical sequence.[2] Although not stated overtly in this article, critical canons are also situated within particular notions of artist and audience identity; as Rilo Kiley sing in their "Absence of God" from 2004 (evoking nothing so much as singer-songwriter Jim Croce's 1972 recording "Operator"), "Folk singers sing songs for the working, baby/We're just recreation for all those doctors and lawyers."

A factor not discussed by Babcock is the basic musical continuity of post–rock 'n' roll popular music: today's listeners can feel and hear a connection in much contemporary popular music to "classic rock"— some of which is more than 40 years old—that simply was not possible in the 1970s and 1980s, when the popular music from 40 years earlier was typified by Bing Crosby and Guy Lombardo. And even if popular music fans 30 years ago expanded their interests into jazz from the 1930s and 1940s, the connection between jazz and 1970s popular music was still relatively weak. Another ramification of the changed sense of history discussed in this article is a shift in academic legitimation: the past 20 years have witnessed an enormous growth in academic societies, conferences, journals, and, yes, courses in the history of popular music.[3]

The Kids Aren't Alright . . . They're Amazing
Jay Babcock

It happened again a few weeks ago. I was checking out Kings of Leon, a band made up of three brothers and one cousin from Tennessee who do an amazing, uptempo '70s Allmans/Faces/gospel/Southern-fried beast of a slurred boogie–rock & roll thing. That these guys were playing this well at 7:45 p.m. on a weeknight to a House of Blues that was at best one-quarter filled was noteworthy. That they had ballads this good and a stage presence this intriguing was special. But it was their ages (16, 18, 21 and 23) that left me in a state of mild shock. I couldn't believe how young these guys are.

Maybe I shouldn't have been so surprised. In the last year and a half, there's been a host of notable debut recordings and performances by other deep-past-

---

2. For a discussion of a related phenomenon, see Greil Marcus, "Death Letters," in *Listen Again: A Momentary History of Pop Music*, ed. Eric Weisbard, 296–305 (Durham, N.C.: Duke University Press, 2007).

3. One could argue that the reference to the past noted in this article as a recent phenomenon had been anticipated by hip-hop's (ir)reverence for history dating back to the 1980s.

influenced youngsters: Starsailor, the Coral, the Cuts, the Black Keys, Devendra Banhart, Whirlwind Heat, Entrance, Jet, Sondre Lerche—young artists looking not just a few years back for inspiration, but decades, to a time before they were even born. This phenomenon seemed counterintuitive—interesting work is rarely done by retro-heads, and artists chasing a strange vintage are usually older, not younger— and perhaps even unprecedented. How and why are these artists, from all across the English-speaking world, arriving on the scene near-simultaneously, playing music rooted in styles templated before their births? How could a kid be so nostalgic for a non-experienced past that he shapes his own art in its image? And why is this happening to the unprecedented degree that it is *right now?*

Well, it wasn't always 2003. In 1987, when I was still in high school and trying to find out about the Sex Pistols, the search was difficult. The songs weren't played on the radio. The record wasn't available at the Wherehouse. There were no books on the subject at the public library or the local B. Dalton. Music magazines like *Rolling Stone, Spin* and *Musician* wrote mostly about contemporary bands, with only the slightest occasional reference to mysterious characters named Johnny Rotten and Sid Vicious, who'd apparently made the most controversial music ever. In Upland, just 50 miles east of Los Angeles, if you didn't have a cool older brother or sister, or didn't know someone else who did, you were stuck—no *Bollocks* for you. The scope of the music you knew about was only what you'd heard on the radio in the previous years, and maybe whatever records your parents had lying around from high school or college. And if you were a musician, that would be where you would start—and the results could be good. As Brit musician-scholar Julian Cope noted recently:

> In those bad old days, it used to be that certain of the more eclectic pop groups had such a wide range of styles that once in a while a song might be released that the public definitely needed more of. But the originators were just so totally on one that it surely weren't gonna be them who provided it . . . [Take] the Zombies' 1964 epic "She's Not There," which the band themselves never even came close to revisiting but whose bass parts, drum parts, keyboard stylings and minor-key melodrama was lifted with extraordinary vision and percipient thoroughness by the Doors for a magnificent (and genuinely exploratory) six-album career of sub-Nietzschean post-Jungian pub-banter.

It had been like that for years. Teenage musicians and music fans would have memories of, at best, the previous five to eight years; everything older than that was kind of mysterious and shadowy and rumorlike. It was like this in 1987, and it had been like that in 1981, in 1977 and so on. The upshot, in rock-music-history terms, was that, generally speaking, you'd get occasional stylistic or formal innovations, followed by a simplified imitation of said innovation, which would eventually fade. Then, a decade or so down the line, you'd hear that style being played again: a revival played by bands making something like the music they'd grown up on; thus you got the god-awful hair-metal of the '80s, a devolution from the glam and glitter of the early to mid-'70s. Sometimes these bands would be good, sometimes they'd be silly, sometimes they'd sell, sometimes they wouldn't. (Late-'60s/early-'70s revivalists in the late '80s to '90s, such as the Black Crowes, Lenny Kravitz or Oasis, managed to do all four of these things.) The point is that their absorption of musical ideas would be pretty much limited to the biggest-selling pop from the 20-year period prior to each band's emergence, because information about music styles earlier than that—and/or less popular than that—was so limited and so arbitrarily distributed. In other words: We all knew about the Beatles and the Stones, but how many of us really knew much about Tim Buckley or Love or the Raspberries or the Voidoids or Gang of Four?

Come 2000, and things have changed. The rapid, broad-based spread of the Internet means that information about bands from all eras, in all styles, whether popular or obscure, has become widely available and easily accessible to the curious young musician. The advent of the compact disc meant that during the '90s both familiar and obscure albums came back into print. A friend in his mid-40s recently reminded me that before the CD appeared, the only way you could hear a lot of music from the '70s—and nearly everything from the '60s—was by borrowing or buying original vinyl copies, usually at great expense and in beat-up condition. Albums by Zappa, Beefheart, the Doors and even the Beatles had the status of antique artifacts—if you saw copies at all. That you can now buy Love's *Forever Changes*, say, in a pristine copy (with extra tracks) is a major development. And, of course, there's file trading and downloading and all that as well.

There is also the classic-rock radio format that is present in almost every substantial radio market in the country, occasionally (as in Los Angeles) on more than one station. If you like guitar-based music but you don't like what's on the "alternative" channel, then your place of refuge is the classic-rock station—to wit, the past. If KROQ is in yet another Korn–Limp Bizkit–Linkin Park–Staind spelling-impaired angry-moper frenzy, there's always KLOS or "the Arrow," where you've got a decent chance of hearing something genuinely good and well-crafted (Beatles, Stones, Zeppelin, Dylan, Hendrix, Bowie, Elton John, Neil Young, Queen, AC/DC) every few minutes, even if the playlists are shamefully narrow.

Then there are the ancillary media that have evolved around rock-music history and culture. There is now a pervasive nostalgia that far outstrips the level of nostalgia in the past, consolidating and enumerating and assessing the substantial, unprecedented artistic achievements of '64–'82, with a special emphasis on that golden period of '66–'74. At the supercultural level, there's VH1 and VH1 Classics; you might not see a program on Love or Captain Beefheart or Television or the Voidoids on VH1's *Behind the Music*, but you might get clues there about them, or about certain histories, styles and lineages. At the minimum, you get the sense that there's a *lot* out there to explore, that current rock styles aren't the only ones to be tapped.

At the midcultural level, there are the "past master" articles that have been running in *Spin* and other music magazines in the last few years, perhaps in response to the success of pop-music nostalgia magazines like *Mojo*, and at the subcultural level there are zines like *Ugly Things* that bring a microscopic, obsessive perspective to all this stuff. Finally, there's the flood of books we've seen over the last decade, published by major houses, available in mega-bookstores in shopping malls across the English-speaking world, devoted to seemingly every band, genre and episode in music history, no matter how minute or obscure. Information that used to be either lost or passed along via word of mouth and low-circulation zines is now out there for everyone.

Something has shifted: You don't need a hip older brother anymore to know about the Sex Pistols; you'll hear about them via any of the aforementioned venues, even the most mainstream ones. Because even if the Velvet Underground, the Sex Pistols, the Ramones and Iggy Pop didn't experience mainstream success in the '60s and '70s, time has been kind to them. Critical consensus has ensured that these giants have earned their place, and music history has been rewritten so that the dross has fallen away. Look back at the music charts of those years and you'll see a million songs you've never heard by thousands of artists you've never heard of. Where did they go, why aren't they talked about, why aren't they played?

The simple truth is that what we call the media—from fanzines to *The New York Times*—like any curators of culture, have seized upon a lot of musical artifacts that were initially passed over and declared that *this* is what was important. So now you get articles saying, "1977: It was the year of *Star Wars* and the Sex Pistols," when, in fact, in the USA the Sex Pistols weren't played on the radio, didn't sell many records and, to the extent that they were regarded at all, were generally seen as a joke/novelty band. But now, after years of magazine articles, feature-length documentaries, books, TV shows, TV commercials, movie soundtracks, concert DVDs and such, we've all got it in our heads that what was culturally significant about '77 was *Never Mind the Bollocks*. Cultural history isn't written by the early victors.

What this means for musicians born since 1980 is that they're being fed the good, fertile stuff from way back when. Critics and fans always go for the art they perceive as pure, authentic, less compromised, and that sort of thing is more likely to exist at the margins than at the center, though as the years go by, the fringe moves from the edge to the mainstream. Nirvana has already been determined to be significant, while Candlebox hasn't even though there was a long period when Kevin Martin, Peter Klett, Scott Mercado and Bardi Martin (Who? Exactly) were outselling Kurt Cobain. The same thing has happened with music from the '60s and '70s: The important, purer sounds (popular or not) have been drawn out, or preserved, and made available.

This is why these young musicians we're seeing now have such seemingly good taste: That taste has been shaped by a media consensus about what was truly of quality back then. Call it the formulation of a rock canon, the imposition of marginal/elitist values on the mainstream—it don't matter none, the outcome is the same: The purer the fertilizer, the stronger the plants that grow in the garden.

But is this interest by young people in the deep past new? Ex-Minuteman/art-punk lifer Mike Watt—the kind of guy who would know—thinks it is. He noted recently in his online tour diary that "The younger folks now are so much more open to music before them than in my days in the '70s. We would've been hard-pressed to dig anything from the '40s or '50s in those days."

So, why exactly does music back-sourced so far in time resonate with the new generation of musicians? Well, consider the crap they grew up inhaling in the pop mediasphere; an Island A&R man observed recently in *The New York Times*, "For young, middle-class, suburban American kids of above-average intelligence, there hasn't been any challenging, soulful music for them, ever. It's all either pop or rap-rock—music with no sensitivity, no intellectual heft." You can see why the young bands might be looking for inspiration to music that hasn't had currency with youths for decades. Also, they're the first generation to grow up with parents who experienced the late '60s and '70s as teenagers. . . .

If you've got a voice like Devendra Banhart's, or James Walsh's of the Tim and Jeff Buckley–inspired Starsailor, it makes no sense to look to contemporary music for ideas. You can page through rock history's encyclopedia and find where you fit in—or, better yet, where you can start. And you have the courage to do it because of the example of others: The White Stripes, the Hives, the Strokes, the Soundtrack of Our Lives, etc., have all emerged in the last few years with sounds derived totally from other than the usual '90s/'00s sources, and they've absorbed and disgorged them with style and success and, most important, via skillful songwriting.

Perhaps it's the willingness of internationally successful bands like the Strokes and the White Stripes to point backward at music more than 20 years old that has inspired, or at least encouraged, so many young artists in the last couple of years to look to other long-abandoned tributaries from that same period. As a rather self-congratulatory Yes keyboardist Rick Wakeman told the *Manchester Guardian* recently, "What's happening is that young people are opening a lot of drawers and finding things that were buried, and going. 'What's this?' Prog-rock used to be the porn of the record industry, and people would almost ask for it in a brown paper bag. But bands are stealing bits of it now, because they want to progress."

The key here is that, Yes aside, there's so much good material to reboot and recombine, and the bands doing it are for the most part proficient enough, that this consciousness-of-rock's-past isn't devolving into mere tribute bands. In L.A. clubs recently, there's been the knockout Raspberries-meet-Television tunefulness of the Cuts at Spaceland; primo Devo–Pere Ubu–Chrome–James Chance art-rock freakazoidery from Whirlwind Heat at El Rey, opening for the White Stripes; Devendra Banhart sharing the Silverlake Lounge stage with the almost comically Tim Buckley-enamored Entrance. Just three months ago, Jet, a young Australian band following in the footsteps of Badfinger, Cheap Trick, AC/DC and *Sticky Fingers*–era Stones, opened a show at Spaceland for the Blue Cheer/Junior Kimbrough/Funkadelic–inflected Black Keys at Spaceland. There were the Kings of Leon that same night at House of Blues, opening for the Coral, a fantastical, charming outfit from Liverpool steeped in Kevin Ayers–era Soft Machine, Scott Walker and Love.

Now, it's not that other bands in rock history haven't looked more than 10 years into the past for inspiration. Bobby Zimmerman was checking out Harry Smith's anthologies of obscure old American music when he was in high school in the '50s. And we all know how the Beatles, the Stones, the Yardbirds and other British musicians studied whatever old blues records they could find in the late '50s and early '60s. But something happened after punk hit in the late '70s. Young musicians were told— or decided, depending on your ideological position—that the old stuff was obsolete. A line was drawn, earth was scorched, babies and bathwater and a lot of bathtubs were thrown out. Somewhere along the line, probably around the time people were digging Johnny Rotten's dismissal of Pink Floyd and the Beatles while simultaneously tuning out his praise for experimental rockers Van Der Graaf Generator and Can, old paths were covered up, paths that are only now being reopened for exploration.

You can call it pop eating itself and say that all we're hearing now is a recapitulation and regurgitation of old gestures and styles—musicians as antique dealers, the pop equivalent of those weird Civil War re-enactors. There's doubtless some truth in that, especially when Starsailor is recording with Phil Spector, but . . . shit, it's Phil goddamn Spector, for crissakes, and watch how goosed your bumps get when you hear the song! (Recorded during sessions that were aborted two months prior to the death of Lana Clarkson at Spector's estate, the thrilling "Silence Is Easy" is the most intense vocal Walsh has ever done.)

Anyway, given the relatively rapid creative exhaustion of various genres and styles during the last decade (grunge, indie rock, alternative rock, electronica, Britpop, post-rock, mainstream hip-hop) and the obvious artistic dead ends of surviving genres (pop-punk, electroclash, rap-rock, emo, nu-metal and underground hip-hop), taking three decadelong steps back to go forward four begins to look like a reasonable artistic strategy, whether it's conscious or unconscious. (In Kings of Leon's case, there's a hint of contrivance, given the presence of Nashville-based songwriter-for-hire Angelo Petraglia in the credits for every one of their songs. So yeah, they're good, but perhaps not as impressive as you might at first think.) Losing the self-defeating straitjacket that is punk-rock ideology—i.e., that technical facility is automatically suspect—has also got to be healthy for artists whose visions can't and shouldn't be confined to two chords (maybe three) and a half-truth. Given the quality of most of these born-after-1979 artists' first records, there really may be no time like the present for the deep past.

You might even say it's been a long time coming.

One final word on the Sex Pistols. With the Internet, VH1, *Mojo, Spin,* the endless books and such, you sure as shit don't need a hip older brother anymore to know about these geezers. In fact, at this point, 26 years after the release of *Never Mind the Bollocks*, you're more likely to have a hip *father*. The Cuts' Andy Jordan laughs, "My dad played me the Sex Pistols when I was like 13 or 14." Perhaps that's the new initiation rite into adulthood for budding musicians in the 21st century: having your pop introduce you to the wonders of "God Save the Queen."

If a new sense of the history of popular music informed its production and reception in the early 2000s, new forms of technology provided a material counterpart. One of these technological innovations, "auto-tune," was first released as a software program in 1997 and reached public awareness with Cher's "Believe," released late in 1998. This recording, with its blend of techno and house that could be described as "dance pop," used the auto-tune effect to enhance the highly electronic and "artificial" quality of the sound, the then-unknown technique lending a mechanical, robotic, otherworldly quality to the music.

In its subsequent rise to popularity and broad dissemination, auto-tune has been used primarily in two ways: (1) to correct deviations from equal-tempered concert pitch, often with little or no discernible effect; (2) to create the audible "auto-tune" effect such as that heard in "I Believe" by setting the pitch correction speed too fast for the signal that is being processed. Almost six years after Cher's recording, the exaggerated auto-tune effect became a pop music cliché following its use by R&B singer T-Pain—the effect is quite audible in his first single, "I'm Sprung" (2005). T-Pain is subsequently credited with influencing the use of the effect in the work of other artists such as Snoop Dogg, Lil Wayne, Ke$ha, and Kanye West. Extreme uses of auto-tune may also be found in the work of the Gregory Brothers, particularly in their use of the effect to "auto-tune the news," in which they manipulate the voices of newscasters to make them sound as if they are singing melodies. Their controversial "Bed Intruder" recording, which features the auto-tuned voice of Antoine Dodson describing the attempted rape of his sister Kelly to a news reporter, became the most-watched video of 2010.[4]

Auto-tune has not been without its detractors, especially in its increasingly subliminal usage: condemned by many musicians, artists such as Allison Moorer have even released CDs with stickers informing consumers that auto-tune was not used in the recording. Perhaps the most prominent critical response from a musician came from Jay-Z upon the release of his "D.O.A. (Death of Auto-Tune)" (2009). Whether or not auto-tune should be used in live performances has also been a matter of debate among performers.

The title of Robert Everett-Green's essay "Ruled by Frankenmusic" captures the spirit of many of the criticisms directed toward auto-tune.

---

4. For more on this production and the rationale of the Gregory Brothers, see Eliot Van Buskirk, "Gregory Brothers of 'Bed Intruder' Fame Discuss TV Pilot, Antoine Dodson," *Wired*, August 13, 2010.

Green suggests that such criticisms often have to do with genre-based aesthetic norms: musicians and critics may imply that it's OK for pop singers, but heresy for a punk band, even if the band is Green Day, whose punk credentials have long been suspect to die-hard punks. That is, pitch variation was formerly an aesthetic choice made by musicians in genres where pitch-bending and creative play with pitch were part of the conventions, and auto-tune tends to be condemned the most when it is used in those genres. Part of the debate also centers around how auto-tune may be conditioning listener expectations, extending a challenge for performers that has existed since the advent of sound recording, in which what is presented as a "performance" to the public in the form of a recording is difficult if not impossible to reproduce in live performance.

Ruled by Frankenmusic
Robert Everett-Green

I was listening to Morrissey sing Dear God, Please Help Me, on his recent album Ringleader of the Tormentors, when I had one of those moments of revelation that sometimes happen in pop music. As that light, vulnerable tenor floated above the song's gliding beat, I realized that I was hearing something that has been banished from whole sectors of the recording industry: a man singing out of tune.

He's not far off the pitch, most of the time, though enough to notice if you have an ear for that sort of thing. One descending line sags a little each time he sings it, especially at the words "track me down," when he slides a full tone flat at the trailing end of the phrase. He goes sharp, too, pushing a bit too high each time he reaches the last and highest-pitched words of the final refrain, "but the heart feels free." At this point in the music, Ennio Morricone's orchestral arrangement has reached its full magnificence, all the tension Morrissey sang about in the opening lines has dissipated, and you're left with the very tactile symbolism of a voice straining upwards as the heart feels its freedom.

Dear God, Please Help Me is one of the most beautiful songs of the year (also one of the most mischievous, since it portrays a sexual tryst as an encounter with divine mercy), and its flaws are part of its beauty. It might not have turned out nearly as well if Moz were up to date, and used Auto-Tune like everybody else.

Auto-Tune, in case you haven't heard, is a top-selling software program that corrects pitch for musicians who can't always do it themselves. It became headline news three years ago, when country singer Allison Moorer attached stickers on her album Miss Fortune that read: "Absolutely no vocal tuning or pitch-correction [technology] was used in the making of this record."

A lot of the discussion since has focused on whether you're cheating if you use Auto-Tune, or programs like it. But at a time when people use samplers and old vinyl to make hit records without singing or playing any instrument themselves, it seems a bit quaint to say that Fatboy Slim is playing by the rules, but Paris Hilton isn't.

What matters more is what auto-tuning software is doing to musical styles and to our experience and expectations as listeners. It isn't just a tool, but an instrument that's reshaping the character of popular music, song by song.

Auto-Tune was introduced in 1997 and has become standard equipment in most recording studios. Run anyone's voice or instrument through it (one at a time-it can't tune a chord), and the program adjusts the pitch of each note to match the nearest comparable value in a preset scale. It's quick and easy to use, and if you listen to popular music, you're hearing its effects every day.

"It's on about 100 per cent of records that you hear on the radio," singer Neko Case said recently on PBS's The Tavis Smiley Show, exaggerating just a wee bit. She was trying to explain to Smiley why he had so often gone to concerts and found that the live thing (as he put it) "doesn't sound anything like the record that you fell in love with." Case told me last year that she asked the engineers at Toronto's Iguana Recording Studios, where she and Darryl Neudorf mixed her latest album, which singers coming through there still don't use the program to tweak their vocals. "They said, 'Just you and Nelly Furtado. Everyone else does,' " she said.

Bob Dylan, Neil Young or Tom Waits probably don't have much use for auto-tuning, because a ragged delivery is integral to their style. To hear one of these performers (whose careers were all well-established before Auto-Tune came along) singing perfectly in tune would be like seeing Dylan with a facelift.

Auto-tuning is audibly rampant in the R&B scene, and among young punk and emo bands. Green Day's hit single Wake Me Up When September Ends is almost a love song to pitch-correction technology. Singer Billie Joe Armstrong delivers this pop-punk ballad about insecurity and pain in an unnaturally steady stream of pitch-perfect vocal sound. It might be an organ playing, except that it's still obviously a human voice, backed by heavily distorted guitars that are also dead in tune from start to finish.

Green Day presents itself as a punk band, and punk has traditionally gone for a messed-up, do-it-yourself aesthetic that scorns overt displays of skill or polish. In that context, the perfectionism of Wake Me Up When September Ends feels like the last nail in Joe Strummer's coffin. Punk used to be about losing control and not really wanting it back; Green Day makes the genre seem as tidy as a golf green. You might say that Green Day was always headed in that direction ("They're not punk, they're plonk," said the Sex Pistols' John Lydon earlier this year), but auto-tuning may have boosted them to the summit of neatness.

American Idiot, Green Day's latest album, has sold almost seven million discs (including legal downloads) and topped the charts on both sides of the Atlantic. The more they and other auto-tuning musicians succeed, the more people become habituated to their kind of pitch perfection. Dead-centre pitch is becoming the new norm. As it does so, a lot of popular music's expressive capacities may wither away.

Sarah Vaughan had a famously good ear, yet she purposely sang away from the centre of the pitch when the music seemed to need it. "You'll dry all my tears," she sings in Lover Man, her voice bobbing below pitch between each of the first words before landing deliberately flat on "tears." She's back in tune by the very end of the phrase, but along the way she has given the line a sexy, needy fluidity that suits the song's dreamy construction of the perfect lover.

Glenn Gould, writing about Barbra Streisand in her prime, said that her singing presented "a seemingly limitless array of available options," one of which was her constant push-pull relationship with the centre of the pitch. You could say the same thing about old-time blues singers such as Leadbelly, whose forceful rise above the "right" pitch on the phrase "your house catch afire!" is as meaningful as the bent "blue" notes of the White Stripes' recording of Little Bird. Much of the expressive power of supposedly reductive forms such as blues and rock comes from all the shade and colour lurking between the "correct" pitches, and it works on you even if you can't consciously detect the deviations.

Antares Audio Technology, which developed and sells Auto-Tune, says that its software doesn't have to strip out expressive details. Only when you put it on the fastest retune setting does it suppress all pitch variations ("the now-infamous 'Cher effect,' " to quote the Auto-Tune manual). That includes vibrato, which from a computer's perspective is just a regularized way of singing out of tune.

"An appropriately selected slow setting can leave expressive gestures intact," says the manual, citing vibrato and portamento (gliding between pitches). You can even use the program to beef up the expressive gestures, adding vibrato or changing its speed or amplitude, "to allow the creation of much more convincing vibratos." Going all the way, you can strip out every distinguishing nuance, add a completely synthetic vibrato, or rebuild from the bottom using the Physical Modeling Vocal Designer, "a radical new vocal tool" whose capacity for virtual redesign of throat, vocal cords, mouth and lips "allows subtle vocal modifications or vocal tract models well beyond limits of physical human anatomy."

Very interesting, Dr. Frankenstein; but most Auto-Tune users are looking for a shortcut, not ways to increase their labours in the studio. They want a gizmo to clean up the one or two takes they've already got, to avoid having to record a dozen more takes and maybe cut and paste between them. Noting the total absence of vibrato in the eerily well-tempered Wake Me Up When September Ends, I'm betting that Green Day ordered something close to the full Cher and called it a day.

And it doesn't stop there. Auto-tuning programs can be used in live performance (including karaoke), with no discernible sound delay. You need never hear how your favourite singer really sounds, unless they forget to switch the thing on, or stray into a situation in which it's not convenient to do so. Michael Bublé is a mediocre song interpreter, but he has a nice sound and on his recordings appears to have a flawless ear. But when he sang his single Home on last spring's Juno Awards broadcast, he was off pitch from beginning to end, and not in a good way (check out the video on YouTube.com). To judge from several other live-performance tapes, that's not unusual for him.

Maybe his fans don't notice. Maybe they do, but accept his shortcomings as part of the immediacy of live performance. I kind of like the fact that he let it all hang out at the Junos. The mask of technology slipped away, and the musician had to show what he could do, and what he couldn't.

"Sometimes on the record I hit notes a little funny," says Neko Case of her recent Fox Confessor Brings the Flood, "but it's kind of like, as my friend Brian Connolly would say, 'Humans were here.' " If you want perfection, try mathematics.

Dating back to the 1920s, successive waves of new technologies have gripped the music industry in a panic. Industry publications in the 1920s fretted over the destructive effect of radio and phonograph on music publishing; in the late 1930s–early 1940s, fears centered on the use of records on radio, which were believed to threaten the livelihood of performing musicians; the use of cassettes for home taping in the late 1970s–early 1980s supposedly portended the collapse of commercial music as we know it; and last, but not least, MP3s, file-sharing and downloading of music stored in digital formats have been blamed for the latest decline in sales figures for recorded music. This is not to say that the fears are always unfounded: revenues for music publishing did decline in favor of mechanically reproduced music; the use of records on radio did cut into the incomes of performing musicians; and the argument for the contributing role of digital copies to the recent precipitous decline of the music industry's fortunes is convincing. The music industry has always recovered in the past by making the new technology work for it or by introducing a new, putatively superior technology that (initially, at any rate) consumers could not control. The crisis over home taping is a fine case in point: the compact disc arrived just in time, with its purportedly better sound quality and its unarguably greater ease of access to individual tracks, to derail the long-term impact of cassettes. The music industry used commercial incentives to hasten the end of the vinyl LP and succeeded in convincing many consumers not only to purchase new CDs, but to replace their entire collection of recorded music.

The CD, however, may now be understood as an intermediate stage in the development of digitally stored music; the digital encoding of tracks on a CD proved to be a "genie in a bottle" that, once unleashed, threatened to erode the centuries-old centralized control of consumable musical objects. Computer software developed during the late 1990s that allowed users to "rip" tracks from a CD onto a computer and then "burn" them onto another CD, enabling virtually unlimited reproduction with minimal sonic degradation. Around the same time, "MP3" technology emerged that permitted the compression of large files with little loss of audio quality (although some would argue this last point), leading to the creation of small, portable MP3 players that could store individualized "mixes" of tracks. This may have looked like home taping retooled in digital form, but another practice soon spread that constituted more of a threat to the music business; it involved circulating digital sound files through the Internet, leading to peer-to-peer file sharing. The "Napster" controversy of 2000–01 pitted music corporations and a few musicians against consumers who were exchanging tracks through the Internet and, in some cases, acquiring access to recordings prior to their official release. Courts in the United States eventually decided that file sharing was an infringement of copyright, and Napster was shut down in its original form. While countless other peer-to-peer networks have sprung up in its place, legal Internet delivery services have also been growing in prominence. In other developments, i-Pods and i-Tunes (and other similar devices and computer programs) have made the digital transfer and storage of individual tracks more common among certain demographic groups than three-dimensional forms of musical storage, and the release of Radiohead's *In Rainbows* (2007) was only the most-publicized case of direct-to-consumer marketing via the Internet. Of course, the more vigorously one attempts to document such a rapidly changing facet of contemporary musical life, the more one risks seeming outdated before the description appears in print.

Unlike the previous cassette-taping controversy, however, few observers of the music industry can doubt that digital duplication and circulation have cut into corporate profits, although some argue that the slump is due to the lack of creativity in an increasingly oligopolistic industry in which four corporations reap the rewards from the sale of music. Furthermore, it could be argued that corporations, in fact, are the only ones hurt by filesharing, and that the Internet has provided access for listeners to lesser-known artists.[5] Indeed, the growing "company store" mentality of record companies has meant that it is increasingly difficult for recording artists to recoup their expenses through sales, and performances and T-shirts have become more lucrative to the vast majority of popular musicians than recording royalties. Yet such utopian arguments also miss how the use of the Internet has broadened the possibilities of surveillance and, therefore, of marketing, into the most intimate recesses of our daily lives.

Eliot Van Buskirk's article complicates some of the most commonly heard arguments about file sharing—namely, that the interests of (what he calls) the "content industry" are unilaterally opposed to those of consumers. He conveys well the imminent sense of crisis that has accompanied this practice since the 1990s, situating this in the context of recent legal challenges. Running somewhat counter to the position suggested by lawsuits against peer-to-peer (P2P) file sharing, his discussion of the Big Champagne company describes how it has tracked file sharing use since the early 2000s while acting as a consultant for the content industry.[6] That is, the content industry tried to use file sharing to its advantage even as it officially fought against the practice in court. The article describes how elements of once-illegal P2P file sharing have now been incorporated into legal, capitalistic practices, for which P2P practices have provided the blueprint for ideas about licensing subscriptions and plans. Van Buskirk also describes the impossibility of completely shutting down illegal P2P practices. The once-rogue practice of file sharing appears to have taught the aboveground industry that it is more efficient to address networks of people than individual users.

Why File Sharing Will Save Hollywood, Music
Eliot Van Buskirk

To hear some tell it, file sharing gutted the music industry by encouraging people to gorge themselves on free, illegal content. Indeed, unless Friday's landmark verdict against The Pirate Bay is overturned, four Swedes will spend a year in jail and owe millions of dollars to entertainment companies for operating a file sharing network.

---

5. See Kembrew McLeod, "MP3s Are Killing Home Taping: The Rise of Internet Distribution and Its Challenge to the Major Label Music Monopoly," *Popular Music and Society* 28 (October 2005): 521–31. For a study of the MP3 from both industrial and psychoacoustic perspectives, see Jonathan Sterne, "The MP3 as Cultural Artifact," *New Media & Society*, 8, no. 5 (2006): 825–42.

6. See Jeff Howe, "Big Champagne Is Watching You," *Wired*, October 2003.

Nonetheless, sites like The Pirate Bay taught—and continue to teach—valuable lessons to the content industry. Even as music labels and movie studios try to sue peer-to-peer networks out of existence, these same networks have been preparing music labels and movie studios for the emerging social-media world, in which sales form only a small slice of the revenue pie, and what really matters is who likes what, and who pays attention to them.

Facebook, MySpace, imeem, YouTube and other social media sites—which the labels now recognize as a major part of their revenue streams going forward—incorporate several aspects of Napster and other early, rogue file sharing networks: buddy lists, user uploads, filtering content by user, viral marketing, ad-supported content and the potential of mining valuable data. The complete DNA of social media was right there, from the very start of P2P.

And even in the early days, the labels were intrigued by the vast pools of user data available on networks like Napster and Kazaa, although they were reticent to take advantage of it.

"It was more than just stigmatized," recalled Eric Garland, CEO of BigChampagne, which measures the popularity of media on file sharing networks. "They feared that to even look at or inquire about what was happening in the file sharing universe would somehow compromise their unflinching stance that this was unauthorized."

But as the initial furor over P2P died down, labels began monitoring file sharing networks through BigChampagne and other services. The data they find there continues to help them in any number of ways, from choosing which leaked song to use as the single, to where a band should tour based on the IP addresses of its fans, to figuring out which artists should perform on the same bill.

The labels beat down Napster, Kazaa, Scour and other P2P networks, and if today's Pirate Bay verdict stands, they will have beaten four Swedes too. Meanwhile, new ways to share files continue to surface, including private and encrypted networks. And The Pirate Bay developers say mirrors exist in other countries, so no matter what happens in Sweden their site will continue to operate. Besides, The Pirate Bay is only one bit-torrent tracker site.

For some, the offense committed by an enabler like The Pirate Bay—as opposed to the people who actually do upload and share copyright material—may be difficult to grasp. You can also find torrents on several other sites—even on Google's search engine. And YouTube hosts pirated copyright material, until and unless it is asked to remove it by the owner, because it is unable to programmatically detect which video clips are pirated.

But the difference is that Google, Yahoo and MSN aspire to catalog everything indiscriminately, while services like The Pirate Bay explicitly cater to practitioners of digital piracy—and are proud of it, to boot.

Even as the content industry celebrates another false victory over file sharing, the world is moving on, to cloud-based, on-demand streaming services—some licensed—where you can hear music and watch videos faster and in a more social way than you can with bit torrent. And as content holders look to monetize those networks, P2P networks provide the only useful template, because they share so many characteristics with today's social-media networks.

Garland, who was there, says tools designed to measure user behavior on file sharing networks led directly to tools that now mine licensed networks like Facebook, imeem, MySpace and YouTube.

When it comes to "where and how people stream, download, watch, listen to, blog about or otherwise make use of or interact with music," said Garland, "file sharing ended up being the blueprint."

And it's a good thing that blueprint was there, from the labels' and studios' perspectives, because today's social-media networks contain even more user data than P2P networks do, and that translates to a bigger opportunity to monetize them through advertising, recommendations and, yes, the occasional sale.

In addition to teaching them how to mine social networks for user data, file sharing taught the content industry that it's often more efficient to address networks than users. On one hand, this sort of thinking led to The Pirate Bay lawsuit. On the other, we have Choruss, Warner Music Group adviser and digital music guru Jim Griffin's plan to license universities, then ISPs, to allow subscribers to download and upload as much music as they want for an overall, royalty-like fee.

"Asserting property rights and attempts at control have cost the sound recording industry over a decade of licensing revenue [and trading] control for compensation," said Griffin during his Digital Music Forum East keynote. "Monetizing friction-free access to music will require swinging to the next vine, and when we make that transition we'll uncover a bigger music service business that's been too-long trapped in the too-small body of an old product-based business of control."

The Choruss plan and the RIAA's official shift away from suing individuals are acknowledgments on the part of the music industry that file sharing will always be a factor, so it could be simpler—and even beneficial—to lump licensed and unlicensed services together under one monthly fee tacked onto users' ISP bills. (ESPN and other video networks already do something similar.) Love Choruss or hate it, Griffin would never have come up with this efficient way of addressing social-media consumption if file sharing networks had never existed.

Finally, P2P accelerated the development of products that people want to purchase when free alternatives exist. Whether music sales are competing with The Pirate Bay or imeem, the answer is the same: Sell ads against free content, and try to sell people something they can't access through the free alternative, be it bonus materials, instant access, concert tickets or whatever. Witness Radiohead's infamous deluxe box set, the recently launched iTunes pass (essentially an album subscription), Josh Freese's crazy album extras, or iPhone apps that deliver an artist's latest creations in near-real time.

File sharing networks forced an industry notoriously set in its ways to acknowledge the enormous power of the internet to distribute music through social channels—if anything, increasing its odds of thriving during the inevitable social-media era.

Lawsuits like this one against The Pirate Bay make sense on the surface. On another level, they're a funny way of saying, "Thanks."

Further Reading

Frith, Simon, and Lee Marshall, eds. *Music and Copyright*. 2nd ed. New York: Routledge, 2004.

Garofalo, Reebee. "I Want My MP3: Who Owns Internet Music?" In *Policing Pop*, ed. Martin Cloonan and Reebee Garofalo, 30–45. Philadelphia: Temple University Press, 2003.

Katz, Mark. *Capturing Sound: How Technology Has Changed Music*. Berkeley: University of California Press, 2004.

Marcus, Greil. "Death Letters." In *Listen Again: A Momentary History of Pop Music*, ed. Eric Weisbard, 296–305. Durham, N.C.: Duke University Press, 2007.

McLeod, Kembrew. "MP3s Are Killing Home Taping: The Rise of Internet Distribution and Its Challenge to the Major Label Music Monopoly." *Popular Music and Society* 28 (October 2005): 521–31.

Middleton, Jason, and Roger Beebe. "The Racial Politics of Hybridity and 'Neo-Eclecticism' Contemporary Popular Music." *Popular Music* 21 (May 2002): 159–72.

Ross, Alex, "Rock 101: Academia Tunes In." *New Yorker,* July 14 and 21, 2003, 87–93.

Taylor, Timothy D. *Strange Sounds: Music, Technology and Culture.* New York: Routledge, 2001.

Théberge, Paul. *Any Sound You Can Imagine: Making Music/Consuming Technology.* Hanover, N.H.: University Press of New England, 1997.

Zak, Albin, III. *The Poetics of Rock: Cutting Tracks, Making Records.* Berkeley: University of California Press, 2001.

Discography

Banhart, Devendra. *Oh Me Oh My . . .* Young God Records, 2002.

Beatles. *Anthology 1.* Capitol, 1995.

_____. *Anthology 2.* Capitol, 1996.

_____. *Anthology 3.* Capitol, 1996.

DJ Dangermouse, Jay-Z, and the Beatles. *The Grey Album.* 2004.

Dylan, Bob. *The Bootleg Series, Volumes 1–3: Rare and Unreleased, 1961–1991.* Sony, 1991.

Freelance Hellraiser. *Waiting for Clearance.* BMG/RCA, 2006.

Go Home Productions (Mark Vidler). *Mixology Mix.* GHP WFMU, 2003.

Kings of Leon. *Youth and Young Manhood.* RCA, 2003.

Linkin Park and Jay-Z. *Collision Course.* Warner Bros./WEA, 2004.

Radiohead. *In Rainbows.* Ato Records, 2007/2008.

Rilo Kiley. *More Adventurous.* Brute/Beaute, 2004.

Starsailor. *Love Is Here.* Capitol, 2002.

Selected Bibliography

Aletti, Vince. "Dancing Madness: The Disco Sound." *Rolling Stone,* August 28, 1975, 43, 50, 56.

Attali, Jacques. *Noise: The Political Economy of Music.* Trans. Brian Massumi. Minneapolis: University of Minnesota Press, 1985.

Bangs, Lester. "Dead Lie the Velvet Underground." *Creem,* May 1971, 44–49, 64–67.

_____. Review of Black Sabbath, *Master of Reality,* in *The Rolling Stone Record Review Volume II,* 308–11. New York: Pocket Books, 1974. First published in *Rolling Stone,* November 25, 1971.

_____. "Bring Your Mother to the Gas Chamber (Part 1)." *Creem,* June 1972, 40ff.

_____. "Bring Your Mother to the Gas Chamber: Black Sabbath and the Straight Dope on Blood-Lust Orgies, Part 2." *Creem,* July 1972, 47ff.

Baraka, Amiri. "The Changing Same (R&B and New Black Music)." In *Black Music,* 180–211. New York: William Morrow, 1967.

Barnes, Ken. "Top 40 Radio: A Fragment of the Imagination." In *Facing the Music,* ed. Simon Frith, 8–50. New York: Pantheon Books, 1988.

Beckett, Alan, and Richard Merton. "Stones/Comment." In *The Age of Rock: Sounds of the American Cultural Revolution,* ed. Jonathan Eisen, 109–17. New York: Random House, 1969. Originally published in *New Left Review* 47 (1968).

Bodroghkozy, Aniko. *Groove Tube: Sixties Television and the Youth Rebellion.* Durham, N.C.: Duke University Press, 2001.

Book, John. "Seattle Heavy." *Goldmine,* April 17, 1992, 46–54.

Brackett, David. *Interpreting Popular Music.* Berkeley: University of California Press, [1995] 2000.

_____. "Music." In *Key Terms in Popular Music and Culture,* ed. Bruce Horner and Thomas Swiss, 124–40. Malden, Mass.: Blackwell, 1999.

_____. "(In Search of) Musical Meaning: Genres, Categories, and Crossover." In *Popular Music Studies,* ed. David Hesmondhalgh and Keith Negus, 65–82. London: Arnold, 2002.

_____. "'Where's It At': Postmodern Theory and the Contemporary Musical Field." In *Postmodern Music/Postmodern Thought,* ed. Judy Lochhead and Joseph Auner, 207–31. New York: Routledge, 2002.

Bradby, Barbara. "Do-Talk and Don't-Talk: The Division of the Subject in Girl-Group Music." In *On Record: Rock, Pop and the Written Word,* ed. Simon Frith and Andrew Goodwin, 341–69. New York: Routledge, 1990.

Bromell, Nick. *Tomorrow Never Knows: Rock and Psychedelics in the 1960s.* Chicago: University of Chicago Press, 2000.

Burroughs, William. "Rock Magic: Jimmy Page, Led Zeppelin, and a Search for the Elusive Stairway to Heaven." *Crawdaddy,* June 1975, 34–35, 39–40.

Campbell, Michael. *And the Beat Goes On: An Introduction to Popular Music in America, 1840 to Today.* New York: Schirmer Books, 1996.

Cantwell, Robert. *When We Were Good: The Folk Revival.* Cambridge, Mass.: Harvard University Press, 1996.

Carby, Hazel V. "'It Jus' Be's Dat Way Sometime': The Sexual Politics of Women's Blues." *Radical America* 20, no. 4 (1986): 9–24. Reprinted in *Keeping Time: Readings in Jazz History,* ed. Robert Walser, 351–65. New York: Oxford University Press, 1999.

Carman, Bryan. *A Race of Singers: Whitman's Working-Class Hero from Guthrie to Springsteen.* Chapel Hill: University of North Carolina Press, 2000.

Cavicchi, Daniel. *Tramps Like Us: Music and Meaning among Springsteen Fans.* New York: Oxford University Press, 1998.

Chang, Jeff. "Word Power: A Brief, Highly Opinionated History of Hip-Hop Journalism." In *Pop Music and the Press,* ed. Steve Jones, 65–71. Philadelphia: Temple University Press, 2002.

Chapple, Steve, and Reebee Garofalo. *Rock 'n' Roll Is Here to Pay.* Chicago: Nelson-Hall, 1977.

Charters, Samuel. *The Roots of the Blues: An African Search.* New York: Da Capo Press, 1981.

Chester, Andrew. "Second Thoughts on a Rock Aesthetic: The Band." *New Left Review* 62 (1970): 75–82.

Chilton, John. *Let the Good Times Roll: The Story of Louis Jordan and His Music*. Ann Arbor: University of Michigan Press, 1997.

Ching, Barbara. *Wrong's What I Do Best: Hard Country Music and Contemporary Culture*. New York: Oxford University Press, 2001.

Christgau, Robert. "Rock Lyrics Are Poetry (Maybe)." In *The Age of Rock: Sounds of the American Cultural Revolution*, ed. Jonathan Eisen, 230–43. New York: Random House, 1969. First published in *Cheetah*, December 1967.

_____. "A Cult Explodes—and a Movement Is Born." *Village Voice*, October 24, 1977, 57, 68–74.

_____. "Jesus, Jews, and the Jackass Theory." *Village Voice*, January 16, 1990, 83–86.

_____. *Any Old Way You Choose It: Rock and Other Pop Music, 1967–1973*. New York: Viking Press, 1973.

Chuck D (with Yusuf Jah). *Fight the Power: Rap, Race, and Reality*. New York: Delacorte Press, 1997.

Cleave, Maureen. "How Does a Beatle Live? John Lennon Lives Like This." *Evening Standard*, March 4, 1966.

Cohen, Ronald D. *Rainbow Quest: The Folk Music Revival and American Society, 1940–1970*. Amherst: University of Massachusetts Press, 2002.

Coleman, Ray. "Would You Let Your Sister Go with a Rolling Stone?" *Melody Maker*, March 14, 1964, 8.

Collins, Matthew. *Altered State: The Story of Ecstasy Culture and Acid House*. London: Serpent's Tail, 1997.

Coon, Caroline. *1988: The New Wave Punk Rock Explosion*. London: Omnibus Press, 1977.

Coppage, Noel. "Troubadettes, Troubadoras, and Troubadines . . . or . . . What's a Nice Girl Like You Doing in a Business Like This?" *Stereo Review*, September 1972, 58–61.

Covach, John. "Progressive Rock, 'Close to the Edge,' and the Boundaries of Style." In *Understanding Rock: Essays in Musical Analysis*, ed. John Covach and Graeme M. Boone, 3–31. New York and Oxford: Oxford University Press, 1997.

Crawford, Richard. *America's Music Life: A History*. New York: W. W. Norton, 2001.

Crowe, Cameron. "Jimmy Page and Robert Plant Talk." *Rolling Stone*, March 13, 1975, 33–37.

Crowther, Bosley. "The Four Beatles in 'A Hard Day's Night.'" *New York Times*, August 12, 1964, 41.

Davis, Angela Y. *Blues Legacies and Black Feminism: Gertrude "Ma" Rainey, Bessie Smith, and Billie Holiday*. New York: Vintage Books, 1999.

DeCurtis, Anthony. "The Athens Scene." In *Rocking My Life Away: Writing about Music and Other Matters*, 21–27. Durham, N.C.: Duke University Press, [1981] 1998.

DeCurtis, Anthony, and James Henke with Holly George-Warren, eds. *The Rolling Stone Illustrated History of Rock and Roll*. 3rd rev. ed. New York: Random House, 1992.

DeVeaux, Scott. "Constructing the Jazz Tradition: Jazz Historiography." *Black American Literature Forum* 25, no. 3 (Fall 1991): 525–60.

_____. *The Birth of Bebop: A Social and Musical History*. Berkeley: University of California Press, 1997.

Eisen, Jonathan, ed. *The Age of Rock: Sounds of the American Cultural Revolution*. New York: Random House, 1969.

_____. *The Age of Rock 2: Sights and Sounds of the American Cultural Revolution*. New York: Random House, 1970.

Ellison, Ralph. "Blues People." In *Shadow and Act*, 247–58. New York: Vintage Books, [1964] 1972.

Ennis, Philip T. *The Seventh Stream: The Emergence of Rocknroll in American Popular Music*. Hanover, N.H.: University Press of New England, 1992.

Erlmann, Veit. "The Aesthetics of the Global Imagination: Reflections on World Music in the 1990s." *Public Culture* 8 (1996): 467–87.

Faludi, Susan. *Backlash: The Undeclared War against Women*. New York: Crown, 1991.

Fariña, Richard. "Baez and Dylan: A Generation Singing Out." *Mademoiselle*, August 1964. Reprinted in *The Dylan Companion*, ed. Elizabeth Thomson and David Gutman, 81–88. New York: Delta, 1990.

Farren, Mick, and Pearce Marchbank. *Elvis in His Own Words*. London: Omnibus Press, 1977.

Fast, Susan. *In the Houses of the Holy: Led Zeppelin and the Power of Rock Music*. New York: Oxford University Press, 2001.

Filene, Benjamin. *Romancing the Folk: Public Memory and American Roots Music*. Chapel Hill: University of North Carolina Press, 2000.

Fitzgerald, Jon. "Motown Crossover Hits 1963–1966 and the Creative Process." *Popular Music* 14 (January 1995): 1–12.

Flippo, Chet. *Your Cheatin' Heart: A Biography of Hank Williams*. Garden City, N.Y.: Doubleday, 1981.

Floyd, Samuel. *The Power of Black Music: Interpreting Its History from Africa to the United States*. New York: Oxford University Press, 1995.

Franklin, Aretha (and David Ritz). *Aretha: From These Roots*. New York: Villard, 1999.

Fricke, David. "Heavy Metal Justice." *Rolling Stone*, January 12, 1989, 42–49.

Frith, Simon. "Beyond the Dole Queue: The Politics of Punk." *Village Voice*, October 24, 1977, 77–79.

_____. "'The Magic That Can Set You Free': The Ideology of Folk and the Myth of the Rock Community." In *Popular Music 1: Folk or Popular? Distinctions, Influences, Continuities*, ed. David Horn and Richard Middleton, 159–68. Cambridge, UK: Cambridge University Press, 1981.

————. *Sound Effects*. New York: Pantheon Books, 1981.

————. *Performing Rites: On the Value of Popular Music*. Cambridge, Mass.: Harvard University Press, 1996.

Frith, Simon, and Howard Horne. *Art into Pop*. London: Methuen, 1987.

Garofalo, Reebee. *Rockin' Out: Popular Music in the USA*. Boston: Allyn and Bacon, 1997.

————. "Setting the Record Straight: Censorship and Social Responsibility in Popular Music." *Journal of Popular Music Studies* 6 (1994): 1–37.

Gendron, Bernard. *Between Montmartre and the Mudd Club: Popular Music and the Avant-Garde*. Chicago: University of Chicago Press, 2002.

George, Nelson. *Where Did Our Love Go? The Rise and Fall of the Motown Sound*. New York: St. Martin's Press, 1985.

Goldstein, Richard. "We Still Need the Beatles, but. . . ." *New York Times*, June 18, 1967, sec. 2, 24.

————. "Pop Eye: I Blew My Cool through the *New York Times*." *Village Voice*, July 20, 1967, 14, 25–26.

Green, Archie. "Hillbilly Music: Source and Symbol." *Journal of American Folklore* 78 (July–September 1965): 204–28.

Greenfield, Robert. "Keith Richard: Got to Keep It Growing." In *The Rolling Stone Interviews, Vol. 2*. New York: Straight Arrow, 1973. First published in *Rolling Stone*, August 1971.

Grossberg, Lawrence. "Same As It Ever Was? Rock Culture. Same As It Ever Was! Rock Theory." In *Stars Don't Stand Still in the Sky: Music and Myth*, ed. Karen Kelly and Evelyn McDonnell, 99–121. New York: New York University Press, 1999.

Guralnick, Peter. *Sweet Soul Music: Rhythm and Blues and the Southern Dream of Freedom*. New York: Harper and Row, 1986.

Hajdu, David. *Positively 4th Street: The Lives and Times of Joan Baez, Bob Dylan, Mimi Baez Fariña, and Richard Fariña*. New York: Farrar, Straus and Giroux, 2001.

Hamm, Charles. *Yesterdays: Popular Song in America*. New York: W. W. Norton, 1979.

————. *Music in the New World*. New York: W. W. Norton, 1983.

————. *Putting Popular Music in Its Place*. Cambridge, UK: Cambridge University Press, 1995.

hampton, dream. "Snoop Doggy Dogg: G-Down," *The Source*, September 1993, 64–70.

Harrison, Daphne Duval. *Black Pearls: Blues Queens of the 1920s*. New Brunswick, N.J.: Rutgers University Press, 1988.

Headlam, Dave. "Does the Song Remain the Same? Questions of Authorship and Identification in the Music of Led Zeppelin." In *Concert Music, Rock, and Jazz since 1945: Essays and Analytical Studies*, ed. Elizabeth West Marvin and Richard Hermann, 313–63. Rochester, N.Y.: University of Rochester Press, 1995.

Hebdige, Dick. *Subculture: The Meaning of Style*. London: Methuen, 1979.

Hentoff, Nat. "The Playboy Interview: Bob Dylan—A Candid Conversation with the Iconoclastic Idol of the Folk-Rock Set." *Playboy*, March 1966; reprinted in *Bob Dylan: The Early Years; A Retrospective*, ed. Craig McGregor, 132–33. New York: Da Capo Press, [1972] 1990.

Heylin, Clinton, ed. *The Da Capo Book of Rock and Roll Writing*. New York: Da Capo Press, [1992] 2000.

Hill, Trent. "The Enemy Within: Censorship in Rock Music in the 1950s." *South Atlantic Quarterly* 90 (Fall 1991): 675–708.

Hirshey, Gerri. *Nowhere to Run: The Story of Soul Music*. New York: Penguin Books, [1984] 1985.

Holden, Stephen. "The Evolution of a Dance Craze." *Rolling Stone*, April 19, 1979, 29.

hooks, bell. "Madonna: Plantation Mistress or Soul Sister?" In *Black Looks: Race and Representation*, 157–64. Boston: South End Press, 1992.

Jackson, John A. *American Bandstand: Dick Clark and the Making of a Rock 'n' Roll Empire*. New York: Oxford University Press, 1997.

Jameson, Fredric. "Postmodernism, or the Cultural Logic of Late Capitalism." *New Left Review* 146 (July–August 1984): 59–92. Reprinted in Fredric Jameson, *Postmodernism, or the Cultural Logic of Late Capitalism*, 1–54. Durham, N.C.: Duke University Press, 1991.

Jatta, Sidia. "Born Musicians: Traditional Music from the Gambia." In *Repercussions: A Celebration of African-American Music*, ed. Geoffrey Haydon and Dennis Marks, 14–29. London: Century, 1985.

Jones, Steve, ed. *Pop Music and the Press*. Philadelphia: Temple University Press, 2002.

Jones, Steve, and Martin Sorger. "Covering Music: A Brief History and Analysis of Album Cover Design." *Journal of Popular Music Studies* 11–12 (1999–2000): 68–102.

Kaplan, E. Ann. *Rocking around the Clock: Music Television, Postmodernism and Consumer Culture*. London: Methuen, 1987.

Keathley, Elizabeth. "Eminem's Murder Ballads." *Echo* 4, no. 2 (Fall 2002), http://www.humnet.ucla.edu/echo/volume4-issue2/keathley/index.html.

Keightley, Keir. "Around the World: Musical Tourism and the Globalization of the Record Industry, 1946–66." Unpublished manuscript, 1998.

Keil, Charles. *Urban Blues*. Chicago: University of Chicago Press, 1966.

Keil, Charles, and Steven Feld. *Music Grooves: Essays and Dialogues.* Chicago: University of Chicago Press, 1994.

Kelley, Robin D. G. "Kickin' Reality, Kickin' Ballistics: 'Gangsta Rap' and Postindustrial Los Angeles." In *Race Rebels: Culture, Politics, and the Black Working Class,* 183–227. New York: Free Press, 1994.

Kopkind, Andrew. "Woodstock Nation." In *The Age of Rock 2: Sights and Sounds of the American Cultural Revolution,* ed. Jonathan Eisen, 312–18. New York: Random House, 1970.

Kruse, Holly. "Subcultural Identity in Alternative Music Culture." *Popular Music* 12 (January 1993): 33–41.

Landau, Jon. "Rock and Art." *Rolling Stone,* July 20, 1968, 18–19.

Latham, Aaron. "The Ballad of the Urban Cowboy: America's Search for True Grit." *Esquire,* September 12, 1978, 21–30.

Lipsitz, George. *Time Passages: Collective Memory and American Popular Culture.* Minneapolis: University of Minnesota Press, 1990.

Macan, Edward. *Rocking the Classics: English Progressive Rock and the Counterculture.* New York: Oxford University Press, 1997.

Magee, Jeffrey. "Before Louis: When Fletcher Henderson Was the 'Paul Whiteman of the Race.'" *American Music* 18 (Winter 2000): 391–425.

Mailer, Norman. "The White Negro: Superficial Reflections on the Hipster." *Dissent,* Summer 1957, 276–93.

Malone, Bill. *Country Music U.S.A.* Rev. ed. Austin: University of Texas Press, 1985.

Manheim, James M. "B-side Sentimentalizer: 'Tennessee Waltz' in the History of Popular Music." *Musical Quarterly* 76 (Fall 1992): 37–56.

Manuel, Peter. *Caribbean Currents: Caribbean Music from Rumba to Reggae.* Philadelphia: Temple University Press, 1995.

Marcus, Greil. *Mystery Train: Images of America in Rock 'n' Roll Music.* 3rd rev. ed. New York: Plume, [1975] 1990.

_____. *Dead Elvis: A Chronicle of a Cultural Obsession.* New York: Doubleday, 1991.

_____. *Invisible Republic: Bob Dylan's Basement Tapes.* New York: Henry Holt, 1997.

_____. "Death Letters." In *Listen Again: A Momentary History of Pop Music,* ed. Eric Weisbard, 296–305. Durham, N.C.: Duke University Press, 2007.

Marsh, Dave. *The Heart of Rock and Soul: The 1001 Greatest Singles Ever Made.* New York: Da Capo Press, [1989] 1999.

_____. "Live through This." *Rock 'n' Roll Confidential,* May 1994, 1–8.

McClary, Susan. "Living to Tell: Madonna's Resurrection of the Fleshy." In *Feminine Endings,* 148–66. Minneapolis: University of Minnesota Press, 1991.

McKeen, William, ed. *Rock and Roll Is Here to Stay: An Anthology.* New York: W. W. Norton, 2000.

McLeese, Don. "Anatomy of an Anti-Disco Riot." *In These Times,* August 29–September 4, 1979, 23.

McLeod, Kembrew. "The Politics and History of Hip-Hop Journalism." In *Pop Music and the Press,* ed. Steve Jones, 156–67. Philadelphia: Temple University Press, 2002.

_____. "MP3s Are Killing Home Taping: The Rise of Internet Distribution and Its Challenge to the Major Label Music Monopoly." *Popular Music and Society* 28, no. 4 (October 2005): 521–31.

McLuhan, Marshall. *Understanding Media: The Extensions of Man.* New York: Signet Books, 1964.

Mercer, Kobena. "Monster Metaphors: Notes on Michael Jackson's *Thriller.*" *Screen* 27, no. 1 (1986). Reprinted in *Sound and Vision: The Music Video Reader,* ed. Simon Frith, Andrew Goodwin, and Lawrence Grossberg, 93–108. London and New York: Routledge, 1993.

Middleton, Jason, and Roger Beebe. "The Racial Politics of Hybridity and 'Neo-Eclecticism' Contemporary Popular Music." *Popular Music* 21 (May 2002): 159–72.

Middleton, Richard. "All Shook Up." In *The Elvis Reader: Texts and Sources on the King of Rock 'n' Roll,* ed. K. Quain, 3–12. New York: St. Martin's Press, 1992.

Modleski, Tania. *Feminism without Women: Culture and Criticism in a "Postfeminist Age."* New York: Routledge, 1991.

Negus, Keith. *Music Genres and Corporate Cultures.* New York: Routledge, 1999.

Oliver, Paul. *Savannah Syncopators: African Retentions in the Blues.* New York: Stein and Day, 1970.

_____. *Songsters and Saints: Vocal Traditions on Race Records.* Cambridge, UK: Cambridge University Press, 1984.

Palmer, Robert. *Deep Blues.* New York: Penguin, [1981] 1985.

_____. *Rock and Roll: An Unruly History.* New York: Harmony Books, 1995.

Pareles, Jon. "How Rap Moves to Television's Beat." *New York Times,* January 14, 1990, sec. 2, 1–2.

Parsons, Michael. "Rolling Stones." In *The Age of Rock: Sounds of the American Cultural Revolution,* ed. Jonathon Eisen, 118–20. New York: Random House, 1970.

Peterson, Richard. *Creating Country Music: Fabricating Authenticity.* Chicago: University of Chicago Press, 1997.

Peterson, Richard, and David G. Berger. "Cycles in Symbol Production: The Case of Popular Music." *American Sociological Review* 40 (1975). Reprinted in *On Record: Rock, Pop, and the Written Word,* ed. Simon Frith and Andrew Goodwin, 140–59. New York: Pantheon, 1990.

Post, Henry. "Sour Notes at the Hottest Disco." *Esquire,* June 20, 1978, 79–86.

Powers, Ann. "When Women Venture Forth." *New York Times,* October 9, 1994, 39.

Pugliese, Stanislao G., ed. *History, Identity, and Italian American Culture.* New York: Palgrave, 2004.

Puterbaugh, Parke. "Anglomania: American Surrenders to the Brits—But Who Really Wins?" *Rolling Stone,* November 10, 1983, 31–32.

Ramsey, Guthrie P., Jr. *Race Music: Black Culture from Bebop to Hip-Hop.* Berkeley: University of California Press, 2003.

Reynolds, Simon. *Generation Ecstasy: Into the World of Techno and Rave Culture.* New York: Routledge, [1998] 1999.

Roberts, John Storm. *The Latin Tinge: The Impact of Latin American Music on the United States.* 2nd ed. New York: Oxford University Press, [1979] 1999

Rockwell, John. "The Artistic Success of Talking Heads." *New York Times,* September 11, 1977, D14, 16.

—————. *All-American Music: Composition in the Late Twentieth Century.* New York: Vintage Books, 1984.

Rodgers, Jeffrey Pepper. "My Secret Place: The Guitar Odyssey of Joni Mitchell." In *The Joni Mitchell Companion: Four Decades of Commentary,* ed. Stacey Luftig, 219–30. New York: Schirmer Books, 2000.

Rodman, Gilbert. *Elvis after Elvis: The Posthumous Career of a Living Legend.* London: Routledge, 1996.

The Rolling Stone Record Review. New York: Pocket Books, 1971.

The Rolling Stone Record Review, Volume 2. New York: Pocket Books, 1974.

Rose, Tricia. *Black Noise: Rap Music and Black Culture in Contemporary America.* Hanover, N.H.: Wesleyan University Press and University Press of New England, 1994.

Rosenthal, David H. *Hard Bop: Jazz and Black Music, 1955–1965.* New York: Oxford University Press, 1992.

Ruhlmann, William. "Joni Mitchell: From Blue to Indigo." *Goldmine,* February 17, 1995; reprinted in *The Joni Mitchell Companion: Four Decades of Commentary,* ed. Stacey Luftig, 21–40. New York: Schirmer Books, 2000.

Rumble, John. "The Roots of Rock and Roll: Henry Glover of King Records." *Journal of Country Music* 14, no. 2 (1992): 30–42.

Ryan, John. *The Production of Culture in the Music Industry: The ASCAP-BMI Controversy.* Lanham, Md.: University Press of America, 1985.

Samuels, David. "The Rap on Rap: The 'Black Music' that Isn't Either." *New Republic,* November 11, 1991, 24–29.

Sanjek, David. "One Size Does Not Fit All: The Precarious Position of the African American Entrepreneur in Post-WWII American Popular Music." *American Music* 15 (Winter 1997): 535–62.

Sanjek, Russell, and David Sanjek. *Pennies from Heaven: The American Popular Music Business in the Twentieth Century.* New York: Da Capo Press, 1996.

Savage, Jon. "Machine Soul: A History of Techno." *Village Voice Rock and Roll Quarterly* (Summer 1993): 19.

Schuller, Gunther. *The Swing Era: The Development of Jazz, 1930–1945.* New York: Oxford University Press, 1989.

Schwichtenberg, Cathy. *The Madonna Connection: Representational Politics, Subcultural Identities, and Cultural Theory.* Boulder, Colo.: Westview Press, 1993.

Shank, Barry. *Dissonant Identities: The Rock 'n' Roll Scene in Austin, Texas.* Hanover, N.H.: Wesleyan University Press and University Press of New England, 1994.

Shelton, Robert. "Bob Dylan: A Distinctive Folk-Song Stylist." *New York Times,* September 29, 1961. Reprinted in *Bob Dylan: The Early Years: A Retrospective,* ed. Craig McGregor, 17–18. New York: Da Capo Press, [1972] 1990.

—————. "On Records: The Folk-Rock Rage," *New York Times,* January 30, 1966, 17–18.

Siegel, Jules. "A Teen-age Hymn to God." In *Rock and Roll Is Here to Stay: An Anthology,* ed. William McKeen, 387–99. New York: W. W. Norton and Company, 2000. First published in *Cheetah,* October 1967.

Silcott, Mireille. *Rave America: New School Dancescapes.* Toronto: ECW Press, 1999.

Slater, Jack. "A Sense of Wonder." *New York Times Magazine,* February 23, 1975, 18, 21–23, 26–32.

Smith, Jeff. *The Sounds of Commerce: Marketing Popular Film Music.* New York: Columbia University Press, 1998.

Smith, Paul, ed. *Madonnarama: Essays on Sex and Popular Culture.* Pittsburgh, Pa: Cleis Press, 1993.

Sontag, Susan. "Notes on 'Camp.'" In *Against Interpretation and Other Essays,* 275–92. New York: Anchor Books, [1964] 1990.

Spector, Ronnie (with Vince Waldron). *Be My Baby: How I Survived Mascara, Miniskirts, and Madness or My Life as a Fabulous Ronette.* New York: HarperPerennial, 1990.

Tate, Greg. *Flyboy in the Buttermilk: Essays on Contemporary America.* New York: Fireside/Simon and Schuster, 1992.

—————. "Diatribe." *Village Voice,* September 3, 1996, 46.

Taylor, Timothy D. *Global Pop: World Music, World Markets.* New York: Routledge, 1997.

Thornton, Sarah. *Club Cultures: Music, Media and Subcultural Capital.* Hanover, N.H.: Wesleyan University Press and University Press of New England, 1996.

Toop, David. *Rap Attack 2: African Rap to Global Hip Hop.* London: Serpent's Tail, 1991.

Touré. "The Family Way: The Hiphop Crew as Center of the World." *Village Voice*, October 10, 1995, 49.

Townshend, Peter. Review of "The Who: *Meaty, Beaty, Big, and Bouncy*." *Rolling Stone*, December 7, 1971.

Trakin, Roy. "Avant Kindergarten [Sturm and Drone]." *Soho Weekly News*, January 26, 1978, 31, 37.

Vincent, Rickey. *Funk: The Music, the People, and the Rhythm of the One.* New York: St. Martin's Griffin, 1996.

Vito, R. "The Chuck Berry Style: A Modern Rocker Pays Tribute to the Master." *Guitar Player*, June 1984, 72–75.

Waksman, Steve. *Instruments of Desire: The Electric Guitar and the Shaping of Musical Experience.* Cambridge, Mass.: Harvard University Press, 1999.

_____. "Grand Funk Live! Staging Rock in the Age of the Arena." In *Listen Again: A Momentary History of Pop Music*, ed. Eric Weisbard, 157–71. Durham, N.C.: Duke University Press, 2007.

Wallace, Michele. "Michael Jackson, Black Modernisms and 'The Ecstasy of Communication.'" In *Invisibility Blues: From Pop to Theory*, 77–90. London: Verso, 1990.

Walser, Robert. *Running with the Devil: Power, Gender and Madness in Heavy Metal Music.* Hanover, N.H.: Wesleyan University Press and University Press of New England, 1993.

_____. "Rhythm, Rhyme, and Rhetoric in the Music of Public Enemy." *Ethnomusicology* 39 (1995): 193–217.

_____, ed. *Keeping Time: Readings in Jazz History.* New York: Oxford University Press, 1999.

Warwick, Jacqueline. *Girl Groups, Girl Culture: Popular Music and Identity in the 1960s.* New York: Routledge, 2007.

Weissman, Dick. *Which Side Are You On? An Inside History of the Folk Music Revival in America.* New York: Continuum, 2006.

Welch, Chris. "Jimmy Page, Part Three." *Melody Maker*, February 28, 1970, 10.

Wenner, Jann. *Lennon Remembers: The Rolling Stone Interviews.* New York: Popular Library, 1971.

Whitesell, Lloyd. "Harmonic Palette in Early Joni Mitchell." *Popular Music* 21 (May 2002): 173–94.

Wilder, Alec. *American Popular Song: The Great Innovators, 1900–1950.* New York: Oxford University Press, 1972.

Willis, Ellen. *Beginning to See the Light: Sex, Hope, and Rock-and-Roll.* Hanover, N.H.: Wesleyan University Press and University Press of New England, 1992.

Willis, Susan. "I Want the Black One: Is There a Place for Afro-American Culture in Commodity Culture?" In *A Primer for Daily Life*, 108–32. London: Routledge, 1991.

Wolfe, Charles. "Presley and the Gospel Tradition." In *The Elvis Reader: Texts and Sources on the King of Rock 'n' Roll*, ed. K. Quain, 13–27. New York: St. Martin's Press, 1992.

Wolfe, Tom. *Electric Kool-Aid Acid Test.* New York: Farrar, Straus and Giroux, 1968.

_____. "The First Tycoon of Teen." In *The Kandy-Kolored Tangerine-Flake Streamline Baby*, 47–61. New York: Pocket Books, 1966.

Young, Charles M. "Rock Is Sick and Living in London: A Report on the Sex Pistols." *Rolling Stone*, October 20, 1977, 68–75.

Zabor, Rafi, and Vic Garbarini, "Wynton Vs. Herbie: The Purist and the Crossbreeder Duke It Out." *Musician*, March 1985, 52–64. Reprinted in Robert Walser, ed., *Keeping Time: Readings in Jazz History*, 339–51. New York: Oxford University Press, 1999.

Zappa, Frank. "Statement to Congress, 19 September 1985." In *The Da Capo Book of Rock and Roll Writing*, ed. Clinton Heylin, 501–08. New York: Da Capo Press, [1992] 2000.

Index

Abbey Road, 315
"ABC," 445
ABC Records, 84, 88–89
ABC's "Primetime Thursday," with Diane Sawyer, 527–33
Abdul, Paula, 539
Abolition movement, 33
Abramson, Herb, 61, 63
Abramson, Miriam, 92
"Absence of God," 546
Abu-Jamal, Mumia, 460
Acardipane, Marc, 509
AC/DC, 411
"Achilles," 306
Acid house, 510
"Acid Tests," 232
Across 110th Street, 275
Activism, 460, 461
Ade, Sunny, 480
Adler, Lou, 263, 264
Adorno, Theodor, 211
Advision Studio, 320
Aerosmith, 291, 423
African American: artist financial issues in 1950's, 80; black power movement, 270; church tradition, 57; cinema, 271, 274; consciousness of 60's, 366; crossover hits by, artists in 1980's, 388; dance music, 390; EDM, 510; migration of, to northern/western cities, 48; music, 34, 57, 426–27, 510; musical authenticity, 517; music and sex, 517–19; musicians, 1, 19, 31; performers commitment to civil rights, 146–49; performers integrating into white society, 97; popular music, 4–5, 57, 170, 424; racial bias in, music, 389; radio,

393; rap and, identity, 425; records advertised, 27; self-respect, 443–44; singing styles copied by whites, 86; songs for Jordan written by, 55; theater, 32–38; TV bandstand programs and, 128; whites listening to, music, 91; women, 37, 518–19
African music, 426–27, 480
Afrocentricity, 444
"After Forever," 298
Aguilera, Christina, 535, 536
AIDS, 434–35, 436
"Ain't Nothin' Goin' On but the Rent," 517
Akon, 542
Alaap, 482, 487
Aladdin Sane, 311
Aldon, 134–36
Aletti, Vince, 333
"Alexander's Ragtime Band," 4–5, 8
"Alfie," 279, 282
Algeria, 483–85
Ali, Muhammad, 288
Alice in Chains, 468
"Alison," 357
"All Along the Watchtower," 167, 241
"All Day and All of the Night," 220
Allegro Barbaro, 317
Allen, Barbara, 164
Allen, Harry, 425–29
"All My Trials," 150
"All Night Long," 390
"All That I Can Say," 516, 518
"All You Need Is Love," 227
Almanac Singers, 145
Alston, Barbara, 139

Altamont, California, December 6, 1969 (Csicsery), 258–60
Altamont "festival," 254, 254n1, 258–60
Alternative rock, 467–71. *See also* Indie rock
American Bandstand, 124–25, 135
American Broadcasting Company, 128
American dream, 539
American Folk Tunes: Cowboy and Hillbilly Tunes and Tunesters, 66
American Graffiti, 378
American Idiot, 553
American Idol, 536–40
American music, courses on, xv–xvi
American Society of Composers and Publishers (ASCAP), 59, 96, 123
Amos, Tori, 491–96, 516
Anderson, Jon, 319–22
Anderson, Orlando, 454
And Justice For All, 400, 403
"And the Band Played On," 434
"Angel," 393
Anso, Sam Gideon, 453–54
Apache Indian, 487–88
Aphex Twin (James, Richard D.), 509, 512
Apocalypse 91 ... The Enemy Strikes Black, 445
Apollo theater, 55, 91, 391
"Aqua Boogie (A Psychoalphadiscobeta-bioaquadoloop)," 283
Arawak Allstars, 420
Arawal Records, 420
Aretha Arrives, 196

Aretha Franklin-"Sister Soul": Eclipsed Singer Gains New Heights (Garland), 195–99
"Arizona," 447
"Arkestra," 284
Armstrong, Billie Joe, 553
Armstrong, Louis, 14, 21–22, 28, 57
Arnold, Eddy, 69, 193
Arnold, Gina, 473
Arranger, 18
Art, 157–59; Beatles and high, 213–14; Beatles cover, 213n1; capitalism and, 386; criticism, popular music and, 158–59; Dylan on, 159; Led Zeppelin cover, 306; mass culture and, 241; music, 245; performance, 220; politically correct, 435; Pop, 341, 353; popular music and, 158–59; rock, 314–22; schools impacting British rock, 219n1; Zappa on education and, 413
Artistic expression, 157–58
ASCAP. *See* American Society of Composers and Publishers
Asch, Moses, 148
Ashburn, Benny, 390
Astaire, Fred, 21
Atlantic Records, 77–79, 81, 84, 88, 170, 171, 173, 192, 195–98, 195n1, 264
Atlantic Sound, 62–63
Attali, Jacques, xv
Authenticity, 38, 316; in African American music, 517; Beatles and, 214; commercialism and, 90; of Dylan, 157–59, 471; in Jazz, 249; popular music, 535; of Springsteen, 380–81, 383–85
Autobiographies, xvii–xviii
Auto-Tune, 552–54
Autry, Gene, 69
Avant-garde Jazz, 231–32
Ayoub, Nina, 537–40
Azor, Hurby, 427
Azpiazu, Don, 25

B-52's, 352–55
The B52's American Graffiti (Holden), 353

Babcock, Jay, 545–52
"Babe I'm Gonna Leave You," 292, 303
Babel, 208
"Baby, Let's Play House," 301
Baby boomers, 545
"Baby It's You", 203
Bacharach, Burt, 132
Backspinning, 423
Backstreet Boys, 534, 536
Bad, 364, 366–67, 370
Bad Boy Entertainment, 452–54
Bad Company, 349
Bad Religion, 474
Badu, Erykah, 461, 516, 519
Baez, Joan, 252, 261, 293, 303; appearance/personality of, 149; death, sings about, 150; Dylan and, 154n2; family of, 151; religion and, 152
The Baffler, 474, 476
Bailey, Buster, 41–42
Baker, Anita, 388, 392–93, 515
Baker, LaVern, 80, 95–96
Baker, Susan, 406, 407, 410–12
Ballads, 167
"Ball and Chain," 236
Bambaataa, Afrika (Donovan, Kevin), 423, 502
Bands Dug By The Beat: Louis Jordan, 52–53
Bangla, Joi, 482
Bangs, Lester, 263, 294, 340, 352
Banjo, 50, 149
Baraka, Amiri (Leroi Jones), 32–39
"Barbara Allen," 150
"The Barbarian," 317
Barbershop quartets, 534
Barbiero, Michael, 403
Barker, Danny, 40, 41
Barn dance, 59
Barnet, Charlie, 16
Barry, Jeff, 136
Bartòk, 317
Basie, William "Count," 19–20, 28, 48, 91–92
"Battle of Evermore," 305
Baudrillard, Jean, 535
B-Beats, 420–21

B-Beats Bombarding Bronx: Mobile DJ Starts Something with Oldie R&B Disks (Ford R.), 420–21
The Beach Boys, 101, 140–44, 348
Beastie Boys, 424, 460
"Beat It," 364
Beatlemania, 202, 208–12
Beatlemania: Girls Just Want To Have Fun (Ehrenreich, Hess, Jacobs), 208–12
Beatles, xvi, 87, 102, 136, 141, 143, 200–230, 342, 343, 348, 534, 541; arrival to U.S. of, 209–10; authenticity, 214; cover art, 213n1; critical review of, 226–30; critics serious view of, 201; Dylan on, 166; early performing repertoire, 201; on Ed Sullivan Show, 209; evolution, 213; fans, 208–12; first movie, 205–8; high art and, 213–14; performances by, 207–8; raga, sound, 215; Rolling Stones compared with, 221, 225–30; sexuality of, 207–8; withdraw from live performances, 217
Beatles (the White Album), 225, 381
"Beatlesaniacs, Ltd.," 210
Beatles For Sale, 213
"Beatles Reaction Puzzles Even Psychologists," 212
Beatnik, 147, 151
Bebop, 477
Beck, Jeff, 301–2
Bee Gees, 329, 333, 338
Beggar's Banquet, 225, 227
Behind the Music, 545
Belafonte, Harry, 146, 480
Bellote, Pete, 329
Benjamin, Benny, 278–79
Berlin, Irving, 1–8, 91, 132, 384
Berns, Bert, 171
Berry, Chuck, 101n2, 102–3, 141–42; learning guitar, 101; style of, 100
Berry Gordy: A Conversation with Mr. Motown (Kubernik), 174–78
Beverly, Frankie, 388, 392
Bhangra, 482, 487, 488–89

*Bias Against "Rock 'n' Roll"
Latest Bombshell in Dixie*
(Roy), 121–22
The Big Band Era, 14–21, 48
Big beat, 252, 503
Big black, 469, 473–74
"Big Bottom," 291
Big Brother, 537
Big Brother and the Holding
Company, 235–40
BigChampagne, 557
The Big Chill, 365
Biggie Smalls. *See*
Notorious B.I.G
(Wallace, Christopher)
Bigotry, denunciation of,
435–36
Big Star, 474
Bikini Kill (band), 532
Billboard, xx, 48, 66–68,
94–95, 545; best selling
album charts, 545; Ford
as writer for, 419–20;
George as writer for, 388;
SoundScan, 521; Top 100,
334
Billboard's Airplay Monitor,
500
"Billie Jean," 364, 369, 370,
393
Billy J. Kramer and the
Dakotas, 219
Billy Ward and the
Dominoes, 80, 82
Björk, 491
Black, Bill, 113
Blackboard Jungle, 324, 325
"Black Dog," 305
Blackface, 32–38
Black Flag, 415–18
*Black Music's on Top; White
Jazz Stagnant* (Freedman),
15–17
Black Panther Pary, 435
Black Panthers, 258, 272, 518
Black power movement, 270
Blacks. *See* African
American
Black Sabbath, 293–99
Black Sabbath, 293
"Black Sabbath," 293
*Black Sabbath Don't Scare
Nobody* (Kelleher), 294–99
Black Star, 460
Blackwell, Bumps, 104–9
Blackwell, Chris, 327
Blackwell, Otis, 112, 116

Blandshaw, Ralph (Van
Silk), 426
Blige, Mary J., 516–19
Blink-182, 536
Blitz. *See* New Music
Blondie, 342, 353
Blow, Kurtis, 421–22
"Blowin' in the Wind," 154,
282
Blue, 266–67
Bluebeat, 480
Blue Cheer, 291, 401
"Blue Moon of Kentucky,"
114
Blue Oyster Cult, 379, 411
Blues, 32–39, 76–77; changes
in, 189–93; Chicago, 220;
country, 44–45, 63, 74;
delta, 45–47; on guitar,
48–49; harmonica, 45;
heavy metal compared
to, 398; instruments, 48;
jump, 53; learning, 32;
lyrics, 58; musicians, 48;
playing, 85–86; singers,
44–45, 75; urban style,
48. *See also* Classic Blues;
Country Blues; Rhythm
and Blues (R&B)
*Blues People: The Negro
Experience in White
America and the Music that
Developed from It* (Jones),
32–39
Bluestein, Gene, 146–49
"Blue Suede Shoes," 115
Blunted on Reality, 462
BMI. *See* Broadcast Music
Incorporated
"Bobby Sox Blues," 49
"Bobby Soxers," 22–24
*The Bobby Sox Have Wilted,
but the Memory Remains
Fresh* (Weinman Lear),
22–24
"Bob Dylan's 115th Dream,"
164
"Bob Dylan's Dream,"
164n2
Body Count, 447
Bomb Squad, 424
"Bongo Rock," 420–21
Bonham, John, 303
Bon Jovi, 400
Bonzo, 305
Boogie Down Productions,
440

Booker T., 190
Boone, Pat, 109
"Boots of Spanish Leather,"
167
"Boppin' the Blues," 115
"Borderline," 374
Born in the U.S.A., 380
"Born in the USA," 387
Born to Run, 378, 379
"Born To Run," 377, 379
*Born To Run: The Bruce
Springsteen Story*
(Springsteen), 378
The Boss. *See* Springsteen,
Bruce
Bottleneck/"slide" guitar,
45–47
Bowie, David (Jones,
David), 307; Beatles/
Rolling Stones and, 313;
on Jagger, 313; on Rock
"n" Roll, 313; on sex,
308–9, 311
Boy bands, 534, 535, 536
Boyz II Men, 534
Bradford, Perry, 26
Brain Salad Surgery, 317
Bratmobile, 474
Braxton, Toni, 518
Break Beats, 423
"Breakbeat Science," 510,
514
Break dancers, 188. *See also*
Hip Hop
Breakdancing, 423
Bream, Julian, 301
Breeders, 473, 475–76
Bricktop, 42
"Bridge Over Troubled
Water," 322
Brill Building, 131–40;
creative flexibility at, 137;
King, Carol and, 262;
songwriters, 131–40; Tin
Pan Alley production
practices revived in, 131
Bringing It All Back Home,
154
"Bring the Noise,"
424, 443
British art schools, 219–24
British invasion, 200–204,
219
Broadcast Music
Incorporated (BMI), 59
Broadus, Calvin. *See* Snoop
Doggy Dogg

Broadway, 1
Brody, John, 334–35
Brooks, Garth, 521–27
Brooks, George, 42
Brother Ray: Ray Charles' Own Story (Charles, Ritz), 83–89
Brower, W. A., 284–90
Brown, Charlie, 180
Brown, Foxy, 457
Brown, James, xvi, 169, 178–89, 192, 286–87, 393; hollering of, 183; indebted to Gospel, 179; Jackson, M., compared to, 365; pop hits of, 188; radio station of, 186–87
Brown, Roy, 106
Brown, Ruth, 74, 77–81; Atlantic Records and, 77–79, 81; dress style of, 80; as Queen of the One-Nighters, 79
Brown, Sharon, 543
"Brown Eyed Handsome Man," 100
"Brown Eyes," 543
Brown Sugar, 515–16
Brown v. Board of Education, 120
Bruce Springsteen and the E Street Band, 378, 381, 385. *See also* Springsteen, Bruce
Bruford, Bill, 320–21
Bryson, Peabo, 391
Bublé, Michael, 554
Buckley, Tim, 547–48, 550
Bunzel, Peter, 125–28
Burdon, Eric, 191
Burke, Solomon, 170, 171
Burnin', 324, 326
"Burnin' Up," 374
Burton, Cliff, 401
Bush Administration, arrogance of, 529
Buskirk, Eliot Van, 556–58
Butler, Terry "Geezer," 295
Buzzcocks, 347, 349
The Byrds, 155, 231, 252, 262, 348
Byrne, David, 343–44

"Cactus Tree," 267
Cage, John, 248
The Cakewalk, 34
Calloway, Blanche, 77

Calypso music, 28, 323
Candid Camera, 534
Cannabis, 323
Cantor, Eddie, 126
Capitalism: art and, 386; hip hop and, 459–60; Springsteen on, 384–85
Capitol Records, 391–92
"The Cardinal," 167
Carey, Mariah, 516–18, 537
Caribbean music styles, 485–87
Carnegie Hall, 210
Carole King: "You Can Get to Know Me Through My Music" (Windeler), 263–66
Carrie, 138
"Cars," 542
Carson, John (Fiddler), 27
Carson, Johnny, 432, 434
Carter, Asa, 120–22
Casablanca Records, 331–32, 336–37
Case, Neko, 553, 554
"Case of You," 493
Cash, Johnny, 530
Cashbox, 91, 95
Cassette tapes, 555
Catch a Fire, 324, 326
"Causing a Commotion," 374
CBGB's, 339–44, 352, 469
CBS Records, 381, 385, 469
CD's, 532, 544, 548, 555
Censorship, xviii, 99, 252, 405–14, 435
C'est Chic, 333–34
Charles, Eric, 293
Charles, Ray, 74, 82–89, 100, 169; accusations of sacrilege in music by, 85; black roots of music by, 85; Franklin, A., similar to, 198; hillbilly music and, 88; songwriting of, 88–89
Cheap Thrills, 236
Checker, Chubby, 132
Cheeba, Eddie, 421
Cheetah, 249–50
Chemical Brothers, 503
Cherry Vanilla, 309
Chess Records, 101–2
Chicago, 220, 330n3
Chicago Defender, 120–22
Chicks Against the Machine (Taylor), 527–33

Child ballads, 150
Child of Mine, 265
"Children of the Grave," 297–98
The Chi-Lites, 273
Choruss plan, 558
Christgau, Robert, 340, 346n1
Christian, Charlie, 48
Christian, Neil, 301
The Chronic, 447–50
Chronology, xix–xx
Chuck Berry: Rock Lives! (Jopling), 101–3
Chuck Berry: The Autobiography (Berry), 101n2
Chuck D (Ridenhour, Carlton), 432n1, 433, 435–37, 441–43, 445–46
Church: African American, traditions, 57; Christian, 33, 37; "Close to the Edge" and, 322; Franklin at, 194–95, 197; Hendrix on, 243–44; Madonna and, 375
"Circus," 543
The City Sun!, 366
Civil Rights movement, 137, 146, 154, 156, 169, 270
Clapton, Eric, 74, 241, 324, 325
Clarence, Paul, 282
Clark, Dick, 123–29
The Clash, 346, 492
Classical Music, 10; heavy metal compared to, 396–97; popular music differentiated from, 7
Classical rock, 317–18, 545, 548
Classic Blues, 29, 32–39; emergence of, 38; first Blues recording as, 37; lyrics of, 35; sexuality in, 39n1; shows, 34; women as best, singers, 37
Classics, 542
Clay, Andrew Dice, 432–35
Clement, Jack, 116
Clemons, Clarence, 385
Cleveland, James, 196–97
Click track, 402
Cliff, Jimmy, 324, 325, 326, 327, 480
Clink, Mike, 403

Clinton, George, 283–90; bands of, 285; barbershop of, 286; on Funkin', 286; on music and politics, 284–90
Close To the Edge, 319–22
"Close To the Edge," 322
"Cloud Nine," 177
Clover, Joshua, 535–36
Clubs: dance, 333–36; disco, 421–22; New York, 513; sound systems of, 509
Cobain, Kurt, 472n4, 474, 475
Cocaine, 508
Cohen, John, 160–68
"Cold Blue Steel and Sweet Fire," 267
Cole, Nat "King," xviii, 48, 85, 121
Collaboration, 5–6
Collier's, 25, 30
Collins, Williams "Bootsy," 187, 271, 283
Columbia Records, 27, 153, 195–98, 326, 458, 459
Combs, Sean "Puffy" (P Diddy), 452–54, 456–57, 459, 461
Come Blow Your Horn, 24
"Come Follow Me," 488
Commercial interests, artistic expression v., 157–59
Commercialism: authenticity and, 90; Disco, 331; in Jazz, 52, 249; The Rolling stones and, 224; songwriters, 493; what is, 93
Commercial power, of Disco, 331
Commercial songwriters, 493
The Commodores, 390
Communal idea, 258
Communications Act, of 1934, 498
Community: disco as glue uniting, 337; hip hop reflecting, 427–28; indie rock, 473; Springsteen's act creating sense of, 383
Como, Perry, 95
Compilation albums, 545
Concept albums, 88, 216

Concert: stage props, 397–98; Tibetan freedom, 460
A Conservative Impulse in the Rock Underground (Wolcott), 341–45
Considine, J. D., 395–99, 441–47
Consumerism. *See* Commercialism
Contemporary Keyboard, 316
The Contortions, 352
Cook, Paul, 347
Cooke, Sam, 75, 169, 197
The Cookies, 135–36
Cool DJ AJ, 421–22
Coon, Caroline, 346–51
Cooper, Alice, 307–8
Cooper, Carol, 429–31
Cooper, Mark, 522–27
Cope, Julian, 547
"Cop Killer," 447, 449
Copland, Aaron, 316, 318–19
"Copper Kettle," 150
Corea, Chick, 317
Corn of Plenty, 68–70
Costello, Elvis, 355–61
Count Basie's Band, 16
Counterpoint, 16
Country Blues, 44–45, 63, 74
Country dweller, musical demand of, 67
Country music, 88, 103, 192–93, 520–21; Euro-American music and, 66; as Folk music/novelty, 65–70; mainstream, 71–73; Nashville-based, industry, 71–72; songs, 66, 521; songwriters, 67–68; from Tin Pan Alley, 66
Country Music Goes To Town (Jarman), 72–73
Cover songs: Dylan, 154–56; by pop names, 96; R&B, 94–97
Cowell, Simon, 539
Crawdaddy, 249
"Crazy Bald Head," 327
"Crazysexycool," 519
Cream, 241, 293
Creem magazine, 340, 378
Crichton, Kyle, 26–29
Criticism, xvii; high art and, 158–59; of Hip Hop/Rap, 425, 440–41; new form of, 214; popular music,

xx, 158–59; rock, 249, 339–40, 378, 380–81; style, meaning and, xvii
Critics: Beatles taken seriously by, 201; on Black Sabbath, 294; crossover, 394; Disco, 333; first female rock, 225–30, 249; Kodwo Eshun, 506; *New York Times*, 153, 432; Pop, 253, 515; react to third Led Zeppelin record, 304; Winchell, Walter, 18
Crosby, Bing, 21–22, 127
Cross, Charles, 469
Crossover, 394; hits by African American artists of 1980's, 388; Prince and critics of, 394
Crowe, Cameron, 308–14
The Crunge: Jimmy Page Gives A History Lesson (Schulps), 300–307
The Crystals, 138–39
"Cry to Me," 327
Csicsery, George Paul, 258–60
Cuellar, Jose, 489
Cultural accreditation, 201n2
Cutler, Sam, 259

"Da Doo Ron Ron," 139
Dale, Dick, 140
Dalhart, Vernon, 27
Dali, 313
Danae, 335–36
Dance: bands, 10, 233; barn, 59; clubs, 333–36; fads, 10, 132, 135; liquid, style, 506; styles, 13
The Dance Band Business: A Study in Black and White (Kolodin), 18–20
Dance music, 373–74; African American, 390; singers, 507. *See also* Electronic dance music (EDM)
"Dance This Mess Around," 354
Dancing age, 233
D'Angelo, 515–16
Dangerous, 367, 370
Daniels, Joe, 16
"Darling Nikki," 406, 410
Date, Terry, 469–70

David Bowie Interview (Crowe), 308–14

Davis, Jimmie, 26, 28

Davis, Meyer, 54

Davis, Miles, 175

Dawson, John William (Rev.), 29

"A Day In the Life," 218

"Day 'n' Nite," 543

"Dazed and Confused," 303

Dead Kennedys, 417

Dead Like Live Thunder (Gleason), 233–35

Dean, James, 309

"Dear God, Please Help Me," 552

Death, 322; Baez sings about, 150; of Cobain, 474; of Notorious B.I.G, 453–56; of 2Pac, 452–56

Death Certificate, 442–44

The Death of Rhythm and Blues (George), 389–94

Death Row Records, 447–49, 452–53

Decca, 28, 55

The Decline of Western Civilization, 415

DeCurtis, Anthony, 466

"Deep Cover," 447, 449

Deep South, 68

Defenders of the Faith, 397

Def Jam Records, 423–24, 444, 459, 542

Dekker, Desmond, 323

De La Soul, 428, 440

Delehant, Jim, 190–93

Delta Blues, 45–47

Democratic populism, 387

Dempsey, David, 211

Denny, Sandy, 305

Denver, John, 408

Desperately Seeking Susan, 374–75

Destiny's Child, 517, 543

Devo, 352

The Dialectic of Disco: Gay Music Goes Straight (Kopkind), 330–39

Diamond, Chuck & Lee, 106

Diamond Dogs, 311, 312

"Diamonds Are a Girl's Best Friend," 372

Diddley, Bo, 100

Digital Music Forum East, 558

Digital sampler, 424

Digital signal processing (DSP), 506

Dike, Matt, 445

DiMartino, Dave, 468

Di Meola, Al, 444

Dirnt, Mike, 476

Disc jockey, 329

Disc jockey (DJ): payola, 128; promotional fees, 60n3, 96; rap, 421–22; role of MC and, 420

Disco, 311–12, 328–39; in big cities, 331–32; clubs, 421–22; commercial power of, 331; critics, 333; dance clubs, 333–36; as a drug, 338; elite, 334; Euro, 329–30, 334; at Flamingo, 332, 335–36; music hurt by, 188–89; in New York, 331–32, 337; Pop, 329–30; as popular music, 328; radio station, 337; R&B and, 329; record companies love of, 188; uniting community, 337

"Disco Queen," 337

Dissent, 529–30

Dixie Chicks, 526–33

Dixieland, 38

DJ. *See* Disc jockey

DJ Hollywood, 421

DJ Kool Herc, 419–20, 420–21

DJ Starski, 421–22

DMX, 460

The D.N.A., 352

D.O.A., 417

Doerschuk, Robert L., 492–96

Doggystyle, 448–50, 452

Domino, "Fats," 100

Don Juan's Reckless Daughter, 267

"Don't Be Cruel," 111–12, 115, 116

"Don't Fear the Reaper," 411

"Don't Pass Me By," 230

"Don't Stop 'Til You Get Enough," 369, 371, 393

Don't Stop 'Til You Get Enough: Bruce Swedien Remembers the Times with Michael Jackson (Easlea), 368–71

"Don't Think Twice, It's Alright," 154

Doowop, 534

Dorsey, Tommy, 28, 30–31

Dot-com bubble, 534–35

Double, Michael, 295

Dowd, Tom, 79

Down Beat, xx, 15, 52–53

Down Hearted Blues, 40, 43

Downing, K. K., 396

Downstairs Records, 420

Dozier, Lamont, 177

Drag queens, sex roles of, 374

Dr. Dre (Young, Andre), 439, 447–50, 464

Dreams, 268

Dreja, Chris, 302

The Drifters, 264

Drum "n" bass. *See* Jungle

DSP. *See* Digital signal processing

DuBois, W. E. B., 388

Duhe, Robin, 392

Dummy groups, 137

Dupri, Jermaine, 449–50

DVDs, 544

Dylan, Bob, xvi, 153–59, 227, 326, 541, 553; albums of, 164–65, 164n2; Art, 159; authenticity of, 157–59, 471; Baez and, 154n2; on ballads, 167; on Beatles, 166; cover songs, 154–56; on folk music, 164; Hendrix indebted to, 241; interviews of, 161–68; lyrics, 160; as major American poet, 251; on muzak, 168; on musical training, 162–63; poetry and, 162, 165; on radio, 168; on Rock "n" Roll, 164; songs of, 164n2; on songwriting, 162, 168; Springsteen and, 377, 384; style of, 154, 155–56, 162; world vision of, 156

Earth, Wind and Fire, 392

"Ease on Down the Road," 371

Easlea, Daryl, 368–71

Easton, Sheena, 406

Easy-E, 439

"Eat Me Alive," 406

Ebony, 194

Ecstasy (MDMA), 502, 508

EDM. *See* Electronic dance music
"The Ed Sullivan Show," 209–10
"Eh, Eh," 543
Ehrenreich, Barbara, 208–12
Eiffel 65, 542, 543
"Eight Miles High," 231
Eivets Rednow, 279
"Eleanor Rigby," 214–16
"Electric Ladyland," 242
Electronica, 503
Electronic dance music (EDM), 502–14; African American music and, 510; creation of, 504–5; drug culture and, 508; feeling and, 507; genres, 502–3, 511–13; Lady Gaga and, 540; musical influences of, 504; spirituality and, 508
Electronic sound, 215
Elektra, 391, 401
Elks Rendezvous, 54
Ellington, Duke, 19–20, 29, 86
Elliott, Missy "Misdemeanor," 457, 516–17, 519
Elman, Mischa, 12
ELP. *See* Emerson, Lake and Palmer
Elvis, 380
The Elvis (Costello, That Is) Interview (Jones), 356–61
Emerson, Keith, 316
Emerson, Lake and Palmer (ELP), 316
Eminem, 464–67
Eminem's Old Words Aren't Hip Hop's Biggest Problem (Graham), 465–67
Empire of the Air (Toomey), 498–501
The Empress of the Blues, 39–43
English folk songs, 28–29
Ennis, Philip, xviii
Eno, Brian, 502, 510
Entertainment, politics and, 539
Entertainment Weekly, 528, 531–32
En Vogue, 519
Epic Records, 468–69
Ertegun, Ahmet, 62–63, 84, 90–93, 264

Essence, 425–31
Estes, John "Sleepy," 28, 29
Ethnic stereotyping, 433
Ethnomusicology, 538
Euro-American music, pre 1950, 66
Evans, Faith, 453, 519
Everett-Green, Robert, 552–56
Everly Brothers, 102
"Everyday I Have The Blues," 49
Exile on Main Street, 343
Experience Music Project, 472
"Express Yourself," 376

Fab 5 Freddy, 428
"Façade," 217
Facebook, 557
The Faces, 379
Failure, 539
Fame, 312
The Fame, 540, 542, 543
Fandom: Beatles, 208–12; new forms of, 21–25
"Fanfare for the Common Man," 316–19
Fanzine, 473
Farley, Christopher John, 458–63
Farrakhan, Louis, 435, 443
Farrow, Mia, 24
Fatback band, 426
Fatboy Slim, 552
Fathead, 86n1
FCC. *See* Federal Communications Commission
Fear of a Rap Planet (Considine), 441–47
Federal Communications Commission (FCC), 498–500
Feller, Sid, 88
The Fellows, 470
Feminism, 372–73, 372n3, 374–76
Femme vocal groups, 96
Festivals, 254–60
"Fewer Media Owners, More Media Choices," 499–500
Field hollers, 77
50 Cent, 464
"Fight the Power," 445
Filesharing, xviii, 554–58

"Final Hour," 461
Fingerpicking, 262
"Fingertips," 278, 280
Fire and Rain, 264
First Piano Concerto, 317
First Wave, 353
Fitzgerald, Ella, 20
"5–10–15 Minutes (Of Your Love)," 80
Five Blind Boys, 31
Flack, Roberta, 391, 457
Flamingo, 332, 335–36
"Flava In Your Ear (Remix)," 459
Flavor Flav, 443
Flipside, 416
Flipside, Al, 416–18
Flo Rida, 542
Flying Lizards, 542
FMC. *See* The Future of Music Coalition
Foley, Red, 71, 72
Folk music, 61–62; American, 144; California, 252; college students interested in, 149–50; country music as, 65–70; Dylan on, 164; English, 28–29; Greenwich village scene, 153; Hillbilly music and, 28–29, 145; in show business, 67. *See also* Urban Folk
Folk rock, 155
Folk Singing: Sibyl With Guitar, 149–53
Fong-Torres, Ben, 278–83
Ford, Lita, 441, 444
Ford, Robert, Jr., 419–22
The Formerly Little Stevie Wonder (Fong-Torres), 278–83
"For No One," 216
For the Roses, 267
Foster, David, 371
Foster, Stephen, 8
Four Tops, 176
Fox Confessor Brings the Flood, 554
Fox trots, 11–143
Frampton, Peter, 332
Frankie Knuckles, 501
Franklin, Aretha, 264, 270, 461, 515, 517–19, 539; awards received by, 196; at church, 194–95, 197; early influences of,

196–97; home life of, 199;
learns piano, 196–97;
similar to Charles, R., 198;
timing in music by, 197
Franklin, Carolyn, 196
Franklin, Erma, 197
Freak Out!, 244–45
Freddie's Dead, 275
Freed, Alan, 124
Freedman, Marvin, 15–17
Freedom, 267
Freese, Josh, 558
Free speech, 409, 412, 413,
435
French popular music,
482–83
Frere-Jones, Sasha, 541–43
Friedman, Kenn, 331–32,
334–36
Friedman, Thomas, 529
Fripp, Robert, 321
Frith, Simon, 381–87
From Here to Eternity, 23
From the Planet Mars, 483
Fugees, 462
"Fugue," 318
Fulfillment, 267
Fulson, Lowell, 49–50, 76
Funk, 178–89, 283
The Funk Brothers, 174
"Funny How Time Flies
Away," 282
Furtado, Nelly, 553
Fusari, Rob, 542–43
The Future of Music
Coalition (FMC), 497–98,
500
Fuzztones, 240

Gabler, Milt, 55
Gaines, Charlie, 54
"Gallows Pole," 305
Gangsta Rap, 406, 439–40,
442, 447, 449
Garcia, Jerry, 232–33
Gardner, Ava, 23
Gardner, Robert, 391
Garland, Eric, 557
Garland, Phyl, 194–99
*Garth Brooks: Meet Nashville's
New Breed of Generously
Stetsoned Crooner*
(Cooper), 522–27
Gay activists, 336
Gay culture, 329–39
Gaye, Marvin, 176, 273, 392

Gay Men's Health Crisis,
436
Gaynor, Gloria, 332
Gay people: indie rock and,
477; in power, 434
Geffen Records, 434–35
Gehr, Richard, 400–405
Gendron, Bernard, 201n2,
352
Generation X, 545
George, Nelson, 388–94, 515
*George Clinton, Ultimate
Liberators of Constipated
Nations* (Brower), 284–90
"Getting Better," 217–18
Gibbs, Georgia, 80, 97n5,
97n5 95
Gibran, Khalil, 165
Gilbert, Jerry, 46–47
Gilbert, William, 126
Gillespie, Dizzy, 57
Gimme Shelter, 254n1
"Gimmie Shelter," 273
Ginastera, 317
Ginsberg, Allen, 162
Girl groups, 131–40
Girls Ain't Nothin' but Trouble
(Cooper, C.), 429–31
Glam rock, 307–8
Gleason, Ralph J., 233–35
Glee, 537
Glen Miller's Band, 16
Global music, 481
Glover, Henry, 61, 105
"G N' R Lies," 436
The Godfather, 274
The Godfather of Soul (Brown,
Tucker), 180–89
Goffin, Gerry, 132, 135, 264
Gold Coast Blues, 27
Golden Gate Quartet, 31
Golden Years, 312
Goldstein, Richard, 214,
216–17, 217n6, 233, 249,
250–53
"Goodbye Earl," 527
"Good Golly Miss Molly,"
109
Goodman, Benny, 19–20, 28
Goodman, Ellen, 410
Goodman band, 18–19
"Good Night Irene," 148
"Good Times," 330
"Good Times Bad Times,"
292
"Good Vibrations," 141n1,
142–43

Google, 557
Gordy, Berry, 173–78, 363–65
Gore, Al, 409–10
Gore, Tipper, 406, 411–12
Gorgeous Gorge, 182
Gospel, 30, 31, 82; battle of,
105; Brown, J. indebted to,
179; numbers by Charles,
84; R&B relationship with,
74; singers, 195; vocal
technique, 169
Gould, Glenn, 553
Grace, Bishop, 180
Grace, Teddy, 238
Graham, Larry, 271
Graham, Renee, 465–67
Grainger, Porter, 35
Grand Funk Railroad, 294
Grandmaster Flash & the
Furious Five, 423, 426
Grand Old Opry, 72–73,
530
Grateful Dead, 232–33
"Great Balls of Fire," 116
Green, Silas, 36, 181
Green, Tuff, 76
Green Day, 473–76, 553
Greene, Bob, 441
Greenwich, Ellie, 133–36
Greenwich Village, 153
Greer, Corny Allen, 28
*Greetings from Asbury Park,
N.J.*, 377
Grieg, Charlotte, 133–40
Griffin, Jim, 558
Griffin, Richard (Professor
Griff), 432–33, 435–36, 443
Grunge, 468, 468n2
Guitar: Chuck Berry
learning, 101; Blues on,
48–49; bottleneck/"slide,"
45–47; electric, 48, 240–44;
fingerpicking, 262; as
multifaceted instrument,
301; sales multiplying,
149
Guitar Player, 49, 316
Guns N' Roses, 402, 405,
432, 435–36
Guralnick, Peter, 366
Guthrie, Woody, 145–46,
148, 153, 261, 384

Hagan, Pat, 211–12
Hailey, K-Ci, 516, 518
Hair-metal, 395
Haley, Bill, xviii, 324–25

Halford, Rob, 396, 397, 398–99
"Hallelujah," 85, 88
Hamer, Fannie Lou, 156
Hamm, Charles, 2
Hammer, 444, 457
Hammett, Kirk, 401–2
Hampton, Mike "Kid Funkadelic," 287
Hardcore, 416–18, 502
A Hard Day's Night, 205–12
The Harder They Come, 324, 325, 326, 480
"Hard Rain," 161–62
Harmonica, 45, 48
Harper's, 17
Harris, Wynonie "Mr. Blues," 57, 62
Harrison, George, 200, 202, 205, 218
Harry Von Tilzer Company, 4
Harvard, 151
HDH. See Holland-Dozier-Holland
"Head," 389
"Headbanger's Ball," 405
Hear Me Talkin' To Ya: The Story of Jazz as Told By Men Who Made It (Shapiro, Hentoff), 40–44
"Heartbreak Hotel," 111, 115
"Heat Wave," 173
Heavy metal, 290–99; aesthetics of, 405–6; Blues compared to, 398; Classical Music compared to, 396–97; of early 1980's, 395–99; feel of, 398; hard/ speed/thrash/death/ pop/glam, 399–400, 405; in late 80's, 99–405; lyrics, 400; on MTV, 396, 405; PMRC and public debate about, 405–14; popularity of, 400, 405; Sex and, 406
Heavy Metal Mania, 405
Heller, Jerry, 442
Hello World, 368
Hell's Angels, 254, 258
Help!, 213
"Help Me Doctor," 401
Henderson, Fletcher, 28, 41
Hendrix, Jimi, xvi, 240–44, 287
Hentoff, Nat, 40–44, 160
Here Ain't the Sonics, 470

Hernandez, Jorge, 488–89
"He's A Rebel," 138
Hess, Elizabeth, 208–12
Hesse, Herman, 320
"He's Sure the Boy I Love," 139
Hetfield, James, 400–405
"Hey Joe," 242
Hilburn, Robert, 324–28
Hilfiger, Tommy, 460
Hill, Lauryn, 457–63, 516–17, 519
Hillbilly music, 25–29, 59, 65, 72; Charles, Ray and, 88; Folk music and, 28–29, 145; independent labels, 61–62; war and, 68
Hilton, Paris, 552
Hinds, Selwyn Seyfu, 454–55
Hip Hop, 188, 439–47, 513; activism, 460; camaraderie in, 427; capitalism and, 459–60; change in social position of, 458; criticism of, 425, 440–41; first female vocalists in, 426; history of, 419, 425–29; progressive, 440, 457; Rap differentiated from, 459–60; reflecting community, 427–28; sampling in, 461; sexism in, 428, 430; stars in movies, 461; subgenres of, 464; violence and, 428. See also Rap
Hip Hop Madness: From Def Jams to Cold Lampin', Rap is Our Music (Allen), 425–29
Hip Hop Nation (Farley), 458–63
Hippies, 258, 337, 472
Historia Electronica Preface (Reynolds), 504–14
HIStory, 370, 371
Hit Parader, 190
Holcomb, Roscoe, 163
Holden, Stephen, 353–55
Holland-Dozier-Holland (HDH), 173, 177, 270, 282
Hollings, Ernest F., 407, 409
Holly, Major "Mule," 197
Hollywood Candy Bars, 128
Hollywood Shuffle, 391

Homophobia, 433–34
Honey Chile, 108
Honkers and Shouters: The Golden Years of Rhythm and Blues (Shaw), 62–64, 75–77
Honky-Tonk music, 65
Hootenanny, 149
Hot Pants, 188
"Hot Pants (She Got to Use What She Got to Get What She Wants)," 187
"Hound Dog," 111–12
House, Son, 46–47
House music, 502, 510
House Un-American Activities Committee, 145–46
Houston, Whitney, 515, 537
Howar, Pam, 410
Howard theater, 55
Howe, Steve, 319–20
"How Many More Times," 292
Human Be-In, 232
Human Be-Ins, 258
Hunter, Alberta, 40, 42–43
"The Hustle," 329

I.A.M., 482–83
I Am...the Autobiography (Nas), 460
Ibo tribe, of Nigeria, 426
"I Can See Clearly Now," 325
"I Can't Stop Loving you," 88
Ice Cube (Jackson, O'Shea), 439, 441–46, 460
Ice-T, 446, 449
Idolized: Music, Media, and Identity in American Idol (Meizel), 537–38
"I Feel Fine," 213
"If the Kid Can't Make You Come Nobody Can," 411
"If You Need Me," 171n3
Iggy Pop, 548
"I Got a Woman," 85
"I Have a Dream" speech, 154
Ike Turner's Kings of Rhythm, 109
"I Like it Rough," 543
"I'll Go Crazy," 182
"I'm Goin' Down," 518

Immigration and Assimilation: Rai, Reggae, and Bhangramuffin (Lipsitz), 482–90

Immigration in Britain, music and, 482–90

I'm White! What's Wrong With Michael Jackson (Gordy), 365–68

Incredible String Band, 166

Independent labels, 58–64, 96, 467; electronic music, 511–12; growth and death of, 93; hillbilly music, 61–62; R&B phenomenon spearheaded by, 61, 90–91

Indian Music, 218

Indie rock, 415; to alternative rock, 467–71; community, 473; gay people and, 477; record company, 58–64; women and, 477

Indies' Surprise Survival: Small Labels' Ingenuity and Skill Pay Off (Simon), 60–62

I Never Loved a Man the Way I Love You, 196

Ink Spots, 30, 82, 534

"In My Life," 315

In Rainbows, 555

Internet, 545, 548, 551, 555–58

Interscope Records, 542

Interview, xvii; Amos, 492–96; Costello, 356–61; Dixie Chicks, 526–33; Dylan, 161–68; with Eminem, 464; of Heller, 442; Meizel, 537–40; Page, 299–307; Phillips, 112–17; with progressive rock musicians, 316

"In The Midnight Hour," 172

In the Studio With Michael Jackson, 368

"In Time," 425

"Into the Groove," 375

Iommi, Tony, 295, 297, 298

I-Phone, 558

I-Pod, 555

Irving Berlin and the Crucible of God (Hamm), 2–5

Island Records, 324, 326

"Israelites," 323

"Is You Is or Is You Ain't (Ma' Baby)," 55

It Might As Well Rain Until September, 264

"It's All About the Benjamins," 459

"It's All Over Now, Baby Blue," 156

It's Getting Better (Kroll), 217–18

I-Tunes, 555, 558

Ives, Burl, 146

"I Wanna Hold Your Hand," 102

Jabs, Matthias, 398

Jackson, Janet, 517

Jackson, Jesse (Reverend), 288

Jackson, Mahalia, 30

Jackson, Michael, xviii, 176, 363–71, 388–90, 393–94

Jackson, Molly, 29

Jackson Five, 363, 534

Jacobs, Gloria, 208–12

Jagged Little Pill, 491

Jagger, Mick, 222–24, 226–28, 258, 326, 348

Jalis, Country Blues and, 44

"Jam," 370

Jamaica, 323

Jamaican culture, in England, 485, 487

Jamerson, James, 175

James, Elmore, 45

James, Etta, 56

James, Harry, 17

James, Rick, 430, 444

"James Brown and the Famous Flames," 179, 183

Jameson, Fredric, 353

Jardine, Al, 141

Jarman, Rufus, 72–73

Ja Rule, 464

Jay-Z, 461, 464, 518

Jazz, 5, 14, 38, 103; age, 10; authenticity in, 249; avant-garde, 231–32; black, 16; celebrities, 19; commercialism and, 52, 249; early, shows, 34; festivals, 195; Gordy on, 174–75; income from, 91; musicians, 16–17, 93; popularization of, 38; popular music and, 21–22;

race and musical style in, 15–16; white style, 16–17

Jazzie B, 486

Jean, Wyclef, 462

Jeff Beck Group, 290

Jefferson, Blind Lemon, 44–45, 76

Jefferson Airplane, 232–33

The Jefferson Airplane Takes Off, 232

"The Jerk," 171

Jive Talking N.Y. Dj's Rapping Away in Black Discos (Ford), 421–22

John, Elton, 465

"Johnny Too Bad," 325

"Johnny Was," 327

Johnson, Billy, 392

Johnson, Enortis, 108

Johnson, Pete, 91

Johnson, Robert, 45, 47

Jolson, Al, 21, 126

Jones, Allan, 355–56

Jones, Brian, 222

Jones, Johnny J., 181

Jones, John Paul, 302, 305

Jones, Leroi. *See* Baraka, Amiri

Jones, Quincy, 363, 369, 370

Jones, Steve, 347

Jones, Wilmore "Slick," 53

Joplin, Janis, 235–40

Jopling, Norman, 101–3

Jordan, Louis, 51–53, 75, 181

Journalism, xvii

Judas Priest, 395–98, 406, 410

Judkins, S., 279

"Judy Is A Punk," 344

Jukebox Culture How I Learned to Stop Worrying and Love the Boy Band (Clover), 535–36

Juke joint, 47

"Jumpin' Jack Flash," 225

Jungle Brothers, 425

"Jungle Love," 411

Jungle music (drum 'n' bass), 502–3, 505, 510, 512–14

Juno Awards, 554

"Just Dance," 542, 543

"Just My Imagination," 177

Kabibble, Ish, 207n3, 208–12

Kansas City Convention Hall, 18

Kapp, David, 28
Kapp, Jack, 22
Kapur, Steve, 487
Kaye, Elizabeth, 112–17
Kazaa, 557
Kazin, Michael, 529–30
Keil, Charles, 366
Keita, Salif, 483
Keith Emerson (Milano), 316–19
Kelleher, Ed, 294–99
Kempton, Sally, 245–49
Kennedy, John F., assassination of, 209, 225
Kennibrew, Dee Dee, 138
Kern, Jerome, 1
Kerouac, Jack, 477
Kesey, Ken, 232
Khaled, Cheb, 484
Khan, Chaka, 515, 516
The Kids Aren't Alright…They're Amazing (Babcock), 546–52
Kiley, Rilo, 546
Kill 'Em All, 401
"Killing Me Softly," 457
Killion, Billy Kay, 125
Kim, Kevin, 453
King, B.B., 48–49, 74–77
King, Carole, 133–37, 261–66
King, Martin Luther, Jr., 147, 154, 225
King, Rodney, beating, 447
King Crimson, 321
"King of Jazz" (Whiteman), 10–11
King of Pop. *See* Jackson, Michael
"The King of Rock," 423
King Records, 61, 184, 185, 185n5, 188
Kings of Leon, 546, 550
Kingston Trio, 146
"King Tim III," 426
The Kinks, 220
Kirschner, Don, 135, 342
Kiss, 291
"Ko Ko Mo," 95–96
Kolodin, Irving, 17–20
Koolhaas, Rem, 535–36
Kootch, Danny, 264
Kopkind, Andrew, 330–39
Kovel, Joel, 433
Kraftwerk, 313, 502
Kreutzmann, Bill, 234
Kris Kross, 449
Kristofferson, Kris, 267

Kroll, Jack, 217–18
KRS-One, 440
Kubernik, Harvey, 174–78

La Bostrie, Dorothy, 107
Lady Gaga, xviii, 540–44
Lady Starlight, 542
"La Isla Bonita," 375, 543
"La Jaula de Oro," 489
Lake, Greg, 315n2, 316, 317
Landau, Jon, 377, 384
Landis, John, 393
Laquidara, Charles, 293
La Raza Studies Department, 489
Larkey, Charles, 265
Latin-American music, 60, 64
Lauper, Cyndi, 372
"Lava," 354
Leadbelly, 146, 148, 238
Lear, Norman, 24
Led Zeppelin, 292–93, 299–307, 349, 493
Led Zeppelin III, 303
Lee, Jerry, 116
Lee, Spike, 391
"Le Freak," 333–34
Leiber and Stoller, 132, 136
Lennon, John, 166, 200–204, 205, 227, 229, 348
Leonard, Harlan, 57
Les Négresses Vertes, 483
"Lesson in Survival," 267
"Less Than Zero," 360
Lester, Richard, 205
"A Letter to the New York Post," 443
Levan, Larry, 501
Lewis, Ted, 19
Lewis, Terry, 394
LFO, 536
Licensed to Ill, 427
Life, 124–25, 209, 255
Life After Death…Till Death Do Us Part, 455–57
The Life and Times of Little Richard: The Quasar of Rock (White), 105–10
"Like a Rolling Stone," 155, 158, 241
"Like a Virgin," 375
Lilith Fair, 491, 516
L'il Kim, 457
lingua franca, 537
Lipsitz, George, 481–89
Lite-metal, 405

Little Earthquakes, 494
Little Egypt From Asbury Park – and Bruce Springsteen Don't Crawl on His Belly, Neither (Marsh), 378–81
Little Esther, 56
Little Eva, 135–36, 264
Little Richard, 86–87, 100, 104–10, 240; crazy image of, 109; first recording session of, 107; performances of, 104; quitting music for ministry, 104; recording of "Tutti Frutti," 107–8; songs, 109
"Little Richard and the Upsetters," 106
Live/1975–85, 380–81, 387
Live at the Apollo, 179, 182–84, 187
Live in New Orleans, 392
L. L. Cool J, 428
"Loco-Motion," 264
"The Locomotion," 135
Lollapalooza, 474–75
Lomax, Alan, 46
Lomax, John, 145, 147
Lombardo, Guy, 10
"Lonesome Road," 150
"Long Tall Sally," 108
"Long Time Gone," 527
"Looks That Kill," 406
"Loosey's Rap," 430
Lopez, Jennifer, 539
Los Angeles punk scene, 416–18
"Lose Yourself," 466
Los Tigres del Norte, 488–89
"Lost Ones," 462, 519
"Louder Than a Bomb," 427
"Louie, Louie," 470
Louis Jordan and His Tympany Five, 54, 181
Love, Darlene, 137–38
Love, Mike, 141–42
"Love Is In Control (Finger On The Trigger)," 369
"Lover Man," 553
"Love's Theme," 332
"Love To Love You Baby," 329
Love Unlimited Orchestra, 332
Lowe, Nick, 360
LSD, 508

Lubbock, Jeremy, 371
Lu Be We, xv
"Lucille," 109
"Lucky Lips," 81
"Lucky Star," 374
"Lucy in the Sky with Diamonds," 218
"Lumpy Gravy," 248
Lunceford, Jimmie, 30
Lunch, Lydia, 352
Luongo, John "T.C.," 333–34, 338
Lydon, John, 553
Lyrics, 97; B52's, 353–54; Blues, 58; censorship, 405–14; "Children of the Grave/After Forever," 298; Classic Blues, 35; Dixie Chicks, 531; Dylan, 160; gangsta rap, 442; hardcore band, 417; heavy metal, 400; Hendrix, 243; Led Zeppelin, 305; Metallica, 401; misogynistic, 407; Joni Mitchell, 266; Rap, 406, 425–26, 446, 448, 450; Rock "n" Roll, 206, 410; sex and, 406, 411; Snoop Doggy Dogg, 448, 450; Springsteen, 385; "Tomorrow Never Knows," 215

"Macho Man," 336
MacManus, Declan, 355
McBride, Mary Margaret, 10–13
McCarthy, Joseph, 145–46
McCartney, Paul, 200–204
McCoy, Van, 329
McKernan, Phil, 234
McLaren, Malcolm, 351
McLuhan, Marshall, 217n6, 250–53
McPhatter, Clyde, 82, 169
Mademoiselle, 146–47
Madison Square Garden, 22
Madonna, 308, 372–77, 541, 543; appearance in 80's of, 376; church and, 375; dancing ability of, 373; feminism and, 372–73, 372n3, 374–76; Monroe compared with, 375; MTV and, 372–74; music videos, 372–74; sexuality of, 373

Mae, Willie, 112
"Maggie's Farm," 158
Magic, 296
"Magical Mystery Tour," 230
Maguire, Martie, 526–31
Mahara, 36
Maharishi, 229
Mahler, Gustav, 201
Maines, Natalie, 526–33
Making the Band, 535, 536
"Mama, He Treats your Daughter Mean," 81
The Mamas and the Papas, 252
Mamie Smith's Jazz Hounds, 26–27
Mann, William, 201–3
The Man Who Fell To Earth, 311–12
The Man Who Sold The World, 309–10
"Many Rivers to Cross," 325
Marcus, Greil, 271–77, 531–32
Marcuse, Herbert, 211
"Marie From Sunny Italy," 4, 6
Market populism, 384–85
Marley, Bob, xviii, 323–28, 462, 541–42
Marley, Rohan, 462
Marsh, David, 378–81
Marshall, Joe, 54
"The Marshall Mathers LP," 465
Martha and the Vandellas, 173
Martin, George, 200
"Mary," 516–18
"Mary, Mary," 424
Mass media, xviii
Master of Puppets, 401, 402–3
Master of Reality, 297–98
Master P, 460, 518
"Material Girl," 372
Matlock, Glen, 347
Matthews, Count Otis, 58
Maximumrocknroll, 474, 478
"Maybellene," 101–3
"Maybe Your Baby," 282
Mayer, John, 318
Mayfield, Curtis, 275
Mays, David, 465–66
Maze, 392
MC5, 291
MCA Records, 436

McCartney, Paul, 348, 369
McCaughey, Scott, 470
MC/DJ, 420
McKinnley, William, 392
MC Lyte, 430
M. C. Solaar, 483
MDMA. See Ecstasy
"Me and Bobby McGee," 236
Media, xx, 250–53, 439–41
Meighan, Elroy, 420
Meizel, Katherine, 537–40
Melisma, 539
Melle Mel (Glover, Melvin), 423, 426
Melody Maker, 221, 241, 304, 346–47
"Memphis," 102
Mendelsohn, John, 292–93
Mento music, 323
Menudo, 534
Mercury Records, 185, 185n5
Merge, 476
Merseybeat, 219
"The Message," 423, 426
Message songs, 160
"Metal Health," 410
Metallica, 399–405, 400n1; lyrics, 401; Osbourne and, 401; recording process of, 402; song structure, 400–401
Metallica (Gehr), 400–405
Metronome, xx
Mezzrow, Mezz, 40, 42
M-G-M, 248
Mickey Mouse Club, 535
Microphones, 368
Mike G, 425
Milano, Domenic, 316–19
Miller, Glenn, 18–19
Miller, Mitch, 151
Milli Vanilli, 536
Mills Brothers, 30, 53–54, 82
Minneapolis scene, 415–16
Minstrel shows, 32–38, 53–54, 179, 181
Minuteman, 415
Miseducation of Lauryn Hill, 458–59, 462, 516–17
Miss Rhythm: The Autobiography of Ruth Brown, Rhythm and Blues Legend (Brown, Yule), 78–81
Mitchell, Joni, 262, 266–69

MK Promotions, 333
Moby, 503
Modern Sounds in Country and Western Music, 83
Mojo, 548
Monkees, 534
The Monkey Chant, 281
Monroe, Bill, 163
Monsters of Rock Tour, 400
Monterey Pop Festival (1967), 190, 236, 241, 254, 254n1
"Moonlight Serenade," 18
Moore, René, 370
Moore, Scotty, 111, 113, 114
Moorer, Allison, 552
Morali, Jacques, 336
Morgan, Al, 53
Morissette, Alanis, 491
Moroder, Giorgio, 501
Morricone, Ennio, 552
Morris Day and the Time, 411
Morrison, Van, 358
Morrison, Walter "Junie," 287
Morrissey, 552
Morse, Tim, 319–22
Morton, Roll, 14
"Mother and Child Reunion," 325
Mothership Connection, 284
Mothers of Invention, 231n1, 244–49
Mötley Crüe, 406, 410
Motor Booty Affair, 284, 288
Motown 25, 393
Motown Museum, 461
Motown Records, 190, 278–79, 282, 363–66; artists, 173–74; Stax compared to, 190, 192; story of, 173; stylistic range of, 174n1–174n2
"Movie Magg," 115
MP3's, 544, 554–55
Mr. Clark and Colored Payola, 128
Neely, 182–83, 188
"Mr. Tambourine Man," 155
MSN, 557
MTV. *See* Music Television Channel
Muddy Waters, 48, 100, 191–92
Mudhoney, 469
Music: American, xvi; in early 21st century, 544; feelings

in, 87, 494; feelings/sex in, 517–19; of past remade, 544–52; portability of, 429; power of, 504; in schools, 429; women in, 490–96, 515–20. *See also* Classical music; Dance music; Popular music
Music, 265
Music Biz Goes Round and Round: It Comes Out Clarkola (Bunzel), 125–28
Music business, 98–99; Costello's lack of respect for, 359; pattern lacking in, 96; race and power in, 14–21; structure, 138; *Variety* attacks, 96–97
Musicians: African American, 1, 19, 31; Blues, 48; jazz, 16–17, 93; swing, 20
Music industry: classification system of, 10; Rock "n" Roll opposed by, 123–29
The Music Man, 202
The Music of Black Americans (Southern), 425
Musicologically... (Strongin), 203–4
Musicological studies, xx
Music Television Channel (MTV), 380; awards show, 374; heavy metal on, 396, 405; Madonna and, 372–74; rap on, 431; "Total Request Live," 497
Music videos, 393; "Bad," 367; dark, 495; indie-alternative, 472; Jackson and, 364; Madonna and, 372–74; primacy of, 540; rap, 441–42
Musique concrète, 231
Muzak, 168
"My Aim Is True," 357
"My Boy Lollipop," 323
"My Claim to Fame," 332
"My Life," 518
MySpace, 557
Mystery Train: Images of America in Rock "n" Roll Music (Marcus), 272–77

Napster, 557
"Napster" controversy, 555
Nas, 460, 461

Nash, Johnny, 324, 325
Nashville, 71–72
The Nation, 478
Nation of Islam, 288
Natty Dread, 324, 326
Naughty By Nature, 445
Nazism, 119
Nebraska, 380
Negro. *See* African American
Nelson, Paul, 157–59
Neudorf, Darryl, 553
"Never Can Say Good-bye," 332
Nevermind, 472
Nevius, Sally, 410
New, Michael, 151
The New Conscious of Pop Music (Powers), 516–20
New Edition, 534
New Kids on the Block, 534
New Music, 519
New Musical Express, 221
Newport Folk Festival, 1965 (Nelson), 157–59
Newport Folk Festival, 1965 (Silber), 156
New Republic, 440, 442
"New Romantic" movement, 415
Newsted, Jason, 401–2
Newsweek, 68–70, 211–12, 217–18, 250, 336, 442
New Wave, 339, 355–61, 417, 475
New York Age, 124n4, 128
New York City, 54; clubs, 513; Disco in, 331–32, 337; punk scene, 350–51, 416–17; rap, 419
New Yorker, 249
New York Newsday, 429
New York Post, on Madonna, 376
New York Times, 118–19, 153, 331, 432, 440, 499–500, 515, 549
The Nice, 242
9/11, 538
Nine Inch Nails, 474–77
"1999," 389
1996 Telecommunications Act, 497–98, 500
1979 BMA conference, 390
Nirvana, 469, 472, 473, 475, 549
Nix, Hammie, 29

Nolen, Jimmy, 186
North Alabama White Citizens Council, 120
North Carolina, 286
"No Scrubs," 517, 519
"Notice," 208
"Not Lookin'," 516
Notorious B.I.G (Wallace, Christopher), 453–56, 459
"Nous Pas Bouger," 483
No wave, 352
No Way Out, 456–57, 461
"No Woman, No Cry," 324
'NSync, 534, 536
Numan, Gary, 542, 543
N.W.A. (Niggas with Attitude), 431, 439, 447

Oberlin Conservatory of Music, 537
"October Song," 166
Off the Wall, 363, 369
"Oh, Joseph," 12
"Oh, What a Dream," 80
Okeh, 26
"Old Folks At Home," 8
One Flew Over the Cuckoo's Nest (Kesey), 232
100 Club (London's), 347, 349
"One in a Million," 433–34
One Nation Under a Groove, 283, 285, 288
On the Road (Kerouac), 477
On Wax (Whiteman, McBride), 11–13
Onyx Club, 29
"Open Your Heart," 375–76
"O.P.P.," 441, 445
Oregon, 468
Organ-Piano combination, used by Springsteen, 386
Originality, 5–6
Osbourne, Ozzy, 294–99, 401, 411, 444
Osmond Brothers, 534, 535
Otis, Johnny, 56–58
Otis Redding Interview (Delehant), 190–93
"O-Town," 535
Over & Out: Indie Rock Values in the Age of Alternative Million Sellers (Weisbard), 473–79
Owen, Alun, 205
Owens, Buck, 530

Owens, Dana (Queen Latifah), 427

Page, Jimmy, 292, 299–307
Page, Patti, 80
Paglia, Camille, 373–77
Palais Royal, 13
Palmer, Carl, 315–16
"Papa Don't Preach," 375
"Papa Was a Rolling Stone," 177, 273
"Papa's Got a Brand New Bag," 185n5, 186
Paradise Restaurant, 18–19
The Paramount, 24
Paranoid, 293, 296
"Paranoid," 298
Pareles, Jon, 372, 432–37, 440
Parental advisory stickers, 408
Parents Music Resource Center (PMRC), censorship and, 405–14, 406n2
Parent Teacher Association (PTA), 406
Parker, Charlie, 49, 175
Parker, "Colonel" Tom, 111
Parker, Graham, 355, 357–58
Parker, Maceo, 186
Parliament-Funkadelic, 283–90, 392
Parton, Dolly, 521
"Party for Your Right to Fight," 435
Party Over (Hinds), 454–55
Patton, Charley, 46
Paxton, Tom, 167
Payola, 60n3, 96, 99, 123–29, 131
P Diddy. *See* Combs, Sean "Puffy"
Pearl, 236
Pearlman, Lou, 535
Peer, Ralph S., 26
Peer-to-peer filesharing, xviii, 554–58
Pee Wee King and His Golden West Cowboys, 69
Pelham Café, 3–4
Penick, Trevor, 536
Penniman Singers, 105
People, 310
People United To Save Humanity (PUSH), 288
Performers: African American, 97, 145–49;

songwriters aligned with, 137–38; Urban Folk early, 145
Perkins, Carl, 115
Perry, Steve, 394
Peter, Paul, and Mary, 154, 156
Petrillo, James C., 60
Pet Sounds, 141–42
Pfeifer, Bob, 468–69
Phillips, Dewey, 114
Phillips, Sam, 62, 110–17
Pickett, Wilson, 170–71, 171n3, 240
"Piece of My Heart," 235
Pierson, Kate, 354
Pig Pen (McKernan, Ron), 233–34
Pink Floyd, 242
The Pirate Bay, 556–58
"Planet Clare," 354
Planet Rock, 423
Plant, Robert, 292, 302, 305
Playboy, 308–14
"Please, Please, Please," 179
Please Please Me, 201
"plug-ins," 506
"Plug Tunin'," 428
PMRC. *See* Parents Music Resource Center
"Poker Face," 542, 543
Polish music, 60
Politics: Clinton, G., on music and, 284–90; Dixie Chicks and, 527, 529–30; entertainment and, 539; Urban Folk and, 145–46, 152
The Polka, 479
Polydor Records, 188–89
Poneman, Jonathan, 469
Pons, Lily, 29
Ponselle, Rosa, 12
Pop, xix; aestheticism, 251; art, 341, 353; censorship of, 252; commerce and, 250; culture, 432–33, 436; culture and B52's, 353; names cover R&B tunes, 96; solo, singers, 21–25; synth, 415; teen, 136, 497; teenagers and, 123–29, 135–36; vocalists, 96; women in, 516–20
Pop Eye: Evaluating Media (Goldstein), 250–53

Pop Eye: On "Revolver" (Goldstein), 214–17

Popular music, 520, 538; African, 480; African American, 4–5, 57, 170, 424; art, and, 158–59; authenticity of, 535; by Berlin, 2–8; black, xviii–xix; categories in, 10; classical music differentiated from, 7; consumption, 544; contemporary social/ political currents in, xv; criticism, xx, 158–59; dawn of modern, 10–13; disco as, 328; endurance in, 541–42; flexibility of, 8; French, 482–83; history courses in, 546; Jamaican, 480; Jazz separated from, in 1930's-1940's, 21–22; Latin tinge in American, 25n2; mass media/trade publications about, xx; 1980's/1990's, xx; post rock "n" roll, 546; Presley impacting, 110–11; segregation of U.S. society mirrored in, 97; what is, xviii–xix; white, xviii–xix; youth and, 545

Popular Press, 118–20

Porn rock, 406, 409

"Positive Vibrations," 326

Poussaint, Alvin, 433–34

Powell, Michael, 499–500

Powers, Ann, 516–20

Prakazrel, Michel "Pras," 462

Pregnancy, teen, 410–11

Prejudice, 436, 518; in Britain, 488; racial/ sexual, 432–35; on radio, 63, 434; Rai music and, in England, 483–84

Presley, Elvis, 91, 110–17, 127, 188, 227, 301; popular music impact of, 110–11; swing and, 119

Presley, Lisa Marie, 367

Price, Vincent, 369

Prince, 388–90, 393–94, 406, 410, 542; critics of crossover and, 394; racial bias and, 389

Prince Albert Tobacco, 72

Princess, 430

"The Prisoner's Song," 26

Professor Griff (Griffin, Richard), 432–33, 435–36, 443

Progressive rock, 314–22

Property rights, 558

Psychedelic rock, 231–44, 252

"Psychedelic Shack," 177

PTA. *See* Parent Teacher Association

Public Enemy, 425, 427, 432–33, 432n1, 435–36, 440, 442–43, 445, 447

Punk rock, 339–55, 415–18, 553; audiences, 350; British, garb, 351; difference between U.S. and U.K., 345–46, 350–51; Los Angeles scene, 416–18; to New Wave, 352–55; teenagers and, 348–51

Punk ska hybrids, 480

Purity and Power – Total, Unswerving Devotion to Heavy Metal Form: Judas Priest and The Scorpions (Considine), 396–99

Purple Rain, 389, 393, 394

PUSH. *See* People United To Save Humanity

Pussycat Dolls, 542

"Put it Right Here or Keep It Out There," 35–36

Queen Latifah, 428, 440, 444

"Quicksand," 542

Quiet Riot, 410

Rabbit Foot Minstrels, 36, 54

"Race man," 30

Race music, 25–30, 48–51, 520

Racism. *See* Prejudice

Radio, 10; African American, 393; classic rock, 545, 548; deregulation, 497–500; Dylan on, 168; first disco, station, 337; format variety, 499–500; 1920's, 554; ownership consolidation, 498–500; prejudice on, 63, 434; public policy in U.S,

496–97; R&B on, 92–93, 94–95; rock on, 497; self-competition in, 500

Radio and Records, 500

"Radio Ga Ga," 543

Radiohead, 555, 558

Radio station: of Brown, J., 186–87; Hot 97, 455–56; KRE of Berkeley, 234; WSM, 69, 72

The Raelettes, 83

Ragamuffin, 489

Rage, 450

Rage Against the Machine, 460

Ragtime, 1, 38

Rai music, 483–84, 487, 489

The Raindrops, 136–37

Rainey, Gertrude "Ma," 30, 36, 42

"Rain is a Bringdown," 78

"The Rain Song," 306

"Rai rebellion," 484

Raising Hell, 427

"Raising Hell" tour, 427

Ramone, Dee Dee, 344

Ramone, Tommy, 344

The Ramones, 344, 352, 548

Ranters and Crowd Pleasers (Marcus), 531

Rap, 419–25; African American identity and, 425; artists, 188; camaraderie in, 427; criticism of, 425; DJ, 421–22; first, record, 426; French, 482–83; Gangsta, 406, 439–40, 442, 447, 449; growing popularity of, 425; Hip Hop differentiated from, 459–60; history of, up to 1991, 419n1; lyrics, 406, 425–26, 446, 448, 450; melody in, 444–45; on MTV, 431; music videos, 441–42; New York, 419; as not music, 444–46; record and talent, 445; sampling in, 461; used in marketing, 459–60; West coast-East coast, feud, 453; women in, 456–63, 518–19. *See also* Hip Hop

Rap dot com, 425

"Rapper's Delight," 330, 419–20, 423, 426, 441

Rappleye, Charles, 453–54
Rap Sheet (Anso, Rappleye), 453–54
Rapture, 392–93
Rare Earth, 296
Rasmussen, Flemming, 402–3
Rastafari movement, 323, 326
Rastaman Vibration, 326
Raves, 502–3, 508
Raygun, 474
R&B. *See* Rhythm and Blues
RCA Records, 470, 531
RCA Victor, 69, 111, 115, 135
Reader's Digest, 211
Ready To Die, 454–55
Reagan, Ronald, 416–17
Reality TV, xviii, 534–35, 536–37
"Real Jazz," 14
"Real Love," 518
The Real Roxanne, 430
"The Real Slim Shady," 465–66
The Real Thing – Bruce Springsteen (Frith), 381–87
Rebels Against the System (Coon), 346–51
Rebels With a Beat (Coleman), 221–24
Record Companies, 97–99, 472; Costello and, 358–59; disco loved by, 188; Indie, 58–64; in1950's analysis, 59n2
Recording: ban, 60; equipment, 107; first, 11; first blues, 37; girl group, 132–33; "Great Balls of Fire," 116; Little Richard, 107–8; major, labels, 476–77; methods in 1950's, 106; process of Metallica, 402; production, 10–13, 334; production speed and volume of (in 1960's), 135; Public Enemy, 425; sales, 60; technology, 12–13; of "Tutti Frutti," 107–8
Record Labeling: Hearing before the Committee on Commerce, Science, and Transportation, United States Senate, 99th

Congress, September 19, 1985, 408–14
Records: Rock, Etc.-The Big Ones (Willis), 226–30
The Red Caps, 75
Redding, Otis, 190–93, 238
RedOne, 543
Reed, Jimmy, 191
Reed, Lou, 343–45
Refugee Project, 461
Regal Theater, 55, 391
Reggae, xviii, 323–28, 332, 487, 513
Reiner, Rob, 396
Reinhart, Django, 301
Religion, 243–44
Religious ring shout, 44
R.E.M., 475
Remixes, 513–14
"Respect," 190–91, 195–99, 430
Retronuevo, 391–94
Retrotrash, 353
Review of Led Zeppelin (Mendelsohn), 292–93
Review of Various Artists, Woodstock (Young), 255–57
"Revolution," 225, 227–29
Revolution of the Mind, 188
Revolver, 213–18
Rexroth, Kenneth, 147
Reynolds, Simon, 504–14
Reznor, Trent, 474–77
Rhymes and Reason, 265
Rhythm and Blues (R&B), 48–51, 56–58, 87, 365–66; changes in, 192; cover songs, 94–97; disco and, 329; divas, 515–20; in early 1950's, 74–77; golden years of, 62–64; Gospel's relationship to, 74; income from, 91; independent labels, 61, 90–91; life in, 89–93; literature on, 62n4; new name for, 169; pop names cover, tunes, 96; popularity of, in 1950's, 94–99; radio and, 92–93; 94–95; Rock "n" Roll to, 100–103; universality of, 93; uptown, 62; weaknesses in, 60
Rhythm and the Blues: A Life in American Music (Wexler, Ritz), 90–93

Richard, Renolds, 84
Richards, Keith, 219, 222–24, 306, 343
Richie, Lionel, 388, 390
Ridenhour, Carlton. *See* Chuck D
Ride the Lightning, 401, 403
Righteous Brothers, 191
Riley, Pebbles (Peeble-Poo), 426
Riley, Teddy, 370
Rilke, Rainer Maria, 542
Riot, 272–73
Riot Girl, 474
Riot Grrrl, 527
Ritz, David, 83–89, 170–72
Riviera, Jake, 356–57
Roach, Max, 429
Roane, Eddie, 53
Robinson, Dave, 358
Robinson, Nat, 427
Robinson, Smokey, 175–76
Robison, Emily, 526, 528, 530
Robles, Jason "Big Jake," 454
Rock, xix; aesthetics of, 249–53; art, 314–22; classical, 317–18, 545, 548; communal, 344; criticism of, 249, 339–40, 378, 380–81; culture, 337–38; first female critic, 225–30, 249; folk, 155; glam/glitter, 307–8; indie to alternative, 467–71; in late 1970's, 339–40; porn, 406, 409; progressive, 314–22; Psychedelic, 231–44, 252; radio stations, 497; revival (of mid 1970's), 350; Schlock, 131, 131n1. *See also* Punk rock; Rock "n" Roll
Rockabilly, 110–17, 520–21
"Rock Around the Clock," 325
Rock Awards, 342
The Rocket, 469
"Rock Lobster," 354
Rock "n" Roll, xix, 86; articles on, 118; beginnings of, 91; as being artistic, 252; Bowie on, 313; Asa Carter on, 121; change in, 348; core values of, 383–84; Dylan on, 164; fans, 56; Jukebox

not playing, 122; listener's innocence, 272; lyrics, 206, 410; music industry against, 123–29; panic surrounding early, 97; popular music post, 546; psychiatrist describing, 118; races brought together by, 109; to R&B, 100–103; "Revolver" as key in creation of, 214; Sinatra berating, 119–20. *See also* Rock

Rock "n" Roll Called Communicable Disease, 118

"Rock of Ages," 156

Rock opera, 220

Rocky Horror Picture Show, 307

Rodgers, Jimmie, 26

Roeg, Nicolas, 311–12

Roeser, Eddie, 477

Rogers, Kenny, 521

Rolling Stone, 229, 232, 296, 313; *Blue* reviewed in, 266; Eminem interview in, 464; Heller interview in, 442; Landau of, 384; Rose on, 435; Sex Pistols in, 346n1; on Woodstock, 255

Rolling Stone Record Review, xv

Rolling Stone Record Review, Volume 2, xv

The Rolling Stones, 101, 219–24, 247, 254, 254n1, 272, 343; Beatles compared with, 220, 225–30; on cigarettes and alcohol, 224; commercialism and, 224; musical preferences of, 223

"Roll Over Beethoven," 102

"Roll the Bones," 442

The Ronettes, 137n3

Ronstadt, Linda, 325

"Roots, Rock. Reggae," 326

The Roots, 461

"Roots 'n' Phuture," 514

Ropin' the Wind, 521

Rose, Axl, 432–33, 436

Ross, Diana, 176

Rotten, Johnny, 346–51, 550

"Roundabout," 319

Route 666: On the Road To Nirvana (Arnold), 473

Roxon, Lillian, 297–98

Roy, Rob, 120–22

Royalties, 85, 88

Rubber Soul, 141, 213n1

"Rubber Soul," 215

Ruffhouse, 459

Ruled by Frankenmusic (Everett-Green), 552–56

The Rumour, 356–57

Run-DMC, 423–24, 425, 426–27

Rush, 442

Rush Management, 449

RZA, 460

Sacramento gangs, in 1960's, 247

Sadler, Eric, 424

Sakamoto, Kyu, 480

Salsa, 56n1

Salter, Mike, 4

Salt "n" Pepa, 424, 427, 430

Sam and Dave, 191

Sam Phillips Interview (Kaye), 112–17

Sampling: in past/present, 457; in Rap/Hip Hop, 461

Samwell-Smith, Paul, 302

Sanday, Peggy R., 434

San Francisco, 228–39, 231–35, 468, 489

San Francisco Chronicle, 232

Sasha & Digweed, 513

Sassy, 474–75

Satanic Majesties, 225, 227

"Satisfaction," 191

Saturday Night Fever, 329, 337, 381

Saturday Night Live, 458, 461

Savage, Jon, 502

Sawyer, Diane and Dixie Chicks, 527–33

Schlock-rock, 131, 131n1

Schneider, Fred, 354

Schonberg, Harold, 23

Schulps, Dave, 300–307

Science News Letter, 212

The Score, 457, 462

The Scorpions, 396

Scorsese, Martin, 393

Scott, Ray "Benzino," 465–66

Scott-Heron, Gil, 392

Scour, 557

Screaming Trees, 469–70

Scrunge, 471–79

Seattle, 467–71, 468n2, 472

A Seattle Slew (DiMartino), 468–71

Second Dimension: Jimi Hendrix In Action (Dawbarn), 242–44

Seeger, Pete, 145, 148, 154, 157–58

Segovia, 301

Seidelman, Susan, 374

Selassie, Haile, 323

The Seventh Stream (Ennis), xviii

Sex: African American music and, 517–19; appeal of Beatles, 207–8; Bowie on, 308–9, 311; in Classic Blues, 39n1; Heavy metal and, 406; lyrics and, 406, 411; Madonna and, 373; in music, feelings and, 517–19; in 1970's, 309; racial/sexual prejudice, 432–35; roles of drag queens, 374; women and, 209, 374

Sexism, 428, 430

Sex Pistols, 346–51, 346n1, 473, 492, 548, 551, 553

Sgt. Pepper's Lonely Hearts Club Band, 216–18, 227

"Shake, Rattle and Roll," 92, 97n5

Shante, Roxanne, 430, 456

Shapiro, Nat, 40–44

Shaw, Arnold, 53–56, 62–64, 75–77

Shea Stadium, 210

Sheet music, 9

Shelton, Bob, 28, 153

Shelton, Joe, 28

Sheridan, Kevin, 48–51

Sheridan, Peter, 48–51

She's Gotta Have It, 391

"She's Out of My Life," 369

Shickler, Aaron, 24

Shider, Guy, 287

Shilts, Randy, 434

The Shirelles, 133, 135, 137

Sholes, Steve, 115

"Shoot to Thrill," 411

"Shout at the Devil," 410

Shuffle rhythm, 52

Siddhartha (Hesse), 320

"Signed Sealed Delivered", 280

Sign "O" the Times, 393

Silber, Irwin, 156

"Silence Is Easy," 550
"Simmer Down," 323
Simmons, Russell, 444, 459, 466
Simon, Bill, 60–62
Simon, Carly, 262
Simon, Marc, 332
Simon, Paul, 261, 324, 325
Simon and Garfunkel, 322
Simulacrum, 535
Sinatra, Frank, 22–24, 119–20
Singers: blues, 44–45, 75; of dance music, 507; Gospel, 195; jalis, 44; solo pop, 21–25; white, picking up on black style, 86; women as best Classic Blues, 37
Singer-songwriter, 261–69, 491
Singles, 390, 545
Sing Out, 155
Sir Mix-a-Lot, 469–70
Sister Act 2, 462
Sitwell, Edith, 217
Ska, 323, 480
Skiffle, 201
"Slave Driver," 326
slavery, of African Americans, 33
"slide" guitar, 45–47
Sly and the Family Stone, 271, 286–87
Sly vs. Superfly, 272–77
Small, Millie, 323
Smith, Bessie, 27–28, 36, 38, 39–44, 54, 238
Smith, Mamie, 26–27
Smith, Patti, 208, 351
Smith, Will, 460
Smith, Willie Mae Ford, 30
Snider, Dee, 408
Snoop Dogg's Gentle Hip Hop Growl (Touré), 448–51
Snoop Doggy Dogg (Broadus, Calvin), 448–51, 453
Social media, 557–58
"So Long," 78
"Somewhere," 176
Sommers, Bill, 234
"Song of India," 12
Song production, Tin Pan Alley's mode of, 7
The Song Remains the Same, 302

Songs: Berry Chuck, 100–103; Country, 66, 521; Little Richard, 109; message, 160; songwriting angry, 494–95; written for Louis Jordan, 55
Songs of the Silent Generation (Bluestein), 146–49
Song to a Seagull, 266–67
Songwriters: Brill Building, 131–40; commercial, 493; Elvis Costello and, 356; Country, 67–68; European American, 1; performers aligned with, 137–38; star, of early 1960's, 134; Tin Pan Alley, 67, 134; white/ black, 55
Songwriting, 549; Amos on, 492–95; angry songs, 494–95; Berry Chuck and, 100–103; Charles, Ray, 88–89; Dylan on, 162, 168; queen of teen pop, 136; and singing split (of early 1960's), 135; Williams Hank on, 73
Son House: Living King of Delta (Gilbert), 46–47
Sontag, Susan, 331
SOS-Racisme, 484
Soul, xix, 169, 173–78; Godfather of, 178–89; queens, 517–19; songs by Otis Redding, 190–91; Southern, 189–90, 270
Soul II Soul, 486
Soundgarden, 469
SoundScan, 521
Sounds of Silence, 261
sound systems, 323
The Source, 465–66
Sources, xix–xx
South, passive resistance movement in (1960's), 147
South Asians, in England, 487–88
South Bronx, 419
Southern, Eileen, 425
Spears, Britney, 535, 536, 542
Specialty Records, 104–5
Spector, Phil, 137–39, 550
Spice Girls, 526
Spin, 442, 472
Spinal Tap, 291
Spirituals, 83–84, 85, 243–44

Springsteen, Bruce, 324, 326, 358, 377–87; authenticity of, 380–81, 383–85; on Capitalism, 384–85; community and, 383; Dylan and, 377, 384; on Led Zeppelin/Marriage and radio, 379; lyrics, 385; message/lyrics of, 385; music sales, 381; physical appeal of, 385; Piano organ combination used by, 386; sense of community and, 383
Squire, Chris, 320–21
Staggerlee, 274
"Stairway to Heaven," 293, 305
Stapp, Jack, 72
Stardust, Ziggy, 311
Starr, Ringo, 200, 204, 205, 230
Starsailor, 550
Star Search, 536–37
"Star Spangled Banner," 241
Station to Station, 310
Stax Records, 170, 173, 190, 192, 270
Steiner, Peter, 498–99
Stereo Review, 262n1, 263
The Steve Harvey Show, 453
Stewart, Rod, 379
Stewart, Sly. See Sly and the Family Stone
Stiff Records, 356–59
St. John Gospel Singers, 75
"St. Louis Blues," 39
Stone, Jesse, 92–93, 105
Stone, Sly, 270–77
"Stop! In the Name of Love," 354
"Stormy Monday," 50–51
Stovall, Natasha, 455–56
"Street Fighting Man," 225, 227–28
Streisand, Barbra, 376
Strobert, Andrei L., 426
The Strokes, 549
Strongin, Theodore, 203–4
Strummer, Joe, 553
Studio 54, 330, 330n2
Sub Pop, 467–70
"Subterranean Homesick Blues," 154
"Sugar," 542
Sugarhill Gang, 330, 419, 426

Suicide, 410–11
"Suicide Solution," 411
"Sukyaki," 480
Sullivan, Arthur, 126
Sullivan, Ed, 203
Sullivan, Maxine, 29
Summer, Donna, 329, 333, 369
Sun label, 62
Sun Ra, 284, 288
Sun Records, 111
"Sunshine of Your Love," 242
"Super Cat," 487
Superfly, 275
"Super Freak," 444
"Superstar," 458
"Surfin' U.S.A.," 141
Surf music, 140–44, 252
Surrealistic Pillow, 232
Survivor, 534
Sutton, Percy, 391
Swedien, Bruce, 368–71
"Sweet Baby James," 264
"Sweet Little Sixteen," 102, 141
Sweet Silence Studios, 402
Swing, 16; bands, 53; Era, 14–21; musicians, 20; Presley and, 119; Western, 65

Talking Book, 278
Talking Heads, 341, 343–44, 352
Tape-edit, 321
Tapestry, 262–65
Tapping technique, 395
Tarkus, 318
Tate, Greg, 365–68, 439–40
Tavis Smiley Show, 553
"Taxman," 216
Taylor, Charles, 527–33
Taylor, Elizabeth, 309
Taylor, James, 264
T-Bone Walker: Father of the Blues (Sheridan, Sheridan), 48–51
"Teardrops from My Eyes," 79
Techno, 502–3
Technology, xviii; electronic music, 504–7; new music, 10–13, 94, 551, 554–55; recording influenced by, 12–13
Ted Snyder Company, 4

Teenage pop stars, 497
Teenagers, 98; of late 60's/70's, 549; pop music and, 123–29, 135–36; pregnancy, 410–11; punk rock and, 348–51; suicide of, 410–11; superficiality of, 311
Teen pop, 123–29, 534, 536
Tee-Tot, 71, 73
Telegraph, 5
Television, 343–44, 351, 534–35, 536–37
"Telstar," 379
Temperton, Rod, 369
The Temptations, 176, 273
"Tennessee Waltz," 67n3
Terrell, Jean, 177
Thank God It's Friday, 337
Thar's Gold in Them Hillbillies (Crichton), 26–29
"That's All Right," 114
"That Thing Called Love," 26
Theater Owners' Booking Agency (T.O.B.A.), 36
There's a New Sound in Pop Music: Bigotry, 432–37
"These Arms of Mine," 191
Things Fall Apart, 461
"Think," 182, 195
"Third-World Theme of Bob Marley," 324–28
This is Spinal Tap, 396
"This Land Is Your Land," 145, 148
Thomas, Arnold, 53
Thomas, Carla, 190
Thompson, Ahmir, 461
Thompson, Steve, 403
Thornton, Willie Mae "Big Mama," 56
"Thou'rt Passing Hence," 126
Three Feet High and Rising, 428, 440
"Three O'clock Blues," 76
Thriller, 363–71, 381
"The Thrill is Gone," 74
Tibetan freedom concert, 460
"Till There Was You," 202
Timbaland, 457
Timberlake, Justin, 535, 536
Time, 117–19, 149–53, 250, 353, 381, 458
Time-Life music catalog, 262n1

Time Passages and Class and Culture in Cold War America, 481–82
Times (London), 201, 211
Time-Warner, 447
Tin Pan Alley, 17, 59; acceptance of, songs, 5; Brill Building revives production practices of, 131; Country tunes, 66; ethnicity and, style, 2; location of, 1; material form of, songs, 7–8; pre Rock "n" Roll music from, 206; songwriters, 67, 134
Tipton, Glenn, 397–98
TLC, 516–17, 519
T.O.B.A. *See* Theater Owners' Booking Agency
"Toccata," 317
"Tomorrow Never Knows," 231
Tone-Loc, 425, 442
"Tonight I Celebrate My Love," 391
The Tonight Show, 432, 434, 476
Toombs, Rudolph "Rudy," 79
Toomey, Jenny, 497–501
"Too Much Monkey Business," 100
Toots and the Maytals, 324
Top Names Now Singing the Blues as Newcomers Roll On R&B Tide, 95–97
Tori Amos: Pain for Sale (Doerschuk), 492–96
Touré, 448–51
Town Criers (Stovall), 455–56
Townsend, Robert, 391
Townshend, Pete, 220, 342
Traffic, 293
Traum, Happy, 160–68
"The Traveling Coon," 34
A Tribe Called Quest, 440
Trilogy, 318
Trouser Press, 300–307
Truth, 292–93, 301–2
Truth or Dare, 374, 376
Tucker, Bruce, 180–89
Tucker, Sophie, 26
Turner, Big Joe, 50, 91–92, 97, 102n5
"Tutti Frutti," 86, 106–8
TV bandstand programs, 128

Twain, Shania, 526
"Tweedle Dee," 95–96, 97
12 West, 332, 334, 336
"Twilo Thunder," 513
"The Twist," 132
Twisted Sister, 408
2 Live Crew, 440
2Pac, 452–56
2 step, 507, 513
Tyler, Steven, 539
Tympany Five, 54

Ugly Things, 548
Ulrich, Lars, 400–405
"Uncle Meat," 248
Uncle Tom's Cabin, 8
Underground Resistance, 509
Understanding Media (McLuhan), 250–51
Under the Pink, 494
United Negro College Fund, 289
Upside Your Head! Rhythm and Blues on Central Avenue (Otis), 57–58
"Up The Ladder To The Roof," 177
Urban Folk: early performers of, 145; female artists in, 148–49; politics and, 145–46, 152; revival, 144–53, 155
Urge Overkill, 477
"U.S.," 377

Vallee, Rudy, 21
Vanguard, 151
Van Halen, 395
Van Halen, Eddie, 369–70
Vanilla Ice, 457, 466
Variety, xx, 96–99, 211; anxiety of, 96; attacks music business, 96–97
Vaudeville. See Minstrel shows
Vaughan, Sarah, 553
Vee, Bobby, 264
The Velvets, 343–44
Velvet Underground, 340–41
Venus of the Radio (Paglia), 373–77
Verlaine, Tom, 343, 344
Verve Records, 244
VH1, 548
Victor Company, 11, 12, 27
Video games, 544

The Village People, 336
Village Voice, 233, 249, 255, 333, 472
Vincebus Eruptum, 401
Vinyl, 555
Violence: Hip hop and, 428; against women, 410
"Virtual studio technology" software, 505
The Voice, 23
"The Voodoo Man," 34

Wah-wah pedal, 240
Wainwright, Loudon, 380
Waits, Tom, 553
Wakeman, Rick, 549–50
"Wake Me Up When September Ends," 553, 554
"Wake Up Little Susie," 102
Waksman, Steve, 294n4
Walker, Frank, 40–41
Walker, T-Bone, 48–51, 74
"Walk This Way," 423
Waller, Fats, 53
Walton, William, 217
"Wanna Be Startin' Something," 370, 393
War, on Iraq, 527, 529–30
Ward, Bill, 295, 297
Ward, Brian, 517–18
Ward, Clara, 197
Warhol, Andy, 341, 353, 542
Warner Music Group, 558
A Warning to the Music Business, 98–99
Warp Records, 512
Wartime, 532
Washington, Booker T., 388, 391–92
Washington, Dinah, 43, 75, 169n1
Washington's Coliseum, 210
"Waste Land," 218
Watch Your Step, 5
Water, Muddy, 46
Waterman, Pete, 133
Waters, Muddy, 45
"Waters of the Minnetonka," 12
Watson, Doc, 163
Watts, Charlie, 222–23
"We Are the World," 364, 387
"Wear My Ring Around Your Neck," 380
The Weavers, 146, 148

Webb, "Chick," 20, 54, 55
Weinman Lear, Martha, 22–24
Weisbard, Eric, 473–79
Wells, James, 332
Wells, Ramon, 470
We Look at Our Parents and... (Hentoff), 237–40
"We Love You," 227
Wenner, Jann, 232
West African music, 44
Western music, 44, 103
Western Swing, 65
West Indian music, 485–86
West Indians, in England, 485–87
Wexler, Jerry, 87, 89–93, 97, 170–72, 198
Weymouth, Tina, 341, 343–44
"What I Say," 87
What is This Thing Called Hardcore? (Flipside), 416–18
"What's My Name?," 449
What Songs the Beatles Sang (Mann), 201–3
Wheatstraw, Peetie, 28
"Whenever You're in My Arms Again," 391
"When You Were Mine," 389
White, Alan, 320
White, Charles, 105–10
White, Georgia, 28
White, Josh, 146
White, Ted, 198–99
White Christmas, 127
Whiteman, Paul, 10–13
White Negro syndrome, 90, 92–93
Whites: African American singing styles copied by, 86; listening to African American Music, 91; songs for Louis Jordan written by, 55
White society: African American performers integrate into, 97; of America, 86; male dominated, 444
The White Stripes, 549, 553
Whitfield, Norman, 177
The Who, 220, 342, 348
"Whole Lotta Love," 293
Who's That Girl?, 374

"Who Wants to Be a Millionaire," 535
Why Don't You Do Right, 41
Why File Sharing Will Save Hollywood, Music (Buskirk), 556–58
"The Wicked Messenger," 167
Wide Open Spaces, 526
The Wild, the Innocent, and the E-Street Shuffle, 377
"Wild Thing," 425, 442
Wilkerson, Donald, 86
Williams, Bert, 27, 40–41, 41n2
Williams, Clarence, 39–40
Williams, Hank, 71, 73, 193
"Willie and the Hand Jive," 56
Willis, Chuck, 80
Willis, Ellen, 225–30, 249
"Will You Still Love Me Tomorrow," 133, 264
Will You Still Love Me Tomorrow? Girl Groups From the 1950's on (Greig), 133–40
Wilson, Brian, 141–44
Wilson, Carl, 141
Wilson, Dennis, 141
Wilson, Frank, 177
Wilson, Jackie, 169, 176–77
Wilson, Teddy, 197
Wilson Brothers, 141
Winchell, Walter, 18
Windeler, Robert, 263–66
Wings, 348
Winslow, Max, 4

Witherspoon, Jimmy, 48–51
"Within You Without You," 218
"Without You," 113
With the Beatles, 201
The Wiz, 363, 369, 371
Wolcott, James, 341–45
Women: African American, in entertainment, 38, 518–19; as best Classic Blues singers, 37; indie rock and, 477; in music, 490–96, 515–20; in pop, 516–20; in rap, 456–63, 518–19; sexual revolution of, 209, 374; singer-songwriter, 261–69; violence against, 410
Wonder, Stevie, 176, 278–83
Wood, Ronnie, 306
Woodstock (1969), 254–58, 254n1
"Woodstock Nation," 254, 255–57
Woollcott, Alexander, 3
Works, Vol. 1, 316–17
Work songs, 44
World music, 479–90
Worrell, Bernie, 283, 287
Would You Let your Sister Go With a Rolling Stone? (Coleman), 221
Wreszin, Michael, 529–30
Wright, Billy, 106
Wu Tang Clan, 452, 460
Wyman, Bill, 222–23

X, 415

Yahoo, 557
The Yardbirds, 220, 301–2
Yauch, Adam, 460
Yeh-heh-heh-hes, Baby, 118n1
"Yellow Submarine," 214, 216
Yes, 319–22, 549
Yesstories: Yes In Their Own Words (Morse), 319–22
"Yesterday," 213, 315
"YMCA," 336
Yoko Ono, 348
"Yo! MTV Raps," 425, 428
"You Can't Keep a Good Man Down," 26
Young, Andre. *See* Dr. Dre
Young, J. R., 255–57
Young, Neil, 553
Young Americans, 312
Your Happiest Years (Clark), 125–26
"You Send Me," 169
"You Shook Me," 292, 301
YouTube, 540, 557
"You Turn Me On (I'm a Radio)," 267
"You've Got the Power," 182

Zappa, Frank, 244–49, 412–14
Zappa and the Mothers: Ugly Can Be Beautiful (Kempton), 245–49
Ziggy, 311
"Zip-A-Dee-Doo-Dah," 139
Zoom, Billy, 415